Practical Heritage Management

PRESERVING A TANGIBLE PAST

Scott F. Anfinson
University of Minnesota

ROWMAN & LITTLEFIELD
Lanham • Boulder • New York • London

Executive Editor: Nancy Roberts
Assistant Editor: Megan Manzano
Senior Marketing Manager: Amy Whitaker
Interior Designer: Ilze Lemesis

Credits and acknowledgments for material borrowed from other sources, and reproduced with permission, appear on the appropriate page within the text.

Published by Rowman & Littlefield
An imprint of The Rowman & Littlefield Publishing Group, Inc.
4501 Forbes Boulevard, Suite 200, Lanham, Maryland 20706
www.rowman.com

Unit A, Whitacre Mews, 26-34 Stannary Street, London SE11 4AB, United Kingdom

British Library Cataloguing in Publication Information Available

Library of Congress Cataloging-in-Publication Data

Names: Anfinson, Scott F., author.
Title: Practical heritage management : preserving a tangible past / Scott F. Anfinson, University of Minnesota.
Description: Lanham, Maryland : Rowman & Littlefield, [2019] | Includes bibliographical references and index.
Identifiers: LCCN 2018012465 (print) | LCCN 2018027350 (ebook) | ISBN 9780759118003 (electronic) | ISBN 9780759117983 (cloth : alk. paper) | ISBN 9780759117990 (pbk. : alk. paper)
Subjects: LCSH: Historic preservation—United States. | Historic preservation—Law and legislation—United States. | Cultural property—Protection—United States. | Cultural property—Protection—Law and legislation—United States. | United States. National Historic Preservation Act of 1966. | National Register of Historic Places. | United States—Cultural policy.
Classification: LCC E159 (ebook) | LCC E159 .A54 2019 (print) | DDC 363.6/90973—dc23
LC record available at https://lccn.loc.gov/2018012465

Printed in the United States of America

This book is dedicated to three generations of national leaders in heritage preservation with Minnesota roots. In the first generation were Vern Chatelain, Charles Peterson, Herb Kahler, and Ronald Lee. All were University of Minnesota graduates who laid the foundations of the National Park Service (NPS) history program. Chatelain (1931–1937), Lee (1938–1951), and Kahler (1951–1964) all served as chiefs of the NPS History Division. Peterson was the first preservation architect for NPS and in 1933 started the Historic American Buildings Survey (HABS).

In the next generation were Russell Fridley and Elden Johnson, who stayed closer to home but made a difference nationally. Fridley was a historian who, as the young director of the Minnesota Historical Society, led the effort to save historic Fort Snelling in the 1950s, the first major historic preservation victory in Minnesota. He served as Minnesota's first state historic preservation officer (SHPO) (1966–1986) and was on the first Advisory Council for Historic Preservation in 1967. Johnson, Minnesota's first state archaeologist (1963–1978), helped develop nationally recognized state heritage preservation legislation in 1963 and wrote the prescient chapter in the 1977 Airlie House archaeological management report (McGimsey and Davis 1977) on improving Indian-archaeologist relations.

In my generation, Charles Nelson, Susan Roth, and Dennis Gimmestad formed the core of one of the best state historic preservation offices in the nation during the late twentieth century. Nelson, a historical architect, served as the first deputy SHPO in Minnesota and pioneered innovative architectural solutions to tax act and Americans with Disabilities Act issues. Roth, a historian, led Minnesota's National Register of Historic Places Program for 30 years, shepherding hundreds of carefully edited nominations through the state review board and assisting with numerous tax certifications. Gimmestad, an architectural historian, served as a survey specialist, department head, and Government Programs head during his 33 years with the Minnesota State Historic Preservation Office (MnSHPO) and was nationally recognized for his skill in implementing Section 106 and crafting agreement documents. As the MnSHPO archaeologist (1990–2005), I received my first focused historic preservation education from Nelson, Roth, and Gimmestad.

The west-central Minnesota hometowns of Peterson, Lee, Gimmestad, and Roth, as well as that of the author of this book, are within about a 100-mile radius of each other: Peterson is from Madison, Lee from Montevideo, Gimmestad from Belview, Roth from Silver Lake, and Anfinson from Benson. There must be something in the water out there promoting a heritage preservation ethic and a public service mentality.

CONTENTS

Figures

Tables

I wrote this book partly for a selfish reason: to provide me with a textbook designed for teaching heritage management at the college level. I needed a book that fit a typical semester schedule (15 teaching weeks), covered basic topics I thought were important, provided diverse information for students of history and preservation architecture, as well as those in archaeology, and gave practical advice to students who may become professionals in heritage management. For the 15 years I taught heritage management in the Department of Anthropology at the University of Minnesota, I was always frustrated by the lack of a textbook that fit my class well.

At about the same time that I started teaching classes in heritage management, Tom King's first edition of *Cultural Resource Laws and Practice* (1998) was published. It was the only textbook that came close to working well for my class. Since then I have relied on King's three updates of the book (2004, 2008, 2013) as my primary text, with some supplemental readings provided by other King books (2000, 2002, 2003, 2005, 2007, 2009, 2011). I also have used portions of other archaeologically oriented heritage management textbooks, such as Neumann and Sanford (2010) and Hardesty and Little (2009). While King's introductory book and the other books noted have much utility to teaching heritage management with an archaeological focus, I still saw a need for a more comprehensive introductory textbook in heritage management, especially when nonarchaeological students began taking my class.

American heritage management is a hybrid. It includes private and public, business and government, professional and avocational. It involves archaeology, history, and architecture, as well as other disciplines, like museology and anthropology. It recognizes the monumental and the ephemeral. It hides the locations of some properties and celebrates the locations of others. Its roots lie in European science and early American values. It considers the heritage of ancient immigrants and much more recent ones. It encourages preservation but necessarily accepts change. Thus, like most things American, it is not only a blend but also a compromise.

I too am a hybrid. American archaeologists of my generation were the first with the potential to work in heritage management as a full-time job for an entire career. Yet we were not trained for it. We were trained to be academics and, upon graduation, found that the only full-time jobs available to most of us were heritage management jobs. We gladly took those jobs as starters for our careers, although many of us felt that we would ultimately return to the academy. But then health insurance and house payments restricted our economic options, and families limited our mobility. Moreover, those jobs in academic archaeology required a PhD and remained in short supply.

We learned heritage management on the job. We rapidly discovered that "new archaeology" did not give us much insight into how to do our day-to-day work. The internet was not available early in our careers, so we could not google our problems. We learned field methods in college that were designed not for site discovery but for site investigation. When we did get to excavate a site for heritage management purposes, it was usually not one we would have chosen for our particular research interests. Development projects chose our sites. To help justify our existence and give us some intellectual satisfaction, we occasionally made unimportant sites seem to be important.

Although the National Historic Preservation Act (NHPA) was six years old by the time I received my undergraduate degree, I was completely unaware of it or any other federal heritage preservation law. There had not been a single course offered in heritage management anywhere at the University of Minnesota. I then had a year off from full-time schooling to decide what to do next. I took a few graduate courses in archaeology as an Adult Special student at Minnesota, including a course from my undergraduate advisor, Elden Johnson, on contract archaeology. The purpose of the course was to prepare students not for a career in heritage management but to bid on and implement contracts in an academic setting. We did not learn much about appropriate field methods, laws, or heritage management agencies, but we did learn how to respond to a request for proposals, how to construct a project budget, and how to do archaeological interpretation in public settings. Some academic archaeologists still consider this the basic heritage management experience necessary to teach all aspects of heritage management.

At graduate school at the University of Nebraska, I was very fortunate to get a job at the National Park Service's Midwest Archaeological Center (MWAC). There I perfected skills in faunal and lithic analysis while writing my thesis on ceramic analysis. I also learned what it was like to work for a federal agency—lots of forms to fill out, lots of acronyms to learn, and lots of diverse resources to manage. I also got some heritage management history. MWAC was the remnant of the Smithsonian Institution's River Basin Surveys, one of the country's first major public heritage management programs. But, once again, I was not able to take a single course in heritage management while at the University of Nebraska.

After obtaining my MA, I went to work leading a highway archaeology survey program in Minnesota. I was essentially a contract archaeologist, although I worked for an institution (the Minnesota Historical Society) rather than a private business. It was mainly a fieldwork job, although winters in Minnesota necessarily provide the opportunity for analysis and writing. Within a few years, I knew how to do the daily work of a cultural resource management (CRM) contract archaeologist, although I didn't fully understand why the work was being done.

While doing my highway archaeology job, I finished my PhD in anthropology/archaeology at the University of Minnesota. This helped me fine-tune my thinking and writing abilities, as well as broaden my intellectual horizons through classes by Guy Gibbon in method and theory, Janet Spector in new archaeological perspectives, Herb Wright in paleoecology, and Fred Lukermann in geography. These classes reinforced the value of an open mind and an interdisciplinary approach, but, once again, I had no opportunity to take a course in heritage management as none were offered.

My second full-time job was as state historic preservation office (SHPO, pronounced "ship-o") archaeologist for Minnesota. My principal concern was with the implementation of the NHPA. It was my first exposure to comprehensive heritage management, although I already had 15 years of full-time experience running a specialized heritage management program. For the first time, I worked closely with historians and architects. I also got to attend training courses under titles such as NRHP Section 106, Section 4(f), NEPA, and comprehensive planning. I obtained insight and advice from my in-house SHPO peers, as well as from those from other states at meetings of the National Conference of State Historic Preservation Officers (NCSHPO, pronounced "nick-ship-o") and on its email list-serve. After 15 years at the Minnesota SHPO, I finally began to understand the width and breadth, as well as the purpose, of American heritage management.

While at the Minnesota SHPO, I also began teaching a course on CRM at the University of Minnesota. It was great to return to a familiar academic setting and start sharing a quarter century's heritage management insider knowledge. As I began teaching, I found I didn't know as much as I thought. I had to learn the history of heritage management. My greatest advantage in teaching was having many personal experience examples, both good and bad, to illustrate how heritage management laws and policies were applied in the real world.

My last full-time job in my formal heritage management career was as state archaeologist for Minnesota. For the first time, I had no federally mandated duties. My focus was on implementing state law. Minnesota has one of the earliest state archaeology statutes and one of the strictest statutes protecting historic Indian burials. When dealing with Indian burials, I no longer worked with tribes directly but with the Minnesota Indian Affairs Council, which represented all the tribes in Minnesota. I had to appear before the state legislature to try to improve the laws, obtain funding for my office, and explain controversial issues. I got to meet my peers at Society for American Archaeology meetings of the National Association of State Archaeologists (NASA), in addition to communicating with them on the NASA email list-serve. Over 10 years, I was exposed to the many aspects of the state side of heritage management, while I continued to teach classes in heritage management and archaeology.

A Note on Purpose

The most important lesson I have learned from over 40 years of doing heritage management is that there is no one right way of doing things, but there are many wrong ways. That is why this book is as much about avoiding the wrong ways as it is about implementing various right ways. It is titled *Practical Heritage Management* because it offers advice on how to get your job done in a manner that is efficient, effective, and consistent with our American heritage management system and laws. The purpose of this book is not to convince the reader that my way is the best way or that my perspective reflects the perspectives of every state but to demonstrate the value of a comprehensive heritage management education and a practical approach to heritage management application. If nothing else, disagreement with my perspective should promote a robust classroom discussion.

This book is principally aimed at advanced college and university students taking a focused course in American heritage management. It assumes that students in this course already know the basics of their chosen profession, be it archaeology, history, architecture, or museum studies. Thus most students will be upper-division undergraduates or graduate students. The book provides a comprehensive overview of the objectives, foundations, players, and methods of heritage management. Although my archaeological bias cannot be overcome because it reflects my personal history and experiences, all heritage management disciplines share the same basic set of laws, many of the same methods (e.g., National Register requirements), and certainly similar objectives.

A secondary audience for the book is made up of the practitioners of heritage management at development and review agencies and in private practice. Although I describe and explain components of the American heritage management system that should be generally familiar to and deemed necessary by most experienced heritage management practitioners, the book may help them fine-tune their skills and understanding.

A big difference between my book and other introductory heritage management textbooks is my emphasis on the historic context of heritage management. I have a full chapter on the history of American heritage management but also provide some historical background particular to each aspect of heritage management in other chapters. As students will come to know and professionals should already know, context is a critical concept for American heritage management. It is the basis for deciding what is worth preserving. I think it is also critical to understanding what is worth learning and doing.

I originally had planned to include chapters covering two topics that I think are important: writing heritage management documents and international aspects of heritage management. They would have been long, and the book is already long enough. The writing chapter would have dealt with critical American heritage management documents, such as reports, management plans, and agreement documents. I will save these for another book and an advanced class. I believe writing is the most important skill to master in heritage management. It is best learned through directed instruction and intensive practice.

As for international aspects, that too is another book and perhaps another class. While this book is about American heritage management, we have been and continue to be influenced by developments abroad, so we cannot completely ignore international aspects of heritage management. We are increasingly part of a global community. The language we speak, the methods we use, and our basic preservation focus is increasingly universal, even though our priorities and detailed purposes will continue to diverge based on political and social necessities.

Book Organization

In its entirety, I have organized this book to fit a 15-week teaching semester. The 14 chapters allow one week for a mid-term examination, two weeks to cover a complex chapter (e.g., chapter 6), or perhaps a week to cover something not included in the book, focusing on an instructor's personal preference (e.g., public history). Based on an instructor's focus and objectives, some chapters could be used only as supplementary reading (e.g., chapters 11–13), especially for an introductory course.

The book starts with some definitions and an explanation of what I think heritage management is. It also covers why I use the term "heritage management" rather than "cultural resource management" familiar to most American archaeologists or "historic preservation" familiar to most historians and architects. Chapter 2 provides an overview of the history of heritage management in the United States, a topic I think is essential to any introductory course. If nothing else, this historical overview reflects the heritage of heritage management professionals. We should be appreciative of our own heritage if we expect others to be concerned with theirs.

I then get to the beef of American heritage management in the next 11 chapters. The first six (chapters 3–8) present the legal and procedural framework of the American federal heritage management system. These aspects are common to all federal agencies, states, and territories. I then provide five chapters concerned with the principal players in the American heritage management system: federal agencies; state, local, and private entities; key professionals; and Indian tribes. In the final chapter, I summarize my "practical" perspective and critically evaluate a few important aspects of the current American heritage management system.

Because the primary purpose of this book is to serve as a college textbook, at the end of each chapter I provide some review questions about what I think are important aspects of the chapter for readers to remember. I also provide recommendations for supplemental readings, most of which were cited in the chapter. Readers can consider Tom King's *Cultural Resource Laws and Practice: An Introductory Guide* (2013) supplemental reading for any heritage management class. Many of the supplemental readings I have included are easily accessible online or through a university library system. Some of the supplemental readings may appear to be quite dated, but they still provide valuable insight, considering the basic federal system has not changed much over the past 50 years, despite Tom King's best efforts to improve it.

I have intentionally tried not to burden the text with too many embedded references, as much of my discussion utilizes well-known information—which I think should be common knowledge in heritage management. I have noted basic sources in the text and/or in the supplemental readings. I have also based much of the text on my personal observations about American heritage management. I also do not use footnotes, as they tend to distract readers and break the rhythm of the writing and the reading. Any references I deem necessary I have tried to put in the text.

The reader will also note that I occasionally repeat something that was present in similar form in an earlier chapter. This is most obvious with respect to historic background. I do this for two reasons. First, I stress throughout the book that laws, regulations, and practice are directly linked to historic context. You can't understand the why without knowing the what and the when. Second, repetition promotes retention. In most instances, I repeat what I think is important and should be remembered.

Finally, much of this book is from a Minnesotan perspective. Although I attended graduate school in Nebraska and have traveled widely in North America and abroad, my full-time jobs have all been in Minnesota. My Minnesota emphasis does not have many adverse implications for most of the chapters, with the possible exception of the state and local chapter (chapter 10) and some elements of the chapters about professional practice (chapters 11 and 12). My perspectives on the history of American heritage management, federal laws, and federal agencies should have universal application. States and agencies share many of the professional practices in heritage management. I have tried to include non-Minnesotan perspectives and examples. My Minnesotan and midwestern perspective may strike some as naive and myopic, especially my basic conclusion that the system we have is usually effective in preserving the most important elements of our tangible cultural heritage.

Final but Important Note

In 2014, the federal government recodified the National Historic Preservation Act from Title 16 to Title 54 of the United States Code (USC) of laws. This recodification also renumbered all the individual sections in the act and put together in Subdivision 5 the two sections most familiar to federal agencies and most practitioners: Section 106 (dealing with agencies' heritage management responsibilities on projects they oversee) and Section 110 (dealing with federal agencies' heritage management responsibilities on properties they manage). Section 106 is now Section 306108 and appears in the middle of Subdivision 5. The rest of Subdivision 5 includes the old Section 110 from Section 306101 to 306114, excepting 306108. The Advisory Council on Historic Preservation (ACHP), most SHPOs, most federal agencies, and most practitioners still use the pre-2014 NHPA section numbers, so I will continue to do so in this book, although I will occasionally note the new section numbers. Tables 3.1 and 4.1 summarize these changes with respect to important heritage preservation laws and the sections of the NHPA.

ACKNOWLEDGMENTS

I have been incredibly fortunate to be associated with bright and caring people throughout my education as a North American archaeologist and my employment as a heritage management professional. At the University of Minnesota for my BA and PhD, Elden Johnson and Guy Gibbon directed my archaeological endeavors, with interdisciplinary support from Herb Wright (paleoecology, glacial geology) and Fred Lukermann (geography). At the University of Nebraska for my MA, my advisor Dale Henning was my principal field and classroom mentor, while Carl Falk of the National Park Service's Midwest Archaeological Center (MWAC) supplied me with a job, lab skills, and professional focus. Dale continues to be a source of knowledge and inspiration.

In my first full-time job at the Minnesota Historical Society, Doug Birk introduced me to historical archaeology, and Les Peterson showed me the basics of being a survey archaeologist. Clem Kachelmyer at the Minnesota Department of Transportation was patient with my initial inexperience and academic divergences. I did my first site mitigation with Mike Michlovic and Julie Stein, two consummate and caring professionals. Mike has continued to lend intellectual and psychological support throughout my career. Craig Johnson, fellow University of Minnesota and University of Nebraska student, has been continually helpful with specialized advice and cautions.

Moving on to the Minnesota State Historic Preservation Office (SHPO), as the staff archaeologist, I was exceptionally fortunate to work closely with three of the most experienced and knowledgeable SHPO professionals in the country: Dennis Gimmestad (architectural historian), Susan Roth (historian), and Charlie Nelson (historical architect). In my last full-time job as Minnesota state archaeologist, my assistant, Bruce Koenen, patiently led me through my first burial authentications and sympathetically smoothed my way through many of the intricacies of the state bureaucracy.

As I started to write this book, I leaned on many of the people listed above for help with various issues. I also got some assistance from Greg Donofrio, Denis Gardner, and Sue Granger for things architectural and historical. I owe a great debt to my former SHPO colleagues in other states through the National Conference of State Historic Preservation Officers list-serve and my state archeologist colleagues on the National Association of State Archaeologists list-serve for their patience with my frequent and sometimes obscure questions. Thanks to three peer reviewers of the first draft of this book for their very helpful and supportive comments.

Bill Beeman and Kara Kersteter of the Department of Anthropology at the University of Minnesota graciously continued my status as an adjunct professor while I wrote this book, allowing me full library and internet journal access. At Rowman & Littlefield, Nancy Roberts and Megan Manzano lent continual editorial support, while Jehanne Schweitzer oversaw the production process and Jen Kelland provided superb copy editing.

Last and certainly most, my wife, Pat, has been incredibly understanding and patient with my archaeological affliction for 40 years. I couldn't have done this book and most other important things in my life without her.

Scott F. Anfinson grew up in the western Minnesota town of Benson, where his father ran the newspaper, his mother was the hospital dietitian, and his five siblings made life interesting. He received his bachelor's degree in anthropology with an archaeology specialty from the University of Minnesota in 1972. After finishing his master's work in anthropology/archaeology at the University of Nebraska in 1975, he was hired by the Minnesota Historical Society to lead the Minnesota Municipal-County Highway Archaeology Survey.

For 15 years he traveled throughout Minnesota, conducting hundreds of reconnaissance and evaluation surveys. After completing an extensive literature search for a proposed parkway along the central Minneapolis riverfront, he coordinated a major survey and salvage effort in the 1980s involving numerous historical archaeological sites. He served on the City of Minneapolis Riverfront Technical Advisory Committee promoting historic preservation on the city's rapidly evolving central xxiv About the Author

riverfront. He entered the PhD program in anthropology at the University of Minnesota, where he was awarded a PhD in 1987.

In 1990, he became the first full-time archaeologist for the Minnesota State Historic Preservation Office (MnSHPO), a job focused on implementing the National Historic Preservation Act. At MnSHPO, he reviewed development projects under Section 106, wrote and edited National Register of Historic Places nominations, helped with preservation planning, served on historic structure reuse and design guideline teams, and led a historic shipwrecks survey. He also helped train and worked closely with some of the first tribal historic preservation officers in the country.

In 1999, Anfinson was asked to develop a course on heritage management for the University of Minnesota's Anthropology Department. Over the next 15 years, he taught graduate and undergraduate students from anthropology, architecture, history, and museum studies. He also served on numerous thesis and dissertation committees in anthropology and architecture.

In 2006, Anfinson became the state archaeologist for Minnesota, a job focused on implementing state laws and maintaining the state's archaeological inventory. In 2008, after the passage of Minnesota's Legacy Amendment, he became a member of the oversight board for the Minnesota Statewide Survey of Historical and Archaeological Sites, developing numerous requests for proposals and guiding over $2 million in research projects. He retired as state archaeologist in 2016.

Anfinson has written and edited numerous publications in his 40 years as a Minnesota archaeologist, including *A Handbook of Minnesota Prehistoric Ceramics* (1978), *The Archaeology of the Central Minneapolis Riverfront* (1989, 1990), *Southwestern Minnesota Archaeology* (1997), and *Manual for Archaeological Projects in Minnesota* (2011). He has served as president of the Council for Minnesota Archaeology and editor of the *Minnesota Archaeologist*.

About the Cover

The cover photo illustrates many of the heritage management topics covered in this book pertinent to archaeology, history, architecture, and museums. It shows a portion of the St. Anthony Falls National Register Historic District in Minneapolis. On the right is the Washburn A Mill, in the center are two sets of grain elevators, and on the left is the Tyrone Guthrie Theater. Hidden beneath the grass in the foreground are multiple ruins of flour mills. When these mills were operating in the late nineteenth and early twentieth centuries, they helped make Minneapolis the flour-milling capital of the world. They are now archaeological sites. Portions have been uncovered as part of Mill Ruins Park, as shown in the author's photo.

When the Washburn A Mill was built in 1878, it was the largest flour mill in the world, becoming the flagship mill of the Washburn-Crosby Company, the parent of General Mills. Two years later, its capacity was eclipsed by the Pillsbury A Mill directly across the Mississippi River. The Washburn A Mill closed in 1965, was listed in the National Register of Historic Places in 1971, and became a National Historic Landmark in 1983. It burned in 1991, destroying most of the building along with the historic milling equipment inside and creating the high-wall ruin that exists today. In 2003, the Minnesota Historical Society opened the Mill City Museum within the ruins, the only major flour-milling museum in the United States. The scaffolding shown on the far-right side of the cover photo demonstrates the continual maintenance issues presented by masonry ruins in temperate climates.

The two sets of grain elevators stored the wheat for the Washburn A Mill to convert into flour. They consist of concrete cylinders capped with a headhouse that contained the equipment to transfer the wheat into the mill. Railroad tracks fed directly into the milling complex, bringing in wheat from the western prairies and shipping out flour to the world. The concrete grain elevator was developed in Minneapolis in 1899 by the Peavey Company with the construction of a single-cylinder structure that still exists on the west edge of Minneapolis. (It too is listed in the National Register as the Peavey-Haglin Elevator.) The larger cylinders shown in the cover photo were built in 1906, with the smaller cylinders to the right completed in 1926. Although such structures are still common, it is almost impossible to find a practical reuse for historic grain elevators.

The Tyrone Guthrie Theater opened in 2006. It replaced a 1963 structure that was located well away from the historic milling district. The new theater was designed by noted French architect Jean Nouvel. The Minnesota State Historic Preservation Office (SHPO) approved the theater's construction within the historic district because it did not destroy any existing historic buildings or significant archaeological sites, and although the design was radically different from the adjacent historic buildings, it contained design elements that invoked the historic structures (e.g., cylinders) without trying to imitate them. The SHPO did oppose the demolition of the old Guthrie Theater, which had been designed by local architect Ralph Rapson.

CHAPTER 1

The Purpose, Structure, and Language of American Heritage Management

Heritage is everything that people want to save.

—Peter Howard

Yesterday's heritage becomes today's history.

—David Lowenthal

You can't understand American **heritage management** without understanding why it is done, how it is organized, and the language it speaks. I will repeatedly examine these three fundamental concepts throughout this book. This first chapter gives you some basics for each.

The "why" requires an examination of the purpose of heritage **management**. Purpose varies by perspective. Everyone is interested in preserving something, but the number and kinds of properties officially "worthy" of **preservation** vary by interest and motive. Cities want to preserve elements of their unique **history** as well as a critical mass of **historic** properties in some neighborhoods and commercial **districts** to maintain their populations and stimulate economic development. The motive of agencies began with fulfilling their legal obligations, but for some, historic preservation has also become mission supportive. Most private groups focus on their particular interests and are often less fretful about authenticity as long as they can satisfy their founding ideals and their current membership. States get caught in the middle between their federal duties and their citizens' demands. Tribes want to preserve their identities.

To understand how American **heritage** management is organized, you need to look at the key building blocks of the system. The basic structure is made up of a number of environmental review laws supplemented by a number of specialty laws. You need to look inside the structure for the key players at various levels. You need to know how the players interact with the structure and with each other.

The language of preservation concerns not only the definitions of key terms and concepts but how they are employed and by whom. **Archaeologists, historians,** and architects speak different professional languages but share a somewhat common preservation vocabulary. Federal agencies developed much of this vocabulary in response to implementation of federal legislation. Embedded in the title and subtitle of this book are many of the key terms: "heritage," "practical," "management," "tangible," and "preservation." Think of how you would define each of these terms prior to reading how I define them.

This book is not a comprehensive study of all potential aspects of heritage management. It does not cover all types of **cultural resources** and is not a textbook for all **cultural heritage** management applications. I have intentionally avoided addressing some of the most controversial issues concerning American heritage management—what some call the intangible aspects. Many of the issues not covered relate to social **impact** assessment (SIA) and environmental justice (EJ). These issues mainly pertain to only one law: the National Environmental Policy Act (NEPA).

I am not avoiding these issues because I am unfamiliar with them or don't think they are important. I don't address them because the great majority of cultural heritage preservation as required and practiced in this country doesn't need to deal with them. They are tangential to the work of most American heritage management agencies, organizations, and professionals as required by law. Dealing with them is not what I did day-to-day as a survey archaeologist, a **state historic preservation office** (SHPO) archaeologist, and a state archaeologist. Read Tom King (2013) if you want an introduction to SIA and EJ issues from a heritage management perspective, as well as a justification for including the less tangible aspects of cultural heritage.

So this book is about those heritage **resources** that are the focus of most of the heritage preservation laws and about what most of the agencies and heritage preservation professionals deal with on a day-to-day basis. Like it or not, this focus is ultimately determined by the **National Register of Historic Places** (NRHP). Like the NRHP, this book addresses only those heritage resources that can be seen and touched. We can refer to them as **tangible cultural heritage**. American heritage management focuses on places and things—places usually containing visible remnants of the past that have definable geographic boundaries and things with a solid substance that can be photographed in the field, analyzed in a laboratory, or collected and conserved in a museum.

This book is about teaching you not to do a perfect job as a cultural heritage manager but only to make an effort that fulfills what our laws require. In the trade this is sometimes known as "a reasonable and good faith effort." This phrase comes from 36 CFR 800, the implementing regulations for Section 106 of the National Historic Preservation Act (NHPA). It doesn't mean doing just an adequate job. It means addressing what the intent and letter of the law require and carrying out your heritage management obligations in a responsible, efficient, effective, and ethical manner.

Dealing with only tangible heritage resources and stressing a reasonable and good faith effort to preserve them is at the core of what I call a *practical* approach. It is an approach that took me a long time to learn and, as an anthropologist, to feel comfortable implementing. It is an approach that is unsatisfying to many. Some of the unsatisfied lack a comprehensive and detailed understanding of how American heritage management was constructed, the functions it is supposed to serve, and what the main players are required to do. Some of the unsatisfied may have unrealistic expectations as to what can be done with existing funding within agencies whose principal mission is not heritage preservation. Some of the unsatisfied strive for an ideal where all **significant** cultural resources, not just the tangible ones, are officially deemed worthy of preservation.

I hope that by the end of the book all readers will come to understand the difference between the practical and the ideal and why this text and American heritage management focus on the tangible. I am not proposing that we abandon investigating a better way of doing heritage management or that we ignore **intangible cultural resources**. I simply stress what is currently required in the day-to-day work and what is currently doable based on resources and obligations. I believe a practical approach can achieve a reasonable level of protection for what we really can preserve, especially in times of limited budgets and unsympathetic politics.

The Purpose of Heritage Management

If you become a heritage management professional, someday you may be asked the "Why do it?" question at a public meeting, by a reporter, or at a legislative committee hearing. The questioners don't really care about your personal interests or your preservation passion. They want to know why tax dollars are being spent on something that seems to have little value for increasing revenue, promoting national security, or improving people's lives. Be prepared to address the purpose of heritage preservation with an answer that isn't about why you personally do it and doesn't rely on a simplistic or generic answer about preserving knowledge or saving the past.

You would think that all textbooks about heritage management, **cultural resource management** (CRM), and **historic preservation** would start by justifying them, or at least explaining why they are done and why they are important. Most don't, implying through their content that we do these things because it is legally required or publicly popular, and that is enough of an explanation. Indeed, we do heritage preservation for both of these reasons, but neither explains the basis of how it became popular, how it became the law, why we should keep doing it, and what inherent value it has for American society.

Robert Stipe's *A Richer Heritage* (2003) is one of the few textbooks to begin with an examination of the "why" of heritage preservation, although his prologue is relatively short and basically repeats a 1972 article he wrote for *Preservation News*. I guess the reasons for doing it haven't changed that much over the half century since the National Historic Preservation Act was passed. The "why" has always included a few fundamental and universal reasons: to preserve our links with our ancestors, to preserve our national identity, to demonstrate to outsiders the essence of our **culture**, and to promote economic development. Heritage preservation is done in most other countries for the same basic reasons as it is done in the United States, although emphasis and terminology may differ based on culture, economic needs, politics, and governmental structure.

All reasons for heritage preservation in the United States necessarily represent a compromise between constitutional rights and community needs. Constitutional rights favor individuals and states, while community needs rely on the actions of federal and city governments. Constitutional restrictions prevent American heritage preservation from taking a truly comprehensive approach, but federal oversight promotes heritage preservation on a national scale, and widely shared community ideals make the system somewhat consistent and understandable.

We can put the reasons for heritage preservation into three basic categories:

- Ideational considerations
- Conservation of resources
- Economic benefits

Like heritage writ large, tangible and intangible aspects make up these categories. Ideational considerations have less tangible objectives, while the other two categories are more tangible. Tangible objectives are easier to justify to politicians and the public and have more immediate impacts, but intangible objectives are perhaps the more important because they support a sustainability not dependent on current legislation, political whims, or economic conditions.

Examples of all three categories appear in Section 1(b) of the NHPA, which declares the congressional intent of the act. The most important of these, by their subsection numbers, are

> (1) the spirit and direction of the Nation are founded upon and reflected in its historic heritage;
> (2) the **historical** and cultural foundations of the Nation should be preserved as a living part of our community life and development in order to give a sense of orientation to the American people;
> . . .
> (4) the preservation of this irreplaceable heritage is in the public interest so that its vital legacy of cultural, educational, aesthetic, inspirational, economic, and energy benefits will be maintained and enriched for future generations of Americans;
> (5) in the face of ever-increasing extensions of urban centers, highways, and residential, commercial, and industrial developments, the present governmental and non-governmental historic preservation programs and activities are inadequate to insure future generations a genuine opportunity to appreciate and enjoy the rich heritage of our Nation;
> (6) the increased knowledge of our historic resources, the establishment of better means of identifying and administering them, and the encouragement of their preservation will improve the **planning** and execution of Federal and federally assisted projects and will assist economic growth and development.

The most common justifications for heritage preservation promoted by SHPOs and national historic preservation organizations are economic, but ideational and conservation aspects dominate archaeological and tribal justifications for doing heritage preservation. Outside of environmental review **mitigation**, most **archaeological sites** and activities are not eligible for tax breaks or development grants. Exceptional **sites** like ruins can promote tourism, but most archaeological sites are modest in scope or visually unexciting. Archaeologists' only real advantage is that their subject matter is interesting to most people, provided that it is visually apparent or presented in an understandable and attractive way. Most tribes don't worry much about justifying their heritage preservation efforts because, to them, the reason is obvious. They are preserving their heritage.

Ideational Considerations

While a few economic benefits are listed in the NHPA declarations of congressional intent in paragraphs 4 and 6 above and a conservation benefit is briefly mentioned as "energy benefits" in paragraph 4, the emphasis of congressional intent was clearly on ideational aspects of preserving our historic heritage. According to Section 1(b) of the NHPA, these aspects

- are the foundation of the spirit and direction of the nation (paragraph 1)
- are a living part of community life that provide a sense of orientation (paragraph 2)
- are a vital legacy of cultural, educational, aesthetic, and inspirational benefits (paragraph 4)
- provide future generations a genuine opportunity to enjoy a rich cultural heritage (paragraph 5)

Ideational consideration is the oldest reason for American heritage preservation. It has its roots more in local pride than in national patriotism, although today it is mostly about the latter when it comes to the places that were first preserved: Mount Vernon and Independence Hall. Early American historic preservation focused on events directly associated with the founding of the United States and preserving places directly associated with the Founding Fathers, especially George Washington. It was geographically and chronologically limited to the cradle of the Revolutionary War from Virginia to Massachusetts.

FIG. 1.1 An originally envisioned perfect past at Colonial Williamsburg—perfectly painted, perfectly clean, and perfectly friendly (Library of Congress).

Through time, local pride has morphed into attempts to preserve an American way of life romanticized into manifestations and justifications that would be largely unrecognizable to the people who lived in the past. Examples are Greenfield Village and Colonial Williamsburg (Figure 1.1). More recently, preservation has become an effort to maintain or improve quality of life. Some perceptions of ways and quality of life, however, are unrealistic and deceptive.

Ideational aspects supporting American heritage preservation include specialized applications such as promoting esprit de corps in the military, where tradition pervades every base and is critical to reinforcing discipline and incentive. The Department of Defense doesn't preserve old **buildings** on bases just because of federal legal requirements. Almost every military base has a museum, not to entertain its soldiers but to support the importance of their mission. Soldiers of all ranks are invested in traditions, including places and objects of historic **significance** to the American military (Figure 1.2).

FIG. 1.2 Building esprit de corps through historic preservation at the 2017 grand opening of the restored historic Long Barracks at Fort Sam Houston in San Antonio, Texas (US Army).

Ideational considerations include educational aspects, although education could be a stand-alone justification for heritage preservation. We can learn just from textbooks, but we learn best and more accurately when the interpreted past is augmented with examples and tangible remnants. The tangible past is also not as subjective as the interpreted past. The words of the original Declaration of Independence and the original US Constitution under glass at the National Archives can't be changed through political will or for convenience. Monticello, by its location and design, is a testament to the worldliness yet Virginia ruralness of Thomas Jefferson's outlook on life and what he thought the nation should be. "Memory and history both derive and gain authenticity from physical remains" (Lowenthal 2015:19).

Ideational considerations also include more generalized and intangible aspects, such as preserving knowledge for knowledge's sake and art for art's sake. Heritage preservation makes the past more understandable, more meaningful, and less remote. Without the past, the present is much less interesting and the future less predictable. To some, like William Faulkner, the present is the past.

Conservation of Resources

Conservation involves the preservation and judicious use of important resources. Resources can be natural, cultural, or a combination of both. In the mid-twentieth century, efforts for the conservation of natural resources broadened beyond concern for pieces of land and species of animals to include all aspects of the natural environment, including water and air. The conservation movement became the environmental movement. In the 1960s, federal legislation blended cultural and natural resources, requiring the consideration of the total **human environment**.

While the focus of the environmental movement was initially, and still is, on natural resources, cultural resource preservation has greatly benefited from inclusion in environmental protection legislation. What is now known as the "green movement" has also been incorporated into heritage preservation by the promotion of the sustainability of vital resources and the reduction of greenhouse gases that cause climatic warming.

The preservation and **rehabilitation** of historic structures promotes sustainability by reusing existing **materials**. This reduces both the need for new materials that deplete important resources and the use of pollution-producing energy for the transformation of resources into usable materials. It further cuts down on pollution by reducing demolition debris in landfills. It promotes efficiency by limiting sprawl, which lessens transportation needs and new construction. Conservation is a progressive yet practical approach to heritage preservation.

Economic Benefits

The economic benefits of historic preservation are of three basic types: local economic development, acquisition of nonlocal income, and community revitalization. These are the aspects of heritage preservation most familiar to architects, cities, and private organizations. They are also the aspects of heritage preservation most widely promoted by **state historic preservation officers**, as demonstrated by their discussions at statewide meetings and the publications featured on many SHPO webpages.

The focus of economic considerations is almost exclusively on urban historic buildings. Not only are the results clearly visible in restored structures, increased tourism, and attractive neighborhoods, but the economic aspects of heritage preservation are the most easily measured in terms of actual metrics. Measurability increases political visibility, increasing legal and financial support. Economic considerations of heritage preservation are also popular because they involve more carrots than sticks.

Economic development focuses largely on communities because needs are most visible and resources most concentrated at the local level. Communities thrive or struggle based on their location, the vitality of their occupants, and their access to resources. We can promote economic development by many methods employed by all levels of government and private heritage preservation organizations. Governments can provide tax incentives and direct grants for rehabilitating historic properties that meet significance and architectural **standards**. Entities can acquire public funds for historic preservation through programs whose principal purpose is to promote something other than heritage preservation, like various transportation enhancement initiatives of the Federal Highway Administration (FHWA). Private organizations can offer expertise and guidance such as that provided by the National Trust for Historic Preservation (NTHP) through its Main Street Program.

The principal acquisition of nonlocal income with regard to heritage occurs through tourism. Tourism is promoted by maintaining districts that have historic character or individual historic buildings or archaeological sites important for their architecture, original occupants, or the historic activities that took place there. House museums were among the earliest heritage tourism sites, giving visitors insight into the lives of important people or a feeling for the way people lived in the past. Heritage tourism has become big business in some communities, such as New Orleans, where entire neighborhoods, like the French Quarter, invoke the past but are accessible in the present.

Maintaining or restoring **historic districts** can not only promote tourism but also help revitalize neighborhoods and commercial districts. This benefits cities by making certain areas more attractive and increasing property values, thereby increasing property tax revenue. This encourages younger and more affluent families to remain in interesting neighborhoods and businesses to remain in viable commercial districts, in addition to increasing the attractiveness of the neighborhoods and commercial districts to potential new occupants.

The Structure of Heritage Management

We can think of the formal structure of American heritage management as an old building with many additions and alterations. Originally built in various styles, it has been renovated to fit the times. Inside it has many rooms of various sizes on several levels, occupied by entities of varying importance. The foundation of the building is made of a key law passed in 1966, although there are some structural remnants of earlier laws. The keystone of the building's main support is our way of determining what is worth preserving. The walls are built of other important laws and the roof of policies and procedures implementing and interpreting those laws. The mortar holding everything together is our legal system.

The building's occupants are the key players in agencies and organizations. The most important of these are found on the ground floor, with others scattered throughout the building, some in big rooms and some in small. The daily work and maintenance is done by professionals, some more experienced and more involved than others. The original occupants of the neighborhood, the newest occupants of the building, have only recently been invited to move in.

In 2016 the building celebrated two anniversaries. Its foundation, the National Historic Preservation Act, had been laid 50 years before, and one of its most important occupants, the National Park Service, had just turned 100. These anniversaries created an opportunity to ask some important questions: What is the building's historic context? Is the foundation adequate? Is the keystone faulty? Are the walls and roof sound? Do the rooms need remodeling? Are the occupants and mainte-nance workers doing a good job? Most importantly, is the building worth preserv-ing, or should we tear it down and build something new?

A major part of this book examines the structure of American heritage manage-ment. It should help you understand how the structure was built, how its compo-nents were meant to function and how they actually do, and what roles its occupants play. By examining these aspects, we can start to address questions about the struc-ture's soundness and propose solutions for repair or replacement. The book may not directly answer all questions, but it should provide the background necessary to frame the right questions and begin to address some of them in a constructive way.

The Language of Heritage Management

To understand American heritage management, you must be familiar not only with its reason for being, its structure, and its principal players but with the language the players use. The words we employ and the meanings we accept for them often deter-mine our focus and our methods. We necessarily use many acronyms, as you may have already noticed. The key terms for understanding the focus of this book are "practical," "heritage," "management," "reasonable," "good faith," "**protect**," and "tangible." I will now define and explain them in what I think is a logical order.

What Is Heritage?

In the United States we have only recently begun to use the word "heritage" with regard to management of our cultural resources. We first referred to resources man-aged by archaeologists, historians, and architects with a different *h* word: "historic." Preserving important parts of the past effectively became "historic preservation" in 1949 with the founding of the National Trust for Historic Preservation. The passage of the National Historic Preservation Act in 1966 established historic preservation as a widespread government endeavor.

In the mid-twentieth century, historic preservation focused mostly on build-ings and places where nationally important people lived or nationally important events took place. It was mainly the practice of historians and **historical archi-tects**, although archaeologists were included when **reconstruction** of a **historic site** was needed from below the ground up or in dealings with in-between **property types** like ruins. Archaeologists at the time didn't complain about being marginal-ized by historic preservation because they were too busy salvaging sites in quickly filling reservoirs or pursuing traditional research interests wholly outside historic preservation.

American archaeologists, with their anthropological education promoting an egalitarian view of society, decided in the mid-1970s to broaden the scope of his-toric preservation to include other types of resources found in the **built environment** (see the glossary in Appendix A for a definition). Since we didn't know peoples' names and rarely could identify important events in prehistoric times, we didn't think much about the level of site significance in national, state, or local terms. The word "culture" was the basis for what our parent discipline studied, and the word "resources" had become popular with the environmental movement of the mid-1960s, so we hitched them together. Historic preservation for archaeologists became "cultural resource management." While we knew cultural resources included much more than archaeological sites, archaeologists initially paid little attention to the broader scope of what CRM implied.

While historic preservationists (i.e., historians and architects) and cultural resource specialists (i.e., archaeologists) continued to drift apart, by the late twentieth century, both groups had also begun to broaden their property-type horizons. Historic preservationists became aware of historic landscapes, and archaeologists became aware of sites from the recent past and **traditional cultural properties**. Suddenly, property types began overlapping as cultural, historical, and part of a nonstructural environment. The natural environment, which had been considered an unbuilt environment, was intruding into historic/cultural property types.

In the late twentieth century, with improved transportation and communication, we increasingly became part of a global society. United Nations organizations and preservationists in other countries had long been using the word "heritage" to refer to what was worth preserving of the past. They also thought of heritage as a blend of the natural and the cultural. The National Trust in England preserves and manages both natural lands and historic sites. If you talk heritage management in Canada, you are talking to educators and managers of both cultural and natural resources.

As postmodern approaches became academically dominant in history, architecture, and **archaeology** in the late twentieth century, new perspectives on the past emerged. Archaeologists became concerned less with cultural processes and more with studying recent societies and all types of people in them in a more collaborative manner. Architects learned how to work outside the modernist box with new designs more compatible with historic settings. Historians began to tell multiple stories of the past, abandoning a single narrative.

Thus, by the end of the twentieth century, American government and American academic institutions had many reasons to start using a more inclusive term for a discipline focused on preserving and interpreting our collective past. Use of the word "heritage" has become common in the federal government and in some university departments that train professionals in the field of preservation. In some ways, heritage, as a broad concept applied to our current heritage management system, has become overused, with a resulting loss of focus for meeting effective and reasonable legally mandated management objectives.

So what is heritage? An archaeologist friend of mine, Mike Michlovic, says, "Heritage is things we like." That is probably how most people think of it, certainly the people at English Heritage or at *American Heritage* magazine. But we also have an important heritage of things we don't like, preserved and interpreted in places like Auschwitz and Wounded Knee. Heritage preservation is not just about attractive places either. We preserve places that lack charm, and we interpret places with mundane functions, such as industrial complexes.

David Lowenthal's *The Heritage Crusade and the Spoils of History* (1998) explicitly looks at heritage from a historian's perspective. As I read the preface, introduction, and first chapters, I searched for his definition of heritage. It wasn't there, which puzzled me. How could he focus on heritage in his title and not explicitly define it? I found many hints early in the book as to what he considered heritage to be or at least how he used the term. "Yesterday's heritage becomes today's history" (p. x). Heritage as a link with the past is joined by "history, tradition, memory, myth, and memoir" (p. 3). Heritage is becoming "more substantial, more secular, and more social" (p. 14). Heritage is "what we hold jointly with others" (p. 60). And finally, "Heritage today all but defies definition" (p. 94).

A common definition of heritage is "things passed down," which implies an intent to preserve something tangible from one's generation or something one inherited by passing it down to the next generation. Much of our material heritage is just left over, discarded, lost, or ignored stuff. Another definition of heritage is "everything that people want to save" (Howard 2003:1). This is heritage made up of what people have intentionally collected, what agencies have inventoried, and what laws are meant to protect. It is all the good stuff from our past, or at least what people, organizations, and governments think is the good stuff.

If we omit the quality judgment of goodness and the requirement of intent to pass down, we are left with a concept of heritage as simply remnants of the past. This is true of both the cultural and the natural. Yellowstone National Park is mostly about natural heritage. A Civil War battlefield is mostly about cultural heritage. Each generation has a different view as to what from the past is important to save and pass down to the next generation. Worthiness ultimately guides heritage preservation.

For American cultural heritage management, properties listed in or eligible for the National Register of Historic Places are those "worthy of preservation" (NRHP 1997a:i). In the federal government's view, what is worthy of preservation in the cultural environment is eligible for the National Register, and what is worthy of recording or evaluating for a public project is potentially eligible. What is worthy of study for a private project is interesting to the principal investigator, the private funder, or the private landowner. What is worthy of preservation as a portable **artifact** is what an archaeologist will put in a bag and a museum will then accept. What is worthy of interpretation is a combination of what the public wants and what interpreters think it should have. Assessment of worth in heritage management is largely based on ownership, interest, and rules.

What Is Tangible Cultural Heritage?

We also base assessment of heritage and its relative worth in the American heritage management system on what is tangible and what is intangible. *Tangible cultural heritage*, for the purposes of most American heritage laws, is made up of remnants of the past that are either places deemed worthy of preservation because they are eligible for inclusion in the National Register of Historic Places, or cultural items such as archaeological artifacts required to be preserved by law, and objects deemed worthy of preservation by museums. Tangible heritage by definition dominates historic preservation and by practice dominates cultural resource management. Buildings, structures, archaeological and historical sites, objects, and assemblages of these property types in districts are examples of tangible cultural heritage.

In addition, these tangible remnants must be from a past that is sufficiently distant to be considered historical. The National Register has set a 50-year minimum for what is sufficiently old enough to be eligible for inclusion in the Register, although it allows exceptions to this **guideline** if a **property** attains exceptional significance in less than 50 years. For archaeological sites, some federal agencies suggest a 100-year guideline, although even these agencies must obey the National Register's 50-year rule when it comes to environmental impact assessments.

Intangible cultural heritage is made up of nonmaterial aspects of cultural behavior, such as religious practices, subsistence-settlement preferences, social institutions, language, oral traditions, ceremonies, morals, values, and performing arts. Behavior associated with these aspects can result in physical (tangible) manifestations such as structures (e.g., a theater) and objects (e.g., a statue). The physical remains of cultural behavior rather than the behavior itself are the focus of our legally mandated preservation efforts.

Much to the regret of Tom King and many others who appreciate and see the value of addressing the entire scope of sociocultural behavior, American heritage preservation as required by federal law focuses only on tangible cultural heritage. Of the broad environmental protection laws, only NEPA could be interpreted to include (but generally doesn't in practice) intangible aspects of our cultural heritage.

So required heritage preservation considers only a small portion of our heritage. It looks at only remnants directly related to the cultural history of a distant-enough past (i.e., at least 50 years), only tangible remnants (i.e., places and things), and only properties that have been deemed significant and have reasonable **integrity** according to National Register rules. Remnants of heritage on public property have a better chance of being preserved than remnants on private property. Remnants affected by public projects have a better chance of being preserved than those affected by private projects. This is a reflection of the constitutional basis for our system of government.

The only major exception to the tangible, age-graded focus of heritage resource preservation laws has to do with Indian religion. The American Indian Religious Freedom Act and Executive Order 13007 require federal agencies to consider the **effects** of their actions on the practice of Indian religion, which would include protecting sacred places on **federal land** and allowing Indian practitioners reasonable access to them. Sacred places, unlike National Register–eligible places, have no age requirement. The believers, not a National Register bulletin, determine what is considered sacred and whether a place maintains sufficient integrity to manifest its sacredness. For non-Indians, the American Folklife Preservation Act encourages preservation of traditional American **cultural practices** but does not require their consideration in most environmental review processes.

In discussing heritage management, this book focuses on preserving places because this is what the laws require. Portable heritage objects present in these places are preferably left in situ, because their removal will harm the integrity of the place. If the place is harmed to the point that it is no longer eligible for the National Register, it may no longer be worthy of preservation. Objects removed from heritage places should be preserved in responsible museums and archives based on federal regulations and each museum's guidelines as to what objects are worthy of preservation and how they should be treated. Objects in museums, however, are not eligible for the National Register due to the loss of integrity of **location, setting,** and **feeling**.

For the purposes of this book and its discussion of cultural heritage resources as they are addressed by federal law as well as by most state and local laws, *heritage consists of tangible remnants of the past that are places deemed worthy of preservation because they are eligible for inclusion in the National Register of Historic Places or are cultural items required to be preserved or protected by law and standard professional practice.* Some, especially anthropologists, may find this definition of heritage very unsatisfying, but it is practical when considering effects to heritage as required by current American heritage preservation law and practice.

It is important to stress that history and archaeology are not heritage; history and archaeology are interpretations of the past, while heritage is the remnant of the past they study. Also, the terms "cultural resources" and "cultural heritage" are not synonymous. While both may include the full range of places and practices associated with human behavior, "heritage" requires a more distant past. Culture has no minimal requirement of antiquity and is constantly changing. A sacred site can be from yesterday, and although the cultural practices associated with it may have originated in a distant past, the place itself can be new. Heritage is usually at least a generation old. History is a view of what was; heritage is what time has left us.

What Is Management?

While writing this book, I would occasionally mention that I was doing so to people to prove to them that I was still working and still being useful. They initially seemed interested, especially if they knew or I had told them that I am an archaeologist. But when I told them the book's topic, heritage management, their eyes glazed over. They weren't really interested anymore. It didn't sound like the archaeology they saw in *National Geographic* or on the news.

I knew it wasn't the *h* word in my topic that caused the lack of enthusiasm, because everyone is interested in heritage. Heritage is recognizable and familiar, although we usually call it by some other name: George Washington's house, an ancient ruin, a shipwreck, a battlefield, an arrowhead, the family farm in Norway. It had to be the *m* word that turned people off. Management sounds necessary but not interesting, except perhaps to people with MBAs.

When I got my first full-time job after finishing my master's, archaeologists had just invented the term "cultural resource management" (soon shortened to CRM) (Lipe and Lindsay 1974). Although I had rarely thought about or been exposed to CRM while in college, when I got my job I thought of myself almost immediately as a CRM archaeologist. I knew what "cultural" meant because I had two degrees in anthropology. "Resources" for my purposes just meant archaeological sites and artifacts. I never thought much about the "management" part of the phrase. To me, CRM was just about doing archaeology in a nonacademic setting, where I didn't get to choose my research locations and I had to write an annual report. I still considered research a big part of what I did. After all, I had to follow a **research design** to do my fieldwork and analysis, and I was still finding familiar objects that I evaluated in familiar ways. I thought I was still doing science, not business.

Not many other archaeologists at the time apparently thought about the *m* word either. If you look at the numerous archaeological books with "management" in the title from the late 1970s, none of them define management unless they tack on "cultural resources" (e.g., Schiffer and Gumerman 1977; McGimsey and Davis 1977; Dickens and Hill 1978). Although cultural resource management had many definitions, the focus was always on the cultural resources (i.e., sites and artifacts), not on how practitioners or the profession managed them. "Management" simply referred to **identification, evaluation,** and sometimes preservation of these resources according to government guidelines.

A notable early discussion of management is Joseph Walka's 1979 *American Antiquity* article "Management Methods and Opportunities in Archaeology," in which he defines management as "planning, directing, and controlling resources toward the achievement of an objective" (p. 576). But his specific application is archaeological research, not cultural resource management, even though the article appears under the heading of CRM in the journal.

A few articles and book chapters in the 1980s paid a little more attention to what management was specifically with respect to CRM. Fowler (1982:21–22) briefly addressed concerns of reconciling management needs with research needs but didn't define management. Knudson (1986:402–404), in a short section titled "The Concept of Management," noted that planning is a key component of management but provided no comprehensive overview of what management is and does.

The absence of concern with what management really means is still lacking in most archaeologically oriented CRM books (e.g., King 2013; Messenger and Smith 2010; Sebastian and Lipe 2009). King (2013:1–3) appears to set up a discussion of what management is as he starts splitting up the three words in CRM. He notes that defining management "is a bit tricky" and that "CRM is always about somehow managing something," but then he retreats to the safe zone of just defining cultural resource management. He relegates management to mere handling of events and processes that affect cultural resources.

One notable exception regarding discussion of management in a recent archaeologically oriented heritage management textbook is Neumann and Sanford's *Practicing Archaeology* (2010). They focus, however, on the tasks of managers in archaeological settings rather than on management as a general concept. "Managerial responsibility is to achieve strategic goals through considered tactical initiatives" (Neumann and Sanford 2010:236). Based on the numerous entries under "management" in their index, tactical initiatives include obtaining contracts, finding and dealing with archaeological sites, guiding laboratory procedures, and completing reports, all for cultural resource management purposes. Their strategic goal could be interpreted as succeeding in business rather than in preserving heritage resources, although, to be fair, they stress that doing a good job is the way to succeed, and doing a good job certainly benefits archaeology and heritage preservation.

Historians and preservation architects haven't worried much about management aspects either, but at least "historic preservation" has no extra word tacked on. When preservation architects and historians occasionally mention management, they assume, just like most archaeologists, that we all know what it means. The subtitle of one of the most widely used historic preservation textbooks, James Fitch's *Historic Preservation: Curatorial Management of the Built World* (1990), does not define management or even list the word in the index. (Fitch also includes a chapter titled "The Heritage as Cultural Resource" with neither "heritage" nor "cultural resource" defined in the text or listed in the index.)

Not much guidance is forthcoming from key federal agencies as to what management is, especially as applied to heritage. A 2001 publication from the Advisory Council on Historic Preservation (ACHP) titled "Caring for the Past, Managing the Future" uses the word "management" multiple times on almost every page of the 100-page document; yet management is never defined. The term is applied to a resource in need of management (e.g., environment, land, facility, historical or cultural site), a resource assisting with management (e.g., personnel, partnership, research, funding), a management action (e.g., plan, program, approach, policy, **treatment**, manual), an issue requiring management (e.g., crisis, disaster, challenge), and a type of management action (e.g., long-term, priority, focused).

The key National Park Service document NPS-28: Cultural Resource Management Guideline uses management not only in the document title but in 6 of the 10 chapter titles. Yet it has no definition of management in the text or in the glossary. The "Selected Management Bibliography" in Appendix F is just a short list of general historic preservation/CRM references.

Although I have done cultural resource management for my whole professional career, I didn't think much about what management meant until I started teaching a university CRM class. Like King, I felt I had to break CRM down into its component parts in order to explain its purpose to students. Not being a business major, I had to do a little research as to what management really meant for cultural resources.

Using dictionary definitions seems lazy or like cheating (like using Wikipedia) and too anonymous. Some dictionary definitions are unsatisfying because they are circular (management: the act of managing), while others focus only on business applications (e.g., maximizing profit). Examining many definitions from multiple dictionaries, online discussions, and a few books (e.g., Drucker 1978; Murray 2010) helped me arrive at a meaning satisfying to me for heritage management purposes.

Common management verbs are "control," "organize," "plan," "direct," "staff," "coordinate," "allocate," "innovate," and "measure." The most common nouns are "plan," "mission," "resource," "objective," "strategy," "personnel," "leadership," "administration," and "result." The most common adjectives are "effective" and "efficient." General sound management advice includes understanding the operating environment, knowing what to do and when, and measuring results to evaluate success. You also need to understand that there is good management and bad. Best practices, due diligence, and risk assessment are popular business management concepts that have application in heritage resource management.

Also be aware that "CRM" is a more universally recognized acronym for "customer relations management." If you google CRM, you won't find the cultural resources variety for the first several hundred hits unless you add another word, like "archaeology" or "cultural," to the search. Many other uses of "CRM" as an acronym include crew resource management, cardiac rhythm management, and cockpit resource management. This may be another reason to use "cultural heritage management" instead of "cultural resource management" if you rely on acronyms in communication. Although not yet a very recognizable acronym for the topic discussed in this book, "CHM" doesn't yet have any better-known competitors (google it).

Putting all of this together, I would suggest this definition for "good" management: *the effective and efficient utilization of an organization's resources to achieve the objectives of the organization's mission.* "Effective" means successful and fulfilling. "Efficient" means competent, well-organized, competitive, and not wasteful. Resources are not just natural or cultural but include people, funding, facilities, and corporate knowledge. We can define the mission by a plan or the legislative intent expressed in a law. In order to evaluate efficiency and effectiveness, you need to constantly and comprehensively assess how resources are being defined and used and whether primary objectives are being accomplished. You also need to prepare for coping with unanticipated difficulties and capitalizing on unanticipated opportunities by promoting and being open to innovation. Your plan needs to be flexible and responsive to change.

So how does my definition of management apply to cultural heritage preservation? First, examine the objectives. Although this can vary somewhat by organization and **agency**, our overall objective is to preserve what is valuable from the past. If we can't preserve a valuable heritage resource, we must try to preserve some record of it or obtain some appropriate mitigation for its destruction.

Second, examine how we can be effective and efficient. We can only preserve what we have identified. We must then focus our efforts on what is truly important. We can best obtain effectiveness and efficiency through knowledge, experience, and innovation, based on the availability of resources such as personnel, facilities, and funding. Furthermore, we cannot find or evaluate all potentially important resources by ourselves; we need to consult with others who may have special knowledge of their location and special insight into their importance.

Finally, we must constantly try to maximize the protection of important heritage resources. We principally rely on environmental review legislation, although all valuable cultural resources on public property, especially federal land, generally have enhanced protection. Maximizing protection also includes carefully examining what we have done to see if we can do it better and more efficiently. Our ability to implement improvements will be limited by our resources and legal restrictions, but even incremental improvements such as reducing natural deterioration (e.g., fixing a roof, limiting erosion) can mean significantly enhanced preservation.

Good heritage management leads to good heritage preservation. If funding becomes more limited and laws less helpful, good management must adapt. Good management is also about knowing what not to do. Good management is ethical, timely, and practical. And yes, good management can be profitable.

What Is Practical Heritage Management?

Being practical means relying on experience and common sense rather than speculation, abstraction, idealism, or the theoretical. Practical applications fit situations in an effective and useful way. Practicality, in my experience, entails examining what has worked and not worked for me as a student of archaeology, a teacher of archaeology, a field archaeologist, a SHPO archaeologist, and a state archaeologist. Practical heritage management attempts to find effective, efficient, economical, and ethical solutions to everyday problems—solutions that address what is necessary and doable, not what is necessarily perfect or ideal.

A practical approach to heritage management examines methods to achieve the overall objective: the preservation of important heritage. When I attempt to fulfill legal requirements, I ask, What is absolutely necessary? What is allowable? Who is the principal client? When I teach a class, I ask, What are the most important takeaways from each class session? What are the most effective ways to help students learn and retain critical information? When in the field, I ask, What methods are reliable, considering constraints imposed by time, funding, and environmental conditions? When in the lab, I ask, What methods are appropriate to the research questions, as well as budgetary and time constraints? When in the office, I ask, What do I need to include in a report that fully yet economically and ethically satisfies stated objectives?

We can apply practical solutions to every aspect of heritage management: office review procedures, property discovery, artifact retention, property recording, property evaluation, property **registration**, reporting, and **consultation**. These solutions must be supportable, balanced, consistent, and reasonable.

Once again, we can apply the concept of worth when looking at a practical approach to heritage management. Not every archaeological site is worth finding. Not every site is worth recording. Not every site is worth evaluating. Not every site is worth registering. You apply worth in consideration of the person or entity you are doing the work for and his, her, or its responsibilities. There are many players in heritage management: agencies, professionals, academics, developers, communities, students, and the public. All have their own assessment of worth.

As you read this book, consider applications of possible practical solutions that I suggest and think of some of your own. Do this for every chapter. Do this for every discrete activity in every chapter. Practical heritage management is all about the everyday implementation of reasonable and effective methods to solve recurrent problems involving heritage preservation.

What Is Preservation?

Although, for the most part, we usually obtain our heritage management successes through **consideration** and consultation, these are not our objectives. Consideration gets our heritage management foot in the door, and consultation helps us to make an accurate and persuasive heritage preservation pitch. Our ultimate objective is to save important heritage resources. We have to sell the saving.

A number of apparent synonyms get used to describe the ultimate objective of heritage management: "saving," "conservation," "preservation," "protection." Yet these terms have slightly different meanings. To save is to rescue or preserve from injury. It requires only one action: the act of saving. It does not guarantee preservation. Additional saving may be needed for the same property in the future. "Save" is not a word used in most heritage management book titles (but note King 2007) or in phrases worthy of a heritage management acronym, but because it is almost synonymous with "preservation," it gets used a lot in discussions.

"Conservation" as applied to heritage management has its roots in nineteenth-century efforts to save the American wilderness from destruction and to keep certain areas indeed as wilderness. To do this, some influential conservationists realized they had to compromise to practically implement the idea through laws. Some of the resources being considered (e.g., certain kinds of wildlife and vegetational associations) were to be *maintained* but also *used* to a degree that they could be restored for use again in the future. Many state departments of natural resources (DNRs) were once called *conservation departments*. They were created not to preserve natural resources for wilderness maintenance or **restoration** but to provide sustainable resources for lumbering, hunting, and fishing.

American archaeological heritage management began to apply the word "conservation" in the early 1970s as an academic alternative to cultural resource management. Academic archaeologists (still the most common type in the 1970s) worried that a strict preservation ethic would discourage all site excavation (e.g., Cunningham 1974), encourage a development mentality that would threaten almost all sites (e.g., Lipe 1974), and not require that CRM archaeology results be utilized for archaeological research purposes. Schiffer and Gumerman (1977:xix), in their edited volume on the topic, emphasized that conservation archaeology entailed not just saving sites but using the results of CRM archaeology "to the fullest scientific and historic extent." The term "conservation" soon went out of fashion in archaeology as the prevention-of-excavation fear was never realized, there were more sites and more protected sites out there than we thought, and the use of CRM-generated results for general research became a matter of individual effort, just as it was in academic archaeology.

Most federal laws and regulations use "preserve" or "protect." It's the National Historic Preservation Act, the Archaeological and Historic Preservation Act, the Archaeological Resources Protection Act, the Native American Graves Protection and Repatriation Act, and the American Battlefield Protection Act. Considering their different meanings, you would think the split is appropriate when it comes to dealing with actions on federal property versus those federally funded or permitted actions off federal property, but based on the title of most acts, the correct verb usage seems to be reversed.

According to the definitions section of the National Historic Preservation Act,

> The term "preservation" or "historic preservation" includes—
>   (1) identification, evaluation, recordation, **documentation**, curation, acquisition, protection, management, rehabilitation, restoration, stabilization, maintenance, research, interpretation, and conservation;
>   (2) education and training regarding the foregoing activities; or
>   (3) any combination of the foregoing activities.

The NHPA "Definitions" section does not include "protection," which is found under Section 101 (now 302501) outlining the duties of certified local governments:

> The term "protection" means protection by means of a local review process under State or local law for proposed demolition of, changes to, or other action that may affect **historic property** designated pursuant to this chapter.

Neither of these NHPA definitions is consistent with standard dictionary definitions, and neither is very satisfying when it comes to federal agency obligations with respect to an act of preserving or protecting a historic property. Preservation as defined in the NHPA refers to all the actions an agency may take as part of a larger process, while protection suggests a type of action that principally takes place at the local level.

For most historic preservationists, "preservation" has both a specific and a general meaning. The specific meaning is a *treatment standard* for historic properties (mostly buildings), defined as "the act or process of applying measures necessary to sustain the existing form, integrity, and materials of an historic property" (Weeks and Grimmer 1995). A general definition of preservation as applied to all historic properties is difficult to find, even in most textbooks containing "preservation" in the title. For example, Glass (1990:ix) circularly defines preservation as "the practice of preserving man-made structures, sites, and objects because of their historical, aesthetic, or architectural importance."

To me, "preservation" as a general term refers to an act of saving something with an expectation of some degree of permanence, thus a sustained effort. "Protection" entails preventing harm to something by reviewing and reacting to the actions that imminently threaten it. I think the intent of Section 106 (now 306108) of the NHPA is to protect properties in the **area of potential effects** from harm due to a specific **undertaking**. It doesn't guarantee long-term preservation of the properties unless preservation measures are stipulated in a mitigation agreement. Remember that Section 106 does not use either "protect" or "preserve," only "consider" and "consult."

On the other hand, the clear intent of Section 110 (now 306101–306114) is long-term preservation. It basically outlines federal agency responsibilities with regard to their own properties. The first sentence in that section states,

> (1) AGENCY HEAD RESPONSIBILITY.—The head of each Federal agency shall assume responsibility for the preservation of historic property that is owned or controlled by the agency.

This means that federal agencies that manage federal properties have an obligation to both protect and preserve historic properties on their land. For undertakings they fund or review off their property, they need only consider temporary protection, with the notable exception of federal transportation agencies subject to Section 4(f) of the Department of Transportation Act (see chapter 7).

Thus we are left with a schizophrenic heritage management structure that sometimes emphasizes long-term preservation and sometimes just short-term protection. We have two lead agencies in the Advisory Council on Historic Preservation and the Environmental Protection Agency. Despite the agency names, neither agency must protect or preserve. They must only take fully into account what their actions mean for the cultural heritage potentially affected by those actions and ask others that may value affected resources for their input, which they must consider but can ultimately ignore.

What Is a Reasonable and Good Faith Effort?

The original subtitle of this book was "Making a Reasonable and Good Faith Effort to Preserve Tangible Cultural Resources," but "reasonable and good faith" got dropped to shorten the title and refine its focus. I do think it is still important to explain here what I think "reasonable and good faith" means, as this phrase is critical to certain aspects of American heritage management and encapsulates what I think is essential to a practical approach.

The phrase "a reasonable and good faith effort" first appeared in 1986 in the third version of 36 CFR 800, the regulations that implement Section 106 of the NHPA. As discussed in chapter 6, Section 106 requires federal agencies to consider the effects of their actions on historic properties and to consult with interested parties about those effects. As stated in 1986 (800.4[b]), the "reasonable and good faith effort" standard specifically applied to agency officials' responsibility to locate historic properties that might be affected by a federal undertaking.

A second use of the phrase appeared in the current 36 CFR 800 regulations, issued in 2004, with respect to an agency official's responsibility to make a reasonable and good faith effort to identify **Indian tribes** and **Native Hawaiian** organizations that might attach religious or cultural significance to any affected historic properties (800.2[c] and 800.2[f]) and thus need to be consulted. The applications of "a reasonable and good faith effort" in terms of Section 106 are discussed in chapter 6 with regard to identification and in chapter 13 with respect to Indian consultation.

I contend that this selective Section 106 language should apply to almost everything we do in heritage management. While the 36 CFR 800 regulations don't exactly define what the phrase means, they have some requirements for implementation, and the ACHP has issued some guidance on how to apply it to both historic property identification and Indian consultation. This guidance provides insight into how to apply it to heritage management as a whole.

In 2010, the ACHP issued a letter to a SHPO on what a reasonable and good faith identification effort entailed, followed up by 2011 general guidance on the ACHP webpage. Even Tom King was impressed by the ACHP response (*Tom King's CRM Plus*, August 25, 2010). The guidance confirmed that (1) you don't always have to do a field survey, (2) a survey report can be short and sweet as long as it contains necessary information, and (3) nonfederal guidance should also be considered. The ACHP's reasonable and good faith identification and consultation guidance as it applies to archaeology is found in the *Section 106 Archaeology Guidance* (2009) document on the council's website. It specifies that a project doesn't have to be delayed if a tribe has been reasonably consulted in good faith and then fails to respond in a timely manner. This was an issue in the recent Dakota Access Pipeline controversy in North Dakota.

"Reasonable" is a term familiar to lawyers and legislators. It is often used in courtrooms and appears in many laws and regulations. It appears several times in 36 CFR 800 not attached to good faith: "reasonable opportunity to comment" (800.1[a]), "reasonable opportunity to identify" (800.2[c]), "reasonable efforts to avoid" (800.13[b]), and "report on the actions within a reasonable time" (800.13[b]). Reasonable means fair, sensible, rational, logical, moderate, just, and practical.

Good faith is also a common concept for lawyers. It has fewer synonyms than "reasonable," as it basically means honest, open, reliable, and sincere. In law it is often used in its Latin version: bona fides. You can see why it has application to consultation.

With regard to overall heritage preservation, I think a "reasonable and good faith effort" basically means a truly professional effort that is fully aware of the intent of law, is within the scope of the law with regard to expected outcomes, utilizes widely accepted and effective methods, honestly and fully reports results, and is ethically grounded. In practical application, it means you don't have to do a 100% survey to find every site and structure, you don't have to preserve every site and structure, and you don't have to consult with every potentially interested group or tribe as long as you make a concerted and transparent effort to consider your effects and consult those with directly applicable knowledge and demonstrated interest.

Welcome to Acronym Land

There are many laws, agencies, procedures, and professional practices with long names in heritage management. To be efficient we, like the military, have had to adopt a shorthand form of communication that necessarily uses lots of abbreviations, mostly for names and phrases that are three or more words long. I have attached a list of common American heritage management abbreviations as Appendix B.

While I will always write out the complete word combination at first use of an abbreviation in every chapter and may sometimes do so several times within a single chapter, there are so many abbreviations that you may occasionally need to refer to the list in Appendix B to remember what I am talking about. You will be expected to know most of these once you become a practicing professional, so be ready to deal with 106 applications of NHPA through an NRHP DOE coordinated with NEPA in case a FONSI is needed. This sentence is perfectly comprehensible (or should be) to most American heritage management professionals.

What We Call What We Do

Although I use "heritage management" in the title of this book to refer to the basic activity that I am discussing, in certain circumstances I will also use "historic preservation," "cultural resource management," and "heritage preservation." For heritage preservation, I have usually dropped the initial word of "cultural heritage preservation." This is for convenience, so usually assume "cultural" is still there unless I state otherwise. I also do not use the "CHM" acronym for cultural heritage management, as it is not commonly recognized as of yet.

"Historic preservation" is the preferred term for historians and architects. It was also the original term for American efforts to preserve the heritage of the built environment. I will use it when dealing with historical and architectural applications (e.g., chapter 12) or when discussing early heritage preservation efforts in this country.

Cultural resource management was a term coined by archaeologists in the mid-1970s to describe what agencies and contract archaeologists were doing with regard to a variety of federal laws, attempting to reduce harm to archaeological sites caused by federal construction. In some ways, it was invented to make—and perhaps keep—us separate from historians and architects. Surprisingly, for the first several decades of its use, it was only applied to archaeological sites and not the wider range of heritage resulting from all cultural behavior. In the 1990s, many federal agencies adopted CRM to partially consider this wider range, but its true range is beyond the scope of most heritage preservation laws. I will still use it to refer to early archaeological heritage management efforts, when taking an archaeological perspective (e.g., chapter 11), and as it applies to some federal laws and procedures.

I will use "heritage preservation" in this book to refer to attempts to preserve and protect a wider range of resources than suggested by "historic preservation" but a narrower range than inferred by "cultural resource management." Remember that heritage preservation is only one aspect of heritage management, although it is the most important aspect when considering legal applications and intent. Heritage management entails the required and justifiable actions that agencies take to preserve important aspects of the past, but it also includes educational and interpretive initiatives that have become the current focus of public archaeology and public history.

Summary

We can justify doing heritage preservation in basic ways, at various levels, and with regard to the various heritage management professions. Archaeologists have the most difficult job of justification because there are few monetary incentives for or direct community benefits from saving an archaeological site. In addition, rural and prehistoric sites are at a disadvantage because they usually lack affiliated community support. Architects and cities have the easiest time justifying what they do for heritage preservation because their efforts are highly visible and usually accessible. They can also directly leverage public funds through grants, tax incentives, and community development programs.

American heritage management is a complex structure, largely built within the last half century. The governmental agencies that implement the laws have become increasingly skilled at doing what the law intends and more supportive of its objectives, in part because younger managers have replaced older ones and regulations have become more understandable and practical through 50 years of trial and error in application.

In order to do, understand, or explain heritage management, you must be familiar with basic definitions, basic concepts, and the jargon of multiple professions and numerous agencies and laws. Heritage management as practiced in the United States is a blend of business, science, and the humanities. It is also a compromise between constitutional rights and community needs. Most university education in archaeology, architecture, and history does not prepare you for a career in heritage management unless you are enrolled in a specialized program or take specialized classes taught by experienced instructors. This book is best used in a specialized program or class focused on cultural heritage management, cultural resource management, or historic preservation. The basic tenet of this book is that to be an effective and successful heritage manager, you need to be both knowledgeable and practical.

Review Questions

1. Why do heritage preservation?
2. What is heritage as it applies to American heritage management?
3. What is management as it applies to attempts to save American heritage?
4. What does it mean to be practical when it comes to implementing our heritage managements laws?
5. What is a reasonable and good faith effort?
6. How does "preserve" differ from "protect"?

Supplemental Reading

To dig deeper into the definition of heritage, the practice of understanding the past, and the philosophy of heritage preservation, you can't do better than David Lowenthal. For in-depth discussions, see his *The Heritage Crusade and the Spoils of History* (1998) and *The Past Is a Foreign Country—Revisited* (2015). For a briefer discussion, see Lowenthal, "The Heritage Crusade and Its Contradictions" (2004).

To see how state or **tribal historic preservation offices** justify heritage management, historic preservation, and cultural resource management in their states or tribes, visit their webpages. The Advisory Council on Historic Preservation and National Trust for Historic Preservation webpages also have sections on the benefits of heritage preservation, but like SHPOs, they tend to emphasize economic and thus nonarchaeological properties.

For dealing with intangible cultural heritage under NEPA and a few other more obscure laws, see *Guidelines and Principles for Social Impact Assessment*, originally prepared by the National Oceanic and Atmospheric Administration (NOAA) in 1994 and updated in 2003. More recently, a federal interagency workgroup produced *Promising Practices for EJ Methodologies in NEPA Review* (Environmental Protection Agency 2016). As mentioned in the text of this chapter, also see various entries under social impact assessment and environmental justice in King (2013).

SIDEBAR

Implementing Heritage Management: A Method for Our Madness

My first graduate school seminar was "Method and Theory in American Archaeology." Dale Henning, my advisor at the University of Nebraska, taught the class. Our textbook was a difficult read for me, Robert Dunnell's *Systematics in Prehistory* (1971). In the first class session, Henning stressed the important difference between **methodology** and **method**, but, as I remember it, he had a different definition of methodology than Dunnell. Dunnell (1971:36) considered methodology "the inquiry into the relationships between the theory of each of the sciences." It therefore was of no real use to us because we were just looking at archaeology. Method, according to Dunnell (1971:199), was "a subsystem of theory which is directed toward the solution of a particular class of problems."

Dunnell's concept of methodology is only one application of *comparative methodology* (see Benjamin 1977). I think Henning saw methodology more like I do today and as expressed by Clough and Nutbrown (2012:25): "Methodology shows how research questions are articulated with questions asked in the field." Dunnell's concept of method is more what I think of as methodology. Methodology to me is the link between theory and method. A method is a technique employed to help answer a research question. Methodology is the justification for using a particular approach and even for the importance of the question.

Method gets more complicated. In archaeology, "the scientific method" was critical to the "new

archaeology" of the 1960s and 1970s and is still important to all archaeologists today. We don't even have to get into debates about factual reality as long as we do careful and defendable work. To historians, "the historical method" is the basis of their profession. Like archaeologists, they are more focused on providing reliable insight into a problem than on absolutely solving it. Historians even have a field of study called historiography to examine how interpretations, emphases, methods, and methodologies have changed over time.

But are the scientific method and the historical method really methods as defined above? I think it is better to think of them as approaches. Users of the scientific approach look at the observable world, while users of the historical approach look at the observed world. Both start with a research problem. The scientist then formulates alternative hypotheses to address the problem, uses carefully chosen and explicit methods to address it, observes and analyzes the results, and comes to some conclusion about the accuracy of one or more of the starting hypotheses. The historian identifies and gathers source material, carefully verifies the reliability of sources to be used to address the problem, analyzes the information contained in the reliable sources, and then synthesizes the findings.

The varying uses of just the terms "method" and "methodology" illustrate some of the confusion that can arise from different definitions or interpretations of a few words. If we want to be unambiguous and understandable in what we do and to promote successful interdisciplinary cooperation, we need to be explicit in our terminology. I have tried to do that throughout this book.

Some final words about terminology. I constantly find my students and even long-term practitioners misusing several homonyms used in heritage management. The first are "principal" and "principle." The most common misuse occurs in statements of who is in charge of a project. In archaeology this person is called the "principal investigator." This is who gets the license, supervises every aspect of the project, and is responsible for the final report. I can't tell you the number of times I have seen it spelled "principle investigator" in proposals, on report covers, and even in books and manuals. "Principal," in the above usage, is an adjective meaning primary, main, or most important. "Principle" is a noun meaning a fundamental idea or basis for a scientific or mathematical theorem. Thus a "principle investigator" could be a mathematician but rarely an archaeologist.

In environmental review, we frequently use the terms "affect" and "effect" when talking about impacts to historic properties. "Affect" is mainly used as a verb: the road project will affect the archaeological site. "Effect" is mainly used as a noun: the road project had an effect on the archaeological site. Agencies make effect findings with some effects being adverse. Archaeologists and archaeological sites are affected by these adverse effects.

Finally, let's look at a usage that I too once had trouble with: "historic" versus "historical." (In prehistoric archaeology we don't have this problem because we just use "archaeological," but not "archaeologic" or "prehistorical.") As the *Oxford English Dictionary* explains, "Historic means 'famous or important in history,' as in a historic occasion, whereas historical means 'concerning history or historical events,' as in historical evidence; thus a historic event is one that was very important, whereas a historical event is something that happened in the past." Historic is a value assessment; we place historic properties in the National Register of Historic Places. Historical is a chronological assessment; if something is old enough, it is historical.

There is one final twist to "historical." A historical archaeologist studies the historical period, traditionally defined as the period of literate societies that could provide primary written texts. This was not a strictly chronological assessment because the timing of "the historic period" varies all over the world. In North America, where there was no formal written language prior to the arrival of the Spanish, the periods after 1492 are now referred to as colonial and postcolonial times. Some SHPOs now call the period prior to European intrusion into their state the precontact period rather than the prehistoric period, concerned that some people might interpret prehistoric as ahistoric (i.e., without a history).

CHAPTER 2

The History of American Heritage Management

A War Story

The past is a foreign county; they do things differently there.

—L. P. Hartley, *The Go-Between*

For the most part, heritage management agencies and professionals have done a poor job telling their own history. Among federal agencies, the National Park Service (NPS) is a clear exception, with historical overviews, chronologies, and links to manuscripts and publications on its webpage. Many of these NPS examples appeared well before the service's 2016 centennial year, so this commemorative effort is not just a recent one. The NPS gets the importance of telling its story as part of carrying out its mission, although most individual park webpages are somewhat deficient in this regard.

Two of the most notable federal agencies failing to document their own histories are the National Register of Historic Places (NRHP) and the Advisory Council on Historic Preservation (ACHP). These two lead agencies in American heritage management have the word "historic" in their names. In order to understand policy and how priorities were set, it would be helpful to know about the people who made major decisions and why changes took place within agencies. The NRHP and ACHP give us nothing for their own historic context.

State historic preservation office (SHPO) webpages rarely provide an overview of the history of historic preservation in their state. Most state comprehensive preservation plans also usually fail to provide the historic context of historic preservation in their state; yet properties can be eligible for inclusion in the National Register because of the role they played in the history of historic preservation at the local, state, or federal level.

In the following overview of the history of heritage management, I found it helpful first to break the story up by what has been written regarding its two traditional component parts: historic preservation from the history-architecture viewpoint and cultural resource management (CRM) from the archaeological perspective. The historic preservation story starts much earlier, although the CRM story eventually becomes more dominant.

Overviews of Historic Preservation History

Charles Hosmer wrote the first substantial history of historic preservation in the early 1960s. What began as his doctoral dissertation at Columbia University

(Hosmer 1961) eventually became a three-volume publication (Hosmer 1965, 1981). In these volumes, Hosmer documented the background of historic preservation events in America in great detail up to the establishment of the National Trust for Historic Preservation (NTHP) in 1949. His research was exhaustive, including original manuscripts, oral interviews, and secondary sources.

Some postmodern historians note Hosmer's efforts but often dismiss them as "holding a narrow view of preservation's undertaking" (Page and Mason 2004:8). However, anyone going into historic preservation, especially in the disciplines of history and architecture, can still benefit from reading Hosmer to get a sense of early achievements and difficulties. Most interestingly, Hosmer's narrative stops well before the passage of the National Historic Preservation Act (NHPA), which many heritage management professionals today think of as the true beginning of historic preservation in this country. Hosmer's view does not rely on comparisons to the National Register of Historic Places or Section 106.

James Glass, also beginning with his doctoral work, picked up where Hosmer left off (Glass 1987, 1990). Hosmer wrote the foreword to the published Glass study. In his *The Beginnings of a New National Historic Preservation Program, 1957 to 1969*, Glass leaves out the eight years between 1949 and 1957, but not much happened during this period that immediately affected historic preservation. On the national scene, the United States was involved in the Korean War, and President Dwight D. Eisenhower was serving his first term. Both of these would later have significant historic preservation effects (see below).

No one has comprehensively summarized developments in American historic preservation between 1969 to the present in any publications similar to those of Hosmer and Glass. Max Page and Randall Mason's edited volume *Giving Preservation a History* (2004) provides some fresh perspectives on historic preservation but mainly cites eastern or western US urban examples. Despite the enticing title, the volume offers very little evaluation or synthesis of the American historic preservation movement as a whole, other than glimpses in the introduction by Page and Mason.

Architecturally oriented historic preservation textbooks do a better job than archaeological ones of presenting historical overviews of their discipline. A somewhat dated but still important volume, *The American Mosaic: Preserving a Nation's Heritage* (Stipe and Lee 1987), includes three chapters discussing the twentieth-century history of historic preservation from national, state, and local perspectives. The volume was produced for the International Council on Monuments and Sites (ICOMOS) general assembly meeting in Washington, DC, in October 1987.

William Murtagh's *Keeping Time* (2006) has two chapters looking at historic preservation before and after World War II, but for the most part the book is concerned with the role of the federal government and the major manifestations of preservation and interpretation inside and outside museums, with scattered early examples and dates. Norman Tyler, in *Historic Preservation* (1994), has a chapter titled "The Historic Preservation Movement in the United States," but it is mainly about how preservation is done there, noting a few early examples. Diane Lea provides a brief overview of American preservation history in the first chapter of Robert Stipe's edited volume *A Richer Heritage* (2003).

Also valuable to the history of historic preservation are overviews concerning the contributions of particular agencies and individuals. As previously mentioned, the National Park Service has done an exemplary job of describing its own historic preservation history (https://www.nps.gov/parkhistory/hisnps/NPSHistory.htm). Of particular note are the writings of Barry Mackintosh, which include an insider's perspective on the National Historic Preservation Act and its effects on the NPS (Mackintosh 1986).

The various journals published by the NPS (*CRM Bulletin*, 1978–1990; *CRM*, 1991–2002; *CRM: The Journal of Heritage Stewardship*, 2003–2011; *Common Ground*, 2003–2011), also available online, contain numerous helpful articles, many sharing insights from the major NPS participants in twentieth-century heritage management, including Ernest Connally, Jerry Rodgers, and Robert Garvey. The *Public Historian* journal ran a series titled "Pioneers of Public History" offering perspectives from early NPS historic preservation leaders (e.g., Spude and Rodgers 2005; Foppes and Utley 2002). The *Public Historian* also published a special issue in 1987 (Volume 9, Number 2) on the NPS and historic preservation.

A common flaw in many of the architecturally oriented texts is a characterization of early historic preservation as a movement, when prior to World War II it mainly consisted of disconnected efforts by private individuals in a few cities and states and eventually, in the 1930s, by the National Park Service in coordination with Depression-era work programs. These textbooks also focus almost entirely on building preservation with limited discussion of the larger scope of heritage management and the myriad nonstructural aspects of heritage.

Overviews of Cultural Resource Management History

As for cultural resource management, archaeology's perspective on heritage management beginning in the early 1970s, historical overviews are limited and often narrowly focused. Understandably, the major textbook authors all have their own priorities. Some discuss the federal heritage management process and tell us what is wrong with it. Others focus on their specialties—fieldwork, site evaluation, engaging a diverse public. In this book I try do a little of each, but I think a historical perspective is critical to understanding almost every aspect of heritage management.

The most commonly used archaeological textbook for university cultural resource management courses is Tom King's *Cultural Resource Laws and Practice* (2013). King devotes 15 pages in the middle of his introductory chapter to a brief discussion of the history of cultural resource management with an archaeological focus on sites rather than structures. The second most common textbook for archaeological CRM is Thomas Neumann, Robert Sanford, and Karen Harry's *Cultural Resources Archaeology* (2010). It provides no synthetic history of archaeological CRM. A third popular CRM textbook is Donald Hardesty and Barbara Little's *Assessing Site Significance* (2009). Although focused on how to determine which sites and structures are worth saving based on their historic contexts, it provides no historic context as to how the current evaluative system came about.

Other recent books about CRM hardly mention the history of the profession except as a few examples with dates. The King-edited *A Companion to Cultural Resource Management* (2011) could have easily included a chapter on CRM history. Hester Davis provides a little history in her chapter in *Archaeology and Cultural Resource Management* (Sebastian and Lipe 2009), edited by Lynne Sebastian and William Lipe, but it is mostly about twentieth-century laws affecting the practice of archaeology. A compilation of writings by Davis's Arkansas compatriot Charles R. McGimsey in the cleverly titled *CRM on CRM* (2004) provides a good perspective from an early state-level insider, but overall it is just a collection of McGimsey's short contributions over his half century of involvement with archaeological aspects of historic preservation.

I think King's 1987 article, "Prehistory and Beyond: The Place of Archaeology," in Robert Stipe and Antoinette Lee's *The American Mosaic* and the history chapter in Thomas King, Patricia Parker Hickman, and Gary Berg's *Anthropology in Historic Preservation: Caring for Culture's Clutter* (1977) are two of the better overviews of the history of CRM, although both are somewhat dated. They discuss how archaeology has had difficulty blending with the architecturally based historic preservation movement, mainly due to the dilemmas posed for archaeology by a strict preservation ethic and the necessity in archaeology of destroying sites in order to analyze what is in them. On the other hand, these publications demonstrate how archaeology has played an often dominant role in heritage management at the federal agency level since the mid-1970s, as the rise of the federal heritage preservation system was concurrent with the rise of a systematic approach in archaeology.

Some focused books and articles discuss important aspects of the early history of cultural resource management archaeology before it was called CRM. The extensive Depression-era archaeology done by federal relief agencies has been discussed in books by Edwin Lyon (1996) and Paul Fagette (1996). Tom Theissen (1999) wrote a nice summary of the reservoir salvage archaeology done along the middle Missouri River from 1946 to 1975. Kimball Banks and Jon Czaplicki (2014) and Jesse Jennings (1985) provide comprehensive overviews of the River Basin Surveys (RBS).

Why Study the History of Heritage Preservation?

It seems a bit silly to ask this question of historians, historical architects, and archaeologists. Studying the past is what we do, and we obviously think it is important. Most of us don't do it for fame or fortune; we do it because we think it is worthwhile and interesting. But we need a more intellectually satisfying justification of the importance of the history of heritage preservation to convince new students and old critics. It is certainly not enough to quote George Santayana (1905): "Those who cannot remember the past are doomed to repeat it." Obviously, people who remember the past have repeated it many times. Look at how many wars France and Germany have fought, even though Alsace-Lorraine is littered with monuments. No one can forget the past there.

Here are some reasons why I think it is important to study the history of heritage preservation:

1. *The past determines why we do heritage preservation and what we preserve.* This is true with regard to legal, political, intellectual, and philosophical perspectives. When laws are passed at the federal or state level, they often have a section titled "Purpose of the Act" or "Legislative Intent." It is important to read these to determine why legislation was enacted. Then consider the way the law is currently applied. Is the current system true to the original intent, or have bureaucrats bent the application to fit their own agency's procedures or priorities? The "Purpose" section in the National Historic Preservation Act is particularly enlightening.

   Laws are passed within political and social contexts and sometimes in response to particular events. The National Historic Preservation Act of 1966 was an element of President Lyndon B. Johnson's "Great Society" program, which grew out of President John F. Kennedy's "New Frontier" program. These programs were efforts to make the country a more prosperous and livable place with equal opportunity for all.

   The policies of President Ronald Reagan in the 1980s resulted in many changes to the practices and procedures of our heritage management system, included requiring owner consent for the National Register listing of privately owned properties and increased dependence on local leadership, a reflection of the new antifederalism. But heritage preservation is not a liberal or a conservative cause. Every state in the nation, be it red or blue, values its heritage. President Richard Nixon was instrumental in enacting many of the strong points of the system we have today.

As discussed in chapter 1, the bottom line of heritage preservation is determining worth. What we deem worthy of preservation changes from generation to generation based on what the country has gone through, economic and social conditions, and the philosophical and intellectual opinions of leadership. As the veterans of both the home front and the battlefront of World War II began to disappear rapidly in the 1990s, the children of "the Greatest Generation" commemorated their parents' contributions and experiences in both the war and the Great Depression. Their grandchildren and great-grandchildren may be more interested in recognizing the entertainment contributions of baby boomers and the technological contributions of Generation X. As chapter 5 will discuss, **historic context** is at the core of determining the historic worth of any individual property. The historic context of heritage preservation is likewise essential in assessing why we do it and what we preserve.

2. *The past determines what heritage preservation has already saved.* A historical perspective is critical to understanding what forces have shaped heritage preservation and how it has evolved. With regard to laws, important elements of the 1906 Antiquities Act are still in effect (at least as I write this). The act gives the president the power to create national monuments. National monuments can have natural or cultural importance. One of the most recent is the Belmont-Paul Women's Equality National Monument in Washington, DC, important as the home of the National Women's Party for 90 years.

This is a very nationalistic country, so places with patriotic meaning are highly valued as heritage sites, even if they are relatively recent. The World Trade Center site in New York was determined eligible for the National Register in March 2004 for the purposes of Section 106 of the National Historic Preservation Act. This determination was based on the site's association with the September 11, 2001, attacks and required application of National Register **Criteria Consideration** G for properties less than 50 years old; this may have been the youngest Criteria Consideration G property accepted for inclusion in the history of the National Register (less than three years from the **significant date**).

3. *Understanding the past helps improve how we do heritage preservation in the present and suggests how we might do it better in the future.* In order to efficiently and effectively carry out the current heritage preservation system, practitioners benefit greatly from knowing strategies and examples of what did and did not work in the past. There is no more powerful teaching tool than an appropriate example, good or bad.

Understanding the past is also critical to plan for more efficient and effective systems in the future and anticipate changes in economic, social, political, and even environmental conditions. Global warming is going to increase flooding in both river systems and coastal areas. Most urban areas are on rivers or oceans, so many historic sites will be threatened. Archaeological sites will be inundated or eroded. Floods of the past have had great impacts on heritage resources, and using what was learned from past disasters helps to focus responses and resources to deal with future ones.

4. *Knowing the history of heritage preservation improves personal skills and opportunities for heritage management professionals.* Understanding how present heritage management systems and priorities came about involves analysis of past political, economic, and social conditions. It also requires

understanding methodological and theoretical changes in heritage studies disciplines. It requires comparing changing intellectual viewpoints like modernism versus postmodernism and processual versus postprocessual archaeology. Critical thinking is a basic element of an advanced education and a successful career.

At the core of heritage preservation is historical knowledge for all the reasons listed above. Demonstrating knowledge of the history of heritage preservation may help you find and perform better in a job in the preservation field. Such knowledge can help you better understand agency policies and build agency loyalty. It strengthens personal and community identity. It should help build a strong ethical foundation. Beyond professionalism, knowledge of your country's heritage can make you a better citizen.

5. *History is interesting.* This is enough of a reason for many heritage preservation professionals, but history is also interesting to the public. That is why there are television channels and magazines dedicated to it. That is why governments fund museums and historical sites and why the public visits them in great numbers. Heritage tourism continues to expand and prosper.

We can enhance our environment by providing tangible remnants of the past. We have lots of parks with greenspace but not many with clearly visible historic **features** (e.g., ruins). We can enhance views of the built environment with interpretation to explain why the view is what it is. My mother told me that when I travel, I should put friends and family in my pictures, because there are postcards for just remembering the scene. More important than the view is the people you shared it with. History and archaeology are all about putting people back into our landscapes. Studying the history of heritage management is both interesting and practical.

Justifying the history of heritage management as outlined above is very different from justifying the relevance of heritage management as discussed in chapter 1. Justifying the history of heritage management is about selling it to professionals and agencies so they can do a better job and better understand the relevance of their professions. Justifying the relevance of heritage management is about selling it to the public and policy makers so they will continue to support it.

The History of American Heritage Management: A War Story

The history of American heritage management is more than a chronology of laws, agency actions, and preservation events. It is a story about not just politics but also social change and shifting intellectual perspectives. We all know that the America of today differs greatly from that of the first Indian settlers who created our most ancient sites, but it is also very different from the America of colonial times, Civil War times, and even our grandparents' time. Some of what we value today is different from what was valued in the past. The present, not the past or the future, determines the heritage management agenda. The present is what we attempt to preserve, satisfying our current needs as well as anticipating our children's and country's future needs.

To me, the history of heritage management is something of a war story. I don't just mean battles won and lost to preserve important historic properties or tales of combatants in modernist versus postmodernist debates. I mean actual war. Just as many medical advances and societal changes are associated with major national and international conflicts, changes in historic preservation and cultural resource management have, to a large degree, also followed the pulses of the country's major wars. Wars are mighty engines of change for many reasons.

First, wars can provide great motivation for historic preservation. Historic preservation can help people deal with loss and hardship by providing direct contact with something familiar and valued from before the war. Wars encourage patriotism and thus the need to preserve patriotic places. Wars can also instill a need to do something positive after they are over. This can entail both destroying and preserving historic sites, depending on what "positive" means to individuals, communities, and governments.

Second, wars have a great economic influence for both preserving and threatening historic properties. Wars cause shortages in money, material, and labor. World War II depleted the History Division staff of the National Park Service, effectively ending the Historic Sites Survey. The Korean War led to the closure of all offices of the River Basin Surveys (Eugene, Oregon; Austin, Texas; and Berkeley, California) except the one in Lincoln, Nebraska. During a war, military needs divert resources from local development, so there may be a hiatus in the normal activity leading to destruction of historic properties. When a war ends, however, there is a great increase in development to put people back to work. There is also a surplus of construction equipment. Note the massive hydroelectric projects on the Missouri and Columbia Rivers after World War II. Postwar development initially focuses on promoting economic development, so arguments for historic preservation are more difficult in the short term.

Finally, war can have many other implications for historic preservation both positive and negative. On the negative side, it can directly destroy many structures and sites; even this country suffered significant property losses during the Revolutionary War (e.g., the Great Fire of New York), during the War of 1812 (e.g., government buildings burned in Washington, DC), and in the South and the border states during the Civil War. The chaos of wars promotes looting, such as what recently happened in Iraq. When wars start, the military acquires and develops new lands. When wars end, many military bases are closed, creating "surplus" historic buildings and sites that overwhelm preservationists.

On the positive side, war (or the threat of it) encourages technological innovations that can greatly benefit heritage preservation. **Light Detection and Ranging** (LiDAR) was developed for submarine detection but has revolutionized the search for surface archaeological sites such as burial mounds and ruins. The Global Positioning System (GPS) was another military development that has revolutionized fieldwork.

Wars create some of our most important historic sites—battlefields, forts, and places associated with generals and heroes. Wars also increase the power of the federal government, especially the executive branch, which has big implications for where, why, and whether sites are preserved, depending on the political climate, economic priorities, and presidential will.

While some might see my organizing this heritage preservation chronology around wars as a bit contrived, beyond the reasons listed above, I think it is helpful to break history up into short periods because small bites of time are easier to chew on and digest. I have found no other divisional scheme to be both compact enough and meaningful in terms of combining significant developments affecting archaeology, history, and architecture as they pertain to heritage preservation.

Certainly each of these professions has its own schemes, with architecture relying on dominant styles (e.g., modernism, postmodernism), history on political trends (e.g., colonial, postcolonial), and archaeology on methodological developments (e.g., processual, postprocessual) or practitioner dominance (e.g., academic,

CRM). These emphases are not mutually understandable and don't fit well together chronologically. Wars have demonstrable political, intellectual, generational, philosophical, and technological effects. They also have occurred with unfortunate frequency during the development of American heritage preservation, breaking up our lives and heritage as well as time.

A Note on Sources

In the overview that follows, I have once again tried not to burden the text with too many citations. Most of the history I present is made up of relatively well-known facts previously presented in many basic historical overviews. Unless otherwise noted, for historic preservation I have mainly relied on Hosmer (1965, 1981) for pre-1950 observations and Glass (1990) for the next 20 years. For the remainder of the twentieth century, Murtagh (2006), Tyler (1994), and various chapters in Stipe and Lee (1987) were my main sources. With regard to archaeological perspectives, King, Hickman, and Berg (1977), Fowler (1986), and King (2013) were major sources. I filled in the nineteenth- and twentieth-century cracks with various lesser-known sources usually cited in the text. For much of the twenty-first-century overview, I relied mostly on my own familiarity and experience.

Post–Revolutionary War: Building a Nation and a Nation's History

It is relatively easy to describe the beginnings of heritage management in the United States if we restrict ourselves to the "built environment," like most historic preservationists do; we just have to look for buildings that were saved from demolition because they were thought to hold historical value by the people of the time. If we apply a broader definition of heritage resources, determining the beginnings of heritage management in the United States becomes more difficult and more interesting. I will present something in between because this book deals with only the tangible aspects of cultural heritage. I will limit my discussion to aspects of heritage that would be recognized by most modern practitioners.

In colonial times, America was one of many provinces of the British Empire. It could not even come close to the home country or the more established colonies in terms of the size, antiquity, or opulence of its buildings. The Indians of the East Coast tribes didn't build with stone, so their villages were ephemeral as far as long-term survival was concerned. To most colonists the Indians themselves were ephemeral, and because they had no written language, they were thought to have no history. Prior to the Revolutionary War, not only the English but also the colonists thought there was little of historical importance in America.

Then in 1776 perspectives changed, as the recent immigrants suddenly became American citizens rather than British colonists. Shots were fired that were heard at least in all 13 colonies and across the northern Atlantic Ocean. Documents were written that are still used as templates for the foundation of new national states. Leaders emerged who have since been difficult to duplicate as a set. Battles were won that should have been lost.

Within a decade, the backwater had become part of the forefront. Suddenly there were places of historical importance worth preserving in America. Each of the original colonies had unique governments and unique attitudes. After the Revolutionary War, American politics did not immediately become national, but they did become more regional, first in the North and South and then in the East and

West. A national perspective took time to realize, as did any recognition of the need to preserve early American history.

The federal government began to build its own buildings in the new capital city of Washington, giving the Treasury Department oversight. In 1790, the Residence Act authorized the construction of the White House and the Capitol Building. President George Washington laid the cornerstone of the Capitol Building in 1793. The designs for these buildings were European in origin, intentionally invoking the classical foundations of democracy.

But the federal government was in its infancy after the Revolutionary War. Some of the new republic's most prominent citizens (e.g., Thomas Jefferson), suspicious of centralized power, carefully scrutinized and criticized even its most minor actions. This was one reason why heritage preservation started at the local level. In 1791, citizens in Boston formed the first state historical society. It was meant to be a repository for important historical objects and a disseminator of historical knowledge. Due to the absence of a national historical institution at that time and the prominent role Massachusetts had played in the American Revolution, the Massachusetts Historical Society took on a role that had implications beyond the state.

With the creation of the Library of Congress by action of that body in 1800, the United States as a country first formally recognized the importance of heritage if not heritage preservation. That heritage was still mainly European, but there was an increasing awareness that history had been made here too, a recognition that something special in world history had occurred. Most of all, there was an awareness that the leaders of the Revolution and their actions were special.

In 1813, the City of Philadelphia purchased Independence Hall with the intent to tear it down to make room for new development. Citizens of Philadelphia soon realized that the building had a historical value that greatly exceeded the land's economic value, so in 1816, the city agreed to save the building. Philadelphia went one step further in 1829, when the steeple of Independence Hall was rebuilt (Figure 2.1), not as an exact replica of the original but in a design that fit the style of its period of historic significance, which in itself was something of a revolution in American architecture.

Also in 1829, Abraham Touro, a wealthy Jewish merchant, left funds in his will for the restoration of a colonial-era synagogue in Newport, Rhode Island. This was not only an early instance of an individual undertaking of historic preservation, a type of action that was to dominate American heritage preservation until after the Civil War, but a demonstration that not all important historic sites were directly linked to the American Revolution or associated with white Anglo-Saxon Protestants.

The federal government first became involved in heritage preservation in the mid-1800s, although heritage preservation was not initially an internal federal initiative.

FIG. 2.1 Independence Hall in Philadelphia with its 1829 restored steeple (Library of Congress).

A wealthy British scientist, James Smithson, left his estate to the US government in 1829 so it could establish an institution (named after him) in Washington, DC, for the increase and diffusion of knowledge. In 1836, Congress formally accepted the gift of $500,000 for this purpose and placed the money in a charitable trust. Finally, an act of Congress in 1846 established the Smithsonian Institution as a building to house an art gallery, a lecture hall, a library, a science museum, a chemical laboratory, and a natural science laboratory. The enabling legislation made no mention of a history museum.

Another mid-nineteenth-century federal action took even longer to result in tangible historic preservation. In 1849, Congress established the Department of the Interior. Its original purpose was not to manage parkland but to consolidate government offices concerned with transfer of public lands into private hands, such as the General Land Office and Indian Affairs Office. Not until 1872 was the first national park, Yellowstone, established. And not until 1892 was the first cultural property, Casa Grande, added to the national park system.

In the second half of the nineteenth century, the pace of historic preservation in the United States quickened, although it was soon halted by the Civil War. In 1850, New York State purchased the Hasbrouck House, which had served as George Washington's headquarters during the final year of the Revolutionary War.

More importantly, in 1853 South Carolina's Ann Pamela Cunningham founded the Mount Vernon Ladies' Association (MVLA) of the Union with the purpose of saving George Washington's home for posterity and restoring it to its appearance at the time of his death in 1799. Initially Cunningham's group only appealed to southern states for funds, but northern newspapers soon took up the crusade, arguing that Washington's legacy belonged to the entire nation. Every state eventually had a chapter of the MVLA. Soon its membership was crusading not just to save Mount Vernon but to keep the Union together.

Raising $200,000 in private funds from across the county, the group purchased the house and 200 acres of the original grounds from Washington's nephew in 1858. Based on the criteria established by Cunningham, the MVLA began to restore the house as a place where George Washington would feel at home. Some architects and politicians proposed that the house and Washington's tomb be upgraded to match expectations of a national shrine, but the ladies of Mount Vernon refused. It was to remain Washington's home.

The purchase of Mount Vernon by a private organization demonstrated once again that the federal government was not ready to do historic preservation. It had multiple opportunities to purchase the Mount Vernon property beginning in the 1840s but never acted. If it had, Mount Vernon would be a very different place today, no doubt "upgraded" to fit political rather than historical expectations. The MVLA still owns and manages Mount Vernon and has never relied on government funding.

These two actions from the 1850s, both elements of what some have referred to as "the cult of Washington," are the first clear manifestations of what we could call an incipient movement in American heritage preservation. Karal Ann Marling has described the wider results of this cultlike activity in her book *George Washington Slept Here* (1988). It was about more than just Washington and more than just preserving places associated with the Revolution. Although interrupted by the Civil War, it would become a revival of the architecture and crafts of America's colonial past.

Other pre–Civil War actions that are important to the history of American heritage preservation include Princeton University's restoration of Nassau Hall in 1855 and the state of Tennessee's acquisition of Andrew Jackson's house (The Hermitage) in 1856. Of importance to the intellectual foundation of historic preservation was the publication of English architect John Ruskin's *The Seven Lamps of Architecture* in 1849, which lists memory as one of the seven lamps. Ruskin decried the intrusion of modern forms into ancient settings and noted that we cannot properly remember the past without the aid of physical remains.

> There are two duties respecting national architecture whose importance it is impossible to overrate; the first, to render the architecture of the day, historical; and, the second, to preserve, as the most precious inheritance, that of past ages.
>
> —Ruskin (1849:148)

There is one pre–Civil War glimmer of archaeological site preservation or at least the preservation of a historic site not containing an intact structure. In 1820, William Pell, a private citizen, purchased the site of Fort Ticonderoga in upstate New York. When Pell bought the land from two local colleges, the fort was a ruin. Fort Ticonderoga was built in 1755 by the French at the beginning of the French and Indian (Seven Years') War. A large British force attacked it in 1758 but was defeated by the French defenders in one of the bloodiest battles on American soil prior to the Civil War. The British finally took Fort Ticonderoga in 1759 and held it until an American force under Ethan Allen captured it in May 1775 in one of the first American military successes of the Revolutionary War. The British retook the fort a few months later, and then the Americans took it again in 1777. The Pell family established a private preservation association that eventually restored Fort Ticonderoga in 1909. The association still manages the property. The National Park Service declared Fort Ticonderoga one of the first **National Historic Landmarks** in 1960.

During the Civil War the destruction of historic sites in the South and the border states was widespread. The burning of Richmond and Atlanta generated especially great losses (Figure 2.2). Military actions caused most of the destruction, although a notable exception is the 1863 demolition of the John Hancock house in Boston. Some incipient historic preservation also took place during the war, more to satisfy immediate wartime needs than out of long-term considerations of heritage preservation. Gettysburg National Cemetery was established in 1863, promoting the preservation of much of the battlefield due to concerns with the setting and feeling

FIG. 2.2 Ruins in Richmond, Virginia, after its capture by Union forces in April 1865 (Library of Congress).

of the cemetery. In 1864 the US Army acquired Robert E. Lee's Arlington House property for a cemetery, thus preserving the building (also known as the Custis-Lee Mansion), with the grounds eventually becoming one of this nation's most sacred places: Arlington National Cemetery.

Post–Civil War: Rebuilding a Nation

As with the period following the Revolutionary War, after the Civil War historic preservation got off to a slow start. The nation and its citizens were too concerned with healing the deep physical, economic, and emotional wounds and dealing with major societal reorganization due to the abolition of slavery. Although Yellowstone became the first national park in 1872, the War Department initially managed it, as it was still in Indian Territory. The National Park Service wouldn't be established until 1916.

Historic preservation didn't really awaken again until the country's centennial celebration in 1876. Some of the state exhibits at Philadelphia's national exhibition reintroduced Americans to colonial-era house interiors and exteriors. Many visitors liked what they saw, resulting in the colonial revival architectural style. Congress was even impressed, authorizing the 1881 construction of a building in Washington, the Arts and Industries Building, to house some of the Centennial Exposition exhibits, another federal baby step toward a national historic preservation system.

The 1876 centennial also inspired other historic preservation activities, as described in Marling's 1988 book. Using the Mount Vernon model, other women's associations took actions to preserve the Old South Meeting House in Boston and the site of Valley Forge in Pennsylvania. The centennial also led to a nationwide obsession with collecting artifacts associated with America's early historic past. Antiques like spinning wheels became part of "modern" home décor, appreciated both for their antiquity and their craftsmanship.

The late nineteenth century witnessed the establishment and actions of a number of associations that would help lay the foundations of historic preservation in America. On the national level in 1884, the American Historical Association (AHA) was founded to promote the study of history. Despite having had little direct effect on historic preservation, the AHA promoted it indirectly by promoting history. The American Institute of Architects (AIA), established in 1857, moved its headquarters into the Octagon House in Washington, DC, in 1898 (Figure 2.3). Designed and built in the late 1790s by Capitol Building architect William Thornton, the house had become the temporary home of James and Dolly Madison in 1814 after the burning of the White House by the British.

At the state level, the Association for the Preservation of Virginia Antiquities, the first preservation organization established in the South after the Civil War, had an immediate effect on historic preservation. Soon after its founding in 1888, it purchased a pre–Revolutionary War building in

FIG. 2.3 The Octagon House in Washington, DC, first home of the American Institute of Architects in the 1890s (Library of Congress).

Williamsburg. It then turned its attention to the preservation of early buildings on Jamestown Island.

In 1895 the Trustees of Scenic and Historic Places and Objects of New York was established, although in 1901 it changed its name to the American Scenic and Historic Preservation Society. The Massachusetts Trustees of Reservations was established in 1890 not to assist Indians but to preserve "natural" landscapes in and near urban areas.

Historic preservation also moved west after the Civil War, leaving colonial and Revolutionary War–era buildings behind and providing a new perspective on what was worthy of saving. The first transcontinental railroad was completed in 1869, and spur lines proliferated throughout the midcontinent, promoting interregional travel. In 1887, the state of Illinois put Abraham Lincoln's Springfield homestead into a trust for preservation. Finally a midwesterner had entered the pantheon of the nation's important historic figures.

The federal government at the time also took some heritage preservation initiatives. In 1889, a presidential executive order (EO) protected the Casa Grande ruins in Arizona from settlement or sale. This was not only the first historic site but the first Indian property and the first archaeological property that the federal government explicitly protected. The US government gave the Spanish Palace of the Governors, built in 1611, to the government of the New Mexico Territory in 1898. It still dominates the central square in Santa Fe.

By the 1890s, the Civil War had become a historical event. In 1890 the Chickamauga Battlefield became the nation's first military park, but the McLean House at Appomattox (where Lee surrendered to Ulysses S. Grant) was demolished in 1893. Gettysburg became the second national military park in 1895. A year later, the US Supreme Court prevented a railroad from going through the Gettysburg Battlefield. Thus, by the end of the nineteenth century, all three branches of the federal government were involved in heritage preservation, but there was still no federal law to this effect.

The World Columbian Exposition in Chicago in 1893 launched the City Beautiful Movement, which was to have a positive effect on some American cities for aesthetics and livability but a very negative effect on historic preservation. It was the first nationwide movement for urban renewal focused on building civic centers, parkways, and monuments. To accomplish this, many historic buildings in urban cores were demolished with little of the regret that characterized 1960s urban renewal.

As America entered a new century, the federal government finally got explicitly involved in heritage preservation on a national scale. In 1906, two important federal actions took place: Mesa Verde became a national park, the first created for cultural reasons, and Congress passed the Antiquities Act. Mesa Verde showcased an aspect of the country's prehistoric past, but the Antiquities Act was the first federal attempt to protect this past on a national scale.

The Antiquities Act benefited heritage preservation in three ways:

1. Anyone damaging historic or prehistoric sites on federal property was subject to a substantial fine and/or imprisonment.
2. A permit was needed to excavate archaeological sites on federal property.
3. The president could establish new national monuments on federal land, including that with historical value.

Ten years later, the year 1916 was also important for heritage preservation for multiple reasons. The passage of the Organic Act established the National Park Service. As specified in the original act, the NPS was to "promote and regulate the use of the Federal areas known as national parks, monuments, and reservations hereinafter specified by such means and measures as conform to the fundamental purposes of the said parks, monuments, and reservations, which purpose is to conserve the scenery and the natural and historic objects and the wild life therein and to provide for the enjoyment of the same in such manner and by such means as will leave them unimpaired for the enjoyment of future generations." The year 1916 was also the fiftieth anniversary of the Civil War and, with life expectancy at the time being about 50 years for men, the nineteenth century's "greatest generation," which had fought the Civil War, was rapidly passing. Unlike the post–Revolutionary War focus on structures associated with famous people, Civil War preservation focused on major battlefields. A year after acknowledging this anniversary, the United States entered World War I.

Post–World War I: Boom and Bust and Boom

With World War I ending in late 1918, the United States didn't take long to get back to normal and then to establish a new normal. Although the country had lost over 53,000 soldiers, its human and financial losses were miniscule compared to those incurred by the European powers. The major impact of World War I on the United States was to transform it into one of the world's leading economies and thrust it into the international spotlight.

Historic preservation was little delayed by the war, with the military taking the initial lead. In 1920, the Army War College sponsored a survey of American battlefields. This was one of the first national attempts to inventory a particular historic property type. When the army completed the survey in 1925, it had identified over 3,400 battle sites in the continental United States. In 1923 Congress created the American Battle Monuments Commission, charging it with commemorating the actions of American soldiers here and in Europe. The War Department also undertook the restoration of Arlington House at the national cemetery in 1929.

The biggest driver of change after World War I was the American automobile industry, which had just started mass production at the beginning of the war. This not only fueled the prosperity of the 1920s but also provided unprecedented mobility for citizens of all income levels. Suddenly historic sites as tourist destinations didn't have to be in major cities or on railroad lines.

Americans' fascination with their early history was facilitated by the new accessibility to historic sites provided by cars and site preservation promoted using funds directly derived from the automotive industry. The restoration of Colonial Williamsburg began in 1926, funded by Standard Oil's John D. Rockefeller. The same year, Henry Ford began work on Greenfield Village near Dearborn, Michigan. Williamsburg utilized a core of surviving pre–Revolutionary War buildings, and then, through intensive historical research and archaeological excavation, much of what had been demolished was reconstructed.

Henry Ford's Greenfield Village was a wholly imaginary early nineteenth-century town assembled by moving in historic buildings from throughout the Midwest and Northeast, including famous buildings such as Thomas Edison's lab from New Jersey, the Wright brothers' shop from Ohio, and Abraham Lincoln's law office from Illinois. Greenfield Village opened to the public in 1933, and Williamsburg opened a year later.

Other events in the 1920s helped shape archaeological contributions to American heritage preservation. In 1921, the National Park Service hired its first professional archaeologist, Jesse Nusbaum, as superintendent of Mesa Verde National Park. A major innovation was California's decision to undertake a statewide historic-sites survey in 1928. Its principal objective was to determine areas to be acquired for the park system, but it nonetheless was the first large-area **inventory** of diverse historic properties, although it did not include prehistoric sites.

The stock market crash of 1929, coupled with the severe mid-continental drought beginning in 1930, had a devastating effect on the American economy. The initial effects on historic preservation were minimal, however, because there was no system to cut back; federal or state governments employed very few historic preservation professionals and provided very little public funding for historic preservation.

Under the leadership of Director Horace Albright, historic preservation within the NPS actually advanced during the waning years of the Herbert Hoover administration, despite the economic crisis. In 1930 NPS acquired Wakefield, the site of George Washington's birth, where archaeological excavations soon found remains of the house. The same year, Congress authorized Colonial National Park to incorporate the sites of Jamestown and Yorktown. Also in 1930, the Library of Congress established its Early American Architecture Division, and NPS hired landscape architect Charles Peterson; both events would soon play important roles in historic preservation. In 1931, NPS hired Vern Chatelain as its first historian and began restoration of the Moore House at Yorktown, the first building restoration undertaken by the service.

In early 1933, at the request of NPS and in one of the last acts of the Hoover administration, Congress authorized Morristown National Historical Park in New Jersey. Hosmer (1981:515) notes that Morristown was successful because NPS recognized that in order to get Congress to establish a national historical site, the site had to have the strong support of a local organization and at least one standing structure associated with a prominent national leader or event. Morristown had both, featuring another George Washington headquarters building. NPS was also beginning to recognize an important factor affecting the success of historical parks: enhanced accessibility by automobile. Morristown was close to New York City.

On the state and local levels, major historic preservation advances were also made in the early 1930s even prior to the Franklin D. Roosevelt administration's federal relief projects and despite the economic crisis. In 1931, California established its State Register of Historic Landmarks. The same year, Charleston, South Carolina, established a heritage preservation commission for planning and zoning and then defined the first urban historic district in America. In 1932, Pennsylvania began archaeological excavations at the site of William Penn's house to aid accurate reconstruction.

A major historic preservation action by the new Roosevelt administration preceded the actual implementation of federal relief employment programs. On June 10, 1933, President Roosevelt issued Executive Order 6166, which transferred control of historic sites from the War Department and the Department of Agriculture to the National Park Service. This gave the NPS a total of 80 historical parks and monuments, representing over two-thirds of all NPS units.

Although NPS had requested the presidential action, the organization was initially unprepared for the massive acquisition of historic sites throughout the country. At this time, NPS was a western-oriented natural lands manager, and even its headquarters personnel had been trained in its western parks. Its role as a steward of historic sites was new, with its three initial national historical parks—Colonial, Wakefield, and Morristown—all established in the early 1930s, all on the East Coast, and all focused on interpreting pre-nineteenth-century events.

The NPS employed only a few historic preservation professionals in 1933, notably historian Vern Chatelain and landscape architect Charles Peterson in Washington, two historians at Colonial National Park, and archaeologist Jesse Nusbaum at Mesa Verde. The need for internal NPS historic preservation expertise and the historical scope of NPS historic properties would soon expand exponentially.

When the Roosevelt administration took office in early March 1933, it recognized the need to provide substantial public employment and restore public faith in government. This resulted in a massive expenditure of federal funds for public works. These included park development and historic site restorations in which archaeological excavations preceded some building restorations. This required the employment of an army of historians, architects, and archaeologists, many of whom assumed supervisory roles within the National Park Service in response to federal relief activities.

Historian Ronald Lee (Figure 2.4), who would become chief NPS historian in 1938, was initially hired at Shiloh National Military Park, fresh out of graduate school in June 1933, to supervise work by new Civilian Conservation Corps (CCC) crews. The same was true for historian Herb Kahler at Chickamauga and Chattanooga National Military Park. Soon Vern Chatelain had 60 historians on his staff.

In late 1933, Charles Peterson proposed using federal relief funds to hire 1,000 architects, draftsmen, and photographers to document in detail important historic structures across the nation. Documentation produced by the project would be stored in the new Early American Architecture collections at the Library of Congress. The government accepted the proposal and created the Historic American Buildings Survey (HABS). By 1935, HABS had 449 employees at the state level. It is one of the few Depression-era programs still in operation today, albeit with much reduced staff and annual production.

Jesse Nusbaum, the original NPS archaeologist at Mesa Verde, became the first department consulting archaeologist (DCA) for NPS in 1933. He was soon dispatching newly hired archaeologists to supervise CCC crews at Yorktown and Jamestown. Under the Federal Emergency Relief Administration (FERA), major excavations began in August 1933 at Marksville, Louisiana, a prehistoric earthworks site. The Civil Works Administration (CWA) established in late 1933 soon had major archaeological efforts underway in California and in multiple southeastern states as salvage work for the Tennessee Valley Authority (TVA). The Works Progress Administration (WPA), established in 1935, took over and expanded the CWA archaeological projects. These federal relief projects continued until American entry into World War II in late 1941.

Other federal relief activities unrelated to park development and construction greatly benefited heritage preservation. The Historical Records Survey of the WPA was an outgrowth of the Federal Writers Project in late 1935. Its purpose was to discover, preserve, and list basic historical research materials for the benefit of officials, historians, and the public. It initially focused on county government records but expanded to include church records, newspaper indexes, maritime records, and even the records at the National Archives and Records Administration (NARA), established in 1934. The original intent had been to publish indexes of all the county records for the entire nation, but only about a third had been published when World War II ended the survey.

FIG. 2.4 Ronald Lee, NPS chief historian from 1938 to 1950 (National Park Service).

Museums also benefited from Depression-era programs. The WPA constructed or improved numerous museums for multiple purposes, including art, natural history, and cultural history. Many buildings built by the WPA for other civic purposes are now used as museums (see https://livingnewdeal.org/new-deal-categories/educational/museums). The WPA's Museum Extension Project (1935–1943) created millions of visual display items, including dioramas, scale models, specimen casts, and artifact replicas for use both within museums and in schools.

Besides the great expansion of historic preservation work directly related to federal relief programs, the other major heritage preservation action of the 1930s was the passage of the Historic Sites Act. As its historic preservation duties began to greatly expand in the early 1930s, the National Park Service recognized the need for broad legal support for historic preservation including actions beyond current NPS properties. The Historic Sites Act became law in August 1935 after intensive lobbying by the NPS and private historic preservationists. It authorized the creation of a survey of nationally significant historic sites, encouraged cooperative agreements between the federal government and private entities for the maintenance of important historic sites, and empowered the secretary of the interior to accept new additions to the system of national historic sites. Within NPS, it promoted research, preservation, restoration, and interpretation.

The Historic Sites Survey began in earnest in the summer of 1936. Its principal purpose was to find and evaluate properties that could eventually come into the National Park Service, so they had to be nationally significant. Four NPS regional historians directed the survey with oversight from Ronald Lee in Washington. An advisory board developed historical thematic categories within which properties could be targeted for survey and evaluated for relative importance. Of course, members of Congress all wanted properties from their home districts represented, and survey requests soon overwhelmed the small NPS staff. By the beginning of World War II, when the survey ended, only 560 properties had been surveyed, of which about 40% were considered nationally significant (Sprinkle 2014:15).

In addition to supervising historic preservation activities associated with federal relief programs and the Historic Sites Survey authorized by the Historic Sites Act, the NPS continued to develop national historical parks. It established the Jefferson National Expansion Memorial in St. Louis in 1935 to commemorate the Louisiana Purchase and the opening of the western United States. Local promoters in St. Louis saw the project primarily as a way to redevelop their aging riverfront, a unique form of urban renewal. Local political pressure to tear everything down in a 91-acre parcel created a major historic preservation dilemma for the NPS. In the end, only three historic buildings were saved: the architecturally prominent courthouse and cathedral and an early stone warehouse (Figure 2.5).

Other national historic areas that came into NPS control in the late 1930s included Salem Maritime in Massachusetts, Hopewell Village in Pennsylvania, Fort Laramie in Wyoming, and the Vanderbilt Mansion in New York, all notable for their lack of strong Founding Fathers associations. NPS attempts in the 1930s to establish national historical parks at Harpers Ferry and several western frontier forts failed.

Nonfederal heritage preservation activities just prior to World War II included the founding of a number of important national organizations. The Society for American Archaeology (SAA) was established in 1934. In 1940, the American Association for State and Local History (AASLH) and the American Society of Architectural Historians (ASAH) were established. Members of these organizations had benefited from the great expansion in the employment of heritage preservation professionals due to federal relief programs.

FIG. 2.5 View of St. Louis looking west from the Gateway Arch. The historic courthouse in the foreground is one of only three historic buildings to survive the post–World War II central riverfront redevelopment (author photo).

With the bombing of Pearl Harbor on December 7, 1941, the United States entered World War II. The need for more military administrative space in Washington, DC, forced the NPS to move to Chicago for the duration of the war, a real and symbolic demonstration of the reordering of national priorities. The war also ended the Great Depression and the need for civilian work programs. The army was soon employing millions.

During the war, there was very little historic preservation activity. The NPS move to Chicago siphoned off funds, key personnel (e.g., Ronald Lee) joined the military, and President Roosevelt didn't want anything to distract Americans from the war effort (Hosmer 1981:718). The shock of seeing what German bombing had done to London created some initial concern that East Coast cities in the United States may also be subjected to war damage. There was some push to expand the efforts of HABS to record additional buildings, but little came of it. In 1943 Independence Hall was finally designated a national historic site, and all existing drawings and plans for the building (done prior to the war) were put in safekeeping in case the building was bombed (Hosmer 1981:768). Military base expansions and even patriotic promotions also led to the loss of historic properties. In Minneapolis, the city tore down a historic bridge over the Mississippi River with the justification that the steel was needed for the war effort.

Post–World War II: Becoming a World Leader

With the end of World War II in August 1945, the country was eager to rapidly recover from the Great Depression and the war. Archaeologists, historians, and preservation architects had gone off to fight, but now these people were back home, some back in their prewar agency positions. The invigoration and expansion of these professions during the 1930s carried over into the 1940s.

Unprofessional aspects of the federal relief archaeology in the 1930s had bothered many senior archaeologists, so in 1939 the National Research Council (NRC) formed the Committee on Basic Needs of Archaeology to review the work done for FERA, CWA, WPA, TVA, CCC, and WPA. The committee recommended some minimum scientific requirements for future federal archaeology programs, that preservation be considered along with excavation, and that the National Park Service have a greater role in coordinating and overseeing federal archaeology.

The federal government began to implement reservoir projects in river basins before the war was even over in accordance with the passage of the Flood Control Act in 1944 to fulfill the desire for hydroelectricity to power postwar industrial, agricultural, and residential expansion. The government had developed basic plans for these projects just before the war, and this had raised concerns from archaeological professionals. As the end of the war neared, Frank Roberts and Julian Steward of the Smithsonian Institution contacted federal agencies involved with the hydroelectric projects to express their concerns regarding the impacts to archaeological sites. These concerns were also discussed at the 1944 annual meeting of the Society for American Archaeology. An SAA committee then met with the NRC archaeological committee, and the Committee for the Recovery of Archaeological Remains (CRAR) was formed in May 1945 to represent all of the professional groups concerned with federal reservoir development.

In October 1945, an interagency agreement between the Corps of Engineers, the Bureau of Recreation, the Smithsonian Institution, and the National Park Service put the Smithsonian in overall charge of archaeological research, with the NPS responsible for obtaining funding and contracting for necessary work. The River Basin Surveys were part of the Smithsonian's Bureau of American Ethnology (BAE) with regional offices at major universities in Lincoln, Nebraska; Eugene, Oregon; Austin, Texas; and Berkeley, California. (**Ethnology** is the study of culture through the comparison of different cultures, while **ethnography** is the description and study of a particular culture.) Over the next 25 years, RBS conducted archaeological surveys, testing, and salvage in 29 states on about 300 reservoirs and recorded over 5,000 archaeological sites. The Missouri River Division based in Lincoln, Nebraska, was the largest and longest lasting of the River Basin Surveys, in operation from 1946 to 1969. The RBS office in Lincoln became the NPS Midwest Archaeological Center when the survey ended in 1969.

The founding of the National Trust for Historic Preservation (NTHP) in 1949 was a major step forward in broadening and focusing American heritage preservation. As a private organization, it had the freedom to promote unpopular causes and challenge government actions. Because it was federally chartered, the NTHP gained instant recognition and status as a national leader in heritage preservation. The federal charter also facilitated access to federal funds.

Just after the National Trust was founded, historic preservationists faced a major crisis. The Housing Act of 1949 promoted "urban renewal" to deal with housing needs due to the postwar influx of people to cities. The Housing Act of 1954, which promoted civic and commercial development of "blighted" areas, reinforced this. Soon blocks and blocks of buildings were demolished in urban cores without consideration of the condition or history of individual buildings; if an area was deemed blighted, the entire area was cleared. Although the 1954 act allowed building rehabilitation, most cities largely ignored this aspect.

During the Korean War (1950–1953), military needs diverted funding and attention from heritage preservation, although existing activities such as the River Basin Surveys continued. The NTHP made its first major purchase in 1952 when it obtained Woodlawn Planation, a post–Revolutionary War property on the original George Washington estate.

Another large federal construction project began in 1956 with the passage of the Federal-Aid Highway Act, which funded the Interstate Highway System. Section 120 of the act authorized states to use highway funds "to the extent approved as necessary" for archaeological and paleontological salvage. It made no mention of buildings and historic sites. Most states took the word "salvage" to mean already well-known sites or major sites encountered (and recognized by construction workers) during construction. Few surveys were done prior to highway construction until after the passage of the National Historic Preservation Act in 1966. The new interstate highways cut massive corridors not only through the countryside but also through older areas of cities, destroying entire neighborhoods and exacerbating the problems of urban historic preservation already caused by urban renewal.

The National Park Service reentered proactive historic preservation in 1956 in an innovative way. Basic maintenance in most national parks had been ignored during the war years due to a lack of funds and labor. Visitorship at the parks also greatly increased after the war with the end of gasoline rationing and an expanding recreational demand due to the baby boom. In response to these needs and in anticipation of its fiftieth anniversary in 1966, the NPS launched Mission 66 in 1956. Besides basic infrastructure improvements, it introduced a new concept of "visitor center" to replace the small and basic facilities built by the CCC in the 1930s (Figure 2.6).

The NPS hired numerous historians and archaeologists to deal with the planning, mitigation, and interpretation needs of Mission 66. Over the 10 years of Mission 66, NPS spent $1 billion on park improvements and the completion of major park projects such as the Gateway Arch in St. Louis. It also established 78 new parks during this period, bringing the total number to 258 by 1966.

With the completion of NPS Mission 66 came the most significant action in American historic preservation: the passage of the National Historic Preservation

FIG. 2.6 Mission 66 project circa 1962 at Chancellorsville Battlefield (National Park Service).

Act. In 1966, many factors—beyond the fiftieth anniversary of the NPS—combined to make this possible.

The United States had a Democratic president and Congress in 1966. It was the middle of Lyndon Johnson's "Great Society" initiative, which included social amenity initiatives such as highway beautification. Massive federal building projects for highways, dams, and urban housing had displaced thousands of people and ripped up cities and the land, energizing the environmental movement. It was a time of civil unrest, with the Vietnam War and civil rights at the top of the news every day. The baby boomers were young and restless. Two influential books had recently questioned government actions: Rachel Carson's *Silent Spring* (1962) and Jane Jacobs's *The Death and Life of Great American Cities* (1961). Another book, *With Heritage So Rich* (1966), though less known to the public, formed the basis of a new preservation movement and directly led to the passage of revolutionary heritage preservation legislation.

The Vietnam War had a greater effect on the country than the Korean War because it was an incremental and unnecessary American offensive action lasting over 10 years. It was thus less popular and more financially and emotionally draining. America was a different place by the time the Vietnam War ended in 1975. However, as during the Korean War and unlike during previous major wars, life in America went on as normal for those not directly involved in the fighting. Heritage preservation continued to rapidly improve.

The National Historic Preservation Act of 1966 in Section 106 required federal agencies to consider the effect of their actions on important historic and archaeological sites and consult with the newly formed Advisory Council on Historic Preservation about these effects. The law established the National Register of Historic Places and state liaison officers, soon to be known as state historic preservation officers. It provided funding for grants to local historic preservation organizations and projects. It made historic preservation a cooperative national, state, and local endeavor, although it took a few years to effectively implement.

Another important law in 1966 also greatly benefited historic preservation: the Department of Transportation Act (DOTA). Section 4(f) of this law specified that all projects receiving federal transportation funding or approval could not use historic sites, public parks, recreational land, or wildlife refuges unless there was no feasible and prudent alternative and all possible planning was done to minimize harm to the resource. This law was about avoidance, not just consideration, of adverse effects.

The National Park Service was reorganized in 1967 to deal with the new heritage preservation legislation. The NPS formed the Office of Archaeology and Historic Preservation (OAHP) to include the new ACHP and NRHP, as well as the existing NPS History, Archaeology, and Architecture divisions. In 1968, the ACHP issued its first regulations to implement Section 106 of the NHPA, although they were nonbinding for agencies.

In 1969 the country's most important environmental protection legislation included consideration of heritage resources in a broader but less focused way than the NHPA. The National Environmental Policy Act (NEPA) once again applied only to federal agencies' actions that were federally funded or subject to federal approval. If such an action had the potential to significantly affect the quality of the human environment, the agency had to briefly yet comprehensively evaluate the effects of the action in an **environmental assessment** (EA). If EA analysis determined that effects would be significant, a detailed **environmental impact statement** (EIS) had to be prepared. As with the NHPA Section 106 process, at the end of the environmental review process the agency did not have to avoid adverse effects; it only had to identify and evaluate them. The human environment potentially included heritage resources beyond the historic properties of Section 106 under social and economic effects, but less tangible aspects of heritage are usually ignored by the EIS process.

In the early 1970s, the procedures used to implement the 1960s heritage preservation legislation were operationalized and fine-tuned. President Nixon issued Executive Order 11593 to address some major deficiencies of the NHPA. Section 106 of the 1966 law only provided for consideration of historic properties actually listed in the National Register of Historic Places. Because the Register was very small at that time and inclusion of new listings was slow (as the burden for submitting new nominations was with the states, which initially had no professional support staff), federal agencies continued to destroy many eligible but unlisted sites. The executive order required agencies to include eligible sites under Section 106 consideration based on consultation with SHPOs.

EO 11593 also required federal land-managing agencies to inventory their lands for historic properties and submit NRHP nominations for eligible sites. In 1974 the Archaeological and Historic Preservation Act (also known as Moss-Bennett) amended the 1960 Reservoir Salvage Act. In some ways it duplicated what NHPA and NEPA required, but it did allow up to 1% of construction funds to be used for archaeological mitigation.

Post–Vietnam War: Rethinking the Past and the Present

Unlike World Wars I and II and Korea, the Vietnam War was discretionary on the part of the United States. It was essentially a continuation of the Korean War, largely due to Western paranoia about the worldwide spread of communism pushed by the Soviet Union and China. The Vietnam War started in the early 1960s, when the United States was at the height of its economic power and international influence. By the time the conflict ended in 1975, the international goodwill created by US actions after World War II had largely evaporated, and the country itself was regionally, generationally, and politically divided.

In 1976, as the country celebrated its bicentennial, there was a burst of federal actions supporting the 10-year-old historic preservation system. Congress amended the NHPA to include the NRHP **eligibility** considerations for Section 106 set forth in Executive Order 11593, make the ACHP an independent government agency, and establish the **Historic Preservation Fund** (HPF) to help finance SHPOs and to provide direct financial support for local historic preservation grants. The National Register of Historic Places provided statutory regulations (36 CFR 60) concerning what was eligible and how to nominate properties.

The Tax Reform Act of 1976 provided tax incentives for the rehabilitation of historic buildings, requiring the secretary of the interior to issue standards for building rehabilitation. Other federal acts of note in 1976 that had important implications for heritage preservation are the Federal Land Policy Act, the National Forest Management Act, and the American Folklife Preservation Act.

During the Jimmy Carter administration (1977–1980), a number of federal actions affected heritage preservation. In 1978 the American Indian Religious Freedom Act (AIRFA) gave Indian people enhanced access to sacred sites on federal lands and allowed some traditional religious practices that had been previously restricted. The same year, the Federal Revenue Act provided additional tax incentives for historic building renovation. An executive memorandum in 1978 gave the ACHP formal rule-making authority, which the ACHP implemented in 1979, issuing 36 CFR 800 pertaining to the Section 106 process.

Due to the *U.S. v. Diaz* Supreme Court decision in 1974, which held the 1906 Antiquities Act to be unconstitutionally vague, the Archaeological Resources Protection Act (ARPA) was passed to strengthen protection of archaeological sites on federal land. Finally, during the last days of the Carter administration, Congress amended the NHPA in 1980 for a second time, adding federal land-management obligations under Section 110 and outlining SHPO duties in Section 101.

A number of other important heritage preservation developments occurred in the late 1970s. The NRHP issued the first National Register bulletin in 1977, describing in detail how to nominate a property. The Supreme Court issued the decision in *Penn Central Transportation Co. v. New York City*, confirming the right of city governments to preserve important historic sites in private ownership. The National Trust started the Main Street Program and the National Council for Preservation Education. In 1978, the internal history and archaeology programs of the NPS were separated from the external ones, ending OAHP and putting the National Register, Grants, Historical and Archaeological Surveys, and Interagency Services into a new non-NPS organization called the Heritage Conservation and Recreation Service (HCRS).

When the Ronald Reagan administration took office in early 1981, it made big changes in federal heritage preservation. The so-called Reagan Revolution attempted to decentralize many aspects of historic preservation and put the responsibility (and the financial burden) on state and **local governments**. An attempt to water down the Section 106 regulations failed, but the HPF was cut by more than half, from $60 million in 1979 to $26 million in 1981. By 1986, the HPF had dropped to its lowest level ever, adjusting for inflation. The HCRS office was eliminated, with all heritage management duties going back to NPS. The Supreme Court's 1983 decision in *Metropolitan Edison Co. v. People Against Nuclear Energy* (commonly referred to as the *PANE* decision) somewhat restricted the application of NEPA for heritage preservation by determining that social and economic aspects alone could not require an environmental impact statement.

All the news was not bad for heritage preservation during the Reagan years. The Economic Recovery Tax Act of 1981 expanded tax credits for renovation and restoration of historic buildings. The *Secretary of the Interior's Standards and Guidelines for Historic Preservation*, issued in 1983, attempted to bring national consistency to the way federal historic preservation was done. In 1986, the ACHP again revised the Section 106 regulations. The Abandoned Shipwrecks Act of 1987 was one of the last congressional actions of the Reagan administration.

The George H. W. Bush administration, which took office in 1989, initially made few major changes in the American heritage preservation system except with respect to the role of Indian tribes. The 1988 Supreme Court decision in *Lyng v. Northwest Indian Cemetery Protective Association* determined that the destruction of sacred sites on federal lands did not violate the First Amendment right to the free exercise of religion. This energized tribal activists and their supporters. There was widespread recognition that tribal participation in federal heritage management needed examination, so in 1989 Congress directed the NPS to examine tribal heritage preservation needs. The NPS published the study as *Keepers of the Treasures: Protecting Historic Properties and Cultural Traditions on Indian Lands* in 1990.

The legislative results of the NPS tribal study were twofold. In 1990, the Native American Graves Protection and Repatriation Act (NAGPRA) required federally supported curational facilities to promptly conduct an inventory of human remains and possible Indian sacred items in their collections, provide the inventories to interested tribes, and return items to tribes where cultural patrimony could be established. It also provided additional protection for cemetery sites on federal land.

Then, in 1992, Congress amended the NHPA to include tribal consultation and the establishment of tribal historic preservation offices (THPOs, pronounced "tip-os") to assume SHPO duties within reservation boundaries. An additional tribal-oriented development was the publication by the National Register of a traditional cultural property (TCP) bulletin in 1992.

Other major federal heritage management developments in the second half of the George H. W. Bush administration included the issuance by NPS of federal curation standards (36 CFR 79) in 1990 and passage of the Intermodal Surface Transportation Efficiency Act (ISTEA) in 1991. ISTEA included provisions for major funding of heritage preservation activities, including purchase of easements on historic properties, rehabilitation of historic buildings, and archaeological planning and research. The 1991 Americans with Disabilities Act (ADA) had important implications for historic preservation in that providing accessibility to public buildings required significant internal and external alterations to many historic properties.

The two terms of the Bill Clinton administration were marked by few legislative actions in support of heritage preservation, but by the 1990s most general procedural needs for historic preservation had been achieved and funding for existing programs was needed. Congress extended the Department of Transportation ISTEA funding provided in 1991 with the Transportation Equity Act for the Twenty-First Century (TEA-21) in 1998. The Clinton administration's contribution to heritage preservation is notable mostly for three laws that focused on particular property types: the National Maritime Heritage Act, the American Battlefield Protection Act, and the National Lighthouse Preservation Act. President Clinton issued a number of executive orders affecting historic preservation: Executive Order 13006 concerned the use of urban historic buildings, EO 13007 extended further protections to Indian sacred sites, and EO 13175 confirmed the nation-to-nation relationship between tribes and the federal government.

Federal agencies during the Clinton administration also focused on particular property types. The National Register finally issued a bulletin on archaeological sites in 1993. In 1996 the secretary of the interior issued updated *Standards for the Treatment of Historic Properties with Guidelines for the Treatment of Cultural Landscapes*. The ACHP finally issued revised 36 CFR 800 regulations based on the 1992 NHPA amendments in 1999 and again in 2001, but these attempts were not legally binding due to lawsuits challenging tribal powers and other aspects of the revision.

Post-9/11 and the War on Terror: A World of Continuous Danger

The "War on Terror" began after the attacks on New York and Washington, DC, of September 11, 2001. It differs from other wars we have fought. There is no one enemy with a country to invade and a capital city to bomb. There is no one entity to defeat. It is a world war without focus, but it is still war. It takes great commitment and resources to fight. It has changed how we travel, how we access buildings, and how we get along with one another. It has affected heritage preservation and not just in areas of site destruction.

The post-9/11 George W. Bush (2001–2008) and Barack Obama (2009–2016) administrations are notable for their lack of significant legislative and executive action in support of heritage preservation. The George W. Bush administration basically followed the Reagan administration's approach by providing funds directly to communities as much for economic development as for historic preservation. The initiative, called "Preserve America," was authorized by Executive Order 13278 in 2003. Also like the Reagan administration, the Bush administration attempted to change policies within the National Park Service through personnel changes. Republican dissatisfaction with some National Register listings perceived as antidevelopment led to the dismissal in 2005 of long-serving Keeper of the National Register Carol Shull. She was replaced with Janet Mathews, an associate director of the NPS under a Bush-appointed director. The ACHP was reorganized and the Denver ACHP office closed.

Other notable heritage preservation events during the George W. Bush administration included final acceptance of the 36 CFR 800 regulations implementing the 1992 NHPA amendments. These regulations reduced ACHP influence on the Section 106 process, so the ACHP attempted to broaden its influence on general historic preservation practice. The ACHP issued guidance on dealing with historic human remains in 2007 and on the practices of archaeology and heritage tourism in 2008.

During the Obama administration, most federal historic preservation activity continued to be internally generated. The ACHP extended its attempts to broadly influence heritage preservation policy, especially with regard to promoting diversity. In 2009, it issued a handbook on Indian consultation as well as expert panel recommendations to improve the structure of the federal historic preservation program. In 2011, it produced a traditional **cultural landscapes** plan and a study of the economic impacts of historic preservation. During the Obama tenure, the ACHP also dealt with Indian sacred sites, Section 106–NEPA coordination, and guidance on preparing agreement documents, on infrastructure projects that may affect historic properties, and on agencies and professionals dealing with THPOs.

A final act affecting heritage management signed by President Obama on December 16, 2016, amended the NHPA to make ACHP chairmanship a full-time position, to make the National Association of Tribal Historic Preservation Officers (NATHPO) chairman a voting member of the ACHP, and to reauthorize the HPF until 2023. Overall, the NHPA's fiftieth anniversary in 2016 saw little change in federal preservation practice. This has basically been true for the last 30 years with the exception of tribal input added by the 1992 NHPA amendment.

As of the end of 2017, despite the initial paranoia of many agencies and professional organizations, the Donald Trump administration had been too distracted with other issues to pay much attention to attacking heritage management. The main concerns were with eliminating or significantly reducing the size of some national monuments and exempting the Department of Defense (DOD) from National Register listing requirements. Still, the lands excised from national monuments would still be federally owned and subject to federal heritage preservation laws. DOD historic properties could still be determined eligible for inclusion in the Register, thus fully subject to Section 106.

Summary

If we examine American historic preservation in the period from the end of the Revolutionary War to the end of the Civil War, a number of trends are apparent. Most importantly, heritage preservation was not a federal initiative and very little of it was even governmental in any form. It was mostly private, local, and individual. Women played a greater role than men, ironically, in preserving and celebrating places publicly associated with men. It was an elitist initiative led by an upper class with upper-class values and priorities, dominated by the preservation of buildings associated with the Founding Fathers, especially George Washington. There was no formal recognition of the value of archaeological sites or places associated with women and minorities. There was no recognition of historic value west of the Mississippi River. There was very little intellectual guidance or insight, with the notable exception of British architect John Ruskin's *The Seven Lamps of Architecture* (1849).

The heritage preservation trends between the end of the Civil War and the beginning of World War I somewhat mirror those of the pre–Civil War period. Individuals, especially women, still dominated heritage preservation, and buildings were still the focus. However, there were some significant differences. The federal and state governments were starting to get involved, the emphasis on the Revolutionary War had shifted to include the Civil War, a few midwestern and western sites had become important and accessible, and Indians, at least ancient ones who built with stone, had become visible.

Heritage preservation between the end of World War I and the onset of World War II began with a national nostalgia for "the good old days." Once again, historic preservation was initially largely a private endeavor; millionaires John D. Rockefeller and Henry Ford led the way, with their golden egg, the automobile, funding their efforts. The automobile also gave the public a way to visit newly recognized historic places. Private organizations acquired threatened historic sites that were clearly of **national significance**, such as Thomas Jefferson's Monticello.

In the 1930s, everything changed. The National Park Service broadened its scope from just western natural areas to include major historic sites throughout the country, beginning with the establishment of three eastern national historical parks. A 1933 executive order giving the NPS historic battlefields, parks, monuments, and cemeteries formerly managed by other agencies made the service's historic scope truly national; its purview now also included some nineteenth-century properties. The federal relief programs of the Roosevelt administration beginning in the summer of 1933 required the NPS and the Smithsonian Institution to hire historians, architects, and archaeologists to supervise hundreds of projects carried out by the new alphabet agencies. Heritage management also took on an archaeological perspective, combining professionalism, legal guidance, and a full range of management activities, including identification, evaluation, treatment, and interpretation.

The 1930s ushered in the professionalization of all heritage preservation as reflected by the creation of professional organizations such as the SAA, AASLH, and ASAH. In this period professionals also awoke to the dilemmas of historic preservation that still plague us: restoration versus reconstruction, interpretation requiring alteration, and archaeological data salvage versus site preservation.

The entry of the United States into World War II soon ended federal relief projects and effectively halted heritage preservation activities. When the war ended, the federal government rapidly reengaged in some heritage preservation activities, such as salvage archaeology associated with the construction of numerous dams in the Southeast, Midwest, and West. These activities largely ignored impacts to standing structures, but the founding of the National Trust for Historic Preservation in 1949 put the history-architecture component of heritage management back on track.

Archaeological site and historic structure destruction rapidly accelerated in the 1950s with federally sponsored interstate highway construction and urban renewal. The passage of the National Historic Preservation Act in 1966 began to address the destruction, but it took a decade to implement an effective heritage preservation system. Archaeologists took the lead in the federal system, with the processual, scientific orientation of the "new archaeology" fitting well with a comprehensive management approach. The National Trust continued to provide leadership for history-architecture matters. Other 1960s laws such as NEPA and DOTA supported the system developed for NHPA.

After the Vietnam War ended in 1975, federal heritage preservation was fine-tuned with several amendments to the NHPA and the adoption of formal regulations implementing Section 106. The federal heritage management system expanded during the Carter administration with peak funding of the HPF. The Reagan administration threatened to erase many of the gains, but the system survived basically intact. By 1990, the need to better protect traditional Indian sites and include tribes in the decision-making process resulted in several federal legislative acts (e.g., NAG-PRA, the 1992 NHPA amendments) and procedural initiatives (e.g., the NRHP TCP bulletin).

Post-9/11 federal legal initiatives have been limited and focused on specialty properties such as maritime resources. Indian consultation continues to be fine-tuned, and THPOs have faced the same learning curve and growing pains that SHPOs faced in the 1960s and 1970s. Political stalemates have politicized and polarized almost all congressional initiatives, leading to legislative stagnation. Concerns with diversity and postmodernist perspectives have broadened the scope of historic preservation but have also distracted some professionals and agencies from focused activities promoting preservation as a whole.

In simplest terms, the history of heritage management in America is a progression and eventual combination of six verbs: "save," "designate," "find," "interpret," "treat," and "manage." (Postmodernists would probably add a seventh: "reinterpret.") There was no national historic preservation movement in the United States until after World War II, just the individual and uncoordinated local efforts of a few individuals, organizations, states, cities, and agencies.

Almost all histories of historic preservation or cultural resource management list the following 13 events as critical to American heritage preservation:

- Saving of Independence Hall by the citizens of Philadelphia (1816)
- Acquisition of Mount Vernon by the Mount Vernon Ladies' Association (1853)
- Passage of the Antiquities Act (1906)
- Establishment of the National Park Service (1916)
- Reconstruction of Colonial Williamsburg (1926)
- Assembly of Greenfield Village (1929)
- Passage of the Charleston zoning ordinance (1931)
- Establishment of Depression-era programs (1930s)
- Passage of the Historic Sites Act (1935)
- Establishment of the National Trust for Historic Preservation (1949)
- Passage of the National Historic Preservation Act (1966)
- Passage of the Tax Reform Act (1976)
- Passage of amendments to the National Historic Preservation Act (1992)

Note that all of the federal actions with broad heritage preservation implications listed above date to the second half of the twentieth century. Also note that two of the most important federal heritage preservation actions are missing from the list: passage of the Department of Transportation Act (1966) and passage of the National Environmental Policy Act (1969). The Native American Graves Protection and Repatriation Act (1990) is often mentioned in CRM (archaeology) overviews but rarely by historically or architecturally oriented historic preservationists.

No actions on the list have occurred in the past 25 years. A comprehensive chronology of heritage preservation (see Appendix C) indicates that over the past quarter century either we have been generally satisfied with the current structure of heritage preservation in this country or there is no political will, or at least consensus, to correct problems with it. The final chapter of this book will present my perspective on the status and needs of American heritage preservation.

Review Questions

1. Why study the history of heritage management?
2. What effects have wars had on heritage management?
3. What are some of the most important events and trends in heritage management and when did they happen?
4. When and why did historic preservation become a movement?
5. Discuss the social and intellectual reasons for heritage preservation.

Supplemental Reading

Any serious student of historic preservation must eventually read the three-volume history of pre-1960s historic preservation written by Charles Hosmer (1965, 1982) and James Glass's 1990 sequel, *The Beginnings of a New National Historic Preservation Program, 1957 to 1969.*

Thomas King's 1987 article "Prehistory and Beyond: The Place of Archaeology" is somewhat dated but a good overview of the role archaeologists played in heritage management up to 20 years beyond the passage of the National Historic Preservation Act. It is unfortunate that King did not provide a chapter on the detailed history of CRM archaeology in the volume he edited in 2011.

The website of the National Park Service provides access to many important foundational documents as well as the historical perspectives of its staff.

SIDEBAR

Implementing Heritage Management: The Electrification of Preservation

When I did my first archaeological field school in 1971, we used nothing electronic at our excavation site. We walked into the site from a county road. We laid out the excavation units, made a topographic map of the surroundings, and tied our datum into the real world with an optical device known as a transit. We wrote our field notes with pencil and paper. Our cameras used film and didn't have batteries. In the field camp lab, we had electric lights and a transistor radio, but that was about it for powered devices. Back at the University of Minnesota, the state site file was kept on 5″ × 7″ index cards.

I took a Paleoindian archaeology course from visiting professor Marie Wormington. She had special punched index cards for all the known Paleoindian points and could mechanically sort them with a special needle. We had mainframe computers, but they weren't accessible to liberal arts undergrads. The most important technological device available to us was a photocopier in the library. As I finished my BA, handheld calculators were beginning to replace slide rules.

By the time I got to graduate school at the University of Nebraska, mainframe computers were accessible to grad students, but you had to use paper punch cards to record and analyze your data. Because statistical analysis was important to the "new archaeology," a big breakthrough was the availability of a software program called the Statistical Package for the Social Sciences (SPSS). I used it to investigate ceramic manufacturing processes at the site I had helped dig in 1971. I typed a rough draft of my master's thesis on a manual typewriter and then hired a professional typist to type the final version.

When I got my first full-time job at the Minnesota Historic Society in 1975, not much had changed with regard to the technology used by my professors at Minnesota and Nebraska when they were university students in the mid-twentieth century. A number of remote-sensing techniques had been developed in the 1950s and 1960s (e.g., soil resistivity and magnetometry), but these techniques were still new and very expensive. Our remote sensing was limited to existing aerial photographs and metal detectors. We still typed up our reports and drew our illustrations in pen and ink.

Then, in about 1980, the world changed. Suddenly desktop computers were widely available with somewhat easy-to-use software. I was two chapters into typing my PhD dissertation when I got a computer at work with WordStar word-processing software. I started keeping track of sites with the dBase program. I got a computer at home, keyboarded those two chapters into it, and saved them on a floppy disk. A big part of my cultural resource management job had suddenly become electrified. I didn't use electric devices in the field, but I sure used them in the office for analysis and communication.

When I joined the Minnesota State Historic Preservation Office in 1990, the electronic revolution was hitting fieldwork. A variety of remote-sensing techniques, including ground-penetrating radar (GPR), had become accessible. Archaeologists were using Total Station survey equipment. Archaeologists were even taking portable computers into the field and loading data directly onto them on-site.

Office work also rapidly advanced in the early 1990s. The World Wide Web (WWW) appeared in 1991, and people started communicating with email. I got to email questions to my SHPO peers in other states through the National Conference of State Historic Preservation Officers (NCSHPO) listserve. People started using PowerPoint on data projectors instead of slide projectors at regional and national professional meetings. They started sharing data in pdf files. Desktop publishing programs made our reports look more professional. By the mid-1990s, digital cameras were replacing film. Geographic information systems (GISs) were not only more user friendly but had digital data available to make them seem like magic.

As we moved into the twenty-first century, cell phones with 3G data-sharing capabilities were common. High-precision GPS allowed fieldworkers to locate themselves with submeter accuracy. Aerial LiDAR could be used to find and map surface features like burial mounds and fortifications. By the early 2010s, field surveys began to use remote cameras on ultralight aerial vehicles, better known as drones, to find and record sites. Apple released the first iPad in 2010, making portable computing really portable.

The electronic revolution in heritage management is not limited to archaeology. Almost all the computer innovations have greatly improved efficiency, accuracy, and communication in history and architecture too. Online resources have dramatically simplified and expanded literature searches. These resources include current and historical aerial photographs, historical maps, General Land Office (GLO) records, US Geological Survey maps, context studies, professional journals, National Register nominations and **Multiple Property Documentation Forms** (MPDFs), historical photographs, and, of course, Google searches on any topic. Many SHPOs have their statewide inventories online. Minnesota has online access to detailed LiDAR information for the entire state.

Most architecture schools continue to first train historical architects as architects, and a few then offer a specialty in historic preservation. Many of their preparatory classes are in design and drawing. Sophisticated computer-aided design applications (e.g., AutoCAD) were introduced in the early 1980s. Current versions of these applications can create 3-D models and even support 3-D printing. Laser scanning of buildings was introduced in the late 1990s, greatly simplifying the recording process and improving accuracy.

CHAPTER 3

The Legal System and Early Heritage Preservation Legislation
Mortar and Some Bricks

The service thus established shall promote and regulate the use of the Federal areas known as national parks, monuments, and reservations hereinafter specified by such means and measures as conform to the fundamental purpose of the said parks, monuments, and reservations, which purpose is to conserve the scenery and the natural and historic objects and the wild life therein and to provide for the enjoyment of the same in such manner and by such means as will leave them unimpaired for the enjoyment of future generations.

—National Park Service Organic Act (1916)

Building our cultural heritage protection system has been a matter of compromise. Almost all of us value heritage, but we also value our essential rights guaranteed in the Constitution: free speech, freedom of religion, and private property rights. We appreciate cultural diversity but value our own cultural identity. We want to preserve aspects of the past but enjoy the freedom to design an interesting future and provide housing and jobs. We understand the right of everyone to have reasonable access to public buildings but realize building ramps in the Mesa Verde ruins would be an unacceptable intrusion. We love nature in our national parks, but there is no restoring their precultural condition, and even if we could do this, we wouldn't want to erase all of the built environment in these parks.

We create laws to regulate our behavior so that our society will be orderly and safe. Our best laws implement compromises that seem fair and reasonable to the majority, without infringing on the basic rights of anyone, including people in the minority. Our system of government gives every citizen a say in what is written in the law and how the law is implemented by public entities, as well as the opportunity for judicial review if they think the law has been misapplied or is unconstitutional.

Bronin and Rowberry (2014:2) point out that American heritage preservation laws have three basic origins: (1) regulation of who has the right to collect **archaeological resources** from public lands, (2) a mandate to protect the environment, and (3) a need to protect significant historic buildings, structures, objects, and sites. We recognize these needs for two basic reasons: inspiration and practicality. Inspirational aspects include patriotism, aesthetics, and commemoration. Practical aspects include economic development, community preservation, sustainability, and education.

As described in chapter 2, heritage preservation in the United States was initially private and local. As our ability to destroy the landscape dramatically increased, so did the need to make preservation of certain aspects of that landscape a national effort, with all that meant with regard to control, funding, and consistency. Our country was well over a century old before we had the collective will to do anything to protect heritage resources on a national scale. It was almost 200 years old before federal preservation caught up with federal destruction.

Prior to 1966, the federal government had focused on the protection of select federally owned historic properties, particularly those of national significance. The only real exceptions were a few federal relief programs during the 1930s and the large reservoir archaeological site salvage efforts after World War II. Both of these were short-term, reactive programs of limited scope. There were, however, some glimmers of the future of American heritage preservation in a few pre-1966 laws. These laws became the first building blocks of our current system. What holds them and the post-1966 laws together is the American legal system.

The American Legal System

In order to understand what is required for heritage management in the United States, you need to first understand how our legal system works. It is a system of laws, regulations, policies, procedures, orders, proclamations, standards, guidelines, agreements, and court rulings. It is a system that varies in its application between federal agencies, states, local governments, Indian tribes, and private entities. It is a system that applies in varying degrees and particular aspects to all three branches of the federal government (Figure 3.1). It is a system that even has some international aspects. Legality is the first test applied to the soundness of any of these aspects.

The Federal Legal System

The basic elements of the federal legal system are the Constitution, treaties approved by Congress, an assemblage of congressionally enacted laws, and judicial and executive agency actions interpreting those laws. The American legal system is hierarchical, and at the top is the Constitution of the United States, ratified in 1789, with its 27 amendments. Next comes treaty law, followed by federal statutes, regulations, judicial decisions (case law), executive orders (EOs), and written agreements that have been appropriately enacted.

There are public laws (PLs) and private laws. Public laws proscribe relationships between governments and individuals, while private laws deal with relationships between individuals or private institutions. Public laws include constitutional law, administrative law, tax law, and criminal law. Private laws mainly deal with business law (e.g., contracts) and property law as part of civil law. Public laws apply to society as a whole, while private laws affect how people interact with each other. All heritage management law is public law, although actions between individuals and private organizations can significantly affect heritage properties and the practice of heritage management.

Constitutional Law

If federal courts deem any federal, state, or local law to be unconstitutional, the law is invalid. The parts of the US Constitution that have particular application to heritage preservation are mostly in the First, Fifth, and Fourteenth amendments. The First Amendment has two areas of application: freedom of speech and freedom of religion. The Fifth Amendment prohibits the taking of private property without just compensation. The Fourteenth Amendment provides equal protection under the law and makes constitutional protections applicable to all the states.

THE GOVERNMENT OF THE UNITED STATES

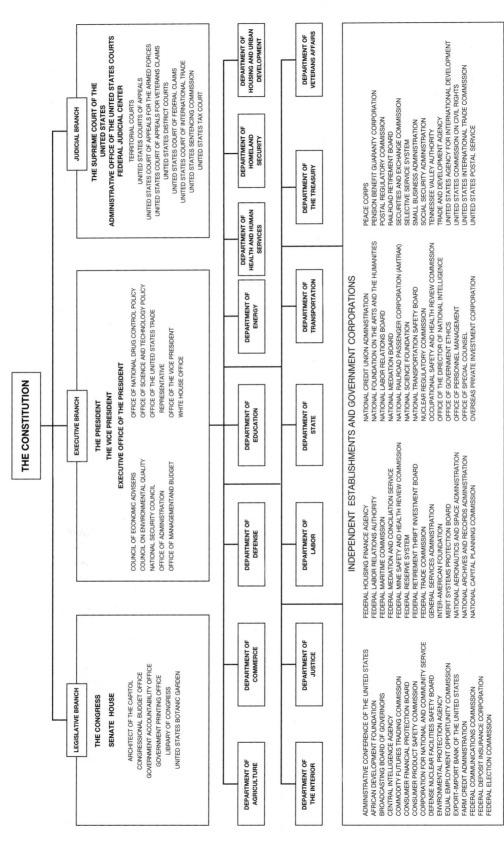

THE CONSTITUTION

LEGISLATIVE BRANCH

THE CONGRESS

SENATE   HOUSE

ARCHITECT OF THE CAPITOL
CONGRESSIONAL BUDGET OFFICE
GOVERNMENT ACCOUNTABILITY OFFICE
GOVERNMENT PRINTING OFFICE
LIBRARY OF CONGRESS
UNITED STATES BOTANIC GARDEN

EXECUTIVE BRANCH

THE PRESIDENT

THE VICE PRESIDENT

EXECUTIVE OFFICE OF THE PRESIDENT

COUNCIL OF ECONOMIC ADVISERS
COUNCIL ON ENVIRONMENTAL QUALITY
NATIONAL SECURITY COUNCIL
OFFICE OF ADMINISTRATION
OFFICE OF MANAGEMENT AND BUDGET
OFFICE OF NATIONAL DRUG CONTROL POLICY
OFFICE OF SCIENCE AND TECHNOLOGY POLICY
OFFICE OF THE UNITED STATES TRADE REPRESENTATIVE
OFFICE OF THE VICE PRESIDENT
WHITE HOUSE OFFICE

JUDICIAL BRANCH

THE SUPREME COURT OF THE UNITED STATES

ADMINISTRATIVE OFFICE OF THE UNITED STATES COURTS

FEDERAL JUDICIAL CENTER

TERRITORIAL COURTS
UNITED STATES COURTS OF APPEALS
UNITED STATES COURT OF APPEALS FOR THE ARMED FORCES
UNITED STATES COURT OF APPEALS FOR VETERANS CLAIMS
UNITED STATES DISTRICT COURTS
UNITED STATES COURT OF FEDERAL CLAIMS
UNITED STATES COURT OF INTERNATIONAL TRADE
UNITED STATES SENTENCING COMMISSION
UNITED STATES TAX COURT

DEPARTMENT OF AGRICULTURE

DEPARTMENT OF COMMERCE

DEPARTMENT OF DEFENSE

DEPARTMENT OF EDUCATION

DEPARTMENT OF ENERGY

DEPARTMENT OF HEALTH AND HUMAN SERVICES

DEPARTMENT OF HOMELAND SECURITY

DEPARTMENT OF HOUSING AND URBAN DEVELOPMENT

DEPARTMENT OF THE INTERIOR

DEPARTMENT OF JUSTICE

DEPARTMENT OF LABOR

DEPARTMENT OF STATE

DEPARTMENT OF TRANSPORTATION

DEPARTMENT OF THE TREASURY

DEPARTMENT OF VETERANS AFFAIRS

INDEPENDENT ESTABLISHMENTS AND GOVERNMENT CORPORATIONS

ADMINISTRATIVE CONFERENCE OF THE UNITED STATES
AFRICAN DEVELOPMENT FOUNDATION
BROADCASTING BOARD OF GOVERNORS
CENTRAL INTELLIGENCE AGENCY
COMMODITY FUTURES TRADING COMMISSION
CONSUMER FINANCIAL PROTECTION BOARD
CONSUMER PRODUCT SAFETY COMMISSION
CORPORATION FOR NATIONAL AND COMMUNITY SERVICE
DEFENSE NUCLEAR FACILITIES SAFETY BOARD
ENVIRONMENTAL PROTECTION AGENCY
EQUAL EMPLOYMENT OPPORTUNITY COMMISSION
EXPORT-IMPORT BANK OF THE UNITED STATES
FARM CREDIT ADMINISTRATION
FEDERAL COMMUNICATIONS COMMISSION
FEDERAL DEPOSIT INSURANCE CORPORATION
FEDERAL ELECTION COMMISSION

FEDERAL HOUSING FINANCE AGENCY
FEDERAL LABOR RELATIONS AUTHORITY
FEDERAL MARITIME COMMISSION
FEDERAL MEDIATION AND CONCILIATION SERVICE
FEDERAL MINE SAFETY AND HEALTH REVIEW COMMISSION
FEDERAL RESERVE SYSTEM
FEDERAL RETIREMENT THRIFT INVESTMENT BOARD
FEDERAL TRADE COMMISSION
GENERAL SERVICES ADMINISTRATION
INTER-AMERICAN FOUNDATION
MERIT SYSTEMS PROTECTION BOARD
NATIONAL AERONAUTICS AND SPACE ADMINISTRATION
NATIONAL ARCHIVES AND RECORDS ADMINISTRATION
NATIONAL CAPITAL PLANNING COMMISSION

NATIONAL CREDIT UNION ADMINISTRATION
NATIONAL FOUNDATION ON THE ARTS AND THE HUMANITIES
NATIONAL LABOR RELATIONS BOARD
NATIONAL MEDIATION BOARD
NATIONAL RAILROAD PASSENGER CORPORATION (AMTRAK)
NATIONAL SCIENCE FOUNDATION
NATIONAL TRANSPORTATION SAFETY BOARD
NUCLEAR REGULATORY COMMISSION
OCCUPATIONAL SAFETY AND HEALTH REVIEW COMMISSION
OFFICE OF THE DIRECTOR OF NATIONAL INTELLIGENCE
OFFICE OF GOVERNMENT ETHICS
OFFICE OF PERSONNEL MANAGEMENT
OFFICE OF SPECIAL COUNSEL
OVERSEAS PRIVATE INVESTMENT CORPORATION

PEACE CORPS
PENSION BENEFIT GUARANTY CORPORATION
POSTAL REGULATORY COMMISSION
RAILROAD RETIREMENT BOARD
SECURITIES AND EXCHANGE COMMISSION
SELECTIVE SERVICE SYSTEM
SMALL BUSINESS ADMINISTRATION
SOCIAL SECURITY ADMINISTRATION
TENNESSEE VALLEY AUTHORITY
TRADE AND DEVELOPMENT AGENCY
UNITED STATES AGENCY FOR INTERNATIONAL DEVELOPMENT
UNITED STATES COMMISSION ON CIVIL RIGHTS
UNITED STATES INTERNATIONAL TRADE COMMISSION
UNITED STATES POSTAL SERVICE

FIG. 3.1 The US government with its three main branches (Government Printing Office).

Miller (2008:18–27) provides a helpful overview of constitutional issues as they affect historic preservation. These issues involve the following areas of law:

- *Police power authority*: Federal and state governments have the authority to make and enforce the law as it applies to the regulation, protection, and promotion of public health, safety, morals, and general welfare. This was an issue in the *Penn Central Transportation Co. v. New York City* ruling confirming the power of New York City to place restrictions on private property for historic preservation purposes.
- *Regulatory taking*: Government has the right to take private property for public use, including physical occupation, as well as to place conditions on development and deny permits. Most heritage preservation court cases deal with permit denials. Regulatory taking also applies to private land containing ancient burials that can't be developed because a state law forbids the disturbance of those burials.
- *Procedural due process and equal protection*: Due process requires that a law must not only be constitutional but applied and enforced in a fair and consistent manner. Equal protection means it must be enacted, applied, and enforced equally.
- *First Amendment*: This amendment has two distinct clauses. The free exercise clause applies to the right of individuals to practice any religion and the restriction on government from promoting any religion. The Free Speech Clause prevents laws that would abridge the freedom to express one's opinions in a reasonable manner. Most heritage preservation issues involve the free exercise of religion, such as building code requirements for churches and Indians' ability to practice their religion.

Treaty Law

The Constitution gives the federal government the exclusive right to make agreements with sovereign entities. These entities include not only foreign governments but states and Indian tribes. The agreements with foreign governments and Indian tribes (prior to 1871) are called *treaties*. Treaty law trumps most federal and all state laws. Relationships between sovereign entities are called "government to government."

Tribes possess all powers of self-government except those retained by the federal government or those ceded to states under federal laws or congressionally authorized agreements. The retained rights include the right to form their own governments, to make and enforce laws, to tax, to determine membership in the tribe, to regulate activities on the reservation, and to forbid certain people or groups from entering the reservation. The excluded rights include the powers to make war, to issue currency, and to engage in foreign relations. States have no authority over Indian tribes within reservations unless that authority is granted by Congress or is in an agreement between the state and a particular tribe as authorized by Congress.

Tribes have to be officially recognized by the federal government to have treaty rights. There are currently 566 recognized tribes. Rights also vary by land status within and outside reservation boundaries. Under the National Historic Preservation Act (NHPA), federal agencies must consult tribes regarding undertakings that may affect properties to which tribes hold cultural patrimony both within and outside reservations. **Tribal historic preservation officers** (THPOs) can assume any or all of the responsibilities of state historic preservation officers (SHPOs), but only within reservations. Landownership may also have implications within reservations as many reservations have substantial nontribal landholdings. Land within reservations that is held in trust by the federal government (i.e., trust land) is considered federal land subject to federal historic preservation laws, such as the Archaeological Resources Protection Act (ARPA) and the Native American Graves Protection and Repatriation Act (NAGPRA), while nontrust land or otherwise nonfederal land within reservations is generally not subject to most aspects of these laws.

Treaty law also has heritage preservation implications for agreements with other countries and international organizations. An example is international admiralty law with regard to historic shipwrecks. Congress attempted to deal with some of these issues with the Abandoned Shipwrecks Act (ASA) in 1987 by transferring sovereignty for shipwrecks in US territorial waters to the adjacent states, but this has caused legal problems when the ship belongs to foreign nationals through law of the sea (i.e., salvage) conditions or to the governments of foreign countries (e.g., naval vessels).

Federal Laws

Next in line of importance are federal laws enacted by Congress, or what is known as *statutory law*. The Constitution gives Congress the right to make certain laws, which, when signed by the president or passed by a two-thirds majority, become public laws and are assigned a number based on when they were passed. Enacted public laws are then assigned a number under the United States Code (USC), which is organized by topic. However, only language that provides direction, authorization, or explanation is codified. This is called *positive law*. In 2014, when Congress recodified 16 USC under PL 113-287, which contained the National Historic Preservation Act (NHPA), it had no effect on NHPA Section 1, "Congressional Findings," as this section had not been codified.

Prior to the 2014 recodification, most heritage preservation laws were under Title 16 (USC), "Conservation." Most of these laws, including the NHPA, the Antiquities Act, the Historic Sites Act, and the Archaeological and Historic Preservation Act (AHPA), are now under Title 54 (USC), "National Park Service and Related Programs." Table 3.1 shows the major heritage management laws that have been transferred from 16 USC to 54 USC.

Some explanations of the changes are contained in "Notes on Title 54 of the United States Code 'National Park Service and Related Programs'" (NPS 2016):

- The creation of Title 54 made no changes to the legal meaning of the statutes that were moved, although Congress made "house cleaning" changes as a part of passing PL 113-287, so there is different language in some places. Consequently, anyone who quotes from NPS-related or federal historic preservation statutes should check the current language.

TABLE 3.1 **United States Code Equivalencies of Major Heritage Preservation Laws Transferred from 16 USC to 54 USC in 2014**

Name of Law	Year Passed	Law Number	16 USC	54 USC
Antiquities Act	1906	59-209	431–433	320101, 320303
NPS Organic Act	1916	(39 Stat. F35)	1	100101–104907
Historic Sites Act	1935	74-292	461–467	320101–320106
Museum Properties Management Act	1955	184-69	18f	102501–102504
NHPA	1966	89-665	470 et seq.	300101 et seq.
AHPA	1974	93-291	469	312501–312508
ARPA	1979	96-95	470aa–mm	Unassigned
Maritime Heritage Act	1994	103-451	74	308701–308707
Battlefield Protection Act	1996	104-333	469k	308101–308103
Lighthouse Preservation Act	2000	106-355	470w-7	305101–305106

- Unlike previous changes to the law, this was not an amendment to existing laws. PL 113-287 repealed the laws and then reenacted their statutory content into Title 54. Title 54 is now the official "positive law" for these provisions.
- In the United States Code format, commonly used terms such as "Section 106" and "Section 4(f)" have never appeared. Common, nonformal usage for historic preservation laws is unlikely to change due to the creation of Title 54.
- Of all the federal historic preservation statutory laws, PL 113-287 moved/repealed some, amended some, and left some unchanged.
- Inconsistent use of terms has been fixed. For example, "prehistoric and historic resources" has been changed to "historic properties" because the NHPA uses "historic properties" elsewhere and the definition of "historic property" includes archeological sites.
- Similar subjects were moved together. For example, Section 106 is now located with other federal agency requirements.
- By reserving certain divisions, subdivisions, and chapters and by assigning six digits to section numbers, the drafters of Title 54 have left plenty of room for expansion. The citations in Title 16 had reached a significant level of complexity and awkwardness.
- Names of individual statutes (e.g., National Historic Preservation Act, Historic Sites Act) have all been removed from the text of the US Code. Some statutory names now appear in the notes to 54 USC 100101.
- Standard changes have been made to eliminate unnecessary words for clarity and consistency. For example, the word "may" is substituted for "is authorized to," "is empowered to," or words of like import. The other standard changes involve the words "shall" and "consider."

A number of other laws critical to heritage preservation were not under Title 16 (USC). The National Environmental Policy Act (NEPA) and the American Indian Religious Freedom Act (AIRFA) are under Title 42 (USC), "Public Health and Welfare." Section 4(f) of the Department of Transportation (DOTA) is under Title 49 (USC), "Transportation." The Native American Graves Protection and Repatriation Act is under Title 29 (USC), "Indians." The Abandoned Shipwrecks Act is under Title 43 (USC), "Public Lands."

Federal Regulations

Federal laws can give federal agencies the power to create regulations to implement laws. Federal regulations provide procedural details and definitions not contained in a law itself. Regulations are numbered and become part of the Code of Federal Regulations (CFR). Approved regulations carry the force of law. This type of law is part of what is called *administrative law*.

Drafts of proposed regulations must be published in the *Federal Register* (FR) for a period of public comment prior to final acceptance. Each time a law is amended, the parallel regulations also need to be amended if there is a substantial difference in the meaning of the revised law. Legal objections to proposed regulations can force long delays in implementation. The regulations that implement Section 106 of the NHPA are 36 CFR 800. After amendments were made to the NHPA in 1992, it took 12 years to fully implement the revised 36 CFR 800 regulations due to legal challenges.

Because regulations can be complex, agencies often issue guidance contained in policy statements, standards, and procedure manuals to assist with uniform implementation of pertinent regulations or laws. Court actions can challenge these guidelines, and courts can accept them as legal documents. The various bulletins that describe how to nominate historic properties to the National Register of Historic Places (NRHP) are examples of agency guidance.

Executive Orders

Executive orders are also part of federal administrative law. Presidents use them primarily to give policy direction to executive agencies, interpreting what is contained in existing statutes or regulations. Executive orders are numbered chronologically, beginning with one issued by President Abraham Lincoln in October 1862. Franklin Roosevelt (1933–1945) issued over 3,500 executive orders.

Executive orders have the force of law, but they cannot make law. In 1952, the Supreme Court ruled that an executive order could only be used to clarify or promote an existing law. They have the force of law unless they are rejected by federal courts or overturned by Congress, although the president can veto congressional actions, and then a two-thirds majority in Congress is needed to override the veto. Executive orders do not expire at the end of a president's term, but subsequent presidents can overturn the executive order of a predecessor, providing its provisions have not been codified by a subsequent law.

In terms of heritage preservation, the most notable executive order is EO 11593 issued by President Richard Nixon in 1971, which made significant clarifications to the National Historic Preservation Act of 1966, including that officially eligible properties are considered the same as listed properties in terms of the National Register for purposes of Section 106. Other notable heritage preservation EOs are EO 6166 (Franklin Roosevelt), which transferred control of historic sites from the War Department and the Department of Agriculture to the National Park Service (NPS), EO 13007 (Bill Clinton) concerning Indian sacred sites, and EO 13287 (George W. Bush) regarding the "Preserve America" initiative.

Presidential Proclamations

Presidential proclamations are of two types: ceremonial and substantive. Like executive orders, they must be published in the *Federal Register*, but Congress must affirm them in order for them to have the force of law. As of May 2017, there have been about 9,600 presidential proclamations.

Ceremonial proclamations are the most common and generally relate to federal policy for commemoration or special observances. George Washington issued the first presidential proclamation in 1789 for a day of national thanksgiving to be observed on a Thursday in November. On May 5, 2017, Donald Trump issued a proclamation for National Hurricane Preparedness Week.

Substantive presidential proclamations mainly relate to the conduct of foreign affairs and other executive duties given to the president by law. The most notable with regard to heritage preservation is the power to create national monuments under the Antiquities Act of 1906. As of 2017, 16 presidents have designated 157 national monuments. The first was Devils Tower, designated by Theodore Roosevelt on September 9, 1906. The most recent is Reconstruction Era National Monument in South Carolina, created by President Barack Obama on January 12, 2017, the day before he left office.

One of Donald Trump's campaign promises was to rescind most of the large national monuments created over the last 20 years by Presidents Clinton, Bush, and Obama. This has never been done by any previous president, although Congress has rescinded presidential proclamations for 11 national monuments and changed the boundaries of many more. The legality of one president rescinding a national monument created by another is unclear. This issue energized many natural and cultural resource preservation groups and professional organizations early in the Trump presidency.

Agreement Documents

An agreement document is basically a written, legally binding contract that spells out legal basis, reasons for need, procedures to follow, and preferred outcomes when a specific policy or project under agency review will affect a significant historic property or when a more general agency action has the potential to affect historic properties. The two most common agreement documents are the memorandum of agreement (MOA) and the programmatic agreement (PA), both implemented under Section 106 of the NHPA.

The Section 106 regulations (36 CFR 800.16) define a memorandum of agreement as a "document that records the terms and conditions agreed upon to resolve the adverse effects of an undertaking upon historic properties." Under the same regulations, a programmatic agreement is defined as a "document that records the terms and conditions agreed upon to resolve the potential adverse effects of a Federal agency program, complex undertaking or other situations in accordance with" the regulations.

NEPA has a less formal process for implementing agreements but can use a memorandum of understanding (MOU) to resolve effects. For nonfederal actions, a simple letter of agreement (LOA) or letter of understanding (LOU) can be used to bind an agency's actions with respect to historic properties.

MOAs, PAs, and MOUs have signature pages that include all the major parties involved in the actions described in the documents. Under Section 106, the two mandatory signatories are usually the federal agency and the SHPO/THPO. Nationwide agreements have federal agency head signatures, as well as those of executives of the National Conference of State Historic Preservation Officers (NCSHPO) and the Advisory Council on Historic Preservation (ACHP).

Agreement documents often have a sunset clause as to when the agreement expires and a clause permitting some signatories to be released from their responsibilities following an appropriate justification notification by one signatory party to other parties. For historic preservation purposes, land-use agreements such as covenants and easements have also been implemented, although with mixed results with regard to effectiveness due to monitoring and enforcement problems.

The Court System

All laws and regulations are subject to judicial review. Court rulings become a part of law known as *common law* unless a higher court overrules them. All lower courts are required to abide by the decisions of higher courts in the same judicial system. A ruling by one federal district court is not binding on another federal district court, but an appeals court ruling has to be obeyed by all of the district courts in the same judicial region. Regardless of jurisdiction, rulings by one court are often carefully examined by other courts for guidance if a similar issue arises. This is called seeking *precedence*.

The rulings by courts provide interpretations of statutory laws and, if upheld, become precedents for future court decisions. These decisions are known as *case law*. Important heritage preservation case law includes the *Penn Central* decision (1978), supporting local historic designations preventing the demolition of privately owned historic properties, and the *Metropolitan Edison Co. v. People Against Nuclear Energy* decision (1983), determining that significant social and economic effects alone cannot require an agency to complete an environmental impact statement (EIS) under NEPA. Most court rulings have upheld the basic tenets of our heritage preservation system.

Federal courts focus on federal laws and constitutional law. There are three levels in the federal court system: district courts, circuit courts, and the Supreme Court (Figure 3.2). The president nominates judges for these courts, and the Senate must confirm them. They have lifelong terms. There are 94 district courts, also known as trial courts, because they deal with initial matters pertaining to civil or criminal

THE UNITED STATES FEDERAL COURTS

SUPREME COURT	UNITED STATES SUPREME COURT
APPELLATE COURTS	U.S. COURTS OF APPEALS 12 Regional Circuit Courts of Appeals 1 U.S. Court of Appeals for the Federal Circuit
TRIAL COURTS	U.S. DISTRICT COURTS 94 Judicial Districts and U.S. Bankruptcy Courts U.S. Courts of International Trade U.S. Court of Federal Claims
FEDERAL TRIBUNALS AND OTHER ENTITIES	Military Courts (Trial and Appellate) Court of Appeals for Veterans Claims U.S. Tax Court Federal administrative agencies and boards

FIG. 3.2 The US federal court system (Administrative Office of the US Courts).

enforcement or application of federal law, treaty law, or constitutional law. Only one federal judge presides at district court trials, but each district usually has multiple judges. There are almost 700 federal district judges, although appointments to these seats may go unfilled for long periods due to political disagreements between the president and Congress.

If there is an appeal of a district court ruling, it first goes to a federal circuit court, also known as an appeals court. There are 13 circuit courts, of which 12 are regionally distributed (Figure 3.2) and 1, the United States Court of Appeals, has national jurisdiction for issues such as patents. Each circuit court has multiple judges, who vary in number from 6 to 29. Appeals are heard by a panel of three judges in a circuit court, although all the judges may be consulted and rule on important issues.

Appeals of the decisions of federal circuit courts or of state supreme courts with implications for the US Constitution are made to the Supreme Court. There are nine judges on the Supreme Court, who are known as justices. The Supreme Court has discretion as to whether or not to hear an appeal from a lower court. The Supreme Court agrees to hear less than 1% of appeals it receives.

Rulings of the Supreme Court are published in *United States Reports*. The case is first given a name with the petitioner (loser in the lower court) listed first and the respondent (winning party) second, with a "v" (versus) between the names. After the name comes the volume of *United States Reports* where the case is found and the initial page number in that volume. Last, in parentheses, is the year of the ruling. An example is *Penn Central v. City of New York*, 48 U.S. 104 (1978). Rulings of lower courts follow a similar tripartite citation style, but the publication is the *Federal Supplement*, cited as "F.Supp."

State Legal Systems

The US Constitution considers states and territories, like Indian tribes, to be sovereign entities. Each state or territory has its own constitution and its own system of laws. These constitutions and laws cannot contradict the US Constitution or federal law. State supreme courts decide if state and local laws are in line with state constitutions. State judicial systems vary considerably, especially in what courts are called, but they typically mirror the federal system, with a trial court, an appeals court, and a supreme court.

As in the federal system, state legislatures pass laws, state agencies can issue regulations or rules implementing these laws, governors can issue executive orders providing agency direction, and state court systems evaluate actions concerning these laws, regulations, and executive orders. States have principal responsibility for criminal and civil law affecting their citizens; thus the majority of legal actions in the United States involve state rather than federal courts.

The laws from state to state can vary considerably, and this is certainly true concerning heritage preservation. Minnesota passed an Antiquities Act in 1939 that, like the federal law with the same name, was principally concerned with regulating artifact collection on state property. The 1963 Minnesota Field Archaeology Act superseded the 1939 law and provided some support for reviewing construction activities on nonfederal property that might affect archaeological and historical sites. State laws determine where the state historic preservation officer is located and if there is a state archaeologist.

Local Legal Systems

State constitutions give local governments, regional agencies, and boards the right to pass their own laws (usually called *ordinances*) and regulations, so long as they don't contradict state or federal law. These laws and regulations apply only to entities and specific actions within their jurisdictional boundaries. It is not uncommon for a person living in a large city to be bound by many layers of law and regulation at the federal, state, regional, county, municipal, and board levels.

The most common local heritage preservation action is an ordinance outlining procedures for reviewing local government actions that may harm historic properties (e.g., building and demolition permits), developing a local historic property designation register, and establishing a **historic preservation commission** (HPC) to review these effects and direct the designation process. Most of these ordinances are at the city level, although a few counties also have them. Chapter 10 discusses local historic preservation ordinances.

Cities and counties also have court systems that mainly deal with violations of the local laws and ordinances within their jurisdictions, such as parking or traffic violations. These court systems have only one level, with appeals going into the state system.

Legislative Intent

Finally, with regard to the legal framework, besides understanding the legal systems at the various levels of government, the practical application of heritage management involves grasping why legislative bodies passed particular laws in the first place. Some of this can be gleaned from historical analysis, but it is instructive to look at the laws themselves and the legislative process that created them. Some laws start with a declarative statement explaining and justifying why the law was passed and the elements it contains. In some state laws (e.g., Minnesota), this is labeled as "legislative intent."

Legislative intent becomes explicit through a process of committee reports and legislative hearings resulting in the actual language eventually contained in a bill for an act. Legislative committees have the principal responsibility of drafting legislation. In order to do this, committee staff conduct research into the topic. If the bill makes it out of committee, a report accompanies the draft bill, describing its purpose and scope. If a committee holds public hearings on the bill, people who appear to testify are asked to provide a written summary of their proposed testimony. These legislative committee documents provide considerable insight into legislative intent and who was for or against a particular law.

Understanding legislative intent is important because agencies implementing the legislation or individuals and organizations supporting or opposing it can skew the intent through their actions or their particular interpretations. Heritage management professionals within government agencies should know the actual legislative intent in order to properly implement a law and determine who supported and who opposed it so as to anticipate agreement or dissent. Other heritage management professionals should know the legislative intent in order to determine if agencies are indeed doing what a law intended and if proponents or opponents of related actions are accurately applying original intent. Interpreting legislative intent can be a key factor in court rulings.

The Early Federal Heritage Preservation Laws

The current American heritage management structure does not rest on a firm footing of pre-1966 federal legislation. There was no national heritage management system prior to 1966, just scattered acts of narrowly intended legislation and a few agency actions focused on particular sites on federal lands or areas taken into federal ownership or proposed federal ownership.

The first federal regulatory action to protect a historic site was for the preservation of the Casa Grande ruins in Arizona (Figure 3.3). An item in an appropriations act in 1889 authorized the president to set aside a federal reservation at Casa Grande to protect the site from "sale or settlement." By executive order in June 1892, President Benjamin Harrison established the 480-acre reservation. As described on the Casa Grande Ruins National Monument website, the site was preserved not because the federal government was previously aware of its importance but because anthropologist Frank Cushing had contacted several influential Bostonians. They convinced one of their senators, George Hoar, to take congressional action to preserve the ruins.

It seems a bit odd to us today that Congress chose Casa Grande for this first federal protective action. It is an unimposing ruin, especially when compared to the great southwestern ruins celebrated today at Mesa Verde, Chaco Canyon, and Navajo National Monument. You have to put Casa Grande into historical and geographic context to understand why it was protected. It is located just southeast of Phoenix, a rapidly growing city in the late nineteenth century, reached by the railroad in 1887. The other great ruins of the Southwest were not on railroad lines, and this was before the automobile and good roads. By 1889, Casa Grande was easily accessible by the public from Phoenix on foot or by horse. It was thus vulnerable to sale, settlement, and vandalism.

The next congressional action to preserve a historic site was the establishment of Chickamauga and Chattanooga National Military Park in 1890. Once again, Congress took this action in response to lobbying by influential citizens, not as part of a comprehensive legislative heritage preservation agenda. Congress gave the War Department control of military parks. The US Army used Chickamauga-Chattanooga as a training ground until the NPS took control in 1933. In 1894, Congress established Shiloh as the second national military park, followed by Gettysburg in 1895 and Vicksburg in 1899.

FIG. 3.3 Casa Grande ruins in Arizona with protective shelter built in 1932, replacing a 1903 roof (National Park Service).

Antiquities Act (1906)

The Antiquities Act of 1906 was the first congressional action aimed at preserving more than a single cultural heritage site, although it focused only on federal land and more on archaeology than on other aspects of cultural heritage. Congress passed the law due to the efforts of New Mexico archaeologist Edgar Hewitt and Iowa congressman John Lacey, working with a very sympathetic president, Theodore Roosevelt (Harmon, McManamon, and Pitcaithley 2006).

The 1906 law contained four important elements:

1. It required that the federal government protect historic and archaeological sites on federal land.
2. It authorized the president to create national monuments "of historic or scientific interest" on federal lands or lands donated to the federal government for that purpose.
3. It prohibited the destruction of such sites without the permission of the head of the federal agency managing the land.
4. It authorized appropriate agencies to issue regulations to implement the act.

The act also emphasized that collection of artifacts on federal property should be for scientific or educational purposes and that public museums should care for the artifacts.

Of the first four national monuments created by President Roosevelt immediately after the passage of the Antiquities Act in 1906, two were basically archaeological: El Morro and Montezuma Castle. Roosevelt added two more monuments showcasing archaeological sites the following year, Chaco Canyon and Gila Cliff Dwellings. Fort Wood (now Statue of Liberty) National Monument, created in 1924, was the first focused on a modern structure. It is also an archaeological site as the base of the statue is set in the remains of Fort Wood, which dates to 1811.

The Supreme Court ruling in *U.S. v. Diaz* in 1974 found the archaeological site protection wording in the Antiquities Act too vague. This defect was taken care of with the passage of the Archaeological Resources Protection Act in 1979.

The enduring legacy of the Antiquities Act is the power of the president to create and enlarge national monuments. Congress can also enlarge national monuments. Some conservative politicians in the western United States not only object to federal government management of a significant portion of their state's lands but also do not want additional restrictions placed on private grazing and mining rights. There have been repeated attempts in Congress to amend the Antiquities Act, taking away presidential power to create national monuments. Beginning in 2017, the Trump administration attempted to reduce or eliminate some western national monuments declared over the past 20 years by Presidents Clinton, Bush, and Obama.

National Park Service Organic Act (1916)

Organic acts are acts of Congress that establish new territories of the United States or new agencies to manage federal lands. The purpose of the National Park Service, as stated in Article 1 of the 1916 Organic Act, was "to conserve the scenery and the natural and *historic objects* and the wild life therein and to provide for the enjoyment of the same in such manner and by such means as will leave them unimpaired for the enjoyment of future generations."

Although the act mentioned "historic objects," it was not a focused *historic* preservation act but rather a *heritage* preservation act. If we consider that the natural landscape is part of our shared heritage, that natural landscapes often contain historic sites and archaeological remains, and that the NPS would become the lead federal agency for cultural heritage preservation, the Organic Act is a critical development in American cultural heritage preservation.

The creation of the national park system did not start with the Organic Act. An act of Congress in 1872 established Yellowstone National Park. Congress established eight other national parks prior to the passage of the Organic Act, of which one, Mesa Verde, was archaeological. The Organic Act also gave the NPS control of national monuments, which by 1916 included the archaeological complexes of El Morro, Montezuma Castle, Chaco Canyon, Gila Cliff Dwellings, Tonto, Tumacacori, Navaho, Gran Quivira, Big Hole Battlefield, and Bandelier.

The Big Hole Battlefield National Monument in Montana, established in 1910, was the first cultural national monument (and thus the first cultural site under the control of the National Park Service) outside the American Southwest. In 1930, Congress authorized the creation of Colonial National Park, containing the sites of Yorktown and Jamestown, the first cultural national park established under the authority of the NPS. Congress authorized the site of the Revolutionary War's Battle of Morristown as the first national historical park in 1933.

Also in 1933, Franklin Roosevelt's Executive Order 6166 transferred all federal historic sites managed by the War Department and the Forest Service to the NPS. This involved 80 properties and meant that, in 1933, the majority of the units within the NPS were primarily cultural.

Historic Sites Act (1935)

With the Great Depression worsening in the early 1930s, the NPS became heavily involved in managing heritage preservation activities associated with federal relief programs instituted by the Franklin Roosevelt administration. The NPS was also instrumental in the passage and implementation of the Historic Sites Act in 1935. The act authorized the creation of a survey of nationally significant historic sites, the first of its kind in its national scope and inclusion of more than just battlefields and southwestern Puebloan ruins.

The act also encouraged cooperative agreements between the federal government and private entities for the maintenance of important historic sites and empowered the secretary of the interior to accept new additions to the system of national historic sites. Within the NPS, the Historic Sites Act promoted research, preservation, restoration, and interpretation, not just the acquisition and management of culturally oriented park units. It also promoted the employment of heritage management professionals.

The NPS was in charge of the Historic Sites Survey put into action in the summer of 1936. The principal purpose of the survey was to find and evaluate properties of national significance that could eventually be national park units. NPS regional historians directed the survey with oversight from historian Ronald Lee in the main Washington office. An advisory board developed thematic categories within which properties could be identified and evaluated for relative importance. By the beginning of World War II, when the survey ended, it had looked at 560 properties and considered less than half nationally significant (Sprinkle 2014:15). The NPS briefly reactivated the Historic Sites Survey in 1957.

After 1935, Congress amended the Historic Sites Act at least eight times under 16 USC 461–467. In 2014, the law largely disappeared with the congressionally mandated reorganization of NPS-related laws into United States Code 54. Exceptions are within four sections of Title 54: "American Antiquities: Policy and Administrative Provisions" (54 USC 320101–320106), "National Park System Advisory Board" (54 USC 102303), "National Park Service Advisory Council" (54 USC 102304), and "Commemoration of Former Presidents" (54 USC 309101).

National Trust for Historic Preservation Act (1949)

After World War II, there was finally a real historic preservation movement in America. This was partially due to the expansion of professionalism in all of the contributing fields during the Depression-era programs, creating leaders and employees both in the private sector and at the NPS. A historic preservation movement was also increasingly necessary due to various aspects of the postwar effect that produced threats and incentives as discussed in chapter 2.

Additionally, the onset of the Cold War encouraged an attitude among many political leaders that they must clearly demonstrate the advantages of a capitalist system over a communist system, such as efficient transportation, home ownership for all, and the benefits of a consumer-based economy. As Hosmer (1981:864) points out, this political attitude was not inherently antipreservation, but it certainly was not supportive of a movement that resisted "progress" by saving old buildings from urban renewal, restricting suburban growth, and delaying interstate highway development, commercialization, and industrial expansion.

A few key government and private historic preservation professionals realized that the postwar threats to historic preservation could not be thwarted by a government agency like the NPS due to political pressures, a restricted mission, and private as well as public needs. These professionals included historians and architects from the NPS (e.g., Ronald Lee, Aubrey Neasham), academic historians and archaeologists (e.g., Guy Stanton Ford, J. O. Brew), museum directors (e.g., David Finley, Frank Roberts), state historical society directors (e.g., Christopher Crittenden, Solon Buck), and private organization leaders (e.g., Horace Albright, George McAneny). These individuals, along with other nationally recognized heritage preservation professionals, met in Washington, DC, in April 1947 to found the National Council for Historic Sites and Buildings (NCHSB). (The photo caption on p. 823 in Hosmer 1981 has a list of attendees.)

The initial purposes of the NCHSB were basically to coordinate preservation efforts nationally and to disseminate information to help promote a national preservation ethic. The council soon developed another purpose, one that would cause its own demise: to develop charter language for a property-owning organization modeled on Britain's National Trust. At the first annual meeting of the NCHSB in October 1947, the goals of that charter organization, the National Trust for Historic Preservation (NTHP), were first fleshed out. The organization could acquire threatened historic properties in order to preserve them and also obtain private funds for special preservation projects beyond the scope of the federal government. Unlike the British National Trust, it would not get involved with the preservation of the natural landscape, as that was the job of the National Park Service.

The NCHSB sent Congress a draft bill for the NTHP charter in early 1949. A congressionally chartered organization had a number of crucial advantages over just a purely privately formed organization. First, it would instantly gain national prominence. Second, as a quasi-governmental organization, it would have tax advantages. Third, it could officially continue the goals of the Historic Sites Act of 1935, such as local organization coordination and a nationwide historic property survey. Finally, it would have direct access to Congress for appeals for federal funding through a required annual report.

Congress passed the NTHP charter act in October 1949, and President Harry S. Truman signed it into law on October 26 of that year. The act included the first official congressional use of the term "historic preservation." In 1953, the NCHSB merged with the National Trust.

Archives and Museums Acts of the 1950s

Congress passed several acts important to heritage management in the 1950s. The Federal Records Act in 1950, the Museum Properties Management Act in 1955, and the Presidential Libraries Act in 1955. The first two acts have broad implications for heritage preservation. The results of the last one are well known to the public

Federal Records Act (1950)

Government records are critical to historians. This 1950 act gave the administrator of the General Services Administration (GSA) authority to oversee management of the records of federal agencies. This duty was transferred to the **archivist** of the United States by a 1984 amendment. The National Archives and Records Administration (NARA), originally established in 1934, maintains the records. The act first governs how government records are to be collected and retained, and then NARA determines which records should be curated or destroyed.

Museum Properties Management Act (1955)

Previous to this 1955 act, the Historic Sites Act of 1935 had directed the secretary of the interior to preserve documents and data of historic and archaeological value, but it only included records, not objects, and did not specify how or where the collections were to be located. The Museum Properties Management Act directed the NPS to increase the public benefits of park museums by preserving and exhibiting historical and archaeological "objects and relics" found on Department of the Interior property. It allowed the NPS to accept donations of, purchase, exchange, accept on loan, or loan these objects. The law (16 USC 18) was amended in 1996 to allow for deaccessioning of objects that had no real historic or scientific value.

Reservoir Salvage Act (1960)

The Flood Control Act of 1944 authorized a massive federal reservoir construction program that threatened to destroy thousands of archaeological and historical sites.

An interagency agreement between the Corps of Engineers (COE), the Bureau of Recreation, the Smithsonian Institution, and the National Park Service in late 1945 committed the federal government to a program of archaeological survey and salvage within the proposed reservoirs. The Smithsonian had overall charge of directing the archaeological research, with the NPS responsible for obtaining funding and contracting for necessary work. The River Basin Surveys (RBS) were a result of this initiative.

Because the River Basin Surveys were part of an interagency agreement and not an act of Congress, funding for the huge survey and extensive data-recovery excavations was inconsistent and confusing. The construction agencies wanted the NPS to fund the archaeological work, while the NPS thought the development agencies should fund it. The federal Bureau of the Budget agreed with the development agencies. The NPS then proposed cost-sharing agreements with the academic entities doing much of the survey work. This arrangement worked for over 10 years but still did not address the unfairness of the development agencies not being fully responsible for the damage they were causing to heritage resources.

The Reservoir Salvage Act, passed in June 1960, directly addressed the funding issue and provided statutory support for the idea of reservoir salvage. The act was basically an extension of the Historic Sites Act of 1935, confirming NPS heritage preservation oversight for large federal undertakings. The Reservoir Salvage Act only applied to large reservoirs unless known archaeological resources were being impacted by smaller ones. The act authorized the secretary of the interior to conduct surveys once he had been notified by the development, licensing, or funding agency about a proposed reservoir project. If "exceptional" historic or archaeological sites were to be destroyed by a reservoir, the secretary could authorize collection and preservation "of the data," providing such collection was "feasible" and done "expeditiously." There were no definitions included in the act, and no regulations were produced to implement the law.

Once again, the cost of the heritage preservation work was not the responsibility of the reservoir development agencies, although that appears to have been the original intent of the legislation (Rosenberg 1981:765). The act only specified that Congress would authorize the funds necessary to carry out the work. The Reservoir Salvage Act was amended in 1974 by the Archaeological and Historic Preservation Act, which addressed the funding responsibility and broadened the scope beyond just reservoirs (see chapter 7).

Summary

The American system of government and legal system determine many of the successes and failures of heritage preservation. Federal laws and court rulings are supplemented by state and local laws and legal systems, as well as private efforts to initiate and continue heritage preservation.

The passage of the Antiquities Act in 1906 was the first national attempt by the federal government to preserve heritage resources on all federal lands. The establishment of the National Park Service in 1916 had a significant effect on implementing a federal system of heritage management and supporting local systems. By the early 1930s, the NPS had acquired direct management responsibilities for the heritage resources present in over 100 parks, national monuments, and historic sites. NPS duties and personnel greatly expanded with federal relief programs during the Great Depression. The Historic Sites Act of 1935 expanded NPS duties to include a nationwide historic sites survey.

A number of significant national laws were passed after World War II, including the act establishing the National Trust for Historic Preservation, the Federal Records Act, the Museum Properties Management Act, and the Reservoir Salvage

Act. The successes and failures of these actions led to the passage of the National Historic Preservation Act in 1966, which became the basis of our heritage preservation and management system today.

Review Questions

1. What federal legal instruments have the force of law?
2. What constitutional amendments have particular application to heritage preservation?
3. Why are court cases important to heritage preservation?
4. What are the basic requirements of the Antiquities Act of 1906?
5. Why was the National Trust for Historic Preservation founded?

Supplemental Reading

A good place to start to learn the fundamentals of our legal system and how it is applied with respect to historic preservation is Miller (2008). Bronin and Rowberry (2014) provides an overview of historic preservation law from a law school perspective, although it provides little historical background on how our heritage preservation laws evolved. For summaries of historic preservation case law, see Kanefield (1996), Richman and Forsyth (2004), and Hutt, Forsyth, and Tarler (2006).

A good source for basic documents and descriptions of our system of government can be found in *The United States Government Manual* (2017) prepared by the Government Printing Office (https://www.gpo.gov/fdsys/pkg/GOVMAN-2017-08-02/pdf/GOVMAN-2017-08-02.pdf).

Other government agencies have helpful information on their websites, such as annual reports, organizational charts, and flow diagrams. A good description of the federal court system is the Administrative Office of the US Courts' *Understanding the Federal Courts* (http://www.uscourts.gov/sites/default/files/understanding-federal-courts.pdf).

For the Antiquities Act and its long-term implications, see Harmon, McManamon, and Pitcaithley (2006). For more information on the application of the Historic Sites Act, see Macintosh (1985).

SIDEBAR

Implementing Heritage Management: Salvaging the Past and Building the Future

When I was in graduate school at the University of Nebraska, Lincoln (UNL), I worked for the National Park Service's Midwest Archaeological Center (MWAC). On one of my first days there, I was asked to help clean out some storage rooms in the basement of the old post office building in downtown Lincoln. When we walked into that basement, I saw rooms filled with shovels, screens, and camping equipment. There was everything you would need to fit out multiple major archaeological excavations. As we started digging through the neatly stacked piles, I noticed everything was marked with hand-painted yellow and red bars, a mark of ownership.

This stuff was a remnant of the River Basin Surveys. We were excavating part of its history.

I didn't know much about the RBS when I came to Lincoln, but I soon was awash in it. The MWAC was a remnant of the RBS. The MWAC building where I worked contained hundreds of boxes of artifacts that came from RBS excavations in the Missouri River region in the Dakotas dating to late 1940s into the early 1970s. A few older guys—Lee Madison, Gaillard Jackson, and Wayne Nelson—occasionally worked for MWAC doing odd jobs; they were RBS veterans. One of my professors at UNL, Warren Caldwell, had once directed the

RBS office in Lincoln. I soon learned that RBS had played a critical role in the development of Plains archaeology and had widespread influences on American archaeology in general.

The RBS had its roots in economic necessity. In the early twentieth century, Americans had been moving west in record numbers. Much of the west was arid, so water was needed for urban populations and crop irrigation. The booming cities also needed electricity, lots of it. Flooding had long been a major problem on main-stem rivers throughout the country. As the end of World War II approached, Congress was very aware of the water, power, and flooding problems, as well as the need to put hundreds of thousands of returning soldiers back to work. One solution to all four problems was the Flood Control Act of 1944.

The Flood Control Act appropriated over $1 billion for almost 300 dams in 29 states. Its scope immediately alarmed archaeologists. They had seen the widespread destruction of archaeological sites caused by the Tennessee Valley Authority (TVA) reservoir projects in the 1930s and the inadequate government response to mitigate this destruction. The leaders of the archaeological community had also recognized the inadequacies of government archaeology in general during the 1930s. While it had employed hundreds of archaeologists, it had no centralized direction, insufficient crew supervision, greatly varying field methods, inadequate artifact curation, and limited publication.

To investigate the problems with relief agency archaeology, the National Research Council (NRC) formed the Committee on Basic Needs in Archaeology in 1939, made up of a number of prominent archaeologists. The committee's report suggested minimum requirements for "scientific" archaeology, called for a national program for the conservation of archaeological resources, and asked that the National Park Service play a greater role in federal archaeological management (Thiessen 1999:2). World War II then intervened, and all large-scale archaeology effectively ended in the country for four years.

With the announcement of plans for the Flood Control Act in 1944, the Society for American Archaeology (SAA) formed the Committee for the Recovery of Archaeological Remains (CRAR). In early 1945, it met with the NRC's Basic Needs committee, as well as a few archaeologists located in the Washington, DC, area. As the war in Europe ended, CRAR released guidelines for a federal archaeological program to mitigate the adverse effects of the reservoir construction, which included the use of qualified personnel and a competent supervisory organization. The guidelines were summarized in *Science* magazine on July 13, 1945.

The federal government responded to CRAR's recommendations by forming the Interagency Archaeological Salvage Program (IASP), made up of the NPS, the Army Corps of Engineers, the Bureau of Reclamation (BOR), the Smithsonian Institution (SI), CRAR, and a number of cooperating educational institutions. The NPS administered the program, which was funded by an initial congressional appropriation of almost $11 million, about $32 million in 2018 dollars (Banks and Czaplicki 2014:15). NPS then transferred about a third of the money to the SI for the RBS, with the other two-thirds going to cooperating institutions that would help carry out the archaeological work in the reservoirs.

The RBS set up five regional offices in cities with major cooperating universities: Lincoln, Nebraska; Eugene, Oregon; Austin, Texas; Berkeley, California; and Atlanta, Georgia. The Lincoln office was in charge of the five main-stem dams on the middle Missouri River, as well as 60 smaller reservoirs on tributaries. The Lincoln office administered about a third of all the RBS funding. Over the next 24 years, the RBS implemented the largest archaeological program ever undertaken in this country. The strengths of the program included a multidisciplinary approach, professional supervision, modern field and lab methods, and consideration of historical archaeological sites. Weaknesses included a focus on only large village sites, no advanced planning for curation or publication, and a lack of consideration for historic architectural resources that would be inundated by the reservoirs.

The legacy of the RBS is huge. It trained many of the next generation of American archaeologists, including notables such as James Deetz and Ray Wood. The findings are still the foundation of many regional cultural histories. More than anything, the RBS established an ethic for the federal government to take responsibility for the harm it did to archaeological sites on federal land and off. This responsibility, initially focused on just salvage, would eventually include preservation and a broad-based program of heritage management.

CHAPTER 4

The National Historic Preservation Act

A Firm Foundation

Be it enacted by the Senate and House of Representatives of the United States of America in Congress assembled, the Congress finds and declares that the spirit and direction of the Nation are founded upon and reflected in its historic past.
—National Historic Preservation Act (1966)

The year 1966 was big for heritage preservation in America, perhaps the biggest year ever. Not only was it the fiftieth anniversary of the National Park Service (NPS), but two laws were passed that radically changed the way the federal government carried out and supported heritage management: the National Historic Preservation Act (NHPA) and the Department of Transportation Act (DOTA). The NHPA was not only proactive but also pertained to more than just the review of federal construction projects and what happened on federal lands. This chapter looks at the origins of the NHPA and the changes it has gone through since 1966.

The NHPA did not amend any previous federal legislation; rather, it was a new law that reflected the changing mood of the American public and good economic times. The heritage preservation needs embedded in this mood were extracted by key individuals and organizations and focused into an aggressive and well-thought-out legislative initiative. By the mid-1960s, not only was the time right for comprehensive heritage preservation legislation, but the right people were in the right places to take advantage of it. James Glass (1990) calls the results "the new preservation."

Origins of the New Preservation

Back to the '50s

Not only was there no firm legislative foundation for comprehensive heritage management by the mid-twentieth century, but the National Park Service had not been providing broad external leadership like it had in the pre–World War II years. The NPS was mainly concerned with correcting the deferred maintenance in the national parks due to the neglect of the war years and dealing with the critical logistical needs brought on by the pressure of a rapidly growing and increasingly mobile population. It was also focused on preparing for the fiftieth anniversary of its founding coming in 1966. The NPS ingeniously compiled these three objectives into what it called Mission 66.

The Mission 66 park revitalization program was implemented by NPS director Conrad Wirth in 1956. Over the next 10 years, Mission 66 not only greatly improved

park infrastructure but introduced the concept of a visitor
center, where the public could
be oriented, educated, warned
about behavioral rules, and
provided amenities like bath-
rooms, drinking fountains,
and a gift shop (Figure 4.1).
Many of the rustic log buildings built by the Civilian Conservation Corps (CCC) were
removed because most were
too small for a visitor center
and lacked modern conve-
niences, although by appearance they seemed historic at
the time; certainly most would
have become officially historic

FIG. 4.1 Mission 66 visitor center at Pipestone National Monument in Minnesota (author photo).

if left in place. (It is ironic that the "modern" structures built to help celebrate the
fiftieth anniversary of the NPS were themselves thought to be outdated for the one
hundredth anniversary in 2016, although they had just achieved the 50-year minimum age requirement for National Register of Historic Places [NRHP] eligibility.)

The adverse effects for historic and archaeological sites from Mission 66 are
often overlooked when compared to other mid-twentieth-century federally supported projects, such as dam construction, interstate highway development, and
urban renewal. Mission 66 was a billion-dollar program, the largest development
ever undertaken by NPS. Besides building 100 park visitor centers, it constructed
hundreds of administrative and service buildings, over 1,000 housing units, and
thousands of miles of roads. Mission 66 also resulted in 78 new parks and monuments being added as NPS units, an increase of 40% over 1955 NPS holdings (http://
mission66.com). While some consideration was given to impacts to heritage properties, most of the projects were not surveyed for unknown archaeological sites, and
large park projects in St. Louis and Philadelphia implemented another form of urban
renewal by clearing entire blocks of older buildings. Many unknown or unevaluated
sites and structures were no doubt destroyed in both urban and rural areas.

There were some benefits to heritage preservation from Mission 66. The Historic American Buildings Survey (HABS) and NPS Historic Sites Survey that had
been abandoned during World War II were restarted in 1957, although on a smaller
scale than in the 1930s (McIntosh 1985). These programs, as well as the need for
interpretation in the new park visitor centers, resulted in the hiring of additional
NPS historians and archaeologists in both parks and the central offices. These activities led to the 1960 establishment of the **National Historic Landmarks** (NHL) Program at NPS, which was a way for NPS both to acknowledge the country's most
important historic sites and to finally admit that not all nationally significant historic sites could be under its direct control.

Talking 'bout a Revolution

Due to the adverse effects of rapid population growth, industrial and agricultural
expansion, and urban sprawl in the 1950s, many Americans began to notice that the
dramatic changes in the world around them were not all positive. A number of popular books in the early 1960s championed the so-called conservation movement, later

called the environmental movement. This movement soon involved not only the protection of natural resources but also the conservation of cultural heritage resources.

The books promoting natural resource conservation included Rachel Carson's *Silent Spring* (1962) and Stewart Udall's *The Quiet Crisis* (1963). George Marsh's prescient 1864 book *Man and Nature* was rediscovered, with a 1965 Harvard University Press reprint. Cultural resource conservation books of note include Jane Jacobs's *The Death and Life of Great American Cities* (1961), Martin Anderson's *The Federal Bulldozer* (1964), and Peter Blake's *God's Own Junkyard* (1964). Archaeologists were fairly quiet conservationists at this time due to the scarcity of heritage management professionals and the beginnings of an internal intellectual revolution that distracted the academic archaeological community during the heyday of environmentalism.

As the NPS began to reassert itself as the federal government's leader in cultural heritage preservation, the National Trust for Historic Preservation (NTHP) gathered up the scattered leadership of the American historic preservation movement for a meeting at Colonial Williamsburg in early September 1963. The purposes of the meeting were to look at the European and American roots of the movement, consider its intellectual basis, evaluate its current effectiveness, and suggest means for its improvement (Short 1966). Few, if any, archaeologists attended the 1963 Williamsburg Conference, although some in-house Williamsburg archaeological staff may have been present.

Several of the 1963 speakers (e.g., Stephen Jacobs, Charles Hosmer) criticized the federal government's lack of leadership in historic preservation, although NPS chief historian Ronald Lee had been instrumental in setting up the conference and compiling the most influential document to come out of the conference: "A Report on Principles and Guidelines for Historic Preservation in the United States." This document, completed a month after the conference, was printed as an appendix to the published essays from the conference (Short 1966). It provided critical guidance for the federal legislative initiative that was soon to follow.

With Heritage So Rich

By 1964, almost all the pieces were in place to pass comprehensive federal heritage preservation legislation. As Glass (1990) points out, the three key elements of the success of this initiative were President Lyndon Johnson's "Great Society" program, the National Park Service's preservation reawakening, and a committee named for and chaired by Albert Rains, a Democratic congressman from Alabama who also chaired the House Subcommittee on Housing.

The Rains Committee was formed in 1964 as the vehicle for a final major legislative initiative for Representative Rains, who was retiring and looking for a lasting legacy. Because urban renewal activities had caused considerable damage to the historic cores of cities, housing advocates and historic preservationists were both aware of the need to come to some mutually acceptable solution. There was, however, considerable resistance within the federal government at the Housing and Home Finance Agency and the General Services Administration (GSA). These agencies opposed the implementation of anything that would impede urban renewal. The objectives of the Rains Committee were guided by a study of how historic preservation was done in Europe, especially after the ravages of World War II. The committee agreed to present its analysis in a report to Congress with recommendations for how historic preservation should be done in the United States.

The Rains Committee was made up of the heads of all the federal government's development agencies, a number of influential members of Congress, and various leaders of the historic preservation movement. The committee's activities, most importantly its trips to Europe and its final report, were sponsored by the National Conference of Mayors and the Ford Foundation. No federal funds were spent on these trips or the report production. The final report, produced in early 1966, was a well-written and well-illustrated book titled *With Heritage So Rich* (Rains and Henderson 1966).

With Heritage So Rich outlined the major elements of an American heritage preservation system. These elements focused on a federal system that could cope with the rapid changes occurring in American society and the American landscape. The publication stressed three critical elements for a successful historic preservation system:

1. A national inventory of historic places maintained by NPS that included properties of national, state, and **local significance**
2. A federal agency focused on guiding federal policy on heritage preservation
3. Incentives for local preservation, including tax breaks for rehabilitating historic buildings and grants to agencies and local governments to assist with preservation

While *With Heritage So Rich* provided the outline and explicit justification for national historic preservation legislation, it was not a comprehensive heritage preservation document. There was little mention of archaeology and nonstructural heritage resources in the book. No archaeologists or tribal members served as consultants or contributors. There was almost no discussion of archaeological site preservation needs. Of the 100 photographs in the book, there was only one of an American archaeological site, Cliff Palace at Mesa Verde, a picturesque prehistoric structural ruin. This lack of a strong archaeological presence in the formative literature of the National Historic Preservation Act was a continuation of the mid-twentieth-century trend separating archaeology from mainstream historic preservation, a separation that continues to this day.

National Historic Preservation Act (1966)

Various groups and agencies within the federal government drafted legislation to implement the recommendations of the Rains Committee. The legislation fit well with the Johnson administration's "Great Society" program, especially Lady Bird Johnson's "Preservation of Natural Beauty" initiative (Figure 4.2). It also had broad congressional support, reflecting the mood of the public with regard to the need to conserve natural and cultural resources. But there was still some resistance from conservative members of Congress and some federal development agencies. There was even discussion as to whether the implementation of the act should be the responsibility of the newly created Department of Housing and Urban Development (HUD) rather than the NPS.

Passage of the act in a form optimally beneficial to heritage preservation required intensive direct lobbying by influential members of the Rains Committee and indirect lobbying by NPS leaders. Various bills were compiled by the Senate, which passed a final version in July 1966. In early October, the House passed an amended version of the Senate bill that the Senate accepted. President Johnson signed the National Historic Preservation Act into law (PL 89-665, 16 USC 470) on October 15, 1966.

Since its 1966 passage, Congress has amended the NHPA over 20 times. Most of these amendments are minor and have to do with funding or the makeup of the Advisory Council on Historic Preservation (ACHP) membership, but major amendments took place in 1976, 1980, and 1992. It is instructive to look in detail at the contents

FIG. **4.2** Lady Bird Johnson and Secretary of the Interior Stewart Udall, leaders of the conservation movement in the 1960s (LBJ Library).

of the original NHPA in order to see what heritage preservation needs were apparent in the mid-1960s, what was done to address those needs, and how the needs and the federal government responses to them have changed over the last half century.

The original NHPA contained two titles subdivided into 13 Sections. Title I outlined the duties of the secretary of the interior, while Title II outlined the organization and duties of a new agency, the Advisory Council on Historic Preservation.

Purpose of the Act

As discussed in chapter 3, it is important to understand the legislative intent of a law in order to properly and practically apply it. In the NHPA, this intent is expressed by both a statement of purpose and the rationale for that purpose. The introduction to the original 1966 act reads,

An Act to establish a program for the preservation of additional historic properties throughout the Nation, and for other purposes.

Be it enacted by the Senate and House of Representatives of the United States of America in Congress assembled, The Congress finds and declares—

(a) that the spirit and direction of the Nation are founded upon and reflected in its historic past;

(b) that the historical and cultural foundations of the Nation should be preserved as a living part of our community life and development in order to give a sense of orientation to the American people;

(c) that, in the face of ever-increasing extensions of urban centers, highways, and residential, commercial, and industrial developments, the present governmental and nongovernmental historic preservation programs and activities are inadequate to insure future generations a genuine opportunity to appreciate and enjoy the rich heritage of our Nation; and

(d) that, although the major burdens of historic preservation have been borne and major efforts initiated by private agencies and individuals, and both should continue to play a vital role, it is nevertheless necessary and appropriate for the Federal Government to accelerate its historic preservation programs and activities, to give maximum encouragement to agencies and individuals undertaking preservation by private means, and to assist State and local governments and the National Trust for Historic Preservation in the United States to expand and accelerate their historic preservation programs and activities.

First, note that the main purpose of the program was to preserve "additional" historic properties, acknowledging that the NPS had already preserved some properties and was acting as steward of those properties. Second, not only was the program to be national in scope, but the properties would be located throughout the nation. Lastly, there were indeed "other" purposes of the program, so it wasn't just about preserving historic properties.

The first two findings of Congress supporting the enactment of the program declared there was great social value to doing historic preservation. The historic past was essential to national "spirit and direction." Furthermore, the physical remnants of the country's historical past were a "living part" of community life, giving the American people a "sense of orientation."

The next finding admitted that there was widespread destruction of historical resources due to urban sprawl, highway development, urban renewal, and commercial and industrial expansion and that existing public and private preservation programs were inadequate to deal with these threats. However, Congress did not admit in this section that the federal government was the main promoter and enactor of these threats.

In the last finding, the act admitted that private organizations had borne the major burden for historic preservation, but the federal government was now obligated to "accelerate" its participation. Thus, in the 1966 act, Congress confirmed the need for and benefits of historic preservation.

Title I: Responsibilities of the Secretary of the Interior

Section 101 stated that the first duty of the secretary of the interior was to "expand and maintain a national register of districts, sites, buildings, structures, and objects significant in American history, architecture, archeology, and culture." This was not initially referred to as the National Register of Historic Places. The Register was not something new, as indicated by the word "expand." The NPS was already maintaining an inventory of historic properties previously documented by the Historic American Buildings Survey, the Historic Sites Survey, and the National Historic Landmarks Program. The new inventory named the National Register was mainly to be expanded by states that were to be given federal grants to undertake surveys.

The next two subsections of Section 101 required matching grant programs for the preservation of historic properties, one for the states and the other for the National Trust for Historic Preservation. The final portion of Section 101 provided definitions of key terms. The definition of "historic preservation" focused totally on the treatment of structures, once again illustrating the dominance of architects and historians during the drafting of the bill and the lack of interest by archaeologists during its passage.

The next four sections (102–105) concerned the financial arrangements made with the states. Section 102 provided the basic guidelines for the grant programs. Grants were to be made in accordance with an approved comprehensive statewide historic preservation plan that was in turn in accordance with a state's comprehensive outdoor recreation plan. The outdoor recreation guidelines had appeared the year before in the Land and Water Conservation Fund Act (LAWCON). Section 103 was concerned with the state apportionment of federal grant money for surveys and plans. The apportionment was at the discretion of the secretary of the interior, although in any year the cost could not exceed half the total historic preservation survey and planning costs in a state. Section 104 dealt with the coordination of funding with other federal funding programs. Section 105 dealt with grant record keeping.

Section 106 was the shortest of the first six sections, containing only two sentences, but it eventually had the most significant effect on historic preservation of the entire act. Most agencies and heritage management professionals recognize it by the section number alone (although it was renumbered in 2014 and is now 54 USC 306108).

> The head of any Federal agency having direct or indirect jurisdiction over a proposed Federal or federally assisted undertaking in any State and the head of any Federal department or independent agency having authority to license any undertaking shall, prior to the approval of the expenditure of any Federal funds on the undertaking or prior to the issuance of any license, as the case may be, take into account the effect of the undertaking on any district, site, building, structure, or object that is included in the National Register. The head of any such Federal agency shall afford the Advisory Council on Historic Preservation established under title II of this Act a reasonable opportunity to comment with regard to such undertaking.

Section 106 meant that any federally funded or licensed project, as well as any project on federal land, had to be carefully reviewed by the federal agency in control of the funds, license, or lands. This federal agency had to consider the effects of the project on National Register–listed properties and consult with the ACHP regarding those effects.

The last two sections of Title I dealt with exclusions and funding. Section 107 excluded from NHPA applicability the White House, the Supreme Court Building, and the Capitol Building. Section 108 was critical in that it designated the yearly funding through fiscal year 1970, appropriating $2 million for fiscal year 1967 (October 1966–September 1967) and $10 million for each of the next three years. Section 108 is the most amended section of the NHPA due to constantly changing appropriations needs.

Title II: Formation of and Responsibilities of the ACHP

Section 201 concerned the establishment and makeup of the Advisory Council on Historic Preservation. It was to have 17 members, of which 6 were heads of federal agencies (Interior, HUD, Commerce, GSA, Treasury, Attorney General), along with the head of the National Trust for Historic Preservation. The other 10 members would be nonfederal individuals appointed by the president for a five-year term. The president also appointed one member to serve as chairman.

Section 202 outlined the duties of the ACHP:

> (1) advise the President and the Congress on matters relating to historic preservation; recommend measures to coordinate activities of Federal, State, and local agencies and private institutions and individuals relating to historic preservation; and advise on the dissemination of information pertaining to such activities;
> (2) encourage, in cooperation with the National Trust for Historic Preservation and appropriate private agencies, public interest and participation in historic preservation;
> (3) recommend the conduct of studies in such areas as the adequacy of legislative and administrative statutes and regulations pertaining to historic preservation activities of State and local governments and the effects of tax policies at all levels of government on historic preservation;
> (4) advise as to guidelines for the assistance of State and local governments in drafting legislation relating to historic preservation; and
> (5) encourage, in cooperation with appropriate public and private agencies and institutions, training and education in the field of historic preservation.

The council also had to send an annual report of its activities to Congress and the president, along with supplemental reports as necessary. The annual reports were to include recommendations for future legislative changes to the act.

Section 203 defined the ACHP's relationship with other federal agencies, which were required to cooperate with the ACHP and provide it with requested information pertinent to carrying out the duties. The agencies were also requested to make suggestions to the ACHP for furthering the purposes of the NHPA.

Section 204 outlined financial compensation for the nonfederal members of the ACHP. Each was to receive $100 per meeting as well as reimbursement for travel and subsistence expenses.

Section 205 located the advisory council within the Department of the Interior for the purposes of budgeting, accounting, and procurement, although the council itself had the power to hire and set compensation rates for its own employees. The director of the National Park Service was to be the executive director of the council; thus the ACHP was effectively located within NPS.

The 2014 recodification of 16 USC resulted in the renumbering of the sections of the NHPA as shown in Table 4.1.

Problems with Initial Implementation

It took almost a decade for the NHPA to be implemented in a manner consistent with its stated purposes. The implementation problems were most acute at the state level, although federal development and property management agencies and Interior Department oversight entities also had difficulties, mainly due to failure by Congress and the Department of the Interior to provide the necessary monetary support for the new program. The implementation problems, especially at the state level, soon made critical flaws with the law itself obvious.

TABLE 4.1   **Selected National Historic Preservation Act Section Equivalencies from 16 USC to 54 USC**

NHPA Area	Law Section	16 USC Section	54 USC Section
National Register	101a	470a(a)	3021
SHPOs	101b	470a(b)	3023
CLGs	101c	470a(c)	3025
Tribal programs	101d	470a(d)	3027
Grant authorization	101e	470a(e)	3029
Federal agency guidelines	101g	470a(g)	3061
Grant requirements	102a–e	470b(a–c)	3029
Apportionment of funding	103a–d	470c(a–d)	3029
Review of federal undertakings	106	470f	306108
Historic Preservation Fund	108	470h	3031
Federal agency programs	110	470h-2(a)	3061
ACHP organization	201a–f	470i(a–f)	304101
ACHP duties	202a–e	470j(a–b)	304102
Definitions	301	470w	3003

The Unsupported States

A major burden for implementing the NHPA fell on the states, and the states were in no way prepared. While the NPS had slowly built up a professional staff of historians, architects, and archaeologists to deal with the needs of its own parks and monuments and had a management structure in place to direct the efforts of these professionals, state governments had few professionals on staff and lacked management systems that could deal with the broad mandates of the NHPA. This included actions to conduct statewide surveys, to register properties in a national inventory, and to distribute funds for the preservation and rehabilitation of historic properties. In addition, the federal funding allocated to the states was slow in coming, with only the National Trust receiving funding by 1968. The states received their first funds in 1969.

To implement NHPA at the state level, the NPS directed the governor of each state to appoint a state liaison officer (SLO) for historic preservation. In most states, state historical societies were state agencies, and their executive directors became the obvious choice for SLOs. Some states (e.g., New York, Missouri, California) preferred to have the SLO reside in their conservation departments because they were already managing natural resources. In a few states (e.g., New Mexico, Rhode Island) housing or other non-preservation-focused agencies captured the SLO. In 1974, state liaison officers became state historic preservation officers (SHPOs).

In the late 1960s, archaeologists in the states were mainly based at universities or museums, where they focused on excavating large multicomponent prehistoric sites. They had no incentive for doing surveys to find new sites because enough "interesting" sites were already known to keep several academic generations of excavators busy. Furthermore, archaeological methods had not yet been developed to efficiently find and record sites, especially small sites in vegetated areas or deeply buried sites. Archaeologists considered all sites to be important, chafing at federally imposed criteria for determining significance and thus which sites were to be registered and determined worthy of preservation. Archaeologists were also suspicious of a national inventory that might become available to unscrupulous artifact collectors (whom they called "pothunters"), providing them with a literal treasure map of site locations.

Historians and architects with the necessary skills and interest in historic preservation were also in short supply after the passage of the NHPA. State historical societies in the 1960s were focused on their libraries and collections, exhibiting samples of their collections in small museums and publishing books on the early Euro-American settlement and formative industries of their states. Historians were busy teaching students their tried-and-true research methods, writing books, and helping museums with public interpretation.

Architects in the 1960s were busy designing new buildings that differed decidedly from those of the past. Most had little interest in preserving the architecture of the past.

The field of preservation architecture was largely limited to the NPS and the National Trust. There were no national standards available at the time for what appropriate restorations should include, and few architectural firms specialized in historic preservation. In Minnesota, the now well-known preservation architecture firm of Miller Dunwiddie was founded in 1966, but the staff specialized in aviation construction until becoming involved with the restoration of historic Fort Snelling in the mid-1970s. Another Minneapolis firm specializing in preservation architecture, Mack and MacDonald, was founded in 1976.

The biggest problem faced by the states in implementing the NHPA had to do with nominating properties for the National Register of Historic Places. This was critical because only listed properties would get development agency consideration and ACHP consultation under Section 106. The states needed to find appropriate properties and then complete nomination forms. To do this, they needed appropriate professionals on their staffs, who in turn needed guidelines as to what was worthy of listing. They also needed an actual form to fill out with instructions on how to do nominations with some consistency.

National Register nomination guidelines and the first nomination form were given to the states in 1968. The initial National Register mostly included historic properties documented by the NPS Historic Sites Survey over the previous 30 years, which had focused on nationally significant properties. Many of these had been listed as National Historic Landmarks by NPS beginning in 1960. The initial Register also included historical or archaeological national parks and monuments. The first National Register list published in the *Federal Register* on February 25, 1969, contained just 960 properties. This meant that almost three years after the passage of the NHPA, Section 106 requirements applied to fewer than 1,000 properties in the entire United States.

Interior Issues: NPS and ACHP

The NPS appointed a committee to deal with NHPA implementation made up of three experienced historic preservation practitioners: Ronald Lee of NPS as historian, J. Otis Brew of Harvard University as archaeologist, and Ernest Connally of the University of Illinois as architectural historian. As discussed in King, Hickman, and Berg (1977:32), the committee recommended the formation of an agency within the Interior Department to oversee all the department's history and archaeology functions except those of the ACHP. This would include the National Register, state grants, the Interagency Archaeological Salvage Program (IASP), the Historic American Buildings Survey, the Historic Sites Survey, and the National Historic Landmarks Program. The original intent of the committee was to make the new agency independent of NPS, but that didn't happen. NPS established the Office of Archaeology and Historic Preservation (OAHP) in 1967 with Connally as its director.

The Interior Department then raided the National Trust leadership to fill two key positions: Robert Garvey became head of the ACHP, and William Murtagh became the first Keeper of the National Register. As OAHP struggled to organize a myriad of internal NPS archaeological and historical activities, the ACHP began to concern itself with building an external nationwide historic preservation system as envisioned by the NHPA. This was hampered by Congress's failure to fund the ACHP in the initial postpassage NRHP appropriation. The ACHP had to rely on squeezing funding out of the existing Interior Department budget.

The ACHP had been given exclusive responsibility for making sure federal agencies complied with their obligations under Section 106. This meant the ACHP staff had to review every development project sent to them by federal agencies as part of the agency consultation clause in Section 106. This included all the roads being built with federal funds provided by the Federal Highway Administration (FHWA), all the urban renewal projects being funded by HUD, all the dams and navigation improvements being undertaken by the Army Corps of Engineers, and every kind of land-disturbing project on millions of acres of federal land managed by the Forest Service, the Bureau of Land Management, the NPS, the Department of Defense, the Fish and Wildlife Service, and a number of other agencies. It was fortunate in some ways that the agencies did not send the ACHP all their projects, as the short-staffed ACHP would have been completely overwhelmed with paperwork.

Just like the states, the ACHP had to build a staff and a management structure from scratch. The sooner it had a qualified staff, the sooner it could review the federal projects it was supposed to receive. The sooner it could provide federal agencies and the states with guidance on how to best fulfill their NHPA obligations, the sooner the congressional intent of the NHPA could be fulfilled. Without adequate funding and internal support, sooner became later and later.

The Feds: Business as Usual

Under Section 106 of the NHPA, federal agencies had the principal responsibility to consider the impacts of all their projects on registered historic properties and were obligated to consult with the ACHP about potential effects to such properties. Agencies were not eager to have to go through a new layer of bureaucracy that could interfere with their missions and cost them funds that they had dedicated to completing their projects. They had little incentive to help the ACHP develop guidelines, so they didn't. Agencies basically ignored the requirements of Section 106 as long as they could get away with it.

The ACHP attempted to fill the federal historic preservation leadership gap left by the inward-focused NPS and Interior Department but was hampered by a number of factors. The council was embedded in a development agency, Interior/NPS, which exposed it to conflict of interest. The ACHP was not directly funded by the NHPA legislation but had to rely on the existing Interior/NPS budget, which was already stretched thin by existing programs within an agency whose main mission was to preserve and provide public access to areas of land valued primarily for their natural resources. The ACHP was a brand-new entity governed by a brand-new law with no implementing regulations, which gave the council little direction as to how to proceed. It was supposed to work with all landowning, development, and permitting federal agencies, but these agencies had little to gain by cooperating with the ACHP and little to lose by not cooperating.

Most of all, the implementation of Section 106, the ACHP's main responsibility, was dependent on a robust and comprehensive National Register, as only effects to listed properties were to be considered by federal agencies and sent to the ACHP. By the end of 1969, only about 1,000 properties were listed in the National Register nationwide. Most of these were well-known landmarks already protected within parks, monuments, or other public lands. Federal agencies did not have the qualified staff or the incentive to add properties to the National Register. State liaison offices were still struggling to assemble qualified staffs and to figure out what their duties were and how to go about them, so few nominations were being forwarded from the states to the National Register in Washington. Thus, federal undertakings continued to destroy important historic properties for the first five years after the passage of the NHPA at a similar rate to prior to the legislation.

Executive Order 11593

In his 1971 Executive Order 11593, titled "Protection and Enhancement of the Cultural Environment," President Richard Nixon addressed the most critical problems inherent in the NHPA that prevented its effective implementation as intended by historic preservationists and Congress. John Sprinkle (2011) has provided the most in-depth history of this important executive order, while Thomas King has scattered insights into its history, application, and current status in his 2013 textbook and an August 31, 2009, post to his *CRM Plus* blog.

Sprinkle and King make clear that the 1969 passage of the National Environmental Policy Act (NEPA; see chapter 7) provided the main impetus for Executive Order 11593. Unlike the ACHP, which was embedded in Interior/NPS, the implementing entity for NEPA, the **Council on Environmental Quality** (CEQ), was an independent agency that received its own funding and reported directly to the president. Due to their similar missions in reviewing federal undertakings that might affect cultural resources, ACHP and CEQ personnel got together soon after the implementation of NEPA to discuss ways to effectively coordinate and implement their reviews.

In July 1970, the CEQ established an interagency workgroup to examine a variety of related problems that could be included in a presidential message on the environment. NPS-based OAHP staff wrote an opinion paper that focused on the need to continue the Historic Sites Survey, especially with regard to federal property. OAHP's main concern at the time was with determining which surplus government buildings were truly important historically. As authorized by the Demolition Act of 1935, the General Services Administration could give historically significant federal buildings to other public entities as long as they were not used for commercial purposes. With the exception of buildings already evaluated by the Historic Sites Survey or HABS, government agencies didn't know which of their properties were indeed historically significant. In addition, ACHP staff thought all types of historic properties needed to be addressed in surveys and evaluated for significance, including archaeological sites.

The NPS-ACHP historic preservation concerns were incorporated into the CEQ recommendations sent to the White House in December 1970. President Nixon delivered his environmental message in February 1971. Included in the message was a directive to agencies that federally owned buildings should not be demolished without an assessment of their historic significance. Executive Order 11593 was then drafted by CEQ staff and issued by the president on May 13, 1971.

Executive Order 11593 required federal agencies to take three major actions to correct deficiencies in the National Historic Preservation Act:

1. It required that all federal agencies survey their lands to identify potentially important sites and structures, evaluate any located sites or structures to determine eligibility for the National Register of Historic Places, and then nominate eligible properties.
2. It required federal agencies "in the interim period" to treat any sites or structures that were determined eligible for the National Register as if they were actually listed in the National Register for the purposes of Section 106 of the NHPA.
3. It required the secretary of the interior (i.e., NPS) to issue explicit guidelines for determining National Register eligibility.

EO 11593 specified that the first action (survey, evaluation, nomination) was to be accomplished by July 1, 1973, a completely unrealistic goal for a comprehensive survey and evaluation of almost one million government-owned buildings and structures and an impossible goal with regard to finding and evaluating all archaeological sites on 640 million acres of federal lands, about one-quarter of the country's total area. Nominating eligible buildings, structures, and known sites to the National Register within a two-year period, although the process was simpler in the early days of the Register, was also totally unrealistic, especially given the scarcity of qualified professional staff at agencies, in state liaison offices, and at the National Register.

While Executive Order 11593 emphasized buildings, applied only to federal property, and had a totally inadequate timetable, it completely altered the way environmental review was done with respect to historic properties, effectively establishing the basis of the system still in use today. Agencies could no longer ignore the ACHP and their responsibilities under NHPA. They had to determine if their undertakings would impact significant historic sites. They could not claim lack of guidance for National Register eligibility, as basic National Register criteria for nomination were developed by OAHP in December 1966 and released to the states and agencies in 1968. In compliance with EO 11593, explicit National Register eligibility regulations (36 CFR 63) for the purposes of Section 106 were published in the *Federal Register* on September 21, 1977. The most important elements of EO 11593 were eventually incorporated into the NHPA by amendments in 1976 and 1980.

Besides establishing the basis for a workable and comprehensive Section 106 process, EO 11593 had other important federal historic preservation implications. As King points out in an August 21, 2009, *CRM Plus* blog post, it integrated historic preservation with federal environmental protection being addressed under NEPA. The staffs of the ACHP and the CEQ had worked closely together to draft EO 11593. Because NEPA required consideration of federal impacts to "important historic, cultural, and natural aspects of our national heritage" (Section 101), it reinforced the intent of the NHPA to protect historic properties.

EO 11593 also fostered the rise of archaeology in historic preservation. This archaeological impact was ironic, given that archaeologists had assisted very little with the passage of the National Historic Preservation Act and paid very little attention to it afterward. Archaeologists at the time were focused on salvage archaeology in the reservoir projects that were the major destructors of prehistoric sites in the 1950s and 1960s. Legislatively they concentrated on the amendment of the Reservoir Salvage Act (RSA) because its revision would broaden archaeological consideration of federal projects beyond just reservoirs and would guarantee full-time employment for many archaeologists.

The NPS responded to EO 11593 by first informing other federal agencies of its historic preservation requirements and implications. King (2013:21–22) notes that NPS sent three archaeologists—Larry Aten, John Young, and Roy Reeves—as evangelists to the major development and landowning agencies. They no doubt stressed the importance of archaeology as well as the new heritage management processes in their agency sermons. In addition, NEPA (Section 102) required an explicitly scientific approach for environmental review, which mirrored the preaching of the new archaeologists of the 1960s.

Amendments to NHPA

In the five years following the 1971 issuance of EO 11593, there were no significant congressional actions affecting the way the National Historic Preservation Act worked, although in 1974 the ACHP issued the first nonbinding guidelines for implementing Section 106. That same year, additional laws affecting historic preservation were passed: the Housing and Community Development Act amended the Housing Act of 1934 and the Archaeological and Historic Preservation Act (also known as Moss-Bennett) amended the Reservoir Salvage Act of 1960 (see chapter 7).

In February 1975, Senator Henry Jackson, chairman of the Senate Committee on Interior and Insular Affairs, requested that the ACHP prepare a report on the status of historic preservation in the United States. In early 1976, the ACHP submitted a report to Senator Jackson titled "The National Historic Preservation Program Today." Jackson had specifically requested that the report not focus on making legislative recommendations but evaluate the strengths and weaknesses of historic preservation in this country.

The report began with an overview of significant historic preservation laws. Under "General Preservation Legislation" it listed the Antiquities Act (1906), the establishment of the National Park Service (1916), the Historic Sites Act (1935), the National Historic Preservation Act (1966), Executive Order 11593, and the National Environmental Policy Act (1969). Under "Archaeological Legislation" it listed the Reservoir Salvage Act (1960) and the Archaeological and Historic Preservation Act (1974). Under "Other Preservation Laws" it listed the Department of Transportation Act (1966), the Federal Property and Administrative Services Act (1949), and the National Trust for Historic Preservation Act (1949). Not listed were the various federal housing acts that had provided incentives for historic preservation with respect to urban renewal.

The next two chapters of the report summarized the basic steps necessary for effective historic preservation: identification, evaluation, and registration. The identification and evaluation chapter had an interesting section providing an international perspective, including the benefits of World Heritage designation and a suggestion that the National Register could be expanded to include "intangible cultural resources." This suggestion and the use of the term "cultural resources" clearly reflected the influence of ACHP archaeologists who had been educated as anthropologists.

The fourth chapter discussed how historic properties were protected by the current federal system but noted (p. 41) that this was the "weakest link" in the current system because no federal authority could require historic preservation and there was no clear mandate that historic properties be identified and evaluated prior to project implementation. The fifth chapter identified the impediments to effective long-term preservation, mainly related to inadequate funding.

The final chapter of the 1976 ACHP Senate report, titled "A Suggestion for Action," was the shortest by far, obviously following Chairman Jackson's directive to limit specific legislative recommendations. These recommendations, however, had been suggested or implied in the various previous chapters in discussions of notable problems. The final chapter briefly stated that the major problems were duplication of effort, lack of agency coordination, a fragmented federal historic preservation program, and a lack of readiness.

The report had six appendixes. The first was a legal analysis of the law citing various court cases that had arisen over the 10 years since the passage of the NHPA. The next five were brief summaries of how historic preservation was done in other countries: Great Britain, the Soviet Union, Japan, the Netherlands, and Canada. The first four countries had experienced widespread destruction of historic sites during World War II and thus had dealt with major restoration issues.

1976 Amendments

While the 1976 ACHP report did not recommend a specific legislative agenda, it led to a direct legislative response in the form of an amendment to the National Historic Preservation Act sponsored by Senator Jackson. The initial congressional action was linked to the Land and Water Conservation Fund Act enacted in 1964. This linkage related to use of the same source of revenue as LAWCON, the Outer Continental Shelf Lands fund. As additional amendment needs beyond funding became apparent, the final language of the 1976 amendment to the NHPA addressed not only the system's deficiencies listed in the ACHP report but also policies first outlined in EO

11593 and other issues made apparent by various interest groups during the drafting of the bill.

With regard to the deficiencies listed in the ACHP report, because so many of the problems with historic preservation were due to inadequate funding, the 1976 amendment established in Section 108 of the NHPA a permanent fund called the Historic Preservation Fund (HPF) to be provided with dollars from outer continental shelf mineral lease fees (mostly related to oil production). The HPF would fund all provisions of the act: for the states, the ACHP, and the National Trust for Historic Preservation. The HPF was to get $24.4 million in 1977, $100 million in 1978, and $150 million in 1979, 1980, and 1981. The ACHP Senate report (p. 52) had recommended a minimum of $180 million a year. Also with regard to funding as recommended in the ACHP report (p. 27), the amendment (Section 102) raised the federal match to the states for survey and planning work from 50–50 to 70–30.

In direct response to the ACHP Senate report, the 1976 amendment (Section 202) authorized the participation of the United States in the International Centre for the Study of the Preservation and Restoration of Cultural Property. The ACHP was to recommend to the secretary of state members for appointment to the delegation from the United States.

As identified in the ACHP report concerning provisions of Executive Order 11593, Section 106 was amended in 1976 to include federal agency consideration of the effects of undertakings on "eligible" as well as National Register–listed properties. EO 11593's "eligible equals in" language with respect to Section 106 reviews had technically expired in 1974, and the Section 106 guidelines issued by the ACHP in 1974 were nonbinding. The ACHP had noted in multiple locations in the 1976 Senate report (e.g., pp. 26, 27, 39) that it was critical to include eligible as well as listed properties in Section 106 consideration. Section 211 of the amendment authorized the ACHP to promulgate rules and regulations to implement Section 106.

While the ACHP Senate report did not say so explicitly, it was clear by 1976 that, due to conflict-of-interest concerns, the ACHP should not be embedded in a federal agency (NPS) that was itself a development agency subject to Section 106. Section 201 was amended to establish the ACHP as an independent agency. It also increased the membership of the ACHP from 17 to 29, adding the heads of nine federal agencies, two more presidential appointments from outside the federal government, and the president of the National Conference of State Historic Preservation Officers (NCSHPO).

As for other NHPA amendment needs brought up by various interest groups, archaeologists had continued to be somewhat paranoid that the locations of archaeological sites, especially ones listed in the National Register of Historic Places, would be made available to the public, leading to increased site vandalism and looting. Language was added to Section 101 allowing exact site locations of National Register properties to be withheld from the public.

1980 Amendments

While the reasons for the timing of the 1976 amendment to the NHPA are fairly apparent—the ACHP Senate report, the expiration of many aspects of EO 11593 in mid-1973, and the tenth anniversary of the act—the reasons for the 1980 amendment are less obvious. They share some historical aspects: both were passed in the final year of a presidential term, Gerald Ford's for the former and Jimmy Carter's for the latter, and both codified aspects of EO 11593 that had proved essential for comprehensive and effective historic preservation.

Looking at the chronology of heritage management (Appendix C), a number of events occurred in 1979 that strengthened the national program. The Archaeological Resources Protection Act (ARPA) improved the protection of sites on federal land in response to the 1974 *U.S. v. Diaz* ruling that had determined Antiquities Act stipulations were too vague. The ACHP had issued legally binding regulations (36 CFR 800) for Section 106. The HPF appropriation of $60 million in 1979 was at the highest level ever, adjusting for inflation ($215 million in 2018 dollars), greatly strengthening federal historic preservation efforts and state programs. Outside the federal system, a third invitation-only NTHP historic preservation conference in Williamsburg focused on nongovernmental historic preservation and setting standards for local historic preservation (see NTHP 1980).

When President Carter signed the legislation amending the NHPA on December 12, 1980, he stated that it was the first major amendment to the National Historic Preservation Act. While it was considerably longer and more detailed than the 1976 amendments, the 1976 legislation had certainly been major in scope, considering it established the Historic Preservation Fund, increased the federal match to the states, codified the National Register eligible-equals-in provision for Section 106 review, and gave the ACHP independent agency status. Although he signed the legislation, Carter was unhappy with several provisions in the act, most importantly the fact that some members of the ACHP were not appointed by the president and that Congress could veto regulations issued by an executive agency (Carter 2013:2802).

Unlike the 1976 amendment, the 1980 amendment to the NHPA added three statements to the legislative intent in Section 1.

1. Stipulation 3 noted that significant historic properties were being lost with increasing frequency.
2. Stipulation 4 listed the many benefits of historic properties beyond just preserving them for posterity, including economic and energy conservation benefits.
3. Stipulation 6 suggested that better knowledge of historic resources would improve federal planning and promote economic growth.

There was also an entirely new declaration of policy in Section 2 that stressed federal leadership in cooperation with the states, local governments, Indian tribes, private organizations, and even other countries.

In Section 101(a) concerning the National Register of Historic Places, the amendment not only provided details on National Historic Landmark designation and National Register eligibility and nomination but allowed private property owners to object to and thus prevent NHL and NRHP listing of their properties. It allowed local governments and private individuals to directly nominate properties. It directed the secretary of the interior to establish or revise regulations for evaluation and nomination of properties. It required the National Register to take action on nominations within 45 days, and if there was no objection by the Register within this period, a nominated property would be automatically listed.

In Section 101(b) concerning state programs, the amendment first directed the development by the secretary of the interior of regulations for certification of state programs, the appointment of a state historic preservation officer, the hiring of appropriate professional staff, the designation of a state review board (SRB), and public participation in state programs. It then required the review of state programs by the secretary at least every four years. Section 101(b)(3) outlined the responsibilities of each SHPO.

Under Section 101(c)(1), the amendment allowed for SHPO certification of local governments to help carry out the purposes of the NHPA and to receive grants passed through SHPOs from the federal Historic Preservation Fund. These entities became known as **certified local governments** (CLGs). The section outlined the certification process and required the establishment of a survey and inventory system at the local level.

The 1980 amendment specified in a number of locations how states should allocate the HPF moneys they received from the federal government. Section 102(c) required states to give at least 10% of their HPF allocation to CLGs. Section 101(d) mandated that states allocate up to 10% of their HPF share for the preservation of properties listed in the National Register. The preservation activities could include training and development of skilled labor to carry out preservation and curation activities. The secretary of the interior could also make grants directly to Indian tribes and minority groups "for the preservation of their cultural heritage."

While several new sections dealt with financial matters—such as Section 105 regarding loans for National Register properties and Section 109 regarding private donations to the federal government to further historic preservation—the most important new section added to the NHPA in 1980 was Section 110. This section outlined the responsibilities of federal agencies with respect to historic preservation on lands and structures owned by the federal government.

Section 110 first concerned itself with buildings, requiring federal agencies to use their historic structures to the fullest extent consistent with their mission, to transfer surplus historic properties out of federal ownership if doing so promoted their preservation, and to fully document any necessary demolition of a historic building. With regard to both structures and archaeological sites, all federal land was to be surveyed for historic properties, all located properties evaluated for their significance, and all eligible properties nominated to the National Register. This repeated what had been included in EO 11593 without any deadline. Federal agencies were to each designate a federal preservation officer (FPO) to coordinate all agency actions under the act.

Under Title II, Section 201 of the 1980 amendment to the NHPA reduced the membership of the ACHP from 29 to 19. Only the secretary of the interior and the secretary of agriculture were retained as mandatory major agency representatives, although "four other agencies" whose activities "affect historic preservation" were also to be on the council. New members were to include a governor, a mayor, and four experts in different fields of historic preservation, all appointed by the president. The president still appointed members at large from the public, but the total was reduced from 12 to 3. The president also appointed a chairman from the public. The only members of the new ACHP not appointed by the president were the NCSHPO president and the National Trust chairman. The term of office of appointed members was changed from five to four years.

Section 202 expanded the duties of the ACHP to include review of federal agency policies and programs with respect to historic preservation. The ACHP was to recommend methods to improve "effectiveness, coordination, and consistency of these policies and programs." The ACHP was also to inform and educate not just federal agencies but state and local governments, Indian tribes, other nations and international organizations, and private individuals and organizations with regard to the council's activities.

The 1980 amendment added a new Title III to the NHPA. Section 301 expanded the definitions previously under Section 101(b), introducing 10 new terms, changing the definition of "historic preservation," and slightly altering the definitions of "state" and "secretary." The term "project" was eliminated.

Under Section 304, the restrictions on releasing data to the general public on the character or location of historic resources was expanded from just National

Register–listed properties to all such properties on federal land. Other notable sections under Title III include Section 306 establishing a National Center for the Building Arts and Section 307 providing for congressional review of new or revised regulations. President Carter was most displeased with Section 307 of the new legislation.

In a strange twist, the 1980 amendments added several appendixes to the legislation that were not formally considered part of the National Historic Preservation Act:

- Section 208 concerned aspects of funding survey and evaluation of historic properties.
- Section 401 concerned US participation in the World Heritage Convention.
- Section 502 required the secretary of the interior, in cooperation with the American Folklife Center, to submit to the president and Congress within two years a report "on preserving and conserving the intangible aspects of our cultural heritage such as arts, skills, folklife, and folkways."
- Sections 503 through 507 required reports from various entities on historic preservation tax laws, the HPF, the Pennsylvania Avenue Development Corporation, **cultural parks**, and fires in historic properties. All of the Section 500 reports appear to concern matters that were not quite ready for prime-time legislation.

1992 Amendments

While only 4 years separated the first two amendments to the NHPA, it was 12 years before the next (and last) major amendment. Once again, the amendment was passed near the end of a presidential term, that of George H. W. Bush.

In the 12 years after the 1980 amendment, there had been significant changes in many aspects of heritage management. In the first year of the Ronald Reagan administration (1981), the HPF was cut in half, and the Heritage Conservation and Recreation Service (HCRS), formed by the Carter administration in 1977 to consolidate historic preservation activities, was disbanded and its duties dispersed within NPS. The *Secretary of the Interior's Standards and Guidelines for Historic Preservation* were released in 1983. The same year, the Supreme Court's decision in *Metropolitan Edison Co. v. People Against Nuclear Energy* put limits on consideration of social effects under NEPA. HPF funding reached its lowest level ever, $24 million, in 1987.

Most significant for the National Historic Preservation Act was a Senate directive in 1989 (Senate Report 101-85) for the NPS to study the funding needs of historic preservation on **Indian lands**. In response to this directive, NPS initiated focused consultation with Indian tribes and broad consultation with federal agencies and SHPOs. In May 1990, NPS produced the required report, titled *Keepers of the Treasures: Protecting Historic Properties and Cultural Traditions on Indian Lands*.

Keepers of the Treasures was a landmark study with far-reaching implications for the way the federal government dealt with heritage management of Indian, Native Hawaiian, and Native Alaskan cultural resources. It demonstrated that these groups viewed heritage preservation differently from mainstream Americans. The most important heritage resources were not physical historic properties but less tangible resources such as language and cultural practices. Preservation of these resources was critical to maintaining tribal identity. In order to find and protect tribal cultural resources, agencies had to first explicitly recognize tribal sovereignty and respect tribal cultural values.

Keepers of the Treasures made 13 recommendations with regard to the preservation of tribal cultural resources. Most of these focused on adapting current federal policies to recognize tribal cultural resource needs and to use existing programs to deal with these needs. There were also specific legislative objectives. Recommendation 8 stated, "As part of developing a consistent American Indian cultural heritage policy, a national approach should be developed regarding the exhumation, display, study, repatriation, and appropriate cultural treatment of human remains, funerary artifacts, and sacred artifacts" (p. 175). This objective rapidly led to the passage of the Native American Graves Protection and Repatriation Act (NAGPRA) of 1990 (see chapter 13).

The last recommendation in *Keepers of the Treasures* was that "the National Historic Preservation Act should be amended to establish a separate title authorizing programs, policies, and procedures for tribal heritage preservation and financial support as part of the annual appropriation process" (p. 177). This recommendation and other observations on tribal needs and priorities within the report were the principal reasons for amending the NHPA in 1992. President Bush signed the amendment into law on October 10, 1992.

The need to include tribal perspectives and participation in the National Historic Preservation Act was added to two Section 2 policy statements (2 and 6) at the beginning of the 1992 amendment. This was implemented in the amendment mainly in Section 101(d)(2) requiring the secretary of the interior to establish a program and regulations "to assist Indian tribes in preserving their particular historic properties." Tribes were given the right to assume any or all SHPO functions on **tribal lands** if they designated a tribal historic preservation officer (THPO), provided the secretary with a historic preservation plan, and were capable of carrying out their responsibilities with respect to the assumed duties.

References to tribal and Native Hawaiian participation in federal policy and programs were then included where appropriate throughout the 1992 amendment. A tribal member was added to the ACHP in Section 201(a)(11), to be appointed by the president. Under the definitions at the beginning of Section 301, the definition of "Indian tribe" was revised and a definition of "tribal lands" was added.

There were other significant changes to the NHPA in the 1992 amendment, including a reduction in the federal match for state programs from 70% to 60% under Section 102(a)(3). Section 103 gave the secretary of the interior more discretion to allocate money to the states "as determined appropriate." Section 110 was reworded, requiring development by each federal agency of a preservation program that included survey, evaluation, and nomination but not the strict preservation of listed or eligible properties, only consideration of actions that could harm them as required in Section 106. The word "all" was dropped with reference to "locate, inventory, and nominate," implying, according to King (2013:234–235), that agencies post-1992 had greater discretion in how they carried out these activities. Section 111 gave agencies more discretion as to how they dealt with leasing or divesting themselves of these historic properties.

Two new sections appeared at the end of Title I. Section 112 required that employees or contractors involved with actions that could impact historic properties meet professional standards developed by the secretary of the interior and that records of these activities be permanently maintained. Section 112 also required the secretary to develop guidelines to assist agencies, SHPOs, and THPOs with encouraging private landowners to preserve historic resources on their property. Section 113 dealt with the illegal trade in antiquities and required the secretary to send Congress a report concerning this trade.

Like the 1980 amendment, the 1992 amendment to the NHPA significantly revised and expanded the definitions at the beginning of Section 301. The only definitions of the previously appearing 13 definitions not revised were "local government," "National Register," and "cultural park." The five added definitions were "tribal lands," "certified local government," "council," "Native Hawaiian," and "Native Hawaiian organization." Section 304 clarified and expanded federal agency and federal grant recipient obligations to withhold data from the public with regard to the location, character, and ownership of certain historic properties.

Finally, Title IV of the 1992 amendment to the NHPA established a new entity, the National Preservation Technology and Training Center. Although it was to be an NPS facility, the legislation required that it be located at Northwestern State University of Louisiana in Natchitoches.

Post-1992 NHPA Developments

There have been few substantial changes to the NHPA since the 1992 amendments. In 1996, Congress reauthorized the funding for the HPF and ACHP through 2000. In 1998, the HPF funding was extended to 2004. There was a concerted attempt in 2005 to weaken the NHPA by allowing Section 106 to pertain only to NRHP-listed properties or properties determined eligible by the Keeper of the National Register. This would have eliminated the streamlining of agency-SHPO/THPO consensus determinations. If private landowners objected to their properties' listing, the process would stop, and the nomination would not be forwarded to the Keeper for a formal determination of eligibility. Responsibility for documentation and analysis for Section 106 projects would have shifted from the project proposers to SHPOs. The 2005 bill would also have expanded the size of, and eliminated a set funding level for, the ACHP.

The 2005 bill did not pass, but a 2006 amendment included some of the proposed 2005 changes. The ACHP was increased from 16 to 23 members. Agencies or private groups were allowed to provide additional funding to the ACHP to help it carry out its duties. Funding for the HPF was extended through fiscal year 2015.

President Barack Obama signed the National Park Service Centennial Act on December 16, 2016. This act amended the NHPA to make the ACHP chairmanship a full-time position, added the chairman of the National Association of Tribal Historic Preservation Officers (NATHPO) as a voting member of the ACHP, and reauthorized the HPF until 2023.

In 2014, the recodification of laws pertaining to the National Park Service was required under Public Law 113-287. This removed the National Historic Preservation Act from United States Code (USC) 16 (Conservation) and put it in USC 54 (National Park Service and Related Programs).

Summary

The roots of a true American historic preservation movement are not deep, and the original federal tending to these roots was insufficient for the movement to thrive. The National Historic Preservation Act of 1966, however, was planted in the fertile soil of the environmental movement. It was pruned and shaped by Executive Order 11593 in 1971 and by major amendments in 1976, 1980, and 1992, until it became a viable structure within the constraints of constitutional requirements and fluctuating funding.

The NHPA provides for much more than just the review of federal construction projects under its well-known Section 106. It defines the duties of state and tribal historic preservation offices. It provides federal matching grants for local historic preservation activities. It requires that federal agencies take the responsibility to find, evaluate, and protect cultural heritage resources on lands they manage. It provides for a listing of all the historic properties that states and agencies have carefully examined and deemed worthy of preservation. These are the branches of a basically healthy American historic preservation structure.

But the branches could not thrive without being attached to a sturdy trunk. That trunk's heartwood is made of the congressional intent of its 1966 planters, who recognized that the vitality of this country rests on its past and that the tangible remnants of that past could not be preserved by just public goodwill and private actions. It was incumbent on the federal government to take the lead in historic preservation and to develop a system that was not perfect but was sufficient to promote cooperation at all levels of government and protect critical elements that continue to define our Americanness.

Review Questions

1. What developments in American history led to the passage of the NHPA?
2. What are the purposes of the NHPA as stated in the act?
3. What are the most important sections of the NHPA?
4. What were some of the problems with implementation of the NHPA?
5. What important amendments have been made to the NHPA?

Supplemental Reading

All serious students of American heritage preservation should look at Rains and Henderson (1966), the study that determined what the original National Historic Preservation Act would look like. Glass (1990) provides the most comprehensive historic overview of the birth of the heritage preservation movement.

For the nascent environmental movement, the rediscovery of George Marsh's 1864 book *Man and Nature* was promoted by a 1965 centennial reprint by Harvard University. There have been several more recent reprints, as well as a 2003 analysis by David Lowenthal with an introduction by William Cronin.

Sprinkle (2011) provides the best background to the development of EO 11593 that was the basis for the first two major amendments to the NHPA in 1976 and 1980. There is no comprehensive overview of all the amendments to the NHPA, but King (2013) and various articles in Banks and Scott (2016) provide helpful background and analysis.

SIDEBAR

Implementing Heritage Management: Rights of Passage

So, of the major heritage management professions, who gets the most credit for our heritage management system as it exists today? Who helped craft the National Historic Preservation Act? Who insured its passage? Who developed the implementation procedures? Much has been written about the origins of the NHPA (e.g., Glass 1990), but proper credit for its passage is buried in the details.

The law's enactment effectively began in September 1963 with a conference sponsored by the National Trust for Historic Preservation in Williamsburg. Many important figures in historic preservation from the United States and Europe were invited, although apparently no archaeologists. The proceedings were published by the NTHP in 1966 (Short 1966). National Park Service senior historian Ronald Lee was charged with writing the final section, titled "A Report on Principles and Guidelines for Historic Preservation in the United States." Strangely, there was no call for comprehensive legislation in any of the papers or in Lee's report.

In the summer of 1964, two more critical meetings took place. One was very informal, between

Carl Feiss, an architectural planner and trustee of the NTHP, and Larry Henderson, a well-known housing lobbyist. Henderson knew a powerful congressman, Albert Rains, was going to retire soon and wanted to sponsor some final important legislation as a legacy. Henderson had also heard the complaints about the destruction of historic properties due to urban renewal and thought there might be a legislative solution. Feiss agreed to help organize the effort. The result was the Rains Committee that would eventually guide the NHPA through Congress.

The second 1964 meeting was between NPS historian Ronald Lee and his boss, George Hartzog, the director of NPS (Figure 4.3). Lee thought the NPS was falling behind as a leader in historic preservation. Hartzog authorized Lee to form an internal committee to investigate the issue. Lee then sent Hartzog a copy of his Williamsburg paper. Hartzog requested that Robert Utley, head of the NPS Division of History, develop guidelines for federal support of local historic preservation. Lee gave Hartzog his advisory committee's report in December 1964, recommending a reassertion of external NPS historic preservation leadership and an NPS reorganization to facilitate it.

Everything began to come together in early 1965. Lady Bird Johnson had her husband, President Lyndon Johnson, deliver a message on

FIG. 4.3 Former NPS directors Newton Drury and Horace Albright (on left) with NPS director George Hartzog and former NPS associate director Conrad Wirth (far right) dedicating a National Historic Landmark in 1964. Wirth had conceived and directed the NPS Mission 66 program, and Hartzog was charged with implementing the National Historic Preservation Act in 1966 (National Park Service).

preserving natural beauty that included consideration of historic sites. In response, Secretary of the Interior Stuart Udall asked the NPS to draft legislation for grants to support local historic preservation. In May 1966, Lee and two handpicked associates, University of Illinois architectural professor Ernest Connally and Harvard archaeologist J. Otis Brew, formed a new committee to study improving current NPS internal operations and anticipated external operations from new heritage preservation legislation. Concurrently, Feiss and Henderson managed to obtain private funding for the Rains Committee to visit historic sites in Europe. The Rains Committee went to Europe in September 1965 and published a report of its findings, titled *With Heritage So Rich*, in January 1966. After intensive lobbying by influential members of the Rains Committee, the NTHP, and the NPS, Congress passed the NHPA in the early fall of 1966, and President Johnson signed it on October 15, 1966.

The law put the NPS in charge of all key elements of federal implementation. Historian Lee organized an internal NPS task force in November 1966 to guide the implementation. It had four historians, one architect, and one archaeologist. They focused on setting up the National Register and finished their recommendations in February 1967. Lee, now retired from the NPS, was asked to organize another task force to write a manual for local grants-in-aid. He served as an advisor to the manual committee. Historians also dominated that group.

In June 1967, a new organization was put in place at the NPS that combined historical architects, archaeologists, and historians all in one division: the Office of Archaeology and Historic Preservation (OAHP). Architect Connally was made its director, historian Robert Garvey was hired away from the NTHP to head the Advisory Council on Historic Preservation, and architectural historian William Murtagh became the first Keeper of the National Register.

Academics largely ignored the new law and new NPS entities. A look at the major professional journals demonstrates this clearly. *American Antiquity* published no articles concerning the federal heritage preservation system until the late 1970s. The *American Historical Review* said nothing on the subject until the mid-1980s. The *Journal of the Society of Architectural Historians* published nothing until 1999.

But professionals in each of the three fields were sorely needed to make the system work, even if there was no educational system to supply appropriately trained workers. The NPS needed more professionals to run its internal and external programs, federal agencies needed professionals to insure their compliance with the law, SHPOs needed professional staff to carry out their many responsibilities, and qualified private consultants were needed to do much of the work.

So, what did the professions contribute to our current system? Architects dominated historic preservation prior to the passage of the NHPA. Historians, mainly at the NPS, dominated the crafting and initial implementation of the law. Archaeologists largely ignored heritage management until after Executive Order 11593 was issued in 1971 and then rapidly became dominant in terms of funding and the number of professionals employed. But none of these professions really gets principal credit for passing the NHPA. That goes to a politician wanting lasting fame, a lobbyist paying a debt, an agency wanting control, a Congress wanting to promote an idealized national image, and a president and his wife promoting a "Great Society." All heritage management professions have benefited from the NHPA, like it or not.

CHAPTER 5

The National Register of Historic Places

Keystone or Cornerstone?

It's not the National Register of Pretty Places.
—Dennis Gimmestad, Minnesota State Historic Preservation Office

The National Register of Historic Places (NRHP) is critical to American heritage management. Tom King (2002:19) calls the National Register "the centerpiece." A centerpiece usually refers to the most visible but least useful aspect of what is on the table. The Register is indeed highly visible to American heritage management agencies and professionals, although to the general public it is largely invisible. A sign on a listed building or on the street of a listed district is all most people see of the Register (Figure 5.1).

While King has noted many of the National Register's inherent flaws, it serves several vital heritage management functions. Those of us in heritage management refer to it constantly, but even most practitioners don't really know its history, its inner workings, or how it can be practically applied to its heritage management functions.

Continuing with my building analogy, I think of the NRHP as a keystone. I was going to call it the cornerstone, but a cornerstone, like a centerpiece, is mostly for show. A cornerstone is commemorative not structural. On the other hand, a keystone is critical for structural integrity. If it fails, the entire structure fails. Like it or not, that is how the National Register works for much of the American cultural heritage management system. There is, however, also a cornerstone aspect, what some call the Register's honor roll function. In this chapter, we will review all of its roles.

The purpose of this chapter is to help you better understand the National Register of Historic Places and make it more visible and understandable by providing practical guidance on how it works within the structure of American heritage management. Tom King doesn't like the Register mainly because of its schizophrenic nature: it tries to be both an honor roll of important historic places and a tool for evaluating property importance for federal environmental review and economic assistance processes (see King 1984, 1987, 2002, 2008, and multiple posts to his *CRM Plus* blog). Much of King's discussion of the Register concerns what it should and shouldn't be. This chapter focuses on what it is and how to use it fairly and reasonably to accomplish its various objectives. I will save some suggestions for how to improve the Register for the final chapter.

FIG. 5.1 Street sign in Wallace, Idaho, demonstrating that National Register listing is a big deal to the town (author photo).

A Note on Chapter Terminology and Focus

While tribal historic preservation offices (THPOs) can assume any and all duties of the state historic preservation office (SHPO) within reservation boundaries, most THPOs have not been actively involved in the National Register nomination process. Rather than list "SHPO/THPO" in every reference to historic preservation office activities in this chapter, I have usually just listed the reference as SHPO. The reader should be aware, however, that in some instances a THPO may also be involved, especially for Section 106 eligibility actions.

National Register bulletins that assist with eligibility determinations and nomination form completion used to have numbers (e.g., 16A), which made reference to them relatively easy, compared to writing out the entire title or using a unique acronym that no one else uses. For reasons never publicly explained, the Register eliminated use of the numbers in 1997. Many experienced National Register practitioners still use the numbers except in reference to the four newest bulletins produced since 1997 that were not assigned numbers. This chapter will occasionally refer to a National Register bulletin by its original number due to ease of reference, although the entire title will always be given at first mention.

Because I am an archaeologist and have written and reviewed mostly archaeological nominations, this chapter tends to emphasize archaeological aspects of the National Register. Nominations for other kinds of properties often require an expertise that is beyond me, although I do allow my history and architecture students to fill out nomination forms for nonarchaeological properties as one of my class assignments. My archaeological emphasis in this chapter is justified not only by my limited knowledge of some property types, especially with regard to building nominations, but by the fact that, in my experience, archaeologists tend to be the most deficient in knowing how to do a proper nomination, so I have a professional obligation to address this deficiency.

Finally, the correct preposition for National Register listing is "in" rather "on." This is a relic of the days when the official National Register was literally kept in a book updated with new entries entered by staff. That book was the literal National Register.

A History of the National Register

For an institution explicitly concerned with history, the NRHP does a poor job of publicly documenting its own. Go to the NRHP website and about the only historical fact you can find pertaining to the NRHP is that it was established in 1966. Its history is not well documented elsewhere either. Search for an article about the history of the National Register on the web and about the best you will do is a short entry in Wikipedia. The Wikipedia entry is more about the history of National Park Service (NPS) history programs than it is about the history of the National Register, and it contains a number of factual errors.

The most detail on the early history of the National Register can be found in Glass (1990), Mackintosh (1986), and Rodgers (1987). It's interesting that William Murtagh (2006) provides very little detail on National Register history in his frequently cited overview of American historic preservation, although he was the first Keeper of the Register. Several articles by other former NRHP employees provide some historical detail on the Register, including those by Shull (1987, 2002), J. Townsend (1994), Keune (1984), and, most recently, Sprinkle (2014). Tom King also provides some insights into the history of the National Register in various publications (e.g., King 1987, 2002).

Most of these sources focus on the establishment of the National Register in 1966 and its early history but provide little detail on its internal workings, such as who staffed it and its post-1980s history. The overview that follows is primarily based on the sources listed above with additional information from my own research and experiences during the 15 years I was the archaeologist for the Minnesota State Historic Preservation Office (MnSHPO). My official title at MnSHPO was National Register archaeologist, although I was the only staff archaeologist and dealt with all program areas.

An understanding of the Register's history is important because it helps us understand not only how the NRHP works today but how it worked in the past, thereby helping explain how decisions were made and priorities set over the last half century of heritage management in the United States. Understanding this history is especially important for archaeologists, as the Register is not particularly friendly toward archaeological sites and deals with archaeology in some strange ways.

In 1966 the passage of the National Historic Preservation Act (NHPA) created the National Register of Historic Places as we know it today. The 1966 law did not explicitly name the NRHP, however, and it did not create the first federal list of the country's important historic places. National monuments, some of which are historic sites, were the first widespread federal acknowledgment that there were historic properties worthy of public preservation. The passage of the Antiquities Act in 1906 allowed for the creation of national monuments, but these sites were indeed of national significance and were exclusively properties owned by the federal government.

The Historic Sites Act (HSA) of 1935 first created a "national register." Although the National Park Service pushed passage of the law in hopes of expanding the national park system, the HSA and several Depression-era programs in the 1930s laid the foundations of our current National Register and created a number of other important building blocks of our heritage management system, as discussed in chapter 3.

The HSA authorized the NPS to "make a survey of historic and archaeological sites, buildings, and objects." This survey complemented the work of the Historic American Buildings Survey (HABS) begun by the NPS in 1933. The HSA took the work beyond just buildings and emphasized preservation of historic properties rather than just documentation. The National Survey of Historic Sites and Buildings, hereafter called the Historic Sites Survey, was formally established by NPS in 1937, although this early national survey emphasized only properties of national significance.

The NPS Historic Sites Survey was guided by 12 prehistoric **themes** placed within geographic areas associated with cultural groups and 23 historical themes placed within three periods. NPS regional historians directed field investigations, often utilizing staff from other programs like the Civilian Conservation Corps (CCC). In addition to importance by theme, location, and period, property selection considerations emphasized historical significance, architectural qualities, and physical condition. A citizen advisory board was established with some members having professional expertise in various fields. No structures postdating 1860 were to be included, invoking a 75-year rule, while the current NRHP minimum age rule is 50 years. Imminent threat of destruction and applicability of public use were also considered for property inclusion in the 1930s Historic Sites Survey.

Although the NPS sites survey was dominated by political and academic interests and emphasized public use rather than general historic preservation needs, it still led to the first official list of nationally significant properties and helped create some government infrastructure to support a long-term historic preservation program. By the onset of World War II, the survey had inventoried over 500 properties and deemed over half archaeological. The war put the survey on hold for almost 20 years, and when it was reactivated in 1957 in association with the NPS's Mission 66 program, the NPS soon conceded that its goal of using the list to significantly expand the park system could not be realized. NPS admitted this defeat by establishing the National Historic Landmarks (NHLs) Program in 1960. NHLs are nationally significant properties documented by NPS staff, but most are not owned by the federal government or targeted for federal acquisition.

Section 101(a)(1) of the 1966 National Historic Preservation Act stated that the secretary of the interior is authorized "to expand and maintain a national register of districts, sites, buildings, structures, and objects significant in American history, architecture, archaeology, and culture, hereinafter referred to as the National Register." Note that the term "expand" refers to the existing NPS list of historic places and that the Register is not named the National Register of Historic Places in the original law. The full five-word name was not used until February 25, 1969, when it appeared in the *Federal Register*. The term was not legally recognized until it appeared in the 1980 amendments to the NHPA.

As pointed out by Mackintosh (1986), the NPS had insisted on use of the word "expand" in the NHPA because it reinforced continued NPS control of the inventory and registration process, building on the NPS survey established by the HSA in 1935. This expansion also inferred inclusion of properties of state and local significance, as the previous NPS surveys had already found many of the properties of obvious national significance.

After the passage of the NHPA, the NPS formed a new department called the Office of Archaeology and Historic Preservation (OAHP) with four divisions: History, **Architectural History**, Archaeology, and National Register. OAHP established a Historic Preservation Task Force consisting of four historians, one architectural historian, and one archaeologist. The task force issued the first draft guidelines for National Register listing in December 1966. After issuing its final report in February 1967, the task force disbanded. The report included definitions, terms, and criteria for evaluation, including the basics still in use today: four significance criteria, seven integrity considerations, and seven criteria exceptions, including properties not meeting the minimum 50-year age requirement.

In 1968 the states received the National Register guidelines and the first nomination form. The guidance document was an amended version of the task force report referred to as the "Grants Manual." It asked that a state's National Register nominations be submitted as a group following a statewide survey that could take up to four years. States were required to have professional staff to complete the survey and nominations. The four-year requirement proved totally unrealistic. States were slow to conduct surveys and complete nominations because few had professional staff in the early days of the program. Furthermore, the National Register office in Washington had limited staffing to review nominations.

Initially, the National Register consisted of all the NHLs, all national parks that were historic sites, and properties documented by the Historic Sites Survey. Only six state nominations were submitted to the National Register in 1968. When the first National Register list was published in the *Federal Register* on February 25, 1969, it included 960 properties. Some were so poorly documented that they did not meet the documentation standards required for new National Register nominations. A revised National Register nomination form was issued in 1969 with only minor changes on the "Significance" page. At the end of 1969, the National Register produced a bound volume with short descriptions of over 1,000 listed sites.

With NPS leadership guiding the National Register, a number of standard NPS policies and procedures were put in place. First, the Register was run by heritage management professionals not only within the NPS but also within states and agencies: state offices were required to have professional staff, **state review boards** were required to have mostly professional members, and federal agency staff who prepared nominations were expected to be professionals. Although not limited to national significance as required by previous NPS initiatives, significance was the key quality for inclusion in the National Register. In addition, integrity had to accompany significance as established by the 1930s National Survey of Historic Sites and Buildings and reinforced by its reactivation in 1957.

There were key differences from the pre-1966 NPS Historic Sites Survey. The first inventory form included in the 1967 task force report had national, state, and local levels of significance, while the survey begun in 1937 and the NHL program begun in 1960 only focused on properties of national significance. As Glass (1990:25) points out, the Register did not require that properties be categorized by **level of significance**, and thus they were not graded as to importance; a locally significant property appeared to be just as important as a nationally significant property. This lack of significance grading based on political level existed until 1980, when NHPA amendments provided additional consideration of nationally significant properties as potential NHLs. Another difference had to do with who conducted the surveys. NPS staff had directed all the pre-1966 surveys, but states were in charge of the new surveys. This created problems for the states because the new state liaison offices had no existing professional staff.

There were also key differences between the 1960s' and today's Register nomination process. There initially was no time limit for National Register staff review of submitted nominations. Properties could be listed without private landowner concurrence. Objects could include those found in museums until 1969, when the formal naming of the National Register of Historic Places established the geographic "in-place" requirement and the need for definable property boundaries.

Throughout the 1970s, the National Register continued to experience birthing problems. There was increasing pressure to list properties, mainly because at the beginning of the 1970s, Section 106 of the NHPA still required that properties actually be listed in the Register in order to receive federal agency consideration under Section 106. This listing pressure was significantly reduced in 1971 when Executive Order 11593 declared that eligible properties would also be considered and allowed agencies and SHPOs to make consensus National Register eligibility determinations for specific projects reviewed under Section 106. Federal Tax Act changes in 1976, however, increased submissions of building nominations, and state professional staffs also felt the need to increase their listings to demonstrate their state's importance in the history of the nation and to meet federal registration guidelines.

Nominations greatly increased after 1969, and by the mid-1970s, over 10,000 properties were listed in the National Register. Despite these listing gains, as of 1975 only 10 states were conducting statewide surveys of historic properties directed by professional staff. The last bound volume describing all National Register sites was issued in 1976 and contained over 13,000 properties. For the period after 1976 and before the appearance of the inventory on the National Register's webpage in the early 1990s, it is almost impossible to find publicly accessible compilations of yearly listings or even yearly totals. The last printed summary published by the NRHP in 1988 stated there were 48,818 listed properties.

The early nomination process was unfamiliar to all professionals, had little formal guidance, and overwhelmed both state staffs and the staff at the National Register. The basic process was the same as today. Nominations were completed by state historic preservation office staff or by heritage preservation professionals under contract with SHPOs, agencies, private entities, or communities. SHPO staff reviewed submitted nominations and, if they met standards, presented them to a state review board (SRB) at regular meetings. If the SRB agreed that they met Register eligibility criteria, they went to the state historic preservation officer (called the state liaison officer until 1974). A SHPO-signed nomination then went to the National Register for staff review, and when the Keeper had signed it, the property was officially listed in the Register.

Federal agencies could also nominate properties on federal land they managed. EO 11593 in 1971 actually required nomination of eligible properties on federal land. These nominations originally used a nomination form different from those used by the states. Agency staff completed the nomination, and it was forwarded to the appropriate agency historic preservation officer (HPO), with a courtesy copy sent to the SHPO for comment. If approved by the HPO, it would be sent to the National Register for staff and Keeper review.

There were also many changes in the mechanics of the National Register in the 1970s. In 1971 the National Register issued the first separately printed instructions for completing the nomination form. In 1974 a third version of the nomination form was sent to the states with many changes, including the addition of archaeology as an area of significance. The revised instructions for this form were issued in 1975. In the late 1970s, the Register issued a number of special bulletins to clarify technical listing requirements, including *Using the UTM Grids to Record Historic Sites* (1977) and *How to Improve the Quality of Photographs for National Register Nominations* (1979), as well as other specialty bulletins, such as *Guidelines for Local Surveys* (1977) and *Guidelines for Evaluating and Nominating Properties That Have Achieved Significance within the Past 50 Years* (1979).

In 1977, the Register made a number of innovations designed to simplify the nomination process and increase the number of listed properties. The first publication of what later became known as Bulletin 16 was issued, providing basic guidance on how to complete a nomination. Multiple resource nominations were also introduced in 1977, allowing nomination of multiple properties at the same time without having to repeat an extended significance statement for each property. For instance, all significant buildings in one city could be listed at the same time as long as the nomination contained an initial historical overview statement as well as a brief statement of each building's significance within the community and a physical description of each property insuring each met basic integrity requirements. The multiple resource nominations were of two types: multiple resource area (MRA) nominations based on a shared geography and thematic resource (TR) nominations based on a shared historical theme. The first multiple resource nominations were listed in the Register in 1979.

Other major 1970s events that affected the National Register included a change in the tax code in 1976 that gave tax benefits for preservation of listed historic structures and provided no economic advantages for demolition of such structures. The tax benefits were of three types:

1. A 20% investment tax credit for depreciable, substantial rehabilitation of structures listed in the NRHP
2. A 10% tax credit for depreciable but nonresidential rehabilitation of NRHP-listed properties built prior to 1936
3. A tax deduction for charitable contributions for conservation of listed historic properties

In 1978, the NPS introduced the Resource Protection Planning Process (RP3) program, which encouraged states to evaluate cultural resources within historic contexts defined by a combination of geography, chronological period, and theme. This replaced original NRHP reliance on property-based state plans, as it had become apparent that state historic preservation plans could not rely on completed inventories due to lagging surveys.

In 1978, the Jimmy Carter administration moved to separate the management of the nation's historic preservation programs from that of the nation's parks and to consolidate some government agency functions. OAHP was subsumed within the Heritage Conservation and Recreation Service (HCRS), which still resided within the Interior Department but not within NPS. HCRS had responsibilities for public recreation as well as historic preservation, as it had also absorbed the Bureau of Recreation. A huge backlog of National Register nominations forced it to hire additional staff. HCRS did not survive much beyond the Carter administration as the Ronald Reagan administration moved external historic preservation functions back into the NPS in 1981, where the National Register has resided ever since.

In 1979, Jerry Rodgers replaced William Murtagh as Keeper of the National Register. Rodgers was a historian and had been the chief of OAHP. In 1980, amendments to the National Historic Preservation Act formally named the National Register of Historic Places. The amendments also attempted to streamline the nomination process and make it less bureaucratic. Once a nomination had reached the NRHP's office in Washington, it was to be automatically listed after 45 days unless the Keeper formally rejected it. This encouraged NRHP staff to only spot-check the bulk of nominations, eliminating a detailed review of most. Nominations from states with poorly run programs were subject to more review than those from "good" states. Most importantly, the 1980 amendments required owner consent for listings of private property. Properties on nonfederal public land could still be listed without owner consent, but these listings required owner consultation.

A number of significant changes affecting the National Register occurred in the 1980s. In 1981, the Economic Recovery Act broadened tax benefits for listed properties, encouraging more building nominations. In 1984, a Multiple Property Documentation Form (MPDF) replaced the multiple-listing MRA and TR nomination forms. The MPDF combined the previous geographic and thematic considerations, adding a dimension of time to fulfill the concept of historic context, encouraged by the RP3 initiative and the 1983 *Secretary of the Interior's Standards and Guidelines for Archaeology and Historic Preservation* (SISG). The MPDF became a way to clarify what property types were eligible within a given context, but no individual property nominations had to be submitted along with an MPDF submission unless a state required it. This gradually reduced the number of multiple property submissions. The Register accepted the last multiple-listing MRA and TR submissions in 1989.

The National Register also made major changes in the individual property nomination form in 1986. In the mid-1980s, the Register began to computerize its listings, with limited online access provided in 1988. It also began encouraging a new kind of large-area property type, landscapes, with bulletins titled *How to Evaluate and Nominate Designed Historic Landscapes* (1986) and *Guidelines for Evaluating and Documenting Rural Historic Landscapes* (1989).

The 1990s began with minor changes in the nomination form, splitting Bulletin 16 into A (individual nominations) and B (MPDF) parts, and the issuance of two important new National Register bulletins: *How to Apply the National Register Criteria for Evaluation* (Bulletin 15) and *Guidelines for Evaluating and Documenting Traditional Cultural Properties* (Bulletin 38). Numerous bulletin updates and new bulletins also appeared in the 1990s, including the 1993 *Guidelines for Evaluating and Registering Historical Archaeological Sites and Districts* (Bulletin 36), the first bulletin dealing exclusively with archaeological properties, although it did not include prehistoric sites. Other 1990s bulletins dealt with properties associated with aviation, mining, battlefields, cemeteries, significant persons, and ships. Carol Shull replaced Jerry Rodgers as the Keeper in 1994. Shull had been the chief historian at the Register.

As the National Register entered the new millennium, Bulletin 36 on archaeological sites was redone in 2000 to include all types of archaeological sites, not just historical archaeological sites. The passage of time for the National Register since its inception in 1966 was reflected in a bulletin focused on residential suburbs and the acceptance of digital photographs. In 2012, the Register released a new nomination form that provided space for summary paragraphs in Sections 7 and 8, eliminated the need for continuation sheets, put the MPDF reference and significance criteria on the first page, and made a number of other minor changes to the form. A new MPDF form was also released in 2012, as were new map and photographic policies promoting digital formats.

There were also organizational changes at the NRHP. In 2005, political pressure led to the replacement of Shull as Keeper and a major staff reorganization. A deputy director of NPS, Janet Mathews, served as Keeper until a new administration in 2009 led to her resignation and the "temporary" reappointment of Shull. Shull continued to serve as interim Keeper until her retirement in 2015. She was replaced as Keeper by Stephanie Toothman, who was also an NPS deputy director and, while not a direct political appointee, subject to direct political influence.

The National Register webpage in May 2017 still listed Toothman as the Keeper and Paul Loether as program manager/National Register chief, but by October 2017, Loether held both jobs. Toothman was replaced in NPS Cultural Resources, Partnerships and Science by an acting associate director (Joy Beasley). As of October 2017, nine NRHP staff were listed as "reviewers," two of whom were "archaeological reviewers." Both archaeological reviewers were historical archaeologists. As of the end of 2017, the NRHP had accepted over 90,000 individual nominations, with almost 1.5 million properties actually listed in the Register, including properties within district nominations. There are just over 2,500 National Historic Landmarks. New York has the most NHLs with 270, while North Dakota has the fewest with 7.

The Roles of the National Register

The National Register of Historic Places fills three basic functions in the American heritage management system:

- It is an official affirmation of and guide to the nation's important historic places.

- It is an affirmation of a property's eligibility for tax incentives and federal grants.
- It is a method to evaluate property significance for the purposes of environmental review.

The first two functions require actual listing of a property in the Register and some action by NRHP staff, but the third only requires an assessment of eligibility by an agency with a SHPO/THPO and rarely requires NRHP involvement.

A fourth function for the NRHP is suggested by National Register staff: it serves as an educational and research tool, but this aspect is minor and would actually form part of the first function if it were indeed fully functional. I have never known a research archaeologist to use the National Register as a research tool. When I was a SHPO archaeologist, I occasionally searched the Register looking for particular property types or MPDFs, but I did this to help me write or evaluate a nomination I was working on, not to answer an archaeological research question.

As of the end of 2017, most National Register nominations were not available online, so as a collection they were not searchable or readily available. The Register has made MPDFs available online since the early 2000s. Furthermore, the archaeological sites listed in the Register are certainly not a representative cross section of archaeological sites and don't even include some of the most important sites in any state. Many important sites on private land are not listed due to landowner objection, and many important sites on federal land are not listed due to agency inaction. At least 21 states are in the process of digitizing their nomination forms for online access. Even if all nominations were accessible online, aiding research would still be a minor Register function.

As for educational purposes, after the politically motivated reorganization in 2005, several senior Register staff, including Keeper Shull, were assigned to educational duties. The Register began to promote travel itineraries to listed sites and educational materials for teachers. Once again, I have never known someone to follow a National Register travel itinerary, and I don't think many teachers use the NRHP educational materials. In Minnesota, the history of the state is taught in sixth grade, so I imagine some Register education materials might be a little too dense. As with most things related to the NRHP, very little self-evaluation is publicly available, so educational initiatives might indeed be very popular, but they probably have little influence on heritage management or preservation.

The Register has expanded the number of sample nominations available on the NRHP website, which can be used as guidance for less experienced nomination writers. In October 2017, there were 46 sample nominations available on the NRHP website; over half involved buildings, 8 involved structures, 7 involved archaeological sites, 13 involved districts, and none involved objects. Of the nominations including archaeological aspects indicated by Criterion D, three had prehistoric components, and five had historic components.

Listing in the National Register only for the purpose of listing is probably the least important function when it comes to actually promoting the preservation of historic properties. The major benefit of listing for nontax, nongrant, and non-environmental-review reasons is it increases the perceived importance of a property to some agencies and the public. This could improve a property's chances of preservation, especially in court cases. Individuals and communities are proud of their listed properties.

Eligibility for tax incentives and grants is very significant financially, having leveraged over the last 50 years more than $45 billion in private investment and grants. Tax incentive and grant eligibility will be discussed in later chapters. By far the most frequent National Register action and arguably the most important preservation tool is the determination of eligibility of a property for the purposes of environmental review. This chapter now focuses on eligibility determinations as well as a brief description of the listing process.

Determining Register Eligibility

Procedures for determining the eligibility of properties to the National Register are found in 36 CFR 60 (National Register of Historic Places) and 36 CFR 63 (Determinations of Eligibility for Inclusion in the National Register of Historic Places). Most formal assessments of eligibility are done for the purposes of Section 106 of the NHPA. Known as consensus determinations, they do not mean a property is eligible or ineligible for all future actions pertaining to its National Register status.

Formal determinations of eligibility (DOEs) are made only by the Keeper of the National Register in the following situations:

- For Section 106 purposes, if an agency and SHPO/THPO disagree on eligibility (36 CFR 800.4[c][2])
- For Section 106 purposes, if a tribe disagrees with a consensus determination by an agency and a SHPO for a property that has religious and cultural significance for its people (36 CFR 800.4[c][2])
- For EO 11593 or NHPA Section 110 purposes, if properties are under the control of a federal agency and the agency requests a DOE from the Keeper (36 CFR 63.6[a])
- For nomination purposes, if a private owner or majority of owners of a private property object to the listing of that property (36 CFR 60.5[n])

The agency submits a disputed eligibility opinion in the case of Section 106 actions or requests for an eligibility opinion for a federally owned property. The SHPO/THPO submits the information to the Keeper in the case of private owner objection. Agencies must submit sufficient documentation on significance and integrity for the Keeper to evaluate eligibility. A completed nomination form is submitted in the case of owner objection. A DOE results in either an eligible or a not eligible determination by the Keeper. For an eligible DOE, the Keeper also determines what significance criteria (A, B, C, and/or D) a property is eligible under.

In any given state, many times more properties are formally considered eligible for inclusion in the National Register each year than are actually listed. Almost all these determinations are for the purposes of project reviews under Section 106 and are the result of consensus determinations made by federal agency agreement with a SHPO or THPO. More result in properties being considered not eligible than eligible.

The National Park Service's Federal Preservation Institute (FPI) in 2007 did a study of 20 years of formal DOEs from 1987 through 2006. The study began with 1987 because prior to this year, the Register would formally confirm consensus actions when a property had been determined eligible. During the 20 years of the FPI study, the Keeper made over 1,400 DOEs. Mainly due to hundreds of Federal Highway Administration (FHWA) bridge issues in Illinois and West Virginia, 1998 was the highest DOE year by far, with 417. Eliminating 1998, the yearly average of the remaining 19 years is about 50 DOEs. Including 1998, FHWA asked for 1,070 Keeper determinations, while the second-closest agencies were the Department of Defense with 137 and the Department of the Interior with 84. Overall, 63% of the Keeper's actions in this 20-year period resulted in an eligible finding. It is difficult to find national statistics for overall ineligible findings for any year or period, although individual states may list these statistics in their annual reports. During the 15 years I was MnSHPO archaeologist, I recommended ineligibility for sites three times as often as I did eligibility.

Despite extensive guidelines issued by the National Register, there is incredible inconsistency from state to state and agency to agency as to the basic question of what constitutes an eligible National Register property. This determination has been increasingly politicized in some states and at the national level. Some evaluators don't strictly apply NRHP guidelines or appear to clearly understand them; deep understanding really only comes with the experience of seeing hundreds of examples.

Only a small percentage of nominations are given a thorough review by NRHP staff prior to listing, but even if all were reviewed, there is limited expertise among current NRHP staff concerning some property types (e.g., traditional cultural properties [TCPs], prehistoric archaeological sites). The recent practice of having an NPS deputy director serve as Keeper, the final arbiter of eligibility, not only demonstrates the vulnerability of eligibility decisions to current political objectives but sets a dangerous precedent of having a nonprofessional or unqualified person making critical decisions that should rest on in-depth understanding and broad experience.

Answering the eligibility question incorrectly leads to a number of critical management problems. If an ineligible property is inappropriately deemed eligible, considerable time and money is wasted at both agencies and SHPOs/THPOs. The agency has to take the environmental review process through unnecessary steps involving close coordination with the SHPO/THPO as well as additional consultation with interested parties. Such a determination may even result in expensive treatment to mitigate adverse effects. An inappropriate determination of ineligibility can lead to loss of a significant property with no serious opposition or mitigation.

Once eligibility is determined, listing properties in the National Register is not a standard objective of the Section 106 process. The objective of Section 106 is to ensure that effects to historic properties are properly considered by federal agencies funding, reviewing, or implementing undertakings. While writing a National Register nomination could be part of a treatment activity, this often doesn't work well. Nominations typically take multiple edits before going to the state review board, and the SRB or even the National Register staff in Washington, DC, can ask for additional changes. This doesn't fit well with the contracting process. It is difficult to leave contracts open-ended, waiting for the review and nomination process to proceed, and to keep focused on something that happened many projects and many months ago.

The most important thing to remember about eligibility versus listing is that if a SHPO has concurred with a determination or considered a property eligible for the purposes of Section 106, the SHPO should not object to that property's being taken through the SRB process and sent to the National Register if an adequate nomination form has been completed. The National Register quality of an eligible property is theoretically no different from that of a listed property. In practice, this is not always the case.

Evaluating a Property

To determine the eligibility of a property you have to go through most of the major steps needed for a nomination, although you don't need to fill out the form and thus don't need to concern yourself with the details of how to correctly fill out most sections on it. The critical elements in determining eligibility are

1. Classifying the property as one of the five *property categories* (building, structure, site, object, district) and as a particular *property type*
2. Determining the property's *significance* under one or more of the four significance criteria (A–D) as well as its *level of significance* (national, state, local) and if any *criteria considerations* apply (A–G)

3. Determining if the property retains sufficient *integrity* under the seven different aspects of integrity (location, **design**, **workmanship**, **materials**, **association**, setting, feeling)
4. Determining the property boundaries as completely as possible considering project restrictions (e.g., no survey outside a project area)

These steps essentially follow the chapter order in National Register Bulletin 15, *How to Apply the National Register Criteria for Evaluation.*

A few other aspects contained in a nomination form are important to understand as they may play a role in evaluating eligibility. According to Bulletin 16A, the period of significance "is the length of time when a property was associated with important events, activities, or persons, or attained the characteristics which qualify it for National Register listing" (p. 42). For archaeological sites, this is the known or approximate time range during which the property was primarily occupied or used and, under Criterion D, the period for which the property is likely to yield important information. There can be multiple periods of significance. If these periods overlap, they should be combined into one longer **period of significance**. For prehistoric archaeological sites, the period of significance is usually estimated based on radiometric dating or diagnostic artifacts.

Bulletin 16A states that a significant date refers to "the year when one or more major events directly contributing to the significance of a historic property occurred" (p. 43). For a building that can be the date of construction or of major additions. There can be more than one significant date. A significant date must fall within the range of a period of significance. Significant dates don't apply to prehistoric sites nominated under Criterion D unless the "has yielded important information" application is associated with past archaeological work (i.e., the date of the archaeological excavation). Criterion A sites that are important to the development of archaeology generally have a significant date, most typically the year or years of primary excavation.

If a property has been identified as possibly eligible for inclusion in the Register, the first essential step is for SHPO staff to review what is known about the property, determine what significance criteria (A–D) best apply, and whether sufficient integrity appears to exist. This is advisable for both federal and nonfederal evaluations and nominations. Applicable NRHP integrity aspects are dependent on applicable significance criteria, although in some cases a property is in such obviously poor condition that it is clearly not eligible under any criteria.

The SHPO may ask for additional information in order to assess eligibility, requiring additional research and/or fieldwork. Meeting this request may be easier for buildings than sites. One reason archaeological sites are so underrepresented in the NRHP is that archaeological fieldwork is expensive and time-consuming, while many architectural properties can be evaluated from the street and in the library.

Classifying a Property

There is a great deal of variety in the kinds of properties nominated for the National Register. Remember that there is a difference between what the Register calls a property category and what it calls a property type. A property category is one of the five basic kinds of places that can be nominated: a building, structure, site, object, or district. Buildings are structures that house human activities. Structures are functional constructions made for purposes other than human shelter. Sites are simply areas of land that have historical significance or contain property types of significance. Objects are small constructions for artistic (e.g., statue), functional (e.g., boundary marker), or commemorative (e.g., plaque) purposes. Districts are assemblages or concentrations of multiple examples of the properties of the other four property categories.

Property types are defined by common physical or associative attributes. They have almost infinite variations. A barn is a property type that is categorized as a building, but barns as a property type can be further subdivided by their shape, architectural style, construction materials, or function. Some property types can be difficult to classify. A ruin of a building is usually classified as a site, but if most of the original structure is still present and it can be relatively easily rehabilitated, it may be listed as a building. A shipwreck is a structure, but if it has an associated scatter of artifacts, it can be listed as a site.

What Is Significance?

According to NRHP Bulletin 15, "To qualify for the National Register, a property must be significant; that is, it must represent a significant part of the history, architecture, archeology, engineering, or culture of an area, and it must have the characteristics that make it a good representative of properties associated with that aspect of the past." The National Register has four basic criteria for determining significance. Properties eligible for inclusion in the National Register must be "associated with events that have made a significant contribution to the broad patterns of our history" (Criterion A), be "associated with the lives of persons significant in our past" (Criterion B), "embody the distinctive characteristics of a type, period, or method of construction," "represent the work of a master," "possess high artistic values," or "represent a significant and distinguishable entity whose components may lack individual distinction" (Criterion C), or "have yielded, or . . . be likely to yield, information important in prehistory or history" (Criterion D).

Most historic sites are eligible under Criterion A (significant event), most houses are eligible under Criterion B (significant person), most commercial buildings are eligible under Criterion C (significant design), and most archaeological sites are eligible under Criterion D (significant data). Some individual properties can be eligible under more than one criterion, and some districts can be eligible under all four. Buildings are the most represented property category listed in the National Register, with Criterion C the most common significance criterion for listing. Over half the properties listed in the National Register have **architectural significance** under Criterion C (Sprinkle 2014:79).

Many archaeologists tend to confuse the concepts of importance and significance as they apply to eligibility. To archaeologists, all sites are important, but for purposes of eligibility, not all sites are significant. Importance is an assessment of a site's value in helping to understand some aspect of the past, while significance is an assessment of which sites are "worthy of preservation" with respect to federal (and some state) law. A site's location is important to predictive modeling even if it contains only a few artifacts or has been completely destroyed. Importance can be measured by an individual archaeologist's research interests or reflect consensus among a group of archaeologists. Significance has only one measure in terms of most cultural resource management (CRM) standards: Is the site eligible for inclusion in the National Register of Historic Places?

Sites, of course, have importance to archaeology beyond research or environmental impact analysis. Sites serve as classrooms to teach the next generation of archaeologists. Sites with features and a variety of artifacts are interesting and instructive, even if they are not eligible. Sites are also places to inform and involve the public. This is especially true with regard to sites from the recent past, where many people can connect with their own origins and see recognizable objects. The excavation of the recent past validates our individual pasts more than ancient sites, where time and sometimes distance render peoples and cultures less understandable and less relatable.

Much has been written about significance with respect to archaeological sites. As early as 1977, Schiffer and Gummerman (1977:239) noted that "the concept of significance . . . has led in a short time to the growth of a fairly large literature." Hardesty and Little (2009) have written an entire book on the subject with more focus on CRM, the Army Corps of Engineers (Briuer and Mathers 1996) has produced a bibliography and historical perspective on significance, and the Florida Archaeological Council (Austin, Hoffman, and Ballo 2002) has held a workshop to examine the issue. National Register Bulletin 36 is the definitive work on archaeological significance with respect to the Section 106 federal review process and most other environmental review applications, although it could use some clarification, especially with regard to certain kinds of sites (e.g., prehistoric **lithic scatter**, historical farmsteads).

A number of archaeological sites can be eligible under National Register Significance Criterion A, a few under Criterion B, and a very few under Criterion C, so most sites tend to be evaluated under Criterion D: "sites that have yielded, or may be likely to yield, information important to prehistory or history." Criterion D significance evaluation asks three critical questions:

1. Has the site already yielded important information?
2. Is the site likely to yield important information?
3. What is important information?

With regard to "has yielded," I contend that this aspect of Criterion D should be moved to Criterion A for two basic reasons. First, "has yielded" suggests the site is important to the history of archaeological research, which is an aspect of Criterion A. Under this consideration, part of the period of significance and perhaps significant dates are associated with the investigation that resulted in the yielded information, dates not appropriate to a Criterion D potential to yield.

"Has yielded" also has implications for the integrity of sites that have been excavated, as opposed to those likely to yield information in a future excavation. Because a site's integrity is adversely impacted by archaeological excavation and perhaps even more by a development where an excavation helped mitigate adverse effects, a site that "has yielded" may have significantly lessened integrity of materials and association, integrity aspects that are critical to a "potential to yield" site.

Furthermore, a site with just the **potential to yield important information** need not have integrity of setting and feeling, while a "has yielded" site should invoke Criterion A requirements, and recent (i.e., post-excavation) activities at the site affecting setting and feeling are important. Bulletin 15 states that partially excavated sites considered under the "potential to yield" aspect "must be shown to retain potential in their remaining portions" (p. 23), but no such requirement exists for "has yielded" sites. It is sort of ironic that a "has yielded" site may be eligible, when the very act of doing archaeology has diminished its integrity, and the archaeology that has been done often makes the site more important under "has yielded" but further diminishes its integrity under "potential to yield."

The second major issue with regard to Criterion D is an appropriate assessment of a site's true potential to yield important information. For CRM archaeology, this is generally accomplished by means of an evaluation (Phase 2) survey. Many evaluation surveys are done by archaeologists with minimal familiarity with the National Register and sometimes even by those with little familiarity with the historic contexts (i.e., cultural components) present at the site. These contractors may favor academic perspectives over heritage management perspectives, confusing significance with importance. They may also be influenced by economic pressure from their companies to keep a project going into another phase.

Even without inappropriate academic or economic bias, most contract archaeologists tend to be overly cautious about suggesting that sites are not eligible. If a site contains multiple components, a reasonable number of artifacts, a diversity of artifact types, and some integrity, most contract archaeologists will say it is eligible even if archaeological testing has been limited and has really only evaluated a small area of a site. That said, the SHPO and the agency make the final determination of eligibility for almost all sites involved in Section 106 undertakings.

As a SHPO archaeologist for 15 years, I regret that too often I concurred with contractors and agencies on site eligibility assessments despite limited evidence to justify an eligibility determination. This was usually because an agency suggested a site was eligible upon the recommendation of its consultant, and I saw no need to disagree because then the Keeper in Washington would have to make the final determination. If the Keeper agreed the site wasn't eligible, we may have lost the opportunity to get some additional archaeology done, even if the site was marginal. Yet I saw a number of sites deemed eligible go into expensive mitigations, and when the results from these mitigations were finally submitted, I wondered why we had bothered and if the money had been well spent. The key issue with regard to "potential to yield" is how to make a realistic Criterion D assessment based on truly *important* and *answerable* research questions at any given site.

What is important information? Bulletin 16A (p. 51) asks whether the information will "broaden" archaeological knowledge and the understanding of a particular culture. Bulletin 15 (p. 21) states that, to be important, information must be evaluated within an appropriate context and have significant bearing on a research design addressing current data gaps, alternative theories, or priority areas in management plans. Furthermore, Bulletin 15 (p. 22) states that "a property is not eligible if it cannot be related to a particular time period or cultural group."

Bulletin 15 states that important information "must be addressed in light of current issues" that are "expressed at professional conferences and in professional literature and journals" (p. 31). The bulletin notes that "a single important question is enough" to satisfy significance with respect to "likely to yield." Questions can deal with either archaeological methods and theory or cultural historical issues such as subsistence-settlement systems. There should be a "clear link between the contexts, the research questions, and the data found" at the site.

The one archaeological bulletin (Revised Bulletin 36) contradicts statements made in Bulletins 16A and 15 about the need for a site to be linked to a historic context or time period: "Precontact sites which lack temporal diagnostics or radiocarbon dates may still be eligible within a context which defines important a-temporal or non-cultural questions, such as those that concern site formation processes or archaeological methodology" (p. 15).

There is a real dilemma in determining what significance criteria to apply when evaluating the eligibility of archaeological sites. The Register's emphasis on applying historic contexts is best suited to Criterion A; it necessarily places the property within a cultural-temporal framework associating the event or pattern of events with its place in history. Most archaeological sites are declared eligible only under Criterion D; yet most research questions link particular aspects of a site (e.g., subsistence, material culture) to a particular **cultural affiliation**. That is why Bulletins 15 and 16A required historic context association for archaeological sites. Only in the more recent Revised Bulletin 36 were eligible sites allowed to lack historic context as long as research questions could be linked to research methods or human behavior in general (e.g., how stone tools are made).

If you do include Criterion A for an archaeological site, almost all aspects of integrity have to be met, including setting and feeling. With regard to prehistoric sites, this integrity standard is difficult to obtain because in most areas of the country, the current setting of a site will rarely be even remotely like what it was during the period of significance. Including Criterion A introduces the further complication of broadening the archaeological impact area of potential effects (APE) for a construction project. APEs for Criterion D are just the construction limits, while Criterion A adds consideration of impacts within a visual APE. This may require additional survey and evaluation testing, as well as increase the need for and scope of any mitigation.

After examining the guidance from the National Register bulletins, we are still left with an open question as to what indeed important information is. Reading between the lines, however, the bulletins suggest that important information is, first of all, based on a consensus among many archaeologists, not just the opinions of one or a few ("in light of current issues"). Second, important information should not be redundant or simply verify what is already fairly well known ("broaden knowledge and understanding"). Third, important information must be based on a regional rather than a site-specific understanding of the past (see Revised Bulletin 36:32), unless a particular site is of exceptional significance (e.g., Cahokia).

The National Register admits that it cannot define what "important" means as this varies according to what archaeologists are interested in at any given time. This is fine in concept, but important information does need some general definitional parameters; otherwise we are left with scientific anarchy or at least a lot of statements of the obvious. As my friend Washington SHPO Allyson Brooks is fond of saying with a sarcastic smile on her face, "If you find white-ware ceramics at a historical site, it may mean people ate off plates." For prehistoric sites, former New Mexico SHPO Lynne Sebastian would say, "They ate corn" in answer to a common research question about past subsistence patterns. (It is common knowledge that corn was a staple of the diet for many Indian groups in the American Southwest.)

We can at least define what isn't important. For example, important information should not be redundant unless it is critical to corroborate something that is not well known or speculative. If another site in the same condition has answered essentially identical research questions or if previous work at the site has already answered the essential research questions, there is little need to examine the site further. For historical sites, the written record may have definitively and better answered a question, so why attempt to corroborate it with less definitive archaeological information? Even considering that there are unanticipated research questions and new research techniques, some sites simply lack potential due to the types, amounts, and condition of the information they contain. Perhaps we need a symposium on "questions that don't count."

A second critical part of solving the eligibility equation for Criterion D "potential to yield" information at archaeological sites is determining if important questions are indeed answerable. While superficial or preliminary testing at a site may suggest its eligibility by the number, type, and cultural affiliation of artifacts present, in some cases only extensive testing can determine integrity of association. A multicomponent prehistoric site may have been so heavily disturbed by natural and/or cultural processes that no discrete cultural horizons still exist, so undiagnostic artifacts cannot be firmly associated with a particular historic context, and datable materials cannot be temporally associated with diagnostic or undiagnostic materials. Potential to yield should be demonstrated prior to determining a site eligible or nominating it under Criterion D.

Harm to sites eligible under Criterion A cannot really be mitigated because the site's physical presence and condition are the important factors of its eligibility. When such sites are destroyed, as they occasionally must be, we simply get some sort of trade-off to make us feel better or the developer worse. For mitigation of sites eligible under Criterion A, we usually just do a Criterion D mitigation by gathering as much data as reasonable. We should also address Criterion A impacts by doing a more creative form of mitigation (e.g., a publication, preservation of a similar site).

One of the biggest problems for CRM archaeology with regard to significance is that many book and journal authors who discuss the topic tend to have little direct role in day-to-day CRM processes and little "skin in the game." They don't really understand what National Register eligibility decisions entail for management or what "a reasonable and good faith effort" implies. For some, their CRM experience is limited to doing a CRM fieldwork contract or teaching an introductory CRM class using standard textbooks. But some of these individuals tend to have the greatest initial influence on the next generation of CRM professionals, who then enter jobs with unrealistic and broad views on significance. Their instructors may be very good teachers who indeed provide students with a good introduction to the field of archaeology, but lacking an in-depth understanding of the true nature of National Register significance and unwilling to miss an opportunity to gain some archaeological information, they are prone to think most sites are eligible and most research questions are important.

Many archaeologists directly addressing the eligibility question for potentially affected sites are consultants who have probably never written a nomination and don't fully understand the financial and management implications of calling a site eligible. Even experienced agency professionals writing on the subject can be influenced by agency priorities (e.g., get the project done as soon as possible, don't let Washington get involved) and may lack detailed knowledge of the NRHP. In general, few archaeologists outside SHPOs have done nominations, read the Register bulletins, and taken National Register training.

NRHP staff are supposedly the experts, but they have selective expertise. Most National Register staff archaeologists have tended to be historical archaeologists who don't know prehistoric sites or current prehistoric research priorities very well. They also tend to be coastal in their experience and training and don't know particular areas of the country very well (such as the Midwest) or are unfamiliar with most states' historic contexts as they pertain to archaeology. Thus, they can't honestly evaluate important research questions or assess if the techniques applied to assess eligibility are regionally appropriate to accurately evaluate a site's true research potential. SHPO staffs probably understand the implications of eligibility the best. They know NRHP rules and state/local historic contexts better than other groups. They are also essentially neutral parties who do understand the management implications of an eligible determination. However, every SHPO is different. Sometimes SHPO staff are inexperienced or have very narrow training and experience. Many SHPOs also have separate National Register and review and compliance (R&C) staff, with the National Register staff having strict rules for nomination, while the R&C staff may apply a lesser standard for consensus determinations.

Understanding Historic Contexts

In the late 1970s, the Heritage Conservation and Recreation Service of the National Park Service began to push the Resource Protection Planning Process (RP3). This eventually became known as comprehensive historic preservation planning, with each state required to produce a comprehensive plan for historic preservation.

Critical to this process was the development of historic contexts. It was an attempt to put "history" back into historic preservation. By the late 1970s, historic preservation had come to emphasize the preservation and reuse of old buildings without really understanding why properties were significant. The RP3 initiative emphasized that historic preservation was more than just restoring buildings or compiling inventories of old-enough properties.

The ascendancy of archaeology in the federal system promoted the RP3 process. By the early 1970s, a mature crop of "new archaeologists" were ready to apply their knowledge of systems and science to historic preservation, a field in which an increasing number of archaeological jobs were located. Planning became a more formal process and archaeologists became more involved in the process, with implications for all kinds of historic properties and all levels of historic preservation.

The need for historic contexts was eventually written into the *Secretary of the Interior's Standards and Guidelines for Archaeology and Historic Preservation* (1983) and into National Register of Historic Places bulletins as the basis for evaluating significance. Historic contexts were originally called "study units" in RP3 documents. Each study unit needed not only an explanatory narrative based on a theme but temporal and geographic limits. By the mid-1980s, the study units were called *historic contexts.*

As defined by the National Register (Bulletin 16A, Appendix 4:2), a historic context is "an organizing structure for interpreting history that groups information about historic properties which share a common theme, common geographical location, and common time period. The development of historic contexts is a foundation for decisions about planning, identification, evaluation, registration, and treatment of historic properties, based upon comparative significance." Thus all aspects of historic preservation, not just evaluation, are subject to contextual considerations.

Additional guidance on historic contexts is provided by the *Secretary of the Interior's Standards and Guidelines for Archaeology and Historic Preservation* (SISC). Historic contexts are considered to be the "cornerstone of the planning process." Standard 1 of the SISG "Preservation Planning" section is "Preservation planning establishes Historic Contexts." Standard 2 is "Preservation planning uses Historic Contexts to develop goals and priorities for the Identification, Evaluation, Registration, and Treatment of Historic Properties."

The general approach to developing historic contexts is to provide a comprehensive summary of all aspects of the history of a particular area; the area can be a state, a local unit of government, or a management area (e.g., national forest). Once the contexts have been defined as to theme, area, and period, information about these aspects is synthesized into a narrative that includes associated property types and information needs.

With regard to the subsequent SISG standards after the planning standards, those for identification, registration, documentation, and treatment activities, there are no standards in most of these sections that explicitly mention historic contexts, but the need for historic contexts is explicit through the guidelines that implement the standards for all these categories. Under the SISG's "Evaluation" section, however, Standard 2 is "Evaluation of Significance Applies the Criteria within Historic Contexts."

By providing an example from Minnesota, I will attempt to demonstrate what historic contexts look like and how historic context development evolved at the state level. In September 1981, the Minnesota State Historic Preservation Office established 15 study units in an unpublished document titled *Minnesota History in Sites and Structures.* The study units were not divided into periods, and there was no discussion of the eventually accepted three-tier system currently applied in Minnesota (statewide, thematic, local).

There were four prehistoric study units (Paleoindian, Archaic, Woodland, and Mississippian), two Indian ethnographic units (Dakota and Ojibwe), three exploration/fur trade–era units (French, British, and American), and six post–white settlement units (St. Croix Triangle Logging, Early Agriculture and River Settlement, Railroad Construction and Agricultural Development, Northern Minnesota Logging, Iron Mining, and Northern Minnesota Resort Industry). In the 1981 SHPO document, all study units except the prehistoric ones included a brief narrative overview, a study unit plan assessing preliminary needs, a list of property types, a list of known examples, and a state distribution map.

By 1985, the MnSHPO was calling the study units "historic contexts." In that year, it produced an overview of the prehistoric contexts completed by the head of the Minnesota Historical Society's Archaeology Department. (The SHPO in Minnesota was based at the Historical Society until early 2018, and the SHPO did not have a full-time archaeologist until 1990.) By 1987, the SHPO had developed a three-tier system of contexts: (1) broad statewide contexts divided into three periods (Prehistoric, Contact, and Postcontact, (2) thematic contexts, and (3) local contexts. In 1987, the SHPO contracted with a private archaeological consultant, the Institute for Minnesota Archaeology (IMA), to produce draft Precontact period (10,000 BC–AD 1650) and Contact period (AD 1650–1837) contexts to deal with the contexts whose property types were principally archaeological in nature.

These contexts were to include the basic requirements of theme, geographic area, and time period but be presented in a robust narrative that included property types, known affiliated sites, research questions, and a bibliography. The SHPO also changed the name of the first period from Prehistoric to Precontact to demonstrate that "prehistoric" did not mean "ahistoric" and that this period was just as important as the succeeding two that happened to have associated written records.

In 1988, the SHPO released narratives for 29 statewide historic contexts associated with the Precontact and Contact periods, along with three "special" contexts (pipestone, rock art, and prehistoric quarries). The statewide Precontact contexts were placed in six stages or periods: preprojectile point (1), fluted point (2), lanceolate point (2), archaic (4), ceramic/mound (11), and late prehistoric (9). The Contact period had eight historic contexts, five Native American and three Euro-American.

In anticipation of the completion of the first comprehensive preservation plan for Minnesota, SHPO staff in 1989 revised the outlines of the Postcontact statewide contexts. Each Postcontact context included a brief narrative overview, a shaded state distribution map, a list of property types, a list of examples drawn from National Register–listed properties, and a bibliography. Two additional Postcontact contexts were added to the original six: Indian communities and reservations, and urban centers. IMA was awarded a second contract in 1989 to refine the Precontact and Contact context documents.

The statewide Postcontact contexts did not include archaeological considerations in the narratives, although the property type lists did include a few archaeological site types (e.g., trading posts, sunken steamboats). The word "archaeology" was not mentioned in the SHPO's 1989 Postcontact context document, demonstrating that even as recently as the late twentieth century, many mainstream preservationists thought archaeology just dealt with premodern property types.

MnSHPO has made no major effort to revise its Postcontact historic contexts since 1989. The IMA draft revision of the Precontact and Contact contexts was submitted to the SHPO in 1990. I attempted to revise a few Postcontact contexts to include archaeological considerations when I was SHPO archaeologist, but these attempts remain in draft form. I also promoted MPDF development for a number of property types that were suggested by the 1988 "special contexts" that are thematic contexts. The SHPO eventually contracted to complete MPDFs for aboriginal earthworks and rock art, while I completed a draft thematic context for lithic scatters (Anfinson 1994).

In the 1980s and 1990s, other states also completed context studies for their state comprehensive plans, although there was great variation in the number of historic contexts, narrative length, and detail provided. Some states never completed comprehensive contexts and currently rely on limited topical contexts completed for particular projects or agencies for evaluation and nomination purposes. Like Minnesota, most states that did complete statewide historic contexts a quarter century ago have never comprehensively revised them.

Understanding Criteria Considerations

The National Register has defined seven criteria considerations that apply to exceptional properties having some characteristic that usually would make them ineligible for the Register. These kinds of properties are (A) religious, (B) moved, (C) birthplace or grave, (D) cemetery, (E) reconstruction, (F) commemorative, and (G) less than 50 years old. Bulletin 15 goes into these criteria considerations in the most detail.

Despite their normal exclusion, many of these kinds of properties are listed in the Register due to "exceptional circumstances" the NRHP has defined. In addition, when such properties appear in and are an integral part of districts, the criteria considerations do not need to be explicitly applied (e.g., cemetery in a ghost town). For individual properties, exceptional building and structure nominations tend to apply Criteria Considerations B, C1, E, and G. For site nominations, the most applicable are Criteria Considerations A, C2, and D. An object nomination may apply Criteria Consideration F.

Criteria Consideration A, or religious, properties are usually excluded because of potential conflicts with what is known as the establishment clause of the First Amendment to the US Constitution: "Congress shall make no law respecting an *establishment* of religion, or prohibiting the free exercise thereof." While most of the religious exceptions defined by the Register are of an architectural or artistic nature as applied to buildings (e.g., churches), there is also an exception for properties that play roles in community life or culture that are broader than just religion. With regard to archaeological sites, Criterion Consideration A would most typically apply to sacred or ceremonial sites associated with Indian tribes. This criterion also has particular application to traditional cultural properties. Examples include medicine wheels and some petroglyph sites.

Criteria Consideration B concerning moved properties mainly applies to smaller buildings (e.g., houses) and structures (e.g., bridges) where integrity of setting and location have been compromised. While location cannot be restored, setting can be somewhat satisfied by placing the moved building or structure in a compatible environment, such as putting a moved house in a residential neighborhood rather than a commercial district or a park. Perhaps the most common retention of eligibility is for buildings or structures eligible under Criterion C (a type of construction), where integrity of design, materials, workmanship, feeling, and association are basically left intact. Sites cannot be moved as integrity of location is critical and cannot be restored.

Criteria Consideration C with respect to birthplaces (referred to here as C1) usually applies to a house or other building where an important person (Criterion B) was born; it is not directly associated with that person's later life or important achievements. Exceptions are made for a person of outstanding importance (such as George Washington) or a building that is the last surviving property associated with an important person. One of the rare archaeological sites meeting this criterion is Wakefield, where George Washington was born in 1732 and lived for the first three years of his life. Extensive archaeology was done prior to the building reconstruction in the early 1930s. The reconstruction follows the footprint of the original house, but the building itself is a "period piece" as no drawings of the original house exist. It is both listed in the National Register and is a national monument.

Criteria Consideration C with respect to graves (referred to here as C2) can be discussed along with Criteria Consideration D regarding cemeteries. Graves are burial places of one individual, while cemeteries contain burials of multiple individuals. Such locations are usually not subject to relocation or significant intrusions, although respect for prehistoric Indian burials and burial grounds is relatively recent. Despite legal and social attitude changes over the last 30 years concerning how prehistoric Indian burials are treated, the federal government and most state governments still consider ancient burials to be archaeological sites. Thus the most common archaeological application of the criteria exceptions for graves and cemeteries would be with respect to prehistoric **burial sites** evaluated under Significance Criterion D (**information potential**). This information could include insight into demography, pathology, mortuary practices, or social status differentiation. In some states, excavation of prehistoric burials has effectively ceased due to legal and ethical considerations, except in salvage or accidental discovery situations.

In most situations, it is perhaps more prudent to nominate a burial site under significance criteria other than D due to the inference that a site's only value is to archaeology, and this value can be best realized though excavation. A mound group could be nominated under Criterion C (design), considering the distribution of the mounds in the group, or Criterion A (historical event) due to its known association with a particular group. A particularly impressive excavated burial site like some of the mounds at the Cahokia site could be nominated under Criterion A (historical event) or Criterion B (important individual). Burial sites can also be **contributing** properties within districts.

Whatever state laws have to say about the treatment of burial sites, if you are doing a Section 106 review and a burial is in the project's area of potential effects, it must be evaluated for its National Register eligibility. Section 106 does not require consideration and avoidance of ineligible burial sites. If a burial site is eligible under more than Criterion D, indirect effects must be carefully considered.

Criteria Consideration E deals with reconstructed properties. National Register Bulletin 15 defines reconstruction as "the reproduction of the exact form and detail" of a "vanished" property as it appeared "at a specific period of time" (p. 37). It does not refer to remodeled properties, although such properties must conform to the *Secretary of the Interior's Rehabilitation Standards* if they want to maintain eligibility for the National Register. Accuracy is critical to a reconstruction. While archaeological excavation may determine the size and foundational structure of a building, the lack of plans or drawings of a building may require the use of a standard or typical design from a period, as was done at Wakefield. The period of significance would conform to the historic period of the original structure rather than the date of reconstruction; thus Criteria Consideration G (less than 50 years old) would not apply.

Criteria Consideration F for commemorative properties usually applies to objects such as markers or small constructions such as statues or obelisks. Although the marker or construction may indeed be at the site of a major historic event or note a major historic figure present at an event, the commemorative object itself is not directly associated with the event or the person. Eligibility would most likely be related to Significance Criterion C (design) or the object's having been at a particular location long enough that it has attained Criterion A significance in its own right.

Criteria Consideration G refers to properties that are younger than 50 years old. This is one of the more commonly used criteria considerations and truly applies to exceptional significance. Examples cited in my copy of Bulletin 15, dated 1991, include National Park Service rustic architecture, Veterans Administration hospitals, and World War II properties, all of which have now largely passed the 50-year-old benchmark. The most recent online version of Bulletin 15, listed as being updated for the internet in 2002, still uses the same examples. Most nominations using Criteria Consideration G apply to buildings associated with Significance Criterion C (design). Frank Lloyd Wright designs were once the standard example, although these too are now largely over 50 years of age. Very few archaeological sites utilizing Significance Criterion D should satisfy Criteria Consideration G, but questions of importance are indeed changing. The issue remains whether a research question could be answered more accurately, more cheaply, and more easily using a nonarchaeological approach (e.g., historical records, oral interviews).

What Is Integrity?

There are two parts to every evaluation of a property's federal importance: significance and integrity. National Register Bulletin 15 (pp. 44–49) has a section on integrity applicable to all property types. Integrity "is the ability of a property to convey its significance. . . . The evaluation of integrity is sometimes a subjective judgment, but it must always be grounded in an understanding of a property's physical features and how they relate to significance" (p. 44). Thus integrity is not evaluated in a vacuum; nor is it simply a judgment of the property's general condition as a construction or a place. It is directly related to which significance criteria are chosen and even what areas of significance are used.

The Register has defined seven aspects of integrity, of which a significant property must "always possess several, and usually, most": location, design, setting, materials, workmanship, feeling, and association. It is interesting that there is no list of integrity aspects to check on the National Register nomination form; these aspects are simply discussed in the text of the Section 7 narrative.

Properties evaluated under Significance Criteria A (events), B (people), and C (design/artistic merit) need to meet more of the integrity aspects than sites evaluated under Criterion D (information). As Bulletin 15 states, "A property possessing information potential does not need to recall *visually* an event, person, process, or construction technique" (p. 23). Thus, setting and feeling are inconsequential for Criterion D sites, and because these two aspects are often the most subjective and because fewer total aspects are needed, the evaluation of integrity for most archaeological sites should be less subjective than for other types of properties evaluated under Criteria A, B, and C.

Guidelines for Evaluating and Registering Archaeological Properties (Bulletin 36) discusses the integrity needs of archaeological sites in some detail (pp. 35–42), although almost every example is for a historic rather than a prehistoric site, reflecting this bulletin's origin as a guideline just for historical archaeological sites and the fact that all the authors are historical archaeologists. The integrity aspects most important for Criterion D sites are location, materials, and association, with design also important if architectural features are present, such as with ruins or earthworks.

Location is "the place where the historic property was constructed or the place where the historic event occurred" (Bulletin 15:44). For archaeological sites, it would be the place where human activity took place and left tangible remnants. Integrity of location is basically assumed for all archaeological sites, as most are indeed the actual place where human activity was undertaken, although complicating factors need to be carefully considered during fieldwork. Artifacts can be transported to new locations by natural forces (e.g., slumping, rapid water movement, ice rafting) or by cultural means outside the period of significance (e.g., filling, discarding, intentional salting). Even considering these activities, the great majority of archaeological sites will have integrity of location, especially those with in situ features. Location can also refer to the vertical or horizontal positions of artifacts within a site, but this is more properly discussed under association.

Bulletin 15 states, "*Materials* are the physical elements that were combined or deposited during a particular period of time and in a particular pattern or configuration to form a historic property" (p. 45). Materials include the basic elements of what a building or structure is made of (e.g., brick) and their particular form (e.g., red fired brick). The integrity of materials for an archaeological site concerns the presence of artifacts and features left by the site's inhabitants during the period of significance, the completeness of the artifacts and features, and the quality of their preservation. The condition of artifacts or features, not their quantity, is evaluated. They should be in as close to original condition as is reasonable.

A property retains the integrity of association if it is "the place where the event or activity occurred and is sufficiently intact to convey that relationship" (Bulletin 15:45). Association is perhaps the most important aspect of archaeological integrity. Unlike with other property types, the vertical rather than the horizontal nature of association is of most importance to archaeological sites.

In order to understand the site environment during the period of significance and the direct linkage of artifacts and features to a particular historic context (i.e., phase, tradition, culture), natural and cultural disturbances to a site are of paramount importance. A site may possess numerous high-quality artifacts (retaining integrity of location, materials, and design), but if those artifacts have been displaced from their original stratigraphic context and if artifacts from multiple contexts have been mixed, the site's value to archaeological research is greatly diminished because the artifacts may not be directly linkable to a particular cultural complex. Horizontal integrity is also an important consideration under association. At some sites discrete areas are apparent, reflecting use-areas for particular activities or time-transgressive site use by different cultures. A number of sites within a National Register district may represent a short-term event such as a butchering area, a stone tool workshop, and a campsite associated with a bison kill.

Setting refers to "the character of a place in which the property played its historical role" (Bulletin 15:45). Integrity of setting considers the basic physical condition of a property as it appeared during the period of significance. It includes not just the area within the site boundaries, but the surrounding environment. With regard to setting, the basic question to ask is, Would a resident of the site during the period of significance recognize the location today?

For archaeological sites nominated under Criterion A or B, integrity of setting and feeling are important, but this is not the case for Criterion D. An archaeological site located beneath a McDonald's parking lot can easily be eligible under Criterion D if it meets the location, materials, and association aspects outlined above, but it is unlikely to be eligible under Criterion A or B, as the setting and the feeling have been too radically altered.

Feeling is the most subjective aspect of integrity. It is closely linked to setting but also incorporates the cultural features of a site that were present during the period of significance. Feeling is more than a consideration of the natural environment of a site; it also involves the site's cultural environment, along with its materials, design, location, association, and workmanship. Feeling is very important to traditional cultural properties.

Integrity of feeling can be more myopic than integrity of setting. Two of the worst examples of integrity of setting for famous historic sites I have visited are the Alamo in San Antonio, Texas (Figure 5.2), and Boot Hill Cemetery in Dodge City,

FIG. 5.2 Aerial view of San Antonio, Texas, with the Alamo in the center, demonstrating impaired integrity of setting (Google Earth).

Kansas (Figure 5.3). The Alamo is in the middle of a city surrounded by parking lots and large, modern buildings; yet if you go into the interior courtyard, you can get a sense of what it was like in 1836 just prior to the famous battle fought there. Dodge City's Boot Hill is also surrounded by a modern city as well as by a clapboard fence that wasn't present during the mid-nineteenth century. If you go inside the fence and view the fake grave markers and concrete path, you will see that the site has clearly lost integrity of both setting and feeling.

All archaeological sites have degraded integrity. Time takes its toll on all seven aspects of integrity both through natural and cultural processes. Climate changes and land-use changes cause setting changes. Rodents,

FIG. 5.3 Knothole view of Boot Hill in Dodge City, Kansas, demonstrating a lack of integrity of feeling even inside the fence (author photo).

plowing, and bulldozers harm association and location by displacing artifacts. Organic artifacts and features rot away, harming design, materials, workmanship, and feeling.

The key to assessing integrity for most archaeological sites is to truthfully answer part two of the Criterion D significance requirement: How likely is the site to yield information that can be clearly used to answer important research questions? Most archaeologists can ask hundreds of what they think are important research questions, but many sites with degraded integrity can't satisfactorily answer any.

Determining Boundaries

Because all National Register listings are properties (i.e., places) and because all eligible and listed properties have federal project review implications, these properties all require absolute locations—not just a point on a map or a general locational description but a line drawn on a map showing the official property boundaries. Determining boundaries for buildings, objects, and structures is generally fairly straightforward as they are obvious and discrete. Boundaries for many recent historic sites are often based on maps and other written records. Determining National Register boundaries for archaeological sites is more problematic. This is true of most prehistoric and many early historical archaeological sites. Boundaries for these types of sites are usually based on the known distribution of artifacts and features.

Known distributions of materials and features, however, are subject to many variables. Surveys related to environmental impact assessments are usually restricted to the project's area of potential effects. This has important implications for both defining the site's actual limits and assessing the site's integrity as a whole. Discretional surveys conducted for SHPOs or THPOs or by researchers in a small area may involve several property owners, some of whom give permission to enter their land and some of whom don't. Some site boundaries can be interpolated by landforms (e.g., islands, peninsulas, major topographic breaks), but the only true determinant is a detailed archaeological survey. Additionally, guidelines for what constitutes a site and a site boundary can vary from state to state.

While National Register nominations require both a firm definition of a site's boundary and a written justification for that definition, the requirements of eligibility evaluations are less strict. If the site clearly extends outside the project's APE and you are prevented by agency policy or lack of landowner permission from determining the complete site boundary, for the purposes of initial site inventory you can combine what your survey told you and make a best guess based on any confining landforms.

When I was a SHPO archaeologist, for evaluation purposes I used a practical approach when confronted with incomplete total site boundaries. If you are dealing with only a portion of a site, you can assess the significance of the entire site by demonstrating that an excavation within the affected and surveyed portion could address important research questions. But if the integrity of a large percentage of the site has not been examined, it is difficult to state that the site as whole retains sufficient integrity to be eligible. As a SHPO archaeologist, in such instances I considered two practical boundaries for a site: a projected complete boundary for the purposes of inventory and a smaller evaluation boundary for the purposes of Section 106 effect assessments. The projected boundary could be used for a state site inventory form, where the "best guess" method based on landform is usually acceptable as long as this is explained on the form. Dashed lines could be used for the projected boundaries of a site and solid lines for boundaries documented by survey or obvious landform or hydrological constrictions.

For assessing effects to potentially eligible sites where I could not assess the integrity of the unaffected portion and perhaps the majority of the site, I basically established an environmental review boundary where I would determine if an important research question could be addressed within the portion of the site to be affected by a project. This allowed me to make a Section 106 determination of eligibility and effect. If the site were ever to be nominated, you would indeed have to determine the absolute boundary, but for the purposes of completing project review under Section 106, a more pragmatic and practical approach was necessary.

Nominating Properties to the NRHP

Most properties nominated to the National Register of Historic Places are identified by statewide surveys, local surveys, tax incentive actions, or initiatives by private individuals or local groups. The need for actual nomination is mainly due to internal pressure within SHPOs to increase the number of listings for their states, local pressure for honor roll acknowledgment, or the need to obtain tax credits for commercial rehabilitations. In my experience, federal agencies rarely do nominations, although both Section 110 of the National Historic Preservation Act and Executive Order 11593 encourage it. The majority of sites considered eligible through consensus determinations (agency and SHPO/THPO) during the Section 106 process are never nominated or formally determined eligible by the Keeper. Federal procedures for listing, revising a listing, and removing a property from the National Register are found in 36 CFR 60.5–60.15.

Generally, if you want to nominate a site, the SHPO is first contacted to assess its basic eligibility. For nonarchaeological properties, this can be done by looking at photographs and reading a brief historic overview of the property that notes why it is important and describes any obvious integrity impairments. Based on the significance criterion selected, the critical submitted information for a building should include the architect, the year built, the years of any major additions or alterations, the building function, and who lived or worked in the building. For archaeological sites, a detailed report from a formal evaluation survey is usually necessary, although some sites are obviously eligible based on just the results of a preliminary field survey.

If the SHPO concurs with a proposal for nomination that a property is indeed eligible, a draft nomination is written. This is usually done by a SHPO staff member or a professional archaeologist, historian, or architectural historian under contract with the SHPO, an agency, or a sponsoring organization or individual. Members of the public can also write and submit nominations, but all nominations require some expertise, and this expertise is not widely present among the general public or avocational historians or archaeologists. The draft nomination is then submitted to the SHPO.

When I was the SHPO archaeologist for Minnesota, I typically went through two drafts before I was ready to take the nomination to the state review board (SRB). SHPOs can also have their own standards for nominations that may exceed or supplement federal requirements. Minnesota has these with respect to items like photodocumentation, word processor formats, sketch maps, and owner verification forms.

Prior to going to the National Register in Washington, DC, nonfederal nominations must first go through an SRB. SRBs are public bodies that are state-appointed (usually by the SHPO) and have duties that go beyond just the review of National Register nominations. This is outlined in 36 CFR 61 (e.g., providing advice on state historic preservation plans). Each state is required to have an SRB if it receives federal historic preservation funds but can determine the number of members, the length of their terms, how members are appointed, and how many meetings to have each year. SRB members must be free of conflicts of interest and must "have demonstrated competence, interest, or knowledge in historic preservation." A majority of SRB members must be qualified professionals in archaeology, history, and **architectural history** or closely related fields. A minimum of five members must be on the SRB, and the SRB must meet at least once a year.

In Minnesota, the SRB consists of 14 members, of which 8 are professionals and 6 are members-at-large. All are appointed to three-year terms by the SHPO, and members can only serve three consecutive terms. The Minnesota SHPO has been diligent in trying to include members who reflect diversity in gender and ethnicity, although the ethnicity part can be challenging, as many members of minority communities are only recently becoming more engaged in historic preservation. The Minnesota SRB currently meets three times a year, although in the past it met quarterly.

Once a SHPO has determined that a nomination is ready to be submitted to the SRB, the property owner and any local governments, including Indian tribes for properties within reservation boundaries, must be notified at least 30 days prior to the SRB meeting. If the property is owned by a private entity, written owner consent must be obtained for listing but not for the nomination process or formal determinations of eligibility. It is essential to consult with private owners of properties prior to even completing a draft nomination if the objective is actual listing, as it is embarrassing to SHPO staff, a waste of contract money, and professionally unfulfilling to have an owner objection letter read at the SRB meeting following presentation of a nomination. Furthermore, federal regulations (36 CFR 60.6[c]) require that landowners be contacted when there is even intent to nominate their property.

If multiple private property owners are involved, each owner gets one "vote," even if an individual parcel is owned by multiple individuals, even if parcels vary greatly in size, and even if one individual owns multiple properties. (I put "vote" in quotation marks because no actual polling takes place; landowners simply have the right to be notified of a proposed nomination of their property and to object to that nomination.) All property owners within a proposed district get to weigh in, even those with **noncontributing** properties. If the majority of private owners object to a listing, the majority rules, and the property cannot be listed in the National Register. In the case of a tie, the property can be listed.

If the SHPO disagrees that a property submitted by the public is eligible, members of the public still have the right to complete a nomination and forward it to the SRB. If the SHPO and SRB disagree on eligibility, the Keeper makes the determination of whether the property can be listed. Even if both the SHPO and the SRB agree about a property's eligibility, a public or private property owner can appeal the decision to the Keeper of the National Register, although that appeal must only address qualities of significance and integrity.

SHPO staff usually make the presentations of nominations at SRB meetings, although professional contractors can be asked to present nominations they have written. Once the nomination has been presented, members of the public attending the meeting are asked if they would like to briefly address the board. Sometimes emotions run high at these meetings. SHPO staff occasionally need to gently remind board members that their only duty is to determine if a property meets National Register criteria with regard to significance and integrity. The board should not be swayed by emotional appeals of preservationists for listing of near and dear properties or by protestations from public property owners of economic hardship if the property is listed.

If a property is determined to be eligible by a majority vote of the SRB, SHPO staff will fix any typos and make minor corrections of factual errors of omission or commission on the nomination form and forward the revised form to the state historic preservation officer. The officer checks the appropriate boxes on page one of the nomination, signs the form, and forwards it to the National Register in Washington, DC.

At the National Register, all nominations are given at least a cursory review by NRHP staff. If there are no major problems with the documentation and the Keeper agrees with the eligibility determination, the Keeper signs the form, and the property is officially listed in the National Register. The property is automatically listed if the Keeper does not act within 45 days of receipt of the nomination. Notice of newly listed properties appears in the *Federal Register* (the US government's official daily publication) along with the state name and official listing date.

If NRHP staff notice minor errors on a submitted nomination form (e.g., acreage of the property), the property can still be listed. Such errors are subject to supplemental listing record (SLR) comments from NRHP staff sent back to a submitting SHPO or federal agency for correction. A SHPO or agency's receiving numerous SLRs is not only embarrassing but may alert NRHP staff to more thoroughly review future nominations from that state or agency. When the NPS was still doing regular three-year audits of SHPOs, excessive SLRs could also result in a finding of deficiency in the National Register program area and lead to a lower Historic Preservation Fund (HPF) allocation to that state.

Listed properties' nomination forms can be amended. Boundary changes are treated like new nominations, as boundary information is kept in a separate database at the National Register. Boundaries are critical to environmental review, tax credits, and grant eligibility. Proposed boundary changes are dealt with in detail in 36 CFR 660.14. Non-boundary-related additional information with regard to a listed property can be sent to the Register at any time, but if it is submitted by an agency, a copy of the information must also be sent to the SHPO.

Properties that cease to meet or truly never met National Register requirements can and should be removed. Usually removal is due to a substantial loss of integrity subsequent to original listing. Removal of archaeological properties from the Register is rare, as effects to integrity are usually less dramatic for them compared to structures, they are often in less visible areas, and there are no implications for tax act or federal grant eligibility. The petition for removal can go directly to the Register, although some states have their own processes, including a vote by the SRB. Any petition for removal submitted by an agency or individual directly to the Register must also be sent to the SHPO. The Keeper has 45 days to respond to removal petitions. Unlike listings, removals are not automatic if the Keeper does not act within 45 days.

Nominations of properties on federal land do not go through the SRB, but federal agencies are required to seek comment from the appropriate SHPO/THPO and local officials regarding nominations. The process for federal nominations is outlined in 36 CFR 60.9. Federal nominations are written by agency staff or private consultants hired by agencies. Once complete, the draft nomination is sent to the SHPO and any appropriate local government officials, and they have 45 days to send comments back to the federal agency. The SHPO has the option of signing the nomination, and SHPO comments are appended to the nomination. If the federal preservation officer (FPO) for that agency signs the nomination, the FPO then sends it along with any SHPO or public comments to the NRHP. If the Keeper signs the form, the property is officially listed. The Keeper must actually sign a federal nomination in order for it to be listed, as there is no 45-day automatic listing rule as there is for nonfederal nominations.

Recently, Republicans in Congress have supported a provision in the Military Lands Act that would amend the National Historic Preservation Act to allow federal land-managing agencies to object to the National Register listing of properties under their control if they can claim a national security reason. It would also allow the removal from the Register of already-listed properties for the same reason. This would set a dangerous precedent, although the national security justification would be a stretch in most instances. Additionally, eligible properties on federal lands receive the same Section 106 consideration as listed properties.

Multiple Property Documentation Forms

The completion of Multiple Property Documentation Forms (MPDFs) is relatively uncommon for most consultants and agencies, so I will not discuss it in much detail here. Heritage management professionals should be aware of the structure and uses of an MPDF, however, as existing MPDFs in any state must be used to evaluate or nominate property types in that state if there is a pertinent MPDF. MPDFs can streamline and simplify the evaluation and nomination process as well as assist with resource management and planning. MPDFs are also the most useful type of National Register document for research purposes.

MPDFs are described in Bulletin 16B. The MPDF was introduced in 1984 and had replaced multiple resource area and thematic resource nominations by 1989. The purpose of MRAs and TRs was to list many properties quickly by using either a common area (e.g., a county) or a common theme (e.g., farmsteads). According to Bulletin 16B (p. 2), an MPDF can be used either to nominate related property types simultaneously or to establish the **registration requirements** for future needs. While the first purpose of an MPDF is a continuation of the MRA and TR tradition to promote numerous individual listings in one submittal, the MPDF today is almost exclusively used for the latter purpose regarding registration requirements. Individual nominations need not even accompany an MPDF submission to the Register unless a state requires it.

Both an MPDF and a directly associated property nomination utilizing the historic contexts, property types, and registration requirements of an MPDF are referred to as a **multiple property listing**. MPDFs must go through the state review board like individual nominations, but no landowner or external agency must be informed except with respect to an accompanying individual property nomination.

Unlike the individual property nomination, the MPDF form is almost entirely a narrative. It has two important sections: Section E ("Historic Contexts") and Section F ("Associated Property Types"). With regard to the other sections, Section A gives the name of the multiple property, Section B simply lists the historic contexts defined in Section E, Section C lists who prepared the form, Section D is for the submitting agency and Keeper certification, Section G defines the geographic area, Section H provides a summary of the identification and evaluation methods, and Section I contains the bibliography.

The Section E ("Historic Contexts") narrative must provide sufficient depth and detail to support the relevance, relationships, and cultural affiliation of the associated property types. Each historic context must have a theme, a geographic area, and a chronological period. The narrative must focus on the theme (e.g., shipwrecks), not on the regional history (e.g., history of the Great Lakes region) or chronological sequence (e.g., the era of wooden ships followed by steel ships). An MPDF must have at least one historic context. Multiple historic contexts should be presented in chronological order and the associated property types named, though not discussed in any detail, in this section. The contexts also have to be linked to appropriate National Register significance criteria (A–D). Contexts should not be defined too narrowly to limit usefulness or so broadly as to diffuse the thematic focus and lead to a plethora of associated property types.

Section F ("Associated Property Types") must first name the property type (one or more), describe its appearance, function, and association, state its significance, and list the registration requirements specific to the property type. The statement of significance must relate the property type to a Section E–defined historic context and discuss the property type with regard to significance criteria, areas of significance, and levels of significance. The registration requirements provide an explicit discussion of all seven aspects of integrity as related to that particular property type and discusses how the property type relates to the historic context and the significance criteria. As with historic contexts, property types should not be defined too narrowly. **Registration requirements** are the most useful elements of an MPDF as they allow a more rapid and accurate assessment of the eligibility of any property that fits the MPDF.

When I was the Minnesota SHPO archaeologist, I guided six MPDFs through the nomination process. These MPDFs were titled "Minnesota's Lake Superior Shipwrecks," "Shipwrecks of Minnesota's Inland Lakes and Rivers," "Precontact American Indian Earthworks," "American Indian Rock Art in Minnesota," "Commercial Logging in Minnesota," and "Portage Trails in Minnesota." They were done either to facilitate nominations arising out of current focused surveys or to deal with common or problematic property types encountered in the environmental review process. I had hoped to complete two additional MPDFs during my tenure as SHPO archaeologist to deal with the property types that caused the most confusion and cost the most money to evaluate in CRM archaeology: prehistoric lithic scatters and historic farmsteads (see sidebar).

An Archaeologist's Perspective on the National Register

In 1993, the National Register issued a bulletin titled *Guidelines for Evaluating and Registering Historical Archaeological Sites and Districts* and assigned the number 36 (Townsend, Sprinkle, and Knoerl 1993). This was the first bulletin issued exclusively for archaeological properties. Unfortunately, it did not include prehistoric sites. This was corrected in a revised and unnumbered version of the archaeological bulletin issued in 2000 and titled *Guidelines for Evaluating and Registering Archaeological Properties* (Little et al. 2000). The expanded bulletin included consideration of prehistoric sites, although most of it still focused on historical sites. I refer to this bulletin as Revised Bulletin 36, although it was technically never numbered.

Currently, only about 7% of individual listings in the Register are archaeological sites or districts. In addition, the growth in interest in traditional cultural properties and **ethnographic landscapes** over the last 20 years has made anthropological properties even more problematic than archaeological ones. The archaeologists among CRM professionals most often have to figure out eligibility recommendations for these often less tangible, complex property types.

Like Tom King, I am generally not a proponent of a need for National Register listing for most archaeological properties, although it is important for archaeologists to understand the basic nomination process in order to honestly and thoroughly assess eligibility. To clearly demonstrate a property is eligible, you should be able to professionally complete a formal nomination form for that property. By going through the basic steps of correctly and completely filling out the nomination form, you can see the strong points and the flaws in an eligibility argument. Broad and deep understanding of the National Register also leads to consistency in property evaluations, not only within a state or agency but between states and agencies.

There are few well-supported reasons to nominate archaeological sites for the National Register of Historic Places despite what Keepers and NRHP staff have said (Shull 2002; Miller 1994; J. Townsend 1994; Sprinkle 1994; Little 1997, 1999). Archaeological sites are relatively expensive and complicated to nominate, landowner permission for archaeological nominations is often more difficult to obtain, archaeological properties often involve large areas of land and multiple owners, there are no federal tax benefits for listing archaeological sites, and archaeological sites are rarely eligible for federal grants.

But there are a few advantages to listing archaeological sites. First, although listed sites are no better protected in federal environmental reviews than simply eligible sites, listing does give sites a higher profile with agencies, the public, and the courts. Serious consideration of listed sites as opposed to just eligible sites during environmental review processes tends to improve.

There are also state environmental review laws that consider only listed sites, not eligible sites. In Minnesota, the state environmental review process requires that an environmental review worksheet (like a federal environmental assessment under NEPA) be completed for "destruction in whole or part" of a property listed in the state or national historic Register. Because the Minnesota State Register process is a cumbersome and rarely used legislative process, listing in the National Register can be essential to the consideration of nonfederal development impacts to significant sites on private property.

It is easy for an archaeologist, especially a midwestern prehistoric archaeologist, to complain about the National Register. Many of the archaeological complaints about the NRHP can be traced to its birth. The Register was really developed for buildings, as clearly illustrated by the fact that Criterion D is inconsistent with Criteria A, B, and C; Criterion D should basically provide additional support for nominations using A, B, and C. The original panel of experts that developed the basic criteria for the Register was dominated by historians (with five historians and one archaeologist). The expectation in the implementation of the initial National Historic Preservation Act that statewide surveys would be completed in four years reflects a clear bias toward standing structures or places easily found and documented. Even after almost 50 years of SHPO-sponsored surveys, environmental-review-mandated surveys, and NHPA Section 110 federal land surveys, many states still have less than 1% of their archaeological properties inventoried, and perhaps only 1% of these known sites have been evaluated for National Register eligibility.

The National Register still has many problems when it comes to archaeological properties. National Register archaeologists have been talented and conscientious professionals, but they tend to be eastern-oriented historical archaeologists. The Keeper as a heritage management professional has always been a historian. There is still only one bulletin dedicated exclusively to archeological properties, and only a few archaeological nominations are provided as examples on the NRHP website.

Problems inherent in the nature of archaeology and archaeological sites also complicate Register applications. Archaeological nominations are more difficult and more expensive to produce due to the need for more than just a visual inspection and library research. Owner objection is more common for archaeological sites, as many properties tend to be in conservative rural areas where there is more government-interference paranoia. Many large sites may have multiple owners. The locations of sites subject to archaeological nominations generally have to be withheld due to pot-hunting, vandalism, and trespassing concerns. Boundaries of archaeological sites are often difficult to define, especially when multiple landowners or multiple land uses are involved.

Like it or not, we are stuck with the National Register as our yardstick for what measures up as worthy of preservation. Only eligible sites are visible to the Section 106 process and most other environmental review processes. If we make too many sites eligible (i.e., viable) for this process, we not only waste time and money but risk changes in the law that will weaken site protection. If we make too few sites visible, we allow actions that irreparably harm important aspects of our archaeological heritage. I will address suggestions to improve the National Register process in the final chapter of this book.

Summary

The National Register of Historic Places was not invented by the National Historic Preservation Act in 1966. A national listing of important places was introduced by the federal government's Historic Sites Survey during the 1930s. The confirmation that some of the places on the list would not come under federal ownership was demonstrated by the National Historic Landmarks Program in 1960. The National Historic Preservation Act did, however, introduce state and local levels of significance to the National Register and utilized the list as a way of determining what would become visible to the federal environmental review process.

It would be nice to save every archaeological site and older structure from destruction just to protect the environment or save us from our own evaluation mistakes, but this is not reasonable or necessary, at least in terms of Section 106. As an archaeologist, I took a while to feel comfortable with the fact that not every site is worth saving. Yet every site is important, and herein lies much of most archaeologists' confusion. We need to be mindful of the difference between importance in an archaeological sense and significance in a National Register sense. In order to do this, we need to minimize our concerns with the National Register as an honor roll and concentrate on thinking about it as an environmental review tool, focusing on what properties and what data are actually worthy of preservation.

The National Register needs to provide better guidance with regard to evaluating archaeological sites. This is especially true of prehistoric sites. No one bulletin deals exclusively with prehistoric property types. Even the one general archaeological bulletin that is available focuses on historical archaeological sites. For prehistoric sites, we could use bulletins on rock art, earthworks, and artifact scatters, to name a few. For historical sites, we could use bulletins for farmsteads, industrial sites, and urban residential areas.

The National Register should consider revising the basic guidelines for eligibility under Criterion D. It should eliminate the "has yielded" clause and move that exclusively to Criterion A. It should also change guidance about research potential to include the word "demonstrated." If the potential hasn't been demonstrated by an evaluation survey, how can we truly say a site is "likely to yield" important information.

I would encourage all archaeologists involved in CRM work to take courses in how to apply National Register criteria. All universities that offer advanced degrees in heritage management, cultural resource management, or historic preservation should include this type of training in their curricula, not just general courses or lectures on archaeological significance in an academic vacuum.

Review Questions

1. What are the early foundations of the National Register?
2. What roles does the National Register play in heritage management?
3. What are the two key factors in determining eligibility?
4. What are historic contexts?
5. What is an MPDF, and what are its key components?

Supplemental Reading

In order to understand National Register eligibility, it is essential for members of all professions to be familiar with National Register Bulletin 16A, *How to Complete the National Register Registration Form* (1997b), and Bulletin 15, *How to Apply the National Register Criteria for Evaluation* (1997a). It is also important to understand Bulletin 16B, *How to Complete the National Register Multiple Property Documentation Form* (1999).

Historians and architects need to be familiar with the specialty bulletins that deal with a number of specific property types pertinent to the properties they are reviewing. Archaeologists should be familiar with Revised Bulletin 36, *Guidelines for Evaluating and Registering Archaeological Properties* (Little et al. 2000), as well as any specialty bulletins that may deal with specific property types they are reviewing (e.g., Bulletin 20 for shipwrecks and Bulletin 38 for traditional cultural properties). The Register also has occasional white papers and other guidance available online dealing with particular issues (e.g., national cemeteries).

Hardesty and Little (2009) provides helpful insights mainly for archaeologists. Sprinkle (2014) gives a good background on the development of the National Register. Critical assessments of the National Register can be found in Tom King's many publications (e.g., 1984, 2003, 2009, 2013) and on his *CRM Plus* blog (e.g., posts for February 16, September 26, and November 28, 2008; January 21 and December 17, 2009; January 5, 2010).

SIDEBAR

Implementing Heritage Management: Lithic Scatters and Scattered Farmsteads

In my many years as both a survey archaeologist and a review agency archaeologist, two archaeological property types were particularly vexing: prehistoric lithic scatters and historical farmsteads. These are some of the most common archaeological sites. Their identification and evaluation have wide-reaching implications for the expenditure of public and private funds, as well as agency and archaeological effort. The National Register has not issued a single bulletin that deals exclusively with specific types of archaeological properties, so we must rely on the general guidance of Bulletins 16A and 15 and Revised Bulletin 36.

Lithic Scatters

Lithic scatters are sites that have yielded almost exclusively the debris or products of stone tool technology. They include sites yielding chipped stone tools, ground stone tools, and/or stone manufacturing debris. Archaeologists commonly use the term "lithic scatter" to describe sites that have no apparent surficial features, lack prehistoric ceramics, contain no significant historical artifacts, and have yielded mainly chipped-stone flaking debris and/or stone tools. If diagnostic stone tools are present (e.g., projectile points), lithic scatters may be assigned to a historic context (e.g., Folsom). Lithic scatters account for over half the recorded prehistoric sites in Minnesota and probably even higher percentages of sites in many other states.

Because most lithic scatters lack clearly diagnostic artifacts, and thus cannot be assigned to a firm historic context and contain only one class of artifacts (stone), this limits the research questions they can address. Most lithic scatters are also in highly disturbed settings, so they have impaired integrity. Based on limited research potential and impaired integrity, most lithic scatters are probably not eligible for inclusion in the National Register. Until Revised Bulletin 36 was released in 2000, a site needed a historic context before it could be considered eligible, and even Bulletin 36 requires that sites lacking a historic context be evaluated within an appropriate thematic context with a *demonstrated* potential to answer *important* questions.

California made a major effort to assess the significance of lithic scatters in the 1980s, using a combination of artifact totals, artifact densities, feature presence, and site size to evaluate research potential (Jackson et al. 1988). Arizona attempted to classify **lithic** sites in the 1990s, using assumed site function (Slaughter et al. 1992). In 1994, I developed a thematic context for lithic scatters in Minnesota utilizing three descriptive property types: single artifact find spots, sparse lithic scatters, and lithic scatters (Anfinson 1994). Single artifact find spots were never eligible. Sparse lithic scatters were not eligible unless they contained unusual raw materials (e.g., obsidian), were in an unusual regional location, or had a probable exceptional special use (e.g., ceremonial). Lithic scatters could be eligible if they retained good integrity, had the same exceptional characteristics listed above for sparse lithic scatters, and were of an exceptional size or had an exceptional density of materials.

More recently, other states and individuals have also investigated the significance of lithic scatters (e.g., Austin 2002). One of the more ambitious studies was based on a colloquium held at the New York State Museum in November 2003 (Rieth 2008). The Rieth volume papers cite numerous other lithic scatter studies that should be examined by anyone interested in evaluation and analysis issues. The Minnesota Department of Transportation (MnDOT) is revaluating the lithic scatters issue in Minnesota.

Farmsteads as Archaeological Sites

Historical archaeological sites from the recent past (i.e., after 1900) have become a major heritage management issue because of their great numbers, widespread distribution, and high visibility on maps and in aerial photographs and written records. Every city block, every farmstead, every industrial site, and every trash dump at least 50 years old could be defined as an archaeological site. This means that tens of thousands of building sites in SHPO history-architecture files could also be included in archaeological site files. If all the known farmsteads in Minnesota were considered archaeological sites, we could add 204,000 sites (the peak number of active farmsteads in 1935) to the archaeological database. Almost every lot on every city block could be considered an archaeological site. With 854 cities in Minnesota, including a major metropolitan area, the number of potential urban historical archaeological sites is overwhelming.

At about the same time I was investigating lithic scatters in Minnesota, I was also examining the archaeological potential of farmsteads. In early 1996, I made a proposal to MnDOT suggesting we undertake a study of farmsteads utilizing a regional framework to look at different types of farms. MnDOT concurred and agreed to provide the major funding. In 2005, the MnDOT study report provided a historical overview of Minnesota farming, property types, and registration requirements for standing structures and landscapes (Granger and Kelly 2005). A separate volume discussed the archaeological potential of farmsteads (Terrell 2005).

Despite all these studies, we still have no clear guidance on how to honestly evaluate lithic scatters and archaeological farmsteads. I think very few lithic scatters that lack a well-established age or historic context are eligible. I also think the great majority of farmsteads that date to the twentieth century have very little archaeological research potential, and if these farmsteads lack significant standing structures, very few should be considered eligible.

Even in the absence of clear guidance on eligibility, I think the greatest proof of the ineligibility of most prehistoric lithic scatters and archaeological farmsteads from the recent past is the fact that so few are currently listed in the National Register. I'm sure that many of these types of sites have been determined eligible through the Section 106 process, but if the SHPOs who promoted or concurred in these determinations thought they really were important, they would have nominated at least some of them. In my 15 years as a SHPO archaeologist, I certainly did not find many examples of these types of sites that I thought were worthy of preservation as demonstrated by listing them in the National Register.

CHAPTER 6

Section 106 of NHPA

The Front Wall

Sometimes I think we should make the whole world eligible and just deal with effects.

—Susan Roth, Minnesota State Historic Preservation Office

Section 106 is one of the shortest sections of the National Historic Preservation Act (NHPA), consisting of only two sentences and 93 words. Yet the implementing regulations for Section 106 (36 CFR 800) are 16 pages long with 16,354 words. Section 106 is the most controversial section in the NHPA, having been the subject of many lawsuits and negative comments since 1966. It is the most recognizable section just by its number. If you ask heritage management professionals or federal agency officials, "Is that project subject to 106?" they will know exactly what you mean. Unlike with "CRM," Google gets "106" right on the first try.

Although Section 106 of the NHPA is the most recognized part of the law, it is also the most misunderstood, certainly by the public and even by some heritage management professionals. Many people think it requires the preservation of significant historic properties. It doesn't. It technically isn't even Section 106 anymore, although the Advisory Council on Historic Preservation (ACHP) and everyone else still calls it that. Amendment of the federal code for National Park Service (NPS) laws in 2014 made it 54 USC 306108, but I can't see many practitioners referring to Section 106 as Section 306108. I will continue to refer to it as Section 106 in this book.

This chapter looks in detail at what Section 106 says and, as implemented by the 36 CFR 800 regulations, what it has come to mean, especially with regard to changes in the regulations over time. Here is the text of Section 106 from 54 USC 306108:

> The head of any Federal agency having direct or indirect jurisdiction over a proposed Federal or federally assisted undertaking in any State and the head of any Federal department or independent agency having authority to license any undertaking, prior to the approval of the expenditure of any Federal funds on the undertaking or prior to the issuance of any license, shall take into account the effect of the undertaking on any historic property. The head of the Federal agency shall afford the Council a reasonable opportunity to comment with regard to the undertaking.

The first sentence basically directs federal agencies to consider the effects on historic properties of any undertaking on federal lands, subject to a federal license or permit, or paid for with federal funds. The second sentence requires the controlling agency to give the ACHP the opportunity to comment on the undertaking. The original language in 1966 required "considering" and "consulting" only with respect to properties listed in the National Register of Historic Places (NRHP). Executive Order 11593 in 1971 expanded this to include properties determined eligible for inclusion in the NRHP, with this requirement codified in the law by the 1976 amendment. The 2014 recodification changed the "listed in or eligible to" language to "any historic property," as historic properties are defined elsewhere in the law as properties listed in or eligible for inclusion in the NRHP.

Besides the consideration of eligible properties, the other major post-1966 change in the implementation of Section 106 is with regard to whom the federal agency must consult. The 1966 language specified consultation only with the ACHP, and this wording has not changed within Section 106. However, the ACHP soon found it more practical and productive for agencies to consult directly with state historic preservation offices (SHPOs), which in effect represent the ACHP. Changes in Section 101 in the 1992 amendment of the NHPA required consultation with Indian tribes, Native Hawaiians, and Native Alaskans, but this is not stated in Section 106.

Although only two sentences long, Section 106 is loaded with implications, and many of the terms used in its application are subject to careful definition and much discussion. These implications and definitions require detailed explication in order for Section 106 to be implemented in a form consistent with congressional intent, in a uniform manner by agencies, and through procedures that are not excessively burdensome. The detailed explication is in the form of legally binding regulations (36 CFR 800).

History of the Section 106 Regulations
Preliminary Guidelines

The 1966 legislation did not give the ACHP or its original parent organization, the Department of the Interior, rule-making authority for the purposes of Section 106 of the NHPA. Yet the infant ACHP needed to rapidly provide some sort of guidance to federal agencies on how to apply Section 106. At the time, most agencies were clearly more than willing to plead ignorance as to the meaning of Section 106 and how to apply it in order to avoid having to deal with it.

The ACHP had no staff for the first nine months after President Lyndon Johnson signed the NHPA into law on October 15, 1966, because there was no accompanying ACHP appropriation for fiscal year 1967. Ernest Connally, head of the newly formed Office of Archaeology and Historic Preservation (OAHP) at NPS, was appointed executive director of the ACHP but was still paid directly by NPS. Furthermore, the council itself was not fully appointed at this time, and there were no ACHP staff other than the executive director.

OAHP staff developed an informal internal procedure for initially implementing Section 106 (Glass 1990:42). Federal agencies would be requested to provide information on projects only near National Historic Landmarks (NHLs). OAHP staff would review the project and then suggest to the agency how to avoid any adverse effects to the NHL. If the agency said it couldn't avoid the adverse effects, the project would be referred to the ACHP for comment. Key OAHP staff making the first major decisions on Section 106 reviews were Robert Utley, the new acting head of OAHP, and Russell Keune, an OAHP historian acting as Keeper of the National Register.

Utley immediately recognized that OAHP staff, who had other duties, could soon be overwhelmed by Section 106 reviews. He thought the solution was to get state liaison officers (SLOs) formally involved in reviewing federal undertakings in their states and have them make initial determinations as to whether there would be adverse effects to National Register properties. This would not only spread out the work but also require agencies to directly work with state officials where the projects were being done. These SLOs were more familiar with their state's historic properties than OAHP staff in Washington and could work more easily with local project sponsors. Utley also encouraged the formation of what would become the National Conference of State Historic Preservation Officers (NCSHPO). OAHP had to provide leadership for that organization until NCSHPO got its first executive director in 1980 (Rodgers 2016:11).

In July 1967 Robert Garvey, executive director of the National Trust for Historic Preservation (NTHP), was hired as the executive secretary of the ACHP. His major responsibilities (as defined by Connally) were to act as the principal contact between NPS and ACHP and to help the ACHP avoid causing any controversies between NPS and Congress (Glass 1990:43). Garvey was in an uncomfortable position between his ACHP boss (Connally) and his NPS employer (Utley). Furthermore, his duties as executive secretary of the ACHP and the duties of Connally as executive director of ACHP were not clearly differentiated.

The first meeting of the ACHP was held in Washington, DC, on July 20–21, 1967, soon after Garvey's hiring. Because the ACHP had no staff of its own separate from NPS, the council empowered OAHP to negotiate on behalf of the ACHP with federal agencies for the purposes of the Section 106 consultation duties and also the agency advisory duties defined elsewhere in the NHPA. Garvey actively sought to balance these two duties when he set up the first meeting of the ACHP, not emphasizing the carrot or the stick.

Garvey set to work immediately after the first ACHP meeting to develop procedures for implementing Section 106, working with OAHP head Utley and the new Keeper of the National Register, William Murtagh, who was appointed in August 1967. Garvey presented the draft procedures at the second ACHP meeting in September 1967, and the council endorsed them. Murtagh discussed the 10 agency project reviews currently being looked at by OAHP under Section 106, including a Department of Health, Education, and Welfare (HEW) project at the Springfield Armory in Massachusetts, a Department of Housing and Urban Development (HUD) urban renewal project in Memphis, Tennessee, and an HEW project in Georgetown.

At the third meeting of the ACHP in February 1968, members took a field trip to the nearby Georgetown site, directly investing the council in the day-to-day review process and demonstrating to federal agencies that it was a real entity. They also voted to have Garvey develop formal rules for Section 106 implementation. Garvey assigned OAHP staff historian Ben Levy to lead the rules project.

Levy delivered his report to Garvey on March 15, 1968 (Glass 1990:48). One of the recommendations that Garvey strongly supported was that the ACHP should take the lead in Section 106 matters and not defer to NPS. Based on the concurrence of Garvey and the council with many of the Levy report recommendations, Garvey was empowered to form an ad hoc committee to draft more formal procedures for implementing Section 106. Included on the committee were representatives of four key government agencies: the Departments of Justice, the Interior, Housing and Urban Development, and Transportation. The committee completed its recommendations in March and April 1968.

The ACHP adopted the following recommendations of the ad hoc committee at its next meeting in May 1968 (Glass 1990:49):

1. Agencies should consult the National Register in the planning stage and determine if any of their projects would affect a property by applying "criteria of effect." The criteria of effect were adapted from National Register evaluations to assess if a change in property characteristics, direct or indirect, would harm eligibility.
2. If there would be an effect, the agency should consult with the state liaison officer with jurisdiction as well as OAHP to determine if the effect would be adverse.
3. The agency should attempt to remove or significantly reduce any adverse effects through application of a "prudent and feasible **alternative**."
4. If the adverse effect could not be resolved by the agency, the matter would be referred to the ACHP for comment.
5. The ACHP would decide which cases needed council review, and the executive director would prepare a report summarizing all of the issues with the assistance of OAHP staff.

In June 1968, ACHP and OAHP staff began implementing the recommendations adopted at the May council meeting, although they realized that the procedures could not be effective until a complete list of National Register properties had been published in the *Federal Register* and the recommended Section 106 procedures had been provided to all federal agencies. OAHP staff were assigned to do both. Additionally, the NPS leadership recognized that control of ACHP staff (i.e., Garvey) by OAHP reduced the council's authority to deal with agencies. So in July 1968 Garvey was promoted within NPS to report directly to NPS director George Hartzog. In addition, a deputy director of NPS, Harthon Bill, replaced Connally as executive director of the ACHP (Glass 1990:49).

The February 25, 1969, issue of the *Federal Register* included the following items:

- A list of the 1,000 properties included in the National Register of Historic Places
- An explanation of NPS authority for the expansion of the National Register in Section 101 of the NHPA
- The National Register criteria for listing a property
- A list of state liaison officers
- The rules for receiving grants under the NHPA
- ACHP procedures for complying with Section 106 of the NHPA

36 CFR 800—1974 Version

Not much more was done to formally implement Section 106 regulations over the next three years. The implications of 1971's Executive Order 11593 stating that eligible properties should be treated the same as those listed in the NRHP for the purposes of Section 106, however, required some timely action. On March 15, 1972, the ACHP published draft "Procedures for Compliance" in the *Federal Register* (37 FR 5430) for agency and public review. Revised drafts of these procedures appeared in the July 15, 1972, February 28, 1973, and November 5, 1973, issues of the *Federal Register*. Finally, on January 25, 1974, the first regulations labeled 36 CFR 800 appeared in the *Federal Register*, converting what had been guidelines into actual administrative regulations, although these regulations were still technically non-binding as the ACHP had not yet been granted rule-making authority.

The procedures for carrying out Section 106 as outlined in the 1974 36 CFR 800 "regulations" did not vary much from the basic procedures developed by OAHP staff soon after the NHPA was passed in 1966. Agencies were responsible for identifying historic properties and assessing potential effects of their undertakings on the properties, then consulting with the ACHP as to the nature of the effects and methods to reduce adverse effects. OAHP decisions and EO 11593 changed what kinds of properties needed to be considered (eligible as well as listed), who needed to be consulted, how to assess eligibility, how to assess effects, and how to proceed if effects were adverse.

The 1974 36 CFR 800 procedures outlined the following basic process:

1. At the earliest stage of planning, the agency should identify all NRHP-listed and NRHP-eligible historic properties within the area to be impacted by an undertaking. The identification and evaluation of properties should be done in consultation with the SHPO.
2. If the agency determines a property not to be eligible, it doesn't need to consider effects to it. If the agency determines a property to be eligible, it can ask the secretary of the interior to confirm this determination. If the agency is unsure of eligibility, it can contact the secretary of the interior to determine final eligibility.
3. In consultation with the SHPO, the agency should determine effects to any listed or eligible properties. If it determines there is no adverse effect, it need only send documentation of its assessment to the ACHP. If there is an adverse effect, the agency should request comment from the ACHP, notify the SHPO, and submit a case report to the ACHP.
4. ACHP staff should review the project and prepare a memorandum of agreement (MOA) if any adverse effect can be avoided or if there is adequate mitigation of the adverse effect.
5. If the agency cannot avoid or adequately mitigate an adverse effect, the undertaking is submitted to the full body of the ACHP. The ACHP first sends comments to the agency and then to the president and Congress.

36 CFR 800—1979 Version

Two years after the release of 36 CFR 800 by the ACHP, the NHPA was amended. The 1976 amendment not only revised Section 106 to include National Register–eligible properties but granted the ACHP rule-making authority in Section 211. In March 1977, determination of eligibility criteria (36 CFR 63) were issued to assist agencies with Section 106 compliance.

On July 12, 1978, President Jimmy Carter issued a presidential memorandum with respect to environmental quality and water resources management, which required the ACHP to promulgate regulations to implement the National Historic Preservation Act by March 1, 1979. This directive and its timetable forced the ACHP to act quickly with the revision of the initial 1974 36 CFR 800 regulations. On March 1, 1979, the ACHP published a revised 36 CFR 800 in the *Federal Register*. In the September 2, 1979, *Federal Register*, the ACHP announced that the revised 36 CFR 800 regulations would go into effect on November 1, 1979.

The 1979 version of the 36 CFR 800 regulations differed from the initial 1974 regulations in a number of ways, although the basic compliance procedures remained unchanged. The regulations were somewhat rearranged and renumbered for greater clarity. The major changes were as follows:

- Section 800.2: definitions added for "consulting parties" and revised for "undertaking," "eligible property," and "area of undertaking's potential environmental impact"
- Section 800.4(a): added guidance on National Register eligibility
- Section 800.5: added SHPO responsibilities in the consulting process
- Section 800.6(d): enabled five-member panel of ACHP to act for full ACHP
- Section 800.7: added consideration of resources found during construction
- Section 800.8: added the use of programmatic agreements for classes of undertakings
- Section 800.9: revised coordination with the National Environmental Policy Act (NEPA) due to new NEPA regulations
- Section 800.11: added provision for counterpart agency regulations
- Section 800.14: added supplementary guidance option
- Section800.15: added public participation by ACHP, agencies, and SHPOs
- Various sections: added time limits for agencies, SHPOs, and the ACHP

36 CFR 800—1986 Version

The third revision of the 36 CFR 800 regulations occurred seven years after the second revision and six years after the 1980 amendments to the NHPA. The 1986 revisions were once again a response more to a presidential directive than to amended language in the law. On February 17, 1981, President Ronald Reagan issued Executive Order 12291 regarding federal regulations in general. The order was designed as part of the "Reagan Revolution" to improve the economy by streamlining or eliminating government regulation, thus reducing the burden on the private sector and decreasing government bureaucracy. The order stipulated that federal agencies minimize duplication in regulations, ensure that regulations were well reasoned, and increase agency accountability for any current or future regulations. These directives were not unique to the Reagan presidency, as President Carter had requested similar agency action in his Executive Orders 12044 ("Improving Government Regulations") and 12174 ("Federal Paperwork Reduction"). Reagan's EO 12291 revoked the two Carter EOs.

While there were no changes to the wording of Section 106 in the 1980 amendment of the NHPA, there were a number of changes in other sections that had implications for the 1986 revision of 36 CFR 800. The definition of "undertaking" had been changed in 1980 to include only government actions that had the potential to affect historic properties, while the previous definition had included all government actions. Several sections of the 1980 amendment stressed the involvement of the public and historic preservation at the local level, allowing private entities to veto nomination of their properties for the National Register, private individuals to directly nominate properties for the Register, and communities to become certified local governments (CLGs).

The 1986 revision of 36 CFR 800 included the following:

- A new definition of "undertaking" (potential to affect historic properties)
- The ability for federal agencies and SHPOs to jointly determine eligibility, and if they agreed, the secretary of the interior need not intervene
- New time frames for the process: 30 days for initial SHPO comment, 15 days for SHPO comment on agency determinations of effect, 30 days for ACHP comment on agency "no adverse effect" determinations, 30 days for ACHP

comments on MOAs, 60 days for ACHP comments on non-MOA submittals regarding effects

- Ability for the ACHP not to participate in the initial Section 106 process unless requested to do so by the agency, a SHPO, or the public
- Ability for the ACHP to declare a project in **foreclosure** if an agency failed to follow the procedures outlined in 36 CFR 800
- An increase in public participation by requiring consultation in several steps
- Additional guidance for resources discovered during construction
- Procedures for emergency situations
- Additional consideration of NHLs by requiring ACHP involvement
- Coordination with related laws—Archaeological Resources Protections Act (ARPA) and Department of Transportation Act (DOTA) Section 4(f) as well as NEPA

A 1986 ACHP publication titled "Working with Section 106" was published the same month that the new regulations took effect (October) and stressed that the keys to making 36 CFR 800 work smoothly and effectively were identification, assistance, and protection. Identification of historic properties had to be done through close agency coordination with SHPOs and carried out not only by agencies but also by communities and the private sector. Assistance was principally the responsibility of the secretary of the interior through grants-in-aid to the states and technical guidance, as well as other federal programs such as tax credits and direct grants. Protection of historic properties had to be integrated into the federal planning process and was guided by obligations specified in Sections 106 and 110 of the NHPA.

The 1986 revision of 36 CFR 800 did not greatly alter the way the Section 106 process was carried out, but it did somewhat streamline the process and provided some new methods for meeting the "consider and consult" objectives, thus fulfilling the goals of EO 12291 (Bell 1987). Better-informed agencies, a streamlined ACHP, and more fully engaged SHPOs settled back to once again implement a now familiar system of historic preservation.

Regulatory Muddle: 1992–2004

The 1992 amendment of the NHPA required revision of the 36 CFR 800 regulations mainly to include the new roles of Indian tribes in the process. While there were other significant changes to the act in the 1992 amendment, most did not impact the Section 106 process. In addition to the 1992 amendment to the NHPA done under the George H. W. Bush administration, in March 1993 the Bill Clinton administration launched a new initiative called the "National Performance Review" in an attempt to reinvent the federal bureaucracy by reforming the regulatory system and making regulations easier to understand through the use of "plain language." The revised 36 CFR 800 regulations had to serve two masters—new legislation and a presidential directive—much like the previous revisions.

To help revise 36 CFR 800, the ACHP sent out a questionnaire to over 1,000 users of the Section 106 process (e.g., agencies, SHPOs, private organizations) and held several meetings with **federal preservation officers** (FPOs) and SHPOs. Based on input from these sources, the ACHP assembled a task force to come up with draft language. The task force adopted five guidelines for the new regulations (63 FR 48580):

- Federal agencies and SHPOs should be given greater authority to conclude Section 106 reviews.

- The council should spend more time monitoring program trends and overall performance of federal agencies and SHPOs and less time reviewing individual cases or participating in case-specific consultation.
- Section 106 review requirements should be integrated with environmental review required by other statutes.
- Enforcement of Section 106 should be increased and specific remedies should be provided for failure to comply.
- There should be expanded opportunities for public involvement in the Section 106 process.

Note that none of the guidelines reference increasing the role of Indian tribes in the process, although the inclusion of tribal involvement in the Section 106 process had been the most significant change included in the 1992 NHPA amendments. On October 3, 1994, the first draft of the revised 36 CFR 800 regulations appeared in the *Federal Register* (59 FR 50396). The ACHP received over 350 comments on the draft, mainly discussing the failure to implement the task force guidelines. The council reinitiated its consultation with major 106 users and in July 1995 sent out a revised draft of the regulations to the commenters on the 1994 draft. Federal agencies made the major objections to this draft, while private industry commenters thought it was a significant improvement over the 1994 version. SHPOs expressed concerns about the ACHP turning over too much responsibility to them and expanding their role in NEPA compliance. Another revised version of the regulations, dated June 5, 1997, was circulated among stakeholders, soliciting additional comments.

On September 13, 1996, a re-revised version of the regulations appeared in the *Federal Register* (61 FR 48580–48594). The draft once again received considerable comment from federal agencies, SHPOs, private industry, and other interested parties such as the Society for American Archaeology (SAA). The ACHP went back to the drawing board, issuing "final" revised regulations on May 17, 1999, to become effective as of June 17, 1999.

When things finally appeared to be going smoothly, the ACHP began instructing agencies and SHPOs on how the new regulations worked and began preparing for the influx of tribal historic preservation officers (THPOs) who would have to be trained in the basics of Section 106 procedures. Then, on February 15, 2000, the National Mining Association filed a lawsuit objecting to several provisions in the regulations, requiring the new 36 CFR 800 regulations to be put on hold. Another lawsuit from a cell tower group followed.

On July 11, 2000, the ACHP published revised regulations based on the lawsuits. Realizing that the legal process would take some time, on September 15, 2000, the ACHP requested that the July 11 version of 36 CFR 800 be temporarily treated as a guideline and suspended the existing 36 CFR 800 rules. Then, on December 12, 2000, the ACHP once again published revised regulations in the *Federal Register* to take effect on January 11, 2001. Federal courts upheld most of these regulations but objected to two subsections: agency obligations after "no adverse effect" determinations and application of Section 106–related state or local regulations subject to federal approval. This required another revision of the regulations.

The ACHP published a notice of proposed rule making on September 25, 2003 (68 FR 55354) and then extended the deadline for comments to November 26, 2003. The final rules were published on July 6, 2004 (69 FR 40544–40555) and took effect on August 5, 2004, after almost 10 years of drafting and redrafting. These 2004 regulations for implementing Section 106 of the NHPA are still in effect.

36 CFR 800—2004 Version

The major policy changes between the 1986 and the 2004 36 CFR 800 regulations are as follows:

- ACHP deference granted to agency-SHPO decisions
- Role of the SHPOs clarified
- Agency responsibilities in identifying historic properties reinforced
- ACHP involvement in the day-to-day process restricted
- Participants' roles better defined
- Tribal and THPO roles clarified, defined, and strengthened
- Role of applicants recognized and given more flexibility
- Early compliance encouraged
- Coordination with other laws, especially NEPA, strengthened
- New procedures outlined for dealing with minor or routine cases
- Public participation clarified
- Archaeological site mitigation considered an adverse effect
- Alternate agency procedures simplified
- Flexibility in programmatic agreements increased

The 2004 regulations also made a number of procedural changes to help simplify and streamline Section 106 implementation:

- Combination of "no historic properties" and "no effect" findings
- Clarification of "undertakings" covered by the Section 106 process
- Increase in flexibility of identification and evaluation steps
- Revision of adverse effect criteria and exceptions
- Elimination of ACHP review of "no adverse effect" determinations
- Determination that failure of agency-SHPO consultation will lead to ACHP involvement
- Determination that head of federal agency must consider ACHP comment provisions
- Clarification of ACHP review of agency findings
- Revision of emergency and inadvertent discovery situations to include assessment of National Register eligibility
- Enhancement of ACHP monitoring of overall Section 106 performance
- Revision of the role of invited signatories
- Modification of documentation standards
- Increase in agency flexibility in tribal consultation on nationwide agreements
- Introduction of the concept of **scope** similar to that in NEPA
- Phased identification of historic properties

Before I proceed with a description and analysis of the current Section 106 process, it is important to first discuss what consideration and consultation mean for the purposes of Section 106, as "consider" and "consult" are the two basic action words of the Section 106 process.

What Is Consideration?

"Consideration" is not defined in the NHPA or in the 36 CFR 800 regulations. It is not discussed in any major cultural resource management (CRM) or historic preservation textbooks. It's one of those words whose meaning the ACHP, agencies, and practitioners assume is so basic and so universally understood that it needs no definition or discussion. Yet it encapsulates everything an agency must do with respect to its obligations under Section 106. An agency must consider not only the impacts of its actions on historic properties but also outside opinions on those actions resulting from consultation.

Consideration of historic properties in the NHPA is more than just the consideration of undertakings required by Section 106. In 54 USC 302304 (old Section 101; 16 USC 470ab3), SHPOs are required to ensure that historic properties are "taken into *consideration* at all levels of planning and development." Under 302505, the secretary of the interior is supposed to develop a program for Indian tribes that will "ensure that all types of historic property and all public interests in historic property are given due *consideration*." Under 306102, federal agencies are required to develop preservation programs that ensure that historic properties under their control are "managed and maintained in a way that *considers* their historic, archaeological, architectural, and cultural values" as well as gives "full *consideration* in planning" to historic properties not under their control but potentially affected by their actions. Under 306131, agencies also need to "*consider* the particular skills and expertise need[ed] for the preservation of a historic property."

Within the 36 CFR 800 regulations, "consider" or "consideration" is used in every section except Section 800.12 ("Emergency Situations") and Section 800.13 ("Post-review Discoveries"). Yet Section 106 requires that agencies must consider actions done in emergencies and with regard to postreview discoveries. The Federal Emergency Management Agency (FEMA) has produced detailed guidelines titled "Integrating Historic Property and Cultural Resource Considerations into Hazard Mitigation Planning" (FEMA 2005). Postreview discoveries are a standard stipulation in Section 106 agreement documents.

Although "consideration" is not defined in 36 CFR 800, some clues as to what the word means to the ACHP can be found throughout the regulations. In 800.1 we find "consideration of alternatives" and "consideration during planning." In 800.2, SHPOs should ensure historic property "consideration at all levels of planning and development," agencies "shall seek and consider the views of the public," and agencies should "consider in their decision-making" the views of tribes and the public. Under 800.4, agencies shall "consider other applicable professional, State, tribal, and local laws, standards, and guidelines." In 800.5 agencies "shall consider any views" concerning effects to historic properties that have been provided by consulting parties or the public. Under 800.8, agencies should include "consideration of project alternatives in the NEPA process."

There are many meanings of "consideration" in dictionaries. Legal definitions focus on contracts where one party agrees to give something of value to another party in exchange for agreeing to some action. Business definitions focus on monetary compensation in exchange for providing a service. Standard dictionary definitions of consideration usually contain a number of common phrases or synonyms: continuous and careful thought, taking into account, being sympathetic, deliberation, evaluation of facts, evaluation of consequences, keeping something in mind when making a decision.

If we combine selected dictionary definitions of "consideration" with how it is used in the NHPA and the 36 CFR 800 regulations, I suggest the following definition:

> Consideration means an agency will fulfill its NHPA obligations by taking into account the full range of potential effects to historic properties in all phases of agency planning, decision making, project implementation, and consultation. This consideration will be carried out in a thoughtful, careful, and continuous manner.

What Is Consultation?

"Consultation" is one of two key words in Section 106 (an agency must consider and consult). The word "consult" is found in some form on every page and in every section of the 36 CFR 800 regulations. The regulations in 800.16(f) provide this definition:

> *Consultation* means the process of seeking, discussing, and considering the views of other participants, and, where feasible, seeking agreement with them regarding matters arising in the section 106 process. The Secretary's "Standards and Guidelines for Federal Agency Preservation Programs Pursuant to the National Historic Preservation Act" provide further guidance on consultation.

With regard to the Section 106 process, the purpose of consultation is straightforward and focused as stated in 800.1(a):

> The goal of consultation is to identify historic properties potentially affected by the undertaking, assess its effects and seek ways to avoid, minimize or mitigate any adverse effects on historic properties.

The regulations specify throughout when and with whom consultation must be done, but with regard to consultation in general for the purposes of Section 106, 800.2(a)(4) states,

> The agency official shall involve the consulting parties described in paragraph (c) of this section in findings and determinations made during the section 106 process.

Almost all of the guidance on consultation available online and in heritage management publications, even that provided by the ACHP, focuses on tribal consultation. Yet required and recommended consultation is broad and deep in 36 CFR 800. The secretary of the interior's standards guidance on consultation cited in the 36 CFR 800 definition above begins with "General Principles" before describing tribal consultation. Standard 5 of this guidance is "An agency consults with knowledgeable and concerned parties outside the agency about its historic preservation related activities." Thus consultation by federal agencies is done for more than just Section 106 purposes and certainly includes groups other than tribes.

This consultation standard and the guidance recommended by the secretary of the interior are based on Section 110 of the National Historic Preservation Act rather than Section 106 and are aimed specifically at federal agencies, as they have the principal responsibility for consultation throughout the process. Section 106 consultation, however, includes a few instances in which initiation of or responsibility for consultation is not vested with the federal agency. In 800.2(c)(4), applicants (e.g., developers) can consult directly with the SHPO/THPO if the agency approves. In 800.6(c)(8), signatories of memoranda of agreement need to consult with each other if one of the parties wants to terminate participation in the MOA. In 800.8(a)(2), consulting parties, tribes, and individuals can initiate consultation with agencies for the purposes of NEPA integration with Section 106. In 800.14(d)(3), the ACHP has to consult with SHPOs/THPOs and tribes about proposed standard treatments.

The *Secretary of the Interior's Standards and Guidelines for Federal Agency Historic Preservation Programs Pursuant to the National Historic Preservation Act* were published in the *Federal Register* on April 24, 1998. The guidelines under the consultation standard (Standard 5) begin with language identical to the 36 CFR 800 definition and then include a basic principle:

Consultation means the process of seeking, discussing, and considering the views of others, and, where feasible, seeking agreement with them on how historic properties should be identified, considered, and managed. Consultation is built upon the exchange of ideas, not simply providing information.

The guidelines go on to instruct that, whether consulting on a specific project or on broader agency programs, the agency should

- make its interests and constraints clear at the beginning;
- make clear any rules, processes, or schedules applicable to the consultation;
- acknowledge others' interests and seek to understand them;
- develop and consider a full range of options;
- try to identify solutions that will leave all parties satisfied.

As specifically applied to Section 106, the guidelines go on to state,

Consultation should be undertaken early in the planning stage of any Federal action that might affect historic properties. Although time limits may be necessary on specific transactions carried out in the course of consultation (e.g., the time allowed to respond to an inquiry), there should be no hard-and-fast time limit on consultation overall. Consultation on a specific undertaking should proceed until agreement is reached or until it becomes clear to the agency that agreement cannot be reached.

Remember that consultation does not require an agency to implement what consulting parties suggest, just as Section 106 does not require agencies to preserve historic properties their undertakings affect. The regulations require agencies to consult broadly and agree with consulting parties "when feasible." Consultation should occur early and often and be respectful and honest. Agency officials should go into consultation with an open mind and maintain that open-mindedness throughout the process.

It is beyond the scope of this book and certainly this chapter to provide an in-depth analysis of consultation. Consultation should be done for almost every aspect of heritage management, not just that required in the Section 106 process. Further discussion of consultation as it specifically applies to tribes will be presented in chapter 13.

How the 36 CFR 800 Process Works

The 36 CFR 800 regulations are divided into three lettered subparts (A–C), 16 sections, and an appendix. Subpart A describes the purposes of Section 106 in Section 800.1 and process participants in Section 800.2. Subpart B outlines the standard process in 11 sections (800.3–800.13). Subpart C contains federal agency program alternatives (Section 800.14), a section (800.15) reserved for state and local program alternatives (not yet completed), and a "Definitions" section (800.16). Appendix A describes when the ACHP gets involved in the review of individual undertakings.

Under "Section 106 Assistance for Users," the ACHP webpage provides considerable helpful guidance for agencies, SHPOs/THPOs, undertaking applicants, and the public. This guidance includes overviews of the entire process, integration with NEPA, working with tribes, writing agreement documents, and the review of a few particular types of projects such as affordable housing construction and shale gas development.

ACHP guidance has greatly proliferated since the expansion of the World Wide Web and the coincidental reduction of day-to-day ACHP Section 106 interaction brought about by the 1992 NHPA amendment. Prior to this, Section 106 guidance was limited to a few printed documents produced by the ACHP in the 1980s, such as *A Five-Minute Look at Section 106 Review* and the more detailed *Working with Section 106*. The second document included a flowchart with four major Section 106 phases: (1) identification/evaluation of historic properties, (2) assessment of effects, (3) consultation, and (4) council comment.

ACHP Flowchart

A standard way to understand the basics of how Section 106 should be implemented through the process detailed in 36 CFR 800 is to look at the current flowchart provided on the ACHP webpage (Figure 6.1). Like earlier ACHP flowcharts, the left-hand column of this chart divides the Section 106 process into four basic phases, although the current phase titles are quite different from those in earlier versions. The new phases involve project initiation, property identification, effect assessment, and resolution. A possible fifth phase, failure to agree, is also present, although this rarely happens.

The right-hand column describes the agency actions (often called *findings*) based on results of the steps under the four phases. The right-hand column for the possible failure-to-agree phase describes the ACHP action. At the bottom of the chart is a short table noting "Key Elements of the Section 106 Process," which includes the role of participants, involving the public, consultation, and documentation. On the ACHP webpage, the flowchart is accompanied by explanatory text, with elements of the flowchart linked to the explanatory material. The explanations are usually the actual language from the pertinent 36 CFR 800 regulation section but occasionally include some helpful guidance.

The ACHP flowchart has a number of problems, however. First, the right-hand column indicates when you have completed the Section 106 process, but the first two phases include multiple steps. One might infer that all of the steps in each phase have to be completed in order to be done with the process (go right on the chart in Figure 6.1) or move to the next phase (go down on the chart). This is not necessarily the case in practice.

In order to better explain the Section 106 process as it is usually—or at least could be—practiced, I have created my own flowchart as shown in Figure 6.2. In both flowcharts I refer to the major action categories as phases that correspond to section numbers in 36 CFR 800 (e.g., 800.3, 800.4). I refer to the subcategories within these phases differently in the two flowcharts. In the ACHP flowchart (Figure 6.1), I call these subcategories "subphases," while in my flowchart (Figure 6.2), I call these subcategories "steps."

In the first phase, "Initiate Section 106 Process," if the agency determines in the first subphase that its action is not an undertaking or has no potential to affect historic properties, it is indeed done. In the second phase, "Identify Historic Properties," the first subphase (determine scope of efforts) actually consists of four steps (shown in Figure 6.2 as Steps 5–8). If, in the second subphase of phase 2 (review existing information about historic properties), the agency determines there is little potential for effects on historic properties, the process ends, and there is no need to complete any of the additional substeps or steps. The process could also end after the third subphase in the ACHP's Phase 2 "Identify Historic Properties" (800.4[b]) if nothing potentially eligible is found, but this is not specified in the regulations.

Second, the ACHP flowchart does not tell us when or with whom to do consultation. Consultation is critical to the Section 106 process. Along with consideration, it is one of the two key processes in Section 106 (the actual language states the agency must provide "a reasonable opportunity to comment," which is implemented

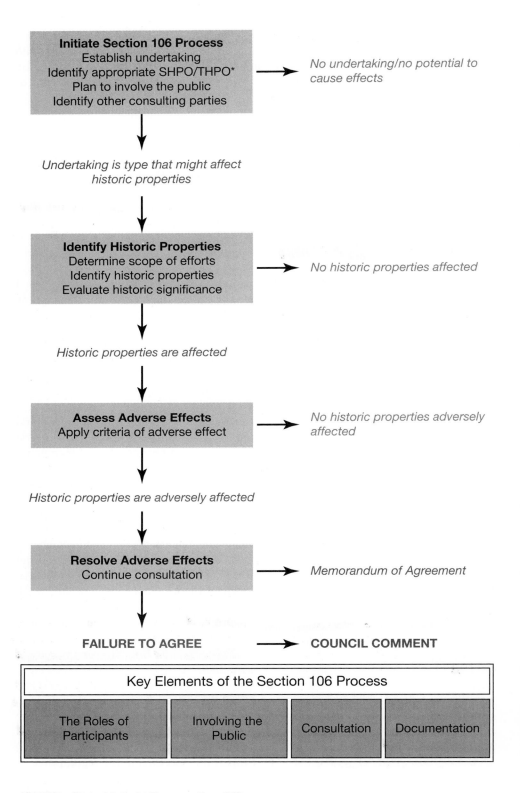

Initiate Section 106 Process
Establish undertaking
Identify appropriate SHPO/THPO*
Plan to involve the public
Identify other consulting parties

→ *No undertaking/no potential to cause effects*

Undertaking is type that might affect historic properties

Identify Historic Properties
Determine scope of efforts
Identify historic properties
Evaluate historic significance

→ *No historic properties affected*

Historic properties are affected

Assess Adverse Effects
Apply criteria of adverse effect

→ *No historic properties adversely affected*

Historic properties are adversely affected

Resolve Adverse Effects
Continue consultation

→ *Memorandum of Agreement*

FAILURE TO AGREE ⟶ **COUNCIL COMMENT**

Key Elements of the Section 106 Process			
The Roles of Participants	Involving the Public	Consultation	Documentation

*SHPO - State Historic Preservation Officer
*THPO - Tribal Historic Preservation Officer
FIG. 6.1 Advisory Council on Historic Preservation Section 106 flowchart (ACHP).

Phases and Steps in the Section 106 Process

Phase 1 – Initiate Section 106 Process (800.3)

Step 1 – *Establish Undertaking* (800.3a–b)

    <u>End of Process Option</u> – No undertaking/no potential to cause effects (800.3a)

Step 2 – *Identify the Appropriate SHPO/THPO* (800.3c–d)

Step 3 – *Plan to Involve the Public* (800.3e)

Step 4 – *Identify Other Consulting Parties* (800.3f–g)

Phase 2 – Determine APE and Identify Historic Properties in APE (800.4)

Step 5 – *Determining and Documenting the Area of Potential Effects* (800.4a)

Step 6 – *Reviewing Existing Information about Historic Properties* (800.4a)

    <u>End of Process Option</u> – No undertaking/no potential to cause effects (800.3a)

Step 7 – *Seeking Information from Parties Likely to Have Knowledge of or Concerns about the Area* (800.4a)

Step 8 – *Gathering Information from Indian Tribes and Native Hawaiian Organizations about Properties to which They Attach Religious and Cultural Significance* (800.4a)

Step 9 – *Identify Historic Properties* (800.4b)

    <u>End of Process Option</u> - No historic properties affected (not in regs; see 800.5b)

Step 10 – *Evaluate Historic Significance* (800.4c)

    <u>End of Process Option</u> - No historic properties affected (800.4d)

Phase 3 – Assess Adverse Effects (800.5)

Step 11 – *Apply Criteria of Adverse Effect* (800.5a–c)

    <u>End of Process Option</u> - No historic properties adversely affected (800.5d)

Phase 4 – Resolve Adverse Effects (800.6)

Step 12 – *Continue Consultation and Execute Memorandum of Agreement* (800.6a)

    <u>End of Process Option</u> - Memorandum of Agreement Enactment (800.6b–c)

Phase 5 – Failure to Agree (800.7)

Step 13 – *Failure to Resolve Adverse Effects* (800.7)

    <u>End of Process Option</u> - Council Comment (800.7a–c)

FIG. 6.2 Author-devised flowchart of the Section 106 process as discussed in this book.

through consultation). There are places where consultation is mandatory and places where it is prudent. In some steps, all consulting parties are involved; in others, just the SHPO/THPO and/or tribes are involved.

Third, it would also be helpful to know deadlines for actions by the agency, by the ACHP, and by the consulting parties. For instance, SHPOs/THPOs have 30 days to respond to the agency after receipt of an initial agency request for undertaking review. These deadlines are critical to all parties concerned. In many cases, if the deadlines aren't met, the agency can proceed with the undertaking without consulting party comment, although the agency still has the responsibility to take the proper action according to the regulations and to make a reasonable and good faith effort to identify historic properties. The ACHP webpage provides additional guidance on time limits in the Section 106 process in a memo dated January 25, 2018.

Finally, some of the phase headings in the ACHP Section 106 chart are misleading or repeat one of several steps contained within the phase. Under the second phase, "Identify Historic Properties," the first subphase is "Determine scope of efforts," which logically belongs under the first phase, "Initiate Section 106 Process," or could be considered a stand-alone phase. Both options would be more in tune with NEPA and many agency project-planning processes, in which scoping plays an important part. Under the "Identify Historic Properties" phase, the second step is "Identify historic properties," and the third step is "Evaluate historic significance." The use of "identification" in the phase title implies both finding all potentially eligible properties in the APE and evaluating their significance to see if they are indeed historic properties. Yet "identify historic properties" also appears in subphase two of this phase in the ACHP flowchart, where it implies just finding potentially eligible properties because it is followed by "evaluate historic significance." This is confusing.

Doing Section 106 Phase by Phase and Step by Step

Due to the inconsistencies and issues with the phases listed in the ACHP flowchart, I have chosen to stress the discrete steps in the Section 106 process and to number them sequentially for the process as a whole rather than by phase (Figure 6.2). I have listed the steps under the phase names as they appear in the flowchart and the regulations. The use of sequentially numbered steps allows a clearer understanding of the process and presents agency options for ending the Section 106 process when these opportunities actually occur after the completion of a particular step.

Before I begin an overview of the step-by-step process, it will be helpful to provide the definitions in the 36 CFR 800 regulations for "agency" and "historic property," two terms that apply to every step in the process. The critical definitions of "consideration" and "consultation" have already been presented. Other important definitions will appear when applicable to a particular step.

> *Agency*, as defined in 5 USC 551: means each authority of the Government of the United States, whether or not it is within or subject to review by another agency, but does not include (A) the Congress; (B) the courts of the United States; (C) the governments of the territories or possessions of the United States; (D) the government of the District of Columbia; or except as to the requirements of section 552 of this title; (E) agencies composed of representatives of the parties or of representatives of organizations of the parties to the disputes determined by them; (F) courts martial and military commissions; (G) military authority exercised in the field in time of war or in occupied territory; or (H) functions conferred by sections 1738, 1739, 1743, and 1744 of title 12;

subchapter II of chapter 471 of title 49; or sections 1884, 1891–1902, and former section 1641(b)(2), of title 50, appendix.

Historic property means any prehistoric or historic district, site, building, structure, or object included in, or eligible for inclusion in, the National Register of Historic Places maintained by the Secretary of the Interior. This term includes artifacts, records, and remains that are related to and located within such properties. The term includes properties of traditional religious and cultural importance to an Indian tribe or Native Hawaiian organization and that meet the National Register criteria.

Phase 1: Initiate Section 106 Process
Step 1: Establish Undertaking
What the regulations say:

800.3(a) Establish undertaking. The agency official shall determine whether the proposed Federal action is an undertaking as defined in § 800.16(y) and, if so, whether it is a type of activity that has the potential to cause effects on historic properties.

To understand this step, it is critical to know the definition of "undertaking" as it appears in 36 CFR 800.16(y):

Undertaking means a project, activity, or program funded in whole or part under the direct or indirect jurisdiction of a Federal agency, including those carried out by or on behalf of a Federal agency; those carried out with Federal financial assistance; and those requiring a Federal permit, license, or approval.

Unlike for NEPA, in determining if an action is an undertaking there are no formal **categorical exclusions** under the standard way (Subpart B) of doing Section 106, although agencies can develop lists as to what they consider to be nonundertakings. Under Subpart C, "Program Alternatives" (800.14[c]), an agency can propose a program or category of undertakings that may be exempt from normal review.

With regard to undertakings, *projects* are the easiest to understand and often have the most obvious and substantial effects for historic properties. Projects usually involve construction or demolition. A highway construction project would be an undertaking if it was receiving any federal funding from the Federal Highway Administration (FHWA).

An *activity* is any type of federal action that could have an impact on historic properties; the root of "activity" is "action," but the action is often by someone other than the agency. If a county highway project involved wetland filling, the US Army Corps of Engineers (COE) would have to *issue* a Section 404 permit, and if the highway project involved US Forest Service (USFS) land, the Forest Service would have to *grant* permission. Permitting and granting permission are both federal actions, and so both are undertakings for the purposes of Section 106.

If multiple federal conditions were met for a single project, each federal agency would decide if the project required Section 106 review as one of *its* undertakings, and one of the agencies might decide to take a lead role in guiding the project through Section 106 review. In the case of a federally funded highway project, this would normally be FHWA as its funding involves the entire project, while a COE permit and USFS land may only involve small portions of the larger project.

It is difficult to find a definition of *program* specifically with respect to Section 106 undertakings. A "federal program" is generally defined as "an organized set of activities directed toward a common purpose or goal that an agency undertakes or proposes to carry out its responsibilities" (General Accounting Office 2005:79). An example of a federal program subject to Section 106 would be the Federal Emergency Management Agency's Flood Mitigation Assistance Grant Program to remove private residences from floodplains, which can result in historic buildings being demolished or archaeological sites being disturbed.

Agency implementation: If an agency action could be defined as an undertaking but has no potential to affect any historic properties, the agency does not have to go through any additional steps of the Section 106 process, and it does not have to document this decision for external review. In addition, the agency may have developed alternative procedures approved by the ACHP that allow it to proceed in a manner not outlined in the remainder of the flowchart.

A few federal agencies may pass their Section 106 review responsibilities to a nonfederal agency for repetitive and frequent projects managed by that agency. This is called *delegation.* The nonfederal agency may or may not be defined as the *applicant* under Section 106. In most cases these transfers are to state agencies, such as when FHWA delegates its 106 responsibilities within a particular state to a state department of transportation. Housing and Urban Development can designate city housing authorities as its representative for doing Section 106 on certain HUD-funded projects in their city, such as those financed by Community Development Block Grants.

Consultation: Determining whether an action is an undertaking is exclusively a federal agency's decision, requiring no formal consultation with anyone, although the agency may ask for advice from the ACHP or from a SHPO/THPO.

Timing: This is not applicable, as an undertaking does not enter the Section 106 process until after an agency has decided that Section 106 indeed applies. An agency may even postpone a project if it anticipates Section 106 issues that it is currently unprepared to deal with, as long as the postponement purpose isn't to allow for a non-agency-reviewed action to change the condition of a historic property prior to the initiation of Section 106 review.

End-of-process option: no undertaking/no potential to cause effects: Although the ACHP flowchart and its explanation seem to imply that you have to minimally finish all of the steps in Phase 1 of the Section 106 process, under 800.3(a)(1) the agency is done with the 106 process if at the end of Step 1 it concludes that an undertaking has no potential to affect a historic property. This conclusion should not be based solely on a visual inspection of the project area or site locational modeling, as most archeological sites, cultural landscapes, and traditional cultural properties (TCPs) are not apparent to casual inspection. Site locational models are subject to varying degrees of error based on changing environmental conditions, imperfectly understood settlement patterns, and poorly known historic contexts. The agency should maintain written documentation of why the "no potential" conclusion was reached, but it does not have to inform any external entity of this decision or send out documentation supporting it.

Issues/observations: During this first step, agencies should also begin coordinating Section 106 compliance with other environmental review statutes and procedures, in particular NEPA and, if it is a transportation project, DOTA Section 4(f). This coordination is completely at the discretion of the agency, requires no external consultation, does not follow a strict timetable, and does not have to be documented.

Step 2: Identify the Appropriate SHPO/THPO

What the regulations say:

> 800.3(c): As part of its initial planning, the agency official shall determine the appropriate SHPO or SHPOs to be involved in the section 106 process. The

agency official shall also determine whether the undertaking may occur on or affect historic properties on any tribal lands and, if so, whether a THPO has assumed the duties of the SHPO. The agency official shall then initiate consultation with the appropriate officer or officers.

The definitions of "agency," "SHPO," and "THPO" are in the "Definitions" section of 36 CFR 800 but are all fairly obvious, so they don't need repeating here. The definition of "tribal lands" does require presenting, as it is more complicated:

Tribal Lands means all lands within the exterior boundaries of any Indian reservation and all dependent Indian communities.

Agency implementation: This step seems fairly simple when it comes to identifying the appropriate SHPO, as an agency certainly knows what state the undertaking is in. If the undertaking is in multiple states, the involved SHPOs may designate a lead SHPO to act for all of them or have the National Conference of State Historic Preservation Officers act for them. If multiple federal agencies are involved in an undertaking, they can designate a **lead agency** to handle consultation with a SHPO or group of SHPOs. In some cases, property owners within an Indian reservation may request that the SHPO also be involved in the Section 106 process. A THPO may also request SHPO involvement in individual undertakings on his or her reservation.

Identifying the appropriate THPO is more complicated. The 1992 amendments allowed THPOs to assume any and all SHPO responsibilities within their tribal lands. The agency must determine if the undertaking could affect historic properties within an Indian reservation and, if so, if the tribe has an NPS-certified THPO that has assumed Section 106 responsibilities from the SHPO.

As of the end of January 2017, there were 171 THPOs in 30 states. The great majority of these THPOs are in states west of the Mississippi River, because tribes were typically removed from most eastern states rather than provided reservations as Euro-American settlement progressed west. Only 36 of 567 federally recognized tribes are east of the Mississippi River; of these, 33 have THPOs. Alaska has 229 tribes, but only 1 THPO. California has 110 tribes and 35 THPOs. Other states with relatively large numbers of tribes and THPOs are Oklahoma (38/19), Washington (29/15), New Mexico (23/11), and Arizona (21/7). Multiple federal agencies have maps and lists of tribal reservations on their webpages. The National Association of Tribal Historic Preservation Officers (NATHPO) has up-to-date lists of THPOs with their addresses on its webpage, as do many SHPOs for THPOs in their state.

If a federally recognized tribe does not have a certified THPO or its THPO has not assumed Section 106 duties, the agency is still required to consult with the tribe if the undertaking is within the boundaries of the reservation or within an area of tribal interest outside the reservation, but that consultation is only legally required to begin in the second major section of the 106 regulations under "Identify Historic Properties." There is no requirement to consult tribes that are only state recognized or that reside in other countries even if they used to live in the United States. Such groups cannot have federally recognized THPOs.

With regard to tribal lands, what are "exterior boundaries" of reservations and "dependent Indian communities"? Definitions of these terms are not included in 36 CFR 800.16 or in the NHPA. It is difficult to find a definition of "exterior boundaries," but it is clear from various statutes and discussions that exterior boundaries are the legally recognized limits of an Indian reservation as established by Congress, by a ratified treaty, or by executive order. Tribes or tribal individuals may only own a small fraction of the land inside the exterior boundaries of a reservation. In many cases, most of the land within a reservation may not be held in trust by the federal government (i.e., technically federal land), but all of the land within the exterior boundaries of a reservation is subject to THPO authority for the purposes of Section 106.

Tribes may also own land outside reservation exterior boundaries, but this land is not always subject to THPO authority under Section 106. It is subject to THPO authority if it is considered tribal land of a "dependent Indian community." The 1998 US Supreme Court decision in *Alaska v. Native Village of Venetie Tribal Government* (522 U.S. 520) held that "dependent Indian communities" refers to a limited category of Indian lands that are neither reservations nor allotments and that must satisfy two requirements: first, they must have been set aside by the federal government for the use of the Indians as Indian land; second, they must be under federal superintendence. This does not include individual tribal allotments that are held in trust outside reservation boundaries, a sore point among many tribes, as the definition of "tribal lands" for the purposes of Section 106 differs from the federal definition of "Indian Country." Additional information on tribes, tribal lands, and THPOs is presented in chapter 13.

In order to determine if tribal lands are involved, most federal agencies and their state or local counterparts begin with state landownership records or reservation maps available online from the Bureau of Indian Affairs (http://www.bia.gov/cs/groups/public/documents/text/idc013422.pdf). They will then need to determine exact boundaries using state or county landownership records, which are increasingly available online.

Consultation: Under 800.3(c) the agency is required to "initiate" consultation with the appropriate SHPO and/or THPO once an undertaking has been established. The consultation usually begins with formal SHPO/THPO notification by the agency in the form of a letter or email requesting SHPO/THPO review. The notice needs to be accompanied by a detailed description of the project and the nature of federal involvement subject to Section 106. If tribal lands are involved and the tribe does not have a THPO that has assumed Section 106 responsibilities, the agency is required to consult directly with the tribe and also with the SHPO.

Timing: The SHPO/THPO has 30 calendar days to respond to the agency with his or her review, with a request for additional information in order to carry out a review, or with a recommendation for survey and evaluation. If the SHPO/THPO fails to respond in any way within 30 days or responds that no further review by him or her is required, the agency can either go to the next step in the process on its own or directly consult with the ACHP. The SHPO/THPO can still reenter the Section 106 process at any time if it is still active.

End-of-process option: There is no end-of-process option listed in 800.3(c–d).

Issues/observations: The 30-day clock can be reset each time a SHPO/THPO reasonably requests additional information if the previous information received from an agency is indeed insufficient to complete a project review. This is one of the indirect powers granted to SHPOs/THPOs and ultimately to the ACHP in 36 CFR 800: the ability to delay or slow down the implementation of an undertaking through reasonable additional-information requests.

It seems rather senseless to continue the process if the agency, the SHPO/THPO, an involved tribe, and the ACHP all agree at the end of this step that there is no need to continue the process. Why "plan to involve the public" (Step 3) and "identify other consulting parties" when the appropriate experts and the major consulting parties have jointly determined that an undertaking has little or no potential to affect historic properties? Thus, there should be an end-of-process option at this point in the regulations.

Step 3: Plan to Involve the Public

What the regulations say:

> 800.3(e) Plan to involve the public. In consultation with the SHPO/THPO, the agency official shall plan for involving the public in the section 106 process. The agency official shall identify the appropriate points for seeking public input and for notifying the public of proposed actions, consistent with § 800.2(d).

Agency implementation: This step does not mean a formal plan has to be prepared, although doing this may streamline the public consultation process and clearly document that the agency actually completed the step. A formal plan is also a good idea if the undertaking is large or has high potential to be controversial. For these large, complex, and potentially controversial projects, some agencies will have a public information page on their websites outlining how the public can provide input.

Consultation: No consultation with any external entity is required in this step, although SHPO/THPO consultation and assistance may be advisable.

Timing: The regulations infer this step has to be completed before the agency issues a Section 106 finding for an undertaking, but there is no set timetable.

End-of-process option: Not applicable.

Issues/observations: As noted above, why complete "a plan to involve the public" when the major consulting parties have jointly determined that an undertaking has little or no potential to affect historic properties? Promoting early public involvement is one of the big differences of Section 106 as opposed to environmental review under NEPA or DOTA 4(f).

Step 4: Identify Other Consulting Parties

What the regulations say:

> 800.3(f) Identify other consulting parties. In consultation with the SHPO/THPO, the agency official shall identify any other parties entitled to be consulting parties and invite them to participate as such in the section 106 process. The agency official may invite others to participate as consulting parties as the section 106 process moves forward.

The regulations go on to specifically note the participation of local governments, applicants, Indian tribes, and, through "written requests," individuals and organizations as consulting parties. With regard to Indian tribes, the regulations under 800.3(f)(2) say that "the agency official shall make *a reasonable and good faith effort* to identify" tribes, but it does not use this language as it applies to identifying other consulting parties.

Agency implementation: The parties to be identified in this step include organizations and individuals with the right to be formally identified as consulting parties under Section 106. This could include Indian tribes, city and county governments, applicants for federal assistance, and private historic preservation organizations. As with Step 3, no formal document is required for Step 4, but documentation of some type may be needed later in the process to demonstrate a concerted effort was indeed made by the agency to identify consulting parties. It also may be advisable to combine the results of Steps 2, 3, and 4 together in a single document that outside parties can review to evaluate appropriateness or completeness before proceeding with steps that require their consultation.

Consultation: This is the second step where the agency is required to consult with an outside party, once again the SHPO/THPO. This step is potentially the most complicated and time-consuming of the four steps in the first phase of Section 106 review, as many obscure individual groups could have an interest in a particular undertaking. This is why the agency is required to consult the SHPO/THPO during this step as he or she may be aware of most of these groups.

Timing: The regulations infer this step has to be completed before the agency issues a Section 106 finding for an undertaking, but there is no set timetable for identifying other consulting parties after the agency has determined that it has an undertaking subject to Section 106 review.

End-of-process option: The ACHP flowchart (Figure 6.1) implies that when this step has been completed, the agency can issue a "no undertaking/no potential to cause effects" finding, providing these conditions have indeed been met and all four steps of 800.3 have been completed. This finding is usually sent by letter to all of the consulting parties, although the regulations do not specify this.

Issues/observations: The first phase of the Section 106 process overall is usually the quickest and easiest to complete. An experienced agency official should be able to rapidly determine if an undertaking holds potential to affect any historic properties and, if it does, to rapidly identify all the mandatory parties that need to be consulted and develop a plan to involve the public. An agency should be able to complete these steps internally in a day or two, although responses from the consulting parties may take weeks to arrive.

Although the Step 4 guidance doesn't say so, agencies should determine if any National Historic Landmarks are in a project vicinity, as any undertaking adverse effects to NHLs will eventually require ACHP involvement and thus add the ACHP as another consulting party. Any agency official can easily identify NHLs by simply looking at the list of NHLs on the NPS website (https://www.nps.gov/nhl/find/intro.htm). There are currently just over 2,500 NHLs, but most states have fewer than 50. My state of Minnesota has only 25, which is about median. New York has the most with 270 and North Dakota the fewest with 7.

Mandatory ACHP involvement in the Section 106 process is discussed in Appendix A of 36 CFR 800. ACHP involvement is automatically triggered by adverse effects in certain instances besides NHLs (e.g., rare, large numbers of eligible properties in the APE), by undertakings that present important questions of policy or interpretation (e.g., foreclosure, anticipatory demolition), by undertakings that have the potential for major procedural problems (e.g., great public controversy), or by undertakings involving significant concerns to tribes (e.g., Dakota Access Pipeline). It is prudent for an agency to consider any of these potential problems early in the Section 106 process and consult the ACHP, although most issues, other than those related to NHLs and tribes, only become apparent after the identification phase. Agencies or SHPOs/THPOs can also request ACHP involvement anytime during the process.

Phase 2: Determine APE and Identify Historic Properties in the APE

If a federal undertaking might have potential to affect historic properties, the second phase of the Section 106 process begins once the agency has identified the consulting parties and can discuss with them its plans to involve the public. Phase 2 in the ACHP flowchart involves three steps—determining the scope of efforts, identifying historic properties, and evaluating significance—although the first step in Phase 2 actually involves four substeps. I treat these substeps as separate steps in this outline.

In the ACHP flowchart, the first step of this phase is labeled "Determine Scope of the Identification Efforts," which has four discrete substeps. The first substep is labeled "Determine and Document the Area of Potential Effects [APE]." As King (2013:121) points out, the ACHP borrowed the concept of scoping from the NEPA process, and it first appeared in the 36 CFR 800 regulations after 1992. "Scope" is not defined in the "Definitions" section of 36 CFR 800, and its meaning is not discussed in the Section 106 flowchart explanatory material. The NEPA regulations (40 CFR 1508.25) defined "scope" as "the range of actions, alternatives, and impacts to be considered in an environmental impact statement."

Scoping in NEPA takes place during the initial project review phase once a project has been designated a **major federal action** significantly affecting the quality of the human environment (see chapter 7). Scoping should logically appear in the Section 106 review process at a similar planning phase, after the project has been determined to be an undertaking, but scoping does not appear until the second phase, labeled "Identify Historic Properties." If, as inferred by the 36 CFR 800 definition of "area of potential effects," the focus is on issues involved with the scale, nature, and kinds of effects, APE determination should take place in the first phase of Section 106 review.

Yet, under Section 106, scoping includes defining the area to be impacted by an undertaking, conducting a literature search to see what historic properties are known to exist in the area, and doing some preliminary consultation with various groups to discover potential historic properties not included in standard inventories. Unlike NEPA, Section 106 scoping does not need to present project alternatives, as the decision to use a preferred alternative usually has already been made by the agency. King (2013:121) states that scoping for the Section 106 process should consist of the agency examining the likely effects of a project and then discussing these effects with the consulting parties identified in the first phase of the process. Scoping thus defines the extent of actions needed for a "reasonable and good faith" identification effort as required in 36 CFR 800.4(b)(1).

Step 5: Determine and Document the Area of Potential Effects

What the regulations say:

> 800.4(a) Determine scope of identification efforts. In consultation with the SHPO/THPO, the agency official shall: (1) Determine and document the area of potential effects, as defined in § 800.16(d).

As defined in 800.16(d),

> *Area of potential effects* means the geographic area or areas within which an undertaking may directly or indirectly cause alterations in the character or use of historic properties, if any such properties exist. The area of potential effects is influenced by the scale and nature of an undertaking and may be different for different kinds of effects caused by the undertaking.

Agency implementation: This is often one of the most challenging and controversial steps in the Section 106 process. In the ACHP flowchart (Figure 6.1), this step is called "determine scope of efforts." In my chart (Figure 6.2) and the discussion that follows, I have avoided use of the word "scope" because the ACHP use of the word is generic and not consistent with its use in NEPA. The word "scoping" only appears in 36 CFR 800 with respect to NEPA coordination. As discussed in Chapter 7 under NEPA, scoping is a detailed and critical process in environmental review.

The ACHP provides no guidance on how to define an area of potential effects in the regulations or the flowchart explanatory material. Scattered APE guidance is present in a few other ACHP documents (e.g., *Section 106 Archaeology Guidance*), but there is no focused ACHP discussion dealing broadly with how an APE should be defined. Some state SHPOs and development agencies have provided guidance on APE definition (e.g., CALTRANS at http://www.dot.ca.gov/ser/vol2/ch4.pdf; South Carolina SHPO at http://shpo.sc.gov/programs/revcomp/Pages/106process.aspx#defining).

With regard to the scale, nature, and kinds of effects on historic properties, APEs include much more than *direct effects* (mostly construction related), such as grading, demolition, vibration, and building. Agencies must consider *indirect effects* (mostly postconstruction), such as changes in the setting (visual), changes in the feeling (auditory, quality of life, olfactory), changes such as zoning and taxation (economic), and impacts to traditional ways of life (cultural). Each of the discrete direct and indirect effects can result in a different boundary for an APE, so an APE can consist of multiple defined areas based on the type and significance of vicinity historic properties.

Agencies also must consider **cumulative effects**, or impacts that accumulate over time due to an undertaking's contribution to long-term changes in the character or use of a historic property. Assessing cumulative effects is complicated and controversial, so for most Section 106 reviews, agencies simply ignore them or only briefly speculate about them. Cumulative effects alone rarely result in a unique APE definition, rarely result in an adverse effect finding, and rarely require mitigation.

Area of potential effects boundaries can also vary greatly in urban versus rural settings. The concentration of historic resources is usually denser in urban areas, certainly with respect to the built environment. In rural areas, the viewshed can be considerably larger as it is not blocked by buildings and structures. A "reasonable and good faith" identification effort in an urban area is often more complicated and expensive because of the density of buildings and the difficulty of assessing below-ground archaeological resources due to access, complex ownership, and utility line issues.

APE definition by agencies usually begins with setting a minimum APE as the area directly impacted by the undertaking, or what project engineers call "the construction zone." This often ends up being the final APE for archaeological impacts. For effects to structures, buildings, landscapes, and traditional cultural properties, the viewshed of the completed project is often the APE, although considerations such as construction/postconstruction vibration impacts to structures and postconstruction noise impacts to settings must also be considered. For archaeological sites, a vertical as well as horizontal APE needs to be defined. This may also apply to potentially eligible structures located below the ground, like millrace tunnels.

Agencies should not define arbitrary APEs but can define them for certain impacts based on **programmatic agreements** (PAs) and standard procedures for projects with consistent footprints and relatively consistent environmental impacts. For example, the Federal Communications Commission (FCC), ACHP, and NCSHPO signed a programmatic agreement in 2004 that defined standard APEs for direct and visual effects for cell towers.

The APE should also include significant project-related impacts that may be quite distant from the project construction zone, such as borrow pits and temporary storage areas. As stated in 800.11, the agency must provide "sufficient documentation to enable any reviewing parties to understand its [the APE's] basis."

Consultation: The agency must consult the SHPO/THPO on APE definition.

Timing: APE definition has to be completed before the agency issues a Section 106 finding or proceeds to identification, but there is no set timetable for consultation or submittal of an initial APE to consulting parties.

End-of-process option: Not applicable.

Issues/observations: Instead of just stating that the APE is the geographical area associated with a project within which the undertaking could affect the integrity of NRHP-listed or -eligible properties, the 36 CFR 800 definition focuses on alterations to the "character or use" of historic properties. "Character" introduces a concept that mixes the NRHP definitions of "integrity" and "condition." "Use" invokes Section 4(f) of DOTA. The 36 CFR 800 definition of "area of potential effects" then focuses on issues involved with the scale, nature, and kinds of effects.

The problem with consideration of property type and significance criteria for APE definition is that this information is only known for NRHP-listed properties and previously evaluated properties when the APE is being defined early in the "Identify Historic Properties" phase. This is well before the survey and evaluation steps in this phase and even before the preliminary review of existing information and consultation with knowledgeable entities substeps in the scoping step. Thus a restrictive APE definition may not include existing but unknown historic properties well outside construction limits, properties that could indeed be impacted by an undertaking.

Most heritage management textbooks do not discuss APE definition, with the notable exception of King (2013:122–125), which devotes several pages to the topic. King advises agencies to use a NEPA-like interdisciplinary approach and not to limit APEs to just the land owned or controlled by the agency. King also presents some discussion of the topic in his June 7, 2014, *CRM Plus* blog post, in which he warns agencies not to define APEs arbitrarily, such as by using a standard numerically defined buffer zone around a project area (e.g., 100 feet). APE definition should only be based on the undertaking's short- and long-term potentials to impact historic properties of all types.

While the scale, nature, and kinds of effects are discussed in most APE guidance, there is little discussion of the kinds of historic properties that may be affected. Yet this is perhaps the most complicated issue related to defining an APE. The kinds of historic sites that may be present involve potential impacts that vary according to NRHP property type and significance criteria under which they may be eligible.

Archaeological sites eligible only under National Register Criterion D (information potential) typically have the most restricted and easily defined APEs. Because effects on Criterion D archaeological sites are limited to direct effects, the APE is usually congruent with the construction limits. Criterion D archaeological sites generally do not sustain indirect effects because impacts to setting and feeling do not impact a site's ability to yield important data. A parking lot may cover an archaeological site, but the site can still retain all of its inherent ability to yield important information (i.e., its eligibility under Criterion D).

APEs for archaeology also need to include a vertical consideration. Putting a trail over an archaeological site can have deep effects if utility lines are put below the trail or a paved trail needs a deep foundation or subgrade correction. A large fill or armored hard-surface area can have implications for future archaeological accessibility.

Landscapes, TCPs, and individual properties eligible under Criterion A or B can have the largest and most complicated APEs because National Register integrity considerations of setting and feeling are critical to their eligibility, and use can be affected by very distant actions. Farmsteads near an unpaved rural road can have their setting and feeling greatly altered if the road is paved, although no buildings or farm-related landscape features are directly impacted by the road project. Any farm-steads along the road should be in the APE, including distant features that are part of an eligible property. A public historic site can be greatly affected by the elimination of a freeway exit, changing the site's use, although the exit is not visible from it. Even if the exit is miles from the historic site, visitorship can be greatly reduced, putting the site in the exit ramp removal's project APE.

It is better for an agency to err on the side of caution when initially defining a nonarchaeological APE. The APE can be narrowed at a later stage, especially following Step 6, "Review Existing Information about Historic Properties," when research and consultation have better characterized the types and conditions of properties that may be present in the general area.

Step 6: Review Existing Information about Historic Properties

What the regulations say: After defining the APE for an undertaking, the next step is as follows:

> 800.4(a) Determine scope of identification efforts. In consultation with the SHPO/THPO, the agency official shall: . . . (2) Review existing information on historic properties within the area of potential effects, including any data concerning possible historic properties not yet identified.

Agency implementation: In the early days of Section 106, this review was limited to the agency's checking the listed properties in the NRHP. Today, basic due diligence for this step includes checking the National Register listings as well as SHPO/THPO inventories for both archaeology and history-architecture. Some states have easily accessible documentation online concerning the location and scope of previous heritage resource surveys and property inventories. Once again, the scope of a review of existing information is not specified in the ACHP flowchart explanation but is standard practice for adequate environmental review in all states and among all agencies.

If any National Historic Landmarks are within or immediately adjacent to the APE, the agency should begin consultation with the ACHP. With regard to archaeological sites, an agency could also do some site locational modeling in this substep to assess the potential for unrecorded sites.

Consultation: The agency must consult the SHPO/THPO regarding the scope of his or her review of existing information.

Timing: A Section 106 finding or an assessment of the needs of the identification and evaluation steps cannot proceed without a review of existing information about known historic properties in the APE, but there is no set timetable for consultation or submittal of an initial APE to consulting parties.

End-of-process option: A review of existing information is usually insufficient for an agency to make a Section 106 finding, unless this information determines that the APE has already been subjected to adequate surveys for historic properties or demonstrates that the APE has been altered to the extent that it is unlikely to contain historic properties of any type. Ending the process at this step would have to be thoroughly documented and justified.

Issues/observations: While most states have extensive inventories of buildings and structures, most have only minimally completed inventories of archaeological sites, historic landscapes, and TCPs. Archaeological site locations can be predicted through the use of geographic information system–based modeling, as can some TCPs if sufficient information has been gathered as to the nature and location of known sites within a region. Potential impacts to historic landscapes can be somewhat assessed using land-use changes over the past 50 years. If these changes are extensive, there may be no cultural landscapes retaining sufficient integrity left within an APE. TCPs can only be determined through intensive literature searches and consultation with communities.

Step 7: Seek Information from Parties Likely to Have Knowledge of or Concerns about the Area

What the regulations say:

> 800.4(a) Determine scope of identification efforts. In consultation with the SHPO/THPO, the agency official shall: . . . (3) Seek information, as appropriate, from consulting parties, and other individuals and organizations likely to have knowledge of, or concerns with, historic properties in the area, and identify issues relating to the undertaking's potential effects on historic properties.

Agency implementation: Such parties are usually identified through consultation with the SHPO/THPO or are familiar to agencies through other historic property review processes. Typical parties include local governments (especially those that are CLGs or have historic preservation commissions), private preservation organizations with a statewide scope, and specialized preservation organizations that have a particular interest in a specific property type (e.g., bridges, barns) that may be present in the APE. Tribes are also critical informants, but this is covered separately in Step 8.

Consultation: The agency must consult with the SHPO/THPO regarding determining parties that are likely to have knowledge of or concerns about the area of potential effects.

Timing: A Section 106 finding or an assessment of the needs of the identification and evaluation steps cannot proceed without consultation with groups or individuals likely to have knowledge or concerns about historic properties in the area of potential effects, but there is no set timetable for the consultation or submittal of an initial APE to identified consulting parties.

End-of-process option: Not applicable.

Issues/observations: Note that the wording in the regulation states that the agency should seek information "as appropriate" about specialized knowledge and particular concerns from groups or individuals that may have such knowledge and concerns. The "as appropriate" suggests to me that these groups are either very knowledgeable or have concerns about a particular area or property type. Remember that this is one of the two "reasonable and good faith" actions, at least with respect to tribes. This means that an agency should discuss this aspect in detail with SHPOs and THPOs, as well as other well-known parties (e.g., local preservation organizations) that may have pertinent information, but they don't have to do a nationwide search for interested parties.

Step 8: Gather Information from Indian Tribes and Native Hawaiian Organizations about Properties to Which They Attach Religious and Cultural Significance

What the regulations say:

> 800.4(a) Determine scope of identification efforts. In consultation with the SHPO/THPO, the agency official shall: . . . (4) Gather information from any Indian tribe or Native Hawaiian organization identified pursuant to

§ 800.3(f) to assist in identifying properties, including those located off tribal lands, which may be of religious and cultural significance to them and may be eligible for the National Register, recognizing that an Indian tribe or Native Hawaiian organization may be reluctant to divulge specific information regarding the location, nature, and activities associated with such sites. The agency official should address concerns raised about confidentiality pursuant to § 800.11(c).

Agency implementation: After the passage of the 1992 amendments, it was very difficult for agencies to assess tribal interest in traditional and religious properties outside reservation boundaries, especially for tribes in states other than the state where the undertaking, agency official, or applicant was located. To deal with the tribal consultation requirement, certain agencies, like the Department of Defense (DOD), looked at ceded lands to determine where tribes lived at the time treaties were signed. While this was helpful in identifying some tribal locations in the recent past, tribes in many areas had undergone significant voluntary and involuntary movement prior to US government acquisition of their lands. In order to reconstruct tribal locations in the more distant past, ethnographic and archaeological studies have to be examined.

Gradually tribes have come forward and made known whether they want to be consulted by various agencies reviewing undertakings in certain states or regions. Most agencies have completed enough reviews since 1992 to have a good sense of which tribes they should contact when a project takes place in a particular state or region. In addition, the NPS, through its Native American Graves Protection and Repatriation Act (NAGPRA) program, has an online database that can provide tribes to consult based on the state or county where an undertaking will occur (https://www.nps.gov/nagpra/onlinedb/index.htm).

The ACHP has considerable guidance on consulting with Indian tribes. This guidance stresses certain points:

- The regulations require federal agencies to consult with Indian tribes when they attach religious and cultural significance to a historic property regardless of the location of that property.
- The presence or absence of federally recognized Indian tribes in a particular state does not absolve the agency of its obligations to make a "reasonable and good faith" effort to identify tribes that once lived in that state and therefore may want to be consulted.
- For identification purposes, the regulations only require consultation with Indian tribes regarding properties of traditional religious and cultural importance that are listed in or have potential to be eligible for the National Register.
- The federal agency is obligated to consult with every Indian tribe that may attach significance to particular historic properties, even properties on another Indian tribe's lands.

Once an agency has identified the tribes that may be interested in a particular undertaking due to its possible effect on religious and cultural properties important to its people, an agency official sends a letter to the appropriate tribal official. If addressed to the executive officer of the tribe, the letter should come from a high-ranking official at the agency in accordance with nation-to-nation protocols. The letter should describe the project in detail, with a map of its location, and ask for the tribe's assistance in identifying properties of traditional and religious importance in or adjacent to the APE. The letter should also ask the tribal official about confidentiality concerns, noting the agency's authority specified in 800.11(c) to withhold certain kinds of information from the public.

Consultation: The agency needs to consult with a SHPO/THPO to help identify tribes that may be interested or have information. In this step, the agency formally initiates consultation with any interested or knowledgeable tribes.

Timing: A Section 106 finding or an assessment of the needs of the identification and evaluation steps cannot proceed without consultation with tribes that are likely to have knowledge or concerns about traditional or religious properties in the area of potential effects, but there is no set timetable for the consultation or submittal of an initial APE to identified tribes.

End-of-process option: Not applicable as this is a consultation initiation step.

Issues/observations: Properties to which Indians attach religious and cultural significance are usually not present in SHPO databases and may not even be listed in THPO inventories. If specific properties of this type are identified at this stage of the Section 106 process, informing the ACHP may be prudent. It is critical for the agency to be "sensitive to any concerns tribes may have about the confidentiality of this information." Tribes may not even provide exact locational information but simply state that such resources are present or immediately adjacent to the APE. Under Section 106 such properties do not have to be avoided, especially if they are determined later not to be eligible for inclusion in the NRHP, although undertakings on federal property are also subject to other laws, such as NAGPRA, ARPA, the American Indian Religious Freedom Act (AIRFA), and Executive Order 13007 (see chapter 13).

Step 9: Identify Historic Properties

What the regulations say:

> 800.4(b) Identify historic properties. Based on the information gathered under paragraph (a) of this section, and in consultation with the SHPO/THPO and any Indian tribe or Native Hawaiian organization that might attach religious and cultural significance to properties within the area of potential effects, the agency official shall take the steps necessary to identify historic properties within the area of potential effects.

Agency implementation: The regulations specify a "reasonable and good faith" *level of effort* to identify potential historic properties in the APE. This effort can include the use of background research, consultation, oral history interviews, visual inspection, and field survey, as well as consider "past planning, research and studies, the magnitude and nature of the undertaking and the degree of Federal involvement, the nature and extent of potential effects on historic properties, and the likely nature and location of historic properties within the area of potential effects." The agency is required to consult with the SHPO/THPO and tribes concerning the appropriate level of effort and their knowledge of historic properties within the APE, but the agency does not have to follow level-of-effort advice it does not deem "reasonable."

If a SHPO/THPO or tribe does recommend a particular type of survey, agencies usually follow this advice. In most cases, the agency will contract with a qualified professional consultant to undertake the survey. Once the survey report is completed, the agency will provide a copy to the SHPO/THPO and, if applicable, the tribe, along with its finding or recommendation for additional analysis.

The 2004 regulations in 800.4(b)(2) allowed for *phased identification*. This basically applies to complex projects with restricted access or large land areas where the scope of the project is initially difficult to define exactly. The phased approach allows agencies to gradually complete identification and evaluation as the undertaking evolves. No formal document is needed to implement this approach, and

SHPO/THPO approval is not required, although the agency should inform all consulting parties. Prior to the 2004 regulations, the phased identification approach could have been used but would have been subject to a programmatic agreement, an approach that is still valid.

Consultation: Consultation is required with the SHPO/THPO as well as any tribe that may attach religious or cultural significance to particular properties located within the APE. This consultation has to do with both known properties within the APE and the level of effort necessary to locate unknown properties.

Timing: As with an initial notification letter or a finding letter submitted later in the process, the SHPO/THPO has 30 days to object to or concur with an agency finding with regard to the identification of historic properties within the APE.

End-of-process option: Although the ACHP flowchart (Figure 6.1) and the 800.4(b) regulations within the identification step do not say so explicitly, if identification efforts find no properties of potential historic or archaeological significance within the APE, the agency official can terminate the Section 106 process at the end of the identification step and issue a "no historic properties affected" finding. If a thorough records search/field survey has come to this conclusion, submittal of this documentation to the SHPO/THPO should suffice to complete the Section 106 process. If any archaeological sites, elements of a nonrecent built environment, or potential TCPs were noted in the APE during identification efforts, the agency is required to assess their eligibility for the NRHP and move to the evaluation step. If, as noted under 800.5(b) for Section 106 Phase 3, "Assess Adverse Effects," the agency alters plans to avoid unevaluated or obviously eligible properties, and if the SHPO/THPO agrees, this too can result in a "no effect" finding.

Issues/observations: This step is one of two in the 36 CFR 800 regulations to use the phrase "a reasonable and good faith effort." The agency must make a reasonable and good faith effort to identify historic properties within the APE. As with APE definition, this step leads to considerable misunderstanding and confusion, so the ACHP has issued guidance on what "a reasonable and good faith effort" means with regard to identifying historic properties for Section 106 undertakings.

In the guidance it is important to pay attention to the verbs "must," "should," and "may" when it comes to identification efforts. The agency *must* "take into account past planning, research and studies; the magnitude and nature of the undertaking and the degree of federal involvement; the nature and extent of potential effects on historic properties; and the likely nature and location of historic properties within the APE." The agency *should* refer to the secretary of the interior's standards and guidelines for guidance on this subject and "consider other applicable professional, state, tribal, and local laws, standards, and guidelines." The agency *may* "include background research, consultation, oral history interviews, sample field investigation, and field survey." A level of effort consistent with the historic property potentials of the APE is enough to satisfy the identification obligations of the agency for Section 106 and to meet the "reasonable and good faith" standard.

The "reasonable" part of the standard for identification basically refers to following best practices and due diligence guidelines for each profession according to national and state guidelines with regard to background research, fieldwork, analysis, and reporting. The "good faith" part of the standard refers to following best practices and due diligence guidelines with regard to consultation, timeliness, thoroughness, adequate funding, and professionalism. "Good faith" should also be measured against the intent of the NHPA as expressed in Section 1 of the act.

"Identify" does not mean a professional archaeological, historical, or architectural field survey has to be done within the APE. If a field survey is done, "identify" does not mean every site has to be found and documented within the APE or that a comprehensive cultural resources report has to be written about the survey. "Identify" does not even require consultation with any outside entity to complete the step and does not require SHPO/THPO approval of the level of effort.

Step 10: Evaluate Historic Significance

What the regulations say:

> 800.4(c) Evaluate historic significance. (1) Apply National Register criteria. In consultation with the SHPO/THPO and any Indian tribe or Native Hawaiian organization that attaches religious and cultural significance to identified properties and guided by the Secretary's Standards and Guidelines for Evaluation, the agency official shall apply the National Register criteria (36 CFR part 63) to properties identified within the area of potential effects that have not been previously evaluated for National Register eligibility.

Agency implementation: If a property of any type is present within the APE that may be impacted by the undertaking and holds some potential to be listed in the National Register of Historic Places, the agency must determine if the property is eligible for inclusion. This determination is made by applying the NRHP significance and integrity criteria (see chapter 5), consulting with the SHPO/THPO, and considering the opinions of groups with special expertise, notably tribes, with regard to properties to which they may attach cultural or religious significance.

The agency can exclude certain kinds of properties from formal evaluation. Buildings and structures that are obviously less than 50 years old and are of a standard type that is common in a region can be eliminated from formal evaluation. Archaeological sites that have been subjected to intensive examination and produced very few artifacts, none of which are clearly diagnostic of age or context affiliation, can usually be eliminated from formal evaluation. The most difficult properties are cultural landscapes and TCPs. If these are identified in the APE, it is usually good to do a formal eligibility analysis utilizing careful consultation and expert analysis unless there are clear integrity impairments.

Following appropriate analysis and consultation, the agency and SHPO/THPO jointly make an eligibility determination. If the agency and SHPO/THPO agree that the property is eligible or ineligible, the process can proceed according to the standard steps outlined in this discussion. This is called a *consensus determination*. If the agency and the SHPO/THPO disagree about eligibility, the agency sends the documentation to the Keeper of the National Register, who makes the final eligibility determination. If a tribe disagrees with a consensus determination pertaining to a property to which it attaches religious or cultural significance, the tribe can ask the ACHP to require a final decision by the Keeper.

The regulations under 800.4(c)(1) do note that "the passage of time, changing perceptions of significance, or incomplete prior evaluations may require the agency official to reevaluate properties previously determined eligible or ineligible." The passage of time usually requires a reevaluation of integrity as site conditions may have greatly altered since the original evaluation due to nonfederal actions or may relate to its now meeting the NRHP 50-year standard. Changing perceptions of significance can relate to properties associated with particular events or people now viewed differently than in the past or to relatively newly recognized property types such as landscapes or TCPs. Incomplete prior evaluations usually refer to properties examined in the early days of the NHPA, when documentation standards were lower, or can relate to the application of new field or analytical methods.

Consultation: Consultation is required with the SHPO/THPO in order to make a consensus determination of eligibility. Consultation regarding eligibility with a tribe may be necessary if there are properties of tribal religious or cultural significance within the APE, but any consensus determination of eligibility is made with the SHPO/THPO and the agency, not the tribe.

Timing: The SHPO/THPO has 30 days to object to an agency's finding of "no historic properties affected." If a SHPO/THPO, tribe, or other consulting party has taken an objection to the ACHP, the ACHP can also object within a 30-day period. If there are no objections, the agency has completed its Section 106 obligations.

End-of-process option: As previously mentioned, *historic properties* are those districts, sites, buildings, structures, and objects listed or eligible for inclusion in the NRHP. According to 36 CFR 800, "*Effect* means alteration to the characteristics of a historic property qualifying it for inclusion in or eligibility for the National Register." Prior to the 2004 regulations, there was a distinction between "no properties" and "no historic properties affected" findings. The 2004 regulations eliminated "no properties" as a discrete finding, rolling it into "no historic properties affected" (or "no effect"), although there still is a distinction between the two outcomes in the process. In Steps 1 and 9, the agency can determine that no potential historic properties are present in the APE. If there are no historic properties, there can't be any effects to them.

In Step 10, the agency evaluates properties in the APE that have potential to be historic. If the agency finds that no property is eligible within the APE or that the undertaking will have no effect on a historic property, the Section 106 process ends after the agency notifies all consulting parties of its decision and provides documentation supporting its conclusion to the SHPO/THPO. The public does not have to be informed. In this step, the agency can also suggest plan alterations to eliminate any effects to eligible properties.

Issues/observations: As discussed by King (2013:137–140), there is no absolute guide to what is and is not eligible for every property within an APE. However, there are NRHP bulletins that deal with specific property types, such as shipwrecks and landscapes, as well as some written guidance available for particular types of properties in particular states. This guidance is usually in the form of a Multiple Property Documentation Form (MPDF), as briefly described in chapter 5. If the agency has any question as to the need for formal evaluation, it should consult with the SHPO/THPO, and exclusion of any properties should be justified in documentation of any identification surveys.

It is interesting that the agency has to make a "reasonable and good faith effort" to identify historic properties in the APE under Step 9, but the regulations do not specify such an effort for evaluation of properties. Evaluation is usually more problematic than identification because finding properties is more straightforward and subject to standard professional procedures than evaluation. This is true of both archaeological and history-architecture properties. Because of all the issues and varying opinions with regard to eligibility, this step can be time-consuming, expensive, and contentious.

The regulations do not address whether a consensus evaluation made by one federal agency and SHPO/THPO for a particular property for one of that agency's undertakings is a valid eligibility determination for another agency with a totally different undertaking affecting that same property at a later date. Logic would suggest that the earlier eligibility determination would not bind a future undertaking done by a different agency. The only evaluations that apply to all federal agencies are for properties listed in the NRHP and properties with eligibility formally evaluated by the Keeper of the NRHP, although these determinations too may be subject to reevaluation due to the passage of time or further analysis. Some properties listed in the National Register during its early days are probably not eligible by today's standards.

In an advanced Section 106 training session held by the ACHP in 2011, I asked the instructor if consensus findings for one agency apply to another for a totally different undertaking by another agency affecting the same property at a later date. She agreed that the earlier finding would not require the same outcome for a subsequent finding. The instructor also stated that 96% of Section 106 reviews do not involve adverse effects to historic properties.

Phase 3: Assess Adverse Effects
Step 11: Apply Criteria of Adverse Effect

What the regulations say: If the agency thinks there may be adverse effects to one or more historic properties within the APE, it must determine this by applying criteria established in the regulations and in National Register guidance. There are no definitions of "adverse effect" or "no adverse effect" in the "Definitions" section of 36 CFR 800, but 800.5(a)(1) states,

> An adverse effect is found when an undertaking may alter, directly or indirectly, any of the characteristics of a historic property that qualify the property for inclusion in the National Register in a manner that would diminish the integrity of the property's location, design, setting, materials, workmanship, feeling, or association. Consideration shall be given to all qualifying characteristics of a historic property, including those that may have been identified subsequent to the original evaluation of the property's eligibility for the National Register. Adverse effects may include reasonably foreseeable effects caused by the undertaking that may occur later in time, be farther removed in distance or be cumulative.

The regulations then go on to give examples of adverse effects:

- Physical destruction of or damage to all or part of the property
- Alteration of a property, including restoration, rehabilitation, repair, maintenance, stabilization, hazardous material remediation, and provision of handicapped access, that is not consistent with the *Secretary of the Interior's Standards for the Treatment of Historic Properties* (36 CFR 68) and applicable guidelines
- Removal of the property from its historic location
- Change of the character of the property's use or of physical features within the property's setting that contribute to its historic significance
- Introduction of visual, atmospheric, or audible elements that diminish the integrity of the property's significant historic features
- Neglect of a property that causes its deterioration, except where such neglect and deterioration are recognized qualities of a property of religious and cultural significance to an Indian tribe or Native Hawaiian organization
- Transfer, lease, or sale of a property out of federal ownership or control without adequate and legally enforceable restrictions or conditions to ensure long-term preservation of the property's historic significance

Agency implementation: The agency must determine if an undertaking will alter the condition of a historic property to a degree that the property will lose its eligibility for the NRHP. An undertaking that restores, rehabilitates, repairs, or makes other changes consistent with the secretary of the interior's treatment standards is not considered to have an adverse effect. In the case of Indian religious or cultural properties, deterioration or neglect, if part of a natural process accepted by a tribe, may not be considered an adverse effect. Property transferred out of federal ownership can be protected from adverse effects through preservation easements or restrictions in the deed.

In the case of archaeological sites eligible only under Criterion D (information potential), prior to the current regulations a "no adverse effect" finding could be issued if the agency agreed to conduct a **data recovery** that would acquire sufficient information from the site to mitigate the adverse effect. This action treated archaeological sites differently from all other property types, where avoidance of impacts was stressed. Data-recovery excavations may still be part of the Section 106 process but now take place after the agency has agreed the effects to a site are adverse and agrees to require a data recovery as specified in a memorandum of agreement. The ACHP webpage has guidelines regarding the treatment (i.e., mitigation of adverse effect) of eligible or listed archaeological sites.

Consultation: The agency must consult with the SHPO/THPO to determine if a historic property within the APE will be adversely affected by the undertaking. If the SHPO/THPO agrees that there will be an adverse effect, the agency must continue to consult this officer if it proposes an alteration of plans that it thinks will eliminate the adverse effect. The agency must notify all consulting parties of a "no adverse effect" finding.

Timing: The SHPO/THPO has 30 days to review and comment on the agency's finding of "no adverse effect." If the SHPO/THPO agrees with the agency finding or fails to comment within the 30-day review period and no consulting party has objected, the agency can proceed with the undertaking. If the SHPO/THPO disagrees or any consulting party notifies the agency in writing of its disagreement, and further consultation fails to yield an agreement, the agency must consult the ACHP. The ACHP has 15 days to comment.

End-of-process option: If the agency determines that historic properties it has identified in the APE will not be adversely affected, it can issue a "no historic properties adversely affected" finding. This finding can be conditional on actions required by the agency, such as alteration of plans or actions taken during undertaking implementation to reduce or eliminate effects on a historic property. If the SHPO/THPO agrees with the "no historic properties adversely affected" finding or a "conditional no adverse effect" finding, the agency has satisfied its Section 106 obligations, although it must make sure that any conditions are fulfilled.

The ACHP does not routinely review "no adverse effect" findings, but ACHP review and comment can be requested by the SHPO/THPO, tribes, or other consulting parties if the request is received by the ACHP within the 30-day review period. ACHP comment is limited to a determination of correct application of the criteria of adverse effect. ACHP comment, if issued, is the final say with regard to whether an undertaking will have adverse effects, although the agency does not have to follow the ACHP recommendations concerning the effects.

Issues/observations: Archaeologists' access should be among effects considered for an archaeological site (its use); if access is restricted in a significant manner, this can be an adverse effect. A public roadway is generally not an accessible area, considering its hard surface and constant use, while a parking lot may allow limited or focused archaeological penetration. When I was Minnesota SHPO archaeologist, I would look at the percentage of the site area that an undertaking would make inaccessible, how long accessibility to archaeology would be denied, and the rarity of the site. I considered long-term inaccessibility of over 50% of any eligible site an adverse effect. I considered long-term inaccessibility of only a small portion of a Paleoindian site an adverse effect.

Phase 4: Resolve Adverse Effects
Step 12: Continue Consultation and Execute Memorandum of Agreement

What the regulations say:

> 800.6 Resolution of adverse effects. (a) Continue consultation. The agency official shall consult with the SHPO/THPO and other consulting parties, including Indian tribes and Native Hawaiian organizations, to develop and evaluate alternatives or modifications to the undertaking that could avoid, minimize, or mitigate adverse effects on historic properties. . . .
>
> (b) Resolve adverse effects. . . . (iv) If the agency official and the SHPO/THPO agree on how the adverse effects will be resolved, they shall execute a **memorandum of agreement.** . . .
>
> (c) Memorandum of agreement. A memorandum of agreement executed and implemented pursuant to this section evidences the agency official's compliance with section 106 and this part and shall govern the undertaking and all of its parts. The agency official shall ensure that the undertaking is carried out in accordance with the memorandum of agreement.

Agency implementation: If at the end of Step 11, the agency finds that an undertaking will result in adverse effects to one or more historic properties, the agency must consult with all consulting parties to attempt to resolve the adverse effects. Any of the consulting parties can also request that the ACHP participate. If the ACHP does decide to participate in the consultation to resolve adverse effects, the ACHP must inform the head of the federal agency. New consulting parties may also enter the discussion if the agency and SHPO/THPO agree. The agency must provide all consulting parties with sufficient documentation to assist their participation.

At this time, the agency must also provide the public with an opportunity to comment. This is the first step in the Section 106 process where the agency is actually required to seek public input. Prior to this, members of the public were allowed to have access to some agency documentation if they were indeed aware of the undertaking. The public is not allowed access to confidential information regarding actual archaeological site locations or about Indian ceremonial sites or TCPs that tribes have requested be held in confidence as specified in Section 304 of the NHPA.

When the agency has agreed that an undertaking will have an adverse effect on one or more historic properties and has initiated consultation with the consulting parties and the public, the resolution to the adverse effects is eventually specified in a memorandum of agreement. The MOA must be signed by the agency and the SHPO/THPO. If the ACHP has been part of the consultation or if ACHP participation is required by one of the conditions specified in the regulations (e.g., NHL involvement), a representative of the ACHP also must sign the MOA.

Consulting parties are invited to sign but do not have to sign in order for the MOA to be a legally binding document. The agency can also invite other parties or individuals to sign, especially entities given responsibilities in the MOA. These entities need not have been consulted prior to the MOA if their responsibilities only became apparent during the writing of the document. For instance, a state archaeologist with burial site responsibilities may be asked to sign if the MOA specifies the possibility of unrecorded burials being encountered during construction, requiring state archaeologist involvement.

Consultation: The agency must attempt to resolve adverse effects through continued consultation with the SHPO/THPO and other consulting parties. The ACHP can be invited to join the consultation by the agency, a SHPO/THPO, or a tribe. ACHP participation is mandatory if an NHL is being adversely affected. Although the agency is required to involve the public in this step, the public is not considered a consulting party; it is simply informed about the undertaking and provided the opportunity to comment.

Timing: The ACHP has 15 days to inform the agency if it will join the consultation if so invited by an agency, a SHPO/THPO, or a tribe. The remainder of this step has no set timetable.

End-of-process option: Once the MOA has been signed by all parties required and invited to sign, the Section 106 process is completed. The agency must ensure that the conditions specified in the MOA are fulfilled. This can take years to complete.

Issues/observations: The regulations do not specify how the agency notifies the public and how the agency receives public opinion on the adverse effects of an undertaking. Prior to wide access to the internet, notice was usually accomplished through a press release sent to print and/or broadcast media that served the specific communities within the APE. This was often accompanied by a notice of a public meeting to be held in the community. This is still a standard way of receiving input, although now announcements also appear on agency or consulting party websites or social media, along with electronic access to some documents and the ability to submit email comments. A SHPO/THPO who has signed a long-term MOA should have policies and procedures in place to monitor progress, compliance, and outcomes.

Phase 5: Failure to Agree
Step 13: Failure to Resolve Adverse Effects
What the regulations say:

> 800.7 Failure to resolve adverse effects. (a) Termination of consultation. After consulting to resolve adverse effects pursuant to § 800.6(b)(2), the agency official, the SHPO/THPO, or the Council may determine that further consultation will not be productive and terminate consultation. Any party that terminates consultation shall notify the other consulting parties and provide them the reasons for terminating in writing.

Agency implementation: If, following consultation with all involved parties, the agency and the SHPO/THPO cannot come to agreement on how to resolve adverse effects of an undertaking to a historic property, there is a formal finding of "failure to agree." This ends consultation with all parties except the agency and the ACHP. The agency requests ACHP comment and provides the ACHP with all necessary documentation as specified in Section 110(1) of the NHPA. If a SHPO terminates consultation, the ACHP and the agency can agree on an MOA. If a THPO terminates consultation, no agreement can be independently enacted for tribal lands.

Consultation: Agency consultation has ended at the beginning of this step with all consulting parties except the ACHP. Consultation ends with the ACHP when it too fails to agree with the agency and decides to terminate the process.

Timing: If the ACHP terminates consultation or if a THPO has terminated consultation, the ACHP has to provide comments to the federal agency within 45 days.

End-of-process option: If the ACHP terminates consultation or if a THPO has terminated consultation, the ACHP has to provide comments to the federal agency and all the consulting parties. This ends the Section 106 process, and the agency may proceed with the undertaking without further consideration or consultation. The agency head is obligated to provide the ACHP with documentation supporting its decision.

Issues/observations: A "failure to agree" finding is a very rare occurrence in the Section 106 process, or at least it is rare in Minnesota, where there have been only one or two instances in the 50 years of the NHPA. Agencies will only get to this step if disagreement is severe because an agreement with the SHPO/THPO or ACHP will be excessively burdensome in terms of project funding, redesign, or delay.

The Cape Wind project in Massachusetts was a failure-to-agree instance that gained national attention. In November 2001, Cape Wind Associates LLC (CWA) proposed building 130 large wind turbines offshore in Nantucket Sound. The permit had to be approved by the federal Bureau of Ocean Energy Management (BOEM) of the Mineral Management Service, a Department of the Interior agency. A COE Section 404 permit was also needed. BOEM became the lead agency for the purposes of Section 106.

After consulting with the Massachusetts SHPO, two Wampanoag tribal groups, various interested organizations, and the ACHP, BOEM determined there were adverse effects to 28 historic districts, a number of individual historic properties, and six properties of religious and cultural significance to the tribes. Two of the districts were NHLs. The final "finding of adverse effect" document was 671 pages long.

The ACHP and other consulting parties concluded that the adverse effects of the project could not be adequately mitigated. When BOEM and the consulting parties failed to agree on project alteration, the Department of the Interior terminated consultation on March 1, 2010. BOEM issued a lease to CWA on October 6, 2010. Construction on the Cape Wind project had not been started as of the end of 2017. It was delayed due to additional BOEM requirements and a CWA request for a lease extension. You can read more about the project on the BOEM and ACHP webpages and in an April 3, 2010, post on *Tom King's CRM Plus* blog.

Other Aspects of 36 CFR 800

In the 36 CFR 800 regulations, there are aspects of the Section 106 process that involve actions that could be taken in multiple steps in Subpart B, and there are procedures that are outside the standard Section 106 process as described in Subpart C.

Coordination of Section 106 with NEPA

Multiple federal laws deal with consideration of development project effects on historic properties. Some are agency specific (e.g., Section 4[f] of DOTA), and some only apply to actions on federal lands (e.g., AIRFA, ARPA). The two laws that apply to all federal actions that may impact historic properties are Section 106 of the National Historic Preservation Act and the National Environmental Policy Act, although NEPA is much broader in its consideration of cultural heritage resources than the NHPA. NEPA considers effects on all elements of the environment, including the sociocultural environment, not just effects on physical properties that are eligible for inclusion in the NRHP.

Coordination of Section 106 with NEPA is outlined in Section 800.8 of the regulations. In 2013, the ACHP produced a handbook for integrating NEPA and Section 106 that is available on its webpage (http://www.achp.gov/docs/NEPA_NHPA_Section_106_Handbook_Mar2013.pdf).
As stated in 800.8(a)(1),

> (a) General principles. (1) Early coordination. Federal agencies are encouraged to coordinate compliance with section 106 and the procedures in this part with

any steps taken to meet the requirements of the National Environmental Policy Act (NEPA). Agencies should consider their section 106 responsibilities as early as possible in the NEPA process, and plan their public participation, analysis, and review in such a way that they can meet the purposes and requirements of both statutes in a timely and efficient manner. The determination of whether an undertaking is a "major Federal action significantly affecting the quality of the human environment," and therefore requires preparation of an environmental impact statement (EIS) under NEPA, should include consideration of the under-taking's likely effects on historic properties. A finding of adverse effect on a historic property does not necessarily require an EIS under NEPA.

The regulations go on to specify details about

- Consulting party roles
- Historic preservation issues
- Actions categorically excluded under NEPA
- Use of the NEPA process for Section 106

The key points to consider about Section 106–NEPA coordination are as follows:

- You must fulfill all the requirements of both laws.
- Almost all undertakings under Section 106 are also actions considered under NEPA.
- Begin coordination of Section 106 and NEPA early in the process.
- Coordination of the two laws and processes promotes efficiency.
- A Section 106 finding of "adverse effect" cannot in itself require an environmental impact statement.
- Most agencies use the results of Section 106 to fulfill parallel NEPA requirements concerning historic properties.

NEPA will be covered in more detail in chapter 7.

ACHP Review of Compliance and Foreclosure

As specified in Section 800.9, the ACHP may review agency compliance with individual undertakings (800.9[a]) or agency performance in general with respect to Section 106 compliance (800.9[b]). The most pertinent definition in this section is with respect to foreclosure.

According to Section 800.16, "*Foreclosure* means an action taken by an agency official that effectively precludes the Council from providing comments which the agency official can meaningfully consider prior to the approval of the undertaking." Foreclosure is usually recommended by a SHPO/THPO to the ACHP on discovery that an agency has not followed the Section 106 process as outlined in 36 CFR 800 or not initiated the process until an undertaking was well underway. Only the ACHP can make a finding of foreclosure. Foreclosure was not uncommon in the early days of Section 106, when agencies lacked staff familiar with Section 106 or thought they could get away with not following it. It is uncommon today, except perhaps in cases where local agencies have assumed Section 106 responsibilities.

Foreclosure can occur at any step within the process but usually occurs when an agency has completely ignored the process for a particular undertaking. The agency has 30 days to comment on the ACHP's notice of foreclosure. If the foreclosure determination is allowed to stand, the ACHP has to make the determination public and inform potential consulting parties. There is no penalty for the agency other than bad public relations and increased scrutiny of future agency actions by the ACHP, SHPOs/THPOs, the media, and the public.

Minimization of Harm to National Historic Landmarks

Section 880.10 discusses agency obligations to minimize harm to National Historic Landmarks. As defined by the National Park Service, NHLs are "nationally significant historic places designated by the Secretary of the Interior because they possess exceptional value or quality in illustrating or interpreting the heritage of the United States." NHLs were first designated in 1960 and consisted of the most obvious historic places associated with events, people, or places familiar to most Americans. Now NHLs are identified in the NRHP process when "national significance" is checked on the NRHP nomination form. There are currently over 2,500 NHLs.

The requirement that agencies minimize harm to NHLs is found in Section 110(f) (now 306107) of the NHPA. When an NHL may be adversely affected by an undertaking reviewed under Section 106, direct ACHP involvement is required, and the secretary of the interior must be notified by the agency reviewing the undertaking. The ACHP must send a report to the secretary and the agency regarding the outcome of consultation through the Section 106 process. As with other historic properties, the NHPA does not require avoiding adverse effects to NHLs.

Documentation Standards

Section 800.11 discusses documentation standards that agencies must meet for various steps in the Section 106 process:

> 800.11 Documentation standards. (a) Adequacy of documentation. The agency official shall ensure that a determination, finding, or agreement under the procedures in this subpart is supported by sufficient documentation to enable any reviewing parties to understand its basis. The agency official shall provide such documentation to the extent permitted by law and within available funds.

General instructions with regard to format and confidentiality are followed by instructions for issuing specific findings and executing a memorandum of agreement. The 800.11 regulations do not require an agency to complete reports or that any completed reports meet certain professional standards (e.g., *Secretary of the Interior's Standards for Documentation*). The SHPO/THPO or the ACHP can inform the agency that its document is inadequate. The agency can then consult with the ACHP if there is a dispute with the SHPO/THPO or another consulting party with regard to the documentation adequacy.

With regard to confidentiality, the 800.11 regulations refer to Section 304 (now 307103) of the NHPA, which states,

> (a) AUTHORITY TO WITHHOLD FROM DISCLOSURE.—The head of a Federal agency, or other public official receiving grant assistance pursuant to this division, after consultation with the Secretary, shall withhold from disclosure to the public information about the location, character, or ownership of a historic property if the Secretary and the agency determine that disclosure may—
> (1) cause a significant invasion of privacy;
> (2) risk harm to the historic property; or
> (3) impede the use of a traditional religious site by practitioners.
> (b) ACCESS DETERMINATION.—When the head of a Federal agency or other public official determines that information should be withheld from the public pursuant to subsection (a), the Secretary, in consultation with the Federal agency head or official, shall determine who may have access to the information for the purpose of carrying out this division.

(c) CONSULTATION WITH COUNCIL.—When information described in subsection (a) has been developed in the course of an agency's compliance with section 306107 or 306108 of this title, the Secretary shall consult with the Council in reaching determinations under subsections (a) and (b).

In most cases, confidential information applies to the exact location of archaeological sites and traditional cultural properties. Other federal laws specify confidentiality with regard to this information for sites found on federal property, such as 16 USC 470hh and 36 CFR 296.18.

Emergency Situations

Some agencies deal with undertakings that require immediate implementation; therefore, going through the standard Section 106 process outlined in 36 CFR 800 Subpart B is burdensome or inappropriate. The Federal Emergency Management Agency is the most obvious, but emergency situations can occasionally occur with other agencies. Section 800.12 of the regulations deal with this, and the ACHP has provided a FAQ document related to this on its webpage.

Examples of emergency situations include natural disasters such as hurricanes and wildfires, unanticipated maintenance on bridges and dams, and military or terrorist actions. The responses to these situations can involve terrain alteration (e.g., dikes, firebreaks), alteration or demolition of structures, and land use generally incompatible with historic resources (e.g., military training in culturally sensitive areas). In most cases, emergency situations apply to responses that will be implemented within 30 days of the disaster or emergency.

Basic ACHP recommendations encourage flexibility and consideration of the broader public interest when examining ways to protect historic properties. A preferred way to deal with emergency situations is for agencies to develop plans that will not impede necessary responses but will include at least some consideration of and consultation about impacts to historic properties. The best way to develop alternative procedures to deal with emergency situations is for an agency to implement a programmatic agreement with applicable SHPOs/THPOs and other consulting parties such as tribes and local governments.

Postreview Discoveries

The Section 106 process flowchart does not take into account the potential for *postreview discoveries*, which are covered in 800.13 of the regulations. Postreview discoveries are previously unidentified historic properties that are encountered during implementation of an undertaking. The agency response to the potential for postreview discoveries and their treatment can be covered in a programmatic agreement enacted between an agency and a SHPO/THPO anytime during the Section 106 process. They can also be addressed in an inadvertent discovery plan attached to an applicant contract.

Postreview discoveries are usually very obvious archaeological sites found within the APE through soil or structure removal or sites encountered by attendant but unreviewed activities in or adjacent to an APE (e.g., utility line relocation caused by a highway project). PAs and inadvertent discovery plans usually specify that all activities affecting such properties must immediately cease, that the properties be evaluated for NRHP eligibility, and that avoidance or adequate mitigation be employed if they are eligible. If there is no PA or plan, the agency is still obligated to make "reasonable efforts" to avoid, minimize, or mitigate effects to historic properties. Inadvertent discovery plans also usually include procedures to follow if human burials are encountered.

A report on any postreview actions must be completed and submitted to interested parties "within a reasonable time after they are completed." If a postreview discovery is made on tribal lands, the agency must comply with any tribal regulations concerning the property. Burials or archaeological sites encountered on non-federal public land may be subject to state laws.

Federal Agency Program Alternatives (800.14)

While most federal agencies follow the steps outlined in Subpart B of 36 CFR 800 to fulfill their Section 106 obligations, 800.14 allows for agencies to develop alternative procedures if such procedures are consistent with the standard procedures. These program alternatives are meant for agencies whose activities do not fit well with standard procedures, causing them excessive expenditures of time and money or unacceptable delays in implementing undertakings. It also allows agencies that have previously established procedures for regulating lands or common actions to adapt the Section 106 process to better fit their established procedures (but see this chapter's sidebar on COE Appendix C).

Agencies must consult with the ACHP as well as NCSHPO or individual SHPOs/THPOs and tribes as appropriate. They must also seek public input. Once the final procedures have been drafted, the agency submits them to the ACHP, which has 60 days to comment on the compatibility of the proposed regulations with 36 CFR 800. The agency must publish notice of the final alternative regulations in the *Federal Register*.

Summary

As stated in the title of 36 CFR 800, the purpose of Section 106 of the National Historic Preservation Act is to promote the protection of important historic places by requiring federal agencies to think carefully about the impacts of their actions on them and to ask for help from knowledgeable entities in identifying, understanding, and reducing any effects. The law does not require agencies to preserve historic properties; nor does it require them to obey the people they consult. It only requires them to reasonably consider the impacts their undertakings have and to acquire and listen in good faith to the external input they obtain.

Over the last 50 years, no other law and no other section of the NHPA has done more to preserve historic properties than Section 106. For archaeology, it has meant that tens of thousands of sites have been found, thousands have been saved from destruction, and research has rapidly accelerated with respect to field methods, data analysis, and understanding of the past. For architecture, it has examined tens of thousands of buildings and structures, led to the preservation and rehabilitation of thousands of properties, and promoted an eclectic view of what's important in the built environment. It has revitalized communities and promoted a greening of the built environment. For history it has promoted a broader view of the past and incorporated a great diversity of viewpoints. Section 106 has also employed thousands of archaeologists, architects, historians, and **curators**.

Laws are products of a purely political process. Regulations are mostly bureaucratic responses to laws but are also subject to complex political pressures and judicial review. When I first taught classes on cultural resource management, I would note the delay between amendments to the NHPA and changes to the Section 106 regulations. It took eight years between the 1966 passage of the NHPA for 36 CFR 800 to first appear in 1974. The 1976 amendment of NHPA, which included the

NRHP-eligible-same-as-listed language added to Section 106, was followed three years later by a new version of 36 CFR 800. The 1980 amendment of NHPA was followed six years later by a new version of 36 CFR 800. The 1992 amendment of NHPA took 12 years to fully implement in revised 36 CFR 800 regulations due to both court challenges and agency dissatisfaction.

In those early classes I failed to stress larger political actions, mainly by presidents, that required language changes and delayed the timing of revisions to the Section 106 regulations. Richard Nixon's Executive Order 11593 in 1971 introduced the eligible-equals-listed consideration, which was incorporated into the 1974 nonbinding ACHP regulations. Jimmy Carter's 1978 Presidential Memorandum on Environmental Quality and Water Resources Management forced the ACHP to issue revised regulations in 1979, incorporating changes to Section 106 from the 1976 NHPA amendment. Ronald Reagan's 1981 Executive Order 12291 concerning reduction of federal regulations was combined with the 1980 amendment to NHPA, resulting in the 1986 version of 36 CFR 800. Bill Clinton's National Performance Review directive in 1993, coupled with the 1992 amendments to NHPA, resulted in the 1999/2004 version of the Section 106 regulations.

The history of the Section 106 regulations once again demonstrates that understanding the way heritage preservation is carried out requires more than compiling a simple chronology of destructive or constructive events, court cases, and focused legislation. Heritage preservation trends even at the regulation level respond to nonlegislative political actions, technological innovations, social changes, and intellectual revolutions.

The most important points to remember about Section 106 are as follows:

- It does not require the protection or preservation of historic properties.
- The principal responsibilities for implementation rest with the federal agency that is providing the funding for an undertaking, licensing or permitting the undertaking, or managing federal land affected by the undertaking.
- The federal agency has two basic responsibilities: consider the impact of the undertaking on eligible historic properties and consult about potential impacts with all entities required by the regulations.
- The federal agency has the final say in whether an undertaking is allowed to proceed even if it adversely affects a historic property.

Finally, this chapter is necessarily complex because the implementation of Section 106 is complex. Even after doing it for over 30 years, I still do not consider myself an expert on Section 106, and I still am asking questions of more knowledgeable people who don't always know the answers. If this is your first encounter with the details of Section 106, be patient. Reread the chapter and look at some of my supplemental reading suggestions below. If you have an opportunity to take an ACHP Section 106 training session, do it, especially if you intend to make a career in American heritage management.

Review Questions

1. Why were regulations needed to implement Section 106?
2. What kinds of federal actions result in regulatory changes?
3. What is consultation for the purposes of Section 106?
4. What two Section 106 actions require a reasonable and good faith effort?
5. What roles do THPOs play in the Section 106 process?

Supplemental Reading

Tom King is certainly one of the experts on Section 106 as he has experience with it since its inception in 1966 both inside and outside the federal government. Look at chapter 4 of King (2013) for a comprehensive summary of his take on its application and effectiveness. There is also lots of helpful information on the ACHP website.

To better understand consultation, its meaning and intent, begin with the secretary of the interior's advice regarding consultation in general by federal agencies. Then look at a 2016 document produced by the American Association of State Highway and Transportation Officials (AASHTO) titled "Consulting under Section 106 of the National Historic Preservation Act." Both of these documents are available online. For a good overview of heritage management consulting from a nonagency perspective, read Nissley and King (2014). King also has some general advice on consultation in his various CRM textbooks and on his *CRM Plus* blog. For the purposes of this chapter, look at the limited guidance on nontribal consultation on the ACHP webpage, such as "Section 106 Consultation Involving National Historic Landmarks."

SIDEBAR

Implementing Heritage Management: But for Appendix C

When I was new at being a SHPO archaeologist, I attended a meeting at the St. Paul District of the Corps of Engineers. I had recommended an archaeological survey of a proposed housing development on an island. The project required a COE permit subject to Section 106 review. Section 404 of the Clean Water Act of 1972 requires federal permits for placing fill in wetlands. The developer had to fill a wetland on one side of the island in order to provide an access road. At the meeting, the COE regulatory guy said the Section 404 permit only covered the fill area; thus the COE could not require a survey of the island as a condition of the permit. The COE archaeologist supported me, however, saying a survey of the island met the "but for" clause in Appendix C. I thought, "What the heck is Appendix C and what is the 'but for' clause?"

In the late 1970s, the Department of the Army began to investigate options in consultation with the Advisory Council on Historic Preservation for streamlining all its permitting actions with respect to Section 106 compliance, including permits processed by the COE. The ACHP's 36 CFR 800 regulations of 1979 had added a provision allowing agencies to develop programmatic agreements for certain classes of undertakings reviewed under Section 106 and encouraging the development of counterpart regulations to make Section 106 application more amenable to individual agency procedures. The army attempted to take advantage of these provisions with respect to its permitting obligations by embedding in "Processing of Department of the Army Permits" (33 CFR 325) an Appendix C titled "Procedures for the Protection of Historic Properties." Although the army failed to get the ACHP to sign a PA accepting Appendix C as a viable alternate procedure for implementing Section 106, the COE began applying Appendix C to its permit review process in the early 1980s.

Despite increased flexibility in 36 CFR 800 alternative procedures, over 35 years of intensive COE-ACHP consultation, numerous court cases, and much public discussion, the COE has still failed to get the ACHP to sign off on Appendix C. The federal Office of Management and Budget (OMB) accepted the adequacy of Appendix C for Section 106 compliance in 1990. The Council on Environmental Quality (CEQ) has approved the COE regulations as they apply to NEPA, but 33 CFR 325 Appendix C is specific to Section 106 of the NHPA, other historic preservation laws, and presidential directives.

Many aspects of 33 CFR 325 Appendix C and the recommendations from the interim guidance issued by the COE in 2005 (see http://www.usace.

army.mil/Portals/2/docs/civilworks/regulatory/InterimGuidance_25apr05.pdf) conform to 36 CFR 800, but there are critical exceptions: the definition of the area of potential effects; the consideration of only listed or previously determined eligible properties located outside the permit area but within a larger project-as-a-whole APE; the scope of effort for identification of historic properties; the limitation of consultation with tribes and other potential consulting parties; the treatment of archaeological sites eligible only under Criterion D; and an optional memorandum of agreement for an adverse effect.

The "but for" clause pertains to the definition of the APE. In Appendix C, the area subject to COE Section 106 review is defined as the permit area: "those areas comprising the waters of the United States that will be directly affected by the proposed work or structures and uplands directly affected as a result of authorizing the work or structures." Appendix C(1)(g) applies three tests that all must be satisfied with regard to the permit area: (1) Such activity would not occur *but for* the authorization of the work or structures within the waters of the United States; (2) Such activity must be integrally related to the work or structures to be authorized within waters of the United States. Or, conversely, the work or structures to be authorized must be essential to the completeness of the overall project or program. (3) Such activity must be directly associated (first-order impact) with the work or structures to be authorized. Thus "but for" asks, Could the project be completed *but for* the action subject to the COE permit?

The Dakota Access Pipeline (DAPL) project is one of the more recent high-profile cases challenging the COE's use of Appendix C. The DAPL is a 1,172-mile, $3.8 billion oil pipeline from the Bakken oil field in north-central North Dakota to existing pipelines near Patoka, Illinois. It traverses parts of North Dakota, South Dakota, Iowa, and Illinois. Unlike natural gas pipelines, oil pipelines are not subject to overall federal review under Section 106, but localized wetland impacts are subject to Section 404 permits. Three COE district offices were involved in DAPL: Omaha, Nebraska; Rock Island, Illinois; and St. Louis, Missouri. Overall, the COE claimed to have jurisdiction over only about 3% of the total pipeline length, treating about 200 wetland incursions (Section 404) under a nationwide permit and navigable river and COE-managed land crossings as separate permits under Section 10 of the Rivers and Harbors Act. The COE required cultural resource surveys of all areas under its direct jurisdiction and consulted with SHPOs, tribes, and other interested parties regarding the various permit applications. The COE concluded there were no adverse effects to historic properties. The key question was, Should 35 miles of a 1,172-mile pipeline federalize the entire project?

If the clear divergences of Appendix C from 36 CFR 800 with regard to MOAs, consultation, treatment of Criterion D sites, and standardized definitions were eliminated and a reasonable compromise reached as to how much of a permitted project to include in the Section 106 APE, the COE would have a reasonable program alternative. Appendix C as currently written and implemented encourages project segmentation, foreclosure, failure to agree, construction delays, and lawsuits. In 2015, the ACHP once again initiated consultation with the COE to address the deficiencies of Appendix C with respect to noncompliance with 36 CFR 800. With regard to the differences between the 36 CFR 800 definition of "area of potential effects" versus the Appendix C definition of "permit area," the ACHP is looking at the issue broadly and has called it part of the concept of projects with "small federal handles" (ACHP 2015). The ACHP recognizes federal agency Section 106 responsibilities are very different for agencies that have limited control over an undertaking (e.g., permitting) as compared to undertakings that take place on federal lands or are done with federal funds.

CHAPTER 7

More Environmental Process Laws

The Other Walls

Come senators, congressmen, please heed the call
Don't stand in the doorway, don't block up the hall
For he that gets hurt, will be he who has stalled
There's a battle outside and it is ragin'
It'll soon shake your windows and rattle your walls
For the times they are a-changin'
— Bob Dylan, "The Times They Are a-Changin'" (1964)

Although the National Historic Preservation Act (NHPA) of 1966 is the foundation of heritage preservation in the United States, many other post-1965 federal laws and executive orders (EOs) complement and supplement it. Some were passed for reasons other than heritage preservation. These laws are a critical part of American heritage management. I referred to them earlier as the other walls of the heritage management structure, with the NHPA as the foundation and Section 106 of that law as the front wall. Almost all heritage management laws rely on NHPA guidance to some degree, certainly to define what heritage resources are considered worthy of consideration and preservation.

Some laws are specific to a particular kind of resource, such as the Abandoned Shipwrecks Act. Some are specific to a particular agency, such as the Department of Transportation Act (DOTA). Some are specific to a particular group, like the Native American Graves Protection and Repatriation Act (NAGPRA). Some only apply to federal land, like the Archaeological Resources Protection Act (ARPA). This book doesn't have room to cover all heritage management laws in detail. Some are too restrictive in scope to be broadly applicable for heritage management, and some are too complex to cover in detail for a survey course.

Like Section 106 of NHPA, a few laws use an environmental review process to assess effects of federal actions on heritage resources and suggest ways federal agencies can help minimize adverse effects to them. Only one other law, the National Environmental Policy Act (NEPA), broadly applies to all types of federal actions that may affect historic properties. Section 4(f) of the DOTA is more restrictive in its scope as it only applies to federal transportation projects, but it is more powerful in its application as it stresses preservation rather than just consideration. The Archaeological and Historic Preservation Act (AHPA) was important to archaeologists in the 1970s but has largely fallen into disuse. In this chapter, I provide brief overviews of NEPA, DOTA 4(f), and AHPA.

National Environmental Policy Act (1969)

Historical Background

Like the National Historic Preservation Act, the National Environmental Policy Act was passed in response to increasing public awareness of environmental degradation in the 1960s. While America was behind the international curve in passing comprehensive historic preservation laws, it was ahead of most countries in environmental protection. Many people know we established the world's first national park (Yellowstone) in 1872, but few know that NEPA, passed almost 100 years later, was the first legislation by any nation to broadly address environmental-quality concerns.

For historic preservationists, the decade of the 1960s began with an old-fashioned, reactive, and narrow type of preservation law, the Reservoir Salvage Act (RSA), but it ended with NEPA, a modern, proactive, comprehensive piece of legislation that included consideration of historic sites as part of the "human environment." The first legislation anticipating NEPA was introduced in the US Senate in 1959, and although it did not pass, it contained aspects that later appeared in NEPA.

Increasing environmental concerns throughout the 1960s climaxed with the introduction of the NEPA legislation in the Senate in early 1969. The Senate bill contained concepts from the 1959 legislation, including a declaration of federal policy, the need for a lead organization in the Executive Office of the President, and the production of an annual report, but it introduced the innovation of a focused analysis called an environmental impact statement (EIS). A similar bill soon followed in the House, with both legislative bodies passing the act in December 1969. President Richard Nixon signed the National Environmental Policy Act into law on January 1, 1970. It is a legislative achievement we can certainly envy today for its completeness, swift enactment, and minimal controversy, despite its scope and potential economic implications for business and government.

The key elements of NEPA, reflecting the intent of the congressional authors and their advisors as summarized in the "Purpose" section at the beginning of the act, were:

- A strong statement of federal policy on the importance of environmental protection. This is expressed in Section 101.
- Inclusion of an "action forcing" provision that required federal agencies to actually implement the government's policy. This is the EIS outlined in Section 102.
- Establishment of an independent agency at the highest level of government that would promote the policy, establish procedures, and monitor compliance. This is the Council on Environmental Quality (CEQ) established in Title 2.
- Mandating of an annual report to Congress from the executive branch assessing the state of the national environment. This is required in Section 201.

In order to provide staffing for the CEQ, Congress unanimously passed the Environmental Quality Improvement Act in 1970. This act established the Office of Environmental Quality to be supervised by the chairman of the CEQ. It also contained a number of additional duties for the CEQ chairman:

> (2) Assisting the Federal agencies and departments in appraising the effectiveness of existing and proposed facilities, programs, policies, and activities of the

Federal Government, and those specific major projects designated by the President which do not require individual project authorization by Congress, which affect environmental quality;

(3) Reviewing the adequacy of existing systems for monitoring and predicting environmental changes in order to achieve effective coverage and efficient use of research facilities and other resources;

(4) Promoting the advancement of scientific knowledge of the effects of actions and technology on the environment and encourage the development of the means to prevent or reduce adverse effects that endanger the health and well-being of man;

(5) Assisting in coordinating among the Federal departments and agencies those programs and activities which affect, protect, and improve environmental quality;

(6) Assisting the Federal departments and agencies in the development and interrelationship of environmental quality criteria and standards established through the Federal Government;

(7) Collecting, collating, analyzing, and interpreting data and information on environmental quality, ecological research, and evaluation.

In 1977, President Jimmy Carter issued Executive Order 11991 requiring the CEQ to develop regulations to implement NEPA. These were produced by the CEQ in 1978 as 40 CFR 1500. Unlike the NHPA Section 106 regulations, which dictated a procedure that applied to all agencies, the NEPA regulations only provided basic guidelines for each federal agency to develop its own regulations. This meant each agency could implement NEPA according to its particular mission and organizational structure.

Overall, the implementation of NEPA over the last half century has been a great success, even though the full intents of its framers have not been achieved and its scope has been watered down by court rulings. The policy of promoting federal environmental protection and the value of an annual report have remained, but the influence of the CEQ has been reduced, and the real-world impact of the EIS is limited.

NEPA Section 202 stipulated that the CEQ was to have three members appointed by the president upon the advice and consent of the Senate; one member was to serve as chairman. Since 1980, presidents have only appointed a chairman and often delayed in doing so. This means there is a "council" in name only. Presidents Jimmy Carter, Ronald Reagan, and Bill Clinton all tried to eliminate the CEQ, but because it was legislatively created, it could only be legislatively abolished. Reagan drastically slashed the CEQ budget as a way of minimizing its influence.

When NEPA went into effect on January 1, 1980, most agencies took no initiative to implement it, much as happened with the NHPA three year earlier. The first court ruling testing NEPA was the Supreme Court's *Calvert Cliffs' Coordinating Committee, Inc. v. United States Atomic Energy Commission* decision in 1971, which said the Atomic Energy Commission's environmental rules were inadequate with respect to NEPA. This win for NEPA was followed by a series of losses that required federal agencies only to perform an adequate assessment of environmental effects, not to mandate a reduction of these effects. These ruling were critical to the severe limitation of what are known as the "substantive provisions" of NEPA, provisions that actually prevent or reduce environmental harm.

NEPA has never been significantly amended since its passage by Congress in 1969. The process that implements it has not been significantly changed since the regulations were issued by the CEQ in 1978, although the Environmental Quality Improvement Act in 1970 gave the chairman of the CEQ additional duties, and the

Clean Air Act of 1970 took away what should have become some of the CEQ's duties.

Also, almost exactly a year after NEPA was passed, two governmental actions had significant implications for its enforcement. In December 1970, the Environmental Protection Agency (EPA) was created by executive order, and the Clean Air Act of 1970 included a provision (Section 309) requiring EPA review of all environmental impact statements. While the CEQ is an advising agency dependent on executive authority, the EPA is a regulatory agency granted autonomous power to determine the appropriateness of other federal agencies' behavior regarding environmental impacts. However, with respect to NEPA, the EPA can only attempt to change agency behavior with respect to following the rules, not with regard to reducing actual impacts to the environment. In some ways, the CEQ is now an "indigent agency," dependent on the EPA to review and assess the adequacy of environmental review documents and on the Department of Energy to maintain the NEPA.gov webpage.

The CEQ's principal responsibility under NEPA is to provide guidance to agencies with respect to complying with NEPA. The CEQ began to offer formal guidance in the mid-1970s mainly in response to newly passed laws and newly issued executive orders. In the 1980s, CEQ guidance focused on the implementation of the NEPA regulations themselves. By the late 1990s, CEQ guidance still included standard aspects of the implementing regulations (e.g., cumulative effects) but also covered more general issues like environmental justice (1997), timely assessment (2005, 2011), and conflict resolution (2012).

The NEPA Process

By the end of the 1970s, a basic federal environmental review legal structure was in place that still exists today. Immediately after passage of NEPA, the CEQ and EPA had to deal with major environmental issues that led to the fine-tuning of the environmental review process as we know it today. These issues included the Trans-Alaska Pipeline, several major canals (Cross Florida Barge Canal, Tennessee-Tombigbee Waterway), the development of the supersonic transport airplane, and controversial nuclear power plants including the Calvert Cliffs plant on Chesapeake Bay. Many of these issues with regard to the application of NEPA were settled in court. Other important environmental protection laws were also passed soon after NEPA, including the Coastal Zone Management Act (1972) and the Endangered Species Act (1973), but NEPA and the EIS process bound them all together.

As with the Section 106 process, it is helpful to look at a flowchart to understand the steps, requirements, and options in the NEPA process. Unlike Section 106, NEPA has numerous flowcharts available on the internet from federal agencies, state agencies, and private entities. Some stress a particular agency's process for dealing with NEPA. Some have a secondary purpose, like emphasizing the public's role in the process. Most are quite complex (see Figure 7.1). For the NEPA beginner, I like to break the process outlined in 40 CFR 1500 down into three key steps described below. Each step can be thought of as a level of analysis.

NEPA Step 1: Determine if an Action Is a Major Federal Action Significantly Affecting the Quality of the Human Environment

The NEPA process for an agency begins with determining (1) if the effects of a particular action are profound enough in environmental impact potential to warrant additional study, and (2) if the agency is indeed the *lead agency* concerning NEPA review of the profound action. The profound actions are called *major federal actions significantly affecting the quality of the human environment*. Although the

The NEPA Process

```
┌─────────────────────────────────────────┐
│  1. Agency Identifies a Need for Action   │
│         and Develops a Proposal           │
└─────────────────────────────────────────┘
                    │
                    ▼
┌─────────────────────────────────────────┐
│   2. Are Environmental Effects Likely     │
│          to Be Significant?               │
└─────────────────────────────────────────┘
```

NO   YES

```
┌──────────────┐    NO    ┌──────────────┐        ┌──────────────┐
│ 3. Proposed  │ ───────▶ │ 5. Significant│        │ 8. Significant│
│ Action is    │          │ Environmental │        │ Environmental │
│ Described in │          │ Effects       │        │ Effects May or│
│ Agency       │          │ Uncertain or  │        │ Will Occur    │
│ Categorical  │          │ No Agency CE  │        └──────────────┘
│ Exclusion(CE)│          └──────────────┘                │
└──────────────┘                │                         ▼
       │                        ▼                  ┌──────────────┐
      YES              YES  ┌──────────────┐       │ 9. Notice of │
                            │ 6. Develop   │       │ intent to    │
                            │ Environmental│       │ prepare      │
                            │ Assessment   │       │ Environmental│
                            │ (EA) with    │       │ Impact       │
                            │ Public       │       │ Statement    │
                            │ Involvement  │       │ (EIS)        │
                            │ to the Extent│       └──────────────┘
                            │ Practicable  │              │
┌──────────────┐           └──────────────┘              ▼
│ 4. Does the  │                  │               ┌──────────────┐
│ Proposal Have│                  │         YES   │ 10. Public   │
│ Extraordinary│                  ▼               │ Scoping and  │
│ Circumstances│          ┌──────────────┐        │ Appropraite  │
│ ?            │          │ Significant  │        │ Public       │
└──────────────┘          │ Environmental│        │ Involvement  │
       │                  │ Effects?     │        └──────────────┘
      NO                  └──────────────┘               │
                                  │                       ▼
                                 NO               ┌──────────────┐
                                  ▼               │ 11. Draft EIS│
                          ┌──────────────┐        └──────────────┘
                          │ 7. Finding of│               │
                          │ No Significant│              ▼
                          │ Impact       │        ┌──────────────┐
                          └──────────────┘        │ 12. Public   │
                                  │               │ Review and   │
                                  │               │ Comment and  │
                                  │               │ Appropriate  │
                                  │               │ Public       │
                                  │               │ Involvement  │
                                  │               └──────────────┘
                                  │                      │
                                  │                      ▼
                                  │               ┌──────────────┐
                                  │               │13. Final EIS │
                                  │               └──────────────┘
                                  │                      │
                                  │                      ▼
┌──────────────────────────────────────┐         ┌──────────────┐
│              Decision                  │         │14. Public    │
└──────────────────────────────────────┘         │Availability  │
                                  │               │of FEIS       │
                                  │               └──────────────┘
                                  │                      │
                                  │                      ▼
                                  │               ┌──────────────┐
                                  │               │15. Record of │
                                  │               │Decision      │
                                  │               └──────────────┘
                                  │                      │
                                  ▼                      ▼
┌──────────────────────────────────────────────────────────────┐
│ Implementation with Monitoring as Provided in the Decision     │
└──────────────────────────────────────────────────────────────┘
```

FIG. 7.1 National Environmental Policy Act flowchart showing coordination with Section 106 (from Council on Environmental Quality 2007).

CEQ does not use an abbreviation for this cumbersome phrase, I have adopted Tom King's MFASAQHE, although it is so long that we almost need an abbreviation for the abbreviation. King does not provide a pronunciation, so you can use whatever comes to mind as you read it, and make it into an acronym.

Determining which actions are major and if they will have a significant effect on the human environment is the important first step in the NEPA process. The MFASAQHE and lead agency determinations rely on multiple definitions and guidance provided in these definitions.

Definitions

There is no "Definitions" section in the act itself, but critical NEPA definitions are included in the 40 CFR 1500 regulations. For Step 1, important definitions include

> *Categorical Exclusion:* "Categorical exclusion" means a category of actions which do not individually or cumulatively have a significant effect on the human environment and which have been found to have no such effect in procedures adopted by a Federal agency in implementation of these regulations and for which, therefore, neither an **environmental assessment** nor an environmental impact statement is required.

> *Cooperating Agency:* "Cooperating agency" means any Federal agency other than a lead agency which has jurisdiction by law or special expertise with respect to any environmental impact involved in a proposal (or a reasonable alternative) for legislation or other major Federal action significantly affecting the quality of the human environment. A State or local agency of similar qualifications or, when the effects are on a reservation, an Indian Tribe, may by agreement with the lead agency become a cooperating agency.

> *Cumulative Impact:* "Cumulative impact" is the impact on the environment which results from the incremental impact of the action when added to other past, present, and reasonably foreseeable future actions regardless of what agency (Federal or non-Federal) or person undertakes such other actions. Cumulative impacts can result from individually minor but collectively significant actions taking place over a period of time.

> *Effects:* "Effects" include:
> (a) Direct effects, which are caused by the action and occur at the same time and place.
> (b) Indirect effects, which are caused by the action and are later in time or farther removed in distance, but are still reasonably foreseeable. Indirect effects may include growth inducing effects and other effects related to induced changes in the pattern of land use, population density or growth rate, and related effects on air and water and other natural systems, including ecosystems. Effects and impacts as used in these regulations are synonymous. Effects includes ecological (such as the effects on natural resources and on the components, structures, and functioning of affected ecosystems), aesthetic, historic, cultural, economic, social, or health, whether direct, indirect, or cumulative. Effects may also include those resulting from actions which may have both beneficial and detrimental effects, even if on balance the agency believes that the effect will be beneficial.

> *Human Environment:* "Human environment" shall be interpreted comprehensively to include the natural and physical environment and the relationship of people with that environment. (See the definition of "effects" [Sec. 1508.8].) This means that economic or social effects are not intended by themselves to require preparation of an environmental impact statement. When an environmental impact statement is prepared and economic or social and natural or physical environmental effects are interrelated, then the environmental impact statement will discuss all of these effects on the human environment.

Lead Agency: "Lead agency" means the agency or agencies preparing or having taken primary responsibility for preparing the environmental impact statement.

Major Federal Action: "Major Federal action" includes actions with effects that may be major and which are potentially subject to Federal control and responsibility.

Significantly: "Significantly" as used in NEPA requires considerations of both context and intensity: (a) Context. This means that the significance of an action must be analyzed in several contexts such as society as a whole (human, national), the affected region, the affected interests, and the locality. Significance varies with the setting of the proposed action. For instance, in the case of a site-specific action, significance would usually depend upon the effects in the locale rather than in the world as a whole. Both short- and long-term effects are relevant. (b) Intensity. This refers to the severity of impact.

There is no definition of "quality" in 40 CFR 1500 with respect to the human environment. As inferred in the definition of "effects," impacts to the "quality of the human environment" with respect to MFASAQHEs can mean both beneficial and adverse effects. NEPA looks at the good outcomes of a federal action as well as the bad.

Discussion

In general, actions that are subject to NEPA analysis as outlined in the CEQ's *A Citizen's Guide* (2004) are of four types:

(1) Adoption of official policy, such as rules, regulations, and interpretations adopted pursuant to the Administrative Procedure Act; treaties and international conventions or agreements; formal documents establishing an agency's policies which will result in or substantially alter agency programs.

(2) Adoption of formal plans, such as official documents prepared or approved by federal agencies which guide or prescribe alternative uses of Federal resources, upon which future agency actions will be based.

(3) Adoption of programs, such as a group of concerted actions to implement a specific policy or plan; systematic and connected agency decisions allocating agency resources to implement a specific statutory program or executive directive.

(4) Approval of specific projects, such as construction or management activities located in a defined geographic area. Projects include actions approved by permit or other regulatory decision as well as federal and federally assisted activities.

The great majority of projects that result in a full environmental impact statement tend to be of the fourth type. These are the projects that are most understandable to the general public and the most controversial.

Determination of the lead agency is obvious for the first three types of projects listed above and is usually pretty straightforward for the fourth type as well, as most projects are funded, initiated, or permitted by a single agency. An agency automatically becomes the lead agency if it is the only federal agency directly involved in an action. *Cooperating agencies* are usually determined by the lead agency. They often have both jurisdiction and expertise with regard to an action, so they must be consulted throughout the process by the lead agency.

To determine if an action is indeed a MFASAQHE subject to additional NEPA analysis, the lead agency most commonly first applies **categorical exclusions** (CATEXes). As seen in the definition, these are actions that pose little risk of affecting the environment. Agencies have a list of CATEXes within their own implementing regulations for NEPA. Examples are personnel procedures, minor existing facility alterations, and reconstruction of small structures in the same location for the same purpose. In most cases, a CATEX action is obvious, but a more complicated CATEX can require use of a checklist to confirmed that additional analysis is not needed. These two types of minor actions are called *automatic* and *checklist* CATEXes.

Agency actions normally subject to additional analysis may also be excluded from the NEPA process if they are considered emergencies, though such actions, depending on their scope, may be subject to additional CEQ or EPA interaction, such as postemergency mitigation or amendment of agency NEPA regulations to anticipate procedures for future emergencies of the same type.

In determining if an action is a MFASAQHE, the lead agency does not have to publish a public notice detailing its deliberations. However, an agency CATEX list would have appeared with the agency NEPA regulations in the *Federal Register*, providing the public a chance to comment on the list itself, if not on subsequent actions subject to it.

Conclusion of Step 1

If an agency determines that an action is classified as a CATEX, its responsibilities under NEPA are completed. No public notice is required. If the action is not subject to a CATEX or otherwise needs additional analysis to determine if it is a MFASAQHE, the agency proceeds to Step 2, requiring the completion of an environmental assessment (EA). If it is apparent through preliminary analysis that an action is clearly a MFASAQHE, the agency proceeds directly to Step 3, requiring an environmental impact statement.

NEPA Step 2: Prepare an Environmental Assessment

The purpose of an environmental assessment is to determine whether an action could have a significant effect on the human environment and, if so, to suggest alternatives or mitigation to lessen effects to the point that they are no longer significant. Critical to this step are three definitions from 40 CFR 1500.

Definitions

Environmental Assessment: (a) Means a concise public document for which a Federal agency is responsible that serves to: 1. Briefly provide sufficient evidence and analysis for determining whether to prepare an environmental impact statement or a **finding of no significant impact**. 2. Aid an agency's compliance with the Act when no environmental impact statement is necessary. 3. Facilitate preparation of a statement when one is necessary.

(b) Shall include brief discussions of the need for the proposal, of alternatives as required by section 102(2)(E), of the environmental impacts of the proposed action and alternatives, and a listing of agencies and persons consulted.

Finding of no significant impact. "Finding of no significant impact" means a document by a Federal agency briefly presenting the reasons why an action, not otherwise excluded (Sec. 1508.4), will not have a significant effect on the human environment and for which an environmental impact statement therefore will not be prepared. It shall include the environmental assessment or a summary of it and shall note any other environmental documents related to it (Sec. 1501.7[a][5]). If the assessment is included, the finding need not repeat any of the discussion in the assessment but may incorporate it by reference.

Mitigation: "Mitigation" includes:
(a) Avoiding the impact altogether by not taking a certain action or parts of an action.

(b) Minimizing impacts by limiting the degree or magnitude of the action and its implementation.

(c) Rectifying the impact by repairing, rehabilitating, or restoring the **affected environment.**

(d) Reducing or eliminating the impact over time by preservation and maintenance operations during the life of the action.

(e) Compensating for the impact by replacing or providing substitute resources or environments.

Discussion

If an environmental assessment is necessary, the lead federal agency is responsible for its completion, but if it is an external action subject only to agency approval, the project applicant usually bears the production responsibility. This includes paying for necessary analytical expertise, writing the text, and printing the document.

The purpose of the EA is to determine if additional analysis in the form of an environmental impact statement is necessary. While the definition stresses that an EA is a "concise document" that requires no set format, many agencies in their NEPA procedures require EAs to use a document structure similar to that used in an EIS. This is often unnecessary for simple projects and just adds paperwork and cost. Although supposed to be "concise," EAs can vary in length from under 100 pages to well over 1,000 pages.

The CEQ *A Citizen's Guide* (2004:11) provides the following guidelines for topics to discuss:

- The need for the proposed action
- Alternative courses of action for any proposal that involves unresolved conflicts concerning alternative uses of available resources
- The environmental impacts of the proposed action and alternatives
- A listing of agencies and persons consulted

The critical discussion in an EA should examine each alternative and how deep and widespread its effects on the human environment would be. This is known as "context and intensity" analysis. *Context* is the geographical, physical, and cultural setting of an action, and *intensity* is the severity of the impact. An EA should also look at possible steps to reduce adverse effects, preferably from the agency's standpoint, obviating the need for an EIS.

As stated in the definition of "human environment," if the EA finds that there will only be significant social or economic effects from the action under review, these effects are insufficient in and of themselves to require an EIS. This "socioeconomic exclusion" has led to a great deal of confusion and been the subject of a number of important court cases. In the most prominent court action, *Metropolitan Edison Co. v. People Against Nuclear Energy*, the Supreme Court decided in 1983 that stated psychological impacts alone were not sufficient to require an EIS.

Other subsequent court rulings have more broadly rejected all social and economic effects from requiring, in and of themselves, mandatory EIS completion. Although tangible historic properties appear to be obvious components of the physical environment, courts have determined that adverse effects to historic properties are considered social effects and thus fit the socioeconomic exclusion (e.g., *Friends of the Astor, Inc. v. City of Reading*, 1998). This even applies to properties already listed in the National Register of Historic Places (NRHP). This finding is supported in NHPA Section 110(i) (now 54 USC 306111).

This doesn't mean that social and economic effects can be ignored in an EA or an EIS, as Tom King has told us time and time again. Social and economic effects must be comprehensively identified and thoroughly analyzed, and mitigation must be suggested to reduce or eliminate adverse effects. Under the socioeconomic category, NEPA looks at more than just historic properties as defined by the NHPA. It also looks at social effects on important cultural resources other than historic properties—in other words, at less tangible aspects of culture.

The NEPA regulations use the term "cultural resources," although they do not define it. In practice, cultural resources have come to include spiritual values, social institutions, community lifeways, historic documents, and artifacts. Because most actions reviewed under NEPA EAs and EISs are also subject to the NHPA, EAs and EISs tend to rely on inventories, surveys, and expertise that stress tangible historic properties to the exclusion of the great diversity of other cultural resources. The NRHP has very specific guidelines as to what is eligible, including only tangible properties that occupy a specific geographic space and generally excluding properties less than 50 years old. Properties excluded from NRHP eligibility may still be important cultural resources and still subject to NEPA.

Social impact assessment (SIA) is a direct outgrowth of NEPA and a heritage management specialty all by itself. It is now worldwide in scope. Social impacts, according to the National Oceanic and Atmospheric Administration (NOAA) Inter-organizational Committee on Principles and Guidelines for Social Impact Assessment (2003), are "the consequences to human populations of any public or private actions that alter the ways in which people live, work, play, relate to one another, organize to meet their needs and generally cope as members of society. The term also includes cultural impacts involving changes to the norms, values, and beliefs that guide and rationalize their cognition of themselves and their society."

Another socioeconomic issue to come to the forefront of NEPA analysis and gain worldwide attention is environmental justice (EJ), a formal American concept that originated in Executive Order 12898 issued by President Clinton in February 1994. This EO basically stated that environmental effects of federal actions on minority and low-income groups should be carefully considered, and these groups should not disproportionately suffer any adverse effects. The NEPA process was singled out as a way to identify and address environmental justice. The CEQ has developed considerable guidance on the matter, with the most recent effort dated March 2016.

Conclusion of Step 2

If the EA determines there are no significant impacts on any non-socioeconomic elements of the human environment, the agency issues a finding of no significant impact (FONSI). The FONSI summarizes the reasons why the agency has concluded that the proposed action under agency review will indeed have no significant impacts.

An increasingly popular option is a *mitigated FONSI*. If the EA has identified one or more significant impacts to the human environment, the agency can propose or agree to mitigative actions that will reduce the effects to a level of nonsignificance, eliminating the need for an EIS. Mitigation can be done in a number of ways. Avoidance of harm or minimization of harm to an acceptable level through plan revision or selection of a different alternative is the best option from environmental and controversy standpoints. Postconstruction restoration of environmental harm is another generally acceptable mitigation option.

Replacement of harmed land and resources through restoration of an approximately equivalent area and resources outside the project area is a standard form of mitigation, but it is often controversial as project opponents may see it as some sort of blackmail to accept a project or token mitigation for substantial environmental harm. The practice is called *mitigation banking*. With regard to cultural resources, this could result in public purchase and protection of an "equivalent" archaeological site or building. Another option for archaeological sites—conducting a data recovery—is applicable to sites eligible only under National Register Criterion D (information potential). For some types of cultural resources, such as traditional cultural properties (TCPs) or truly unique historic properties, there is no reasonable data-recovery or replacement option.

Mitigated FONSIs are popular because they eliminate the need for an EIS. Having to do an EIS increases project costs and can result in project delays. An EIS is more public than an EA, potentially resulting in more controversy that can further increase costs and project delays. The key to an acceptable mitigated FONSI is that it truly reduces effects to acceptable levels and is enforceable in its mitigation strategy.

Examples of standard and mitigated FONSIs can be found on the NEPA webpage (https://www.energy.gov/nepa/listings/findings-no-significant-impact-fonsi). A standard FONSI is typically 5 to 10 pages in length. If it relies on the EA itself for basic justification language, the FONSI will often be in letter format with the EA attached. The letter should refer to the critical pages in the EA.

As with Step 1, the opportunity for public involvement in Step 2 is limited and largely dependent on a public that is diligent and savvy when it comes to the NEPA process. The only public involvement required by the NEPA regulations is publication of a notice of availability (NOA) of a FONSI in the *Federal Register* with a 30-day comment period, but this is only required if the action under agency review is unusual or would normally require an EIS. Some agencies are more proactive with regard to public involvement. They put all EAs and FONSIs on a project page on their websites or publish notices in a local newspaper.

If the EA finds significant impacts to at least one non-socioeconomic element of the human environment, the agency needs to complete an EIS.

NEPA Step 3: Prepare an Environmental Impact Statement

Environmental impact statements are expensive, time-consuming, and often controversial. They can consist of intensive analysis resulting in thousands of pages of documentation. As a state historic preservation office (SHPO) archaeologist and a state archaeologist, I reviewed a number of EISs that individually stacked over 3 feet high. Appendices tend to make up the vast majority of pages. While it often takes only months to complete an EA, an EIS can take up to five years. There are 10 times as many EAs done as EISs, with an average of about 500 EISs done each year nationally, according to the CEQ webpage.

Definitions

Note that "environmental impact statement," the concept that in practice takes the most time, costs the most money, and is the most controversial, is subject to the shortest definition in 40 CFR 1500.

Environmental Impact Statement: "Environmental impact statement" means a detailed written statement as required by section 102(2)(C) of the Act.

Notice of Intent: "**Notice of intent**" means a notice that an environmental impact statement will be prepared and considered. The notice shall briefly:
(a) Describe the proposed action and possible alternatives.
(b) Describe the agency's proposed scoping process including whether, when, and where any scoping meeting will be held.
(c) State the name and address of a person within the agency who can answer questions about the proposed action and the environmental impact statement.

Scope: Scope consists of the range of actions, alternatives, and impacts to be considered in an environmental impact statement. The scope of an individual statement may depend on its relationships to other statements (Secs.1502.20 and 1508.28). To determine the scope of environmental impact statements, agencies shall consider 3 types of actions, 3 types of alternatives, and 3 types of impacts. They include:

(a) Actions (other than unconnected single actions) which may be:

1. Connected actions, which means that they are closely related and therefore should be discussed in the same impact statement. Actions are connected if they: (i) Automatically trigger other actions which may require environmental impact statements. (ii) Cannot or will not proceed unless other actions are taken previously or simultaneously. (iii) Are interdependent parts of a larger action and depend on the larger action for their justification.

2. Cumulative actions, which when viewed with other proposed actions have cumulatively significant impacts and should therefore be discussed in the same impact statement.

3. Similar actions, which when viewed with other reasonably foreseeable or proposed agency actions, have similarities that provide a basis for evaluating their **environmental consequences** together, such as common timing or geography. An agency may wish to analyze these actions in the same impact statement. It should do so when the best way to assess adequately the combined impacts of similar actions or reasonable alternatives to such actions is to treat them in a single impact statement.

(b) Alternatives, which include:

1. **No action alternative.**

2. Other reasonable courses of action.

3. Mitigation measures (not in the proposed action).

(c) Impacts, which may be: (1) Direct; (2) Indirect; (3) Cumulative.

Special Expertise: "Special expertise" means statutory responsibility, agency mission, or related program experience.

Discussion

When beginning an EIS, the preparers will first need to establish a *purpose and need* that basically justifies the action. It answers the question: What public purpose is served by whatever action is the subject of the EIS, and why does this purpose need to be served? If the action involves the damming of a river, the purpose and need statement will focus on flood control and recreation, not on the building of the dam. Reasonable alternatives are those that meet the purpose and need.

Once the purpose and need have been established, the agency will publish a notice of intent (NOI) in the *Federal Register* and optionally in a local publication or on the lead agency webpage. The NOI includes a basic description of the project and the scoping process the agency will follow, including anticipated public participation in the scoping process. The NOI should identify a person at the lead agency who can be contacted for additional information on the project and the NEPA process.

"Scoping" has the longest and most detailed definition in the regulations (see above). The basic purpose of scoping is to identify "the range of actions, alternatives, and impacts to be considered in an environmental impact statement." For a savvy public, it is an opportunity to enter the process early and provide initial recommendations for completion of an EIS.

As outlined in the NEPA *A Citizen's Guide* (2007:14), the scoping process should

- Identify people or organizations who are interested in the proposed action;
- Identify the significant issues to be analyzed in the EIS;
- Identify and eliminate from detailed review those issues that will not be significant or those that have been adequately covered in prior environmental review;

- Determine the roles and responsibilities of lead and cooperating agencies;
- Identify any related EAs or EISs;
- Identify gaps in data and informational needs;
- Set time limits for the process and page limits for the EIS;
- Identify other environmental review and consultation requirements so they can be integrated with the EIS;
- Indicate the relationship between the development of the environmental analysis and the agency's tentative decision-making schedule.

The people and organizations identified in the first step or who come forward in response to an NOI must be invited to participate in the scoping process. The method of participation is not made explicit in the NEPA regulations, but it will need to be justified as appropriate in the EIS.

The agency now begins work on completing a draft environmental impact statement (DEIS). Unlike for an EA, the NEPA regulations (40 CFR 1502.10) do have a "recommended" format for an EIS, which should consist of

- Cover sheet
- Summary
- Table of contents
- Purpose of and need for action
- Alternatives including proposed action
- Affected environment for each alternative
- Environmental consequences
- List of preparers
- List of agencies, organizations, and persons to whom copies of the statement are sent
- Index
- Appendixes (if needed)

The core of the EIS deals with establishing the affected environment for each alternative and determining the environmental consequences of implementing each alternative. This analysis requires a diverse group of experienced specialists. It also usually requires extensive fieldwork, state-of-the-art research, and careful scientific analysis of the results of the fieldwork and research.

Most EISs divide the environment into discrete areas that each require special expertise to assess effects. A typical division is

- Noise
- Air quality
- Safety
- Soils and water
- Biological resources
- Cultural resources
- Land use
- Infrastructure
- Hazardous materials and waste
- Socioeconomics
- Environmental justice

Note that in this example cultural resources are separated from socioeconomics, although judicial rulings put cultural resources under socioeconomics when it comes to determining the need for an EIS. The separation of the two within the EIS itself is helpful in fulfilling the needs of other laws such as the NHPA and in establishing that cultural resource analysis is not limited just to tangible aspects of the physical environment.

All alternatives that reasonably meet the stated and justified purpose and need of the action must be evaluated in the EIS. Included among the alternatives must be a "no action alternative," often called the "no build option." The EIS must explain what will happen if the action is not taken. The EIS usually identifies a preferred alternative, and although the effects of all alternatives must be evaluated, an EIS may concentrate on mitigating any adverse effects of the preferred alternative.

Once the DEIS is completed, the agency sends a copy to the EPA and other consulting parties. The EPA then publishes a notice of availability in the *Federal Register* with a minimum 45-day comment period. An agency will often also advertise the availability of the DEIS in local media outlets and conduct public hearings on the contents of the DEIS. The agency is required to ask for comments from federal, state, local, and tribal agencies that may have some jurisdiction with regard to the action under review. Because the availability of a DEIS is usually well advertised and contains the complete summary of the action and probable effects, this is the most public action taken in the NEPA process.

After the public comment period ends, the agency is obligated to carefully consider all comments received, both public and private. Sometimes these comments are simply corrections of fact, and sometimes they are long sermons on why the project is an environmental disaster. Any substantive comments should be addressed by the agency. The submitted comments and agency responses are included in the final EIS. When the final EIS is completed, the EPA once again publishes an NOA in the *Federal Register*.

Conclusion of Step 3

At least 30 days must pass before the agency issues its **record of decision** (ROD), which is the final agency step in the NEPA process. As stated in the NEPA *A Citizen's Guide* (2007:19), "The ROD is a document that states what the decision is; identifies the alternatives considered, including the environmentally preferred alternative; and discusses mitigation plans, including any enforcement and monitoring commitments. In the ROD, the agency discusses all the factors, including any considerations of national policy, that were contemplated when it reached its decision on whether to, and if so how to, proceed with the proposed action. The ROD will also discuss if all practical means to avoid or minimize environmental harm have been adopted, and if not, why they were not." Although there is no requirement to publish an agency ROD, it is made available to members of the public if they request a copy. RODs occasionally appear in the *Federal Register* or on agency websites. The EIS itself is usually so extensive that printed copies are not made available to everyone upon request, but electronic copies are available on the EPA website, and a printed copy may be available in a public library near the project.

If a substantial amount of time (e.g., five years) passes after the completion of an EIS and the actions covered in it have not been implemented, if there are substantial changes to an action, or if there are substantial changes in environmental circumstances where an action is to take place, an agency may prepare a *supplemental EIS* (SEIS). The SEIS follows the same process as an EIS, except it doesn't have to go through scoping. If the SEIS is supplemental to a DEIS, both have to be addressed in the final EIS.

The EPA reviews all DEISs, commenting to the lead agency on the adequacy of the analysis. To streamline the review process and make the reviews consistent, the EPA uses a standardized rating system, looking at both the intensity of the environmental effect of the action and the adequacy of the EIS. If it deems the DEIS unsatisfactory, it notifies the agency and the CEQ. Neither the CEQ nor the EPA can require the agency to redo a DEIS or EIS deemed unsatisfactory.

NEPA from an Archaeological Perspective

Because NEPA is basically a scientific process, archaeologists educated in the 1970s and 1980s found it familiar. The postprocessual archaeologists educated in the 1990s, with their skepticism of science, and post-post archaeologists educated in the twenty-first century, with their focus on diversity and social justice, find the NEPA process too rigid and myopic. Postmodernist historians share the scientific skepticism. Architects, who are basically innovative and imaginative engineers, tend to be more like processual archaeologists; they just do their job when asked to contribute to completing an EIS without worrying about varying social and intellectual perspectives.

Some archaeologists within agencies and consulting firms have actually found themselves doing more than just archaeology for NEPA endeavors, while other heritage management professionals have continued just to contribute to their narrowly defined sections. Although consideration of cultural resources is part of NEPA, the law goes beyond NHPA in considering impacts to the larger cultural environment. Social and environmental justice concerns promote an anthropological approach, another reason archaeologists can broadly contribute to the NEPA process, as most are educated in departments of anthropology.

Department of Transportation Act of 1966 Section 4(f)

Historical Background

Some states as early as the 1930s had provisions in their highway construction specifications that allowed for "salvage" of archaeological sites hit by road construction (e.g., Nebraska in 1937). Most of these specifications did not pay for or sponsor the salvage; they just temporarily suspended construction at the site location until university or museum archaeologists completed the salvage as soon as possible. In Minnesota the destruction of habitation and burial sites in the 1930s, most notably the Minnesota Woman site (21OT1) in 1931, required a number of major site salvage operations. In 1951, the Minnesota Highway Department issued a memorandum directing all project engineers to report "evidences of Indian occupation" to the chief engineer. New Mexico started the first proactive highway archaeological survey in 1954 (Wendorf 1962).

The Federal Highway Administration (FHWA) began to pay more attention to cultural resources when it started to build the Interstate Highway System in the late 1950s. The Federal-Aid Highway Act of 1956 provided funding for the construction of this system. Section 120 of the act authorized the use of funds as approved by state highway departments for archaeological and paleontological salvage. The federal-state match for these funds was the same as for the road construction, 90% federal and 10% state. Consideration for nonarchaeological historic properties was not included in the 1956 act.

Although the 1956 law did not mention preconstruction surveys, some state universities and state historical societies began to be more proactive by requesting yearly updates of state highway plans so that some consideration of known sites could be included prior to the beginning of construction. Minnesota did this in 1957 (Anfinson and Peterson 1979).

Interstate highway construction soon became one the most notorious destroyers of historic properties, especially in cities where large corridors were cleared through older neighborhoods and commercial districts. The interstate construction's effect on archaeological sites, especially in rural areas, has never been comprehensively measured, as sites were less visible and advocates more dispersed. The widespread destruction of urban buildings and structures promoted the passage of the National Historic Preservation Act as well as several highway acts.

In order to save a popular park in San Antonio from destruction by highway construction, Senator Ralph Yarborough of Texas proposed that a parkland preservation provision be added to the 1966 Federal-Aid Highway Act. The amendment was expanded to include historic sites and added to the Senate bill along with a policy statement that the secretary of commerce (later transportation) should make maximum efforts to preserve public parklands and historic sites with respect to highway development. The law passed and was enacted as 23 USC 138.

At the same time, another Senate committee was working on the parallel Department of Transportation Act, whose main objective was to put all federal transportation agencies, including the Federal Highway Administration, under one cabinet-level agency, the Department of Transportation (DOT). The Yarborough amendment was also added to DOTA with even stronger language not only mandating minimization of harm but requiring that the Department of Transportation not approve any harm to parks and historic sites if there was "a feasible and prudent alternative." It also included consideration of recreation areas and wildlife refuges. DOTA was passed by Congress in late 1966, with the Yarborough amendment's preservation policy requirement appearing as Section 2(b)(2) and the land and historic site preservation requirements as Section 4(f); this became 49 USC 1653(f). President Lyndon Johnson signed DOTA with its Section 4(f) into law on the same day as the National Historic Preservation Act, October 15, 1966.

Section 4(f) has been amended several times since 1966, but the substance of what the law requires has remained intact. In 1968, Congress addressed the different wording in the DOTA versus the Federal-Aid Highway Act, with the DOTA 4(f) wording retained for both acts. However, the Federal-Aid Highway Act (23 USC 138) only applies to FHWA. In 1983, codification was amended, and DOTA 4(f) became 49 USC 303; thus Section 4(f) is now Section 303. As with Section 106 of NHPA, however, most practitioners, including DOT agencies, still use the term 4(f).

In 2005, a substantive change was made to simplify the 4(f) process in the case of projects that had only minimal impacts to included resources; this is now known as **de minimis impact** analysis. The 2005 amendment also required the US DOT to issue regulations to clarify the "feasible and prudent" requirement in considering alternatives. In the 2005 amendments, there was an attempt to eliminate Section 4(f) consideration of historic properties if Section 106 of NHPA applied, but this effort failed. The first regulations implementing 4(f) were issued as 23 CFR 771.135 in 1981. The current regulations for 4(f) were issued in the *Federal Register* on March 12, 2008, as 23 CFR 774.

The courts have been largely sympathetic to the congressional intent of Section 4(f). The Supreme Court's 1971 decision in *Citizens to Preserve Overton Park v. Volpe* set a high standard for compliance with Section 4(f), stating that Congress intended the protection of parkland to be of paramount importance. The Court also made clear that an avoidance alternative must be selected unless it would present "uniquely difficult problems" or require "costs or community disruption of extraordinary magnitude." Many legal actions DOT agencies face are due to 4(f), but the majority of these are related to wildlife land and park concerns, not historic sites.

Legislative Language and Definitions

In the amended version of DOTA (49 USC 303), the original Section 2(b)(2) and Section 4(f) have been put into three subsections of Section 303. Section 4(f) as originally written in 1966 consists of 303(b) and 303(c). Minor changes have been made to the wording of 4(f) in the 303 version:

§303. Policy on lands, wildlife and waterfowl refuges, and historic sites

(a) It is the policy of the United States Government that special effort should be made to preserve the natural beauty of the countryside and public park and recreation lands, wildlife and waterfowl refuges, and historic sites.

(b) The Secretary of Transportation shall cooperate and consult with the Secretaries of the Interior, Housing and Urban Development, and Agriculture, and with the States, in developing transportation plans and programs that include measures to maintain or enhance the natural beauty of lands crossed by transportation activities or facilities.

(c) Approval of Programs and Projects. Subject to subsections (d) and (h), the Secretary may approve a transportation program or project (other than any project for a park road or parkway under section 204 of title 23) requiring the use of publicly owned land of a public park, recreation area, or wildlife and waterfowl refuge of national, State, or local significance, or land of an historic site of national, State, or local significance (as determined by the Federal, State, or local officials having jurisdiction over the park, area, refuge, or site) only if (1) there is no prudent and feasible alternative to using that land; and (2) the program or project includes all possible planning to minimize harm to the park, recreation area, wildlife and waterfowl refuge, or historic site resulting from the use.

Key definitions in the 23 CFR 774 implementing 4(f) include

All possible planning. All possible planning means that all reasonable measures identified in the Section 4(f) evaluation to minimize harm or mitigate for adverse impacts and effects must be included in the project. (2) With regard to historic sites, the measures normally serve to preserve the historic activities, features, or attributes of the site as agreed by the Administration and the official(s) with jurisdiction over the Section 4(f) resource in accordance with the consultation process under 36 CFR part 800.

De minimis impact. (1) For historic sites, de minimis impact means that the Administration has determined, in accordance with 36 CFR part 800 that no historic property is affected by the project or that the project will have "no adverse effect" on the historic property in question.

Feasible and prudent avoidance alternative. (1) A feasible and prudent avoidance alternative avoids using **Section 4(f) property** and does not cause other severe problems of a magnitude that substantially outweighs the importance of protecting the Section 4(f) property. In assessing the importance of protecting the Section 4(f) property, it is appropriate to consider the relative value of the resource to the preservation purpose of the statute. (2) An alternative is not feasible if it cannot be built as a matter of sound engineering judgment. (3) An alternative is not prudent if: (i) It compromises the project to a degree that it is unreasonable to proceed with the project in light of its stated purpose and need; (ii) It results in unacceptable safety or operational problems; (iii) After reasonable mitigation, it still causes: (A) Severe social, economic, or environmental impacts; (B) Severe disruption to established communities; (C) Severe disproportionate impacts to minority or low income populations; or (D) Severe impacts to environmental resources protected under other Federal statutes; (iv) It results in additional construction, maintenance, or operational costs of an extraordinary magnitude; (v) It causes other unique problems or unusual factors; or (vi) It involves multiple factors in paragraphs (3)(i) through (3)(v) of this definition, that while individually minor, cumulatively cause unique problems or impacts of extraordinary magnitude.

Historic site. For purposes of this part, the term "historic site" includes any prehistoric or historic district, site, building, structure, or object included in, or eligible for inclusion in, the National Register. The term includes properties of traditional religious and cultural importance to an Indian tribe or Native Hawaiian organization that are included in, or are eligible for inclusion in, the National Register.

Section 4(f) Property. Section 4(f) property means publicly owned land of a public park, recreation area, or wildlife and waterfowl refuge of national, State, or local significance, or land of an historic site of national, state, or local significance.

Use. Except as set forth in §§ 774.11 and 774.13, a "use" of Section 4(f) property occurs:

(1) When land is permanently incorporated into a transportation facility; (2) When there is a temporary occupancy of land that is adverse in terms of the statute's preservation purpose as determined by the criteria in § 774.13(d); or (3) When there is a constructive use of a Section 4(f) property as determined by the criteria in § 774.15.

Some critical terms are not found in the 4(f) "Definitions" section, yet are used throughout the process and play critical roles in 4(f) implementation. Some of these terms do not have the same meaning as they do with respect to Section 106 of NHPA and NEPA.

Significance

The terms "significant" and "significance" are used throughout the Section 4(f) regulations and the FHWA's *Section 4(f) Policy Paper* (2012). "Least overall harm" is partially determined by the "relative significance of each 4(f) property." Properties associated with the Interstate Highway System (e.g., rest areas, bridges) are not to be considered 4(f) properties unless they are of "national or exceptional significance." Included in "constructive use" determinations are "enjoyment of a historic site where a *quiet setting* is a generally recognized feature or attribute of the site's significance" and "examples of substantial impairment to visual or esthetic qualities would be the location of a proposed transportation facility in such proximity that it obstructs or eliminates the primary views of an architecturally significant historical building." Most importantly, only the *use* of *significant properties* means a 4(f) evaluation has to be done.

For parks, recreation areas, and refuges, "significance" means the property must play an important role in fulfilling the mission of the public management entity. The management entity (i.e., the official with jurisdiction) makes this decision, and any determination of insignificance by that official must apply to the entire parcel. FHWA can review the reasonableness of an official's determination of significance and find a park, recreation area, or refuge insignificant for 4(f) if FHWA thinks the determination was "unreasonable."

With regard to historic sites, "significance" has almost the same meaning as it does in Section 106 of the NHPA. A historic property is significant and thus subject to 4(f) if it is listed or eligible for inclusion in the National Register of Historic Places. However, eligibility for the National Register under NHPA is determined by a combination of meanings of significance under one or more criteria as well as a property's integrity. For 4(f) purposes, "significance" for historic sites has the same general meaning as "listed in or eligible for the NRHP."

There is also the issue of properties to which tribes attach "religious and cultural significance." Although this phrase originated with the Section 106 regulations, it also appears in the definition of "historic site" in the 4(f) regulations. Some of these properties may not meet National Register criteria mainly due to age and religious exception considerations, but a noneligible property of this type could still be a 4(f) property. In addition, Part II of the FHWA policy paper states under "Historic Sites Question 2A" that if a property is determined not eligible by the SHPO or the tribal historic preservation officer (THPO), FHWA can still consider it a "significant" 4(f) property if requested to do so by a local official with authority (e.g., a mayor).

Identification

"Identification" for Section 106 of NHPA involves finding any potentially eligible properties in the area of potential effects (APE) of an undertaking. For Section 4(f), "identification" involves two separate steps. The first entails finding if any public parks, recreation areas, refuges, or public or private registered historic sites are in or immediately adjacent to a project. This is done through a literature search and consultation with officials with jurisdiction. The first three types of greenspace properties are already known and have been mapped by officials with jurisdiction, while listed and already-determined-eligible historic properties, especially buildings and structures, are contained in SHPO or THPO inventories.

The second step of 4(f) identification involves, like Section 106, determining if there are any unknown but potentially eligible historic properties in or immediately adjacent to the project area. Like Section 106 of the NHPA, this involves fieldwork, usually in two phases: a thorough **reconnaissance survey** to locate any previously unidentified historic properties within the project area and an evaluation survey to determine if any known or recently identified properties are eligible for inclusion in the National Register.

If the transportation agency and the SHPO/THPO agree that an inventoried property is eligible, it becomes a 4(f) property if it will be *used* (see Step 1 below) by a transportation project. Any listed or eligible historic properties should be identified as early as possible in the 4(f) planning process (23 CFR 774.9), but most 4(f) historic property determinations await the completion of Section 106 identification and evaluation efforts. This means that Section 106 Step 10 (see chapter 6) is completed prior to the completion of Step 1 in the 4(f) process.

Evaluation

"Evaluation" for Section 106 means making a determination of eligibility for the National Register. For Section 4(f) it means undertaking and documenting the entire process used to determine if 4(f) applies to a particular project and how that project is dealing with it. Evaluation for 4(f) has a similar function as an environmental assessment for NEPA. An evaluation needs to consider the *net benefit* (see below) of a project on a 4(f) property.

There are two types of 4(f) evaluation: *programmatic* and *individual*. Programmatic evaluations utilize one of the five nationwide programmatic agreements (PAs) that FHWA has implemented. Programmatic evaluations require minimum documentation. Three of the FHWA programmatic agreements apply to historic sites:

- Programmatic Section 4(f) Evaluation and Approval for FHWA Projects That Necessitate the Use of Historic Bridges
- Final Nationwide Section 4(f) Evaluation and Approval for Federally Aided Highway Projects with Minor Involvements with Historic Sites

- Nationwide Programmatic Section 4(f) Evaluation and Approval for Transportation Projects That Have a Net Benefit to a Section 4(f) Property.

Individual evaluations require more extensive documentation and go through a process similar to approving an EIS.

Net Benefit

The 4(f) regulations under 774.3(d) allow for programmatic evaluations as "time-saving procedural alternatives" to preparing individual Section 4(f) evaluations. The FHWA has issued five programmatic agreements to accomplish this. One, first issued in 2002 and approved in 2005, is for projects that result in a *net benefit* to a 4(f) property. The net benefit determination for a 4(f) property is basically an alternative to a de minimis finding.

According to the net benefit programmatic agreement, "A 'net benefit' is achieved when the transportation use, the measures to minimize harm and the mitigation incorporated into the project results in an overall enhancement of the Section 4(f) property when compared to both the future do-nothing or avoidance alternatives and the present condition of the Section 4(f) property, considering the activities, features and attributes that qualify the property for Section 4(f) protection. A project does not achieve a 'net benefit' if it will result in a substantial diminishment of the function or value that made the property eligible for Section 4(f) protection." Thus, if a *use* is determined for a historic property by a transportation project, and the proposed project includes all appropriate measures to minimize harm and subsequent mitigation necessary to preserve and enhance those features and values of the historic property that originally qualified it for Section 4(f) protection, the net benefit programmatic agreement applies.

For historic properties this means:

> The project does not require the major alteration of the characteristics that qualify the property for the National Register of Historic Places (NRHP) such that the property would no longer retain sufficient integrity to be considered eligible for listing. For archeological properties, the project does not require the disturbance or removal of the archaeological resources that have been determined important for preservation in-place rather than for the information that can be obtained through data recovery. The determination of a major alteration or the importance to preserve in-place will be based on consultation consistent with 36 CFR part 800, and consistent with 36 CFR part 800, there must be agreement reached amongst the SHPO and/or THPO, as appropriate, the FHWA and the Applicant on measures to minimize harm when there is a use of Section 4(f) property. Such measures must be incorporated into the project.

Proximity Impacts

"Proximity impacts" are reviewed under the concept of constructive use of 4(f) properties (776.15). Proximity impacts are basically the same as indirect effects under Section 106. They consist of effects on historic properties due to audible, visual, atmospheric, and access factors. These proximity impacts expand the project area beyond the direct construction zone.

In order to be determined a constructive use of a property considered under 4(f), the proximity impacts must "substantially impair" the critical features of a property. For historic properties, this means they must impair integrity aspects, such that the property's eligibility for the National Register is compromised. For archaeological sites, this would be rare because most are eligible only under National Register Criterion D and do not have public access, although archaeologists' access could be impaired (i.e., impervious covering, deep burial by filling).

The FHWA policy paper (2012:3) suggests that any proximity impacts be determined in "coordination" with officials with jurisdiction, but unlike with eligibility, the determination is made not by consensus but solely by the transportation official. Under 776.15(f)(6), "Proximity impacts will be mitigated to a condition equivalent to, or better than, that which would occur if the project were not built, as determined after consultation."

The 4(f) Process

It is important to remember that Section 4(f) only applies to the 11 DOT agencies, including the Federal Highway Administration, the Federal Aviation Administration (FAA), the Surface Transportation Board (STB), the Federal Railroad Administration, and the Maritime Administration. It applies to all projects receiving DOT funding or approval *and* using any of the four kinds of 4(f) properties.

Unlike the 36 CFR 800 regulations implementing Section 106 of NHPA and the 40 CFR 1500 regulations implementing NEPA, the 23 CFR 774 regulations for Section 4(f) of DOTA do not clearly outline the sequential process agencies should follow in applying the law. The 4(f) regulations have sections that separately discuss approvals, coordination, documentation, timing, exceptions, and applicability as to how they apply to the 4(f) process as a whole, as well as the meaning of "constructive use." Additional explanations of how various concepts from the law are to be applied in the process appear in the "Definitions" section (e.g., "de minimis," "all possible planning," "feasible and prudent alternative").

The Department of Transportation website and most DOT agency websites provide substantial information on Section 4(f), but most give little help with actually applying the process in an easy-to-understand way, especially for the general public. The FHWA website has the most extensive information on applying 4(f), presented as a "toolkit." The toolkit includes a policy paper that originally appeared in 1987 and was updated in 2005 after the de minimis amendment to the law.

The most recent version of the *FHWA 4(f) Policy Paper* is dated July 20, 2012. It is issued as a supplement to the 4(f) regulations and is based on the law, the regulations, court decisions, and FHWA experience in applying the law. Its primary purpose is "to aid FHWA personnel with administering 4(f) in a consistent manner" and to assist state DOTs and other applicants. FHWA also has an online tutorial to explain 4(f) (https://www.environment.fhwa.dot.gov/strmlng/newsletters/jun13nl.asp). The American Association of State Highway and Transportation Officials (AASHTO) also provides helpful 4(f) guidance. Standard Section 4(f) flowcharts are presented in Figure 7.2. One shows the entire process and the other de minimis situations.

Although there may be some variation between DOT agencies as to how the 4(f) process is carried out, the process outlined below is how it is applied by the FHWA, which has the most experience in applying the law and provides the most detailed information on 4(f). While 4(f) applies to public parks, recreation areas, and wildlife and waterfowl refuges as well as historic sites, historic sites are treated substantially differently in the regulations. Historic sites affected by transportation projects can be on public or private land, while the other types of 4(f) properties are limited to those only on public land. Historic sites as 4(f) properties are primarily determined by the process outlined in the Section 106 regulations, which requires them to be listed in or determined eligible (by agency-SHPO/THPO consensus or Keeper decision) for the National Register. The other types of properties are automatically given 4(f) status if they are publicly owned, designated as parks, recreation areas, or refuges by federal, state, or local authorities, and deemed significant by their management officials.

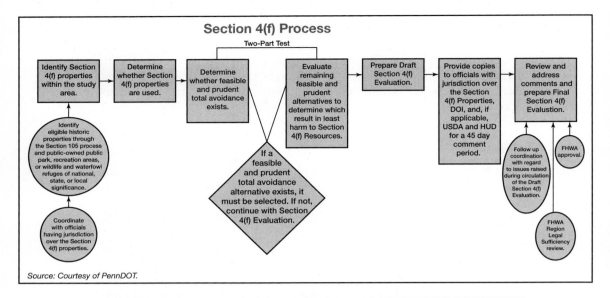

Section 4(f) Process

Two-Part Test

| Identify Section 4(f) properties within the study area. | → | Determine whether Section 4(f) properties are used. | → | Determine whether feasible and prudent total avoidance exists. | → | Evaluate remaining feasible and prudent alternatives to determine which result in least harm to Section 4(f) Resources. | → | Prepare Draft Section 4(f) Evaluation. | → | Provide copies to officials with jurisdiction over the Section 4(f) Properties, DOI, and, if applicable, USDA and HUD for a 45 day comment period. | → | Review and address comments and prepare Final Section 4(f) Evalustion. |

Identify eligible historic properties through the Section 105 process and public-owned public park, recreation areas, or wildlife and waterfowl refuges of national, state, or local significance.

Coordinate with officials having jurisdiction over the Section 4(f) properties.

If a feasible and prudent total avoidance alternative exists, it must be selected. If not, continue with Section 4(f) Evaluation.

Follow up coordination with regard to issues raised during circulation of the Draft Section 4(f) Evaluation.

FHWA approval.

FHWA Region Legal Sufficiency review.

Source: Courtesy of PennDOT.

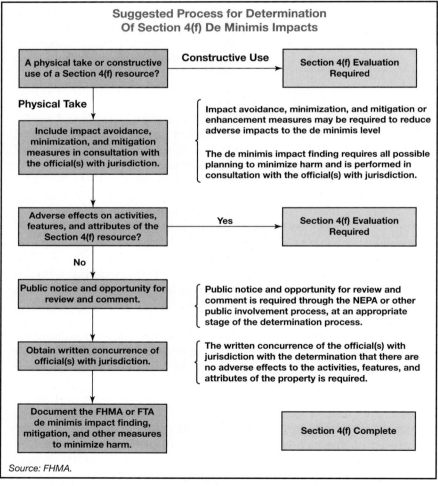

Suggested Process for Determination Of Section 4(f) De Minimis Impacts

A physical take or constructive use of a Section 4(f) resource? → **Constructive Use** → **Section 4(f) Evaluation Required**

Physical Take

Include impact avoidance, minimization, and mitigation measures in consultation with the official(s) with jurisdiction.

{ Impact avoidance, minimization, and mitigation or enhancement measures may be required to reduce adverse impacts to the de minimis level

The de minimis impact finding requires all possible planning to minimize harm and is performed in consultation with the official(s) with jurisdiction.

Adverse effects on activities, features, and attributes of the Section 4(f) resource? → **Yes** → **Section 4(f) Evaluation Required**

No

Public notice and opportunity for review and comment.

{ Public notice and opportunity for review and comment is required through the NEPA or other public involvement process, at an appropriate stage of the determination process.

Obtain written concurrence of official(s) with jurisdiction.

{ The written concurrence of the official(s) with jurisdiction with the determination that there are no adverse effects to the activities, features, and attributes of the property is required.

Document the FHMA or FTA de minimis impact finding, mitigation, and other measures to minimize harm.

Section 4(f) Complete

Source: FHMA.

FIG. 7.2 Department of Transportation Section 4(f) flowcharts showing standard process (top) and de minimis determination (bottom) (Federal Highway Administration).

With regard to historic sites, the 4(f) process, if fully implemented, goes through six basic steps:

1. Identify any historic properties that will be used by a federal transportation project.
2. Assess the NRHP eligibility of any used properties.
3. Determine if any impacts are de minimis or subject to a programmatic agreement.
4. Evaluate potential adverse effects to historic properties.
5. Develop prudent and feasible alternatives.
6. Select the alternative that will do the least overall harm.

4(f) Step 1: Identify Potential Historic Properties That Will Be Used

There are three types of use of a historic property subject to Section 4(f). "Permanent incorporation" means the property will be acquired outright for the transportation project. "Temporary occupancy" means the use of the property is only temporary, but project implementation may have adverse effects on the property. "Constructive use" means there are significant proximity impacts to unacquired property such that its activities, features, or attributes are substantially impaired. Constructive use would be more commonly applied to the historic properties of the built environment (e.g., buildings, structures) as opposed to most archaeological sites (see my definition of "built environment" in Appendix A).

Although Section 4(f) has no formal designation of a project area, the Section 106 area of potential effects is often used, as almost all projects subject to 4(f) are also subject to Section 106. Standard literature searches and field surveys consistent with Section 106 application are used to determine if any potentially eligible properties are within or adjacent to the transportation project. Because transportation agencies usually require that Section 106 be completed prior to 4(f), all necessary identification and documentation of the effort will have been completed for a 4(f) decision with regard to historic properties. Potential historic sites include the full range of properties eligible for inclusion in the National Register, including traditional cultural properties.

If a transportation project is found to be using no 4(f) properties of any kind, the project can proceed as planned. FHWA procedures require the agency to make a *determination of nonapplicability* that states why 4(f) does not apply to the project. The project can then proceed. There is no required public, tribal, or external agency consultation, although communication and consultation with the SHPO/THPO would have been necessary to coordinate any Section 106 findings.

4(f) Step 2: Assess the NRHP Eligibility of Any Used Properties

If a transportation project is found to be using potential historic properties, the agency issues a *determination of applicability* that states why 4(f) does apply. The properties must then be evaluated for National Register eligibility. Once again, because 4(f) is usually done after or at least in parallel with Section 106, the eligibility finding done for one law also applies to the other.

The process to determine National Register eligibility for 4(f) purposes is identical to that for Section 106. The transportation official consults with the SHPO/THPO, and if all parties agree the site is eligible, it is eligible for the purposes of Section 4(f). If they disagree on the eligibility, the transportation official sends the documentation to the Keeper of the Register, who makes the final determination. If a property to be used is determined ineligible, the 4(f) process does not apply to that property, and if it is the only 4(f) property under consideration, the 4(f) process ends for a particular project.

One variation in the 4(f) process concerning historic sites is that a site pre-viously determined ineligible, but still historically important to a community, can, upon request by a prominent local official, be considered by the transportation offi-cial as significant for 4(f) purposes, and if there is a use of that property for the transportation project, it will be considered a 4(f) property.

4(f) Step 3: Determine if Any Impacts Are De Minimis or Subject to a Programmatic Agreement

If a listed or eligible historic site will be used by a project, the next step is to deter-mine if the impact is de minimis. As indicated by the definition given above, an impact is de minimis if it has been determined through the Section 106 analysis to have no adverse effect on a historic property based on a consensus finding of the agency and the SHPO/THPO. Thus the transportation agency is required to consult with the SHPO/THPO to complete this step for de minimis determinations.

For a programmatic agreement determination, the transportation official can apply one of the existing FHWA PAs specific to historic properties (e.g., historic bridges) or the net benefit PA. The documentation of a programmatic determination must support the specific criteria contained in the PA. The FHWA webpage has examples of application of de minimis to historic properties (https://www.environment. fhwa.dot.gov/section4f/projects_deminimis.aspx).

If the de minimis or programmatic determination is made that no historic sites are being used by a project, the 4(f) process is over with respect to that property.

4(f) Step 4: Evaluate Potential Adverse Effects to Historic Properties

If a de minimis or PA determination cannot exclude an eligible or listed historic property from use by a transportation project, the agency must do an in-depth eval-uation as to what the potential adverse effects will be. This results in an *individual evaluation*. The individual evaluation presents results from the combination of two findings: (1) there is no feasible and prudent alternative that completely avoids the use of a Section 4(f) property, and (2) the project includes all possible planning to minimize harm to the Section 4(f) property resulting from the transportation use.

An FHWA policy paper provides the following format for an individual evalua-tion. This format was presented in an FHWA technical advisory dated October 30, 1987, and has not changed:

1) Applicability or non-applicability of Section 4(f) to the park, recreation, ref-uge or historic property proposed to be used by the project;
2) Whether or not there is a use of Section 4(f) property;
3) Activities, features, and attributes of the Section 4(f) property;
4) Analysis of the impacts to the Section 4(f) property;
5) Records of public involvement;
6) Results of coordination with the officials with jurisdiction;
7) Alternatives considered to avoid using the Section 4(f) property, including analysis of the impacts caused by avoiding the Section 4(f) property;
8) A least overall harm analysis, if appropriate;
9) All measures undertaken to minimize harm to the Section 4(f) property;
10) Comments submitted during the coordination procedures required by 23 CFR 774.5 and responses to the comments; and
11) Results of the internal legal sufficiency review.

The draft evaluation contains a description of the 4(f) properties, the particulars of their use, an alternatives analysis, and the measures proposed to minimize harm. The draft does not contain an in-depth discussion of why there are no prudent and feasible alternatives, what possible planning has been done to minimize harm, and what specific alternative would result in the least overall harm. These three elements are discussed in the final 4(f) evaluation document. The draft evaluation document is sent by FHWA to the Department of the Interior and to all officials with jurisdiction. It is also included in the DEIS, if there is one. There is a minimum 45-day comment period for the draft.

4(f) Step 5: Develop Prudent and Feasible Alternatives

Based on the preliminary assessment of the effects of use on a historic property, the agency must examine all "feasible and prudent alternatives" as options to the alternative causing the adverse effect. Note the definition of "feasible and prudent avoidance alternative" listed above. The purpose of this analysis is to completely avoid all adverse effects to a historic property and, if that is not possible, to minimize the harm.

The first part of this step is to develop a reasonable range of alternatives, including at least one that avoids all adverse impacts to the subject historic property. The alternatives must include a no-build or no-action alternative. Alternatives examined by the NEPA process can be used if they will avoid or minimize impacts to the property, but additional alternatives may need to be developed exclusively for the 4(f) process. Alternatives generally include looking at alignment shifts and design changes, such as using curbs and gutters instead of ditches.

Next, the alternatives have to be examined to see if avoiding an effect on one type of 4(f) property will result in adverse impacts to another type of 4(f) property. When I was a highway archaeologist working in wildlife refuges, I called this being "between the devil and the deep blue sea." Archaeological sites were generally on uplands, so to avoid an archaeological site you might have to fill a wetland, adversely impacting a waterfall production area (see chapter 8 sidebar).

The initial alternatives analysis should also examine the relative significance of the properties being impacted. For historic sites, this is difficult when you are comparing listed or eligible properties of local, state, and national significance. All are significant in terms of the National Register, but properties of national significance that are National Historic Landmarks (NHLs) are treated as more valuable in the Section 106 process. Uniqueness is also a factor in determining relative significance. A rock art site may be more important to save than a prehistoric habitation site from a well-known historic context.

After the kinds and importance of adversely affected properties have been determined, the feasible and prudent standards are applied separately. *Feasible* basically looks at engineering soundness. *Prudent* looks at issues such as not fulfilling the project's purpose and need, the project design's becoming unsafe, adverse community impacts, social justice concerns, significantly increased building and/or maintenance costs, or any combination of these factors, which may not be significant individually but become so together.

Unlike other historic property types, eligible archaeological sites are not all treated equally by Section 4(f). If an archaeological site will be adversely impacted by a transportation project and is only eligible under National Register Criterion D (i.e., valuable only for its information potential), it does not require "preservation in place" and therefore is not considered a 4(f) property. Data recovery (i.e., mitigation excavation) to obtain the information contained in the site is not required by 4(f) but is encouraged. A data recovery would be the subject of a memorandum of agreement under Section 106 due to an adverse effect determination. The eligibility determination including the Criterion D–only assessment has to be made in consultation with a SHPO/THPO. Criterion D archaeological sites also had second-class status under Section 106 prior to the 1992 NHPA amendments. Apparently the authors of the 2005 amendments to DOTA didn't get the memo.

If the agency chooses an alternative that will avoid the adverse effects, the final evaluation document is then prepared; it addresses the comments received on the draft and includes an in-depth discussion justifying the selection of a prudent and feasible alternative. The final evaluation also must consider *legal sufficiency*, which is done by the agency's legal counsel and basically substantiates that the agency has followed and documented the required steps in the 4(f) process. The final evaluation document can be issued 15 days after the 45-day draft comment period has ended. The final 4(f) evaluation is included in a final NEPA EIS if there is one. Once the final 4(f) evaluation has been submitted to the transportation agency district office and legal sufficiency has been confirmed, the project can proceed if other legal requirements have been met.

4(f) Step 6: Select the Alternative That Will Do the Least Overall Harm

After all alternatives have been examined and the agency has determined that it can't find a feasible and prudent one that avoids harming the historic site or other types of 4(f) properties, it must determine which alternative will cause the least overall harm. This determination is based on seven factors:

1. The ability to mitigate adverse impacts to each Section 4(f) property (including any measures that result in benefits to the property)
2. The relative severity of the remaining harm, after mitigation, to the protected activities, attributes, or features that qualify each Section 4(f) property for protection
3. The relative significance of each Section 4(f) property
4. The views of the officials with jurisdiction over each Section 4(f) property
5. The degree to which each alternative meets the project's purpose and need
6. After reasonable mitigation, the magnitude of any adverse impacts to resources not protected by Section 4(f)
7. Substantial differences in costs among the alternatives

The first four factors consider the net harm each alternative would cause. The final three allow FHWA to take into account any substantial problems with any of the remaining alternatives that are basically beyond Section 4(f) considerations.

The final evaluation is then written. It must address the comments received on the draft evaluation as well as contain an in-depth discussion of why there are no prudent and feasible alternatives, what possible planning has been done to minimize harm, and what specific alternative would result in least overall harm based on the seven factors listed above. The final evaluation document can be issued 15 days after the 45-day draft comment period has ended. The final 4(f) evaluation is included in a final NEPA EIS if there is one. Once the final 4(f) evaluation has been submitted to the FHWA district office and legal sufficiency has been confirmed, the project can proceed if other legal requirements have been met.

Conclusions Regarding Section 4(f)

There are four paths for compliance with Section 4(f):

1. Finding of no use
2. De minimis determination
3. Programmatic evaluation
4. Individual evaluation

With regard to historic properties, 4(f) applies to those that are publicly or privately owned if they are listed in or determined eligible for the National Register. All major steps in the 4(f) process must be documented in writing and be available for public inspection, although the exact locations of sensitive resources (e.g., archaeological sites, TCPs) can remain confidential.

The 4(f) process essentially requires *coordination* rather than *consultation*; coordination is more about letting other entities know what you are doing, while consultation entails a formal process for discussing your plans with other entities, requiring attention to the timing, intensity, and nature of the contact and, if possible, integration of its results into the implementation of your plans. For 4(f) much of the coordination is with the SHPO/THPO and local government officials with jurisdiction with regard to historic sites.

Formal consultation for 4(f) with the SHPO/THPO is only required for eligibility assessments and de minimis determinations for historic sites, unless it is required for another action as specified in an applied programmatic agreement. Formal tribal coordination is required only if a historic property is located on a reservation, but it does not include portions of the project outside the reservation limits or mandate consultation with nonresident tribes that may have an interest in the area of the project.

Archaeological and Historic Preservation Act (1974)

The one piece of heritage preservation legislation talked about when I was getting my master's degree was the Archaeological and Historic Preservation Act of 1974. We first knew it as the Moss-Bennett Bill, so named for its two congressional sponsors. Ironically, after 40 years of practicing heritage management, I have never used the AHPA and rarely encountered it. Compared to the other late-twentieth-century environmental protection legislation affecting heritage management, it was and still is a very minor player. In retrospect, archaeologists talked about it in the mid-1970s because it was about jobs for archaeologists. If anything, the AHPA is a clear demonstration that in the 1970s many archaeologists were not initially involved or interested in the big three environmental laws with cultural heritage implications: the National Historic Preservation Act, the National Environmental Policy Act, and the Department of Transportation Act.

Based on the name of the act, the AHPA appears to be broadly targeted heritage preservation legislation, but it was basically written by archaeologists almost exclusively for archaeological benefit. The AHPA amended the 1960 Reservoir Salvage Act (RSA). Because the AHPA expanded the scope of the RSA beyond just reservoir construction and provided a dedicated funding source, the amended version was also initially known as the Archaeological Recovery Act or the Archaeological Data Protection Act. There is no official title for the act in the law. It was originally cited as Public Law 93-291 (16 USC 469–469c) but is now 54 USC 3125.

As discussed in chapter 3, the RSA itself was basically an extension of another law, the Historic Sites Act of 1935. The RSA specified that if a federally funded reservoir or construction activities associated with it destroyed "exceptional" historic or archaeological sites, the secretary of the interior could authorize collection and preservation "of the data." Paying for the preservation work was not the responsibility of the reservoir development agencies (i.e., Corps of Engineers, Bureau of Reclamation) but was dependent on congressional appropriation of funds necessary to carry out the work.

The RSA was amended in 1974 by the AHPA not only to better address funding responsibility and amounts but to broaden the scope beyond just reservoirs. The AHPA's chief proponents were Charles McGimsey of the Arkansas Archaeological Survey and Carl Chapman, an archaeologist at the University of Missouri. When first proposed in 1969, it generated considerable excitement in the archaeological community, but there was little coordination with nonarchaeological professionals despite the inclusion of "historic sites." The emphasis was clearly on the preservation of data, not sites, and the included "historic" sites were inferred to mean historical archaeological sites, not historical buildings and structures. With its focus on data preservation, AHPA ignores nonarchaeological heritage resources, as few elements of the built environment are considered significant just for their information potential (National Register Criterion D).

Like the Reservoir Salvage Act, the AHPA

- calls for the collection and preservation of important archaeological and historical data,
- applies to all major reservoir construction,
- requires implementing agencies to provide the secretary of the interior notice of and plans for construction projects,
- requires a preconstruction survey,
- considers both the collection and the preservation of data and artifacts,
- puts the secretary of the interior in charge of implementing the act,
- allows the implementing agency to do the archaeological work itself or have the Department of the Interior do it, and
- includes an appropriation clause for "necessary" funds to carry out the act.

The AHPA makes the following major improvements on the RSA for heritage preservation:

- The RSA only applied to reservoir construction, while the AHPA includes "any alteration of the terrain caused as a result of any Federal construction project or federally licensed activity or program."
- The RSA only included the preservation of historical and archaeological data of "exceptional value," while the AHPA includes "significant scientific, prehistorical, historical, or archeological data."
- The RSA had no archaeological reporting requirement, but the AHPA allows funding for the production of analytical reports, requires that all reports be sent to the secretary of the interior, and mandates that the secretary make received reports "available to the public."
- Section 469(c) of the AHPA requires the secretary to submit an annual report to the Committee on Natural Resources of the House of Representatives and the Committee on Energy and Natural Resources of the Senate "indicating the scope and effectiveness of the program, the specific projects surveyed and the results produced, and the costs incurred by the Federal Government as a result thereof."
- The RSA authorized the appropriation of funds to carry out the purposes of the act, while the AHPA not only authorizes appropriation of funds but allows agencies to transfer up to 1% of the total project cost to the Department of the Interior to help cover the costs of "survey, recovery, analysis, and publication."

While a significant improvement over the RSA, the AHPA still has a number of flaws:

- The RSA required construction monitoring, but the AHPA only allows for data recovery from sites encountered during construction. Without experienced, independent professionals on-site during major terrain disturbance, the likelihood of finding previously unknown sites decreases significantly.
- The AHPA doesn't include any real consideration of nonarchaeological cultural resources like structures and TCPs.

- The exclusion for "activities undertaken in anticipation of a natural disaster" could exclude AHPA application to flood-control projects designed to prevent future flooding.
- It requires allowing public access to archaeological reports without redacting exact site locations.
- It does not consider indirect or cumulative impacts.
- It lacks definitions except for "state"; it doesn't define "significance" or "appropriate historical or archaeological authorities."
- It does not require coordination with NHPA, NEPA, and DOTA 4(f).
- It does not require congressional appropriation.
- It does not require that agencies actually provide funding for survey and data recovery.
- There is confusion about the use of 1% of project costs for archaeological mitigation, although Section 208(3) of the 1980 amendment of NHPA provides a means for agencies to get a waiver of the 1% limit.

The AHPA Process

The National Park Service (NPS) is the agency within the Department of the Interior charged with AHPA implementation. There are no broad regulations implementing AHPA, although the 36 CFR 79 curation regulations issued by NPS in 1990 are a direct result. A statement of program approach for AHPA was issued by the Department of the Interior in 1975, followed by proposed regulations (36 CFR 66) in the *Federal Register* on January 28, 1977. These regulations were never finalized, and 36 CFR 66 has disappeared from the active list of NPS codified federal regulations. These 1977 draft regulations focused on data-recovery operations, curation of data and materials, and reporting. They also included definitions of key terms, although "significant data" was defined but not "significant site." Elements of 36 CFR 66 were incorporated into later Advisory Council on Historic Preservation (ACHP) archaeological guidance, including *Treatment of Archaeological Properties: A Handbook* (1980).

Because almost all federal agency actions would be included under NHPA, NEPA, and/or DOTA 4(f) reviews, NPS and agencies generally follow the procedures outlined in the regulations implementing those laws for the implementation of AHPA. Because the focus of AHPA is archaeology, the departmental consulting archaeologist (DCA) at NPS handles cases that come under AHPA. The DCA also reviews and approves any requests for archaeological funding exceeding 1% of project costs.

The process for development or permitting agencies to comply with the AHPA were not clearly outlined in the draft regulations in 1977, but the law outlines what is needed. I have never seen an AHPA flowchart, but the process should consist of the following steps.

AHPA Step 1: Agency Determines if AHPA Is Applicable to a Project

The law states that a federally funded or permitted project is subject to AHPA if it "may cause irreparable loss or destruction of significant scientific, prehistorical, historical, or archeological data." For historical and archaeological resources, such a determination is contingent on three factors: the nature of the project, the nature of the area affected, and the potential of the area to contain any of the significant types of data.

If the project involves major natural soil disturbance, it meets the first condition. If the area has not been previously disturbed to a level where all the significant data has been destroyed or seriously impaired, it meets the second condition. The area's site/

data potential is assessed using three methods: examining existing standard inventories of archaeological sites (e.g., SHPOs), using predictive modeling to assess the area's potential to contain significant sites/data, and conducting a reconnaissance survey. The agency can determine that the area has archaeological data potential without doing a survey, but if the area has potential, it can't prove a site isn't there without doing a survey. For very large projects, agencies generally assume site potential.

AHPA Step 2: Agency Informs the Secretary of the Interior

If the area has significant data potential, the agency must notify the secretary of the interior in writing and provide "appropriate information concerning the project." This usually means providing a detailed description of the project and including plans that clearly show the area to be impacted and the nature of the impact. At this time, the agency may

1. request that the secretary determine if the area indeed has significant data potential or if a known site in the area may contain significant data;
2. if the area does have potential, request that the secretary undertake a survey of the area or, if there is a known significant site that will be harmed, undertake the data recovery and reimburse the secretary for the cost using up to 1% of project funds; or
3. notify the secretary that the agency will complete the necessary archaeological work using its project funds. If this latter approach is used, the agency is not restricted to 1% of the project funds.

The survey or data recovery must be initiated within 60 days of the notification.

AHPA Step 3: Necessary Archaeological Work Is Completed

If the Department of the Interior does the work, the secretary must keep the implementing agency informed as to findings and progress. Regardless of who does the work, it must meet professional standards, and a detailed report also meeting professional standards must be completed and submitted to the agency and the secretary. Whoever does the archaeological work is also responsible to make sure the recovered material and archaeological records are properly curated. Once the secretary confirms that the necessary archaeological work has been completed, he or she notifies the agency that work on the project can proceed.

Reports to Congress

In 1968, the National Park Service, under its Archaeology Division of the Office of Archaeology and Historic Preservation (OAHP), began annual reports to Congress on the federal archaeology program (Knudson and McManamon 1992). The main focus of the Archaeology Division at that time was managing contracts under the RSA. This reporting obligation was reinforced in 1974 when AHPA amended the RSA. The DCA in OAHP's Interagency Archaeological Services division took responsibility for writing the reports. The first secretarial report under AHPA was produced in fiscal year 1975. The Archaeological Resources Protection Act of 1979 broadened the NPS congressional reporting role to include the archaeological activities of all federal agencies. The reports became biennial in 1988 and then quadrennial in 1998.

AHPA Conclusions

When I was in graduate school in the mid-1970s, the AHPA was a big deal, as it was expected to be an "archaeological full-employment act." Today, it receives little attention from agencies or archaeologists due to its overlap with NHPA, NEPA, and DOTA 4(f), its focus on data salvage rather than site preservation, and the fact that few large reservoirs, still a main focus of the act, are being built. Today it seems strange that archaeologists in the late 1960s and early 1970s were seemingly so unaware of the requirements and potentials of the existing NHPA, DOTA 4(f), and NEPA. Yet the 1974 passage of the AHPA is often credited with increasing the awareness of archaeologists and federal agencies of the needs and requirements of federal heritage preservation.

Tom King (2013:280) has pointed out that AHPA has some strengths often ignored by archaeologists and cultural heritage preservationists. The fact that AHPA doesn't define "significant" as equal to "eligible" allows some room to consider impacts on ineligible sites that are dismissed by the other major laws. AHPA procedures for dealing with unanticipated discoveries allow for an alternative method to that outlined in Section 106.

Finally, the inclusion of the "scientific data" consideration in AHPA leads most to think of paleontological finds, but it can include acquiring environmental data that could be lost due to a construction project, including pollen sites, animal bone beds, and pack rat middens. King (2013:281) also notes AHPA is rarely used in litigation.

A congressional appropriation for funding AHPA was last made in 1983.

Summary

NEPA

The CEQ advertises NEPA as "informed decision-making." The NEPA process is basically a scientific process. It requires identifying possible impacts, understanding them, performing rigorous and repeatable tests to examine their implications, carefully analyzing the results of the tests, and writing up the results. To do the first four tasks requires familiarity with the scientific process, internal expertise, and consultation with external experts. The final task requires consideration of outside expert opinions as well as the opinions of those who are potentially affected by the outcome (e.g., the public).

The NEPA process outlined in 40 CFR 1500 is similar in many ways to the Section 106 process outlined in 36 CFR 800. The regulations of both laws specify and encourage cooperation to streamline processes and come to similar conclusions. Other similarities between NEPA and Section 106 of NHPA include allowance for agencies to develop alternative procedures, consideration of effects to historic properties, emphasis on doing environmental effect assessment early in the agency planning process, consideration of direct, indirect, and cumulative effects, and completion of the review process prior to authorization of any work. Most importantly, the federal agency under both laws makes all the important decisions, and only consideration, not preservation or protection, is required.

There are, however, significant differences between NEPA and NHPA both in terms of process and subject matter. These include definition of the project area, the timing and intensity of public and tribal consultation, the types of resources included for consideration, procedures for developing agency alternatives, documentation requirements, and timing. The Section 106 process does not require identification of all historic properties in all NEPA alternatives, emphasizing identification of properties in only the NEPA preferred alternative.

While NEPA has done much to increase governmental, agency, and public awareness of the environmental impacts of a wide range of federal government actions, it cannot prevent environmental degradation, including the destruction of important cultural resources. The "P" in NEPA stands not for "Protection" or "Preservation" but for "Policy."

DOTA 4(f)

Unlike Section 106 and NEPA, DOTA 4(f) is focused on the preservation of historic properties, not just their consideration by a rigorous review process. It requires avoidance of adverse effects if a feasible and prudent alternative is available and minimization of adverse effects if they cannot be completely avoided. Unlike Section 106 and NEPA, 4(f) is property specific, not project specific. Section 4(f) reviews must be coordinated with Section 106 and NEPA. The Section 106 process is generally completed prior to much of the 4(f) process.

Section 4(f) of DOTA, while more powerful for actual preservation than NEPA, is limited only to projects that come under the jurisdiction of the Department of Transportation. Because 4(f) goes beyond Section 106 in offering protection to heritage resources, it has been a target of conservative congressional action to make it consistent with Section 106 or even weaker.

AHPA

To most archaeologists, archaeology is more about understanding the past than preserving it. Due to the priorities of the modern versions of NHPA and NEPA, as well as the intellectual influences of postprocessualism and postmodernism, many archaeologists and some federal agencies now focus on strategies that avoid impacting sites, supposedly promoting site preservation. This includes not collecting artifacts during surveys. Agencies also promote noncollect policies, as curation responsibilities are greatly increasing in cost, and there is increasingly limited space available in curation facilities.

Despite current trends, AHPA promotes artifact collection through preconstruction surveys and data-recovery excavations. This is good for archaeology as a science because it increases our understanding of the past, furthering archaeology's primary purpose. Accessible collections in public repositories give future researchers an artifactual library to continue or reexamine past studies. Under AHPA, a reservoir can't be filled and most developments can't be built without collecting artifacts and excavating sites. Although these activities destroy or partially destroy sites, the reservoir or project itself will ultimately destroy most of the sites it impacts in addition to making many of them archaeologically inaccessible. Furthermore, the AHPA-mandated process saves in a scientific and public manner vital data that may be lost through future activities that aren't under federal review and the AHPA mandate.

Review Questions

1. What forces led to the passage of the National Environmental Policy Act?
2. What is a MFASAQHE?
3. What is a FONSI?
4. What types of properties are covered by DOTA Section 4(f)?
5. What is de minimis with respect to 4(f)?
6. What laws did the AHPA amend?

Supplemental Reading

NEPA has been the subject of numerous books and articles from various perspectives, including Clark and Canter (1997). The CEQ provides considerable guidance on its webpage, such as *A Citizen's Guide to the NEPA* (2007). Some agencies also have NEPA guidance on their webpages. For a heritage management perspective on NEPA, see chapter 2 of King (2013). Weiland (1997) notes deficiencies in the current version of NEPA.

Section 4(f) of the Department of Transportation Act has lots of analysis available through national and state transportation agency webpages (e.g., FHWA's *Section 4[f] Policy Paper*), as well as from transportation specialty organizations like the American Association of State Highway and Transportation Officials. King (2013:243–246) provides a brief cultural resource management perspective on 4(f).

There aren't many in-depth analyses available for AHPA. Look at King (2013:278–281) and McManamon (2000) for brief overviews.

SIDEBAR

Implementing Heritage Management: The Times Were Indeed a-Changin'

When I was a kid, leaded gasoline, DDT, and nuclear power plants were celebrated as examples of human progress. By the time I got to college, the first two were in disfavor. By the time I got my first full-time job, DDT had been banned, and leaded gasoline was being phased out. Before long the construction of nuclear power plants virtually ceased. All were victims of the environmental movement. Of the major social movements of the 1960s, the environmental movement often gets less attention, but its effects had the widest scope and benefits.

The environmental movement was a reaction to trends that began with the Industrial Revolution in the late 1700s but greatly accelerated after World War II: population growth, urbanization, and industrialization, all dependent on fossil fuels. This caused widespread conversion of natural lands to agricultural production and greatly increased coal and oil production for power generation. This decimated many plant and animal species and led to a rapid reduction in air and water quality. Between 1950 and 1970, the US population grew by almost 40%, while gross domestic product and energy consumption more than doubled. The end of gasoline and rubber rationing after World War II, coupled with rising personal incomes, meant almost everyone could have a car. Suburban sprawl had the dual effect of converting open land into a built environment and making middle-class suburban dwellers more aware of the need to slow degradation of the adjacent environment.

The principal environmental concern of the 1950s was nuclear radiation, although some large cities (e.g., New York, London) were experiencing killer smog events. In the 1950s, degradation of animal populations and wild lands was more of a concern than the direct effects of pollution on human health. This led to the founding of the Nature Conservancy in 1951 and the rapid expansion of the national park system. By the 1960s, environmental concerns focused on air and water pollution and their negative effects on people. Rachel Carson's *Silent Spring* (1962) is perhaps the most influential literary work to affect any modern social movement. It galvanized public and private efforts to improve all aspects of the natural environment. This happened at the same time as the flowering of the historic preservation movement.

There was not much interchange between the natural and cultural preservation movements in the 1960s. If you look at the major concerns of each, there just wasn't much overlap. Air pollution, water pollution, the loss of species, and radiation threats had little direct impact on tangible cultural resources. Urban renewal had little effect on the natural environment. The two principally had in common the adverse effects of reservoir construction and interstate highway construction. For the most part, each movement fought against these developments without asking for or receiving significant help from the other.

This had not always been the case. When the Trustees of Reservations was founded in Massachusetts in 1891, its members were concerned with preserving both natural and cultural resources. The organization actually served as a model for the founding of the English National Trust three years later (McMahon and Watson 1992). The English National Trust remained true to its natural and cultural resource preservation mission for an entire country, but the Trustees of Reservations and their cultural-natural approach didn't spread beyond New England.

Then, in 1965, the two conservation movements were brought together in the Johnson administration's "Great Society" initiative. Although it was called the White House Conference on Natural Beauty, Lady Bird Johnson made sure historic resources were included in the initiative to preserve the environment. This "natural beauty" initiative led directly to the passage of the National Historic Preservation Act in 1966, soon followed by the Clean Air Act of 1967 and the National Wild and Scenic Rivers Act of 1968. It also had a significant influence on promoting the addition of Section 4(f) to the Department of Transportation Act in 1966.

Advocates for environmental protection and historic preservation speak a similar language. "Conservation," "protection," "stewardship," "heritage," and "management" are words common to both vocabularies. The core missions are also the same: improving or maintaining quality of life for people. The Johnson administration's blending of the two movements climaxed with the passage of the National Environmental Policy Act in 1969 in the first year of the Richard Nixon administration.

The inclusion of social impact effects in NEPA rapidly led to the consideration of intangible cultural resources not included in the NHPA, but the complexity and subjectivity of social impact assessment and environmental justice encouraged agencies to gradually retreat to just consideration of effects to tangible cultural resources. The courts did not discourage this retreat and even supported it by declaring in 1998 that social impacts alone could not require an environmental impact statement. Today, the SIA of an EIS relies almost exclusively on the processes and findings of Section 106 of NHPA.

The current implementation of NEPA has gone much beyond what Congress intended to protect even for the natural environment. An EIS was envisioned as providing enough data for an agency to alter a project if it indeed had a significant adverse effect on the human environment. The eight-page initial EIS for the Trans-Alaska Pipeline and the three-page Corps of Engineers EIS for dredging in the Great Lakes in 1970 were a bit too short on detail, but no one in the 1969 Congress, and certainly not President Nixon, envisioned EIS documents that were multiple feet high and cost millions of dollars. With the election of 2016, the times may be a-changin' again, but this time it may be to the detriment of natural and cultural resources.

CHAPTER 8

Federal Specialty Laws
The Rest of the Structure

> The heads of all Federal agencies shall assume responsibility for the preservation of historic properties which are owned or controlled by such agency.
> —Section 110, National Historic Preservation Act

Besides environmental review laws, there are a number of federal laws that deal with particular actions and particular kinds of heritage resources. They can be divided into five basic types according to application:

- Laws for federal properties
- Laws for urban renewal and redevelopment
- Laws for museums and curation
- Laws for special properties and areas
- Laws for Indian heritage resources

This chapter deals with the first four types: laws based on who owns the land, how older parts of cities are rehabilitated, portable heritage resources, and special kinds of heritage properties. Indian laws will be dealt with in chapter 13.

A number of other federal laws that have some application to heritage management (e.g., Amtrak Improvement Act of 1974) fit into one or more of these categories, but they are not discussed because their application is so limited and narrow. They are not critical to understanding the main structure of American heritage management and actions that could result in major losses of heritage resources.

The paths to the preservation of historic buildings and structures are very different from those taken for archaeological sites. Constructed properties and sites each have distinct property types often found in very different settings. Archaeological preservation laws over the years tended to focus on the rural environment, but structure preservation laws have focused on urban areas. Archaeological sites are often invisible on the surface, while you can find and even partially evaluate historic structures without getting out of your car. Most sites don't need maintenance, but all structures do. Structures can serve broad economic and social purposes, while most archaeological sites as heritage resources are pretty much limited to research and interpretation. Historic structures can get federal tax credits, but archaeological sites are not eligible. A building can be "surplused," but a site cannot. A building can be fully documented before it is destroyed, but this is almost impossible for an archaeological site.

Many modern federal laws, regulations, and executive orders (EO) have implications for cultural heritage resources on federal lands or with regard to federal buildings. In the discussion that follows, I split these categories of federal ownership into two sections, one concerning land and the other buildings. Some laws, like the Marine Protection, Research, and Sanctuaries Act of 1972, the Coastal Zone Management Act of 1972, the Amtrak Improvement Act of 1974, the Mining in National Parks Act of 1976, the Federal Lands Management Act of 1976, the National Forests Management Act of 1976, and the Department of Defense Appropriations Act of 1991, have some aspects of federal land management that apply to cultural heritage resources, but their overall focus is on unrelated aspects, so they won't be dealt with here. They are worthy of notice, however, and have been included in the chronology in Appendix C. A number of important federal land laws focus on Indian cultural resources (e.g., Native American Graves Protection and Repatriation Act [NAGPRA], American Indian Religious Freedom Act [AIRFA]), but they are discussed in chapter 13.

Laws Focused on Federal Lands

There are two laws primarily focused on federal lands rather than federal buildings and structures built on those lands. The majority of these lands are undeveloped, and they contain relatively few buildings or structures that could be considered historic properties. Therefore, heritage management on large areas of federal land focuses on archaeological properties. One of these laws, the Archaeological Resources Protection Act (ARPA), is focused on protecting archaeological sites on federal lands from the actions of outsiders, while the other, Section 110 of the National Historic Preservation Act (NHPA), is focused on the preservation responsibilities of the federal land manager.

Archaeological Resources Protection Act (1979)

Like the Archaeological and Historic Preservation Act (AHPA) of 1974, the Archaeological Resources Protection Act of 1979 was a big deal for a lot of archaeologists when it was passed, but unlike AHPA, it still is a big deal. ARPA basically amended the 1906 Antiquities Act. This was required by the federal court decision in *U.S. v. Diaz* in 1974, which found the wording of the Antiquities Act too vague to prosecute a federal lands cultural resources site looter and artifact seller in Arizona. ARPA is one of the laws and acronyms best known to federal archaeologists, but most nonfederal archaeologists know little about its application other than the requirement to get an ARPA permit for archaeological work on federal property.

The basic purpose of ARPA was to reduce looting of archaeological sites (Figure 8.1). To do this, it provided definitions and more detailed descriptions of prohibited actions on federal land (the main faults in the Antiquities Act), proscribed more substantial penalties for violations, set up a more rigorous permitting process for excavations on federal land, and set penalties for illegal interstate trafficking in artifacts, including artifacts obtained illegally under state and local laws. It also broadened the scope of the Antiquities Act to include certain Indian lands not held in trust by the federal government.

Two amendments to ARPA in 1988 were passed within a week of each other. The amendment of October 28, 1988 (Public Law 100-555) added a Section 14 concerning archaeological survey of federal lands and the reporting of violations. The amendment of November 3, 1988 (Public Law 100-588) made a minor punctuation

FIG. 8.1 Sign noting closure of a rock-art site in Capital Reef National Park citing the Archaeological Resources Protection Act (author photo).

change in 3(3), inserted the word "deface" in 6(a), lowered the felony threshold from $5,000 to $500 in 6(d), and added a public education provision to Section 10.

NHPA Section 106, AHPA, the National Environmental Policy Act (NEPA), and the Department of Transportation Act (DOTA) Section 4(f) are basically *process* laws: they outline a process federal agencies must follow with regard to reviewing actions they take part in that might have adverse effects on cultural resources. ARPA is a *policy* law. Its main policy objective is to protect in situ archaeological resources by proscribing significant penalties for those who violate the policy.

The Sections of ARPA

Because ARPA is not a process law, the best way to understand it is not to look at a flowchart but to examine its various sections. The original act (Public Law 96-95) was divided into 13 sections. The amendment of October 28, 1988, added Section 14 to the law. When the law was codified into 16 USC 470, the original Section 1 short title, which gave the law its name, was put at the end of Section 2 (470aa). The 13 codified sections are numbered 470aa through 470mm. Although part of 16 USC, ARPA has not been moved to 54 USC, probably because it applies to all federal agencies, with the National Park Service (NPS) just having the overall congressional reporting responsibility.

ARPA Section 470aa—Congressional Findings and Declaration of Purpose

This section begins with four findings noting the accessibility, increasing vulnerability, and inadequacy of existing statutes and the need to engage private collectors who "have a wealth of archaeological information." It then states the reason for the act:

> The purpose of this Act is to secure, for the present and future benefit of the American people, the protection of archaeological resources and sites which

are on public lands and Indian lands, and to foster increased cooperation and exchange of information between governmental authorities, the professional archaeological community, and private individuals having collections of archaeological resources and data which were obtained before October 31, 1979 [the date of the enactment of this Act].

ARPA Section 470bb: Definitions

The "Definitions" section defines "archaeological resource," "federal land manager," "public lands," "Indian lands," "Indian tribe," "person," and "state." The meanings of most of the terms are fairly obvious or identical to their usage in other laws already mentioned, except for the following two:

> *Archaeological resource* means any material remains of past human life or activities which are of archaeological interest, as determined under uniform regulations promulgated pursuant to this Act. Such regulations containing such determination shall include, but not be limited to: pottery, basketry, bottles, weapons, weapon projectiles, tools, structures or portions of structures, pit houses, rock paintings, rock carvings, intaglios, graves, human skeletal materials, or any portion or piece of any of the foregoing items. Non-fossilized and fossilized paleontological specimens, or any portion or piece thereof, shall not be considered archaeological resources, under the regulations under this paragraph, unless found in an archaeological context. No item shall be treated as an archaeological resource under regulations under this paragraph unless such item is at least 100 years of age.
>
> . . .
>
> *Indian lands* means lands of Indian tribes, or Indian individuals, which are either held in trust by the United States or subject to a restriction against alienation imposed by the United States, except for any subsurface interests in lands not owned or controlled by an Indian tribe or an Indian individual.

With regard to "archaeological resource," it is important to note that such resources must be at least 100 years old for the purposes of ARPA. This is very different from the 50 years set by the NHPA as the standard for any historic property, as well as from NEPA standard practice, which often uses 45 years because the environmental impact statement (EIS) process can take five years or more to complete. A number of advantages to the 100-year rule specifically for archaeology will be discussed later.

As for "Indian lands," trust lands are clearly federal lands that are held in trust by the federal government for a recognized tribe. They are administered by the Bureau of Indian Affairs (BIA). The Indian lands that are "restricted against alienation" are more complicated. This is restricted fee title land where an individual member of an Indian tribe holds legal title but is not allowed to sell without the permission of the secretary of the interior. This land is usually within a reservation but was allotted to an individual member of that reservation after passage of the Dawes Act in 1887.

ARPA Section 470cc: Excavation and Removal

This section could also be titled "Permitting" as it describes the process for obtaining a permit to "excavate or remove" archaeological resources from federal land. The ARPA permit form is fairly standardized, but each major land-management agency may have its own instructions and requirements. To obtain a permit, you must apply to the federal land manager. According to the law, the application must include "the time, scope, and location and specific purpose of the proposed work." The land manager is obligated to "notify" any Indian tribe "which may consider the site as having religious or cultural importance." Even tribal members have to get an ARPA permit for excavations on tribal lands, unless their reservation has a tribal law regulating the excavation or removal of archaeological resources.

The ARPA permit may be issued if

(1) the applicant is qualified, to carry out the permitted activity,

(2) the activity is undertaken for the purpose of furthering archaeological knowledge in the public interest,

(3) the archaeological resources which are excavated or removed from public lands will remain the property of the United States, and such resources and copies of associated archaeological records and data will be preserved by a suitable university, museum, or other scientific or educational institution, and

(4) the activity pursuant to such permit is not inconsistent with any management plan applicable to the public lands concerned.

ARPA Section 470dd—Custody of Archaeological Resources

This section requires the secretary of the interior to promulgate regulations for the "ultimate disposition" of archaeological resources obtained under an ARPA permit, as well as under the AHPA (54 USC 3125) and the Antiquities Act (54 USC 3203). This was done in 1990 as 36 CFR 79. The law allows exchanges between the federal government and "suitable universities, museums, or other scientific or educational institutions." If the archaeological resources are from Indian lands, the tribe must consent to any exchange.

ARPA Section 470ee—Prohibited Acts and Criminal Penalties

As the title states, this section specifies what actions are illegal under ARPA and the suggested criminal penalties for various types of prohibited actions. There are three basic types of prohibited acts:

(a) Unauthorized excavation, removal, damage, alteration, or defacement of archaeological resources

(b) Trafficking in archaeological resources the excavation or removal of which was wrongful under Federal law

(c) Trafficking in interstate or foreign commerce in archaeological resources the excavation, removal, sale, purchase, exchange, transportation or receipt of which was wrongful under State or local law

The first two acts are direct violations that apply to federal lands, while the third attempts to discourage looting for profit on nonfederal lands by restricting interstate commerce.

For criminal penalties, the law specifies,

Any person who knowingly violates, or counsels, procures, solicits, or employs any other person to violate, any prohibition contained in subsection (a), (b), or (c) of this section shall, upon conviction, be fined not more than $10,000 or imprisoned not more than one year, or both: Provided, however, That if the commercial or archaeological value of the archaeological resources involved and the cost of restoration and repair of such resources exceeds the sum of $500, such person shall be fined not more than $20,000 or imprisoned not more than two years, or both. In the case of a second or subsequent such violation upon conviction such person shall be fined not more than $100,000, or imprisoned not more than five years, or both.

The decrease from $5,000 to $500 for the value of the artifact and the cost of "restoration and repair" was changed by the 1988 amendment. This made the over-$500 infraction a felony. The increasing fines and imprisonment for multiple violations is indicative of the fact that most looters are habitual criminals. The 1988 amendment made a lot of looters sit up and take notice, but also complain about violation of their constitutional rights for what they considered minor infractions.

As a nod to "minor infractions," in 470ee(g), the law states that the "removal of arrowheads located on the surface of the ground" is not a prohibited act and not subject to criminal penalties. However, if the arrowheads are part of an archaeological resource, their unpermitted collection would be subject to ARPA under the definition of "archaeological resource," including burial sites and certain features associated with other types of sites. In addition, the removal would violate other laws (e.g., 18 USC 641) applicable to taking federal government property without permission.

ARPA Section 470ff—Civil Penalties

Individuals who violate ARPA are subject to civil penalties in addition to any criminal penalties. Penalty amounts were to be established in regulations implementing the law. The factors to be taken into consideration were the archaeological or commercial value of the artifact as well as the costs of restoration and repair of both the artifacts and the site.

Hutt (1994) points out a number of advantages in pursuing civil as opposed to, or in addition to, criminal penalties:

- The burden of proof for civil cases is lower than for criminal ones.
- Civil cases involve nonjury trials.
- Some civil cases don't need lawyer involvement.
- There is no set limit on civil fines.
- Civil fines can go to the agency or other entities, while criminal fines go to the general fund.
- Agencies have more discretion as they don't have to involve a US attorney.

ARPA Section 470gg—Enforcement

This section was originally titled "Rewards; Forfeiture," as these are the two subjects discussed in the section. Any person who provides information leading to the successful criminal or civil conviction of a violator of ARPA can receive up to half the amount of the fines imposed, not to exceed $500. Penalties for violation of ARPA can include the forfeiture of equipment used to commit the crime, including vehicles. If the infraction took place on Indian lands, the tribe can receive all the fines and forfeited equipment.

ARPA Section 470hh—Confidentiality of Information Concerning
Nature and Location of Archaeological Resources

As with NHPA and AHPA, ARPA requires that information about the "nature and location" of archaeological sites be withheld from the public. However, the governor of any state can request this information from an agency, and the agency must comply if the written request includes the following:

1. The specific site or area for which information is sought
2. The purpose for which such information is sought
3. A commitment by the governor to adequately protect the confidentiality of such information to protect the resource from commercial exploitation

Because federal lands comprise significant percentages of the land in many states and because extensive archaeological surveys have usually been done on these lands, the information about federal site locations, site types, and site contents is critical to understanding the cultural history of a state. This information is also essential for any site locational modeling. Although many federal agencies report site locations to state historic preservation officers (SHPOs) and state archaeologists so that official state site numbers can be tallied, in order to legally make federal site information readily available to contract archaeologists, research archaeologists, and local planning agencies, it may be advisable for a state to officially obtain permission to selectively distribute federal site information through a governor's ARPA request.

ARPA Section 470ii—Rules and Regulations; Intergovernmental Coordination

This section, first of all, authorizes the secretaries of the interior, agriculture, and defense, along with the chairman of the board of the Tennessee Valley Authority (TVA), to promulgate regulations to carry out the purposes of ARPA. This is known as the act's *uniform regulation*; it was first issued in 1984 and amended in 1995. The second subsection authorizes each federal land-managing agency, including the ones named above, to develop regulations specific to its "functions and authorities."

The third subsection refers to public education initiatives that were added by one of the 1988 amendments. It states:

> Each Federal land manager shall establish a program to increase public awareness of the significance of the archaeological resources located on public lands and Indian lands and the need to protect such resources.

Many ARPA initiatives by some large federal land-management agencies (e.g., Bureau of Land Management [BLM]) focus on public education. This supports both their mission and public support for their mission.

ARPA Section 470jj—Cooperation with Private Individuals

Artifact collectors are the biggest violators of ARPA; yet they have considerable information about the location of archaeological sites and what these sites contain, information valuable to management and archaeology. This section encourages the secretary of the interior to communicate, cooperate, and exchange information with "private individuals having collections of archaeological resources and data which were obtained before the date of the enactment" of the law. It also encourages cooperation between agencies and with professional archaeologists to "expand the archaeological data base for the archaeological resources."

ARPA Section 470kk—Savings Provisions

This is an odd section title, except to lawyers, who know that *savings provisions* are special exceptions contained in laws to avoid constitutional or other legal challenges. In the case of ARPA, exceptions apply to the following:

- Mining, mineral leasing, reclamation, and other multiple uses already granted
- Private collecting of any rock, coin, bullet, or mineral which is not an archaeological resource
- Collecting or excavation on private lands embedded within public lands

Most archaeologists would object to the inclusion here of coins and bullets, especially if they are over 100 years old. As with surface collections of arrowheads discussed earlier, if the coins or bullets are part of an *archaeological resource*, they will be subject to ARPA under the definition of "archaeological resource," including burial sites and certain features associated with other types of sites. As with arrowheads, the removal of the coin or bullet from federal lands would violate other laws (e.g., 18 USC 641) applicable to taking federal government property unless the collector could prove he or she had recently lost the item at that location.

ARPA Section 470ll—Annual Report to Congress
As part of the annual report required to be submitted by the secretary of the interior specified in AHPA Section 469a-3(c), this section of ARPA requires the secretary of the interior to

> comprehensively report as a separate component the activities carried out under the provisions of this chapter, and he shall make such recommendations as he deems appropriate as to changes or improvements needed in the provisions of this chapter. Such report shall include a brief summary of the actions undertaken by the Secretary under section 470jj of this title, relating to cooperation with private individuals.

This report has been discussed under AHPA in chapter 7.

ARPA Section 470mm—Surveying of Lands; Reporting of Violations
This is the new section added by the 1988 amendments. It requires the secretaries of the interior, agriculture, and defense and the chairman of the board of the Tennessee Valley Authority to

> (a) develop plans for surveying lands under their control to determine the nature and extent of archeological resources on those lands;
> (b) prepare a schedule for surveying lands that are likely to contain the most scientifically valuable archeological resources; and
> (c) develop documents for the reporting of suspected violations of this chapter and establish when and how those documents are to be completed by officers, employees, and agents of their respective agencies.

This is a duplication of survey requirements specified in Section 110 of the NHPA. Like Section 110, ARPA does not require agencies to complete archaeological surveys of their lands according to any set timetable or in a specified chronological manner (e.g., timely). The annual reports to Congress completed by the NPS usually have tables that list how many acres of land each agency has surveyed during the reporting period, but it is difficult to determine what total percentage of each agency's land has been surveyed to date and if all those surveys were done to the same standards.

Regulations Implementing ARPA

The ARPA Uniform Regulation
As required in Section 470ii, the secretaries of the interior, agriculture, and defense, along with the chairman of the board of the Tennessee Valley Authority, are required to promulgate regulations to carry out the purposes of ARPA. This final uniform regulation was issued on January 6, 1984 (49 FR 1027), and revised on January 26, 1995 (60 FR 5260). The 1984 version is called Part I and the 1995 version Part II. The ARPA Uniform Regulation (36 CFR 296) includes 21 sections:

2961 Purpose
2962 Authority
2963 Definitions

2964 Prohibited Acts and Criminal Penalties
2965 Permit Requirements and Exceptions
2966 Application for Permits and Information Collection
2967 Notification to Indian Tribes of Possible Harm to, or Destruction of, Sites on Public Lands Having Religious or Cultural Importance
2968 Issuance of Permits
2969 Terms and Conditions of Permits
29610 Suspension and Revocation of Permits
29611 Appeals Relating to Permits
29612 Relationship to Section 106 of the National Historic Preservation Act
29613 Custody of Archaeological Resources
29614 Determination of Archaeological or Commercial Value and Cost of Restoration and Repair
29615 Assessment of Civil Penalties
29616 Civil Penalty Amounts
29617 Other Penalties and Rewards
29618 Confidentiality of Archaeological Resource Information
29619 Report
29620 Public Awareness Programs
29621 Surveys and Schedules

The ARPA Uniform Regulation basically provides more detail on how all federal agencies are to carry out the provisions of the act without changing any of the basic requirements of the law. The regulation considers the experience of putting the law into practice, the addition of new federal land-use laws such as AIRFA and NAGPRA, newly defined types of cultural resources (e.g., sacred sites), and new federal policy laws like the Paperwork Reduction Act.

Of the 21 sections in the regulation, eight (5–12) deal with ARPA permitting, and five (4, 14–17) deal with enforcement. The permitting sections provide a great deal more detail with regard to actions that don't need permits (Section 5), what permit applications should include (Section 6), how to undertake and respond to notification of tribes of permitted activity that they may have an interest in (Section 7), professional qualifications necessary for work at various kinds of sites (Section 8), the terms and conditions attached to permits (Section 9), suspension and revocation of permits (Section 10), an appeals process for application rejections, suspensions, and revocations (Section 11), and the fact that permit issuance in itself is not subject to Section 106 of NHPA (Section 12).

With regard to the enforcement of ARPA, Section 4 of the uniform regulation is basically the same as Section 6 (470ee) of the law, dealing with criminal actions and penalties. Section 14 of the regulation provides methods to determine the commercial value of artifacts and assess the costs of restoring and repairing damaged artifacts and sites, something not contained in the law. Sections 15 and 16 provide great detail on the process of bringing civil actions and the civil penalties, including dollar amounts. Section 17 of the regulation, "Other Penalties and Rewards," blends aspects from Sections 6 and 8 of the act.

As for the eight nonpermit, nonenforcement aspects of the uniform regulation, Section 1 summarizes the "Purpose" section of the law, adding a little of Section 12 ("Savings Provisions"). Section 2 ("Authority") recapitulates Section 10 of the law regarding the need for regulations. Section 3 ("Definitions") has two definitions not included in the law, "arrowhead" and "act," but spends most of its time providing examples and explanations of "archaeological resource." Section 13 of the regulation deals with custody of archaeological resources, with a new section related to NAGPRA. Section 18 of the regulation deals with keeping site locations and site descriptions confidential, like Section 9 of the act. Section 19 concerns congressional reporting, like Section 13 of the act. Section 20 of the regulations, titled "Public Awareness Programs," concerns the final subsection of Section 10 of the act added by a 1988 amendment. Finally, Section 21 of the regulation talks about surveys and schedules, like Section 14 of the act, but includes reference to the *Secretary of the Interior's Standards and Guidelines for Archaeology and Historic Preservation.*

Agency ARPA Regulations

ARPA Section 10 (470ii) also authorizes federal land managers to develop regulations specific to their "functions and authorities" as long as they are consistent with the law and the uniform regulation developed by the four lead agencies. Most agencies just use the uniform regulation, but the Department of the Interior (DOI), the Bureau of Indian Affairs, the Tennessee Valley Authority, the Minerals Management Service (MMS), and a few other agencies have promulgated their own ARPA regulations.

The DOI regulations (43 CFR 7) have definitions for "site of religious or cultural importance" and "allotted lands" as well as additional details on permitting procedures and civil penalties. There is also a section labeled "Determination of loss or absence of archaeological interest." The BIA ARPA regulations (25 CFR 262) have definitions for "funerary objects," "scared objects," "Indian individual," "lands of Indian tribes," and "lands of Indian individual," as well as sections on consultation with tribes for permits, activities of Indian tribes or individuals that require a permit, and other permitting details on reservations. The MMS issued ARPA regulations (30 CFR 250) specific to archaeological surveys for outer continental shelf leases; they include a definition of "archaeological resource," stating such have to be "at least 50 years old," differing from the 100 years of the act and the uniform regulation, as well as a definition of "significant archaeological resource" that requires National Register of Historic Places (NRHP) eligibility.

Conclusions Regarding ARPA

More books and articles have probably been written on ARPA, especially its criminal and civil penalty aspects, than on any other cultural resource management (CRM) archaeology topic (e.g., Friedman 1985; Hutt 1994; Hutt, Jones, and McAllister 1992; Carnett 1991; McManamon 1991; Bronin and Rowberry 2014:339–350). It is also the most common federal archaeological training offered by land-management agencies, especially for their own heritage management employees. Yet you rarely hear ARPA mentioned outside federal land-management circles. I don't remember ever discussing ARPA with other staff in my 15 years at the Minnesota SHPO.

There are a number of misconceptions about ARPA. ARPA permits are not required for walkover archaeological surveys that do not excavate or collect surface artifacts, although it is usually good to contact the federal land manager to let him or her know what you are doing on the property, and certain federal lands (e.g., those of the Department of Defense) have restricted access. With regard to surface collection of arrowheads, bullets, and coins, although specifically mentioned in ARPA and its uniform regulation as not subject to an ARPA permit, implying that it is legal for private collectors to collect these types of artifacts, their collection can be subject to an ARPA permit if they are part of an *archaeological resource*, and even if they are not, they are still subject to federal property laws.

Although ARPA is a big deal for all federal land-management agency archaeologists, it is not as big a deal in the eastern United States as it is in the western part of the country. West of the Mississippi River there are extensive federal lands, much of them subject to erosion, exposing artifacts on the surface, and in the Southwest there are large late-prehistoric sites containing things like complete pottery vessels that are worth a lot of money. Western archaeological sites are more likely to be on federal land, they are more easily found and easier to loot, and the artifacts are more lucrative for looters than those on eastern sites. Most ARPA violations and prosecutions are out west.

But site looting on federal lands has also been a problem in the East. Some Civil War battlefields have been picked clean of bullets and other metal objects by people using metal detectors. In the Upper Midwest, many logging camps and fur posts have suffered the same fate. Most rock shelters along the major rivers in Wisconsin and Illinois have been looted. Looting of burial mounds was once a major problem, but most states now have laws that make disturbing them illegal on public and private land. While plowed fields are avidly scoured by arrowhead hunters, it is generally unproductive for collectors to dig for artifacts, as digging and screening dirt is hard and slow work, as well as being very obvious and frowned upon by landowners.

The effectiveness of ARPA in the reduction of site looting is hard to gauge. There is a substantial criminal and civil case history with numerous convictions. Treasure hunting magazines have published articles discussing the law. But the prices of some artifacts continue to go up, and new methods such as Light Detection and Ranging (LiDAR) and the use of aerial drones make finding some sites easier. There is no doubt ARPA is an important CRM tool, but how much it has reduced looting on a national scale has yet to be determined.

Finally, ARPA should not be used by overzealous federal bureaucrats to hamper or prevent legitimate archaeological research. Although it is easier for some land managers to restrict all excavation, especially on Indian-related sites for political and "preservation" reasons, most Indian-related sites do not have "religious or cultural importance" to specific Indian groups. Most of them don't meet the definition for this type of site, and most prehistoric sites cannot be attributed to a particular tribe. ARPA requires the "notification" of tribes regarding permit applications if they have an interest in certain kinds of sites in certain areas. Smart agencies should go beyond notification and do true consultation. But tribes do not have veto power over ARPA permits except on tribal lands. Both agencies and tribes should promote sound archaeological research with public reporting. It benefits them both, as well as the American people in general.

Section 110 of NHPA

It is important to stress that Section 110 of the National Historic Preservation Act is about much more than federal agency responsibilities with regard to properties they manage or control. Some of the other aspects Section 110 covers are discussed elsewhere in this book (see chapters 4 and 9). More than anything, Section 110 is about federal agencies embedding heritage management considerations into every aspect of their very diverse missions, not just the properties they oversee. Section 110 emphasizes *planning* to preserve heritage resources.

In this part of the chapter, I discuss the federal agency responsibilities originally outlined in the first major subsection of Section 110. The 1980 amendment to NHPA designated this subsection as 110(a)(1–2). It was amended and renumbered in the 1992 amendment under 110(1)(A–B) and was reordered and recodified in 2014 as 306101 through 306114, excepting 306108 (old Section 106).

What Section 110 Says

Section 110 had its origins in the fourth stipulation in the preamble of the original NHPA in 1966: "It is necessary and appropriate for the Federal Government to accelerate its historic preservation programs and activities." Federal land-management implications were made explicit five years later in Executive Order 11593:

> Sec. 2. Responsibilities of Federal agencies.
>
> (a) no later than July 1, 1973, with the advice of the Secretary of the Interior, and in cooperation with the liaison officer for historic preservation for the State or territory involved, locate, inventory, and nominate to the Secretary of the Interior all sites, buildings, districts, and objects under their jurisdiction or control that appear to qualify for listing on the National Register of Historic Places.

Issued May 15, 1971, EO 11593 required federal agencies to survey their lands to identify potentially important archaeological and historical sites and structures, evaluate any located properties to determine their eligibility to the National Register of Historic Places, and then nominate eligible properties to the Register. Survey, evaluation, and nomination were to be completed by July 1, 1973.

This was an impossible two-year goal, considering there were almost a million government-owned buildings and structures, as well as 640 million acres of federal lands, of which most had not been surveyed for archaeological sites. The provision in the 1976 amendments to NHPA that eligible as well as listed properties were to be considered under Section 106 reviews took some pressure off agencies and SHPOs by eliminating the time limit to nominate properties.

The 1980 addition of Section 110 to the NHPA reinforced the EO 11593 inventory-evaluate-nominate directive to federal land managers and added other federal historic property protections. It specified no time limit. Section 110(a) from the 1980 amendment to NHPA reads,

> (1) The heads of all Federal agencies shall assume responsibility for the preservation of historic properties which are owned or controlled by such agency. Prior to acquiring, constructing, or leasing buildings for purposes of carrying out agency responsibilities, each Federal agency shall use, to the maximum extent feasible, historic properties available to the agency. Each agency shall undertake, consistent with the preservation of such properties and the mission of the agency and the professional standards established pursuant to section 101(f), any preservation, as may be necessary to carry out this section.
>
> (2) With the advice of the Secretary and in cooperation with the State historic preservation officer for the State involved, each Federal agency shall establish a program to locate, inventory, and nominate to the Secretary all properties under the agency's ownership or control by the agency, that appear to qualify for inclusion in the National Register in accordance with the regulations promulgated under section 101(a)(2)(A). Each Federal agency shall exercise caution to assure that any such property that might qualify for inclusion is not inadvertently transferred, sold, demolished, substantially altered, or allowed to deteriorate significantly.

This was revised in the 1992 NHPA amendments to read,

> (2) Each Federal agency shall establish (unless exempted pursuant to section 214), in consultation with the Secretary, a preservation program for the identification, evaluation, and nomination to the National Register of Historic Places, and protection of historic properties. Such program shall ensure—

(A) that historic properties under the jurisdiction or control of the agency, are identified, evaluated, and nominated to the National Register;

(B) that such properties under the jurisdiction or control of the agency as are listed in or may be eligible for the National Register are managed and maintained in a way that considers the preservation of their historic, archaeological, architectural, and cultural values in compliance with section 106 and gives special consideration to the preservation of such values in the case of properties designated as having National significance.

With the 2014 recodification of NHPA, the federal land responsibilities in Section 110 (54 USC 3061) are under three subsections and now read,

306101. Assumption of responsibility for preservation of historic property
(a) IN GENERAL.—
(1) AGENCY HEAD RESPONSIBILITY.—The head of each Federal agency shall assume responsibility for the preservation of historic property that is owned or controlled by the agency.
(2) USE OF AVAILABLE HISTORIC PROPERTY.—Prior to acquiring, constructing, or leasing a building for purposes of carrying out agency responsibilities, a Federal agency shall use, to the maximum extent feasible, historic property available to the agency, in accordance with Executive Order No. 13006 (40 U.S.C. 3306 note).
(3) NECESSARY PRESERVATION.—Each Federal agency shall undertake, consistent with the preservation of historic property, the mission of the agency, and the professional standards established pursuant to subsection (c), any preservation as may be necessary to carry out this chapter.
(b) GUIDELINES FOR FEDERAL AGENCY RESPONSIBILITY FOR AGENCY-OWNED HISTORIC PROPERTY.—In consultation with the Council, the Secretary shall promulgate guidelines for Federal agency responsibilities under this subchapter (except section 306108).
(c) PROFESSIONAL STANDARDS FOR PRESERVATION OF FEDERALLY OWNED OR CONTROLLED HISTORIC PROPERTY.—The Secretary shall establish, in consultation with the Secretary of Agriculture, the Secretary of Defense, the Smithsonian Institution, and the Administrator of General Services, professional standards for the preservation of historic property in Federal ownership or control.
306102. Preservation program
(a) ESTABLISHMENT.—Each Federal agency shall establish (except for programs or undertakings exempted pursuant to section 304108[c] of this title), in consultation with the Secretary, a preservation program for the identification, evaluation, and nomination to the National Register, and protection, of historic property.
(b) REQUIREMENTS.—The program shall ensure that—
(1) historic property under the jurisdiction or control of the agency is identified, evaluated, and nominated to the National Register;
(2) historic property under the jurisdiction or control of the agency is managed and maintained in a way that considers the preservation of their historic, archeological, architectural, and cultural values in compliance with section 306108 of this title and gives special consideration to the preservation of those values in the case of property designated as having national significance;
306106. Review of plans of transferees of surplus federally owned historic property
The Secretary shall review and approve the plans of transferees of surplus federally owned historic property not later than 90 days after receipt of the

plans to ensure that the prehistorical, historical, architectural, or culturally significant values will be preserved or enhanced.

Section 110 Regulations

Unlike for Section 106, there is no overarching federal regulation resulting from Section 110 of the NHPA; nor was any required by the law. In 1985 (50 FR 7590), the Department of the Interior issued regulations (36 CFR 78) titled *Waiver of Federal Agency Responsibilities under Section 110 of the National Historic Preservation Act*. These regulations were updated in 1997 (62 FR 30235). The waiver pertained to 110(j), which required the secretary of the interior to promulgate regulations to waive Section 110 responsibilities "in the event of a major national disaster or an imminent threat to the national security."

There was some apprehension on the part of historic preservationists that this waiver could be broadly interpreted to apply to any activity that may prevent a natural disaster (e.g., flooding) or enhance national security (e.g., military training). The 36 CFR 78 regulations damped down this apprehension somewhat by using terms like "extraordinary circumstances," "major," and "imminent" and required that a waiver applied only to a specific geographic area.

In 1988, the DOI published the *Secretary of the Interior's Standards and Guidelines for Federal Agency Historic Preservation Programs Pursuant to the National Historic Preservation Act* (53 FR 4727–4746). They were updated in 1998 (64 FR 20496–20508) to incorporate the changes required by the 1992 amendments to NHPA and were also reformatted. The original had gone through the various subsections of 110 and provided guidance on how to implement each subsection. The 1998 version established seven basic standards, followed by guidelines to implement each standard. These are not regulations but only provide guidance to federal agencies.

Four of the seven standards apply to lands and historic properties under "agency jurisdiction and control."

> *Standard 2.* An agency provides for the timely identification and evaluation of historic properties under agency jurisdiction or control and/or subject to effect by agency actions.
> *Standard 3.* An agency nominates historic properties under the agency's jurisdiction or control to the National Register of Historic Places.
> *Standard 6.* An agency manages and maintains historic properties under its jurisdiction or control in a manner that considers the preservation of their historic, architectural, archeological, and cultural values.
> *Standard 7.* An agency gives priority to the use of historic properties to carry out agency missions.

Many agencies provide additional guidance for Section 110 in their own management manuals. An example is the *National Cultural Resources Handbook* (2003) of the Natural Resources Conservation Service (NRCS). Guidance specific for Section 110 appears in Subpart D. For federal property NRCS manages, the focus is on buildings. Because NRCS is one of the few federal agencies whose activities are dominated by work on private land, the handbook stresses preservation partnerships and fostering preservation within communities in order to effectively carry out the heritage management part of its mission.

Section 110 Application by Federal Land Management Agencies

In the original 1980 version, Section 110 first concerned itself with buildings. It required federal agencies to use their historic structures to the fullest extent consistent with their missions. Surplus historic buildings could be transferred out of federal ownership if the transfer promoted the building's preservation. When a historic building had to be demolished as the result of federal action or assistance, the agency had to ensure that the action was fully documented, as stipulated in Subsection 101(b) (now 306103); this applied to both federal and nonfederal buildings.

With regard to finding and nominating eligible properties on federal land, the 1980 version of Section 110 required inventory, evaluation, and nomination, but without the time limit of EO 11593. With regard to both structures and archaeological sites, all federal land was to be surveyed for historic properties, all located properties evaluated for their significance, and all eligible properties eventually nominated to the National Register.

The 1992 amendments did not substantially change any of the federal building use or federal land survey/evaluation requirements, but in Tom King's opinion (*CRM Plus* blog, November 18, 2014), the 1992 amendments did change the National Register nomination provision by deleting the word "all." King (*CRM Plus* blog, August 27, 2008) also states that the requirement for agencies to nominate *all* federal properties was removed at the request of the BLM and the United States Forest Service (USFS), which manage vast tracts of federal land.

The 1998 guidelines provided NPS expectations as to how federal agencies should implement Section 110 with regard to their own properties. Standard 2, the "timely" identification and evaluation of historic resources on federal lands, first stressed the need to look at "the full-range of historic properties," including traditional cultural properties (TCPs), cultural landscapes, and linear features like roads and trails. In order to effectively manage historic resources, they have to be identified and evaluated for significance.

The Standard 2 guidelines give agencies a lot of wiggle room in carrying out identification and evaluation on their own property. "The level of identification needed can vary depending on the nature of the property or property type, the nature of the agency's management authority, and the nature of the agency's possible effects on the property." Furthermore, for particular purposes it "may not be necessary to identify exhaustively every historic property or historic property type." However, identification for a particular area "is not complete until all historic properties have been identified," and due to changes in field methods and property type recognition, "even when an area has been completely surveyed for historic properties of all types it may require reinvestigation if many years have passed since the survey was completed."

Some agencies request formal Section 110 determinations of eligibility (DOEs) from the Keeper of the National Register, while others work with SHPOs and tribal historic preservation officers (THPOs) to make consensus determinations of eligibility. Although the properties in question may not be threatened with any imminent adverse effects, Section 110 eligibility assessments help agencies determine which of their properties are worthy of preservation, streamline Section 106 actions that may eventually threaten those properties, and sort out which properties the agency may want to nominate to the National Register. Unlike Section 106, Section 110 does not formally address consensus determinations of eligibility.

Standard 3 addresses nomination of federal properties to the National Register. First of all, an agency should determine "what role nomination will play in the agency's overall preservation program." For the NPS, where the National Register program resides and which manages numerous public historic sites, this is necessarily a high priority, but for most large land-management agencies, nomination is low priority. Also, an "agency that controls relatively few historic properties may find it realistic to nominate them all," while an "agency with an excellent internal program for identifying and preserving historic properties may find that other determinants, such as whether a property is to be managed and interpreted as a site of public interest, are more useful in establishing nomination priorities."

Standard 6 for federal land-managing agencies declares that practices regarding historic properties should consider "the preservation of their historic, architectural, archeological, and cultural value." Thus agencies should "endeavor to retain historic buildings and structures in their traditional uses and to maintain significant archeological sites and landscapes in their undisturbed condition." If it isn't feasible to do this, "the agency should consider an **adaptive use** that is compatible with the historic property." Any modifications should meet the *Secretary of the Interior's Standards for the Treatment of Historic Properties*. Importantly, unevaluated properties "should be maintained so that their preservation is ensured."

Standard 7 is the last standard listed in the guidelines, but it concerns what was listed first in the 1980 addition of Section 110 to the NHPA—namely, that agencies should give priority to use of their own historic properties in carrying out their missions. This applies more to buildings and structures than to other property types, as properties such as archaeological sites and some TCPs (e.g., plant-gathering areas) could be used in education and interpretation but generally not for more practical applications like housing agency activities. Agencies should "provide for regular inspection of the properties and an adequate budget for their appropriate maintenance." In the end, the "agency's responsibility is to balance the needs of the agency mission, the public interest in protecting historic properties, the costs of preservation, and other relevant public interest factors in making such decisions."

Definitions: The NPS Section 110 guidance ends with a "Definitions" section. Most definitions it contains have been presented elsewhere in related laws and regulations. One definition notably missing is that of "professionally qualified individuals." Under the Standard 2 guidelines, agencies are required to use such individuals to carry out identification and evaluation activities, but the guidelines do not specify if the individual has to meet the professional qualification standards established in 1983 by the secretary of the interior. Most of the federal agencies I worked with when I was a SHPO archaeologist had a supervisor who met the secretary's professional qualification standards, but a few didn't. This has gradually changed through retirements and the hiring of qualified personnel. It would now be difficult to find an agency whose survey and evaluation activities were supervised by someone not meeting the *Secretary of the Interior's Professional Qualifications Standards*.

An Archaeologist's Perspective on Section 110

Section 110 is second only to Section 106 in its numerical notoriety among federal agencies and heritage management professionals. These two sections are probably the only two sections of the NHPA that are immediately recognizable to most practitioners by their numbers alone. With regard to Section 110, most practitioners would say the law is about the obligations of federal agencies on their own property, although its scope is much broader. Section 106 is more familiar to most heritage management practitioners, but Section 110 lies at the heart of every federal agency's heritage management program.

While the number of acres surveyed by federal agencies in a given period is included in the NPS-produced report to Congress, it is difficult to determine any agency's total percentage of surveyed land and evaluated buildings. I would guess that most buildings have been evaluated, as their retention and maintenance needs are partially driven by their eligibility. Archaeological surveys of the hundreds of thousands of square miles of federal lands lag behind because of the expense involved and the lack of threats to most sites on these lands due to their remoteness.

As for nomination, I fully agree with Tom King's numerous sermons that nomination to the National Register is not reasonable or necessary for most federal archaeological sites. "Eligible equals in" for the purposes of environmental review pretty much put an end to a need for listing in that process, especially for federal properties. Because federal properties are not subject to tax benefits or state laws, benefits derived from these aspects are also moot.

Laws Focused on Buildings and Structures

Federal building and structure preservation laws have been reactions to two major forces: federal government property priorities for federal buildings and urban renewal for the promotion of economic development and livability. These forces are interrelated, and with regard to the second, a legislative initiative labeled for one purpose (e.g., preservation) is actually intended for another (e.g., economic development).

Preservation of Federal Government Buildings

The federal government's preserving its own historic properties was the first driver of building preservation on a national scale. The federal government owns a lot of buildings and structures, perhaps a million. Military bases alone account for hundreds of thousands. Most of these buildings and structures were built for specific purposes. Needs change, buildings deteriorate, and structures are damaged by fires or natural disasters. As new purposes arise and buildings begin to fail structurally, demolition and replacement are often necessary. When federal facilities are closed, buildings are abandoned and no longer maintained, gradually falling into ruin.

One of the first historic buildings to come under federal government protection was Robert E. Lee's Arlington House in 1864, when the US Army acquired the larger property for a Civil War cemetery, thus unintentionally preserving the building that is also known as the Custis-Lee Mansion. The War Department undertook the restoration of Arlington House in 1929.

The first large-scale intentional federal historic building preservation was connected with the 1930 NPS acquisition of Colonial National Park, which incorporated the sites of Jamestown and Yorktown. Yorktown contained historic buildings, including the Moore House (Figure 8.2), the earliest restoration project undertaken by NPS soon after acquisition. Also in 1930, the Library of Congress established an Early American Architecture Division, preserving and promoting the study of building plans with the related Historic American Buildings Survey (HABS) established three years later.

Executive Order 6166 in 1933 transferred control of historic sites managed by the

FIG. 8.2 Author in front of the Moore House at Yorktown. The Moore House was the first building restoration by the National Park Service in the early 1930s (author photo).

War Department and the Department of Agriculture to the National Park Service, giving NPS a total of 80 historical parks and monuments, which included some historic buildings. In 1935, the Historic Sites Act formally launched a federal government program to preserve historic buildings throughout the country.

Historic Sites, Buildings, and Antiquities Act (1935)

As discussed in chapter 2, the Historic Sites, Buildings, and Antiquities Act, better known as the Historic Sites Act (HSA) of 1935, authorized a survey of nationally significant historic sites, encouraged cooperative agreements between the federal government and private entities for the maintenance of important historic sites, and allowed the secretary of the interior to acquire new historic sites. Within NPS, the lead agency for implementation of the law, the HSA promoted research, preservation, restoration, and interpretation, as well as the acquisition and management of historic sites. In 1935, the two most prominent types of historic sites were buildings and archaeological sites (i.e., antiquities), with each featured in the official title of the act.

With regard to buildings, Sections 1 and 2 of the act stated,

Section 1
  It is hereby declared that it is a national policy to preserve for public use historic sites, buildings, and objects of national significance for the inspiration and benefit of the people of the United States.
Section 2
  The Secretary of the Interior (hereinafter in sections 1 to 7 of this Act referred to as the Secretary), through the National Park Service, for the purpose of effectuating the policy expressed in section 1 of this Act, shall have the following powers and perform the following duties and functions: . . .
(d) For the purpose of sections 1 to 7 of this Act, acquire in the name of the United States by gift, purchase, or otherwise any property, personal or real, or any interest or estate therein, title to any real property to be satisfactory to the Secretary.
(e) Contract and make cooperative agreements with States, municipal subdivisions, corporations, associations, or individuals, with proper bond where deemed advisable, to protect, preserve, maintain, or operate any historic or archaeologic building, site, object, or property used in connection therewith for public use, regardless as to whether the title thereto is in the United States.

The HSA could protect historic structures in two ways: (1) the federal government could acquire structures that were nationally significant for incorporation into the national historic sites system managed by the NPS, or (2) the federal government could make available through lease or sale its own historic structures to other entities as long as the historic structure was used for a public purpose and its historic integrity maintained. The law did not require the federal government to take any action and emphasized national importance only, but it did result in some building preservation and established the federal government as the standard-bearer for heritage preservation.

The HSA's application to federal buildings was reinforced by 40 USC 1303 concerning actions of the General Services Administration (GSA), the agency that manages nonmilitary government property:

(c) DEMOLITION.—The Administrator may demolish any building declared to be surplus to the needs of the Government under this section on deciding that demolition will be in the best interest of the Government. Before proceeding with the demolition, the Administrator shall inform the Secretary of the

Interior in writing of the Administrator's intention to demolish the building, and shall not proceed with the demolition until receiving written notice from the Secretary that the building is not an historic building of national significance within the meaning of the Act of August 21, 1935 (16 U.S.C. 461 et seq.) (known as the Historic Sites, Buildings, and Antiquities Act). If the Secretary does not notify the Administrator of the Secretary's decision as to whether the building is an historic building of national significance within 90 days of the receipt of the notice of intention to demolish the building, the Administrator may proceed to demolish the building.

Executive Order 11593 (1971)

As previously discussed, President Richard Nixon's Executive Order 11593 in 1971 corrected many critical deficiencies of the 1966 NHPA, some of which were put into law by the Section 110 amendment of NHPA in 1980. With regard to buildings, Section 2 of the Executive Order read,

> Sec. 2. Responsibilities of Federal agencies. . . .
>
> (c) initiate measures to assure that where as a result of Federal action or assistance a property listed on the National Register of Historic Places is to be substantially altered or demolished, timely steps be taken to make or have made records, including measured drawings, photographs and maps, of the property, and that copy of such records then be deposited in the Library of Congress as part of the Historic American Buildings Survey or Historic American Engineering Record for future use and reference. Agencies may call on the Department of the Interior for advice and technical assistance in the completion of the above records.

Public Building Cooperative Use Act (1976)

The Public Building Cooperative Use Act of 1976 amended the Public Buildings Act of 1959. It required the administrator of the General Services Administration (GSA) to

> (a) 1. acquire and utilize space in suitable buildings of historic, architectural, or cultural significance, unless use of such space would not prove feasible and prudent compared with available alternatives;
>
> 2. encourage the location of commercial, cultural, educational, and recreational facilities and activities within public buildings;
>
> 3. provide and maintain space, facilities, and activities, to the extent practicable, which encourage public access to and stimulate public pedestrian traffic around, into, and through public buildings, permitting cooperative improvements to and uses of the area between the building and the street, so that such activities complement and supplement commercial, cultural, educational, and recreational resources in the neighborhood of public buildings; and
>
> 4. encourage the public use of public buildings for cultural, educational, and recreational activities.

This 1976 law has not been amended, but it was reinforced by Executive Order 12072 two years after enactment.

Executive Order 12072 (1978)

President Jimmy Carter issued Executive Order 12072 on August 16, 1978, "for the planning, acquisition, utilization, and management of Federal space facilities." The sections pertinent to building preservation stated,

1-101. Federal facilities and Federal use of space in urban areas shall serve to strengthen the Nation's cities and to make them attractive places to live and work. Such Federal space shall conserve existing urban resources and encourage the development and redevelopment of cities.

1-102. Procedures for meeting space needs in urban areas shall give serious consideration to the impact a site selection will have on improving the social, economic, environmental, and cultural conditions of the communities in the urban area.

1-105. Procedures for meeting space needs in urban areas shall be consistent with the policies of this Order and shall include consideration of the following alternatives:

(a) Availability of existing Federally controlled facilities.

(b) Utilization of buildings of historic, architectural, or cultural significance within the meaning of section 105 of the Public Buildings Cooperative Use Act of 1976 (90 Stat. 2507, 40 U.S.C. 612a).

(c) Acquisition or utilization of existing privately owned facilities.

(d) Construction of new facilities.

(e) Opportunities for locating cultural, educational, recreational, or commercial activities within the proposed facility.

NHPA Section 110 (1980)

The original 1980 version of NHPA Section 110 first concerned itself with buildings, requiring federal agencies to use their historic structures to the fullest extent consistent with their mission. Transfer of unneeded historic properties out of federal ownership was allowed if it promoted a building's preservation. Section 110 required the full documentation of any federal building to be demolished. The demolition aspect actually applied to both buildings the government owned and buildings affected by federal actions or federal assistance.

Section 110(a) from the 1980 amendment to NHPA reads,

> (1) The heads of all Federal agencies shall assume responsibility for the preservation of historic properties which are owned or controlled by such agency. Prior to acquiring, constructing, or leasing buildings for purposes of carrying out agency responsibilities, each Federal agency shall use, to the maximum extent feasible, historic properties available to the agency. Each agency shall undertake, consistent with the preservation of such properties and the mission of the agency and the professional standards established pursuant to section 101(f), any preservation, as may be necessary to carry out this section.

Executive Order 13006 (1996)

On May 21, 1996, President Bill Clinton issued Executive Order 13006. It reinforced earlier federal actions to preserve historic buildings owned by the federal government. The pertinent sections read,

> Section 1. Statement of Policy. Through the Administration's community empowerment initiatives, the Federal Government has undertaken various efforts to revitalize our central cities, which have historically served as the centers for growth and commerce in our metropolitan areas. Accordingly, the Administration hereby reaffirms the commitment set forth in Executive Order No. 12072 to strengthen our Nation's cities by encouraging the location of Federal facilities in our central cities. The Administration also reaffirms the commitments set forth in the National Historic Preservation Act to provide leadership in the preservation of historic resources, and in the Public Buildings

Cooperative Use Act of 1976 to acquire and utilize space in suitable buildings of historic, architectural, or cultural significance. To this end, the Federal Government shall utilize and maintain, wherever operationally appropriate and economically prudent, historic properties and districts, especially those located in our central business areas. When implementing these policies, the Federal Government shall institute practices and procedures that are sensible, understandable, and compatible with current authority and that impose the least burden on, and provide the maximum benefit to, society.

Sec. 2. Encouraging the Location of Federal Facilities on Historic Properties in Our Central Cities. When operationally appropriate and economically prudent, and subject to the requirements of section 601 of title VI of the Rural Development Act of 1972, as amended (42 U.S.C. 3122), and Executive Order No. 12072, when locating Federal facilities, Federal agencies shall give first consideration to historic properties within historic districts. If no such property is suitable, then Federal agencies shall consider other developed or undeveloped sites within historic districts. Federal agencies shall then consider historic properties outside of historic districts, if no suitable site within a district exists. Any rehabilitation or construction that is undertaken pursuant to this order must be architecturally compatible with the character of the surrounding historic district or properties.

Sec. 3. Identifying and Removing Regulatory Barriers. Federal agencies with responsibilities for leasing, acquiring, locating, maintaining, or managing Federal facilities or with responsibilities for the planning for, or managing of, historic resources shall take steps to reform, streamline, and otherwise minimize regulations, policies, and procedures that impede the Federal Government's ability to establish or maintain a presence in historic districts or to acquire historic properties to satisfy Federal space needs, unless such regulations, policies, and procedures are designed to protect human health and safety or the environment. Federal agencies are encouraged to seek the assistance of the Advisory Council on Historic Preservation when taking these steps.

EO 13006 emphasizes initial consideration of historic properties in historic districts when locating federal facilities in particular cities. It stresses that construction or rehabilitation of federal buildings should be architecturally compatible with the surrounding historic properties and directs federal agencies to examine and revise regulations and procedures that hamper the location of federal facilities in historic properties or districts. More than anything, Executive Order 13006 reaffirms the requirement that federal agencies not just preserve historic buildings but provide leadership for historic preservation in general.

Building Preservation in Response to Urban Renewal and Redevelopment

The first nationwide efforts to "revitalize" aging cities are associated with the City Beautiful Movement beginning in the last decade of the nineteenth century. It was urban renewal focused on building civic centers, parkways, and monuments. Chicago was the heart of this movement, epitomized by the World Columbian Exposition in 1893 and Daniel Burnham and Edward Bennett's *Plan of Chicago* in 1909. The City Beautiful Movement had a positive effect on the look of some American cities but a very negative effect on historic preservation. To accomplish its objectives, it needed space to work, so many older buildings in urban cores were demolished with little of the historic preservation regret that characterized post–World War II urban renewal.

FIG. 8.3 Urban renewal in Philadelphia in the late 1950s (Library of Congress).

With the passage of the Housing Act of 1949, government-promoted "urban renewal" became widespread (Figure 8.3). The purpose of the act was to deal with massive housing needs for the influx of people to cities after World War II, but the housing ideal was hijacked by commercial developers and city planners. Urban renewal as an economic stimulus was further promoted by the Housing Act of 1954, which advocated development of "blighted" areas in cities; blighted usually meant "old."

Although the 1954 Housing Act had made some allowances for historic building rehabilitation, this aspect was largely ignored. Two years later, the Federal-Aid Highway Act funded the Interstate Highway System. The new interstate highways cut massive corridors through cities, destroying or dividing entire neighborhoods and exacerbating the problems of urban historic preservation caused by the housing acts. By the early 1960s, block upon block of older buildings were being demolished in urban areas without consideration of the historical value of individual buildings or historic districts; if an area was deemed blighted or needed for a freeway, the entire area was cleared, even if individual buildings had architectural, historic, or community-cohesiveness merit.

In 1966, a number of laws radically changed things for the better as far as historic preservation in cities was concerned. The NHPA required all federal agencies to start considering the effects of their actions on historic structures, Section 4(f) of the Department of Transportation Act required federal transportation officials to find prudent and feasible alternatives to harming historic sites, and the Demonstration Cities and Metropolitan Development Act included the preservation of historic sites as vital to livable cities.

Demonstration Cities and Metropolitan Development Act (1966)

The Demonstration Cities and Metropolitan Development Act of 1966 amended the Housing Act of 1949. Its principal purpose was to "improve the quality of urban life" by providing federal financial and technical assistance to help cities "plan, develop, and carry out" projects that demonstrated improved living conditions in multiple and comprehensive ways. One way was to encourage cities to maintain "historic sites and distinctive neighborhood characteristics." The act fostered what became known as the Model Cities Program, part of President Lyndon B. Johnson's "Great Society" initiative. It ended in 1974.

Title 6 of the act was labeled "Preservation of Historic Structures" and encouraged the preservation of historic structures as part of urban renewal projects. To accomplish this, it authorized Department of Housing and Urban Development (HUD) grants to the National Trust for Historic Preservation (NTHP) for building restoration and surveys of historic structures. Grants were also made available to local governments for historic property surveys.

Title 7, "Open Space Land, Urban Beautification, and Historic Preservation," started with the following statement: "The Congress further finds that there is a need for timely action to preserve and restore areas, sites, and structures of historic or architectural value in order that these remaining evidences of our past history and heritage shall not be lost or destroyed through the expansion and development of the Nation's urban areas." It required HUD to consult with the Interior Department to provide "(1) appropriate information on the status of national and statewide recreation and historic preservation planning as it affects the areas to be assisted with such grants, and (2) the current listing of any districts, sites, buildings, structures, and objects significant in American history, architecture, archeology, and culture which may be contained on a National Register maintained by the Secretary of the Interior pursuant to other provisions of law." Grants were to be made available to states and local governments to "assist in the acquisition of title to or other permanent interests in areas, sites, and structures of historic or architectural value in urban areas, and in their restoration and improvement for public use and benefit, in accord with the comprehensively planned development of the locality."

Housing and Community Development Act (1974)

The Housing and Community Development Act of 1974 recognized there were "critical social, economic, and environmental problems facing the Nation's urban communities." This was due to rapid urban growth, the concentration of lower-income groups in central cities, inadequate investment to combat blight, and increasing energy costs. To deal with these problems, concerted efforts were needed by government at all levels. One of the objectives stressed in the act was "the restoration and preservation of properties of special value for historic, architectural, or esthetic reasons." Restoration and preservation of historic properties was one of the eligible categories for HUD grants through this act. Up to 20% of the grant money authorized by the act could be used on historic properties.

Section 5320 of the act is labeled "Historic Preservation Requirements." It empowered the secretary of the interior, the Advisory Council on Historic Preservation (ACHP), and SHPOs to help administer the grant program by developing regulations and reviewing properties for their eligibility for the National Register. SHPOs had 45 days to review applications.

Tax Reform Act (1976)

Following intensive lobbying by multiple private and public historic preservation groups, Congress passed the Tax Reform Act in 1976 by a 94–2 vote in the Senate. President Gerald Ford signed it into law on October 4, 1976. The act assisted historic building preservation in two ways: (1) it provided tax incentives for rehabilitating historic buildings, and (2) it eliminated incentives for demolishing buildings. The tax incentives applied only to buildings that were "depreciable" for tax purposes or, in other words, income-producing buildings used for commercial purposes. The building had to be listed in the National Register, a contributing element in an NRHP-listed historic district, or located in a local historic district whose evaluation criteria were approved by the NPS.

The act allowed a five-year accelerated depreciation deduction of rehabilitation expenses for commercial buildings that were rehabilitated in accordance with standards set by the secretary of the interior. This required the NPS to have written standards that developers could use to guide rehabilitation and that SHPOs and NPS could use for certification. Standards had already been developed for the NHPA-established Historic Preservation Fund (HPF) grant-in-aid program in 1973.

These were revised in 1976 specifically for HUD grants and rehabilitation tax credit (RTC) applications. *The Secretary of the Interior's Standards for Rehabilitation* were codified as 36 CFR 67 in 1977 and a year later were included in the revised 36 CFR 67, labeled "Preservation Project Standards." The most recent guidelines for rehabilitating historic buildings were issued by NPS in 2011.

Revenue Act (1978)

The Revenue Act of 1978 added another category to tax breaks for building rehabilitation. Earlier Revenue Acts in 1962 and 1975 had allowed investment tax credits for business equipment improvements but not for building improvements. The 1978 Revenue Act added a 10% investment tax credit for commercial building rehabilitation. It did not require older buildings to meet any eligibility standard other than being at least 20 years old, but buildings that did meet the secretary of the interior's historic building standards (e.g., listed in the National Register) could choose to use either the five-year depreciation of the Tax Reform Act of 1976 or the 1978 investment tax credit.

Not only did the 1978 Revenue Act allow a set tax credit, but it also established basic conditions that still apply to RTCs. It required "substantial rehabilitation" of a "major portion" of a building. If over 25% of a building's exterior walls were replaced, the project wasn't eligible. It limited the credit only to direct expenditures for rehabilitation. It also stipulated that if a rehabilitated building was demolished or had subsequent rehabilitation done outside the historic preservation standards within the five-year amortization period, the developers had to pay back the full tax credit previously received.

Economic Recovery Tax Act (1981)

The Economic Recovery Tax Act (ERTA) of 1981 is a major federal historic building preservation tax act. It was part of the Ronald Reagan administration's tax reform initiative but had strong bipartisan support. Like the 1978 Revenue Act, it focused on RTCs. It used the basic eligibility guidelines in the 1976 and 1978 tax acts, although it added a more detailed description of what "substantial rehabilitation" entailed. It also allowed the inclusion of residential as well as commercial properties.

The 1981 act had three basic components:

- 15% credit for nonresidential buildings at least 30 years old
- 20% credit for nonresidential buildings at least 40 years old
- 25% credit for NPS/SHPO-certified historic buildings

ERTA's basic purpose was not to further historic preservation or even neighborhood revitalization but to spur a stagnant national economy. The inclusion of older buildings that did not meet National Register standards broadened its use, but the higher credit (25%) for certified historic buildings clearly encouraged historic preservation and soon proved to be a significant historic preservation tool for buildings. A historic preservation downside to ERTA was that it reintroduced some tax incentives for demolition.

Tax Reform Act (1986)

The rapid success of ERTA soon threatened its existence. Tax revenue losses amounted to hundreds of millions of dollars each year (Ryberg-Webster 2015:212), but the Deficit Reduction Act of 1984 allowed the three-level ERTA credits to stand and even reduced demolition incentives. However, some congressional and executive opposition to ERTA as originally enacted persisted.

The Tax Reform Act of 1986 left ERTA in place but did scale back the types and amounts of the tax credits. There was now a 20% credit for NPS-certified historic building rehabilitation and a 10% credit for rehabilitating uncertified buildings built before 1936. The 1936 date for the 10% credit reflected the application of the NRHP 50-year rule for the 1986 legislation. This date has never been corrected, so the 10% credit as of 2016 only applies to buildings that are at least 80 years old. The other provisions of the 1986 act also remain in place. Republican tax code reform proposals in late 2017 included elimination or reduction of tax credits for historic building rehabilitation.

Application of Building-Rehabilitation Tax Breaks

To receive the 20% tax credit, a developer of an unlisted property would have to hire an architectural historian to complete a National Register nomination, hire a historic preservation architect to come up with a certifiable rehabilitation plan, and have an accountant to deal with a complex tax law. Despite these hurdles, the NPS estimated that as of 2015, the federal rehabilitation tax credit program has encouraged over $120 billion in private investment, rehabilitated over 40,000 historic buildings, and been directly responsible for creating or rehabilitating over a half million housing units (NPS 2015).

Since 1976, NPS has administered the tax certification program in cooperation with the Internal Revenue Service (IRS) and the SHPOs. According to a 2011 NPS brochure, the discrete duties of the three entities are as follows:

- SHPO
  - Serves as first point of contact for property owners.
  - Provides application forms, regulations, and other program information.
  - Maintains complete records of the State's buildings and districts listed in the National Register of Historic Places, as well as State and local districts that may qualify as registered historic districts.
  - Assists anyone wishing to list a building or a district in the National Register of Historic Places.
  - Provides technical assistance and literature on appropriate rehabilitation treatments.
  - Advises owners on their applications and makes site visits on occasion to assist owners.
  - Makes certification recommendations to the NPS.
- NPS
  - Reviews all applications for conformance to the Secretary of the Interior's Standards for Rehabilitation.
  - Issues all certification decisions (approvals or denials) in writing.
  - Transmits copies of all decisions to the IRS.
  - Develops and publishes program regulations, the Secretary of the Interior's Standards for Rehabilitation, the Historic Preservation Certification Application, and information on rehabilitation treatments.
- IRS
  - Publishes regulations governing which rehabilitation expenses qualify, the time periods for incurring expenses, the tax consequences of certification decisions by NPS, and all other procedural and legal matters concerning both the 20% and the 10% rehabilitation tax credits.
  - Answers public inquiries concerning legal and financial aspects of the Historic Preservation Tax Incentives, and publishes the audit guide, Market Segment Specialization Program: Rehabilitation Tax Credit, to assist owners.
  - Insures that only parties eligible for the rehabilitation tax credits utilize them.

SHPO guidance on tax act programs, including on state tax breaks, can be found on each office's website. The NPS maintains a robust website on historic preservation tax guidance. IRS specifics can be found in the Internal Revenue Code, Section 47.

Besides tax credits for rehabilitation of buildings, several other tax breaks can be applied to certified historic buildings. Historic preservation easements are covenants that permanently protect a historic property. A restriction is placed in the deed that prevents certain changes to the property no matter who owns it. The easement is typically donated to an organization that is sympathetic to the restrictions. It is considered a charitable contribution and is tax deductible by the original owner on income or estate taxes. Originally, the restriction typically applied to only the front facade of a historic building but now includes the entire exterior. Another potential tax break is for use of a historic building for low-income housing.

Main Street and Other Programs

Federal urban renewal and tax incentive initiatives have focused on urban core areas, where the majority of historic buildings and historic districts exist and where economic and housing programs are most needed and have the most telling effect. The National Trust for Historic Preservation recognized that smaller towns were largely ignored by these federal programs, so in 1980 it started the Main Street Program to help revitalize commercial historic districts in small towns. Some historic building preservation has also been promoted by the Intermodal Surface Transportation Efficiency Act (ISTEA) of 1991 and its successors. Privately developed Leadership in Energy and Environmental Design (LEED) standards for "green" buildings also promote the rehabilitation of historic buildings.

Laws for Museums and Curation

With the creation of the Library of Congress in 1800, the United States as a country first formally recognized the importance of heritage, although that heritage was considered largely foreign. The library was established to assist Congress's lawmaking process, not as an archive of American heritage. When British troops invaded Washington in 1814, they burned the library. Thomas Jefferson then sold his own personal library to the federal government to restart the national collection. Many of the books and manuscripts in the Library of Congress eventually became historic resources, in part for their association with Jefferson. In 1930, the library established an Early American Architecture Division and soon became the repository for the Historic American Buildings Survey.

The Great Depression in the 1930s fostered the development of multiple object and manuscript preservation efforts. The National Archives and Records Administration (NARA) was established in 1934 to retain important federal government documents and materials. Today, NARA is the home of the Declaration of Independence, the original US Constitution, and census data, as well as millions of more mundane documents valuable to history and the country's heritage.

The Historic Sites Act of 1935 directed the secretary of the interior to preserve documents and data of historic and archaeological value, but it only included records, not objects, and did not specify where the collections were to be located. The Historical Records Survey of the Works Progress Administration (WPA) was an outgrowth of the Federal Writers Project in late 1935. Its purpose was to discover, preserve, and index basic historical research materials for the benefit of officials, historians, and the public. It initially focused on county records but expanded to include records from churches and newspapers.

The WPA constructed or improved numerous museums throughout the country, including those for cultural history. Many WPA buildings built for other civic purposes are now used as museums. The WPA's Museum Extension Project (1935–1943) created millions of displays, including dioramas, scale models, specimen casts, and artifact replicas for use both within museums and in schools. With the onset of World War II, most Depression-era programs ended, with the notable exception of HABS.

Museum Properties Management Act (1955)

Several acts important to heritage management were passed in 1955. The Presidential Libraries Act established publicly accessible repositories for collections of papers and objects directly related to particular presidents of the United States. More important, however, was the Museum Properties Management Act. The act directed the National Park Service to increase the public benefits of park museums by preserving and exhibiting historical and archaeological "objects and relics" found on Department of the Interior property. It allowed the NPS to accept donations of, purchase, exchange, accept on loan, or loan these objects. The law (16 USC 18) was amended in 1996 to allow for deaccessioning of objects that had no real economic or scientific value.

36 CFR 79 (1990)

In response to requirements listed in the Antiquities Act of 1906, the Reservoir Salvage Act of 1960, the National Historic Preservation Act of 1966, the Archaeological and Historic Preservation Act of 1974, and the Archaeological Resources Protection Act of 1979, in September 1991 the National Park Service issued regulations (36 CFR 79) titled *Curation of Federally Owned and Administered Archaeological Collections*. These regulations set the standard for collections not only from federal lands but from nonfederal lands made in response to federal agency actions taken to comply with federal laws and regulations.

The 36 CFR 79 curation regulations address the following issues:

- Responsibility for federal collections
- Procedures and guidelines to manage and preserve collections
- Terms and conditions for federal agencies to include in contracts, memoranda, agreements, or other written instruments with repositories for curatorial services
- Standards to determine when a repository has the capability to provide long-term curatorial services
- Guidelines for collections access, loan, and use

    According to the regulations, basic "proper care" requires that a repository

- provide a catalog list of the collection contents to the responsible party (i.e., federal agency official, Indian landowner, or tribal official);
- periodically inspect the physical plant to monitor physical security and environmental conditions;
- periodically inspect the collection and associated records to monitor their condition;

- periodically inventory the collection and associated records;
- provide a written report of the results of inspections and inventories to the responsible party;
- make the collection available for inspection by the responsible party.

To meet these standards, a repository must be climate controlled, secure from theft and natural disasters, reasonably accessible to researchers, and under the supervision of a trained museum professional. The materials in the collection include not only artifacts but records associated with the acquisition of the artifacts (e.g., field notes, artifact catalogs, excavation maps). The repository need not be a federal facility, but the federal land manager of the lands of collection origin is still responsible to make sure all conditions of 36 CFR 79 are and continue to be met.

Proposed revisions to 36 CFR 79 were published in the *Federal Register* on November 18, 2014, but no final revised regulations had been published as of the end of 2017. As stated in the *Federal Register* (79 FR 68840), the purposes of the revisions were to "establish definitions, standards, and procedures to dispose of particular material remains that are determined to be of insufficient archaeological interest. This rule would promote more efficient and effective curation of these archeological collections."

Laws for Special Properties and Areas

A number of laws protect certain types of cultural resources that have been singled out as needing specialized protection. Many of these have to do with properties associated with our maritime and military heritage. Others have to do with less tangible and more recent aspects of our past.

American Folklife Preservation Act (1976)

Cultural resources consist of much more than archaeological sites and historic buildings. Although early historic preservation laws focused on the tangible aspects of our past as expressed and preserved in artifacts and structures, recognition of the importance of less tangible cultural resources spread to this country from England in the late nineteenth century in the form of folklore studies. The American Folklore Society was founded in 1888. Government recognition of this aspect of our heritage came in 1928 when the Library of Congress established the Archive of Folk Culture within its Music Division.

In 1976, the American Folklife Preservation Act expanded the scope of folklife preservation by establishing the American Folklife Center at the Library of Congress. The intent of the center, as expressed in the act, was to recognize

(1) that the diversity inherent in American folklife has contributed greatly to the cultural richness of the Nation and has fostered a sense of individuality and identity among the American people;
(2) that the history of the United States effectively demonstrates that building a strong nation does not require the sacrifice of cultural differences;
(3) that American folklife has a fundamental influence on the desires, beliefs, values, and character of the American people;
(4) that it is appropriate and necessary for the Federal Government to support research and scholarship in American folklife in order to contribute to an understanding of the complex problems of the basic desires, beliefs, and values of the American people in both rural and urban areas;

(5) that the encouragement and support of American folklife, while primarily a matter for private and local initiative, is also an appropriate matter of concern to the Federal Government; and

(6) that it is in the interest of the general welfare of the Nation to preserve, support, revitalize, and disseminate American folklife traditions and arts.

"American folklife" is defined in the act as "the traditional expressive culture shared within the various groups in the United States: familial, ethnic, occupational, religious, regional; expressive culture includes a wide range of creative and symbolic forms such as custom, belief, technical skill, language, literature, art, architecture, music, play, dance, drama, ritual, pageantry, handicraft; these expressions are mainly learned orally, by imitation, or in performance, and are generally maintained without benefit of formal instruction or institutional direction." Folklife is reflected in almost everything about us as individuals, as members of families, communities, ethnic groups, and regions, and as citizens of this country. Our names, our home furnishings, the way we do things, and the way we speak are all elements of folklife. Unlike with historic sites, there is no age limit for determining the significance of folklife; some of it is ancient, and some of it is recent. Some elements are more important to us as individuals or small groups. We cannot comprehensively preserve folklife in place because it is always evolving. We can only record it to better understand ourselves and our cultural surroundings.

The American Folklife Center at the Library of Congress is concerned with both preserving elements of folklife and interpreting it. More than anything, it celebrates the diversity of American culture. In order to understand that diversity, it has an international collection of materials. It is supervised by the director of the center and managed by a 15-member board.

As King (2013:295) points out, the American Folklife Act is not a regulatory act as it does not require federal agencies to consider impacts of their actions on folklife, although elements of folklife are certainly included under the social impact analysis of NEPA, and under the NHPA, tangible aspects of folklife that are eligible for inclusion in the National Register must be considered in the review of a federal undertaking. The 1980 amendments to the NHPA required the NPS, in cooperation with the American Folklife Center, to report to Congress on "preserving and conserving" aspects of folklife. The report *Cultural Conservation: The Protection of Cultural Heritage in the United States* (Loomis 1983) recommended further study by the federal government to identify important aspects of American folklife, but that study has not yet been completed.

For the purposes of this book, the elements of folklife that are applicable to most American heritage preservation laws are the tangible elements. These are places associated with important aspects of folklife that still retain meaning, the integrity to convey that meaning, and physical artifacts of folklife behavior that can and should be preserved in situ or in museum collections.

Abandoned Shipwrecks Act (1987)

In 1987 Congress passed the Abandoned Shipwrecks Act (ASA), and President Reagan signed it into law in April 1988. It gave individual states authority over certain historic shipwrecks on state-owned bottomlands. It attempted both to defederalize shipwreck disputes in these waters and to clarify when maritime salvage laws and historic preservation laws applied to particular shipwrecks. To understand the ASA, you have to know something about water law and the law of the sea.

An aspect of water law affecting all states is *riparian law*. Riparian law concerns itself with *riparian rights*—use and ownership of inundated or intermittently inundated areas associated with lakes, streams, and oceans adjacent to upland property. Riparian rights are dependent on many factors, such as whether the waters are navigable, border an international boundary, are tidal, or are subject to state laws. Ownership of tidal lands and the land beneath navigable waterways generally goes to the adjacent or encompassing state. Private landowners adjacent to bodies of water own the land to the ordinary high watermark in some states and to the ordinary low watermark in other states.

For coastal areas, the federal government has sovereignty over "territorial waters," which extend out 12 miles from the ordinary low watermark. The Submerged Lands Act of 1953 gave states ownership of natural resources within three miles of their ocean shores but did not include cultural resources. Some coastal states (e.g., Virginia) claim ownership of the seabed in the entire territorial waters zone (12 miles), while others only claim the first 3 miles (e.g., Massachusetts). Like the oceans, all the Great Lakes except Lake Michigan contain an international boundary. All the Great Lakes states except Illinois and Indiana (they are only on Lake Michigan) own the bottomlands off their shores out to the international boundary with Canada.

The law of the sea is known as *maritime law* or *Admiralty law*. It governs both navigation and shipping. Each country has its own maritime laws, although the United Nations has a Convention on the Law of the Sea that most countries abide by. The United States has signed the UN maritime convention, but Congress has not ratified it, so it is not legally binding for the United States.

In the United States, Admiralty courts that deal with maritime law are at the same level as federal district courts. Agreements between countries with respect to maritime law fall under *treaty law*. In the United States, international treaties must be ratified by Congress and are approximately equal in force of law to acts of Congress. Like congressional acts, treaty provisions cannot conflict with the Constitution.

With regard to shipwrecks, the aspects of maritime law that traditionally applied were under what are called the *law of finds* and the *law of salvage*. Under the law of finds, if ownership of a shipwreck cannot be established, finders can claim ownership unless the claim contradicts another law with precedence. Under the law of salvage, all vessels have an obligation to assist other vessels that are in distress. If the owners of one vessel save another vessel from sinking, they can claim salvage rights to that vessel. For sunken vessels, ownership has usually passed from the owner at the time of sinking to an insurance company. Thus, for many historic shipwrecks the law of finds assumes ownership has been abandoned, while the law of salvage assumes ownership still applies.

The ASA, first of all, corrected the deficiency of the Submerged Lands Act of 1953 by including cultural resources. It asserted federal government ownership for all resources within territorial waters and then transferred the ownership of the bottomlands to the adjacent states within the three-mile coastal limit and beneath inland navigable waters. The federal government retained its ownership of shipwrecks and other cultural resources between the 3- and 12-mile coastal limits.

The ASA then defined three types of "abandoned" shipwrecks that federal ownership and the state transfer of ownership applied to:

- Shipwrecks embedded in submerged lands
- Shipwrecks embedded in coral formations
- Embedded shipwrecks that were eligible for or listed in the NRHP

If one or more of the above conditions applied, the jurisdiction for disputes arising for shipwrecks in the ASA-defined state waters were now subject to state courts and not federal courts. This effectively eliminated the application of the law of finds and salvage with regard to historic shipwrecks unless the shipwreck could be proven to belong to a foreign country.

The ASA required that the NPS issue "guidelines" (not regulations) to help implement the law; guidelines are advisory and not legally binding. These guidelines were first issued by the NPS in December 1990 (55 FR 50116), with a corrected version issued in February 1991 (56 FR 7875).

The guidelines are divided into four parts: Part I contains definitions of key terms, Part II contains guidelines for the management of shipwrecks under state and federal agency ownership or control, Part III contains the Abandoned Shipwreck Act as passed by Congress, and Part IV lists the 142 shipwrecks listed in or determined eligible for the National Register as of December 4, 1990. The list has greatly expanded since 1990 but has not been updated in the ASA guidelines.

The ASA guidelines expanded and clarified critical definitions from the act. These include

Abandoned shipwreck means any shipwreck to which title voluntarily has been given up by the owner with the intent of never claiming a right or interest in the future and without vesting ownership in any other person. By not taking any action after a wreck incident either to mark and subsequently remove the wrecked vessel and its cargo or to provide legal notice of abandonment to the U.S. Coast Guard and the U.S. Army Corps of Engineers, as is required under provisions in the Rivers and Harbors Act (33 U.S.C. 409), an owner shows intent to give up title. Such shipwrecks ordinarily are treated as being abandoned after the expiration of 30 days from the sinking.

Embedded as defined in the Act means firmly affixed in the submerged lands or in coralline formations such that the use of tools of excavation is required in order to move the bottom sediments to gain access to the shipwreck, its cargo, and any part thereof. Tools of excavation would include, but not be limited to, hydraulic, pneumatic, or mechanical dredges; explosives; propeller wash deflectors; air lifts; blowtorches; induction equipment; chemicals; and mechanical tools used to remove or displace bottom sediments or coralline formations to gain access to shipwrecks.

Historic shipwreck means a shipwreck that is listed in or eligible for listing in the National Register of Historic Places.

Shipwreck as defined in the Act means a vessel or wreck, its cargo, and other contents. The vessel or wreck may be intact or broken into pieces scattered on or embedded in the submerged lands or in coralline formations. A vessel or wreck includes, but is not limited to, its hull, apparel, armaments, cargo, and other contents. Isolated artifacts and materials not in association with a wrecked vessel, whether intact or broken and scattered or embedded, do not fit the definition of a shipwreck

Submerged lands as defined in the Act means the lands that are "lands beneath navigable waters," as defined in section 2 of the Submerged Lands Act (43 U.S.C. 1301). Examples of submerged lands to which the Abandoned Shipwreck Act applies would include, but not be limited to, the bottomlands of navigable inland waters (such as rivers and lakes), tidal and offshore marine waters (such as sounds, bays, and gulfs) seaward to a line three geographical miles from the coastline, and lands that formerly were navigable but have since been filled in, made or reclaimed (such as former river beds where courses have meandered or been filled in and former harbor areas that have been reclaimed to create non submerged land). However, abandoned shipwrecks embedded in

FIG. 8.4 The shipwreck of the USS *Essex* in Duluth, Minnesota (Minnesota SHPO photo taken by Elmer Engman).

formerly submerged lands would, under common law, belong to the owner of the land. (There are additional provisions that apply to submerged lands in U.S. territories and with respect to the laws of particular states.)

The ASA not only gave states jurisdiction over shipwrecks and provided some protection for them if they were indeed abandoned, embedded, and historic, but also required that states provide reasonable public access to these shipwrecks for recreational and educational purposes. SHPOs can use HPF funds to help implement the ASA. Minnesota did this in 1990, initiating a 10-year study of shipwrecks in Lake Superior and inland waters (Anfinson 1993, 1997b). The *USS Essex* (Figure 8.4) was one of the shipwrecks studied (Anfinson 1996).

The ASA has been challenged many times in state and federal courts. Most decisions have supported the law and allowed states to restrict access to historic wrecks for salvage purposes. It should also be noted that military vessels and aircraft remain the property of the nation of origin no matter where they are found. For US military wrecks, the Sunken Military Craft Act of 2004 (10 USC 113) confirms that the military still owns its sunken ships and aircraft.

National Maritime Heritage Act (1994)

In the 1980s, historic preservationists and archaeologists from maritime states lobbied NPS and Congress to do more for maritime cultural resources. In 1984 Congress asked the NPS to "conduct a survey of historic maritime resources, recommend standards and priorities for the preservation of those resources; and recommend appropriate Federal and private sector roles in addressing those priorities"

(*Congressional Record*, October 10, 1984, p. 11922). In 1987 NPS created the National Maritime Initiative within its History Division to survey, evaluate, and develop preservation methods for historic maritime resources. This effort also resulted in the passage of the Abandoned Shipwrecks Act of 1987 and the National Maritime Heritage Act of 1994.

The National Maritime Heritage Act established a grants program to foster the preservation of historic maritime resources. The program is funded by the sale of obsolete vessels from the National Defense Reserve Fleet. To be eligible for grants, a maritime property must be listed in or determined eligible for the National Register of Historic Places. Although Section 8 of the act required NPS to develop regulations to carry out the act, no regulations have been forthcoming, although NPS does have a grants manual. In November 2014, the National Conference of State Historic Preservation Officers (NCSHPO), NPS, and ACHP signed a nationwide programmatic agreement pertaining to their roles in the maritime heritage grants program.

Historic maritime properties are historic properties bordering the ocean or inland waters or historic properties related to waterborne navigation or commerce. Although maritime resources are not defined in the act, according to the NPS Maritime History Grants webpage, the major categories of historic maritime resources are

- *Maritime Districts* which make up a geographically definable area possessing a significant concentration, linkage or continuity of maritime sites, buildings, structures or objects united by past events or by plan or physical development.
- *Maritime Sites* such as submerged or terrestrial maritime-related archeological sites or other maritime sites which are the location of a significant event or activity, buildings or structures where the location itself maintains historical or archeological value regardless of the value of any existing structure.
- *Maritime Buildings* such as lighthouses, lifesaving stations, custom houses, warehouses, hiring hall, sailors homes, marine hospitals or other maritime buildings created to shelter any form of human activity, or maritime buildings comprising a historically related complex such [as] light stations or lifesaving stations;
- *Maritime Structures* where a work is made up of interdependent and interrelated parts in a definite pattern of organization such as stationary waterfront cranes, locks, canals. Maritime structures, constructed by man, are often large-scale engineering projects; and
- *Maritime Objects* such as vessels, shipwrecks and hulks, floating drydocks, piers or cranes, or other maritime objects that are by nature moveable yet related to a specific setting or environment.

The NPS National Maritime Initiative Office

- Maintains inventories of historic U.S. maritime properties including Large Preserved Historic Vessels, Historic Light Stations, Historic Life-Saving Stations, Shipwrecks and Hulks, and Small Craft
- Provides preservation assistance through publications and consultation
- Educates the public about maritime heritage through [its] website
- Sponsors maritime heritage conferences and workshops
- Funds maritime heritage projects through grants

A number of publications are available to assist with the documentation and evaluation of maritime resources, with the emphasis on vessels (e.g., Delgado 1992; Delgado and Foster 1992; Anderson 2004). The inclusion of inland waters in the

Maritime Heritage Act meant features promoting river navigation and systems of historic canals were included as maritime resources. The inland aspect of the act has been underutilized both with respect to publications and grants.

American Battlefield Protection Act (1996)

Battlefields and battle sites have long been a focus of American historic preservation efforts. In 1890, the Civil War Chickamauga Battlefield became the first national military park. In 1895, Gettysburg became a national military park, and a year later the Supreme Court prevented a railroad from cutting through the Gettysburg Battlefield. A private group began the restoration of Fort Ticonderoga in 1908.

One of the first national attempts to comprehensively inventory a particular historic property type began in 1920 when the Army War College sponsored a study of American battlefields. When the preliminary survey was completed in 1925, it had identified over 3,400 battle sites in the continental United States. In 1926 Congress passed the Act for the Study and Investigation of Battlefields, which formalized a national survey of battlefields, eventually completed in 1932. Federally owned historic battlefields were consolidated under NPS management by Executive Order 6166 in 1933. The American Battle Monuments Commission created by Congress in 1923 was given responsibilities for battlefield-related cemeteries here and abroad, as well as for placing monuments at foreign battlefields commemorating American activities.

In 1988, battlefield preservation became the focus of national attention when a private developer purchased 550 acres of the Manassas (Bull Run) Battlefield in Virginia for residential and commercial development. Responding to nationwide protests from Civil War history buffs and historic preservationists, Congress condemned the land and purchased it for over $130 million. It was a hard lesson in "reactive preservation" (Gossett 1998; Zenzen 1998).

In order to be more proactive, Congress authorized the Civil War Sites Advisory Commission in 1990. A year later, the NPS started the American Battlefield Protection Program (ABPP). These organizations had to assess significance, evaluate interpretive potential, and prioritize preservation efforts for over 10,500 Civil War battle sites. The 384 most significant Civil War sites, including sites already in public ownership, were field-surveyed. Of these sites, 78 were well protected, 50 were in immediate need of major protection, 105 needed some protection, and 135 did not retain sufficient integrity to be "worthy of preservation."

The mission of the ABPP was congressionally supported in 1996 with the passage of the American Battlefield Protection Act. It was amended by the Civil War Battlefield Preservation Act in 2002. The purpose of the act is "to assist citizens, public and private institutions, and governments at all levels in planning, interpreting, and protecting sites where historic battles were fought on American soil during the armed conflicts that shaped the growth and development of the United States, in order that present and future generations may learn and gain inspiration from the ground where Americans made their ultimate sacrifice." In order to carry out the purpose of the act, NPS, through its Battlefield Protection Program, was authorized to "encourage, support, assist, recognize, and work in partnership with citizens, Federal, State, local, and tribal governments, other public entities, educational institutions, and private nonprofit organizations in identifying, researching, evaluating, interpreting, and protecting historic battlefields and associated sites on a National, State, and local level." An annual appropriation of $3 million was authorized to carry out battlefield protection in the form of cooperative agreements, grants, and contracts. Based on the definitions, eligible sites did not have to be listed in or eligible for the NRHP, and they could not be current NPS sites.

National Historic Lighthouse Preservation Act (2000)

The National Historic Lighthouse Preservation Act (NHLPA) of 2000 (54 USC 305101–305106; formerly 16 USC 470w-7) is basically an amendment to the National Historic Preservation Act. It provides for the disposal of federally owned historic light stations that no longer serve the needs of the current management agency. The NHLPA allows these surplus light stations to be transferred at no cost to federal agencies, state and local governments, nonprofit corporations, educational agencies, and community development organizations as long as these entities agree to comply with conditions set forth in the NHLPA and are financially able to maintain the property. The receiving entities also must make the property available for education, recreation, cultural, or historic preservation activities.

Only those light stations listed in or deemed eligible for the National Register of Historic Places can be conveyed under this program. The nomination for listing, or determination of eligibility, is prepared by the US Coast Guard. Light stations that are not eligible for listing will be disposed of through other processes. Prior to the NHLPA, historic lighthouses could be transferred to state or local agencies through the National Park Service's Historic Surplus Property Program or the Federal Lands to Parks Program.

The NHLPA is managed by the NPS Maritime Heritage Program. Each year the NPS publishes a list of light stations available under the act. Each time a light station is deemed eligible for the NHLPA, the General Services Administration issues a notice of availability (NOA) for the property. Applications are reviewed by an NPS committee, and final decisions are made in consultation with SHPOs.

Summary

Federal agency actions that may impact heritage resources are reviewed not only by environmental protection legislation but by specialty laws that apply to federal lands, federal efforts to rejuvenate cities, laws that require special care of portable heritage resources in federal ownership, and laws that apply to particular kinds of historic places under federal control.

For properties owned by the federal government, Section 110 of the National Historic Preservation Act is the go-to legislation. Section 110 outlines the process agencies must follow in the day-to-day management of properties under their control to ensure important heritage resources on those properties will be preserved. While Section 106 is reactive, Section 110 is proactive.

The Archaeological Resources Protection Act sets policies and penalties concerning the disturbance of archaeological sites on federal land. Legitimate archaeological work by nonagency personnel requires an ARPA permit, while illegitimate activities (e.g., looting) are subject to severe criminal and civil penalties.

Historic building preservation has benefited greatly from federal government policies regarding the use of federal historic buildings, HUD-related grants for the purposes of urban renewal, and federal tax incentives. Federally owned building preservation initiatives began in the 1930s with federal relief programs and greatly accelerated after the passage of the National Historic Preservation Act in 1966.

Tax initiatives began after the passage of NHPA, with National Register listing setting the standard for eligibility. Federal tax incentives benefiting building preservation appeared over a 10-year period from 1976 to 1986. They initially were a response to an economic downturn, reduced availability of federal funds for urban renewal initiatives, and a Republican strategy to give local governments more control over their own growth by stimulating private investment in cities. The tax incentives received broad bipartisan support in Congress.

Economic development was initially a driver of historic building demolition, but in the 1970s it also assisted historic building preservation. This is most commonly implemented through tax laws. Tax-incentive programs have been not only a very successful federal historic preservation initiative but also a critical and cost-effective community revitalization tool. Many states have copied and expanded the tax program, making the entire tax-incentive effort all the more important as a preserver of historic buildings and the social fabric of cities.

Special care of portable heritage resources is subject to federal oversight if the materials come from federal lands or are housed in federal facilities. In response to a number of laws, the National Park Service developed regulations (36 CFR 79) specifying the kind of care federal collections require.

Recently, the federal government has paid particular attention to battlefields and historic maritime resources as historic properties in need of special care. Over a 12-year period in the late 1980s and 1990s, a number of laws were passed promoting the preservation of these heritage resources.

Review Questions

1. To what kinds of properties do federal specialty laws apply?
2. What does ARPA require?
3. What are other laws that apply to federal land?
4. What laws promote the preservation of historic federal buildings?
5. What effects have urban renewal had on historic preservation?
6. What maritime resources are given some protection by federal law?

Supplemental Reading

For more information on Section 110 of the National Historic Preservation Act, see Sprinkle (2015).

Almost every federal land-managing agency has information on its website concerning the Archaeological Resources Protection Act. Also see Bronin and Rowberry (2014:339–350) and McManamon (2000).

For a general overview of archaeological laws prior to the 1992 NHPA amendments, see Carnett (1991).

For more information on housing and tax laws as they apply to heritage preservation, see Ryberg-Webster (2015).

For more information on specialty laws concerning particular property types, the National Park Service has considerable information on its webpages. Also see various sections in King (2013) as suggested in its index. For American folklife, see Hufford (1991). For social impact assessment, see Hutt, Jones, and McAllister (2003).

Implementing Heritage Management: Between the Devil and the Deep Blue Sea

Sometimes you need to deal with multiple federal laws and multiple federal agencies for the same project. This can make federal environmental protection processes for cultural heritage resources very complicated. The example below illustrates this complication as well as the use of common heritage management terms and acronyms. This is an example of how much you may have to know to be a competent heritage management professional.

In my first full-time heritage management job, I did a Phase 1 (identification) archaeological survey on a county highway project that was receiving federal funds and going through a national wildlife refuge (NWR). To do the survey, I first had to get an Archaeological Resources Protection Act (ARPA) permit from the Fish and Wildlife Service (FWS). I found a prehistoric archaeological site, and it was adjacent to a wetland.

The site could be avoided by filling part of the wetland, but I did a Phase 2 (evaluation) survey of the site in case it couldn't be avoided. The site was considered eligible for the National Register of Historic Places (NRHP) by the FWS and the state historic preservation office (SHPO). A decision had to be made by the FWS to allow the county to impact the wetland or the site or not to allow either. If the wetland was going to be impacted, an Army Corps of Engineers (COE) Section 404 permit was required. I told the refuge manager that he was "between the devil and the deep blue sea." As an archaeologist, I was the devil, and the wetland was the deep blue sea. His agency's primary mission was to protect nature, but my primary mission was to protect culture. The county's mission was to improve the road.

The situation was complicated by the need to address the requirements of multiple laws applicable to three federal agencies and also laws that pertained specifically to one agency. All the agencies had to address the archaeological impact under Section 106 of the National Historic Preservation Act (NHPA) and the National Environmental Policy Act (NEPA). The Federal Highway Administration (FHWA) was funding the project with federal dollars, the FWS managed the federal land, and the COE was potentially issuing a federal permit.

NEPA requires federal agency consideration of project effects to both the cultural and the natural environments. NEPA somewhat favors natural resources over historic resources because the courts have considered effects to historic resources as part of the sociocultural environment. Sociocultural effects alone can't trigger an environmental impact statement (EIS).

In Minnesota, the state Department of Transportation (MnDOT) acts for FHWA for Section 106 and NEPA. MnDOT also has to fulfill responsibilities under Section 4(f) of the Department of Transportation Act (DOTA). Section 4(f) protects both historic sites and wildlife refuges and is stronger in its protection of historic sites than Section 106 of NHPA. Section 4(f) requires all possible planning to avoid harm to historic sites, parks, and wildlife refuges. Transportation projects cannot harm such properties unless there is no prudent and feasible alternative. Two types of 4(f) properties were involved with the road project—once again, the devil-and-the-deep-blue-sea dilemma.

Because the project was on federal land, Section 110 of NHPA was applicable. Section 110 requires federal land managers to preserve historic properties on their land. The land manager is also obligated to consider the broader site protection requirements of ARPA as well as the Archaeological and Historic Preservation Act (AHPA). If the site was found to contain burials or objects of cultural patrimony, the Native American Graves Protection and Repatriation Act (NAGPRA) and perhaps the American Indian Religious Freedom Act (AIRFA) and Executive Order 13007 could be involved. The FWS had to address all these federal requirements.

These types of projects have many issues. With multiple agencies involved, who takes the lead? All heritage management laws specifically tied to the federal land (e.g., ARPA) give the responsibility for heritage resources to the land manager. For Section 106 purposes, under 36 CFR 800.2(a)(2), the federal agencies involved in the road project can agree to have one take the lead. The lead agency basically runs the Section 106 process, determining the area of potential effects (APE) and who will be accepted as consulting parties, interacting with the state historic preservation officer (SHPO) and/or tribal historic preservation officer (THPO), and doing the consultation with any interested tribes as well as other identified consulting parties.

Because the land was federal and most of the effects would be dealt with by the land manager, the FWS was designated the lead agency for Section 106 purposes. MnDOT (acting for FHWA) and the COE were still responsible for their own compliance with Section 106. MnDOT was also in charge of completing its DOTA Section 4(f) responsibilities. For NEPA, like 106, multiple agencies can agree to designate a lead, while the others become cooperating agencies. FWS was the designated lead. If an EIS had needed to be completed, the county would have had to pay for it.

As already mentioned, under NEPA natural effects are given precedence over cultural effects.

Because of its mission to "conserve, protect, and enhance fish, wildlife, plants, and their habitats," the FWS also tends to favor preservation of the wetland over the archaeological site, unless the impacts to the wetland are minor and the effects to the archaeological site are major. It is also a matter of cost. If the wetland was filled, an equivalent amount of wetland needed to be created as mitigation, probably a minor cost. If the archaeological site needed major mitigation, the FWS would make the county responsible for excavation costs that could run into hundreds of thousands of dollars. The developer, the agencies, and the consulting parties had to balance the needs of both the devil and the deep blue sea, as well as the needs of the traveling public.

CHAPTER 9

Federal System Players

The Ground Floor of Heritage Management

The first duty of government is to see that people have food, fuel, and clothes. The second that they have means of moral and intellectual education.

—John Ruskin (1876)

In the previous chapters, we have seen how federal agencies are given heritage management responsibilities by general environmental review laws, agency-specific or property-specific management laws, various executive orders, and Section 110 of the National Historic Preservation Act (NHPA). These responsibilities are linked to the lands and buildings they manage, the projects they fund or carry out, and the permits and licenses they issue. There are also federal agencies that have responsibilities to help other agencies fulfill their heritage management duties.

In this chapter I discuss the obligations, procedures, and roles of the major federal players in heritage management. By major, I mean the agencies that are responsible for providing guidance, that manage the most property, that fund or do the majority of the construction, and that issue the majority of the permits with implications for harming heritage properties. These agencies can be identified by determining which are given management responsibilities in law, which are in charge of the most property, which do specific activities, and what each spends on cultural heritage management each year, if such can be determined. At the state level, we can also examine how many state historic preservation office (SHPO) reviews are done each year for various federal agencies under Section 106 of NHPA.

What Are Agencies and What Do They Do?

Federal agencies are entities of the federal government in all three of its branches. They are given responsibilities by laws, regulations, and executive orders to carry out official governmental duties. Agencies can also be called departments, services, bureaus, commissions, offices, authorities, committees, councils, organizations, programs, centers, corps, and corporations, among other names.

Most federal agencies are under the executive branch. The highest-level executive agencies are at the cabinet level and are called departments. Each cabinet department is led by a secretary nominated by the president and confirmed by the Senate. There are currently 15 cabinet-level agencies. A cabinet-level agency can have numerous subagencies. Under the Department of the Interior (DOI) are the National Park Service (NPS), the Bureau of Indian Affairs (BIA), the Bureau of Land Management (BLM), the Bureau of Ocean Energy Management, the Bureau of Reclamation, the Bureau of Safety and Environmental Enforcement, the Office of Surface Mining Reclamation and Enforcement, the US Fish and Wildlife Service (FWS), and the US Geological Survey. There are also independent executive agencies, most of which report directly to the president, like the Advisory Council on Historic Preservation and the Council on Environmental Quality (CEQ).

A few agencies report directly to Congress, such as the Library of Congress, the Architect of the Capitol, and the Congressional Budget Office. The Supreme Court's agencies include the Administrative Office of the United States Courts, the Federal Judicial Center, and the Judicial Conference of the United States. There are also "independent agencies" that operate independently of the three branches of government. Examples are the Central Intelligence Agency, the Federal Reserve, and the US Postal Service (USPS). Most are governed by a board or a commission.

For the purposes of the following discussion, some cabinet-level agencies are better discussed at their subagency level because the parent departments are so large and their subagencies have very diverse missions. The Interior Department agencies discussed here include the National Park Service, the Fish and Wildlife Service, the Bureau of Land Management, the Bureau of Indian Affairs, and the Bureau of Reclamation. The Agriculture Department includes the US Forest Service (USFS) and various farm-related agencies, including the National Resource Conservation Service, the Farm Service Agency, and Rural Development. The Defense Department includes the US Army (with its Corps of Engineers), the US Navy (including the Marine Corps), and the US Air Force. Since 9/11, the US Coast Guard has been part of the Department of Homeland Security.

The federal government owns about 672 million acres of land (Figure 9.1). This is 28% of all the land within the United States. The big land managers in order of percentage of federal land are the Bureau of Land Management (40%), the US Forest Service (29%), the Fish and Wildlife Service (14%), the National Park Service (12%), and the Department of Defense (DOD) (3%). Other large federal land managers include the

FEDERALLY OWNED LAND

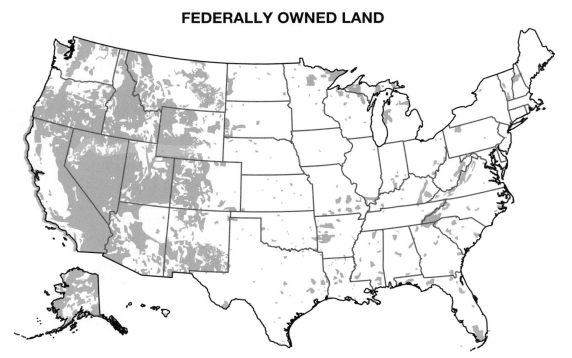

FIG. 9.1 Map of federally owned land in the United States (US Geological Survey).

Bureau of Reclamation and the Department of Energy. The Bureau of Indian Affairs has management authority over 55 million acres of Indian land held in trust by the federal government, but this is not included in the federal land totals or percentages.

There are about 500,000 buildings and about the same number of structures in federal ownership. As defined by the National Register of Historic Places (NRHP), buildings house human activities, while structures are built for activities that don't require human shelter. The largest federal building/structure manager is the Department of Defense, which has about 275,000 buildings, 178,000 nonlinear structures, and 107,000 linear structures (roads, railroads, trails, ditches, etc.), accounting for over half the federal building/structure total. Most military bases are in the South or along the coasts. Other large federal building managers include the US Postal Service, the General Services Administration (GSA), and the Department of Energy (DOE). The second-largest structure owner is the Department of the Interior with about 102,000.

The heritage management importance of project developers can be evaluated by both the number and the scale of projects. The Department of Housing and Urban Development (HUD) and the Natural Resources Conservation Service (NRCS) fund a great many projects. HUD projects are focused on building rehabs or small-footprint developments in urban areas. NRCS projects involve small grants to many rural landowners, once again with generally small footprints. The Federal Highway Administration (FHWA) funds thousands of road projects throughout the country, although the size and scope of most projects have significantly declined since the completion of the Interstate Highway System.

The Army Corps of Engineers (COE) dominates the permit issuers in most states, usually for Section 404 permits related to wetland filling under the Clean Water Act. Other major permitters are the Federal Communications Commission (FCC) for cell towers and the Federal Energy Regulatory Commission (FERC) for natural gas pipelines and hydroelectric reservoirs. All federal land-managing agencies can issue Archaeological Resources Protection Act (ARPA) permits for archaeological work on their lands, but ARPA permits in and of themselves are not subject to external environmental impact review under Section 106 or the National Environmental Policy Act (NEPA).

For 15 years I participated in Minnesota State Historic Preservation Office (SHPO) Section 106 reviews as the staff archaeologist. SHPO reviews can vary significantly from state to state in terms of overall numbers and numbers by individual agencies. For federal land management, Minnesota has two large national forests (Chippewa and Superior). It has one large national park (Voyageurs), as well as several smaller NPS units. The FWS has 13 national wildlife refuges in Minnesota, as well as hundreds of waterfowl production areas. Minnesota has 11 Indian reservations, but the great majority of reservation land is not held in federal trust. BLM is the largest federal land manager in the country but has very little land in Minnesota and very little land east of the Mississippi River in general. Minnesota has no major military bases, so its SHPO has limited DOD interaction. Compared with other states, Minnesota has the smallest percentage of land (.01%) managed by the DOD (see Figure 9.2).

In an average year in Minnesota when I was the SHPO archaeologist, about 20 different federal agencies submitted a total of 4,000 projects for Section 106 review. Of these reviews, about three-quarters were related to agency-sponsored or -funded development. HUD always led the pack with typically over 2,000 reviews each year. Various farm-related programs for the Department of Agriculture were usually second, followed by state and local highway construction funding from the FHWA/Minnesota Department of Transportation. The other reviews were mostly for federal permits, led by 200 to 300 COE permits and 200 to 300 FCC permits.

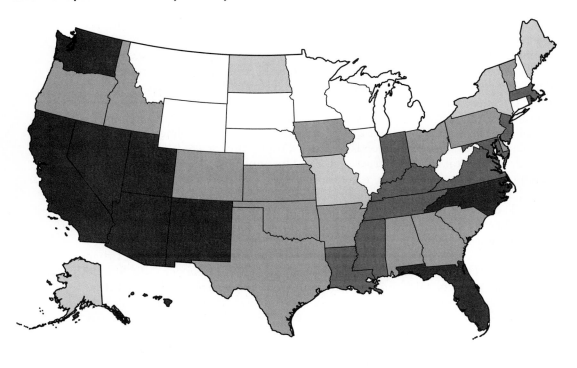

FIG. 9.2 Percentage of land in each state used for military bases (Kiersz 2014).

Finding yearly Section 106 review totals for individual SHPOs is difficult. The Minnesota SHPO used to publish an annual report summarizing all of its activities but quit doing this in 2001. In 2017, the only SHPO annual report I could find online was for Montana, but it did not provide a "review and compliance" breakdown by agency, type, or whether reviews were mandated by the federal government or the state. SHPOs do annually report general Section 106 summaries to the NPS, but these are not publicly available.

Section 110 of NHPA

It is important to begin a summary of individual agency heritage management activities with a discussion of the responsibilities of all federal agencies with regard to heritage management as stipulated in Section 110 (54 USC 3061) of the National Historic Preservation Act. These are internal agency responsibilities not dependent on the environmental review processes required in Section 106, NEPA, or other laws. Overall, Section 110 responsibilities are more proactive than reactive, although the eighth subsection of Section 110 essentially repeats the Section 106 requirement of agencies to "consider and consult" with regard to their undertakings.

The basic responsibilities of federal land-managing agencies with respect to their lands and buildings have already been discussed in chapter 8. As noted there, Section 110 of NHPA did not appear until the second round of amendments to the act in 1980. It had its philosophical origins in the preamble of the original NHPA in 1966 and its application origins in Executive Order 11593 in 1971.

There are very few articles and no books focusing on Section 110 in contrast to the many publications on Section 106. For written materials on Section 110, notable but short-length exceptions are Sprinkle (2015), a July 2015 series for the National Trust for Historic Preservation's (NTHP) Preservation Leadership Forum, and posts on *Tom King's CRM Plus* blog (August 27, 2008; November 18, 2014). John Sprinkle discusses the origins and overall purposes of Section 110. The NTHP forum looks at historic, legal, and specific agency applications. Tom King examines the meanings of each subsection. King also stresses that Section 110 is concerned with much more than federal agencies' responsibilities on lands they manage and does not absolutely require that all eligible historic properties on federal land be nominated to the National Register.

Perhaps the most important part of Section 110 of NHPA is the requirement that federal agencies develop comprehensive management practices with respect to historic properties as stated in the 2014 recodification of Section110:

§ 306102. Preservation program
(a) ESTABLISHMENT.—Each Federal agency shall establish (except for programs or undertakings exempted pursuant to section 304108[c] of this title), in consultation with the Secretary, a preservation program for the identification, evaluation, and nomination to the National Register, and protection, of historic property.
(b) REQUIREMENTS.—The program shall ensure that—
(1) historic property under the jurisdiction or control of the agency is identified, evaluated, and nominated to the National Register;
(2) historic property under the jurisdiction or control of the agency is managed and maintained in a way that considers the preservation of their historic, archeological, architectural, and cultural values in compliance with section 306108 of this title and gives special consideration to the preservation of those values in the case of property designated as having national significance;
(3) the preservation of property not under the jurisdiction or control of the agency but potentially affected by agency actions is given full consideration in planning;
(4) the agency's preservation-related activities are carried out in consultation with other Federal, State, and local agencies, Indian tribes, Native Hawaiian organizations carrying out historic preservation planning activities, and the private sector; and
(5) the agency's procedures for compliance with section 306108 of this title—
(A) are consistent with regulations promulgated by the Council pursuant to section 304108(a) and (b) of this title;
(B) provide a process for the identification and evaluation of historic property for listing on the National Register and the development and implementation of agreements, in consultation with State Historic Preservation Officers, local governments, Indian tribes, Native Hawaiian organizations, and the interested public, as appropriate, regarding the means by which adverse effects on historic property will be considered; and
(c) provide for the disposition of Native American cultural items from Federal or tribal land in a manner consistent with section 3(c) of the Native American Graves Protection and Repatriation Act (25 U.S.C. 3002[c]).

In 1988, the Department of the Interior published the *Secretary of the Interior's Standards and Guidelines for Federal Agency Historic Preservation Programs Pursuant to the National Historic Preservation Act* (53 FR 4727–4746). They were updated in 1998 (64 FR 20496–20508) to incorporate the changes required by the 1992 amendments to NHPA and were also reformatted. The 1998 version established seven basic standards, followed by guidelines to implement each standard.

Standard 1 concerns agency preservation programs. The standards related to land-ownership (2, 3, 6, 7) were discussed in chapter 8. Standards 4 and 5 basically refer to Section 106 duties discussed in chapter 6.

Standard 1 states, "Each Federal agency establishes and maintains a historic preservation program that is coordinated by a qualified Preservation Officer, and that is consistent with and seeks to advance the purposes of the National Historic Preservation Act. The head of each Federal agency is responsible for the preservation of historic properties owned or controlled by the agency." As outlined in the *Guidelines for Agency Programs* under Standard 1, federal agency historic preservation programs should

- include, to the extent feasible given the agency's mission and mandates, the full consideration and appropriate preservation of historic properties under the agency's jurisdiction;
- be embodied in agency-wide policies, procedures, and activities;
- hold identification, evaluation, and preservation of historic properties as the fundamental goal of the program;
- manage and maintain properties in a manner that takes into account their historic significance;
- seek and use historic properties to the maximum extent feasible in carrying out the agency's activities;
- ensure that historic preservation issues are considered before budgetary decisions are made that foreclose historic preservation options;
- ensure that the historic preservation program itself is adequately funded;
- engage, where possible, in public education and interpretation.

An agency is required to have a federal preservation officer (FPO) if its activities are subject to any of the provisions of the NHPA. This is true for all cabinet-level agencies and many of their subagencies. The Advisory Council on Historic Preservation (ACHP) website lists 77 FPOs. Of the 15 cabinet-level federal departments, 12 FPOs are based in the departmental secretary's office. Of these, Defense, Homeland Security, Justice, Transportation, and Treasury also have FPOs at the subagency level: Defense has 5, Homeland Security has 4, Justice has 1, Transportation has 11, and Treasury has 2.

The three cabinet-level departments that do not have a departmental-level FPO are Agriculture, Commerce, and Interior. The Department of Agriculture has seven subagency FPOs: Agricultural Research Services, Farm Service Agency, Forest Service, Natural Resources Conservation Service, Rural Business Cooperative Service, Rural Housing Service, and Rural Utilities Service. The Department of Commerce has one FPO in the National Oceanic and Atmospheric Administration. The Department of the Interior has nine FPOs: Bureau of Safety and Environmental Enforcement, Fish and Wildlife Service, US Geological Survey, Bureau of Indian Affairs, Bureau of Land Management, Bureau of Ocean Energy Management, Regulation, and Enforcement, National Park Service, Bureau of Reclamation, and Office of Surface Mining.

Under the Section 110 guidelines, the FPO is the person in the agency responsible for coordinating the entire agency preservation program. An FPO should have substantial experience with carrying out federal historic preservation activities and/or supervising staff who have experience. Federal preservation programs should have adequate agency-wide authority, staff, and other resources to effectively carry out Section 110 responsibilities. The preservation officer must be empowered to review and comment "meaningfully" on all agency programs and activities to influence decisions that could affect historic resources.

The guidelines go on to specify that when significant preservation responsibilities rest with regional or field offices, an agency should also appoint qualified preservation officials at those levels. These officials should make sure that their historic preservation actions are coordinated and consistent with those of the preservation officer for the agency. These individuals should be identified as preservation officials by agency personnel management, and their preservation responsibilities should be listed in their position descriptions. The agency should also provide ongoing training in historic preservation for all agency personnel with preservation responsibilities.

NHPA Section 110 requires agencies to have a historic preservation program and historic preservation personnel but not a historic preservation plan. As far as I am aware, the only federal agency-level historic preservation plan similar to the comprehensive plans that SHPOs are required to have is the 2013 *National Park Service Cultural Resource Challenge*. As part of their historic preservation programs, most agencies do have specific policies and guidelines.

NPS and ACHP: The Federal Cultural Heritage Leaders

Two federal agencies are designated as the leaders in American heritage management, the National Park Service and the Advisory Council on Historic Preservation. The NPS is a century old, has many duties besides cultural heritage management, and contains numerous subagencies. The ACHP is exactly half the age of NPS, but it has no subagencies, and its entire mission is focused on the preservation of historic properties. The NPS is subject to ACHP guidance for Section 106, and the ACHP promotes NPS guidance for heritage management elements such as consulting with Indian tribes.

National Park Service

The National Park Service is the only federal agency that performs all of the major actions subject to heritage preservation review: resource management, building, permitting, and providing heritage management guidance to other agencies. The NPS is the country's fourth-largest land manager and one of the largest building/structure managers. It gives out grants for maritime resource preservation, certified local government activities, and heritage area development. It issues permits for various kinds of work on its lands. It became the lead agency for heritage preservation with its founding in 1916, immediately supplemented by duties required by the Antiquities Act passed a decade earlier. Since the enactment of the National Historic Preservation Act in 1966, its cultural heritage management duties have greatly expanded, both for internal NPS activities and for external assistance. Today NPS is involved in so many heritage management activities, it would take multiple books to cover them in detail.

Historical Background

The passage of the Organic Act in 1916 established the NPS "to promote and regulate the use of the Federal areas known as national parks, monuments, and reservations . . . which purpose is to conserve the scenery and the natural and historic objects and the wild life therein and to provide for the enjoyment of the same." In its early days, NPS focused on the natural first in its large, inherited, landmark western parks: Yellowstone (1872), Yosemite (1890), Mount Rainier (1899), and Glacier (1910).

The conservation of "historic objects" on the landscape in an organized manner was slow to develop within NPS.

In 1921, the NPS hired its first professional archaeologist, Jesse Nusbaum, to help care for, explore, and interpret the prehistoric ruins at Mesa Verde. Nusbaum became the first NPS department consulting archaeologist (DCA) in 1933. In 1930, NPS undertook archaeological excavations at Wakefield, George Washington's birthplace, and Congress authorized Colonial National Park, incorporating the sites of Jamestown and Yorktown, which were largely archaeological. This initiated NPS eastern region and historic period attention.

Also in 1930, Charles Peterson, a landscape architect, was hired by NPS to assist with the development of Colonial National Park. A year later, Elliot Cox and Vern Chatelain were hired as the first NPS historians, with Chatelain soon becoming the first chief historian for NPS. Along with Peterson, the new historians worked on the restoration of the Moore House at Yorktown, the first building restoration undertaken by NPS. Peterson effectively became the first historical architect for NPS and was instrumental in establishing the Historic American Buildings Survey (HABS) in 1933.

The first major reorganization of the NPS also occurred in 1933. President Franklin D. Roosevelt issued Executive Order 6166, which transferred control of historic sites from the War Department and the Department of Agriculture to the National Park Service. This gave the NPS a total of 80 historical parks and monuments, representing over two-thirds of all NPS units, although a relatively small percentage of total acreage.

NPS was unprepared for the massive acquisition of historic sites throughout the country. It had only a few historic preservation professionals in 1933, one historian in Washington, two historians at Colonial National Park, and one archaeologist at Mesa Verde. New Deal programs also included park development and historic site restorations preceded by archaeological excavations. This required the employment of many historians, architects, and archaeologists. Some of these professionals soon had supervisory roles within the NPS to help manage the army of cultural heritage workers.

In 1933, Ronald Lee, who would replace Chatelain as chief NPS historian in 1938, was hired to help with interpretation at Shiloh National Military Park. Besides acquiring all military parks and national monuments and supervising various history-architecture-archaeology New Deal projects, NPS played a major role in implementing the Historic Sites Act in 1935. The act required a survey of nationally significant historic sites and empowered the secretary of the interior to accept new additions to the system of national historic sites. National historic areas that came into NPS control in the late 1930s included Jefferson National Expansion Memorial in St. Louis, Salem Maritime in Massachusetts, Hopewell Furnace Village in Pennsylvania, Fort Laramie in Wyoming, and the Vanderbilt Mansion in New York.

World War II put most NPS cultural resources activities on hold and ended the employment of most NPS heritage management professionals. It took a decade after the war to somewhat recover. In anticipation of its fiftieth anniversary in 1966, the NPS launched the Mission 66 program in 1956. Basic infrastructure improved in most parks, and the "visitor center" concept emerged to replace very basic public facilities built by the Civilian Conservation Corps (CCC) in the 1930s. Numerous historians and archaeologists were again hired to deal with the planning, mitigation, and interpretation needs of Mission 66. Park improvements and the completion of park projects such as the Gateway Arch in St. Louis cost $1 billion. During this period, 78 new parks were also established, bringing the total number to 258 by 1966.

The NPS was reorganized in 1967 to deal with the NHPA, passed the year before. The Office of Archaeology and Historic Preservation (OAHP) was formed to include the new Advisory Council on Historic Preservation and National Register of Historic Places, as well as the existing NPS History, Archaeology, and Architecture divisions. In 1978, OAHP was replaced with the Heritage Conservation and Recreation Service (HCRS), a new non-NPS Interior Department organization that took over NPS OAHP and Bureau of Outdoor Recreation responsibilities. HCRS was disbanded in 1981, and the cultural heritage management offices returned to NPS.

In 2000, all NPS heritage management programs, internal and external in focus, were reorganized under an associate director for cultural resource stewardship and partnerships. Political pressure during the George W. Bush administration in 2005 resulted in replacement of the Keeper of the National Register (Carol Shull) with a politically appointed NPS associate director (Janet Mathews). Shull returned as interim Keeper in 2009 after the Barack Obama administration took office. In 2012, an NPS reorganization put all heritage management programs under a new Cultural Resources, Partnerships, and Science Directorate.

Current NPS Heritage Preservation Activities

As of 2017, there were 413 NPS management units of 19 different types, including national parks (59), national monuments (84), national historical parks (50), national historical sites (78), national battlefields (11), national military parks (9), national preserves (19), national recreation areas (18), national seashores (10), national lakeshores (4), national rivers (15), national trails (3), and national parkways (4). While some units like battlefields, historical parks, and historical sites focus on cultural resources, almost every NPS unit has some kind of cultural resource. The larger units have thousands of cultural properties.

NPS headquarters is in Washington, DC, where staff are housed in several buildings collectively known as the Washington Support Office (WASO). The director of NPS is appointed by the president. Under the director are three deputy directors, one each for operations; congressional and external relations; and management and administration. Under the deputy director for operations are nine associate directors and seven regional directors. One of the associate directors in operations leads the Cultural Resources, Partnerships, and Science Directorate.

There are 32 separate programs within the Cultural Resources, Partnerships, and Science Directorate. These include the American Battlefield Protection Program, Archeology, Cultural Anthropology, the Federal Preservation Institute, the Historic American Buildings Survey, the Historic American Engineering Record (HAER), the Historic American Landscapes Survey (HALS), the Maritime Heritage Program, the National Register of Historic Places, Park History, and the Tribal Historic Preservation Program.

About a third of these programs are internal NPS programs (e.g., Park History), while other programs deal with mostly external activities (e.g., Federal Historic Preservation Tax Incentives). Some programs overlap: the Heritage Documentation Program manages HABS, HAER, and HALS, while Technical Preservation Services for Historic Buildings oversees the Tax Incentives and Historic Surplus Property programs. A few of the NPS programs, like the American Battlefield Protection Program, are a direct response to federal legislation (Public Law 104-333, 16 USC 469k/54 USC 308101–308103), while others, like the Tribal Historic Preservation Program (started in 1990), address specific needs reflecting the evolution of heritage preservation in this country.

Most NPS cultural heritage programs are narrowly focused on particular types of properties (e.g., lighthouses), particular groups (e.g., tribes), or particular duties (e.g., internships). Three broad NPS cultural heritage programs are critical to the implementation and success of heritage management in this country: Federal Historic Preservation Tax Incentives, Historic Preservation Fund Grants, and the National Register of Historic Places. Five other broad NPS programs provide important guidance to help heritage preservation operate efficiently and effectively: Archaeology, Cultural Anthropology, the Federal Preservation Institute, Historic Preservation Planning, and the National Center for Preservation Technology and Training.

Besides the Washington offices, the NPS has a major service center in Denver that is in charge of planning, design, and construction for all NPS units. There are seven regional NPS offices: Alaska (Anchorage), Pacific West (San Francisco), Intermountain (Denver), Midwest (Omaha), Southeast (Atlanta), Northeast (Philadelphia), and National Capital (Washington, DC). There are also five NPS centers that provide specialty services for NPS units: the Midwest Archaeological Center (Lincoln, Nebraska), the Southeast Archaeological Center (Atlanta, Georgia), the Submerged Resources Unit (Lakewood, Colorado), the Olmsted Center for Landscape Preservation (Boston, Massachusetts), and the Harpers Ferry Center for Media and Museum Conservation (Harpers Ferry, Virginia).

NPS is the largest employer of heritage management professionals in the United States, with over 1,000 heritage management personnel. According to a 2014 online database search, most professional employees are in the fields of archaeology, anthropology, history, architecture, archives, and museology.

The 2014 database lists 219 NPS employees under "archaeologist," with 192 archaeologists and 27 supervisory archaeologists. Most archaeologists are based in national parks or monuments that have significant archaeological resources (e.g., Mesa Verde, Chaco Canyon) or at the three archaeological service centers (Midwest, Southeast, Submerged). The chief archaeologist for NPS, called the departmental consulting archaeologist, is located in Washington, DC. Archaeologists are also based at the regional offices and at the various WASO facilities, including one or two at the National Register of Historic Places. There are at least 28 cultural anthropologists in NPS, with most located in WASO or at the regional offices. Of its almost 78 million acres, the NPS has archaeologically surveyed about 10%. There are about 69,000 recorded archaeological sites on NPS lands.

There are 163 historians according to the 2014 NPS database search but 266 historian positions listed in the 2009 NPS Directory of Historians (https://www.nps.gov/parkhistory/NPShistorians06.pdf). The discrepancy seems to entail whether employees consider themselves historians, even if that is not their position description. The majority are supervised by the chief NPS historian. NPS historians are in parks (165), regional offices (54), the Washington offices (40), and specialty service centers (7). They principally work with the Parks History Program and the HABS-HAER-HALS programs. There are 8 to 10 historians at the National Register.

The 2014 database lists 16 historical architects and 35 historic landscape architects. Most historical architects work in the Washington office or the regional offices or are associated with the HABS and HAER programs. Historic landscape architects are mostly based at the main NPS offices or at the Olmsted Center in Boston or work with the HALS program. The NPS has about 27,000 historically significant buildings/structures in its units.

The NPS has over 300 museums, the world's largest museum system. This is reflected in the numbers of personnel listed under museums (342), curation (19), and archives (121). There are three general types of NPS museum collections: **archival collections** consisting of personal papers, manuscripts, and resource management records; cultural collections consisting of archeological, ethnological, and historical objects; and natural history collections consisting of biological, geological, and paleontological objects. NPS has over 120 million objects in its museum collections. Curators and other museum specialists work mainly in parks with large collections as well as at the specialty professional service centers.

As with all federal agencies, it is difficult to determine overall NPS heritage spending. Individual management units (e.g., parks) pay for their own heritage management staff out of unit budgets. There are also private contracts for various heritage management activities. The fiscal year 2015 NPS overall budget was $2.615 billion.

NPS's basic mission has not changed significantly since the service's founding in 1916: preserve resources and make them available. NPS activities are still dominated by the "park" mission on its own lands. Most people still think of the NPS as preserving natural resources, although the majority of units (60%) were obtained as archaeological and historic resources. There is also a new awareness of less tangible cultural features on natural lands such as traditional cultural properties (TCPs) and cultural landscapes. NPS's most important external heritage management jobs are overseeing the funding and performance of SHPOs and tribal historic preservation officers (THPOs) and the Tax Incentives program. Other important external programs run by NPS include the National Register of Historic Places and the HABS-HAER-HALS programs.

Advisory Council on Historic Preservation

The Advisory Council on Historic Preservation is an agency whose only mission is to promote cultural heritage preservation as outlined in the National Historic Preservation Act. The ACHP is the primary federal policy advisor on heritage preservation to the president and Congress. It recommends preservation actions, promotes consideration of cultural heritage values in decision making, and reviews programs and policies to promote effectiveness, coordination, and consistency. The ACHP also works with nonfederal entities by encouraging public involvement in heritage preservation and advising state and local governments, as well as Indian tribes, Native Hawaiian organizations, and Native Alaskan organizations.

Historical Background

The ACHP was created by the National Historic Preservation Act in October 1966. The original council had 17 members: 6 federal agency heads, the director of the National Trust for Historic Preservation, and 10 members appointed by the president.

Five general duties of the ACHP were defined in Title 2 of the 1966 legislation:

(1) advise the President and the Congress on matters relating to historic preservation; recommend measures to coordinate activities of Federal, State, and local agencies and private institutions and individuals relating to historic preservation; and advise on the dissemination of information pertaining to such activities;
(2) encourage, in cooperation with the National Trust for Historic Preservation and appropriate private agencies, public interest and participation in historic preservation;
(3) recommend the conduct of studies in such areas as the adequacy of legislative and administrative statutes and regulations pertaining to historic preservation activities of State and local governments and the effects of tax policies at all levels of government on historic preservation;

(4) advise as to guidelines for the assistance of State and local governments in drafting legislation relating to historic preservation; and

(5) encourage, in cooperation with appropriate public and private agencies and institutions, training and education in the field of historic preservation.

What soon became the most important duty was not explicitly mentioned in the Section 202 duties of the NHPA, but it was included in the second sentence of Section 106: "The head of any such Federal agency shall afford the Advisory Council on Historic Preservation established under title II of this Act a reasonable opportunity to comment with regard to such undertaking."

The ACHP office was initially located in the Office of Archaeology and Historic Preservation within the Department of the Interior. The ACHP didn't have any staff until July 1967, when Robert Garvey became executive secretary and the lone staff member. The first meeting of the council took place in Washington in July 1967. At the third meeting of the council in February 1968, the ACHP asked Garvey to develop formal procedures for Section 106 implementation. Preliminary procedures were adopted by the ACHP in May 1968.

Because the Department of the Interior is a federal development and land-managing agency, there was a basic conflict of interest with housing the ACHP at NPS. The first step to reduce the conflict of interest was taken in July 1968, when the ACHP executive secretary was promoted within NPS to report directly to the NPS director. The conflict of interest was eliminated in 1976 when amendments to the NHPA made the ACHP an independent federal agency no longer under the secretary of the interior.

The 1980 amendments to the NHPA added two additional duties for the ACHP:

(6) review the policies and programs of Federal agencies and recommend to such agencies methods to improve the effectiveness, coordination, and consistency of those policies and programs with the policies and programs carried out under this Act; and

(7) inform and educate Federal agencies, State and local governments, Indian tribes, other nations and international organizations and private groups and individuals as to the Council's authorized activities.

The last duty expanded the assistance mission of the ACHP beyond just federal agencies to include state and local governments, Indian tribes, other nations and international organizations, and private groups and individuals. The inclusion of assisting Indian tribes in 1980 anticipated the 1992 amendments to the NHPA that allowed tribes to assume (on their reservations) the same NHPA powers as SHPOs.

Although the 1992 NHPA amendments did not specify any major changes in the duties of the ACHP, they did require revision of the 36 CFR 800 regulations with regard to implementation of Section 106. Based on input from federal agencies in the early stages of regulation revision, the ACHP recognized it should give federal agencies and SHPOs greater authority to conclude Section 106 reviews without ACHP review when there was little potential for controversy.

In the final version of the 36 CFR 800 revised regulations issued in 2004, there was greater ACHP deference to agency-SHPO decisions, ACHP involvement in the day-to-day Section 106 process became more restricted, alternate agency procedures were simplified, and there was increased flexibility in programmatic agreements (PAs). As implemented, this included combining "no historic properties" and "no effect" findings into one "no effect" finding. In addition, the identification and evaluation steps became more flexible, adverse effect criteria and exceptions were revised, ACHP review of consensus "no adverse effect" determinations was eliminated, and ACHP review of agency findings was clarified.

ACHP involvement was still required if there was a failure to agree after agency-SHPO/THPO consultation, if a federal agency failed to follow the required process (foreclosure), if an undertaking was highly controversial with the public or tribes or involved an important policy or interpretation question, if a National Historic Landmark (NHL) or other highly important historic property was adversely affected, or if ACHP involvement was requested by an agency or a SHPO/THPO. The 2004 regulations also required more vigilant ACHP monitoring of overall Section 106 performance by agencies and SHPOs/THPOs.

With implementation of the new 36 CFR 800 regulations, the day-to-day work of ACHP became somewhat less focused on Section 106 duties and more inclusive of general historic preservation guidance and broad social issues (e.g., encouraging diversity). This is demonstrated by the type and number of ACHP publications. Only two ACHP publications from prior to 1992 are listed among current ACHP publications on the council's website: *Balancing Historic Preservation Needs with the Operation of Highly Technical or Scientific Facilities* (1991) and *Balancing Assessing the Energy Conservation Benefits of Historic Preservation: Methods and Examples* (1979). A few other ACHP publications prior to 1992 have been withdrawn because they are out of date, such as *Treatment of Archaeological Properties: A Handbook* (1980).

Since 1992, there have been almost 50 ACHP publications. About half focus on Section 106, but the rest are various guidelines and position papers on other topics. They include

- *In a Spirit of Stewardship: A Report on Federal Historic Property Management* (2015)
- *Preserving Historic Post Offices: A Report to Congress* (2014)
- *Managing Change: Preservation and Rightsizing in America* (2014)
- *Measuring Economic Impacts of Historic Preservation* (2013)
- *Celebrating Asian American/Pacific Islander Heritage* (2013)
- *Traditional Cultural Landscapes Action Plan* (2012)
- *Get Youth Involved to Build a Better Preservation Ethic—and Nation* (2011)
- *Becoming Better Stewards of Our Past: Recommendations for Enhancing Federal Management of Historic Properties* (2004)
- *Heritage Tourism and the Federal Government: Summit I—Report of Proceedings* (2002)
- *Caring for the Past, Managing for the Future: Federal Stewardship* (2001)
- *America's Historic Legacy* (2001)

The Current Council

Over the 50 years since the ACHP was created, the makeup of its membership was changed by amendments to the NHPA in 1976, 1980, 1992, 2006, and 2016. Membership was increased to 29 members in 1976, decreased to 19 members in 1980, increased to 20 in 1992 with the addition of a tribal member, and increased to 23 in 2006. President Obama signed the National Park Service Centennial Act on December 16, 2016 (Public Law 114-289). The act amended the NHPA to make the chairmanship of the ACHP a full-time position and added the chairman of the National Association of Tribal Historic Preservation Officers (NATHPO) as a voting member of the ACHP. This changed the ACHP membership from 23 to 24 and a voting quorum from 12 to 13.

At the end of 2016, the council had 10 federal agency heads (Defense, Transportation, Housing and Urban Development, Education, Veterans Administration, General Services Administration, Homeland Security, Interior, Agriculture, Architect of the Capitol), the head of the National Trust for Historic Preservation, the head of the National Conference of SHPOs, the chairman of NATHPO, and 11 nonfederal members appointed by the president, including a governor, a mayor, and a Native American.

Current ACHP Staff

At the end of 2017, the ACHP had 40 professional staff members in eight "offices," all located in the Washington, DC, headquarters. The Office of the Executive Director includes three other offices: the Office of the General Council, the Office of Administration, and the Office of Information Technology. Other, smaller ACHP offices are the Office of Native American Affairs, the Office of Preservation Initiatives, and the Office of Communication, Education, and Outreach. The largest office is the Office of Federal Agency Programs (OFAP), with 22 staff members divided into two sections: Federal Property Management and Federal Permitting, Licensing, and Assistance. OFAP is focused on Section 106 "to address program and policy development in key areas."

Within OFAP, staff members are assigned to particular federal agencies. The staff assignment chart lists 52 agencies. Most staff members are assigned to multiple agencies, with a few having as many as six under their responsibility. Four staff members have only one agency: BLM, NRCS, FHWA, and GSA. These staff handle agency undertakings that come under ACHP authority. They also answer general questions the particular agencies may have and assist with writing agreement documents.

The Property Managers

The federal property managers can be divided into two groups: land managers and building/structure managers. Four federal agencies (Figure 9.3) control over 90% of federal lands: the Bureau of Land Management (37%), the US Forest Service (28%), the Fish and Wildlife Service (14%), and the National Park Service (12%). The largest federal building/structure manager is the Department of Defense, which has over half the federal building/structure total. Other large federal building/structure managers include the Department of the Interior, the US Postal Service, the General Services Administration, and the Department of Energy. The NPS is one of the largest land managers and one of the largest building/structure managers, as discussed in the previous section of this chapter. The DOD, with all of its

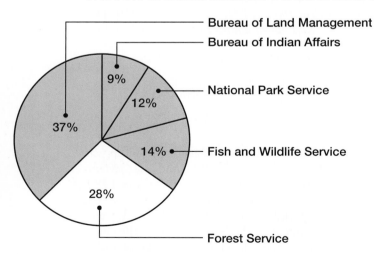

Total = 700 million acres

☐ Forest Service
▨ Interior agencies

Sources: GAO analysis of Forest Service and Interior data.

FIG. 9.3 Major federal land-management agencies (General Accounting Office).

branches, is the fifth-largest federal land manager as well as the largest building/structure manager.

The Land Managers

Bureau of Land Management

BLM Historical Background

The Bureau of Land Management manages 12% of all the land in the United States and about 37% of all federal land, encompassing about 250 million acres. BLM was established in 1946 under President Harry S. Truman's Reorganization Plan 3, which merged the General Land Office (GLO) and the 1934-established Federal Grazing Service. In 1976, the Federal Land Policy and Management Act (FLPMA) consolidated and better defined the BLM's responsibilities, in addition to declaring that the public lands BLM managed were to be retained in public ownership for multiple uses. The FLPMA is often referred to as BLM's Organic Act.

The BLM's mission is "to sustain the health, diversity, and productivity of America's public lands for the use and enjoyment of present and future generations." BLM staff are housed in the central office in Washington, DC, 12 state offices, 6 national support centers, 5 interpretive centers, and 132 field offices; 11 of the state offices are in the western United States, where all but 3 manage lands just in their own state. The Montana Office also includes North Dakota and South Dakota, the Wyoming Office includes Nebraska, and the New Mexico Office includes Kansas, Oklahoma, and Texas. All 31 other states are in the one eastern office. Each state office has a deputy preservation officer.

BLM Cultural Heritage Management

BLM began to hire professional cultural resource management (CRM) staff in the mid-1960s. CRM staff greatly expanded after 1974 following the implementation of regulations for both NEPA and Section 106 of the NHPA. In 1976, BLM California archaeologist Rick Hanks became the first cultural resource national program leader (Douglas 1999:26). By 1978, there were 120 CRM staff members in BLM, almost all of whom were archaeologists, as most BLM lands do not contain historic buildings and structures, and BLM museums had not yet been established. In 2007, there were 195 BLM archaeologists (NPS 2010). The number of BLM historians is not readily available, although in 2016 one historian appeared on the staff list for the Washington, DC–based BLM Office of Cultural and Paleontological Resources and Tribal Consultation.

BLM also has **curators** and other museum staff who help manage millions of archaeological, historical, and paleontological objects, as well as documents, in its collections. Some of these staff members work in BLM's three cultural heritage interpretive centers: the Anasazi Heritage Center in Colorado, the Billings Curation Center in Montana, and the National Historic Oregon Trail Interpretive Center in Oregon. Most collections from BLM lands and facilities are housed in over 150 non-BLM facilities scattered throughout the United States.

BLM claims to have inventoried cultural resources on about 35% of its lands (NPS 2010). Current BLM totals for the various types of cultural resources are not readily available online, but at the end of fiscal year 2013, BLM reported that it managed a total of 358,515 cultural properties (BLM 2014), the great majority of which are archaeological sites. The NPS *Federal Archaeology Program Report* in 1995 listed 187,028 recorded archaeological sites on BLM lands (Hass 1998, Table D4), and the NPS total for 1996 is 202,403. The 2014 BLM *Preserve America*

Progress Report (the most recent available online at the beginning of 2017) notes about 10,000 cultural properties were recorded each year in 2011, 2012, and 2013. Because there are so few buildings under BLM control, BLM doesn't even appear in most federal real property summary reports.

The BLM budget for CRM was $16.2 million in fiscal year 2016. In the early 2000s, CRM funding averaged about $15 million per year, with a low of $13.5 million in 2008. The NPS 2004–2007 report to Congress (NPS 2010) on federal archaeology estimated the BLM should have an optimal number of 2,918 archaeologists, 15 times more than the 195 listed in the NPS report.

Most BLM state offices have close working relationships with their respective SHPOs for data sharing and Section 106 compliance. The agency provides CRM guidance to its employees in what is known as its *Manual 8100* (BLM 2004). In 1997, BLM signed a nationwide programmatic agreement with the ACHP and the National Conference of State Historic Preservation Officers (NCSHPO). This agreement was amended in 2012 due to the 2004 finalization of the revised 36 CFR 800. The agreement led to the establishment of a BLM Preservation Board, which provides heritage management policy and procedure advice to the agency.

The 1997 BLM nationwide programmatic agreement dealt with establishing program alternative Section 106 procedures based on individual PAs established between SHPOs and the BLM state-level offices. The 2012 amendments to the nationwide PA focused on revising the BLM CRM manual and existing state agreements to be consistent with 2004 36 CFR 800 definitions of "consulting parties" and "adverse effect" as well as procedures for consulting with the public and tribes. All of the western state BLM offices have drafted or implemented revised state protocols; the 31-state eastern BLM office was not included in the PA (see https://www.blm.gov/wo/st/en/prog/more/CRM/historic_preservationx.html).

Tom King received a copy of the proposed revision of the California-BLM PA and was not happy with it (*Tom King's CRM Plus*, June 18, 2013). His major complaints were (1) inadequate tribal and public consultation prior to drafting the revised protocol, (2) inadequate and confusing guidance on how to actually implement the protocol, and (3) inadequate attention to inventorying and determining effects to nonarchaeological cultural resources.

In 2014, the BLM extended the time for amending state-level PAs, but the Utah office still had not implemented a comprehensive statewide protocol by the end of 2017, although it does have a PA for small-scale undertakings. The three state offices that have multiple states under their jurisdiction (Montana, New Mexico, and Wyoming) only included their home states in the protocols.

US Forest Service

USFS Historical Background

In 1876, an office was created in the US Department of Agriculture (USDA) to assess the condition of forested land in the country. This office became the USDA Division of Forestry in 1881. A decade later, Congress gave presidents the power to create federal forest reserves with the passage of the Forest Reserve Act. The General Land Office initially administered these reserves under its Division of Forestry. The first forest reserve was established in 1891 surrounding what was to become Yellowstone National Park. In 1897, Congress passed legislation (now referred to as the Forest Service Organic Act) requiring that new forest reserves meet certain requirements for forest and watershed protection as well as timber production.

In 1905, the GLO Forestry Division was combined with the USDA Forestry Division to become the US Forest Service within the USDA. At the time, there were

55 million acres in federal forest reserves, which were renamed national forests in 1907. In 1911, Congress authorized the expansion of the national forests through the purchase of private land, and by 1919 over 100 million acres had been added to the original 55 million acres of federal forests (Gorte 2005).

In 1916, in response to the newly created National Park Service, the Forest Service established its first national forest campground (Williams 2005:42). At the request of Aldo Leopold, a USFS employee and early conservationist, the first wilderness area was created in Gila National Forest in 1924. During the drought of the 1930s, the federal government began to purchase marginal agricultural land in the Great Plains to help control erosion. These lands were originally under the Soil Conservation Service (SCS), but in 1954, 5.5 million acres were transferred to the USFS. In 1960, 3.8 million of these acres were included in 19 national grasslands under the management of the USFS.

Today, the mission of USFS is "to sustain the health, diversity, and productivity of the nation's forests and grasslands to meet the needs of present and future generations." The USFS manages about 193 million acres of land, most of which is included in 154 national forests and 20 national grasslands. About 37 million acres are considered wilderness. These lands have 4,300 campgrounds, 122 ski areas, and 158,000 miles of trails.

The Forest Service is organized into four basic levels. The headquarters is in Washington, DC. Its chief executive, called the chief forester, is almost always a forestry professional. The chief forester reports to the undersecretary for natural resources and environment at the Department of Agriculture. At this level are also an Albuquerque Service Center for Budget and Finance and a Forest Management Service Center in Boulder. At the next level are nine regional offices led by a regional supervisor. Seven of the nine regions are in the western United States. At the third level, each national forest and national grassland has a main office led by a forest supervisor. Finally, national forests and grasslands have district offices led by district rangers. There are over 600 districts with staffing that varies from 10 to 100 people. The Forest Service also has seven research laboratories scattered across the country.

USFS Cultural Heritage Management

The Forest Service federal historic preservation officer (HPO) is the Heritage Program manager based in the Washington, DC, central office in the Recreation, Heritage, and Volunteer Resources Division. This office also houses a History Program manager, an Interpretive Services program manager, and a Heritage Program specialist. Each region and most individual forests and grasslands have cultural heritage resources staff, usually just archaeologists.

Archaeologists were the first cultural heritage professionals hired by the Forest Service beginning in 1970 in several western regions. As in the BLM and many other federal agencies, the 1974 issuance of regulations for NEPA and Section 106 of NHPA immediately led to a great expansion in CRM professionals in the Forest Service. The Forest Service's "archaeology program" was renamed the Cultural Resource Management Program in 1976.

The first national forest archaeologists were rapidly overwhelmed by the need to do surveys for new logging areas and the road construction that served them. The USFS CRM Program was basically a reactive program with little general inventory survey or heritage management planning. To deal with the survey work overload, a paraprofessional program was developed in the mid-1970s, teaching other Forest Service employees basic archaeological skills so they could assist with archaeological survey work.

The addition of Section 110 to the NHPA in 1980 required the USFS to adopt a more proactive approach to finding, evaluating, and managing cultural resources. A decade later, the Forest Service began to adopt an "ecosystems" approach to forest management. This de-emphasized the view that the forest was a commodity and promoted a view that it was a reservoir of interdependent systems, both natural and cultural. The USFS CRM Program became the Heritage Program in 1992. This not only expanded the focus of heritage to include natural aspects but also expanded cultural heritage aspects beyond just archaeological sites and standing structures.

Besides the heritage management responsibilities found in the general cultural heritage laws outlined in previous chapters, the USFS has specific responsibilities described in the Wilderness Act of 1964 (16 USC 1131–1136) and the National Forest Management Act of 1976 (16 USC 1600; 36 CFR 219). Forest Service regulations pertaining to heritage management are found in 36 CFR 200. Internal guidelines for heritage management are in chapter 2360 of the *Forest Service Manual*. Six of the nine USFS regions have entered into programmatic agreements with the ACHP and various SHPOs for the management of cultural heritage resources.

As of 2008, the Forest Service had inventoried about 350,000 cultural heritage properties, of which most are archaeological sites. The 2016 USFS heritage management budget was $28.3 million. Today, the activities on Forest Service land that pose the greatest threat to cultural resources and come under Section 106 review are timber harvesting, road construction, and campground development. In 2013, there were almost 400 archaeologists within the USFS, as well as a much lower number of historians, historical architects, and museum professionals. A USFS history museum is under construction in Missoula, Montana. Although being built by a private organization, the museum will include some USFS collections.

A 2008 National Trust study evaluated the effectiveness and deficiencies of Forest Service cultural heritage management (Jarvis 2008). The NTHP report noted that earlier internal USFS reports focused on the need to simplify and reduce regulatory burdens rather than discuss management responsibilities under the NHPA. The NTHP suggested that a new management approach and additional funding were needed to better protect cultural resources on lands managed by the USFS

US Fish and Wildlife Service

FWS Historical Overview

The US Fish and Wildlife Service, as its name implies, has a diverse origin. The fish part traces its beginnings to 1871, with the founding of the US Commission on Fish, which was reorganized in 1903 as the Bureau of Fisheries. The wildlife part dates to 1886 with the establishment of the Division of Economic Ornithology and Mammalogy within the US Department of Agriculture, which became the Division of Biological Survey in 1896. In 1903, the first national wildlife refuge was established as a federal bird reservation on Pelican Island in Florida. The modern version and current name of the FWS came about in 1940, when the Bureau of Fisheries and the Biological Survey were combined into the US Fish and Wildlife Service after they were moved into the Department of the Interior.

The mission of the FWS is "to conserve, protect, and enhance fish, wildlife, and plants, and their habitats for the continuing benefit of the American people." The FWS has three principal types of properties: wildlife refuges, waterfowl production areas, and wildlife coordination areas. There are also 34 national fish hatcheries as well as other fisheries facilities managed by the regional FWS offices through 65 field offices. The wildlife refuges are the largest part of the FWS system in terms of acreage, with the majority of FWS-managed land in 550 national wildlife refuges (NWRs) scattered across the country, within territorial waters, and in trust territories.

Waterfowl production areas (WPAs) consist of about 7,000 parcels concentrated in the prairie pothole region of the north-central United States within 38 wetland-management districts. The WPAs cover a total of about 677,000 acres, with an average of 100 acres each. They are open to public hunting, fishing, and trapping. Wildlife coordination areas are managed by states under a lease agreement with FWS but are owned by the federal government.

The director, deputy directors, and most assistant directors are in the FWS Headquarters Building in Washington, DC, with most other national executives based in a large service center in Falls Church, Virginia. There are nine regions, each with a regional director: Pacific (1), Southwest (2), Midwest (3), Southeast (4), Northeast (5), Mountain Prairie (6), Alaska (7), Pacific Southwest (8), and Washington Office (9). Each field region has a number of district offices.

FWS Cultural Heritage Management

While the FWS is the third-largest federal landowner, its cultural heritage management footprint in the federal government is surprisingly modest. The first CRM professional was hired in 1977 in the Alaska office. By the early 1980s, the central office as well as each regional office had a CRM professional. Today, there are only about 20 CRM professionals in the entire FWS, most of whom are archaeologists, but there are also a few historians and curatorial staff.

The FWS cultural heritage program is supervised by the chief of the Visitor Services branch within the Division of Visitor Services and Communications. This individual is also the federal historic preservation officer for the FWS. Each FWS region has a regional HPO who is often the only CRM professional within the region. According to the 2014 FWS *Preserve America Update* report, all of the regions but Region 8 (Pacific Southwest) have an archaeologist as the regional CRM manager/ preservation officer; Region 8 has an architectural historian. In 2014, Region 1 (Pacific) had the most CRM employees with eight. Three employees are listed in Regions 5 and 6, with the other regions typically having one professional heritage management employee. The Alaska Region (7), which accounts for over 76 million acres, or about 85% of FWS lands, had one CRM professional on staff in 2014.

The 2014 FWS report lists the total number of archaeological sites at 15,419 and the total number of "acres surveyed for archaeological sites" as 1,565,960, or about 2% of FWS management area. The total number of buildings/structures is listed as 1,814. The FWS in 2014 had about 4.5 million objects in its museum collections, which include materials related to archaeology, ethnography, history, manuscripts, biology, paleontology, and geology. About 28% of these collections are housed in 114 FWS facilities, while the rest are at 175 nonfederal locations. About half these collections are archaeological, and about a third are written materials.

Funding for the CRM staff involved in compliance with federal heritage preservation laws comes from program dollars within each region. Nonprogram budgets are used to cover the costs of outside contracts that complete almost all the survey and evaluation work on FWS land with respect to both NHPA Section 106 and Section 110 responsibilities. Funding for the museum and curation programs comes from FWS Arts and Artifacts funding, which amounted to $362,659 in fiscal year 2013.

Policies for FWS cultural heritage management are found in several sections of the FWS *Service Manual* (https://www.fws.gov/policy/manuals). Chapters 1 to 4 of Section 614 cover general policy and procedures for cultural heritage management and compliance with NHPA, chapter 5 deals with public interpretation of cultural resources, and chapter 6 covers tribal consultation. Chapters 1 to 3 of Section 126 provide policies and procedures for documentation and preservation for the FWS museum property program.

The major internal FWS undertakings that impact cultural resources on FWS lands are access roads, trails, parking lots, and facility construction. External undertakings include nonfederal roads that pass through refuges or WPAs, as well as nonfederal construction activities such as cell towers built on FWS lands. The 2014 FWS *Preserve America* report noted a national total of 1,878 completed Section 106 reviews in fiscal year 2013.

The Building/Structure Managers

Not only is the federal government the country's largest land manager, but its agencies also manage the largest number of buildings and structures. There are about 500,000 buildings and about the same number of structures under federal ownership. Once again, for heritage management purposes, buildings house human activities, while structures are built for activities that don't require shelter. Buildings include residences, barns, factories, stores, and offices, while structures include roads, dams, farm outbuildings, and even ships.

Buildings and structures have very different requirements for discovery, evaluation, treatment, and interpretation when compared to archaeological sites, cultural landscapes, and traditional cultural properties. Buildings and structures are almost always visible, so they are easily found and mapped. Because they are so visible and their importance is known locally without formal evaluation, direct impacts from construction are often avoided if the property is deemed historically important to the National Register, the agency, or the local community.

Many buildings and structures can be inventoried and even formally evaluated for significance without ever being entered, although the National Register is increasingly considering interior significance and integrity. Treatment with regard to mitigating adverse effects can be much cheaper than archaeological mitigation, but archaeological sites usually require very little maintenance, while buildings and structures can be very expensive to maintain. Furthermore, the National Register of Historic Places provides numerous bulletins focused on specific building and structure evaluation (6) compared to archaeological sites (1). The National Park Service has explicit guidelines for building and structure treatment when it comes to tax credit and grant eligibility.

Department of Defense

DOD Historical Overview

The largest federal building/structure manager is the Department of Defense, which has about 275,000 buildings, 178,000 nonlinear structures, and 107,000 linear structures such as roads, railroads, trails, and ditches. The DOD manages over half of the federal building/structure total. It also has a huge land base, ranking fifth among federal agencies with over 25 million acres. The mission of the DOD is "to provide the military forces needed to deter war and to protect the security of our country."

The DOD includes the US Army, Navy, Air Force, and Marine Corps, as well as the Army Corps of Engineers. The US Coast Guard was moved into the Department of Homeland Security following the 9/11 terrorist attacks. With regard to buildings, the Marine Corps and COE are relatively minor players and won't be discussed here. The COE is a major player with regard to federal permits and will be discussed in the next section with the permitters.

The DOD was originally called the War Department. In 1947, all branches of the military were consolidated into what was known as the National Military Establishment under a secretary of defense, with the air force becoming a separate entity from the army. The army, navy, and air force each had secretaries at the cabinet level. In 1949, the Department of Defense was established with only one cabinet-level position retained for the secretary of defense.

The army as an entity of the federal government originated in 1775, when a Continental Army was established by the Second Continental Congress to help fight the British in the War of Independence. It was rapidly reduced in size after the war ended, retaining several small units to help deal with Indian conflicts caused by western expansion and to guard the national arsenal at West Point. Congress made West Point a military academy in 1801, but initially it focused only on engineering.

Prior to the Civil War, most construction activity of the army was associated with western forts. At the beginning of the Civil War in 1861, the army had about 16,000 soldiers scattered across the country at 79 posts. By the end of the Civil War in 1865, the federal army had over 2.5 million soldiers. The Civil War shifted most construction back east, but a western focus resumed after the Civil War and lasted until near the end of the 1800s. The units of the regular army were formally named the United States Army in 1896.

The US entry into World War I created a need for the rapid expansion of training facilities for the army, which resulted in a proliferation of bases. Most of these facilities remained after World War I, although personnel numbers were greatly reduced. These bases were again invigorated by US entry into World War II in late 1941. After the end of World War II, many bases were closed and thousands of their buildings and structures abandoned. Regional conflicts since the mid-twentieth century have led to the maintenance of a relatively large standing army with about 500,000 active-duty personnel.

The distribution of military bases and the percentage of land in bases varies greatly by state and region (Figure 9.2). Army bases tend to be located in the Southeast and Southwest, where weather conditions are more amenable to year-round training and maintenance. Naval bases tend to be located on the coasts for obvious reasons. Air force bases are widely dispersed, as airborne threats can come from any quarter. Bases are concentrated around Washington, DC. States thus have greatly varying historic preservation responsibilities with regard to the Department of Defense. In the Upper Midwest, bases are almost exclusively run by the air force, represent relatively small parcels of land, and are usually located adjacent to or within commercial airports. In the Southwest, where there is considerable federal land, bases are huge and often distant from population centers.

Today, there are about 70 active army bases in the United States with another 40 bases in other countries. There are over 150 abandoned army bases in this country. The largest army base in terms of size is Fort Bragg in North Carolina at 163,000 acres. The largest army base with regard to population is Fort Hood in Texas with about 65,000 active-duty personnel. Overall, the army is the largest DOD real property owner with over 138,000 buildings and over 134,000 structures, as well as about 11.2 million acres of land.

The navy also dates its beginning to 1775 and, like the army, was subject to similar fluctuations in personnel between the Revolutionary War and Civil War. The Annapolis Naval Academy was established in 1845. The great expansion of the navy and naval bases took place in the late nineteenth century with the ascent of the battleship and other steam-powered steel vessels. The US Navy played a minor role in World War I, although by the end of the war, it was the largest navy in the world in terms of personnel, with a Pacific and an Atlantic fleet.

Unlike the army, the navy maintained a strong force between the world wars. Like the army, the navy rapidly expanded after the attack on Pearl Harbor in December 1941. During World War II, American naval power became unrivalled. The navy continued to maintain its world-leading naval presence after World War II due to the Cold War with the Soviet Union and, more recently, the rise of China as a naval power.

The current navy has the world's largest fleet. It has about 80 bases in the United States and 32 bases in other countries. The largest naval base is at Norfolk, Virginia, which covers an area of approximately 3,400 acres and has 149,000 personnel. It was established in 1917. Overall, the navy manages over 61,000 buildings and over 50,000 structures, as well as about three million acres of land.

The air force began as the Air Service, established as a separate unit within the military when America entered World War I in 1917. The Air Service was put under control of the army in 1920 and was renamed the Army Air Corps in 1926. It was significantly increased in size in 1941 just prior to American entry into World War II and renamed the Army Air Force (AAF). There was a great expansion of bases during World War II. After the war, many AAF bases were closed or abandoned. The National Security Act in 1947 reorganized the military, and the AAF became an independent branch of the military renamed the US Air Force. The Air Force Academy in Colorado Springs was established in 1955.

Because state National Guard units receive federal funding but their properties are not owned by the federal government, active National Guard facilities in states and cities are subject to Section 106 but not Section 110 of the NHPA. After World War I, most moderate to large towns had a National Guard unit, but the number of municipal armories still in federal service has greatly declined. There are currently about 2,500 armories (now called readiness centers) still in service with the National Guard. Many of the former and current facilities are important local historical buildings. The National Guard also has 110 major bases (training centers) scattered across the country, consisting of about two million acres of land containing over 12,000 buildings.

Today the air force has about 70 bases in the United States and 40 overseas. There are also almost 90 Air Force Reserve and Air National Guard bases, most of which share space with public airports around the country. There are over 100 closed or inactive air force bases. Overall, the air force manages about 51,000 buildings and over 71,000 structures, as well as about 8.6 million acres of land.

DOD Cultural Heritage Management

The military began assuming historic preservation duties with the establishment of national military parks in the late nineteenth century. These duties were reduced in 1933 when the military parks were transferred to the NPS. Prior to the issuance of Executive Order 11593 in 1971, DOD historic preservation was basically an internal program limited to the Center for Military History (started in 1943 to record World War II history) and the army museum program, although a museum was started at West Point in 1854.

Modern cultural resource management within the DOD began in the Army Corps of Engineers. In 1947, the federal Bureau of the Budget ruled that only the NPS could undertake archaeological investigations on federal works projects, so in 1951 the COE requested that NPS deal with all Antiquities Act permit applications on army lands. The passage of NHPA and NEPA forced the DOD to start developing its own agency-wide historic preservation program. The first archaeological professional was hired by the COE's Tulsa District in 1970.

The COE considered the issuance of Executive Order 11593 in 1971 as a directive to fund and undertake its own archaeological work (Ramirez 1997:6). Once again, the Tulsa District led the way with contracts for archaeological survey for a proposed dam in Texas. In the mid-1970s, the COE consulted with NPS about initiating a CRM program. Resulting stipulations in Engineering Regulation 1105-2-460 laid the foundation for COE CRM. By the late 1970s, the COE had a staff of over 20 heritage management professionals scattered throughout its district offices, including archaeologists, historians, and architects. These professionals received technical assistance from the COE's Construction Engineering Research Laboratory.

The army also included heritage management considerations in its initial environmental regulations issued in 1974. Consultation with the ACHP in 1976 led to the hiring by army headquarters in 1977 of the first heritage management professional, Constance Ramirez. Individual army bases began to hire consultants to help survey construction, inventory base buildings, and develop heritage management plans. Army Regulation 420-40, issued in 1984, directed all army installations to prepare historic preservation plans. The navy began to develop its historic preservation program in 1979, followed by the air force in the early 1980s. The DOD developed uniform heritage management regulations for all the services in 1985.

By the end of the 1980s, the DOD and all its branches were fully involved in cultural heritage management. However, as Ramirez (1997:9) points out, the DOD efforts still lacked consistent, centralized funding and were often given low priority in military budgeting. This was addressed by Congress in 1990 when $10 million was appropriated to set up the DOD Legacy Resource Management Program, which included both cultural and natural resource considerations. This led to increased and regular DOD funding for heritage management activities, just as the national heritage management structure began to radically change. It also led to a change of military attitude toward cultural resources as assets rather than burdens (e.g., US DOD 1994).

In the same year that the DOD legacy program was established, the Native American Graves Protection and Repatriation Act (NAGPRA) was passed, the NPS issued new federal curation standards (36 CFR 79), and the Base Realignment and Closure Act (BRAC) was passed. Two years later, the NHPA was amended to include tribal consultation, and the National Register issued Bulletin 38 on traditional cultural properties. Additional direction for the DOD legacy program was included in the National Defense Authorization Act in 1997. By the end of the twentieth century, the DOD was utilizing new technologies and new guidelines to fulfill its considerable and diverse heritage management responsibilities.

The current DOD Cultural Resources Program is within the Office of the Assistant Secretary of Defense for Energy, Installations, and Environment and directly under the deputy assistant secretary of defense for environment, safety, and occupational health, who is the DOD historic preservation officer. Each branch of the military, as well as the COE, also has a federal preservation officer and a deputy preservation officer. In 2001, the ACHP approved the army's alternate procedures for Section 106 compliance.

With regard to heritage management personnel, in 2007 the army had 132 archaeologists, the navy had 27 archaeologists, and the air force 19 archaeologists. Current numbers of historians, historical architects, and museum professionals are not readily obtainable. The Office of the Secretary of Defense has had a Historical Office since 1949. A number of historians also work in the Army Center of Military History. Historical architects play a critical role in DOD CRM, with so many historic buildings and structures to manage, especially since the implementation of

BRAC. In 2005, the ACHP established a task force to help deal with the BRAC process.

With regard to museums and curation needs, American military history is interpreted in almost 300 facilities in the United States. The DOD itself operates 91 museums worldwide, utilizing about 350 buildings for museum purposes. In fiscal year 2013 alone, the DOD budgeted over $91 million for museums. In 1999, the DOD issued *Guidelines for the Field Collection of Archaeological Materials and Standard Operating Procedures for Curating Department of Defense Archaeological Collections*.

The 2014 DOD *Preserve America* report lists the following statistics:

- Total archaeological sites recorded: 123,641
- Total acres surveyed: 9,343,447 (44% of surveyable land)
- Total buildings not yet evaluated: 265,828
- Total buildings determined not eligible: 43,661
- Total buildings determined NRHP eligible: 17,033
- Individual buildings NRHP listed: 206
- Buildings contributing to NRHP districts: 1,821
- Individual NHLs: 89
- Total museum collection items: 1,244,846
- Legacy project spending, fiscal year 1991–2013: $140 million (about 40% on cultural resources)

DOD support for cultural heritage preservation has been discussed in numerous DOD publications and other external publications describing DOD heritage preservation activities. The military has always recognized that honoring and promoting tradition plays a significant role in establishing and maintaining esprit de corps by fostering discipline, dedication, and positive attitudes among its personnel. Visible and well-preserved historic properties on military bases play a major role in maintaining traditions. The DOD also recognizes that the reuse of historic buildings and structures brings cost savings and environmental benefits. While DOD efforts at preserving "legacy" resources have been understandably focused on buildings, battlefields, and bastions, the department has made a substantial effort to consider prehistoric and nonmilitary resources on its many bases.

US Postal Service

USPS Historical Overview

The US Postal Service is an independent federal agency. The original Post Office Department traces its origins to 1775 when the Continental Congress appointed Benjamin Franklin the first postmaster general. The US Constitution, ratified in 1788, in Article I, Section 8 gave Congress the power "to establish Post Offices and Post Roads." Congress established an executive office of the postmaster general in 1789.

Most early post offices were in private residences or commercial buildings. Dedicated post office buildings, often combined with federal court buildings, began to be constructed in the mid-1800s. Free city mail delivery began in 1862, with free rural delivery starting in 1896. Rural delivery required that roads be improved, leading to the first great expansion of the American road system. Many new post office buildings were constructed during the 1930s. A 1% allowance for art led to extensive use of interior murals in post offices painted by WPA-supported artists.

The Postal Reorganization Act passed in 1970 led to the USPS becoming an independent agency in 1971. Today it operates about 31,000 postal facilities, of which 8,900 are federally owned buildings and the remainder are privately owned buildings leased by the Postal Service. The USPS is one of the largest employers in the United States with over 600,000 workers. In terms of square footage, it ranks fifth among federal agencies with over 270 million square feet owned or leased.

USPS Cultural Heritage Management

Because the USPS is primarily a municipal building owner-leaser, it manages few other types of historically significant property types (e.g., archaeological sites). The USPS federal preservation officer is based in Washington, DC, and is under the vice president for facilities. The USPS has only one cultural heritage professional on staff, a historian.

The USPS role in cultural heritage management has been controversial since the Postal Service was partially privatized in 1971. In 1982, the USPS Board of Governors issued a resolution that the service would "voluntarily comply" with NHPA Sections 106, 110, and 111. Beginning in 2008, the USPS increased the rate at which it was disposing of its buildings, many of which were historically significant. This led to public controversy, as many historic post offices are landmark buildings in cities and towns.

Because many post offices are such visible and important historic buildings in communities, in 1984 the National Register of Historic Places issued Bulletin 13 titled *How to Apply the National Register Criteria to Post Offices*. A revised version of this bulletin was issued in 1994. In 2012, the USPS was beginning to feel the heat of public criticism of its sale of historic post offices, so it hired a private contractor (URS Corporation) to complete a report titled *USPS Nationwide Historic Context Study: Postal Facilities Constructed or Occupied between 1940 and 1971*. The time period was chosen because pre-1940 post offices were more obvious when it came to historical significance, and 1971 was the year the USPS became an independent agency. The NRHP bulletin and the 2012 USPS report provide a sound basis for evaluating the historical significance of most federally owned post offices.

Responding to public controversy regarding post office closures, in 2014 Congress required the ACHP to report on how the USPS would comply with federal historic preservation laws and regulations. At the same time, the Office of the Inspector General for the USPS examined the same issue. Both agencies issued reports in 2014, and both reports concluded that the USPS was doing an inadequate job of ensuring full consideration of impacts to the historic character of post offices if they are put up for sale.

The ACHP and USPS 2014 reports specified that the USPS

- does not have a comprehensive inventory of historic properties under its control;
- does not know the costs involved in preserving its historic properties;
- did not collaborate with the ACHP to improve compliance with the NHPA;
- did not notify the senior curator at the National Museum of Art regarding the potential impact on New Deal art of the sale of 10 post offices between 2010 to 2013;
- had not completed a program alternative to help implement Section 106;
- used historic preservation covenants that were insufficient to ensure preservation;
- inappropriately rejected consulting party requests by community groups during the Section 106 process;
- had not issued *Preserve America* reports for some years.

The ACHP made the following recommendations for improvement of the USPS's compliance with the NHPA:

- Congress should clarify USPS responsibilities with respect to the NHPA.

- The USPS should suspend the sale of historic post office facilities until the USPS has fully implemented the recommendations in the ACHP report.
- The USPS should expand and reorganize its historic preservation program.

General Services Administration

GSA Historical Background

The mission of the General Services Administration is to "deliver the best value in real estate, acquisition, and technology services to government and the American people." GSA assists federal agencies in building construction and leasing office space, as well as obtaining supplies and services necessary for day-to-day office operations. Another important aspect of the GSA mission is monitoring the adequacy of historic preservation implementation with respect to federal properties, especially buildings. Within the GSA, the Public Building Service manages federal buildings.

GSA was established in 1949 during the Truman administration. It immediately absorbed numerous other federal agencies, including the National Archives Establishment, the Federal Works Agency, the Public Buildings Administration, the Bureau of Federal Supply, the Office of Contract Settlement, and the War Assets Administration. Its basic purpose then was the same as now: to serve as a central source for workplaces and office supplies for federal agencies. Besides federal office management, GSA was given other related duties. For instance, the agency was in charge of emergency preparedness, including stockpiling strategic materials to be used in case of war, a big concern after the Soviet Union tested its first hydrogen bomb in 1953.

As the federal government continued to grow after World War II, it scrambled to provide enough office space. The Public Buildings Act of 1959 gave GSA responsibility for federal building construction. Many of the new Washington, DC, office buildings were constructed in the 1960s, including the Rayburn House Office Building, the Housing and Urban Development Building, and the Department of Energy Building. As technological improvements rapidly proliferated, the GSA had to apply these to federal government operations. In 1960, GSA created the Federal Telecommunications System, a government-wide intercity telephone system in the nation's capital. In 1972, GSA established the Automated Data and Telecommunications Service, which later became the Office of Information Resources Management.

As budgets became tighter during the Vietnam War, GSA attempted to promote better management practices and introduced innovative funding strategies. In 1973, GSA created the Office of Federal Management Policy. In 1974, it began to charge federal agencies rent on their office space. In 1984, GSA introduced the use of credit cards for federal payment for office services.

In the 1990s, further innovations were introduced by GSA to streamline government operations. GSA's policy functions were merged into the Office of Government-wide Policy, which sets policy in the areas of real property, travel, transportation, information technology, regulatory information, and use of federal advisory committees. In the late 1990s, GSA's Courthouse Management Group oversaw the largest courthouse construction project in a half century, resulting in the renovation or rebuilding of many federal courthouses.

More recently, initiatives have been introduced by GSA "with the goal of transforming federal buildings into high-performing green buildings," which include mechanical upgrades, new lighting, window replacements, cool or green roofs, water-saving fixtures, on-site renewable energy, and enhanced recycling. In 2008, the American Recovery and Reinvestment Act authorized $1.7 billion for modernization of 150 historic buildings managed by GSA.

According to its website in 2017, the GSA "provides workspace to more than one million federal civilian workers, oversees the preservation of more than 480 historic buildings, and facilitates the federal government's purchase of high-quality, low-cost goods and services from quality commercial vendors."

GSA Cultural Heritage Management

GSA's historic preservation officer is the director of the Center for Historic Buildings based in the Office of the Chief Architect. GSA also has 11 regional preservation officers. Most regional centers have historic preservation specialists, mainly related to architecture or art history. According to the GSA and the ACHP websites, one-third of GSA's 1,500 buildings are over 50 years old, and 464 of these are eligible for or listed in the National Register of Historic Places. GSA also leases space in another 175 historic buildings. The historic properties include courthouses, customhouses, and federal buildings that are important landmarks in Washington, DC, as well as many other cities.

In the early 1950s, one of the first historic-preservation-related tasks of the GSA was to supervise a major remodeling of the White House. Some preservationists are of the opinion that in the 1960s and 1970s GSA did major harm to the historic landscape of the nation's capital by introducing large "brutalist" office buildings such as the Health, Education, and Welfare Building (Hubert Humphrey Building) and the Department of Energy Building (James Forestall Building) (Figure 9.4). More recently, GSA's Public Building Service in 1994 introduced the Design Excellence Program to streamline the way it selects architects for major construction projects and also to promote "enduring examples of federal architecture." GSA states this program was inspired by the *Guiding Principles for Federal Architecture* written in 1962 by Senator Daniel Moynihan.

Because it manages so many historic buildings, GSA has become a critical player in compliance with a number of federal laws concerning historic preservation, including the NHPA and the Public Cooperative Use Act, as well as multiple executive orders (12072, 13006, 13287). It provides technical advice, strategies, publications, and training to help accomplish historic preservation objectives through its Center for Historic Buildings. GSA regional centers have implemented programmatic agreements with the ACHP and various SHPOs. Two GSA publications in 1999 and 2005 outline the GSA strategy with regard to historic buildings.

FIG. 9.4 Bartholdi's 1876 *Fountain of Light and Water* at the US Botanic Garden in Washington, DC, with the 1977 Hubert Humphrey Building (right) and the 1965 Rayburn House Office Building (left) in the background (Library of Congress).

The Builders

The federal government is the principal implementer, funder, and facilitator of large-scale construction projects in this country. Federally funded construction projects often carried out by nonfederal entities (e.g., state and local highway departments) have done extensive damage to cultural heritage resources over the last 200 years.

The first federal construction projects were fairly modest in terms of geographic scope. The earliest projects included the first national road west from the Cumberland Gap begun in 1811, as well as military forts and government buildings in Washington, DC. Beginning in 1789, customhouses were the first nonmilitary federal buildings constructed outside Washington. The Army Corps of Engineers, originally charged with building and repairing military fortifications, began undertakings to improve river traffic on the Mississippi River in 1824.

By the mid-1800s, post offices and federal court buildings were being built in cities across the nation. After the Civil War, railroad expansion led to urban growth and the consolidation of military bases. The creation of the US Forest Service and National Park Service in the early twentieth century promoted road development on public land. The automobile boom in the 1920s led to the building of federally funded highways to connect cities and rural roads to facilitate postal delivery.

The first big boom in federally funded construction occurred with the Franklin Roosevelt administration's Depression-era programs. It incorporated a wide array of construction, including infrastructure, public buildings, public lands amenities, recreational facilities, and housing. US entry into World War II ended this broadly distributed building boom but caused a more focused boom in military base construction.

The second national building boom occurred after World War II. Federally funded reservoir and interstate highway construction began to radically alter the American landscape. Federally funded urban renewal projects decimated entire city neighborhoods.

Of the three agencies featured below, the Federal Highway Administration and the Natural Resources Conservation Service are both big funders of projects but manage very little land of their own. The Department of Housing and Urban Development impacts primarily urban cultural resources, NRCS impacts mostly rural ones, and FHWA can impact both rural and urban cultural resources. HUD activities primarily impact buildings, and NRCS activities primarily impact archaeological sites, while FHWA's activities impact all types of cultural heritage resources.

Federal Highway Administration

FHWA Historical Background

In 1806, Congress appropriated funds for a road to connect Cumberland, Maryland, with the Ohio River to support and promote western settlement. Construction began in 1811, and the National Road finally reached its western terminus at Vandalia, Illinois, in 1834. It was known by various names, including the Cumberland Road and the National Pike, but because it served as the main street for the towns along its route, the National Road was also known as America's Main Street. Early in the automobile age, it became US Route 40.

With the exception of the National Road, road construction for the first century of the United States was done by private entities and local authorities. The first federal agency charged with assessing the need for national road construction was the Office of Road Inquiry (ORI), created in 1893 in the Agriculture Department. The ORI originated with the Good Roads Movement, privately founded for the needs of bicycles not automobiles. In 1899, it was renamed the Office of Public Road Inquiries (OPRI). In 1904, OPRI began an inventory of all the existing rural roads in the country.

The Agriculture Appropriation Act of 1906 renamed OPRI the Office of Public Roads (OPR). The first focus was internal, with the OPR helping build roads in the newly created national forest reserves and national parks. The Postal Service also needed assistance with providing better roads for rural delivery. The Federal Road Act of 1916 began a federal-state partnership with the creation of and funding for the Federal-Aid Highway Program to build and improve rural post roads. Two years later, the OPR became the Bureau of Public Roads (BPR).

With the 1920s came the boom in automobile travel. A National Highway Research Board was formed to develop better road-building techniques to deal with motorized traffic. A national highway map was published in 1922 showing important routes to assist travel in case of war. A numbered highway system was introduced in 1925 to replace the names highways had been given by state and private groups (e.g., Lincoln Highway).

The Depression-era New Deal programs initially suspended funding for the federal-aid highway system as the federal government focused on a diverse program of public works that included roads. Construction began on the Blue Ridge Parkway in 1935. That same year, US Route 30 was completed, making it the first coast-to-coast paved highway. In 1939, BPR was renamed the Public Roads Administration (PRA) as part of the Federal Works Administration. The PRA sent Congress the first concept plans for an Interstate Highway System, having taken note of Nazi Germany's autobahn. This system was approved in 1944 along with a system of federal-aid secondary roads.

After World War II, planning began for the first 40,000 miles of the interstate system. The PRA was transferred from the Department of Agriculture to the Department of Commerce, with its name reverting to the Bureau of Public Roads. Congress authorized the first funding for the interstate road system in 1952. Interstate highway funding greatly increased with the Federal-Aid Highway Act of 1954. In 1956, President Dwight D. Eisenhower, having seen the German road system, pushed through legislation that created the Highway Trust Fund as a way of providing continuous and substantial funding for the federal highway system. The trust fund had to be reauthorized every six years.

Construction of the Interstate Highway System immediately caused controversy in cities. A conference in Hartford, Connecticut, in 1957 called for the suspension of all metropolitan interstate highway construction until comprehensive land-use plans were developed. Criticism of the impacts of the interstate highway construction was invigorated by the environmental movement of the early 1960s. In 1966, the passage of the National Historic Preservation Act and inclusion of Section 4(f) in the Department of Transportation Act (DOTA) stemmed in large part from the adverse impacts of interstate highway construction.

The DOTA also consolidated federal transportation agencies into a single cabinet-level department and created the Federal Highway Administration as one of these agencies. The Bureau of Public Roads became one of three bureaus within FHWA, although it was finally eliminated in 1970. The Interstate Highway System as originally planned was completed in 1992.

The year before FHWA announced the completion of the interstate system, the Intermodal Surface Transportation Efficiency Act (ISTEA) was passed by Congress. It restructured the Federal-Aid Highway Program by eliminating the four traditional federal-aid systems (interstate, primary, secondary, urban) and placing them all within the National Highway System (NHS).

The NHS, made up of designated federal, state, and local roads, includes about 22% (847,000 miles) of the total public road network. Only about 5% (181,000 miles) of the nation's nearly four million miles of public roads are on federal land.

State-managed roads account for about 20% (800,000 miles), while locally managed roads account for over 70% (2.7 million miles).

The FHWA has three primary tasks with regard to the federal-aid highway system:

1. It distributes congressionally appropriated funds to the states.
2. It provides policy and guidance with regard to adequate highway design and construction standards.
3. It develops regulations to implement federal laws regarding federal-aid highways.

States administer the federally funded NHS. The states determine which projects are funded, they do the contracting for construction and maintenance, and they oversee project implementation. States are given federal funding according to a complex allocation formula based on system miles, the number of deficient bridges, safety needs, and other factors. States must use some of their own funds in order to use federal dollars. The federal-state match is 90–10 for interstate highways and 80–20 for other NHS roads. Federal spending on highways totaled $46 billion in 2014.

Most states pay their share for NHS projects as well as assist non-NHS road projects through state highway trust funds financed by state gas taxes. In Minnesota, about 90% of road construction is paid for exclusively with state and local funds. This funding is not subject to federal Section 106 or 4(f) review, although all state trunk highway projects are considered Section 106 undertakings because federal planning funds have been used to develop them and all are eligible for federal construction funds.

FHWA Cultural Heritage Management

As previously discussed in chapter 7, although some state highway departments had archaeological salvage initiatives in place as early as the 1930s, highway planning at the federal level didn't begin to consider impacts to cultural resources until the building of the Interstate Highway System started in the late 1950s. Section 120 of the Federal-Aid Highway Act of 1956 authorized the use of federal funds, as approved by state highway departments, for archaeological and paleontological salvage. Consideration of nonarchaeological historic properties was not included.

As the interstate highway construction increasingly destroyed entire historic neighborhoods in cities and important archaeological sites in both urban and rural areas, the passage of the National Historic Preservation Act and Section 4(f) of the Department of Transportation Act in 1966 required the newly formed FHWA to develop a more comprehensive and proactive approach to assessing and fulfilling historic preservation needs. The Yarborough amendment to DOTA that created Section 4(f) required not only minimization of harm to important historic and archaeological sites but no harm at all if there was "a feasible and prudent alternative" (see chapter 7).

In 1991, the Intermodal Surface Transportation Efficiency Act did more than reorganize the federal-aid highway system; it also emphasized environmental protection in lieu of highway expansion. ISTEA required that 10% of federal transportation funding be dedicated to transportation enhancements (TEs). These enhancements included substantial funding for cultural heritage preservation. Of the 12 eligible categories for TE funds, seven specifically benefited heritage management:

- Acquisition of scenic easements and scenic or historic sites (including historic battlefields)
- Scenic or historic highway programs (including the provision of tourist and welcome center facilities)
- Historic preservation
- Rehabilitation and operation of historic transportation buildings, structures, or facilities (including historic railroad facilities and canals)
- Preservation of abandoned railway corridors (including the conversion and use of the corridors for pedestrian or bicycle trails)
- Archaeological planning and research
- Establishment of transportation museums

The basic concepts of ISTEA were reauthorized in 1998 by the Transportation Equity Act for the Twenty-First Century (TEA-21) and again in 2005 by the Safe, Accountable, Flexible, Efficient Transportation Equity Act (SAFETEA). Dedicated funding for TEs was eliminated by Congress in 2012 in the Moving Ahead for Progress in the 21st Century Act (MAP-21), although states are still allowed to spend any remaining funds from earlier TE appropriations, and some activities eligible for TE funding are now eligible under the MAP-21-created Transportation Alternatives Program (TAP). Eligible activities affecting cultural heritage preservation under the TAP Community Improvement area include (1) historic preservation and rehabilitation of historic transportation facilities, and (2) archaeological activities relating to impacts from implementation of a transportation project.

Because federal-aid funding is implemented at the state level, individual states provide much of the leadership for highway cultural heritage preservation required by federal laws. Under 36 CFR 800.2(a), FHWA can delegate basic Section 106 duties to state agencies like departments of transportation (DOTs). Most, if not all, state DOTs have assumed these 106 duties. There are some Section 106 responsibilities that FHWA can't delegate to the states, like consultation with tribes, although state DOTs can sign programmatic agreements with tribes to help streamline the Section 106 review process and allow for direct consultation.

For all agencies in the federal Department of Transportation, the chief historic preservation officer is the director of the Office of Safety, Energy, and Environment. Each federal DOT agency (e.g., FHWA) also has an agency preservation officer. The FHWA has a good working relationship with the ACHP, helping to develop templates for state-level programmatic agreements, implementing an interstate highway exemption for most 106-applicable construction, and undertaking research to improve the Section 106 review process.

SHPO FHWA project reviews in many states have slowed considerably in recent years due not only to a reduction in major highway projects but to programmatic agreements concerning bridge replacements and other common aspects of highway construction. The Minnesota SHPO did only 15 FHWA reviews in 2016 compared with 287 reviews in 2001.

Department of Housing and Urban Development
HUD Historical Background
The federal government's first foray into public housing began in 1937 with the passage of the Housing Act, which authorized cities to build residential units financed with federal bonds. The act created the Federal Home Loan Bank System and the Federal Housing Administration (FHA). As with later federal housing efforts, the purpose of this first initiative was more to stimulate local economies than to provide

low-income housing. When housing was created, early FHA initiatives tended to "red-line" areas within cities, promoting housing segregation according to income level and race.

After World War II, there was a great influx of people into American cities. To help deal with housing needs, Congress passed the Housing Act of 1949, which also promoted "urban renewal." The urban renewal aspects of federal housing policy were reinforced by the Housing Act of 1954, which promoted redevelopment of "blighted" areas and urban planning. Hundreds of historic buildings were demolished in urban cores with little consideration of the historic significance of individual buildings. Although the 1954 act allowed for building rehabilitation, this aspect was largely ignored by most cities, which were just eager to demolish entire blocks to promote economic revitalization and get rid of "slums."

The Department of Housing and Urban Development was created in 1965 as one of the "Great Society" initiatives of the Lyndon Johnson administration. This was a cabinet-level department tasked with implementing the Housing and Urban Development Act passed a month earlier. This included funding for low-income housing and various public works initiatives. As its title indicates, HUD has a dual role: to provide affordable housing and promote community development.

The Housing and Community Development Act of 1974 made some major changes in the way HUD implemented its mission. It consolidated a great variety of grant programs into a single program called Community Development Block Grants (CDBG), providing more flexibility in implementation by cities but also a more formal planning process. The 1974 act also amended the 1937 Housing Act to create the Section 8 program in order to help subsidize the difference between a renter's income and a HUD assessment of fair market rent.

HUD's mission as currently stated is "to create strong, sustainable, inclusive communities and quality affordable homes for all." HUD implements its mission through a great variety of agencies and programs. The most prominent programs are CDBG, Section 8 public housing, and FHA mortgage insurance. HUD has district offices across the country, with at least one in every state. The federal government currently subsidizes 1.3 million public housing units and 1.9 privately owned housing units. HUD annual budgets often approach $50 billion.

HUD Cultural Heritage Management

HUD's programs subject to cultural heritage review can be broken down into three major areas: Community Planning and Development, Federal Housing Administration, and Public and Indian Housing. Most grants are subject to Section 106 review, while federal rent subsidies, loans, and mortgage subsidies are not. However, if a HUD loan is in default and the property reverts to HUD ownership, the property becomes federal, and any rehabilitation, demolition, or sale of it is subject to Section 106.

Examples of some of the types of HUD projects subject to Section 106 review were recently summarized in a memorandum from the Texas SHPO to local and state officials receiving HUD funds (Wolfe 2014):

- Rehabilitation projects that affect structures or buildings forty-five (45) years of age or older;
- Community improvement projects in an established neighborhood forty-five (45) years of age or older (e.g., where trees, sidewalks, or other streetscape features may be added, altered, removed, or demolished to accommodate the project);
- Infrastructure projects affecting previously undisturbed soil (e.g., utility lines, curb and gutter installation, etc.);

- New build/infill projects;
- New construction in undeveloped natural areas;
- Construction of public housing units;
- Commercial rehabilitation or development projects;
- Transfer, lease, or sale of historic properties;
- Construction of new government facilities; and
- Any project that may affect a property included in or eligible for inclusion in the National Register of Historic Places, designated as a Recorded Texas Historic Landmark or State Antiquities Landmark, or located within a locally designated historic district.

In terms of numbers of individual Section 106 reviews, few agencies can match HUD. In 2016, the Minnesota SHPO did 1,653 HUD reviews, just over half the total reviews it did for that year. Many reviews are accomplished through the use of what HUD calls responsible entities (REs). HUD's environmental review responsibilities, including with regard to Section 106 and NEPA, are codified in two basic sets of regulations: 36 CFR 50 covers review responsibilities retained by HUD, while 36 CFR 58 covers the responsibilities delegated to REs. The use of REs for certain aspects of Section 106 review is also allowed under 36 CFR 800.2(a). The ACHP has also developed guidelines (72 FR 7387) for reviewing affordable housing projects that include both HUD and USDA's Rural Development.

While FHWA is the most prominent example of federal agency delegation of Section 106 responsibilities at the state level, HUD is the most prominent example at the local level. Many communities that have assumed HUD authority for Section 106 have implemented programmatic agreements. Examples of these are available on the HUD website. The most controversial part of HUD delegation of Section 106 authority to REs has been with respect to Indian consultation. The ACHP objected to this soon after the 2004 revised 36 CFR 800 regulations were fully implemented, but case law has supported HUD and confirmed its validity under 24 CFR 58.

HUD compliance with Section 106 was spotty during the first 30 years of the NHPA, especially with respect to the actions of its local REs. When I was at the Minnesota SHPO, the Minneapolis Community Development Agency (MCDA) destroyed most of the archaeological remains of an early railroad complex to build a HUD-subsidized housing complex in the St. Anthony Falls National Register District. Because the damage had already been done and MCDA/HUD was in foreclosure with regard to Section 106, the Minnesota SHPO developed an after-the-fact mitigation strategy that included Section 106 training for MCDA staff and required MCDA to fund and publish a study of early railroading in the historic district (Hofsommer 2009).

HUD has greatly improved its Section 106 compliance over the last 20 years. HUD's federal preservation officer is located in its main Washington, DC, office within the Office of Environment and Energy, Environmental Planning Division. The HUD website provides confirmation of its intent to preserve cultural heritage resources and provides considerable guidance on how to implement this through worksheets, examples, toolkits, and publications.

Some fact sheets demonstrate various aspects of the HUD historic preservation program:

- HP Fact Sheet 1: Summary of Section 106 Compliance
- HP Fact Sheet 2: Ten Questions on Section 106 Compliance
- HP Fact Sheet 3: Compliance Options for the Section 106 Review Process
- HP Fact Sheet 4: Criteria for the National Register of Historic Places

- HP Fact Sheet 5: Secretary of the Interior's "Professional Qualification Standards"
- HP Fact Sheet 6: Guidance on Archeological Investigations in HUD Projects
- HP Fact Sheet 7: Historic Property Searches

HUD also has worked with the ACHP and tribes to develop a government-to-government consultation policy with respect to impacts to Indian cultural heritage resources. Although HUD has delegated some consultation responsibilities to REs, it still retains considerable responsibility for some of its programs under 24 CFR 50 and for all of its actions under Executive Order 13175.

Natural Resources Conservation Service

NRCS Historical Background

The Natural Resources Conservation Service traces its beginnings to the establishment of the Division of Agricultural Soil within the USDA's Weather Bureau in 1894. The name was changed to the Division of Soils in 1899 and the Bureau of Soils two years later. In the mid-1920s, the USDA soils unit was moved out of the Weather Bureau and merged with the Chemistry Bureau within the USDA. The soil surveys so familiar to most late-twentieth-century archaeologists were a product of the USDA soils unit beginning in the early twentieth century, eventually becoming known as the National Soil Survey as part of the USDA's Agricultural Research Administration in 1942.

A competing soils agency, called the Soil Erosion Service, was established within the Department of the Interior in 1933 to help deal with the massive soil erosion in the Great Plains caused by devastating droughts of the early 1930s. The Soil Erosion Service was moved by President Roosevelt to the USDA in March 1935, and a month later the Soil Conservation Act of 1935 created the Soil Conservation Service (SCS). The original limited mission of the SCS as defined in the 1935 legislation was to "provide permanently for the control and prevention of soil erosion."

During the 1930s, the SCS made extensive use of CCC and WPA labor to assist not only with soil surveys but with massive soil stabilization efforts to reduce erosion. These efforts included planting grasses and trees on marginal agricultural lands purchased by the federal government as well as assistance to private landowners with revegetation, drainage control, and irrigation. The SCS also began to foster the creation of local soil conservation districts. The districts would establish priorities and direct actual work, while the SCS would provide funding and guidance.

After World War II, SCS efforts increasingly focused on watersheds, emphasizing the need for flood-control structures near headwaters to lessen soil erosion into streams and rivers. In 1952, the National Soil Survey was officially subsumed within the SCS. The SCS mission expansion beyond soil erosion control began in the 1960s with the creation of the Resource Conservation and Development Program in 1962. This promoted initiatives for rural economic development and recreation, as well as erosion control.

Increasing concern about environmental degradation in the 1960s and 1970s forced SCS to take a hard look at the methods and objectives of its programs. A farm economic crisis in the 1980s also increased emphasis on promoting the economic health of farmers. The Conservation Reserve Program paid farmers to put marginal land into noncrop vegetation reserves.

In 1994, Congress directed the USDA to streamline its programs. One of the results of the reorganization was the creation of the Natural Resources Conservation

Service, mainly made up of the old SCS. The modern mission of the NRCS is to "improve the health of our Nation's natural resources while sustaining and enhancing the productivity of American agriculture." This has moved much beyond the original mission of just preventing soil erosion.

NRCS Cultural Heritage Management

The NRCS heritage management program began as the SCS CRM program. There is very little comprehensive information available online or in publications regarding the founding or condition of either program with regard to the implementing personnel. Furthermore, the NRCS's main website provides little guidance on how NRCS implements Section 106. It contains a few links to ACHP material, a copy of the cultural resources section of the NRCS *General Manual*, and a copy of the NRCS *Cultural Resources Procedures Handbook*. The handbook is helpful for internal personnel in implementing their NHPA duties but provides little insight into the day-to-day workings of the NRCS CRM program.

The historic preservation officer for the NRCS is the national cultural resources specialist in the Ecological Sciences Division under the deputy chief for science and technology, who is under the associate chief for conservation. The NRCS has four regional offices: Northeast, Southeast, Central, and West. Under the regional office is a state office for each state. Each state has local service centers or what used to be SCS district offices, usually at the county level. SCS had over 3,000 of these local offices.

Other than the HPO in Washington, NRCS professional CRM staff are usually based only at the state offices. Most NRCS CRM staff are archaeologists. NRCS does not maintain any museums or interpretive centers and curates its object collections with private repositories.

NRCS has been a leader in providing CRM training for its personnel, especially personnel at the local level who undertake fieldwork to evaluate, approve, and monitor NRCS-funded activities. When I was Minnesota SHPO archaeologist, I participated in several NRCS summer training sessions that were well attended by enthusiastic and attentive NRCS employees. The objectives of the NRCS training programs are to:

- define what cultural resources are;
- explain why NRCS considers impacts to cultural resources;
- describe NRCS policy and procedures for identifying and protecting cultural resources;
- locate and receive assistance from NRCS cultural resources specialists and coordinators and other sources;
- appropriately incorporate cultural resources information into conservation plans;
- identify cultural resources by conducting a review and survey;
- develop, maintain, and safeguard cultural resource information files;
- document actions that can be taken to protect cultural resources;
- describe steps to be taken when cultural resources are encountered during program/project implementation or construction.

Employees who complete the training are not qualified to undertake CRM surveys or evaluations but can make preliminary assessments as to the possible presence of cultural resources within an NRCS project area.

In 2014, NRCS worked with the ACHP to develop a prototype programmatic agreement for dealing with cultural resources. Since implementation of the prototype PA program, 21 states, one territory, and four tribes have completed NRCS

PAs. Minnesota does not have a formal PA following the prototype, but it does have a state-level agreement that was implemented in the mid-1990s.

Section 106 reviews of NRCS projects in Minnesota are based on a NEPA-like categorical exclusion list. NRCS activities in Minnesota involve 116 different standard "practices." Each practice has a specific NRCS code number. After careful consultation with the SHPO, it was determined that only 70 of these practices would be considered undertakings under Section 106. Examples of practices that are considered undertakings are the building of access roads, ponds of various types, dikes, trails, drains, and ditches and wetland restoration.

The Minnesota SHPO typically reviews about 500 NRCS projects each year. NRCS personnel field-survey about 10% of these based on their internal assessment of the potential of each project to involve cultural resources, mainly archaeological sites. Each year in Minnesota 5 to 10 archaeological sites are found within or adjacent to NRCS projects.

The Permitters

The 36 CFR 800.16(y) definition of undertakings subject to Section 106 review includes projects, activities, or programs "requiring a Federal permit, license or approval." A permit is short-term or limited permission from a regulating agency to an individual or entity to do something. A license is a long-term and sometimes permanent action by an agency allowing a person or entity to undertake specific activities. Both permits and licenses are a form of official regulation allowing government to control, monitor, and even gain revenue from private actions. Approval is a less formal process and can be in the form of a letter.

Most activities subject to federal license or permit do not require Section 106 review because they don't pose a threat to cultural resources. ARPA permits are only subject to Section 106 review if an archaeological survey or excavation poses an anticipated threat to cultural resources due to the use of unconventional methods (e.g., mechanical soil stripping).

The Army Corps of Engineers issues permits for wetland filling and for actions affecting navigable waters. If you are going to do mining or drill on federal offshore lands, you need a permit from the Bureau of Safety and Environmental Enforcement. The Federal Communications Commission licenses cell tower construction and colocation of antennas on existing structures. The Federal Energy Regulatory Commission issues licenses for hydroelectric facilities, which require dams and reservoirs. I refer to all the permitters, licensers, and approvers as permitters within this section.

Because all the permitters, with the exception of the COE, are not big property managers or big project funders, they tend to have only a few heritage management professionals on staff and often give low priority to their heritage management obligations. This can lead to both over- and underreaction when it comes to responding to some heritage management issues.

Army Corps of Engineers

COE Historical Background

The Army Corps of Engineers was established in 1802 to assist with the construction and management of the military academy at West Point. It soon was involved with building East Coast military fortifications as tensions with Great Britain increased early in the nineteenth century. After the War of 1812, most military forces were drastically reduced, but COE personnel numbers actually increased as

Congress recognized the need to maintain a strong national defense based on key forts on the East and Gulf Coasts. The COE expanded military fort construction to the West Coast beginning in 1848.

As American settlement pushed west, the COE moved with it, not only to help build frontier forts but to aid the movement of military forces and new settlers. Transportation initially focused on rivers. By the mid-1820s, the COE was removing snags and sandbars from the Ohio and Mississippi Rivers. They also became proactive, deepening channels and building wing dams to help keep channels open. Beginning in 1825, the COE took over construction management on the National Road from the Cumberland Gap to Vandalia, Illinois.

During the Civil War, COE efforts once again concentrated on eastern military needs, but as soon as the war ended, the COE turned its attention to civil works, including the improvement of eastern canals and building locks and dams on the Ohio River. To control flooding on the lower Mississippi River, the COE began to construct massive levees. It assisted with western railroad expansion by undertaking route surveys. It was also given responsibility for building and maintaining parks, bridges, and monuments in Washington, DC, when the Office of Public Buildings and Grounds was placed under the COE in 1867.

In the late nineteenth century, the COE began to get involved with dam construction to provide hydroelectricity in the East and irrigation in the West. The Rivers and Harbors Acts of 1890 and the Rivers and Harbors Appropriation Act of 1899 required COE approval of new dams on major waterways. Section 10 of the 1899 act also gave the COE the power to regulate all potential obstructions to navigable waters, thus beginning the COE regulatory program with Section 10 permits. Most dams continued to be built by private interests, but the first Mississippi River lock and dam was built by the COE in St. Paul just prior to World War I. It included a hydroelectric power station later leased to the nearby Ford automobile plant.

COE civil works construction briefly ceased in 1917 when the United States entered World War I. After that conflict ended, the COE focused on flood control, especially along the lower Mississippi River. The massive Mississippi River flood of 1927 clearly demonstrated that levees alone could not prevent flooding. The Flood Control Act of 1935 declared that flood control was a responsibility of the federal government, but any reservoir construction had to have economic benefits exceeding the construction cost. The COE began extensive construction of reservoirs and flood diversion control structures. The Flood Control Act of 1944 required that reservoirs have multiple purposes, such as flood control, hydroelectric power generation, agricultural irrigation, city water supply, and recreation. The act also authorized the first large reservoirs on the middle Missouri River.

The COE also was responsible for one of the largest water transportation initiatives in US history. The Rivers and Harbors Act of 1930 authorized a 9-foot navigation channel on the Mississippi River between St. Paul and St. Louis. From 1930 to 1940, the COE constructed 27 locks and dams on the Mississippi River. The system of locks and dams was also extended up the Illinois River. An unexpected benefit of this project was the ability to build smaller oceangoing vessels on the upper stretches of the river for service in World War II.

Anticipating the US entry into World War II and the role airpower would play, the COE was empowered to start a massive program of Army Air Corps base construction in 1940. Immediately after the Pearl Harbor attack, the COE was tasked with acquiring land for, managing construction of, and maintaining all army facilities, including training camps, munitions plants, bases, hospitals, and depots. Construction of military facilities peaked in 1942, and by the end of that year, the army had housing for 4.5 million personnel, had constructed 149 manufacturing facilities, and had over 200 million square feet of storage space. During World War II, the COE also worked in Canada on a highway connecting Alaska with the continental United States.

After World War II, civil works once again took precedence over military works for the COE, although it had some military responsibilities, such as Veterans Administration (VA) hospitals and antimissile defense bases. Dam construction for major reservoirs on the Missouri River and in the Pacific Northwest resumed in earnest. Locks and dams on the Mississippi River were rebuilt and enlarged. For the federal government, the COE built post offices and National Aeronautics and Space Administration (NASA) launch facilities. The COE had the primary responsibility for disaster relief until the Federal Emergency Management Agency (FEMA) was established in 1988.

The biggest expansion of COE nonconstruction responsibilities occurred in 1972 with the passage of the Federal Water Pollution Control Act Amendments of 1972, commonly known as the Clean Water Act. Section 404 of the act authorized COE to issue permits for the discharge of fill into wetlands. A decade later, the Defense Environmental Program in 1983 put the COE in charge of removing hazardous materials and unsafe buildings on active and inactive bases.

Today, the COE is not only a major permit issuer but also a major builder and land manager. It controls over 12 million acres of land, mainly adjacent to and under reservoirs. This includes about 55,000 miles of shoreline. It has 3,600 boat ramps, almost 2,000 campgrounds, and over 11,000 miles of trails. The current COE mission is to "deliver vital public and military engineering services . . . to strengthen our Nation's security, energize the economy, and reduce risks from disasters." The COE in the United States has eight major geographic divisions, which are divided into 41 districts. Each division and district is commanded by an army officer, but the great majority of COE employees are civilians.

COE Cultural Heritage Management

The Army Corps of Engineers is one of the few federal agencies subject in a major way to all three aspects of Section 106 compliance: property management (including buildings and land), construction, and permitting. While the COE or its army parent carry out most construction and property management aspects of COE undertakings involving Section 106, permitting applies to actions carried out by others.

Most of the COE's undertakings are carried out by the Civil Works Directorate. With regard to construction, major nonmilitary projects are along waterways (e.g., navigation improvements, environmental enhancement, flood-control structures, streambank protection), as are most recreation projects (e.g., campgrounds, boat landings). COE regulatory responsibilities pertain to actions affecting "waters of the United States." Most of these actions involve Section 404 permits for wetland filling in compliance with the Clean Water Act. Other actions involve Section 10 permits for projects affecting navigable waterways in compliance with the Rivers and Harbors Act and Section 103 permits pertaining to ocean discharges under the Marine Protection, Research, and Sanctuaries Act.

There are two basic types of COE permits, general and individual. General permits cover actions that have minimal potential to impact waters of the United States and are not project specific. The three varieties of general permits are nationwide, regional, and programmatic. Activities under general permits are not subject to many aspects of environmental review, including individual project public notifications and, in the case of Section 106, consultation with SHPOs or tribes. However, the COE requires district engineers to carefully review individual actions done under general permits to see if they hold potential for harming significant historic properties. Examples of general permits are Nationwide Permit 12 for construction on and maintenance of utility lines and Nationwide Permit 51 for construction and maintenance of renewable energy facilities in nontidal waters. Decisions on issuing nationwide permits are made at the COE headquarters level, while regional and programmatic permit decisions can be made at the division or district level.

Individual permits are project specific and involve activities that can have major impacts on waters of the United States. These permits are subject to environmental review and public comment. Examples are road projects or housing developments filling a wetland (Section 404) and a pipeline crossing a navigable waterway (Section 10). All decisions with regard to individual permits are made at the district level. A district engineer can also issue a letter of permission (LOP) for a minor project with little chance of having an adverse environmental impact.

In the late 1970s, the Department of the Army began to investigate options in consultation with the ACHP for streamlining permitting actions with respect to Section 106 compliance, including permits processed by the COE. The ACHP's 36 CFR 800 regulations of 1979 had added provisions allowing agencies to develop programmatic agreements for certain classes of undertakings reviewed under Section 106 and encouraging the development of counterpart regulations to make Section 106 application more amenable to individual agency procedures. The army attempted to take advantage of these provisions with respect to its permitting obligations by embedding in 33 CFR 325, "Processing of Department of the Army Permits," an Appendix C titled "Procedures for the Protection of Historic Properties." Although the army failed to get the ACHP to sign a programmatic agreement accepting Appendix C as a viable alternative procedure for implementing Section 106, the COE began applying Appendix C to its permit review process in the early 1980s.

The ACHP issued revised 36 CFR 800 regulations in 1986 and 2004 that continued to encourage agencies to develop alternative procedures for complying with Section 106. This is presented in the 2004 regulations under "Federal Agency Program Alternatives" (800.14). Despite increased flexibility in alternative procedures, over 35 years of intensive COE-ACHP consultation, numerous court cases, and much public discussion, the COE has still failed to get the ACHP to sign off on Appendix C. The federal Office of Management and Budget (OMB) accepted the adequacy of Appendix C for Section 106 compliance in 1990. The CEQ has approved COE regulations as they apply to NEPA, but 33 CFR 325 Appendix C is specific to Section 106 of the NHPA, other historic preservation laws, and presidential directives.

Currently, the COE uses a version of Appendix C published in the June 29, 1990, *Federal Register* as well as interim guidance documents from April 25, 2005, and January 31, 2007, issued after the revised 36 CFR 800 regulations were accepted by the ACHP in 2004. The interim guidance was needed to apply changes required by the 1992 amendments to NHPA, particularly with regard to tribal consultation.

Appendix C has been highly controversial and has been criticized by many SHPOs as well as the ACHP. In 2015, the ACHP once again initiated consultation with the COE to address the deficiencies of Appendix C in terms of compliance with 36 CFR 800. With regard to the differences between the 36 CFR 800 definition of "area of potential effects" versus the Appendix C definition of "permit area," the ACHP is looking at the issue broadly and has termed it part of the concept of projects with "small federal handles." The ACHP recognizes that federal agency Section 106 responsibilities are very different for undertakings over which the agencies have limited control (e.g., permitting) as compared to undertakings that take place on federal lands or are done with federal funds. For additional discussion of COE Appendix C, see the sidebar in chapter 6.

The COE hired its first CRM professional, archaeologist Larry Banks, in the Tulsa District in 1970. This was a direct response to the 1969 passage of NEPA, not the 1966 passage of NHPA (Banks 1976). Banks was the only COE archaeologist until 1974, when passage of the Archaeological and Historic Preservation Act (AHPA) became the second incentive for the COE to expand its heritage management program. Beginning in 1974, the number of COE archaeologists rapidly rose to about 70, where it remained for much of the rest of the twentieth century.

In 2007, there were 113 COE archaeologists, with most located in district offices. As far as divisional total, the Lower Mississippi Valley, North Central, Southwest, Missouri River, North Atlantic, North Pacific, South Pacific, and South Atlantic divisions each have the most, with an average of 10 per division. Only about a third of the divisions have a historian, and they have only one historian per division in one district office. There is also a History Office within the COE headquarters in Washington that "collects, documents, interprets, disseminates, and preserves the history and heritage of the U.S. Army Corps of Engineers."

The COE historic preservation officer is based in the Pentagon and is the assistant for environment, tribal and regulatory affairs in the Office of the Assistant Secretary of the Army (Civil Works). The COE deputy federal preservation officer is also in Washington in the Civil Works Directorate.

The COE currently lists a total of 56,000 inventoried sites and buildings on land it manages. This includes 1,500 properties listed in the National Register and 9,800 that have been determined eligible for inclusion in the NRHP. The COE started building interpretive centers at its facilities, especially the locks and dams, in the 1960s. The COE Mandatory Center of Expertise in St. Louis has a central curational facility called Curation and Management of Archaeological Collections. This center maintains artifact collections from sites on COE lands. It also provides expertise to other federal agencies concerning forensic issues and archival and cartographic needs.

Federal Communications Commission
FCC Historical Background
The Federal Communications Commission (FCC) is an independent federal agency that reports directly to Congress. The Radio Act of 1912 began regulation of wireless transmission that became necessary to designate both private and public frequencies for dedicated use. The Federal Radio Commission was established in 1926 to help with regulation. The FCC was established by the Communications Act of 1934. It took over responsibility for wire-dependent communication (telegraph, telephone) from the Interstate Commerce Commission and for wireless communication from the Federal Radio Commission.

After World War II, television licensing became a major aspect of FCC regulation. The next big wireless breakthrough occurred half a century later with the explosion of cell phone technology. The Telecommunications Act of 1996 encouraged the rapid growth of wireless communication. Today, the FCC regulates radio, television, wire, satellite, and cable communication.

FCC Cultural Heritage Management
The principal FCC activity subject to Section 106 is the review of cell phone antennas involving both new cell tower structures and colocation of antennas on existing buildings and structures. The advent of widespread cell phone technology clearly

shows up in Minnesota SHPO annual federal Section 106 review totals. The Minnesota SHPO reviewed no FCC actions in 1995, 4 in 1996, 2 in 1997, 14 in 1998, 41 in 1999, 252 in 2000, and 344 in 2001. It reviewed 145 FCC submittals in 2016, less than half of peak reviews.

Numbers of FCC Section 106 reviews have remained high since the early 2000s, although they have declined significantly as the wireless grid has filled in, satellite usage has increased, and nationwide and state-specific Section 106 programmatic agreements have proliferated. In 2000, the ACHP agreed that the FCC could delegate some Section 106 responsibilities to its licensees and applicants, such as initiating consultation with SHPOs and THPOs.

A nationwide programmatic agreement in 2002 dealt with the colocation of antennas, excluding from review most colocation on buildings and structures under 45 years of age outside National Register historic districts. A nationwide PA in 2004 dealt with new construction of cell towers, excluding most reviews if a tower was being replaced in the same location, the tower was less than 200 feet tall and located in a commercial or industrial area, or the tower location was in an area previously determined by a SHPO/THPO to have no historic properties. The 2002 colocation PA was amended in 2016 to exempt colocation of small or concealed antennas on all existing buildings and structures if they were not NHLs or in or adjacent to historic districts. It also exempted antennas placed in building interiors.

The FCC federal preservation officer is based in Washington, DC, in the Wireless Telecommunications Bureau. The FCC does not have regulations, comprehensive written guidance, or a comprehensive alternative procedure for implementing Section 106. It has developed standardized forms that applicants must complete and submit to SHPOs/THPOs to complete the Section 106 process for projects that are not exempt under the PAs.

Summary

Prior to the passage of the National Historic Preservation Act in 1966, most federal agencies had little obligation to consider, consult about, and protect cultural heritage resources. The major exception was the National Park Service, which was required by its Organic Act in 1916 to conserve historic objects and scenery. NPS involvement in heritage management outside its parks and monuments greatly expanded with Depression-era public works programs in the 1930s. The Historic Sites Act in 1935 also established a survey to find and document historical and archaeological sites of national importance.

With the passage of the NHPA exactly 50 years after the founding of NPS, all federal agencies not only had to consider impacts to significant heritage properties under Section 106 but under Section 110 had to plan for the discovery and protection of historic properties they managed. This included archaeological sites on over 600 million acres of federal land and about 500,000 federal buildings and structures.

Federal agencies in this chapter were divided into leaders, property managers, builders, and permitters. The NPS and Advisory Council on Historic Preservation, as leaders, give direction and provide assistance to the other three types of agencies whose heritage management obligations are tacked on to their primary missions.

Property managers include those agencies that principally manage lands, such as the Bureau of Land Management and the US Forest Service, and those that principally manage buildings, such as the General Services Administration and the US Postal Service. The property managers are concerned more with their day-to-day NHPA Section 110 duties than with their Section 106 responsibilities.

Builders are basically agencies that distribute federal funds to state and local agencies such as the Federal Highway Administration and the Department of Housing and Urban Development, as well as agencies assisting private individuals, such as the Natural Resources Conservation Service.

Permitters are agencies, like the Corps of Engineers and the Federal Communications Commission, that regulate certain actions of individuals and nonfederal entities. Builders and permitters are concerned more with their heritage management obligations under Section 106 than with those under 110.

Besides heritage management requirements stipulated in the NHPA, agencies must also follow specialty laws, regulations, and guidelines specific to their own agencies. For example, the FHWA must follow Section 4(f) of the Department of Transportation Act, which is more stringent in its requirements to actually avoid harming heritage resources. All federal agencies must also adhere to heritage resource requirements in the National Environmental Policy Act, which often run parallel with Section 106 of the NHPA.

Review Questions

1. What kinds of federal agency activities are subject to heritage preservation laws?
2. What laws apply to all federal property-managing agencies?
3. What are the roles of the NPS and the ACHP in federal heritage management?
4. What agency manages the most federal land, and where is this land?
5. What agency manages the most buildings and what kind of buildings?
6. What agencies provide the most funding for external construction?
7. What agency issues the most federal permits subject to Section 106?

Supplemental Reading

As already mentioned at the end of chapter 8, for more information on Section 110 of the National Historic Preservation Act, see Sprinkle (2015).

Most federal agencies have considerable information on their webpages as to how they fulfill their heritage management obligations. The NPS and ACHP as leaders provide considerable guidance. King (2013) has some information on federal agencies in the beginning of chapter 9 and scattered through the text; King divides federal agencies into two basic types, action and review.

For a general overview of a number of federal agencies, see Baldwin (2005).

SIDEBAR

Implementing Heritage Management: R. F. Lee and the Battle of Washington

As I was writing this book, I kept running into familiar Minnesota names. The anthropology building at the University of Minnesota was named Ford Hall after Guy Stanton Ford, a professor of history and president of the University of Minnesota before he became the executive secretary of the American Historical Association and a founding member of the National Trust for Historic Preservation. Solon Buck was superintendent of the Minnesota Historical Society (MHS) in the 1930s and later became the national archivist and head of the Manuscript Division at the Library of Congress. Conrad Wirth, a landscape architect who grew up in Minneapolis (his father was superintendent of parks), was head of the National Park Service (1951–1964), where he implemented the Mission 66 program. Russell Fridley, my first boss when he was director of MHS, was on the first Advisory Council on Historic Preservation.

Then I started running into unfamiliar Minnesota names: Vern Chatelain, Charles Peterson, Herb Kahler, and Ronald Lee. Like me, all were University of Minnesota graduates. Chatelain was chief of the NPS History Division from 1931 to 1937. Kahler served in that position from 1951 to 1964. Peterson was the first preservation architect for NPS and in 1933 started the Historic American Buildings Survey. Lee had been chief of the NPS History Division from 1938 to 1951, between Chatelain and Kahler.

While the names of some of these Minnesotans were initially unfamiliar to me, some of their birthplaces were not. I am from Benson, a small town in western Minnesota. Ronald Lee was born in Montevideo, Minnesota, a year before Charles Peterson was born in Madison, Minnesota. Montevideo is 30 miles south of Benson, and Madison is 50 miles southwest. Montevideo was in my high school athletic conference. I went to teenage dances at Madison Armory. Of all those individuals with Minnesota roots mentioned above, I soon discovered Ronald Lee had made the most significant contributions to American heritage preservation.

Ronald Freeman Lee was born on September 18, 1905, the year before the federal Antiquities Act was passed. He attended the University of Minnesota, graduating with an economics degree in 1927. Lee went on to get a master's degree in American history from the University of Chicago in 1929. He then went back to the University of Minnesota to get his PhD in history. He was a teaching fellow in the History Department along with Herb Kahler. One of Lee's history professors was Theodore Blegen, who was also a professor of Vern Chatelain's. When Chatelain was at the University of Minnesota getting his PhD in the late 1920s, he had also been the assistant superintendent of MHS under Solon Buck.

In 1931, Chatelain was asked by NPS director Horace Albright to be chief historian for NPS. As New Deal programs began to proliferate, Chatelain and the NPS were given supervisory responsibilities for work in historical parks. Chatelain contacted Theodore Blegen looking for assistance. Blegen recommended Ronald Lee and Herb Kahler, as well as several other University of Minnesota graduate students.

Ronald Lee was hired and sent to the Shiloh National Military Park in June 1933, where he was the resident historian and supervisor of Civilian Conservation Corps crews doing restoration and interpretation work. His supervisory skill and insight soon came to the attention of key people in Washington, DC. Lee was transferred to the central history office in the fall of 1934. In Washington he also excelled, so Conrad Wirth, head of the CCC State Parks Department (CCCSPD), in the spring of 1935 made Lee the head of his History Division within CCCSPD. Lee supervised all CCC history projects going on in the country's state parks. His administrative and historian skills played a crucial role in the drafting of the bill and the writing of the implementing regulations for the Historic Sites Act (HSA) of 1935. As the newly appointed assistant to Chatelain in 1936, he helped set up the Federal Survey of Local Archives and the Survey of Historic Sites and Buildings. In May 1938, Lee became chief historian for NPS. He took over management of history projects resulting from the HSA, as well as those being done for various New Deal programs. Then NPS history projects were put on hold for almost a decade with the onset of World War II. Lee volunteered for the Army Air Force, serving as an instructor in England for use of the Norden bombsight but also getting a chance to see England's National Trust up close.

Lee resumed his duties as chief historian for NPS after the war. Within a year, he was warning historical organizations about the major threats to historic properties posed by construction of highways, dams, and urban renewal, as well as less obvious threats such as army base closings. In 1947, he helped found the National Council for Historic Sites and Buildings (NCHSB), and then helped it become the NTHP in 1949, serving as its first secretary. In 1951, he became an assistant director for NPS. In 1960, he started the National Historic Landmarks Program just before becoming the northeastern regional director for NPS. Before his retirement at the end of 1966, he helped write and pass the National Historic Preservation Act,

even accompanying the Rains Committee on its tour of European historic sites. Lee remained a critical advisor to NPS until his death in 1972, helping to write the grants manual and Section 106 regulations for the implementation of the NHPA.

Ronald Lee, in many ways, is the father of American historic preservation. He helped write key laws as well as their regulations and guidelines. He sounded the alarm after World War II, recognizing the need for both a strong private preservation organization and external initiatives by NPS. He created NHLs as an attempt to protect privately owned historic sites. He developed the concept of National Register Criterion C significance for architectural properties. He was instrumental in establishing heritage management professionalism in the NPS. As both an innovator and an implementer, he was ahead of his time, but thank goodness he was in his time.

CHAPTER 10

Nonfederal Heritage Management

The Building's Other Occupants

Public sentiment is everything. With public sentiment nothing can fail, without it nothing can succeed.

—Abraham Lincoln

This chapter is about heritage preservation at the grassroots level—the work done by states, by communities, and by private entities. This is heritage preservation that is truly publicly accessible, publicly supportable, and, to a large degree, publicly understandable. Many federal processes are complicated, mainly regulatory, and largely invisible to the public, although prominent examples are nationally showcased.

Success and failure in heritage preservation off federal lands is often a matter of local and private will, not necessarily a result of environmental review or agency compliance. Although adverse impacts to a historic property might initially be avoided due to an environmental review requirement for a major undertaking, that property remains vulnerable once the undertaking is completed. A private initiative or an unreviewed state or local initiative may later destroy it unless there is local heritage preservation vigilance.

While all types of American heritage management textbooks discuss federal aspects, most cultural resource management (read archaeological) books pay little attention to the state, local, and private aspects of heritage preservation. Most historic preservation (read history-architecture) books pay considerable attention to particular cities (e.g., New York) and particular private (e.g., National Trust) aspects, but these publications talk little about state-level efforts, unless it is to discuss state implementation of the federal program (e.g., Lyon and Brook 2003).

Some of the lack of attention to broad state and local heritage preservation efforts is due to the complexity and diversity of the topic. There are great differences in preservation laws, practices, and situations between states and communities as opposed to the largely standardized federal system. Each state has a different set of laws and each community a different set of ordinances. Each state has different professional guidance. Each community has a unique set of heritage resources and unique attitudes as to their relative value.

While the federal government is now the undisputed leader in funding, guiding, and implementing cultural heritage preservation in the United States, this was not the case prior to 1966. Private entities provided the first leadership in American historic preservation. Historic preservation prior to the Civil War was dominated by private efforts to preserve places like Fort Ticonderoga, Mount Vernon, Princeton's Nassau Hall, and the Newport Synagogue. A few notable state efforts include New York's preservation of Hasbrouck House and Tennessee's preservation of Andrew Jackson's Hermitage. The citizens of Philadelphia, not the city, the state, or the nation, preserved Independence Hall.

After the Civil War, historic preservation at any level was largely absent, with the exception of efforts on a number of levels to preserve the Gettysburg Battlefield. Finally, in the late 1880s, some broad historic preservation was again apparent. In 1887, Illinois preserved Abraham Lincoln's Springfield Home. A year later the Society for the Preservation of Virginia Antiquities began to buy historic buildings in Williamsburg. In 1891, the American Institute of Architects acquired the Octagon House in Washington, DC.

Private efforts continued to dominate heritage preservation until the mid-1920s. One notable exception was the federal Antiquities Act of 1906, but it only applied to federal lands and effectively to only prominent archaeological ruins. In 1925, New Orleans formed the first heritage preservation commission. In 1928, California started the first statewide survey for historic sites and, three years later, started a state register of historic landmarks. Also in 1931, Charleston started the first historic preservation district and the first planning and zoning commission concerned with historic sites. Louisiana passed a constitutional amendment in 1936 to help preserve the French Quarter in New Orleans.

As the federal government began to enter historic preservation in a big way on a national level in the mid-1930s, state and local efforts had already created a strong preservation ethic, although it was geographically patchy and topically focused on buildings. The significant Depression-era efforts of the federal government were about employment and economic recovery more than heritage preservation, with almost all the programs terminated by the onset of World War II. The most important heritage preservation legacy of the 1930s was the establishment of federal professionalism.

After World War II, the federal government was once again slow to take up historic preservation, with the notable exception of the archaeologically focused River Basin Surveys. Private entities took up most of the postwar slack, with the predecessor of the National Trust for Historic Preservation (NTHP) established in 1947 and transitioning into the National Trust two years later. The trust sponsored a conference at Williamsburg in 1963 that established principles and guidelines for historic preservation in the United States (see Short 1966:243–256).

At the state level, Pennsylvania started a statewide historic sites survey in 1947 that included archaeological sites. Many states began to pass heritage preservation legislation in the 1950s and 1960s. The National Conference of Mayors sounded the loudest historic preservation alarm in 1965, leading to the passage of the National Historic Preservation Act (NHPA) in 1966.

The States

Like Indian tribes, states and territories are considered sovereign entities under the US Constitution. Each state and territory has its own constitution and its own system of laws. These constitutions and laws cannot contradict the US Constitution or federal law. Mirroring the federal system, state legislatures pass laws, state agencies can issue regulations or rules implementing those laws, governors can issue executive orders providing agency direction, and state court systems evaluate the legal standing of actions concerning these laws, regulations, and executive orders. State supreme courts decide if state and local laws are in line with state constitutions. States have the principal responsibilities for criminal and civil law affecting their citizens; thus the majority of legal actions in the United States involve state rather than federal courts.

State Heritage Resources Laws

State Historic Preservation Legislation

State laws vary considerably, and this is certainly true concerning state heritage preservation laws. State laws determine where the state historic preservation office (SHPO) is located and if there is a state archaeologist. They define what historic and archaeological sites are, what the penalties are for harming them, and to what types of properties the laws apply. For an overview of early state historic preservation legislation, nothing published compares to the analysis of state archaeological legislation in McGimsey (1972). A year prior to McGimsey, Wilson and Winkler (1971), in an article on state historic preservation legislation, offered some valuable historical perspective but did not provide a comprehensive review of state statutes. Both of these studies are valuable historically but are way out of date for overviews of current legislation and procedures.

In 1998, the National Conference of State Historic Preservation Officers (NCSHPO) hired historian Jeffrey Shrimpton to compile a database of state historic preservation legislation. It was originally available online through several sources, but now all internet links to it appear to be broken. As I remember it, this database provided no historical background information on the development of the statutes, just a summary of what state legislation covered as of 1998.

States were typically slow to enact general historic preservation legislation. A number of states had pre-1966 legislation aimed at acquiring and caring for important historic sites (e.g., Indiana, Vermont) or enabling legislation to encourage the creation of local preservation districts (e.g., Louisiana, Massachusetts). Another popular state activity was placing historical markers at significant site locations. State centennial or bicentennial celebrations often provided the incentive for these limited state historic preservation initiatives. By 1964, at least 40 states had historical marker and/or historic site programs (Lyon 1987:83).

Most states did not enact broad historic preservation legislation until after passage of the 1966 NHPA. Minnesota is one exception, but barely. In 1965, Minnesota passed a Historic Sites Act that included the establishment of a state register of historic places and prohibited state and local agencies from harming registered historic sites without the permission of the Minnesota Historical Society (MHS). The "Policy" section states, "It is in the public interest to provide for the preservation of historic sites, buildings, structures, and antiquities of state and national significance for the inspiration, use, and benefit of the people of the state." The inspiration for Minnesota's Historic Sites Act was not the pending national historic preservation legislation but state initiatives for tourism and recreation resulting from the federal Land and Water Conservation Fund Act (LAWCON) of 1965.

Today, all states have legislation to help protect some aspects of their cultural heritage resources. Many states have separate statutes pertaining to archaeological sites, burial sites, structures, and less tangible aspects such as folklore. These laws include different protective mechanisms such as state environmental review of certain types of projects, state tax breaks for certain types of properties, listing of historic properties in state registers, acquisition of important sites by the state, and criminal and civil penalties for disturbing certain kinds of sites. MacDonald (2008) compared state historic preservation laws, noting that 18 states had "laws equivalent to NHPA," meaning that they had laws with aspects similar to Section 106 of NHPA. No state has an NHPA equivalent with provisions for state agency historic preservation planning, inventory, and evaluation (Section 110), as well as undertaking consideration and consultation (Section 106).

Another aspect of environmental review at the state level is cultural resource consideration in state variations of the National Environmental Policy Act (NEPA) or Section 4(f) of the Department of Transportation Act (DOTA). State environmental protection/policy acts (SEPAs), sometimes referred to as mini-NEPAs, that closely mirror NEPA are more common than full state 4(f) equivalents, although the "prudent and feasible" language from 4(f) has been adopted by a number of states in their general historic preservation legislation or their environmental protection laws.

State Archaeological Legislation

Based on a query I sent to all state archaeologists in early 2017, Alabama appears to have the earliest archaeologically focused state heritage preservation law. The Alabama Antiquities Act dates to 1915, nine years after the federal Antiquities Act. Alabama's law reserved the state's exclusive right and privilege to explore, excavate, and survey mounds, earthworks, burial sites, and other types of sites and declared state ownership of the artifacts from these sites. It also prohibited nonresidents from exploring Alabama sites and from transporting artifacts out of Alabama. Arizona was second, passing an Antiquities Act in 1927. It was administered by the Arizona State Museum and protected archaeological and paleontological sites on lands owned or controlled by the state, subdivisions of the state, counties, and municipalities.

A number of states passed Antiquities Acts in the mid-1930s, including three in 1935: Oklahoma, Oregon, and Wyoming. Oregon's was the result of the proposed construction of the Bonneville Dam on the Columbia River, which threatened hundreds of sites, while Oklahoma's was an attempt to stop looting at the nationally important Spiro site. Wyoming's law required permits for archaeological or paleontological excavations on state or federal lands. It also required approval for the removal of archaeological remains, with failure to comply resulting in a fine or imprisonment. North Dakota and Minnesota passed Antiquities Acts in 1939. Both states' laws were principally concerned with regulating artifact collecting on public property.

There appears to be a gap during the 1940s and 1950s in passage of state archaeological laws, with the pace picking up again about 1960, perhaps inspired by federal laws, especially the Reservoir Salvage Act of 1960 and the National Historic Preservation Act of 1966. At first, most of these state laws shared much in common with the earlier federal and state archaeological laws being called Antiquities Acts, focusing on permits for archaeological activities on public land and covering both archaeological and paleontological resources. A few states (e.g., Illinois, Idaho, Arkansas) established statewide archaeological surveys. States passing archaeological laws during this period included Kentucky (1960), Texas (1965), Florida (1965), Colorado (1967), and Kansas (1967). One of the innovations found in some of these laws was the establishment of a state archaeologist. Iowa established an Office of the State Archaeologist in 1959 but did not pass a more comprehensive Antiquities Act.

States that had passed earlier laws also began revising them in the 1960s, including adding a provision for a state archaeologist. Arizona revised its Antiquities Act in 1960, Minnesota in 1963, and North Dakota in 1965. The 1963 Minnesota Field Archaeology Act superseded the 1939 law and provided some provisions for reviewing construction activities on nonfederal public property that might affect archaeological and historical sites. Unfortunately, the project review provisions were vaguely worded and put the review burden on the landowning entities, not on funding or permitting agencies. By 1966, 19 states had specific archaeological legislation, although only 5 states required excavation permits and only 7 had a state archaeologist (Lyon 1987:85).

Most states have a statement of legislative intent associated with their archaeological statutes, with some giving first priority to site preservation and others (including Minnesota) giving first priority to regulating the practice of archaeology. At least two of the states besides Minnesota that give priority to archaeological regulation based their initial statutes on Minnesota's 1963 Field Archaeology Act. In most states, archaeological regulation is not even discussed in the legislative intent. In a few states, the intent includes other elements, such as making archaeological information available to the public.

In at least 40 states, a permit or license must be obtained to do archaeological work. In most of the states that do issue permits/licenses, this applies to state or other nonfederal public land only, but in four states (North Dakota, Oregon, Washington, Oklahoma) a permit/license is also needed on privately owned land. The state archaeologist acts alone in issuing permits in only two states, Michigan and Massachusetts. In Minnesota, the Minnesota Historical Society actually issues the license, while the state archaeologist certifies the qualifications of applicants; this is a relic of the days when the state archaeologist was a staff member at the University of Minnesota with no official office attached.

Private lands protection for nonburial archaeological sites beyond permitting/licensing requirements is part of statute in only a few states. Wisconsin has perhaps the most workable private lands protection, offering tax breaks for protecting significant archaeological sites, although very few landowners in Wisconsin have taken advantage of the program. The most common private lands protections mentioned in state statutes are forbidding trespassing on privately owned sites and forbidding state agencies to sell land containing sites to private interests without taking appropriate measures to protect the sites (e.g., easements).

With regard to nonfederal project review for broad heritage preservation, by the early 1980s about half the states required some form of state project review (Lyon 1987:95). Some of these reviews involved public lands, some public funding, and some public permits, but few involved all three of these actions. Even today, very few states have laws that require a true 106-like process with definitions, comprehensive provisions, and regulations/rules to help implement the laws.

Illinois is perhaps the closest to having a state-level 106-like process with a few elements of DOTA 4(f). Passed in 1989, the Illinois Historic Resources Protection Act has definitions similar to NHPA and 36 CFR 800, applies to projects with state funding and state lands, and requires consideration rather than protection. The state review process is referred to as the "707 process" after the law number. Permits for private projects are considered if they are in state-defined high-potential areas. In some ways the Illinois law is stronger than Section 106, as the director of historic preservation can require (not just recommend) surveys of state projects that may threaten significant historic resources. The director has the unilateral authority to declare something a historic resource, although "reasonable and prudent" alternatives regarding adverse effects are consensus determinations with the agency. A mediation committee of state agency officials rules on disputes between the director and an agency. Unlike federal Section 106, the Illinois law does not have a tribal consultation requirement, although there are no federally recognized tribes or Indian reservations in Illinois.

With regard to environmental review processes, Douglas MacDonald (2008) provides some insight into the effectiveness of states' historic preservation legislation, although overall he focuses on the protection of traditional cultural properties (TCPs). According to MacDonald, with respect to nonfederal state undertakings (funding, permitting, land), 18 states have historic preservation laws approximately equivalent to NHPA Section 106 requirements, 22 require consideration of historic property impacts only on state land, 8 don't require any state project consideration, and 2 are unclear.

Possible flaws in MacDonald's analysis are that he doesn't account for important variations in each state law or analyze how strictly review provisions are enforced. For example, in Minnesota, the Field Archaeology Act requires all public agencies to submit development plans to the state archaeologist and the Minnesota Historical Society if developments on their land could harm "a known or scientifically predicted" historic resource. Most agencies, especially local ones, do not know about this requirement, to say nothing of knowing site locations and how to assess site potential. The state archaeologist and MHS/SHPO do not push enforcement because there are hundreds of times as many local projects as federal projects, and the federal projects alone already overwhelm review agencies. Requiring all public entities to obey the Minnesota law, considering today's political climate, would no doubt result in a legislative backlash that could not only eliminate the review requirement but weaken other parts of the current law.

State penalties for harming archaeological sites by and large deal with willful destruction of sites on public land. Most states treat this action as a gross misdemeanor, although several states (e.g., Michigan, Oregon) can treat it as a felony. Archaeological excavation without a permit is treated similarly in most states, although if professional archaeologists were guilty of such an action, they would rarely be charged in most states if they could provide a reasonable explanation. Few states are even willing to aggressively pursue prosecution of nonarchaeologists who harm public sites, unless burials are involved.

Some states (e.g., Wisconsin, New Mexico, Arizona) have state boards of archaeology. In New Mexico, the seven-member Cultural Properties Review Committee is made up exclusively of professionals. In Wisconsin, the Archaeological Review Board has only three members, a professional archaeologist, an avocational archaeologist, and a member of the Historical Society Board. In Arizona, the 11-member Archaeology Advisory Commission has a mixed membership, but all members must have a "demonstrated interest or expertise" in archaeology or closely related fields. The governor appoints board members in New Mexico and Arizona, while the director of the historical society appoints them in Wisconsin. No set term of office is present in Wisconsin; it is three years in Arizona and four years in New Mexico. The boards in Wisconsin and New Mexico meet every three months, and the board in Arizona meets as needed.

Professional archaeological qualifications are defined in state law in only a few states' statutes. States with qualification standards set them out in licensing requirements or in state survey manuals issued by the state archaeologist or the SHPO. Most states use the federal professional qualification requirements found in *The Secretary of the Interior's Standards and Guidelines for Archaeology and Historic Preservation*, although a few states (e.g., Minnesota) have more strict qualification standards, such as requiring regional experience.

Underwater archaeological sites are discussed in exclusive sections of the laws of some states, in particular those that border the ocean or the Great Lakes. Underwater sites are included in almost all states' statutes under general provisions for sites on public lands because river, lake, and coastal ocean bottoms are usually considered property of the state. Several states (e.g., Wisconsin, Michigan) have underwater preserves to provide special protection where concentrations of cultural resources exist. Federal marine protection areas can include natural and cultural resources.

Very few states explicitly deal with Indian sacred sites or traditional cultural properties in their historic preservation legislation, although at least 15 deal with TCPs in their survey manuals (MacDonald 2008). Some of these states have guidelines for locating and treating these sites, while others rely on National Register of Historic Places (NRHP) Bulletin 38 (Parker and King 1990). Most of the states that deal with this kind of site are west of the Mississippi River, where Indian reservations and recognized resident tribes are more common. New Mexico has explicitly designated TCPs on its historic sites register under its Cultural Properties Act.

The confidentiality of archaeological site information is mentioned in the archaeological statutes of at least eight states. In some states where it is not explicitly mentioned (like Minnesota), site confidentiality has been established by legal opinions utilizing other laws, such as data privacy acts. Burial sites usually have stricter data confidentially requirements than nonburial sites. Exact locational information concerning sites on federal property that are included in state inventories can be withheld from the general public based on several federal laws, as discussed in earlier chapters.

Most states have a state historic site register that is similar to the National Register of Historic Places. All of these registers include consideration of archaeological sites. At least five states (South Dakota, California, Idaho, Arkansas, Massachusetts) have state archaeological site registers to provide additional protection for and acknowledgment of archaeological sites.

Formal awareness and treatment of historical archaeological sites are increasing nationwide and are thus becoming an important cultural resource management problem. At least two states (Washington, Oregon) explicitly discuss and define historical archaeological sites, while at least two additional states (California, Massachusetts) pay some attention to them in statute. In Washington, a historical archaeological site must be at least 30 years old, and in Oregon such a site must be at least 75 years old—a significant chronological discrepancy for these two adjacent states.

Indians rarely play a major role in general state archaeological legislation, although most states require their input when Indian burials are involved. Only a few states (e.g., Minnesota, Washington, Oregon, Arizona) give Indians a role in general archaeological legislation. In Minnesota, the Minnesota Indian Affairs Council (MIAC) is consulted for the appointment of the state archaeologist, and the state archaeologist is required to consult with the MIAC regarding various archaeological matters concerning Indian-related sites. In Oregon and Washington, consultation with Indian groups is done prior to issuing permits to excavate Indian-related sites. In Arizona, Indians serve on the State Board of Archaeology.

Other provisions of state laws of interest include prohibition of artifact forgery (South Dakota, Montana, Arizona), prohibition of the use of metal detectors on public sites (Michigan), archaeological certification requirements (Illinois), prohibition of the sale of artifacts (Arkansas), an underwater archaeology board (Massachusetts), and provisions for state agency historic preservation officers (New York).

State Historic Burial Site Legislation

The federal government and almost all states consider historic and ancient burial sites to be archaeological sites. In the 1970s and 1980s, an internal debate raged in American archaeology as to the appropriateness of excavating burials and retaining human skeletal materials in archaeological repositories, especially those of American Indian ancestry. While most archaeologists immediately conceded that burials clearly related to modern Indian groups were off-limits, most still deemed prehistoric burials that could not be closely affiliated with modern groups appropriate for scientific research. The passage of new state and federal laws restricting burial excavation and repatriating skeletal collections ended much of the debate by the early 1990s.

A number of states have legislation explicitly dealing with protecting unregistered, unplatted, or private cemeteries. As with general archaeological legislation, there is a great deal of variety in who serves as the lead agency. Responsibilities for protection lie with the state archaeologist in some states or with the SHPO, the state historical society, or public health agencies or the coroner in others. The state archaeologist is officially involved with human burials in multiple states (e.g., Minnesota, South Dakota, Iowa, Arkansas, Massachusetts, Oklahoma) and unofficially involved in a few others.

In Minnesota, the state archaeologist has sole authority to authenticate burial grounds if the burial is determined to be at least 50 years old. The medical examiner, county coroner, state police, or sheriff's department have roles in most states, especially in the preliminary stages of verification and authentication. The state archaeologist in Minnesota can issue a permit to qualified archaeologists to authenticate burial grounds. At least two other states, Wisconsin and Illinois, have a formal burial authentication process. The Minnesota state archaeologist consults with the Indian Affairs Council if a suspected Indian-related burial ground may be identified by the authentication (e.g., suspected burial mound site). The state archaeologists in Illinois and Wisconsin are not required to consult with an external entity at the authentication stage.

Most states have to issue a formal permit for burial excavation. In Minnesota, only the Minnesota Indian Affairs Council can authorize the relocation of an Indian burial, and only the state archaeologist can authorize the removal of non-Indian historic burials from unplatted cemetery locations. Landowners must also consent. Indian tribes or representative groups are consulted in most states if an Indian burial is to be excavated or removed. In Wisconsin and Montana, tribal members serve on the state burial boards.

Some states (e.g., Wisconsin, Montana, Kansas, Missouri) have established boards to deal with archaeological/historic burials. New Mexico's Cultural Properties Review Committee deals with burials as well as other types of archaeological sites. In all these states, the boards are made up of seven members, and they generally meet quarterly. The governor appoints the boards in Montana and New Mexico, but the director of the Historical Society appoints the Wisconsin board. The terms of the board members vary from two to four years. In Wisconsin, the board is made up of three Indian members and three professional archaeologists with a representative of the Historical Society serving as the seventh member. In Montana, the board has a mixed membership of Indians, archaeologists and other professionals, and members of the public. In New Mexico, all of the board members are professionals.

Every state has legal penalties for burial disturbance. Most states have a penalty for failure to report an exposed burial; this is usually a misdemeanor. If archaeologists excavate burials without a permit, it could be treated like willful destruction in most states, although this would rarely occur as all professional archaeologists are well aware of burial site excavation/disturbance prohibitions, especially with regard to Indian burials. Willful destruction of human burials is a felony in almost every state.

Minnesota allows its state archaeologist right of entry (even if a landowner objects) to authenticate a burial if a suspected burial ground has been disturbed on private property. In most other states, a court order would have to be obtained. Other private land provisions regarding burial sites in states include property tax breaks in Wisconsin, Illinois, and Minnesota.

Special burial site inventories are maintained in Wisconsin, Illinois, Minnesota, and Montana. In every state, prehistoric or historical burial sites are added to the state archaeological site file, and historic burials are defined as archaeological sites in all of the study states. Minimal ages for historic burials are set in Minnesota (50 years), Iowa (150 years), Illinois (100 years), Wisconsin (after 1889), Arizona (50 years), and Massachusetts (100 years). In most states, local law enforcement officials are first contacted when burials are accidentally encountered and then they make a decision to bring in archaeologists if they think the burial is old enough.

The State Heritage Preservation Players

The State Historic Preservation Office

The acronym "SHPO" can refer to either the state historic preservation officer or the state historic preservation office. The SHPO as an official defined in the 1966 National Historic Preservation Act was originally called a state liaison officer (SLO). By popular acclaim the SLOs changed their title in 1974 to "state historic preservation officer" because "liaison officer" was too amorphous (i.e., liaison for what?), or perhaps they didn't like the way the acronym "SLO" was pronounced. The documentation for this name change is on the revised National Register of Historic Places nomination form dated June 1974, where state historic preservation officer replaces state liaison officer in the signature block.

In 1969, the state historic preservation officers decided to form a national association that would become the National Conference of State Historic Preservation Officers. According to the NCSHPO webpage, "The NCSHPO is a 501(c)(3) corporation registered in the District of Columbia. The NCSHPO acts as a communications vehicle among the SHPOs and their staffs and represents the SHPOs with federal agencies and national preservation organizations." NCSHPO is guided by a 15-member board made up of SHPOs elected by all SHPOs. The president of the board is also a required member of the Advisory Council on Historic Preservation (ACHP). There are three full-time NCSHPO staff members, all based in Washington, DC. The NCSHPO president is a required signatory on nationwide programmatic agreements completed for the purposes of Section 106 of the NHPA.

The 1992 amendments to the NHPA gave recognized tribes the right to have their own historic preservation officers with jurisdiction within their reservations. I will discuss tribal historic preservation officers (THPOs) in the next chapter. THPOs also have a national organization called the National Association of Tribal Historic Preservation Officers (NATHPO).

As I use the term "SHPO" in this book (and as most agencies use the term in general), it usually means the office that includes the officer. All states have a designated SHPO (officer) with the location of that person specified in each state's laws. There are also SHPOs for the District of Columbia, Puerto Rico, the Virgin Islands, and each of the six Pacific Island trust territories.

In about half the states, the appointment of the official known as the SHPO is automatic, as the position is attached by law to the holder of another state title, usually the head of the state historical society, the state museum, or the state heritage commission. In five states, there is a stand-alone historic preservation office whose executive reports directly to the governor. In the other states, the SHPO (officer) is employed within a larger state agency. With regard to state agency SHPOs, 11 are in natural resources/state parks departments, 2 are in economic development departments, 2 are in departments of state, 2 are in recreation and tourism departments, 2 are in housing departments, 1 is in a planning department, 1 is in an environmental protection agency, and, as of March 1, 2018, Minnesota's SHPO moved from its Historical Society to its Department of Administration.

In a few states, the appointment of the official known as the SHPO is almost honorary or even political, as that person does very little of the day-to-day work of the office. After the passage of the NHPA, the director of the Minnesota Historical Society, a person hired by a private board, was designated the SHPO. The MHS is a private organization, not a state agency, although state law gives it a number of official duties, such as maintaining the state archives and housing the office known as the SHPO. When I was at the Minnesota SHPO (MnSHPO), years would pass without a visit from the SHPO (officer) to the SHPO (office), although we were in the same building. The SHPO (officer) only got involved if a situation was potentially politically volatile or publicly unpopular.

The requirements for state historic preservation programs are outlined in 54 USC 3023, or what was 16 USC 470a(b) prior to the 2014 recodification. Subsection 302301 requires that the secretary of the interior promulgate regulations that provide for

1. the designation and appointment of a SHPO by the state's governor or the appointment of professionally qualified staff as may be necessary;
2. an adequate and qualified state historic preservation review board; and
3. adequate public participation in the state historic preservation program, including the process of recommending properties for nomination to the National Register.

The regulations for federally supported state programs are in 36 CFR 61. The regulations include additional definitions and declare that the National Park Service (NPS) is the federal administrator of the state programs. They specify that NPS can allow state, tribal, and local programs to use their own financial auditors for day-to-day accounting, but the NPS must ensure that those audits are accurate and that certain staff of programs and boards meet the secretary of the interior's professional qualifications standards.

The 1980 amendments to the NHPA required that NPS assess the adequacy of state preservation programs every four years. Sorry to say, this came about partially due to some inappropriate use of federal historic preservation funds by the Minnesota Historical Society to pay non-SHPO MHS staff. When I first started there in 1990, MnSHPO was preparing for one of these quadrennial NPS audits. It was a thorough, top-to-bottom review of each program area and required that all SHPO staff dedicate much time each day to audit preparation for several months prior to the one-week visit by NPS audit staff.

These audits found most program areas at the MnSHPO adequate or exemplary, except for review and compliance, which always was a little behind on timeliness for a small percentage of 30-day Section 106 reviews. If the audit determined multiple areas of a SHPO's program were deficient, NPS could reduce the amount of federal funds the SHPO received. If the whole program was really deficient, the NPS could suspend all funds, contracts, and agreements.

After many complaints from overworked SHPOs and NPS audit staff (who also had other duties), the quadrennial NPS on-site review requirement was eliminated in 1995. The current law and regulations both still mention four-year reviews, but the 1992 amendments to NHPA allowed for alternative audit procedures. SHPOs now essentially self-evaluate their performance, although they must submit end-of-year (federal fiscal year) summary reports to NPS that briefly summarize basic performance measures such as Section 106 reviews, number of new National Register nominations, number of properties added to state inventories, and number of tax-incentive certifications. Unfortunately, SHPOs do not put these annual NPS reports online, so there is no way for the public, agencies, or professionals to consistently and comparatively track SHPO workload and performance.

SHPO Duties

SHPOs are the ombudsmen of American heritage preservation. They are the interface between federal agencies and the ACHP. They are the link between local governments and the federal government. They provide guidelines and standards of practice for state agencies and private contract heritage management. They are the local experts, local enforcers, and local advocates.

SHPOs deal with every type of historic property. Their staffs include historians, archaeologists, architects, and grant managers. They facilitate and oversee National Register nominations and tax act certifications. They maintain inventories of a state's archaeological sites and historic structures/buildings. They are required to develop comprehensive plans to efficiently and effectively guide heritage preservation in their state. They help train tribes and THPOs in the intricacies of heritage management. Without SHPOs, the federal historic preservation system could not operate.

The NHPA (54 USC 302303) outlines the following responsibilities for SHPO implementation of a state historic preservation program:

(1) in cooperation with Federal and State agencies, local governments, and private organizations and individuals, direct and conduct a comprehensive statewide survey of historic property and maintain inventories of the property;
(2) identify and nominate eligible property to the National Register and otherwise administer applications for listing historic property on the National Register;
(3) prepare and implement a comprehensive statewide historic preservation plan;
(4) administer the State program of Federal assistance for historic preservation within the State;
(5) advise and assist, as appropriate, Federal and State agencies and local governments in carrying out their historic preservation responsibilities;
(6) cooperate with the Secretary, the Council, other Federal and State agencies, local governments, and private organizations and individuals to ensure that historic property is taken into consideration at all levels of planning and development;
(7) provide public information, education, and training and technical assistance in historic preservation;
(8) cooperate with local governments in the development of local historic preservation programs and assist local governments in becoming certified pursuant to chapter 3025;
(9) consult with appropriate Federal agencies in accordance with this division on—
(A) Federal undertakings that may affect historic property; and
(B) the content and sufficiency of any plans developed to protect, manage, or reduce or mitigate harm to that property; and
(10) advise and assist in the evaluation of proposals for rehabilitation projects that may qualify for Federal assistance.

Most SHPOs put these 10 responsibilities into eight program areas: survey and inventory (1), National Register (2), planning (3), grants (4), review and compliance

(5, 6, 9), education (7), local government assistance (5, 8), and tax certification (10). The review and compliance program area is focused on the ninth duty required in the law, namely Section 106 responsibilities, but it also overlaps with the fifth and sixth duties. At the Minnesota SHPO, the review and compliance program area is part of government programs and compliance, reflecting this overlap.

In Minnesota and a number of other states, the SHPO carries out not only the federal duties assigned in the NHPA but state-related heritage management duties as well. This involves the review of certain state and local undertakings as required by state law, the maintenance of state historic site registers, and oversight of state tax certification programs.

Most SHPOs set state standards for professional qualifications and guidelines for doing heritage preservation fieldwork. Some states' professional qualification standards (e.g., Minnesota's) exceed the federal standards. Many SHPOs also maintain lists of historic preservation professionals and companies available to do contract work for agencies and private entities. Most SHPOs also participate in the National Trust's Main Street Program to help smaller cities preserve their downtown commercial districts.

SHPO Funding

The 1976 amendment of the NHPA created the Historic Preservation Fund (HPF), a federal trust fund that receives its money from outer continental shelf oil and gas revenues. The HPF is authorized at $150 million annually, but the amount actually available for historic preservation activities each year depends on a congressional appropriation. Because the trust fund is not cumulative from year to year and can be used for other federal, non-historic-preservation purposes, the full HPF authorized amount has never been appropriated.

HPF appropriations increased steadily for the first three years in the late 1970s and then steadily declined until the late 1980s, when they began to gradually increase again (Figure 10.1). Another change in the early 1980s was the elimination of grants to acquire and preserve historic properties (known as bricks-and-mortar projects). SHPOs then focused their activities on survey and planning.

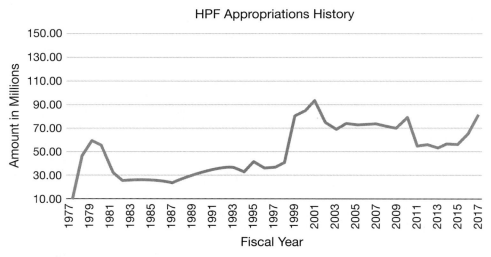

HPF Appropriations History

*Excludes $128 million in supplemental funding that was appropriated over the years for natural disaster relief and job creation.

FIG. 10.1 Historic Preservation Fund appropriations from 1977 to 2017 (NCSHPO).

In the late 1990s, there was a significant increase in appropriations for the HPF. The amount fell dramatically in 2002 and 2003, and then gradually rose again. The 2016 funding was $56.4 million. Adjusting for inflation, the 1979 amount of $60 million represents the actual peak HPF funding over the past 40 years, with the past 30 years of funding remaining essentially flat.

While the states get about 85% of the HPF allocation each year, THPOs and tribes get about 15%, with the remainder going to various activities such as under-represented-community grants. Some years the HPF funds even disaster-relief activi-ties, such as after Hurricane Sandy hit the East Coast in 2013. Prior to the National Trust for Historic Preservation's cutting its federal funding strings in 1998, it too got a share of the HPF.

The HPF state share is allocated to individual states according to a three-tiered formula. Each state gets a base award of about $357,000, which is the Tier 1 amount of $20 million divided equally between the states, with some consider-ation of the territories. The next part of the allocation is based on population, land area, and number of recorded and registered historic resources. The overall amount available to the states to divide in Tier 2 typically varies from $20 million to $50 million. Tier 3 is based on preservation initiatives proposed by individual SHPOs, but allocations from this tier have never been made due to the annual appropriation ceiling's being reached by Tier 1 and Tier 2 allocations.

Currently, states must provide a 40% match for federal funds received from the HPF, an increase from the original 1976 30% HPF match requirement. This match can be in-kind (e.g., equipment costs, office space) or actual nonfederal dollars obtained by the SHPO for state historic preservation purposes. At least 10% of the state allocation must be passed through to certified local govern-ments (CLGs) as grants. SHPOs use the other 90% for staff salaries, contracts for National Register nominations, contracts for survey and inventory work, and various office needs.

State financial support of SHPOs varies greatly, with some states contributing two to three times as much to SHPO operations as they receive from the HPF. Other states struggle to meet their 40% match requirement. For instance, in 2007 three states (Alabama, Louisiana, Rhode Island) contributed more than 70% of what they received in HPF allocation, but 11 states (Kansas, Kentucky, Massachusetts, Missouri, Nebraska, New Hampshire, North Dakota, Tennessee, Texas, Virginia, West Virginia) contributed less than the required 40% in order to obtain their full federal HPF allocation. As one would expect, due to population factors in Tier 2, in 2007 California was allocated the highest amount at $1,004,702, with New York second at $928,863, while at the low end $454,591 went to Delaware and $480,661 to Vermont. Due to land area, Alaska received $730,638, an above-aver-age amount.

Some SHPOs charge fees to help make up for tight budgets or to help provide their federal match. The most typical fee is for records searches in association with development projects to determine potential effects to known historic properties for Section 106 purposes. Other SHPOs may get direct personnel hiring assistance from state agencies, like a state department of transportation's paying half the salary of one of the review and compliance staff.

SHPO Staffing and Program Implementation
The number of staff members and their individual duties at each SHPO vary greatly. The regulations (36 CFR 61.4[e]) require that every SHPO have at least three full-time professionals who meet the *Secretary of the Interior's Professional Qualifi-cations Standards*: an archaeologist, a historian, and an architectural historian.

Many SHPOs also have a historical architect to assist with tax act projects and provide guidance to grant recipients who are rehabilitating historic structures or buildings. Most SHPOs will have a manager for each of the eight standard program areas, although the managers can serve as one of the required professionals in the National Register (historian), review and compliance (archaeologist), and tax incentives (architectural historian) areas.

The California SHPO has almost 40 employees divided into six program areas, of which five have some environmental review responsibilities; only grants and information management were excluded. In 2016, it had at least 13 historians, 8 archaeologists, and 2 restoration architects.

The New York SHPO is part of the Division of Historic Preservation, which has three bureaus: Community Preservation Services, Technical Preservation Services, and Historic Sites and Parks. The SHPO functions are handled by the first two bureaus. The Community Preservation Services Bureau has a CLG unit, a National Register unit, and an outreach unit. The Technical Preservation Services Bureau has units for technical assistance and compliance, tax credit, archeology, and information resources. The New York SHPO has 30 full-time staff, but individual qualifications and specific duties are not listed on its webpage.

Among smaller states, the Rhode Island SHPO has 16 staff members mostly dedicated to federal program activities. The staff appear to include two architectural historians, two archaeologists, and one historian. There are no formal program areas listed on the website, but based on the staff list, the standard SHPO program areas are present. The Delaware SHPO is part of the Division of Historical and Cultural Affairs within the Department of State. The Historic Preservation Unit is led by a deputy SHPO and has three historians, three archaeologists, two architectural historians, and an information research specialist.

The Minnesota SHPO has 14 employees. For professional staff, MnSHPO has one archaeologist, one historian, one architectural historian, and one historical architect. The archaeologist deals with all the program areas, with most time spent on review and compliance. The historian and architectural historian spend most of their time doing National Register work, much of it related to evaluating and nominating buildings for federal and state tax incentives. The historical architect is focused on implementing the tax incentives for buildings. MnSHPO has 10 other staff members whose work is mostly dedicated to federal programs: a deputy SHPO who is chief executive for the office, a survey and inventory manager and assistant, a grants manager, a government programs and compliance manager with two assistants, a local preservation programs manager, and an office manager.

Review and compliance for agency undertakings is the most time-consuming and potentially controversial aspect of every SHPO's day-to-day work, although most of it is invisible to the public as most reviews are routine and most agencies comply with the law. It is the controversial projects that get attention, like the Dakota Access Pipeline (DAPL) in North Dakota, where the SHPO was unfairly criticized for not requiring a more thorough archaeological and traditional cultural properties survey. The SHPO can't require anything; it can only recommend certain actions and try to ensure that an agency fully complies with 36 CFR 800. In the case of DAPL, the Army Corps of Engineers (COE) fully complied with SHPO survey recommendations, required avoidance of potentially eligible properties, and made a reasonable and good faith effort to identify historic properties and consult with interested tribes. It should also be noted that SHPOs rarely get credit for saving historic properties through the review and compliance process.

Based on NPS *Historic Preservation Fund Annual Reports* and the publication *Back to the Future: A Review of the National Historic Preservation Program*

(Hodsoll, Leighty, and Morgan 2007), since 2000 the nation's SHPOs typically have reviewed over 100,000 federal undertakings each year, with about four million reviews total since NHPA was passed in 1966. Although programmatic agreements have significantly reduced the number of SHPO reviews for certain agencies (e.g., Natural Resources Conservation Service), other types of reviews have increased due to post office closings, cell tower construction, army base closings, and various agency reviews associated with the constant sprawl of cities and infrastructure.

Due mainly to federal undertaking reviews and surveys done for them, a total of over 100,000 previously unrecorded properties are typically added to inventories each year, of which over half are evaluated for eligibility and one-quarter found eligible. Most states no longer have sufficient budgets to support internal or private contract surveys to increase coverage of their proactive statewide historic property inventories. This is most apparent with regard to archaeological sites in states with limited federal land. While buildings and structures are visible and thus easily documented for basic inventory and evaluation needs, most archaeological sites are surficially invisible, and evaluation is time-consuming and expensive. In Minnesota, we have 20,000 recorded archaeological sites, which is probably less than 1% of the state's total. Of the recorded sites, only a very small percentage has been evaluated for National Register eligibility.

With regard to the National Register program area, of the 20,000 or so properties nationally considered eligible each year, only a small fraction is actually nominated to the National Register of Historic Places. In 2015, 999 properties were added to the National Register, bringing the total individual listings to 91,475, with 1.8 million properties contributing to districts. Most of these nominations were not due to the Section 106 process. Most Minnesota nominations these days are related to tax incentives, as a building has to actually be listed to receive federal or state tax benefits, while eligibility is enough to force federal agencies to consider adverse effects to a property.

Each state is required by the NHPA (SHPO duty 3) to have a statewide historic preservation plan that guides its work and focuses efforts on problem areas. There is no required format or update schedule for these plans, so they vary greatly from state to state. Other reasons for state variations include percentage of federal/public land (review and compliance implications), dominant property types (e.g., urban versus rural), tribal presence (TCP implications), nature of threats to historic properties (e.g., mining versus agriculture), and even politics.

In my estimation, an effective and useful statewide plan should include the following:

- Statement of purpose
- Brief overview of the state's history
- History of heritage preservation in the state
- Overview of historic contexts and **resource types** associated with each context
- Status and statistics for survey and inventory
- Major threats to resources and how the SHPO expects to deal with them
- Priorities (e.g., what resources are most threatened, which ones should be preserved)
- Accomplishments since last statewide plan
- Challenges and discrete objectives for the current planning period
- Principal players and partners in the state's heritage management
- A list of SHPO staff by program area

Overall, most SHPOs are overworked and underfunded. Federal agency compliance with Section 106 has greatly improved over the last 20 years, but in some states this has increased the SHPO workload. Despite workload increases and budget stress, much of a SHPO's efficiency and effectiveness is based on how experienced and dedicated staff are. These aspects vary greatly from office to office and decade to decade.

The most important person on the SHPO staff is the head of the office, whether that is the actual SHPO or a deputy SHPO. This person must not only understand all program areas but have the respect of agencies, the dedication of staff, and professional standing among the state's heritage management practitioners. SHPOs can only be successful by forging broad partnerships and being aggressively proactive as well as appropriately reactive. SHPO performance is the most critical factor in a state's heritage preservation effectiveness.

State Archaeologists

How states implement nonfederal aspects of their heritage preservation efforts is even more variable than federal implementation by SHPOs. This is especially true with regard to archaeology, as the archaeological resources of each state, or at least each region, are more problematic than standing structures. Archaeological sites are much more expensive to find and assess, effects to archaeological sites are more difficult to determine and more expensive to mitigate, and treatment of archaeological resources usually is more subject to tribal input as there are reservations in some states and not in others.

Most states do not have a state historian or a state architect who is broadly involved in heritage management. State architects usually deal with architectural licensing or overseeing public building construction. State historians generally guide educational initiatives concerning a state's history or oversee public archives and are also known as state archivists.

Most states do have a designated state archaeologist who provides leadership for finding, recording, investigating, saving, interpreting, and publicizing archaeological resources. Twelve states do not have an official state archaeologist designated by statute, but a high-ranking archaeologist in some other state office often acts as the de facto state archaeologist in these states to provide leadership and represent the state in the National Association of State Archaeologists (NASA). In at least three states in 2017 (Massachusetts, Nevada, and Vermont), the state archaeologist was also the SHPO. In at least four states (Alaska, California, Colorado, Idaho), the state archaeologist was also a deputy SHPO.

In 35 states, the state archaeologist (or the de facto substitute) is in the same state department as the SHPO, although in a few cases this individual is in a different division within that department. The most common location (19) is in a state historical society, state heritage commission, or state museum. Universities are the second most common location for state archaeologists (8), followed by natural resources/state parks departments (7) and stand-alone executive agency historic preservation departments (6). The other 10 state archaeologists are in various departments, including departments of state (2), tourism (2), housing and community development (2), planning (1), administration (1), environmental review (1), and trade and economic development (1).

The staffing, activities, and budgets for offices of the state archaeologist (OSAs) vary greatly. In Minnesota, the OSA has two state civil service employees, the state archaeologist and an assistant, with an annual budget of about $210,000 from a general fund legislative appropriation to the commissioner of administration. The Minnesota OSA does not charge a fee for any services and does not do any contract work, so the office has little flexibility in dealing with emergencies or new initiatives.

The Minnesota state archaeologist has 30 discrete duties mandated by six separate laws, as well as at least 10 traditional duties that have evolved since the office was established in 1963. The major duties of the Minnesota state archaeologist are

- approving license applications and monitoring the activities of the licensees, including reviewing submitted archaeological reports;
- reviewing site inventory forms, issuing official state site numbers, and maintaining the inventory of known and suspected sites;
- reviewing development plans submitted by government agencies and private entities to evaluate the potential for harm to archaeological sites in project areas;
- promoting and undertaking research in Minnesota archaeology;
- providing public education and answering archaeological questions from the public;
- ensuring burial sites protection through careful record keeping, development plan review, interaction with MIAC, consultation with experts, and fieldwork;
- guiding the Statewide Survey of Historical and Archaeological Sites.

In Iowa, the OSA has 25 full-time staff members who all are employees of the University of Iowa. The University of Iowa provides about 15% of the funding for OSA's statutory activities, with the other 85% coming from contracts and grants from state and federal agencies dedicated to specific survey, research, or educational projects. The annual budget varied between $3.9 million and $1.6 million between 2007 and 2017. The Iowa OSA charges fees for most of its services. The statutory duties of the Iowa state archaeologist include

- discovery, location, and excavation of archaeological sites;
- recovery, restoration, and preservation of archaeological remains in and for the state;
- coordination of activities through cooperation with the Iowa Departments of Transportation and Natural Resources, as well as other state agencies concerned with archaeology;
- discretionary publication of educational and scientific reports relating to the responsibilities and duties of the office;
- establishment of a cemetery on existing state lands for the reburial of ancient human remains found in the state;
- authorization or denial of permission to disinter human remains that have state and national significance from an historical or scientific standpoint.

In California, there is no statutorily defined state archaeologist. All archaeological employees of the state are considered "state archaeologists," classified hierarchically as assistants, associates, seniors, or a supervisor. The supervisor is the archaeologist who is the head of the Cultural Resource Program in the California Office of Historic Preservation, which is part of State Parks. The Cultural Resource Program is also the Archaeology and Environmental Compliance Division, one of five divisions under the California state historic preservation officer. There are five associate state archaeologists under the supervisory state archaeologist.

One of the ways state archaeologists promote public support for the preservation of archaeological sites is to sponsor or participate in state archaeology days, weeks, and months. Arizona started the first Archaeology Week in 1983, an event publicized by an NPS *Technical Brief* (Hoffman and Lerner 1988). Minnesota

FIG. 10.2 A demonstration of flint knapping to make stone tools at Minnesota's 2015 Archaeology Week Archaeology Fair (author photo).

held its first Archaeology Week in 1995 and, like many states, has recently moved to an Archaeology Month. These events feature public lectures, demonstrations (Figure 10.2), and the production of educational materials, most notably posters that compete in an annual contest sponsored by the Society for American Archaeology (SAA).

State Historical Organizations

States began efforts to preserve their histories as early as 1791, when the parent organization of the Massachusetts Historical Society was founded in Boston. The need for state historical societies moved west with Euro-American settlement. Many states established such organizations at the same time as their constitutions or even before. These organizations served as early libraries, museums, genealogical repositories, and curation centers. Most initially were indeed more like societies than state institutions, with a small, elite membership generally run by a few of the state's most prominent citizens.

Today, every state has a statewide historical organization. Some are still called societies, while others are called commissions, associations, or state museums. The Ohio Historical Society recently changed its name to the Ohio History Connection. In almost all states, the statewide historical organization is part of state government and serves various official capacities for the state. In Minnesota and Ohio, the organizations are still private but are given public duties such as serving as the state archives. The Minnesota Historical Society is classified as a public corporation, while Ohio's is a 501(c)(3) nonprofit.

State historical organizations gradually expanded beyond being elite book and object depositories with small museum displays to becoming true public interpretive centers, research and publication organizations, and managers of state historic sites. About half of these organizations house their state's SHPO. Nineteen state historical organizations house their state's Office of the State Archaeologist.

Community-Level Heritage Preservation

All the major historic preservation textbooks (e.g., Stipe 2003; Tyler, Ligibel, and Tyler 2009; Stipe and Lee 1987) have a chapter or at least a section dedicated to historic preservation as implemented by local governments. Some textbooks, such as Page and Mason (2004), even focus so exclusively on city historic preservation efforts as to imply that cities are both the heart and soul of American historic preservation. This is a narrow view based on a myopic vision of historic preservation as being mostly about historic districts, mostly about buildings, mostly about urban areas, and mostly not involving archaeology. It also ignores the fact that the main source of money, guidance, incentives, and preservation activity is the federal government.

There is no doubt that city governments have played and continue to play a critical role in heritage preservation. As noted in the introduction to this chapter, successful early-twentieth-century city historic preservation efforts in Charleston and New Orleans laid the foundations for modern urban historic preservation efforts. Late-twentieth-century court cases in New York and Philadelphia confirmed that historic preservation serves a valid public purpose and is within the constitutional scope of a local government.

Prior to the passage of the NHPA in 1966, city historic preservation efforts were largely isolated and reactive to localized threats. Threats to major historic and character-defining areas of particular cities led to the establishment of historic districts and preservation commissions, while threats to major individual buildings led to landmark designations and landmark commissions. These reactions by cities were not part of any federal government historic preservation initiative and, for the most part, were in response to private development.

Widespread and intensive federally initiated threats to city historic properties began after World War II. Interstate highways were cutting wide corridors through urban centers, and federal urban housing/urban renewal programs encouraged the destruction of entire neighborhoods. In 1966, the urban world of historic preservation changed radically with the passage of the National Historic Preservation Act, Section 4(f) of the Department of Transportation Act, and the Demonstration Cities and Metropolitan Development Act (DCMDA). Both of the first two acts required federal development project review, with the NHPA also bringing local historical significance to the forefront and allowing grants to local governments for historic preservation. The DCMDA allowed the Department of Housing and Urban Development (HUD) to provide two-thirds of the cost of historic preservation surveys in cities, though few cities used this provision.

The 1966 federal laws brought about the current carrot-and-stick historic preservation approach used by cities. The stick is made up of federal and state environmental review laws, as well as city historic preservation ordinance restrictions regarding demolitions, alterations, and new construction within designated historic districts. The carrot consists of federal incentive programs of grants and tax credits supporting appropriate historic preservation activities tied to housing and economic development.

While HUD and its urban development and housing predecessors were initially thought of as foes of historic preservation, by 1966 HUD had gotten some preservation religion, even publishing a brochure that year titled *Preserving Historic America*. HUD's preservation zeal faded in 1974 when the Housing and Community Development Act created Community Development Block Grants (CDBG). City redevelopment authorities were given Section 106 responsibilities without much clue as to what those responsibilities entailed. HUD programmatic guidance and oversight of historic preservation implementation was largely eliminated.

The world changed again in 1980, with amendments to the NHPA. As part of the "Reagan Revolution" and the "New Federalism," local governments were given more control over their own federally supported historic preservation programs. Certified local governments were authorized to help guide these efforts. Landowner permission was needed to list a privately owned property in the National Register. Federal funding for the HPF was cut drastically, including grants to cities. On the positive site, the National Trust initiated the Main Street Program in 1980 to promote historic preservation of commercial districts in smaller cities and towns.

HPF funding started to increase in the late 1980s and then flattened out over the last 20 years. It is now shared by more cities, and since 1992 THPOs have competed for funds. There are now almost 2,000 CLGs. Many cities obtained significant funding for historic preservation activities from the 1991 Intermodal Surface Transportation Efficiency Act (ISTEA) and its successors, although transportation-enhancement funding effectively ended in 2012.

Local Laws and Ordinances

It is not uncommon for a person living in a city to be bound by many layers of law and regulation, including those passed by federal, state, regional, county, and municipal governments and even specialized boards. State constitutions give local governments, regional agencies, and some public boards the right to enact their own laws (usually called ordinances) and implement their own regulations (e.g., building codes), so long as they don't contradict state or federal law. These laws and regulations apply only to specific entities and specific actions within their jurisdictional boundaries.

Just as the federal and state governments are given legal authority by their constitutions, county and city governments are given authority by their charters. Charters provide the structure of the local government and a description of its powers. There are two basic types of charters: *general law* and *home rule*. General law charters are more common. They allow local governments to produce ordinances that basically supplement state laws. In Minnesota, the resulting "statutory cities" make up over 90% of the city governments in the state. Home rule charters are more stand-alone instruments, more comprehensive in scope, and have the force of state law within the local government boundary, although they can't contradict state law.

Ordinances are the local legal equivalent to a state statute. Like federal and state laws, ordinances are codified by assembling them into chapters of related subjects (e.g., parks and recreation, health and safety). Ordinances passed early in a city's history may never have been codified and may not appear in current city code books, but some may still have the force of law or provide necessary historical background to understand city development.

Heritage Preservation Commissions and Certified Local Governments

Ordinances for local heritage preservation outline procedures for reviewing local government actions that may harm historic properties (e.g., construction and demolition permits), for developing a local historic property designation register, and for establishing a heritage preservation commission (HPC) to review these effects and direct the designation process. Once an ordinance and an HPC are in place, local governments can apply to the SHPO of their state to become a certified local government eligible for federal HPF grants.

HPCs have been around for almost a century. They were not an invention of the federal government but were instituted as local necessities to preserve the essential character of this country's first cities. Charleston, South Carolina, had an incipient HPC initiated with a published survey of the city's houses in 1917 (Smith and Smith 1917), followed by the formation of the Preservation Society of Charleston in 1920. Eleven years later, Charleston passed an ordinance establishing a Board of Architectural Review and designating a 183-acre historic district. The first formal HPC was established in New Orleans in 1925 to protect the Vieux Carré District, now known as the French Quarter.

Although the National Historic Preservation Act of 1966 recognized the importance of local governments, it recommended no formal historic preservation organization for cities and outlined no procedures to provide federal grants to cities until the 1980 NHPA amendments. These amendments specified that local governments were given the authority to nominate properties to the National Register, were required to receive from SHPOs notification of all NRHP nominations within their boundaries, were provided a process for certifying access to federal funds, and were guaranteed 10% of the HPF allocation to each state.

In Section 201(c)(1) of the NHPA, the 1980 amendments stipulated that one of the requirements for local government grant eligibility certification was the establishment of "an adequate and qualified historic preservation review commission." The other requirements for becoming a CLG, as stated in the 1980 version of the NHPA, were to

- enforce appropriate state or local legislation for the designation and protection of historic properties;
- maintain a system for the survey and inventory of historic properties;
- provide for adequate public participation in the local historic preservation program, including the process of recommending properties for nomination to the National Register;
- satisfactorily perform the responsibilities delegated to it under the NHPA.

Since 1980, states have developed their own manuals for obtaining and maintaining CLG status that provide more detail regarding the NHPA requirements. To obtain CLG status, a local unit of government must first pass a historic preservation ordinance in compliance with the NHPA, the SHPO guidelines, and the state statute authorizing such ordinances. There is considerable guidance available from the NPS, SHPOs, and the NTHP on what model historic preservation ordinances should contain. Most ordinances have five basic elements, according to Miller (2008:9):

1. Establishment of an HPC
2. Procedures and criteria for local designations
3. Procedures and criteria for reviewing impacts to designated properties
4. Considerations for exceptions (e.g., hardship, emergencies)
5. Provisions for enforcement and appeals

The local government must then appoint members to serve on the HPC to carry out the stipulations in the ordinance. The membership of the HPC preferably will include several historic preservation professionals, but in smaller communities this is not possible. In larger cities, there is often a full-time staff person in the local government to coordinate historic preservation activity. It is most important that the HPC have a balanced membership that does not overly represent either development interests, which will give priority to economic development over historic preservation, or historic preservation interests, which will do the opposite.

Once an ordinance is passed and an HPC in place, the SHPO and the NPS can certify the local government. The CLG is then eligible for the federal pass-through grants administered by the SHPO. The first major task of an HPC, which it can do with a grant, is to conduct a historic properties survey within its jurisdictional boundaries. The survey is done by qualified personnel and the results recorded on SHPO-approved inventory forms. Once the survey has been completed, the HPC determines which properties meet its eligibility requirements to become locally designated as historic sites. Once the designated list is in place, the HPC can focus on reviewing the local government actions that may harm historic properties, as well as promoting policies and programs that benefit historic preservation in the community. Most CLGs are required to submit an annual report to the SHPO summarizing their activities.

While most CLGs fairly rapidly survey their jurisdiction for buildings, relatively few undertake comprehensive archaeological surveys. Archaeological surveys not only require specialized professional expertise but are expensive and difficult in urban settings with complex ownership, multiple underground utility lines, limited surface exposure, deep modern fill, and serious logistical implications of having to dig holes in people's yards, city streets, and private parking lots. They can be accomplished more readily in undeveloped areas or during some construction activities. Detailed literature searches, along with land-use histories, can help locate areas with high site potential and high historic interest.

Some cities and even a few counties (e.g., Riverside County in California, Broward County in Florida, Anne Arundel County in Maryland) have a staff archaeologist who reviews development plans and deals with accidental discoveries. City archaeologists are primarily found in eastern cities where Euro-American settlement dates to colonial times (e.g., Boston, New York, Alexandria, St. Augustine) or in western cities with extensive prehistoric remains (e.g., Phoenix). City and county archaeologists are usually in planning departments, as are city HPC staff, although in New York archaeology is part of the Landmarks Preservation Commission.

Cities that have done significant archaeology have found that it complements other historic preservation activities that promote a city's unique character and thus civic pride and tourism. In Minneapolis, the city park board agreed to do a major archaeological survey prior to the construction of a parkway along the Mississippi River through the heart of the original city. Over 100 archaeological sites were documented, and many were extensively explored (Anfinson 1989, 1990). The eventual parkway construction was designed to avoid major important sites, and the route is now lined with ruins and historic markers celebrating and displaying the city's early history. It has become a major tourist attraction.

Incentives for Local Historic Preservation

A city's historic preservation initiatives should move beyond just restricting certain activities in an ordinance to promoting other activities that offer enhanced financial, educational, and inspirational benefits. If you attend a state preservation conference, the featured speaker often talks about incentives rather than restrictions. There are two ways to classify incentives: *benefit type* and *government level*. Benefit types are financial, educational, civic identity, and environmental, while government level can be federal, state, or local. I will classify incentives first by government level and then by benefit type.

Federal Incentives

Federal historic preservation incentives to local governments are mainly financial and come in two forms: tax credits and grants. As discussed in chapter 8, federal tax incentives began in 1976 and were revised in 1979, 1981, and 1986. Their basic purpose is to stimulate private investment in cities while preserving the historic character of those cities. To receive a 20% federal tax credit, a rehabilitated building has to be listed in the National Register of Historic Places, the developer has to follow the *Secretary of the Interior's Guidelines for Restoration*, and the project has to obtain the proper certification from the SHPO and NPS. According to NPS, as of 2016 federal tax incentives have leveraged over $78 billion in private investment to preserve 41,250 historic properties.

Grants come in two basic forms: those designed specifically to promote historic preservation and those aimed at providing housing or neighborhood revitalization. The first kind of federal assistance comes from the HPF in the form of pass-through grants administered by the SHPO. Originally they could be used for a wide range of activities, including historic building acquisition and rehabilitation, but now they can only be used for survey and planning efforts.

The second form of federal grants to cities is from HUD, as discussed in chapter 9. These grants are for the Office of Community Planning and Development, the Federal Housing Administration, and the Office of Public and Indian Housing. This type of incentive was introduced in the Housing Act of 1954 but not extensively utilized for urban historic preservation until passage of the Housing and Redevelopment Act of 1974.

State Incentives

Like federal incentives, state-originated historic preservation incentives in most states are basically financial in nature. The most common state initiative is to offer redevelopment tax credits for commercial properties like the federal tax credit. States usually require use of the same rehabilitation standards as federal projects. One of the major differences is that listing on a state or local historic property register could qualify a property, not requiring listing in the National Register. Some states offer the tax credits to owner-occupied historic properties as well as commercial structures. According to the NTHP, there were 31 states offering a state tax credit in 2017.

States can also offer state appropriation grants to local governments, to historic preservation organizations, or to individual historic properties in cities for historic building preservation, building rehabilitation, or other cultural resource preservation activities. Minnesota currently has what are called legacy grants from a constitutionally created fund appropriated by the legislature and administered by the Minnesota Historical Society. About 1,700 grants exceeding $31 million have been awarded to almost 700 organizations since the grant program was started in 2009. In 2016, grants to local organizations went for the preservation of museum collections (e.g., fire trucks), interpretive exhibits, village hall restorations, historic resources surveys, and National Register nominations.

Florida has a Historic Preservation Grants Program that allocates state funds for the preservation and protection of the state's historic and archaeological properties. The program is administered by the Bureau of Historic Preservation. Eligible entities include state agencies, state universities, nonprofit organizations, units of local government, cities, towns, and counties but not private property owners. Iowa has grants for general operating support for nonprofit arts and culture organizations with budgets under $150,000.

Local Incentives

Beaumont (1991) provides an overview of the various types of local incentives available for historic preservation. These tend to be much more diverse than most federal and state incentives. These incentives include tax breaks, grants, regulatory exclusions, zoning benefits, and technical assistance. Tax breaks at the local level are usually with respect to property taxes, not income taxes. Regulatory exclusions can include exemptions from parking requirements and building codes. Zoning incentives can include the sale of development rights (e.g., air rights) for a historic building owner to use at a different location or exemptions from certain zoning rules for historic structures. Technical assistance can be in the form of architectural and engineering advice or "old house" workshops.

Benefits of Local Historic Preservation

Besides preservation of historic resources just for the sake of heritage preservation, there are numerous other benefits of historic preservation for local governments and local residents. Politicians and the general public are constantly reminded of these benefits by public and private historic preservation organizations. Usually at the top of the list are financial benefits. These include job creation, stabilizing or increasing property values, small business support, investment attraction, improving existing public investments, revitalizing main streets, and increasing tourism.

Next among the commonly cited historic preservation pluses are livability benefits. These include strengthening neighborhoods, improving blighted areas, and creating affordable housing. Restoration of historic buildings makes a city more attractive by fixing up properties and promoting attractive designs for in-fill and adjacent structures. Attractive neighborhoods create and improve civic pride and optimism. Historic properties provide unique educational opportunities.

There are numerous environmental benefits. Building-rehabilitation costs are about the same as for constructing an entirely new structure. This reuses older materials, resulting in less expenditure of energy and raw materials, as well as less demolition debris for landfills. Revitalizing an entire neighborhood reduces urban sprawl, with attendant savings in air pollution, water pollution, traffic congestion, and energy use.

The Private Sector

Almost all historic preservation is privately inspired. Concerned citizens form groups, establish basic principles, and lobby political organizations. Today the regulations and programs that have resulted from that private inspiration, concern, and action are manifested in organizations such as the National Park Service, the Advisory Council on Historic Preservation, SHPOs, and local historic preservation commissions, in laws such as the National Historic Preservation Act and Section 4(f) of the Department of Transportation Act, and in programs such as Save America's Treasures, Main Street, and Preserve America.

Beginning in the mid-nineteenth century and continuing into the mid-twentieth century, private groups provided the leadership and guidance for American historic preservation. Almost every history of historic preservation begins with the story of the Mount Vernon Ladies' Association. Nineteenth-century private groups like the Association for the Preservation of Virginia Antiquities, the Society for the Preservation of New England Antiquities, and the American Institute of Architects took the lead in protecting regional, state, and city historic properties. John D. Rockefeller and Henry Ford initiated substantial private preservation and restoration efforts in the 1920s. It wasn't until the Great Depression of the 1930s that the federal government finally began to exhibit national preservation leadership. Nationwide private historic preservation began after World War II with the founding of the National Trust for Historic Preservation, still the principal national private historic preservation organization.

National Organizations

The National Trust for Historic Preservation

With the onset of rapid development after World War II, it became clear to the NPS, the government leader in historic preservation, and to influential leaders of private preservation organizations that the government alone could not protect, much less acquire, all important American historic sites. Many historic properties were privately owned and were unlikely to be gifted to NPS. Some were isolated in rural locations where historic preservation commissions were not readily established.

In 1948, a historic mansion and eighteenth-century farming complex called Hampton Plantation was threatened by development north of Baltimore. Its proximity to Washington, DC, its largely intact suite of buildings and land, and the fact that the Georgian mansion was one of the earliest and best-preserved examples of that architectural style brought the small preservation community together in an attempt to save it (Lee 1970). Threats to other prominent historic properties also created an atmosphere of urgency; James Monroe's Oak Hill House in Virginia, 1730s Washington Square row houses in New York, and Castle Clinton, an early nineteenth-century fort at the south end of Manhattan Island, are notable examples.

Hosmer (1981) discusses the beginnings of the National Trust for Historic Preservation as the necessary combination of NPS professionalism and private organizations' public support. Ronald Lee, chief historian of the NPS, took the lead in creating a private national historic preservation organization. The first version started in 1947 when a small group of preservationists held several meetings in Washington, DC, and formed the National Council for Historic Sites and Buildings (NCHSB). The group included historians, architects, archaeologists, and planners.

The members of the NCHSB continued to meet and correspond throughout 1948 and 1949. It soon became clear that just a confederacy of existing preservation organizations could not effectively deal with the many preservation crises across the country. A new entity with a professionally staffed central office was needed to bring focus to preservation efforts, effectively raise funds for operating and acquisition costs, and own and manage historic properties. Leaders of the NCHSB looked at England's National Trust as a model. By early 1949, they had the basic framework for an American trust worked out. They also had a full-time executive director with an office in Ford's Theater in Washington, DC.

In order to gain national recognition and eventually the ability to receive federal funds, the NCHSB sought a congressional charter in 1949 for a National Trust for Historic Preservation. Congress passed the legislation in October 1949, and President Harry S. Truman signed it. The charter outlined the mission, authority, and activities of the organization. The NCHSB was soon dissolved, with its membership merging with the NTHP. The National Trust was initially completely reliant on private funding. Its principal initial purpose was to preserve important historic properties by purchasing them.

While the NTHP now had a federally sanctioned organization and a dedicated professional staff, it needed to build a national membership base for financial support and to gain widespread public backing for its efforts. In 1951, the NTHP acquired its first historic property, Woodlawn Plantation near Mount Vernon. In 1952, the organization began publication of a magazine called *Historic Preservation* (later shortened to just *Preservation*).

The NTHP became a major player in American historic preservation with the passage of the National Historic Preservation Act in 1966. Its membership had lobbied hard for the legislation. The 1966 NTHP publication *Historic Preservation Today* had influenced the professional rationale for and support of the NHPA, as much as the publication of *With Heritage So Rich* (Rains and Henderson 1966) the same year had influenced public and political opinion. *Historic Preservation Today* presented papers from a 1963 conference at Williamsburg that had examined international preservation practices and established basic principles for American historic preservation.

The NHPA not only authorized federal funding for the NTHP but officially acknowledged the organization's importance. The declaration of purpose of the NHPA mentioned the vital role the NTHP played in historic preservation. Section 101(a)(3) authorized the secretary of the interior to establish a program of matching grant-in-aid to the NTHP. Section 201 made the director of the NTHP a member of the Advisory Council on Historic Preservation. Funds that went to the NTHP and were given as a grant could then be used for the "maintenance, repair, and administration" of historic properties.

Energized and partially funded by the NHPA, NTHP began to promote its mission and vision for the preservation of historic resources. It started a Preservation Services Fund in 1969 to handle distribution of both its federal and its private grants to local organizations. It opened a field office in San Francisco in 1971, giving a West Coast presence to what had been largely an East Coast organization. In 1973, the National Trust promoted the first national Preservation Week.

The 1976 amendments to the NHPA didn't change anything for the NTHP. In 1977, increasing deterioration of central business districts in small towns led the trust to try three demonstration projects in Hot Springs, South Dakota; Galesburg, Illinois; and Madison, Indiana. These projects were so successful that the NTHP started its Main Street Program in 1980. The same year it started a state demonstration project to promote historic preservation at the state level. In 1988, it initiated its Most Endangered List to highlight critical threats to nationally significant properties. A year later, it began to actively promote heritage tourism.

By the 1990s, the National Trust was firmly entrenched as the private leader of American historic preservation. Its efforts were now guided by the eight Charleston Principles adopted in 1990:

> Principle I: Identify historic places, both architectural and natural, that give the community its special character and that can aid its future well-being.
> Principle II: Adopt the preservation of historic places as a goal of planning for land use, economic development, housing for all income levels, and transportation.
> Principle III: Create organizational, regulatory, and incentive mechanisms to facilitate preservation, and provide the leadership to make them work.
> Principle IV: Develop revitalization strategies that capitalize on the existing value of historic residential and commercial neighborhoods and properties, and provide well-designed affordable housing without displacing existing residents.
> Principle V: Ensure that policies and decisions on community growth and development respect a community's heritage and enhance overall livability.
> Principle VI: Demand excellence in design for new construction and in the stewardship of historic properties and places.

Principle VII: Use a community's heritage to educate citizens of all ages and to build civic pride.

Principle VIII: Recognize the cultural diversity of communities and empower a diverse constituency to acknowledge, identify, and preserve America's cultural and physical resources.

Note that archaeology is not mentioned in these principles. The focus is clearly on urban settings and buildings. Although archaeologists had been included on the original NCHSB, the NTHP drifted away from archaeological concerns, and archaeologists drifted away from the NTHP. You would be hard-pressed to find a symposium focused on archaeological matters at a National Trust annual meeting. Relatively few archaeologists are members of the trust. None of the National Trust–owned properties are recognized as archaeological sites.

In 1998, the NTHP was well enough positioned and funded that it no longer needed to be part of the federal grant process. It voluntarily declined additional federal funds. Today the National Trust provides leadership, training, political advocacy, and legal assistance to help preserve important American historic properties. It has over 300 staff members distributed in 10 offices throughout the United States. The annual budget in 2015 was over $60 million, largely supported by individual and foundation contributions. The quarter-million members only supply about 8% of the operating budget. The trust now owns 27 historic properties, over half of which are in the mid-Atlantic region near or in Washington, DC, or New York City.

The Archaeological Conservancy

While the National Trust for Historic Preservation focuses almost exclusively on buildings and includes some purchase of threatened historic properties, the Archaeological Conservancy focuses exclusively on archaeological sites and buying threatened sites. Since its founding in 1980, the conservancy has purchased over 500 sites. The 10 to 12 staff members operate out of five offices in Albuquerque, New Mexico; Columbus, Ohio; Frederick, Maryland; Marks, Mississippi, and Wheatland, California. In 1997, it began publishing *American Archaeology* magazine. Income from memberships, donations, and educational initiatives brought in about $4 million in 2016.

Preservation Action

Preservation Action is a nonprofit created in 1974 to serve as "a national grassroots lobby for historic preservation." Its small Washington-based staff lobbies the federal government with regard to historic preservation policy and programs such as tax incentives, the Historic Preservation Fund, and review-process streamlining, with the overall purpose of improving the federal historic preservation program. It has 21 state coordinators who work for a variety of other organizations, including the National Trust, state preservation offices, and educational institutions. Their efforts are mainly focused on historic buildings.

State Organizations

Almost every state has a private organization to provide leadership, advocacy, and monitoring of historic preservation issues in its state without being part of state government. For example, the Preservation Alliance of Minnesota (PAM) was founded in 1981. Its mission is to "lead and inspire people to connect with historic places, promoting community vitality." PAM is the only preservation-based nonprofit in Minnesota, with offices located in St. Paul and Granite Falls. It works closely with the SHPO, the Minnesota Historical Society, and the National Trust for Historic

Preservation. PAM has a full-time executive director and a number of other staff members.

Local and Context-Specific Private Organizations

Some cities have private organizations dedicated to preserving the local historic fabric. Examples are the Floral City Heritage Council in Florida and the Historic Kansas City Foundation. Some of these organizations mainly focus on running a local museum. In addition, an almost uncountable number of private organizations advocate for a particular type of cultural resource or one particular historic property. Some examples are City Lore for the preservation of New York urban folk culture, the Canal Society of New Jersey, the American Truck Historical Society, and the Fort Delaware Society.

Summary

Most heritage preservation begins and ends at the local level. Off federal property, it is what citizens value that receives enough attention to be considered worthy of preservation by organizations. Even if federal laws and assistance are important in identifying and initially preserving a building or archaeological site, once environmental review attention fades, threats to the properties will continue, and most of these threats will not be subject to further environmental review. The implications of cumulative effects are usually poorly analyzed in the environmental review process, and long-term neglect is not usually subject to review. Individual vigilance at the local level is usually what leads to long-term preservation.

If community action is the first line of defense for nonfederal heritage preservation, state historic preservation offices are the second line. While initially reliant on federal financial support and guidance, SHPOs are becoming increasingly self-reliant in conducting their operations, and their roles have expanded beyond the duties outlined in the National Historic Preservation Act. Most SHPOs are designated the key players in state environmental protection and heritage preservation legislation.

In most states, the third line of defense lies with entities defined by state statutes, created to fill gaps in addressing public preservation needs. State archaeologists and state historical societies are the most widespread of these entities. Many states enacted laws that attempted to protect archaeological sites long before general historic preservation legislation. Like the federal Antiquities Act of 1906, many of these early state laws focused on protecting public sites by requiring state oversight of excavations and state ownership of artifacts. Today, state archaeologists play a vital role in archaeological education and research, as well as the protection of historic burial sites on private and nonfederal public land. State historical societies and other statewide historic preservation organizations are active in most states, preserving individual historic sites, promoting state legislation (e.g., state tax incentives), and assisting communities.

The final line of defense for heritage preservation is once again local, but in formal organizations rather than individual action. City historic preservation commissions keep an eye on developments in their communities that could harm important resources, and they constantly add to their inventories of known historic properties. Most HPCs tend to focus on just buildings or assemblages of buildings called districts in their communities, but urban archaeology is becoming more prevalent and worthier of consideration by HPCs.

Review Questions

1. What kinds of laws have states passed to promote heritage preservation?
2. What duties are SHPOs given by the NHPA?
3. What is the HPF, and how does it work?
4. What do state archaeologists do?
5. What are HPCs and CLGs?
6. How does the NTHP support heritage preservation?

Supplemental Reading

For early overviews of state heritage preservation legislation and initiatives, see McGimsey (1972) and Wilson and Winkler (1971). For a somewhat more recent overview of state perspectives, see Lyon (1987) and Carnett (1995). Most state archaeologists and SHPOs have extensive information pertinent to their state's heritage preservation laws and programs on their webpages.

For overviews of historic preservation at the local level, see Beaumont (1991) and Cofrise and Radtke (2003). The National Trust for Historic Preservation has numerous discussions and publications about local historic preservation, although you have to be a member to get access to some of these. Cities with active HPCs usually provide information about local ordinances and initiatives on their webpages. SHPOs also have information about their state's CLGs.

SIDEBAR

Implementing Heritage Management: States' Rights (and Wrongs)

As a state archaeologist, I was constantly thinking about the problems with and inadequacies of Minnesota's heritage preservation legislation. The Minnesota Field Archaeology Act had been passed in 1963, with only minor changes since. The legislative intent emphasized state regulation of doing "archaeology" on nonfederal public property. This meant regulating not only pothunters but professional archaeologists. The unstated purpose was to protect "state sites." The law established the Office of the State Archaeologist, required state-issued licenses to do archaeological work on nonfederal public land, asserted state ownership of all artifacts from these lands, provided some basic procedures for review of developments on these lands, and established penalties for violations of the act.

Minnesota passed a separate Historic Sites Act in 1965. This law described official historic sites to be managed by the Minnesota Historical Society, established a state register of historic places, and defined obligations of state agencies for protecting

historic sites listed in the state or federal registers. There was no provision for consideration of eligible sites. It is notable that both of Minnesota's heritage preservation laws were passed prior to the National Historic Preservation Act of 1966.

While I frequently considered what I thought were necessary changes to these two laws, in my 10 years as state archaeologist I never went to the legislature to try to change them. I did initiate some changes in the state burial law, but they were of a more logistical than substantive nature. Each legislative session, either I was too busy or my parent agency wouldn't allow me to make an amendment effort for the broader laws. Coordination with stakeholders is complicated, and the legislature was too focused on fighting about the state budget.

As to what should be in a state heritage preservation law, some general advice: First, state heritage management laws should attempt to follow the intent, definitions, and basic procedures of the NHPA. This reduces confusion and promotes understanding. That said, a full Section 106 or Section 110 process will not be possible to enact and implement in most states. Second, as with the NHPA, I think all types of historic properties should be included in one statute, unlike in Minnesota, where historic sites and archaeological sites are the subject of two different statutes. Almost all historic sites are also archaeological sites, both can be listed in the state register, and environmental review has to consider both, so why not combine them in one statute. Third, don't include duplications of federal law, such as listing SHPO duties and federal definitions. Fourth, stick to the protection of tangible resources. Don't include consideration of sacred sites as it involves First Amendment issues and is too complicated and fraught with emotion. Sacred sites are indeed important, but any consideration of them will probably become the focus of public, agency, and legislative turmoil, threatening the passage of the entire bill. Let them be addressed in another form of legislation. Finally, include some consideration of ancient burial sites as they are archaeological sites regardless of whether archaeologists can excavate them. Leave most of the details of their protection and treatment to state burial statutes. As with sacred sites, burial site protection and consideration can get very complicated and very emotional.

When it comes to the actual details of state heritage preservation legislation, here are some of my observations as to what should be included:

Policy: Like all well-crafted legislation, a state heritage preservation law should begin with a statement of legislative intent. This intent should be focused on heritage preservation and the reasons for it. Intent is important for judicial interpretation.

Definitions: Good definitions are critical to implementation. One of the reasons I pushed for the amendment of Minnesota's burial law was that state law contained no definition anywhere of what a burial was. If you use terms from the NHPA or 36 CFR 800, you can just refer to them rather than repeating them, unless their state usage differs

significantly. Definitions to include are "agency" (state or all public?), "archaeological site" (what's included, how old?), "archaeology" (what needs regulation?), "artifact" (how old, any exclusions?), "consideration" (if different from federal), "consult" (if different from federal), "historic property" (if different from federal), "qualified professional" (include archaeologist, historian, preservation architect), "protect" (does it mean preserve?), "significant" (what determines that a historic property is worthy of protection or consideration?), "treatment" (more than architectural?), and "undertaking" (if different from federal).

Office of the State Archaeologist: I think every state should have a designated state archaeologist even if that person is in a SHPO. SHPOs are principally defined by federal law. List the duties and responsibilities of the state archaeologist and an office location.

Permit/license: This is usually limited to nonfederal public land, although some states (e.g., North Dakota) also require one on private land. Does it include only archaeology? Will it be issued yearly or by project?

Review of undertakings: What kinds of undertakings need review: on public land, with public money, and with public permits? What is the process? If subject to federal Section 106, does it also need state review? Include the need for consultation and with whom. Provide state agencies and local governments with tools so they can do preliminary reviews (e.g., access to databases).

Private lands protection: Private lands are subject to limited government authority under the Constitution, but some attempt should be made to protect these historic properties. In most states this is limited to burials or public actions. Easements or tax deductions could be considered.

State register: This is generally needed only if consideration of eligible properties is required for environmental review and state register eligibility criteria differ from federal law. It can also be included if a state honor roll is deemed desirable.

CHAPTER 11

Among the Professionals
Archaeology

Archaeology is the only branch of anthropology where we kill our informants
in the process of studying them.

—Kent Flannery (1982:275)

Archaeology is the study of the past through the analysis of material culture. For
understanding the prehistoric past, archaeological methods are supplemented with
ethnographic analogy (looking at the recent past to see how known people behaved
in similar settings with similar technologies) and environmental reconstruction (suggesting behavioral possibilities based on climate and biota and noncultural reasons for
behavioral change). Archaeological study of the historical past is assisted with examination of written records and even oral accounts for the more recent past. Archaeologists
do not have to dig to find remnants of material culture. Some of these remnants are
still clearly visible and conveniently accessible as structures, machines, and collections.

Most archaeologists become archaeologists because they want to study the past.
These days, most archaeologists are cultural resource management (CRM) professionals who occasionally get to study the past as part of their jobs in government
agencies or at contracting firms. Most of the time, CRM archaeologists study the
present, assessing how preserving parts of the past fits into it and planning for how
these pieces will fit into the future.

This chapter presents a brief history of American archaeology, stressing how
methodological changes in the mid-twentieth century positioned archaeologists to
play a key role in modern heritage management. It then looks at how archaeology
is practiced in heritage management, discussing the terminology, standard procedures, and objectives of the various CRM phases responding to staged environmental review needs. As noted in the preface, this discussion should benefit not only
archaeological students and practitioners but other heritage management professionals by familiarizing them with the intellectual roots, language, and procedures
of CRM archaeology to improve interdisciplinary understanding and promote multidisciplinary cooperation.

A Brief History of Heritage Management Archaeology
The Beginnings of American Archaeology

American archaeology is different from other Western archaeologies in its intellectual origins and theoretical basis. European archaeology, because of its initial

focus on early Mediterranean civilizations that had a written history, is part of the academic tree of history. Because early cultures in North America didn't have a written language, American archaeology grew from an anthropological base and is still rooted in that base. Early American anthropologists almost exclusively studied Native Americans, so their archaeological understudies did the same.

Professional American archaeologists were not only anthropologists but also scientists more than humanists. Their anthropological roots were grafted onto the scientific method. Thomas Jefferson undertook one of the first scientific archaeological excavations in America. His 1784 excavation of a burial mound on his property in Virginia not only used careful methods but also resulted in a 1785 publication of his results. Rigorous methods and public presentation of results are two of the key elements of doing science.

The earliest intensive explorations of America's distant past were not archaeological because they were not scientific or professional. Beginning with the founding of the American Antiquarian Society in 1812, examination of the Indian past was the realm of antiquarians—people curious about the past but not seeking or trained to truly understand it in a comprehensive manner. These antiquarians tended to be well educated and well-off. Most dug to find things, not explain things. American archaeology for most of the nineteenth century was a hobby, not a job or a profession.

The focus of antiquarian endeavors was trying to determine who built the thousands of burial mounds found throughout most of the eastern United States. Because ethnographically known Indian tribes did not build mounds and didn't use the more elaborate artifacts found within, it was assumed that a lost, non-Indian race had built them. So began the myth of the Mound Builders, mostly focused on murky Old World origins of lost tribes and peoples. Antiquarian interest in the Mound Builders increased as white settlement pushed west of the Appalachians,

FIG. 11.1 Grave Creek Mound in West Virginia, one of the largest burial mounds in North America (author photo).

encountering the large and relatively rich mounds of the Hopewell complex centered on Ohio (Figure 11.1). The best of the antiquarians did document their finds. One of the more notable examples is *Ancient Monuments of the Mississippi Valley* by Ephraim Squier and Edwin Davis published in 1848.

Things began to change for archaeology in the second half the nineteenth century. At the same time that Squier and Davis were exploring mounds in Ohio and Kentucky, researchers in Denmark were beginning to make a closer, more scientific examination of early cultures in northern Europe. Christian Thomsen defined a three-part chronological organization scheme for premedieval cultures: a Stone Age, followed by a Bronze Age, followed by an Iron Age. His work was translated into English in 1848. Thomsen's student, Jens Worsaae, began careful excavations in Denmark in an attempt to answer specific research questions, keeping track of the positions in which artifacts were found in relation to other artifacts at the same site (Worsaae 1843).

The Smithsonian Institution in Washington opened in 1855 and the Peabody Museum at Harvard in 1866, providing institutional bases for American archaeology. In 1879, the Smithsonian started its Bureau of American Ethnology (BAE), and the Anthropological Society of Washington and the Archaeological Institute of America (AIA), professional organizations focused on the scientific study of the past here and abroad, were founded.

There were still no professional archaeologists, however. Professionals are individuals who are educated as archaeologists and pursue archaeology as a full-time career. Some employees of the Smithsonian's BAE (William Holmes, Cyrus Thomas) and Harvard's Peabody Museum (Frederick Putnam) were incipient professionals, laying the methodological foundation. Cyrus Thomas's *Report on the Mound Explorations of the Bureau of Ethnology*, published in 1894, finally dispelled the myth of the Mound Builders by demonstrating that the mounds had been built by the ancestors of modern American Indians. True archaeological professionalism finally appeared at the same time the Mound Builders myth was put to rest. Harvard University issued its first PhD in archaeology in 1894.

Federal government protection of archaeological sites began about the same time archaeology became a profession. Congress passed an act to preserve the Casa Grande ruins in Arizona in 1889, followed by an executive order in 1892 providing additional protection for Casa Grande (Figure 11.2). In 1906, the Antiquities Act was passed, requiring some protection of archaeological sites on federal property and empowering the president to declare national monuments at places of "historic or scientific interest" on lands already owned by the federal government. Of the first 10 national monuments, half were archaeological: El Morro (1906), Montezuma Castle (1907), Chaco Canyon (1907), Gila Cliff Dwellings (1907), and Tonto (1907). All of these monuments were prehistoric sites, but all focused on architectural ruins.

Employment opportunities were very limited for professional archaeologists in the early twentieth century. Most were at a few academic institutions (e.g., Harvard, University of Chicago) or at large museums (e.g., Smithsonian, American Museum of Natural History). The National Park Service (NPS) hired its first archaeologist in 1921 at Mesa Verde. In 1930 the NPS undertook archaeological excavations at Wakefield, George Washington's birthplace in Virginia.

When the Depression-era work programs kicked-in in 1933, federal archaeology blossomed. Soon widespread excavations were being undertaken by the Civil Works Administration (CWA), Civilian Conservation Corps (CCC), and Works Progress Administration (WPA). There was so much federal work that the NPS needed a full-time archaeological supervisor. The position of departmental

FIG. 11.2 The Casa Grande ruins in Arizona circa 1890 (National Park Service).

consulting archaeologist (DCA) was established in 1933 at NPS. There was also a need for a professional organization, so the Society for American Archaeology (SAA) was founded in 1934.

Most of the Depression-era archaeology was funded more for employment than for science. This led to rapid excavation of major archaeological sites with limited attention paid to careful field methods, detailed analysis, and published reports. In 1939 the Committee on Basic Needs of Archaeology of the National Research Council (NRC) reviewed the work done by the federal relief agencies and recommended minimal professional requirements for future federal archaeology. It also recommended that preservation of archaeological sites be considered along with excavation and that oversight of federal archaeology be vested with the National Park Service.

Federal relief archaeology ended with the onset of World War II. The employment of federal archaeologists went from hundreds to just a few at NPS and the Smithsonian Institution. Four years later, with the end of the war in sight, another federal initiative began to concern professional archaeologists. The plans for massive hydroelectric projects on the Missouri and Columbia Rivers, proposed just prior to the start of the war, were revived. At the 1944 annual meeting of the SAA, Frank Roberts and Julian Steward of the Smithsonian raised concerns about impacts to archaeological sites by reservoir inundation.

The resulting Committee for the Recovery of Archaeological Remains (CRAR) was formed in May 1945 just as the war in Europe ended. Six months later, with Japan defeated and the large dam projects set to begin, the Corps of Engineers (COE) and the Bureau of Reclamation (BOR) signed an interagency agreement with the Smithsonian Institution and the NPS. The agreement put the Smithsonian in overall charge of archaeological research, but the NPS was responsible for obtaining necessary funding and contracting for the archaeological work. The result was the River Basin Surveys (RBS). Over the next 25 years, RBS teams conducted archaeological survey, testing, and salvage in over half the states on hundreds of reservoir projects, large and small (Figure 11.3). Funding for RBS was improved by the passage of the Reservoir Salvage Act in 1960.

FIG. 11.3 Excavated prehistoric house floor at the Medicine Crow (39BF2) site in South Dakota, excavated by the River Basin Surveys program (NPS Midwest Archaeological Center).

Archaeology and Historic Preservation

Just as the River Basin Surveys began to wind down, a broader and more proactive federal heritage management approach began to wind up. At the time, this was commonly known as historic preservation. The passage of the National Historic Preservation Act in 1966 initially didn't have much of an effect on federal employment of historic preservation professionals, as no one really understood the implications until after Section 106 regulations were in place in 1968 and Executive Order 11593 was issued in 1971.

In the early 1970s, three archaeologists under federal contract first explained the new federal review requirements to federal agencies. This began a Section 106 focus on archaeological aspects (King 2013:21–22). It also began turning what had been a friendly divide between archaeologists and other heritage management professionals into a more formal one.

The divide between archaeologists and historic preservationists (i.e., historians, architects) widened after World War II. The first big recognized threat to historic properties was reservoir construction in rural areas, so that is where archaeologists focused their attention. The next big threat was to buildings in cities due to urban renewal and interstate highway construction, so that is where historic preservationists concentrated their activity. Archaeologists also tended to focus on individual sites, while historic preservationists in cities relied on the tried-and-true district approach. We lived and worked in different worlds.

While historians and architects had taken the lead in historic preservation and have retained it in the private sector and in communities, archaeologists gradually took the lead in federal cultural heritage management and have, to a large degree, retained it. This had not been due to aggression on the part of the archaeologists. Archaeology, with its jargon and rural isolation, was largely invisible to the public, while urban historic preservation was very visible and very reliant on public support. Archaeology had not been treated equally when the National Historic Preservation Act (NHPA) was passed in 1966, but that was largely due to archaeological inattention. Archaeologists were simply in the right place at the right time with the right tools when federal environmental review began to take effect in the 1970s.

The River Basin Surveys of the 1950s and 1960s necessarily tipped the federal funding and employment balance in favor of archaeologists. This wasn't at the expense of historians or preservation architects, who retained a steady level of federal employment. It did, however, support the expansion and entrenchment of a major archaeological presence in the federal government. This was enhanced by archaeological dominance of the early and continued application of Section 106, where history-architecture properties are more obvious and thus more easily taken into account in the planning process for federal undertakings. It is also generally much cheaper to do history-architecture surveys and mitigations compared to archaeological ones. Among historic preservation historians and architects, the new archaeological dominance of the federal preservation structure became known as "the archaeology problem."

A New Archaeology and Cultural Resource Management

Federal environmental review needs were not the only reason archaeologists came to dominate federal heritage management. They were methodologically better positioned. Beginning in the 1960s, a long-anticipated revolution swept through American archaeology. Walter Taylor had attempted to start the revolution with the publication in 1948 of *A Study in Archaeology*. Taylor said American archaeology was not being true to its anthropological and scientific roots. But throughout the 1950s, few listened. The country was too focused on getting over World War II, and archaeologists were too focused on salvaging sites in the rapidly filling reservoirs.

As the Vietnam War began to flare and a mood of social unrest swept the country in the early 1960s, archaeologist Lewis Binford attempted to rekindle Taylor's revolutionary fire with the 1962 publication of his article "Archaeology as Anthropology." Binford stressed the need for archaeology to transcend merely describing artifacts and developing cultural-historical frameworks. Archaeology needed to put material culture back into its societal framework by attempting to explain cultural processes and the reasons for cultural change. In order to do this, archaeologists had to use a more systematic method and a more overtly scientific approach, utilizing more sophisticated field (e.g., sampling on a regional scale) and analytical (e.g., statistics) techniques. The "new" archaeology was soon referred to as *processual archaeology* for its emphasis on examining cultural processes.

Binford's "revolutionary" approach not only found a ready audience among students of archaeology but could be applied with emerging revolutionary methods. Radiocarbon dating, first introduced in 1949, was finally becoming readily available to archaeologists by the early 1960s. Sophisticated statistics were more easily applied using computers commonly available in universities by the mid-1950s. Flotation recovery employed at excavations beginning in 1962 retained seeds and charcoal, allowing botanical analysis to complement faunal analysis. **Historical archaeology** began to develop as a discrete subfield with formal training and specialized methods, allowing a text-supplemented and text-formulated examination of human behavior and societal change. Palynological analysis of sediment cores from lakes allowed detailed and datable regional environmental reconstructions.

The "new archaeology" emerged just as federal agencies needed a new type of employee: cultural resource managers. The emphasis on formal research designs for archaeological projects to explicitly examine processes stressed a need for planning and a need for a systematic approach. The emphasis on regional studies in archaeology looked beyond individual communities and emphasized the need for broad historic and geographical perspectives to evaluate significance. The anthropological perspective looked beyond just structures and sites to include less tangible aspects of cultural heritage that were inferred by the National Environmental Policy Act (NEPA). NEPA fostered interdisciplinary cooperation, as did processual archaeology.

Comprehensive planning was essential for effective management, and the "new archaeology" had planning at its core. In 1974, archaeologists had even come up with a new term for their participation in historic preservation: cultural resource management. Embedded in the new term was a broader perspective on what was worthy of preservation, certainly much broader than what was inferred and practiced by historic preservation. CRM was probably a bit too broad a term in practical application, so it soon came to be focused on just archaeological sites.

The forced marriage of archaeology and historic preservation had a rocky start, as noted in King (1987). Archaeology had greatly expanded in the 1950s and 1960s with the salvaging of data from archaeological sites, while historic preservation emphasized actual preservation of properties. Historic preservation was dominated by a historically based perspective emphasizing the documented events, people, and relationships of one American society, while the "new" archaeology had an anthropological perspective that was largely focused on multiple societies and a prehistoric past lacking firm dates and famous people.

As CRM (archaeology) diverged from historic preservation (history-architecture) in the 1970s, CRM archaeologists also began to diverge from academic archaeologists. Because the 1950s reservoirs were planned with large lead times, reservoir salvage archaeologists could be based at universities and museums, where a summer-only field season fit well with their teaching schedules. The restricted field season didn't work well for most federal undertakings covered by Section 106 and NEPA, where rapid and year-round field responses were often required. Private consulting firms began to emerge to provide timely and focused archaeological services.

Many academic archaeologists were immediately suspicious of for-profit archaeology, contending it was being done by less qualified individuals who were more responsive to the needs of their employers and development interests than the needs of their profession. But some of Binford's disciples adapted their research-oriented methodology to doing CRM archaeology (King, Hickman, and Berg 1977:28). They did their CRM surveys and excavations according to explicit research designs that considered expected results (hypotheses), clear objectives, and appropriately focused methods. They used regionally oriented approaches where possible to place individual sites into larger contexts, both culturally (i.e., phases and traditions) and organizationally (i.e., settlement systems). They considered all types of sites to have archaeological value, not just large villages. They applied sophisticated, interdisciplinary analytical methods. The inclusions of broad research objectives and the use of scientific rigor by CRM archaeologists somewhat dampened academic criticism, but there remained a good deal of disdain among many ivory tower archaeologists for their private contracting and agency cousins.

Another academically based reaction was for CRM archaeology to adopt and adapt a basic historic preservation philosophy. This was promoted as *conservation archaeology*. But it was an overreaction with respect to understanding the extent of the threat to archaeological sites. William Lipe (1974:20) considered all archaeological sites to be threatened and thought salvage archaeology was an archaeology of last resort: "If our field is to last beyond a few more decades, we need to shift to resource conservation as a primary model." Lipe also called for public education to stress the societal value of archaeology, for archaeologists to get involved in planning at all levels, and for the establishment of archaeological preserves.

Over 40 years after Lipe's and other conservation archaeologists' call to arms, most sites in the country are still preserved, although there remains a concern about the finite nature of archaeological resources (e.g., Surovell et al. 2017). Most of us still agree that salvage should be a last resort and that planning, education, and formal preservation of some sites are all key components of successful CRM archaeology, but in order for American archaeology to remain viable and vital, a robust excavation program must remain. Not all sites can be avoided.

The gap between CRM archaeologists and their historic preservation cousins in history and architecture still remains quite broad. Most historic preservation textbooks fail to even mention archaeology, or at least fail to give archaeology equal billing with architectural preservation. You will rarely hear an archaeological presentation at a National Trust conference and rarely see a historian or an architect at an archaeological conference. There is still a huge gap between the amount of federal money and number of employees dedicated to archaeology as opposed to history and architecture. But I think everyone has come to understand the federal pie is divided by professional need, not professional greed. Archaeology's financial demands are simply greater to accomplish the same basic consideration and preservation objectives.

Much of our failure to interact is due to the fact that we each mostly go down one-way streets to practice our heritage preservation professions. Archaeologists focus on federal agency actions that implement federal environmental review processes (e.g., Section 106), while preservation architects and historians tend to focus on local and private incentives (e.g., tax credits, grants). Archaeological activity is still mostly rural and concerned with single sites, while architectural preservation is mostly urban and focused on districts. Archaeologists still call it cultural resource management, while it is still historic preservation to architects and historians.

King (1987:239) also notes personality differences between archaeologists and historians/architects that may inhibit close interaction. Archaeologists tend to have more rugged and rough-edged personas, probably due to a greater reliance on having to do extensive remote fieldwork, often getting dirty. We tend to favor jeans and khaki shirts even in the office, while architects and historians like slacks and dress shirts. Even when archaeologists do dress up, you rarely see one wearing a tie, much less a bowtie. We drink beer and coffee, they drink wine and tea.

The "New" Historical Archaeology

The "new archaeology" sweeping the country in the 1960s and 1970s focused primarily on prehistoric cultures, the people we could only really know through archaeology. Exploration of sites associated with "historical" people had been done in North America in a very limited way since the 1850s, but it greatly expanded with the federal government programs of the 1930s. This early historical archaeology focused on nationally famous people and nationally important events: Washington's birthplace, the Jamestown settlement, and Colonial Williamsburg. It also concerned itself mostly with early Euro-American history: those people and events associated with the country's initial white settlement, early wars, and frontier expansion. A primary purpose of this archaeology was to help with architectural reconstruction at colonial sites.

Most nonreconstruction historical archaeology in the first half of the twentieth century proceeded in a less purposeful fashion. Historic sites were dug by people trained in prehistoric archaeology. Historical archaeology was considered as a supplement to the written record. Things began to change in the early 1960s. The first Conference on Historic Sites Archaeology was held in Florida in 1960. Three years later, a session at the Society for American Archaeology annual meeting was titled "The Meaning of Historic Sites Archaeology." Lew Binford was one of the panelists. Bernard Fontana chaired the session and later wrote up some of its results (Fontana 1965).

At the Central States Meeting of the American Anthropological Association in 1965, historical archaeologists decided to form their own organization. The Society for Historical Archaeology (SHA) was founded in 1967, publishing the first issue of its journal, *Historical Archaeology*, that same year. Its first articles focused on early American sites and artifacts, but a few articles hinted at what was soon to come: "Post-1800 Historic Indian Sites" by Roderick Sprague, "Post-1800 Mining Camps" by Franklin Fenenga, and "The Archaeology of Post–18th Century Ranches in the United States" by Bernard Fontana. The use of "post" seems almost like an apology for looking at anything younger than 1800 or at least a qualifier indicating an aberrant topic for historical archaeology.

In order to better define the scope of research and escape being thought of as just a supplement to history, the archaeologists of historical sites, now that they had their own society and their own journal, implemented two additional important changes in the 1960s. Robert Schuyler discussed both in his 1970 article "Historical and Historic Sites Archaeology as Anthropology: Basic Definitions and Relationships." He, first of all, clarified why the practice should be called "historical" archaeology; "historic" inferred "important," while historical referred to the time period being studied.

Second, Schuyler stressed that historical archaeology must move beyond just correcting historians' errors, confirming their conclusions, or filling in gaps in the written record. Historical archaeologists must do like their "new" prehistoric archaeologist brothers and sisters by investigating aspects of the past often not well documented in writing, such as basic economic and social aspects of cultures in the historic period. Schuyler's call for an anthropological perspective was taken up by Binford's undergraduate classmate Stanley South in his influential 1977 publication *Method and Theory in Historical Archaeology*.

By the 1970s, historical archaeology had moved away from studying famous men and events to a focus on "the undocumented" (Orser 2017:41). The most obvious example of this illustrated by Orser (2017:44) is a study of the slave quarters on a southern plantation rather than the manor house. While earlier definitions of historical archaeology had focused on sites belonging to a vaguely defined period when places and people were partially documented by texts, historical archaeology now focuses on investigating the "modern" past. This is the past of the last 500 years when great societal changes were worldwide in scope due to global exploration, large-scale urbanization, industrialization, the spread of capitalism, widespread literacy, and colonialism (Orser 2017:14). This refinement led to the growth of subfields of historical archaeology such as industrial archaeology (the Society for Industrial Archaeology was founded in 1971) and urban archaeology (e.g., Dickens 1978).

New Methods and New Technology

Not only did the theory and methodological approaches change greatly in the second half of the twentieth century, but so did basic field and analysis methods. The archaeological techniques and technology I used for my first CRM job in 1975 are very different from today's standard practices. Beyond historical interest, understanding the evolution of methods helps explain and evaluate the adequacy of archaeology done in the past. Past surveys may not meet today's standards for site identification, past recovery techniques may have missed important artifacts classes that could influence significance evaluation, and past analysis may have limited the research questions asked and addressed.

Field Methods

We excavate sites today much as we did 50 years ago at the beginning of comprehensive CRM. We slowly dig square units with careful vertical and horizontal control, utilizing shovels, trowels, and whisk brooms. We screen the dirt, save all the artifacts, and carefully document our progress.

Just prior to the flowering of CRM archaeology in the late twentieth century, most sites were excavated differently, and many were not found due to inadequate discovery methods. To be more scientific, we moved from English measurements to the metric system. I dug my first test unit in 1971 as a 5-foot square in 3-inch levels. Five years later, I was using 1-meter squares and 10-centimeter levels. Screening the soil from excavation units did not happen routinely prior to 1960; soil from excavation units was removed slowly by troweling or shovel skimming.

There were multiple reasons for the failure to screen the dirt. First, in the salvage-oriented archaeology of the 1930s to the 1950s, time was of the essence; the project had to be completed during the academically governed summer field season, it needed to get done in a timely manner, and the filling reservoir was soon going to inundate lots of sites. Time was also money, and screening takes more time. Second, the traditional excavation practice was to piece-plot artifacts to record their relative relationships for later analysis. Relying on screening lost the exact nature of the relationship. Finally, archaeological analysis focused on features and large, carefully manufactured artifacts (e.g., projectile points, ceramic rim sherds) with little concern for faunal or botanical remains; it didn't matter if seeds, small animal bones, and lithic debris were not recovered.

All of this changed in the mid-1960s with increasing criticism of salvage archaeology, attention to nonreservoir developments, the availability of year-round contract archaeologists, and the "new archaeology" focusing on the entire scope of past human behavior.

With regard to site discovery, we still find many non-surface-feature sites in places where there is good soil exposure; we walk over the area and scan the surface for artifacts. This is implemented broadly in the western United States, where exposed soils and deep erosional cuts are common. It is implemented selectively in the eastern half of the country, where agricultural practices have exposed a considerable amount of soil, but there are still extensive vegetated areas with poor surface soil exposure. In the late 1970s, we began to find sites in vegetated areas using shovel testing, a simple but innovative technique that relies on excavating regularly spaced, small test units and screening the soil (Figure 11.4).

While shovel testing and surface survey are still the two most common techniques to find previously unrecorded archaeological sites, two other methods became popular in the 1970s for finding certain kinds of sites in special situations: deep testing and remote sensing.

FIG. 11.4 Archaeologist recording information about an excavated shovel test in a new state park in northern Minnesota (Minnesota Department of Natural Resources).

Deep testing: Although all archaeologists were familiar with deeply buried archaeological sites, reconnaissance surveys for the first decade of CRM archaeology relied on methods that mostly looked for near-surface sites. The one notable exception was examining terrace edges where stream cuts or erosion had exposed deeply buried soils. Most archaeologists also assumed their knowledge of soils was sufficient to understand where sites might be located in the soil column and the soil contexts associated with cultural horizons.

This began to change in the mid-1970s, when the word "geomorphology" entered the mainstream archaeological lexicon. I used my first geomorphologist, Julie Stein, in 1976 to help me interpret the soils of a Glacial Lake Agassiz beach ridge at a known archaeological site in northwestern Minnesota (Anfinson, Michlovic, and Stein 1978). I first learned about geomorphologists helping to find deeply buried archaeological sites at a conference I helped organize in 1980 (Bettis and Thompson 1981).

For reconnaissance survey purposes, deep testing and geomorphological assistance may be required if soils with high or moderate potential to contain significant archaeological materials in the project area exist below 1 meter. The assessment of site potential should be based on known deeply buried sites in the project vicinity or landform suitability analysis such as that used by the Minnesota Department of Transportation's (MnDOT) MnModel predictive model (https://www.dot.state.mn.us/mnmodel/about/phase.html). MnDOT also has guidance on deep testing protocols (https://www.dot.state.mn.us/culturalresources/deeptest.html).

Remote sensing: The use of various kinds of electronic remote sensing to define the presence/absence and extent of buried archaeological sites during reconnaissance surveys also became a mainstream technique in the 1970s. I was introduced to it by John Weymouth while at the University of Nebraska in the mid-1970s. Today soil resistivity, magnetometers, and ground penetrating radar (GPR) are commonly used techniques, although care must be taken when interpreting the results. Remote sensing must be used in combination with excavation to verify and better define most results.

Light Detection and Ranging (LiDAR) is one of the newest and most valuable archaeological remote-sensing tools for finding and mapping surface features. These features include burial mounds, fortification ditches, and architectural expressions such as ruins, house depressions, or linear features (e.g., railroad grades). LiDAR can also be used to better topographically characterize an area to help determine in the office what areas need not be subject to survey, such as steep slopes. While archaeologists have long relied on aerial photographs to find, document, and interpret sites, the recent availability of small drone aircraft equipped with digital cameras has made aerial photography more flexible, immediate, and easy to employ.

Improved Data-Recovery Methods

Improved excavation methods have also greatly benefitted site discovery and site interpretation. Stuart Struever of Northwestern University introduced flotation in 1962 to recover charcoal and seeds from archaeological contexts (Struever 1968). This allows for analysis of plant use and provides materials for radiocarbon dating.

Flotation is often used in combination with fine-mesh water screening to recover very small artifacts that would go through a quarter-inch dry screen. Water screening is used to recover small animal bones (e.g., fish) and microdebitage for both site discovery and site analysis. Use of the technique started about 1970, initially for features and then for general excavation. Besides in the recovery of small artifacts, it is also useful in clay-rich soils that don't dry-screen well.

New Analytical Techniques

Dendrochronology had been used as early as 1929 to date late prehistoric Puebloan sites in the American Southwest, but the technique was limited in its geographic and chronological scope. The availability of radiocarbon dating in the 1950s completely revolutionized archaeological chronology. Accelerator mass spectrometry (AMS) dating was introduced in 1977 but not widely used by archaeologists until the mid-1980s. AMS dating produces not only more accurate dates but dates on much smaller samples.

The analysis of plant remains from archaeological sites greatly improved with the introduction of flotation recovery in the early 1960s. The study of ancient plant remains from archaeological sites is called paleoethnobotany. Once the importance of plant foods to prehistoric cultures was demonstrated, some archaeologists began calling them gatherer-hunters instead of hunter-gatherers. We also were able to determine when various domesticated plants became important in various parts of the country. Seeds are also useful for accurate radiocarbon dating; wood charcoal can be from a 200-year-old tree, but a seed is from an annual plant.

Lithic analysis is the study of stone tools and their manufacturing processes. By the early 1960s, American archaeology was moving away from just describing artifacts, determining basic function, or defining historical index types. It began to provide detailed insights into the manufacturing sequence of a stone tool and the reasons for variation within assemblages of the same time period and locality. This opened the potential for deeper and broader insights into past human behavior. By the late 1970s, the study of lithic technology focused on two avenues of research: (1) use-wear analysis to better understand tool function, and (2) the replication of classic tool types (e.g., Folsom points) to better understand the manufacturing process. Finding the original sources of regional raw materials also grew in importance, moving beyond just general categories (e.g., chert, chalcedony) to specific types of stone associated with specific source localities (e.g., Hixton quartzite).

Computers and Software

Most universities began using mainframe computers in the mid-1950s. They became accessible to some university students about a decade later. In 1968, Statistical Package for the Social Sciences (SPSS) software was released, allowing widespread application of advanced statistics promoted by the new archaeologists. I used SPSS applications for my master's thesis in the mid-1970s, tediously punching paper cards for mainframe use.

Personal computers (PCs) became widely available by the early 1980s, with the Apple II introduced in 1977 and the IBM PC in 1981. I had to hire a typist to do the final version of my master's thesis in 1977 and used a typewriter for the drafts of the first two chapters for my PhD dissertation in the late 1970s. I switched to a PC word processor in the early 1980s, over the years moving from WordStar to WordPerfect to MS Word. PC database software was introduced in 1980. I compiled the first database of Minnesota archaeological sites in 1983. Use of desktop publishing software became widespread in the late 1980s. Photoshop 1.0 was introduced in 1990, followed a year later by MS PowerPoint and portable document files (PDF) a year after that, improving digital enhancement and information sharing.

The geographic information system (GIS) revolution for spatial analysis began in the late 1960s will the development of SYMAP software at Harvard University. Mike Michlovic of Moorhead State University used SYMAP to produce a density map of Minnesota burial mounds for an article of mine in the early 1980s (Anfinson 1984). The first version of Esri's ARC/INFO program was released in 1982, allowing widespread GIS accessibility to PC users. I took my first ARC/INFO training in the mid-1990s.

Recording and Communication Advances

Photocopiers were a great boon to archaeological research and data sharing, allowing cheap and easy reproduction of single articles, chapters, and pages from library copies of journals and books. I had library access to wet-process, pay-by-the-page photocopiers during all my university years. Large-batch photocopying was soon available for use for class material or reproducing theses. Photocopiers as introduced by Xerox first became widely available in the 1960s, with improvements in the 1970s featuring a dry process, the use of single-sheet typing paper, and the ability to reproduce color.

Digital cameras began to replace film cameras in the late 1990s. I took my first digital photos in 1999 and my last color slides in 2003. Digital photos could not match the quality of film until very recently, but they greatly reduced costs and greatly improved image sharing. Over the last 10 years, digital cameras in cell phones have made photo taking more portable and photo sharing almost instantaneous. Cell phones became widely used in the early 2000s, with smartphones and iPads appearing about a decade later. Smartphones and iPads are internet connected and have applications that allow texting, GPS, worldwide web browsing, and various forms of digital recording in remote locations.

Total Station electronic surveying devices were first introduced in the early 1970s but were not widely used by archaeologists until the 1980s. I was taught to use an optical transit when mapping the first site I helped excavate in 1971. The biggest pain was tying our excavation grid into the real world. We had to manually link our datum to a bridge corner over a mile away. Tying my highway surveys into the real world was an issue throughout my first CRM job (1975–1990). The public availability of portable, precision GPS by 2000 completely changed locating project areas and field mapping sites.

Perhaps the most significant technological advance for all fields of science and humanities was the introduction of the World Wide Web (WWW) in 1991. I began using email almost immediately after taking my Minnesota State Historic Preservation Office (SHPO) job in 1990, receiving messages from the NPS, the Advisory Council on Historic Preservation (ACHP), and the National Conference of State Historic Preservation Officers (NCSHPO). Internet resources rapidly improved, allowing for quick and comprehensive access to all types of information, including journal articles and government documents. I don't know how I could have written this book without it.

Doing Heritage Management Archaeology
Becoming a Heritage Management Archaeologist

When I was an undergraduate in archaeology/anthropology in the early 1970s, there were no courses, much less degree programs, in heritage management archaeology. For our archaeology degrees in anthropology departments, we took an introductory course in archaeology that provided a world perspective, followed by courses in regional prehistoric archaeology (e.g., North American, Mesoamerican, European), a method and theory class, and perhaps analytical specialties (e.g., ceramics, lithics, faunal analysis). We took a field school one summer where we were taught site excavation and basic artifact recognition and analysis. We had the option to take a few Mediterranean archaeology classes in the classics department and some related courses in the "hard" sciences (e.g., soils, glacial geology).

By the time I got to graduate school for my master's degree in the mid-1970s, my university (Nebraska) still had no focused CRM class. We began to hear the term "CRM" being used, but that was with respect to a possible summer job. The only textbook that touched on the subject was Charles McGimsey's *Public Archaeology* (1972), but it focused mainly on setting up state programs. There was no realization at the time that we needed a specialized education for doing CRM work. We were simply taught the basics that all archaeologists were taught: how to dig a site, how to analyze artifacts, and how to interpret what we found. Completing a thesis was supposed to demonstrate we could do all these things, as well as follow a research design and write an academically acceptable manuscript.

A few universities began to offer classes in CRM archaeology in the early 1970s, although most only featured one specialized class. The first CRM master's degree programs appeared in the mid-1970s. These included programs at the University of Arizona (Woodbury 1973:316), Idaho State and Washington State universities (Peebles 2013:37), and the University of South Carolina (South 2005:290). Of these, only Arizona's CRM master's program survives today.

Many "old" and "new" archaeologists in universities resisted devising CRM specialty graduate programs, although as early as 1974 Raymond Thompson had presented a cogent argument for developing such programs with diverse CRM-focused courses (Thompson 1974:18). Schiffer and Gumerman (1977:13) took the shortsighted academic view that standard archaeology courses should be the only required courses for the education of CRM archaeologists:

> There has been a tendency in some universities to design graduate programs in cultural resource management that seemingly will produce only cogs for bureaucratic machines. The overemphasis in these programs on courses in law

and management is quite alarming. It is already quite clear that most conservation archaeologists either will be doing innovative archaeological research or will be evaluating proposals or reports of such research. If that is the case, then the primary responsibility of training programs must be to insure that cultural resource management students acquire the basic background and skills in archaeological research needed to implement and evaluate efficient, realistic, and sound scientific management studies. Many "real-world skills" can be acquired on the job, but archaeological competence can only be acquired in a university setting.

This view has clearly been proved deficient, as I can attest from my own experience and as demonstrated by this book. I was unprepared for the first CRM job I got after leaving graduate school, although I was well prepared to be a professional archaeologist. My lack of specialized CRM knowledge initially hurt my performance in both the field and the office. I had been taught to excavate sites, not find, evaluate, or preserve them. I had been taught to write for my graduate school peers and instructors, not for my agency employers, project developers, or the public. I knew nothing of heritage management laws, history, or practice.

In CRM I indeed needed many of the archaeological skills I had learned in college: how to develop a research design, how to do a controlled excavation, how to map a site, how to describe and analyze artifacts. I had polished my expository writing skills by taking writing courses in the English Department. My university education gave me the essential ethical and methodological foundation for being an archaeologist, but the book I am writing doesn't dwell on any of my college-learned skills. It is focused on the "real-world skills" I learned "on the job" doing CRM for 40 years and the fine-tuning that only came from teaching classes in CRM in the second half my career.

Overviews of CRM in general archaeological textbooks are almost nonexistent or, when present, are narrowly focused and misinformed. I use the CRM overview in one popular general archaeology textbook as a class exercise: I have my students critique it to see how many important CRM elements are missing or just plain wrong. There are many textbooks specifically on archaeology in CRM (or on CRM in archaeology). The most popular are King (2013), Hardesty and Little (2009), and Neumann, Sanford, and Harry (2010). Most such textbooks are aimed not specifically at university students but at all types of CRM practitioners.

As noted in the preface, competent CRM university programs and the best textbooks should provide the skills and knowledge you need to do a good job beginning on day one of your CRM employment. Doing a great job will only come with experience, additional training, and motivation to improve.

With regard to professional qualifications, most states and agencies focus on just the qualifications necessary for the principal investigator of an archaeological project as regards projects involving public money or public land. Most states rely exclusively on the 1983 *Secretary of the Interior's Standards and Guidelines for Archaeology and Historic Preservation* (SISG). The standards with respect to archaeological principal investigators are as follows:

The minimum professional qualifications in archeology are a graduate degree in archeology, anthropology, or closely related field plus:
1. At least one year of full-time professional experience or equivalent specialized training in archeological research, administration or management;
2. At least four months of supervised field and analytic experience in general North American archeology, and
3. Demonstrated ability to carry research to completion.

In addition to these minimum qualifications, a professional in prehistoric archeology shall have at least one year of full-time professional experience at a supervisory level in the study of archeological resources of the prehistoric period. A professional in historic archeology shall have at least one year of full-time professional experience at a supervisory level in the study of archeological resources of the historic period.

These professional qualification standards reflect an academic bias by requiring an advanced degree, a requirement not found for the other heritage management professions (history, architectural history, or historic architecture). They are also very vague when it comes to the more critical aspect of archaeological experience as it relates to doing competent fieldwork on particular types of projects in particular parts of the country. Furthermore, there are no definitions of critical terms like "supervisory," "closely related field," or "demonstrated."

Under the first SISG category, the one year of full-time professional experience can be in research, administration, or management. What if none of this experience involves fieldwork? In the second category, the four months of supervised experience can be a combination of fieldwork and analysis. What if it is almost all analysis? In the last paragraph, the one year of full-time experience at the supervisory level must be in "the study of archaeological resources." This studying could all be done in the library or in the lab.

The bottom line is that an archaeologist could meet the SISG without knowing much about how to find sites, how to assess their significance and integrity, or how to excavate them. Furthermore, as far as regional experience, the SISG specifies only that it needs to be in North America, suggesting that the archaeology of Maine is not significantly different from that of California.

For Minnesota, the *SHPO Manual for Archaeological Projects in Minnesota* (Anfinson 2001) and the *State Archaeologist's Manual for Archaeological Projects in Minnesota* (Anfinson 2011) require professional qualifications significantly beyond the SISG for the principal investigator. They require specific kinds of archaeological experience for each major phase of archaeological fieldwork: identification survey (Phase 1), evaluation testing (Phase 2), and intensive excavation (Phase 3). All phases require one year's supervisory experience in either prehistoric or historical archaeology, with at least three months of supervisory experience doing field archaeology in the Midwest. Some demonstration of familiarity with midwestern historic period artifacts, features, and contexts is expected, but, especially for field survey, prehistoric experience is essential. They also require specific standards for doing burial authentication and underwater archaeology.

The Minnesota standards provide some critical definitions not in the SISG. "Supervised experience" means work done under the direction of a person meeting the Minnesota basic professional qualification standards. "Demonstrated ability to carry research to completion" means evidence of timely submittal of professional-quality reports and other documents. "Supervisory experience" is comprehensive project supervision, which means providing principal direction for all aspects of an archaeological project, including planning, agency coordination, records search, fieldwork, artifact analysis, and reporting. "Supervisory experience" does not mean simply being a field supervisor, lab supervisor, or crew chief.

In addition to meeting basic professional qualifications, in Minnesota principal investigators for evaluation (Phase 2) surveys must also meet the following qualifications:

4. The applicant must clearly demonstrate familiarity with evaluating the historic contexts expected at the location.

5. The applicant must possess the appropriate regional, topical, and managerial experience to direct, analyze, and report the results of a complex archaeological investigation.
6. The applicant must have demonstrated experience with evaluation criteria of the State (Minnesota) or National Register of Historic Places (NRHP).

In Minnesota, principal investigators for excavations (Phase 3) must also meet the following qualifications:

1. The applicant must have demonstrated experience designing and implementing data-recovery plans.
2. The applicant must clearly demonstrate familiarity with the historic contexts known to exist at the site.
3. The applicant must clearly demonstrate the appropriate regional, topical, and managerial experience to direct, analyze, and report the results of a complex archaeological investigation.

Qualifications for archaeological project personnel other than the principal investigator are not covered in the SISG and most state standards. Most states and agencies expect other project personnel to be qualified to carry out their assigned tasks. The principal investigator is ultimately responsible for ensuring that all personnel are qualified. Requests for proposals (RFPs) or scopes of work will sometimes specify qualifications for necessary specialists. The professional competence of all project personnel is one of the critical components in evaluating proposals submitted in response to RFPs.

Doing an Archaeological Project

Once you have met the professional qualification standards for the state you work in and the agency you are working for, you are ready to begin doing a CRM project. Beyond understanding all the legal requirements and management objectives of the project, doing good archaeology is essential. Preparing for and doing fieldwork, analyzing artifacts, and reporting what you find should sound like the archaeology you learned in college and why you went into the profession in the first place. There is a great deal of variety, however, in what agencies and states consider adequate archaeological work. Many agencies and most states have their own guidelines for doing archaeology, especially with regard to appropriate fieldwork.

There are no national standards for doing archaeological projects, but numerous textbooks have been written on the subject. In my undergraduate days and prior to the flowering of CRM archaeology, Robert Heizer was the big-name fieldwork guy (e.g., Hole and Heizer 1965; Heizer and Graham 1967). His texts focused on the large-scale excavation of late prehistoric villages or multicomponent prehistoric sites with complex stratigraphies and features. There was no mention of CRM and very little discussion of historical archaeology, regional surveys, remote sensing, predictive modeling, or fine-scale recovery. These texts were worldwide in scope. It was a one-method-fits-all archaeology that was strictly university or museum based and done almost exclusively for research purposes.

Tom King (1978) presented one of the first guides for CRM field methods. Today there are many specialized texts for doing just American archaeology, including texts on artifact recovery methods, historical archaeology, underwater archaeology, and regional survey. Some of the newer textbooks even discuss methods used specifically for CRM archaeology (e.g., Burke, Smith, and Zimmerman 2009; Neumann and Sanford 2010; Collins and Molyneaux 2003; Carmichael, Lafferty, and Molyneaux 2003; White and King 2007). For the purposes of CRM archaeology, the only guidelines that matter are those used by the state where you are working and the agencies you must please and those specified in your contract.

Because there are no national standards and guidelines for doing archaeological fieldwork, most states and some agencies have their own survey manuals. State standards and guidelines for archaeological projects may be issued by offices of the state archaeologist (OSAs), state historic preservation offices, or state professional organizations. As discussed in chapter 10, the OSA and SHPO are the same office in about half the states, which makes agency pleasing a more pleasant task.

There is great variation in state terminology and standards for doing fieldwork. The biggest flaw I saw in new out-of-state applicants for work in Minnesota was their unfamiliarity with Minnesota's field standards and terminology. They would simply cite the 1983 federal SISG, seemingly unaware that it provides no field guidance, only vague directions on how to classify types of projects (not following Minnesota's standard archaeological phase designations) and general guidelines on how to prepare a report (not following Minnesota's specified guidelines). Most sections of the SISG are really meant only to guide federal agencies and SHPOs, especially with planning. They are also somewhat outdated, especially with regard to archaeological aspects. The 1983 version is very "new archaeology," reflecting the flavor of the times but also demonstrating the movement's continued survival into "postprocessual" times and beyond.

CRM Archaeological Project Terminology

The SISG defines four basic levels of archaeological projects: *identification, evaluation, documentation/treatment*, and *registration*. Registration means nomination to the National Register of Historic Places or to a state register as discussed in chapter 5, so it will not be discussed here. Furthermore, registration is not a critical activity in day-to-day archaeological heritage management. Identification, evaluation, and documentation/treatment refer to everyday archaeological activities in American heritage management, although they are often called by other names.

The SISG divides identification into *archival research* and *field survey*. It then subdivides field survey into *reconnaissance* and *intensive* categories. The original focus of reconnaissance survey was to help refine historic context development, while intensive survey was intended to determine what historic properties existed within a particular area. Thus reconnaissance was basically for planning purposes, while intensive was basically for environmental review purposes. In this chapter I focus on environmental review.

These very different management objectives of reconnaissance versus intensive surveys infer very different geographical scopes and very different field methods. Reconnaissance surveys as defined in the SISG were meant to characterize a region's historic properties, while intensive surveys were to find and describe all historic properties within a specific area. To characterize a region, a field survey relies on scattered sampling to look at particular settings based on probabilistic modeling or archaeological intuition. Reconnaissance survey field methods tend to emphasize locating large property types found by low-intensity methods like surface walkovers. Regional boundaries are usually generalized and inexact.

To characterize one particular area in an intensive survey, thorough and intensive sampling of the entire area is required. To do this, archaeologists must utilize methods that make a reasonable and good faith effort to identify all potentially significant properties within the tightly defined area. Although it is often stated that adequate intensive surveys must find all archaeological properties within a specified area, this ideal is usually not realistic, because all field surveying relies on sampling and can miss small or unusual sites even when using very rigorous methods.

The SISG evaluation step is less complicated to understand and apply. Evaluation is meant to determine if a property is worthy of consideration in the Section 106 process, if it should be preserved because it is on federal land or may be affected by a federal undertaking, and if it can be federally registered, should registration be required (i.e., grant eligibility) or desired. In other words, is the property being evaluated eligible for inclusion in the National Register of Historic Places?

Documentation and treatment appear in the same section of the SISG. Documentation appears first, although logically the order should be reversed. The purpose of treatment, according to the SISG, is to attempt to preserve or protect eligible or listed historic properties. If preservation is not possible, the purpose of documentation is to retain as much information about affected sites as reasonably possible. For buildings and structures, treatment is generally some form of aggressive architectural intervention classified as rehabilitation, restoration, or reconstruction, and documentation prior to destruction is done by compiling a detailed history and visual record (e.g., sketches, measured drawings, photographs) of the building or structure. Documentation includes reporting at any level of preservation activity.

For most archaeological sites, treatment resulting in preservation is usually accomplished by avoiding a site with terrain-disturbing activities, and if you can't avoid the site, a mitigation excavation is done to recover as much data as reasonable. Prior to the 1992 amendments to the National Historic Preservation Act, for the purposes of Section 106, treatment and documentation were often automatically blended for archaeological sites by moving directly to data-recovery excavation during the Section 106 process if the site was only eligible under National Register Criterion D (information potential). This resulted in a "no adverse effect" determination, eliminating the need for a memorandum of agreement (MOA) and effectively reducing needed consultation. This suggested to agencies that you could always destroy a significant site in a project's area of potential effects (APE) as long as you did a data recovery. After the 1992 amendments, archaeological sites are now treated the same as architectural properties, with avoidance being the treatment preference. As with architectural properties, archaeological documentation includes reporting any level of preservation activity.

Most states do not formally use the four-part SISG division of archaeological projects, especially with regard to the fieldwork identification category. Most states east of the Mississippi River use "phase" designations for fieldwork activities meant to fulfill discrete management objectives. In most eastern states, the purpose of a **Phase 1 survey** is identification of historic properties within a discrete area. The purpose of a **Phase 2 survey** is to assess the National Register eligibility of all or selected properties located in that area. The purpose of a **Phase 3** archaeological project is data recovery at eligible sites that an undertaking cannot avoid. These "phase" states do not assign a discrete phase name or number to the SISG prefield "archival research" category, calling it by the various names listed below. I sometimes refer to it informally as Phase 0.

A few eastern "phase" states (e.g., Iowa, New Hampshire) blend the archival research and the initial part of a standard identification/Phase 1 survey into what they call a Phase 1A. The purposes of a Phase 1A survey is to assess the archaeological potential of an area and find any obvious sites to help determine if an intensive survey (Phase 1B) is needed. Fieldwork is generally limited to pedestrian walkovers, with some coring or small-unit testing to determine soil stratigraphy and the extent of disturbance vertically and horizontally. As they do not use methods causing significant soil disturbance, Phase 1A surveys should not be subject to most state or federal permitting requirements unless artifacts are collected or archaeological feature mapping is done in a systematic manner. You still would have to travel to the project area and obtain landowner permission to go on the property to complete a Phase 1A.

Because small-area, complete Phase 1 surveys can often be accomplished in a single day (e.g., cell tower surveys), distant travel for a separate Phase 1A survey by a private contractor or agency archaeologists is often an unnecessary expense. With up-to-date aerial photographs and soil surveys now available online for most areas, you can get a good sense of the terrain and degree of previous disturbance without actually going into the field. The agency or developer description of the APE should also include a current setting description based on a staff visit to the location. For the most part, when I was SHPO archaeologist and state archaeologist in Minnesota, I didn't think most Phase 1A surveys were very practical and economical unless they were for large-scale projects, small projects within a day's journey of the project area, or projects otherwise well justified in a research design.

The origin of the phase system appears to be with the Bureau of Public Roads in an instructional memorandum dated November 18, 1964. It stated that work done under archaeological and paleontological salvage fell into three phases:

1. Reconnaissance surveys to locate sites on or along proposed routes
2. Preliminary site examinations for evaluation of sites to determine the necessity of salvage
3. Salvage work for excavation resulting in the removal and preservation of objects of value and related data when preservation in place was impractical

The Bureau of Public Roads may have gotten the idea from state practices, as Illinois appears to have been using a phase system for archaeological work, possibly tied to highway planning phases, as early as 1960 (Thomas Emerson, personal communication). Minnesota archaeologists began using the phase system in 1975.

Most western states have adopted the Bureau of Land Management (BLM) "class" strategy for archaeological identification purposes (BLM 2004). This system was developed more for large-area assessments such as Section 110 inventories. In this system, a Class I survey is an augmented archival research project. Like standard archival research, it begins with a thorough literature search, but it then goes into extensive detail analyzing what is known about the environment, previously known archaeological manifestations in the area, and data reliability in order to help construct site locational models and frame research questions.

Class II surveys are limited field surveys within a parcel of land or an APE utilizing limited sampling in areas thought to have site potential based on statistically supported probability modeling. Class III surveys are equivalent to Phase 1B or intensive surveys, where the ideal outcome is to find all historic properties in the designated area. In the BLM system, there is no class designation for evaluation (Phase 2) surveys or treatment activities (Phase 3). BLM also has a survey level just called "reconnaissance," which is like a Phase 1A in that it is neither intensive nor formally probabilistic.

At least 12 states do not use the standard phase or class categorization for their heritage management archaeological projects. Most of these states (Alaska, Arizona, Hawaii, New Mexico, Oklahoma, South Carolina, Texas) appear to use just the language of the SISG. A few states have their own unique terminology. South Dakota uses three survey "levels" that somewhat mirror the BLM classes, although Level 1 is more like standard archival research, Level 2 is called a "sample survey" to look at long but narrow utility corridors, and Level 3 blends the methods and objectives of reconnaissance and intensive survey. Kansas uses its own phase terminology, with the first phase similar to a Class II or Phase 1A, the second phase like Class III or Phase 1B, and the third phase like a standard Phase 2. California, Nebraska, and Washington appear to have no guidelines for preferred survey terminology.

Most agencies adopt the survey terminology and procedures of the state they are working in, although most western states have done the reverse by adopting BLM terminology and procedures. The BLM adoption is due to the fact that many of these western states have much of their land under BLM management. Many contractors adopt the terminology of their home state and perhaps inappropriately apply it to other states in which they are working. In most states and agencies, the phase and class system has not been applied to nonarchaeological projects.

In the discussion that follows, I will use the Phase 1-2-3 system without the subdivision of Phase 1 into A and B. This is the system used in about half the states, including Minnesota, so it is the system most familiar to me and to most archaeologists.

Research Designs

Before any level of archaeological project can proceed, the principal investigator should prepare a research design. A research design defines the objectives of the proposed work and carefully considers the methods to be used in both the field and the lab to obtain the stated objectives. The research design provides the focus for an archaeological project to ensure that it efficiently and adequately fulfills the contract, management needs, and research goals. Research designs can be very simple for archival research and very complicated for data recovery.

For any archaeological field project, the research design clearly links archival research, field procedures, laboratory analysis, and reporting. The research design determines the focus and extent of archival research. It is critical to choosing the appropriate field methods. The materials gathered in the field must be analyzed in such a way as to address the questions posed in the research design and any new questions that have arisen based on results. Specialists may need to be employed to do some of the fieldwork and analysis. Reporting must describe the procedures in enough detail to demonstrate that the research design was properly followed, the results are clearly applicable to the research questions posed, and management needs can be adequately addressed.

For most archaeological purposes, research designs for all phases of archaeological work should contain the following:

Objectives. Research designs must address the objectives of an archaeological project usually outlined in a *scope of work* (SOW) or a *request for proposals* (RFP). The research questions should not simply be a generic list of potential questions, but include only *important* and *answerable* questions that focus the fieldwork, analytical methods, and staffing requirements to obtain necessary information. Questions should not be trivial, but anticipate answers that will add significant insight to our understanding of the past or the objectives of the project. Research designs should not repeat questions that have already been adequately answered by previous investigations at a site, unless these questions justifiably require validation or additional insight. The objectives must also include a critical assessment of the relevant historic contexts and property types in the project area, the physical extent of the area to be investigated, and the amount and kinds of information to be gathered.

Methods. The project's research methods must be clearly related to the research question(s) identified in the *Objectives* section. Any proposed archival research, field techniques, or analytical methods should be carefully explained so that others using the gathered information can understand how and why the information was obtained. The methods selected should be compatible with the geographical area, historic contexts, and the kinds of properties most likely to be present. They should describe in detail field and laboratory methods such as the testing intervals and soil processing (e.g., screen size). The type of personnel and their professional qualifications must also be carefully considered in order to insure that appropriate expertise is available to attain the objectives.

To some new archaeologists and the creators of the 1983 SISG, research designs are also supposed to contain a formal section titled "Expected Results." This concept was consistent with doing scientific archaeology focused on hypothesis testing; you stated what you expected to find, and if you didn't find it, an alternative hypothesis was needed to explain the results. Over the years, the "Expected Results" section of research designs, rather than serving as an essential component of a practical research approach, simply became a rote exercise in demonstrating that you were being scientific and a proper "new" archaeologist.

For most surveys, the expected results are pretty obvious. For a Phase 1 survey, you either find potentially eligible sites or you don't, while for a Phase 2 survey a site is either eligible or it isn't. For a few complicated or large-area Phase 1 surveys, especially those involving site locational modeling, the expected results can be more complicated, such as predicting what types of sites will be present in the research area and where. Expected results are also a reasonable component of a Phase 3 excavation. Be aware that some states and agencies still require a formal "Expected Results" section in research designs at all levels of archaeological and historical work.

Most SHPOs and state archaeologists generally do not preapprove research designs for archival research or identification (Phase 1) archaeological surveys, unless the proposed methods deviate significantly from standard state or agency procedures or the project is especially complex, such as a large-area survey in which site locational modeling and stratified sampling may be important. Final reports for all archaeological projects, however, should contain a section clearly labeled "Research Design." Evaluation (Phase 2) surveys that are subject to state licensing or federal agency review often need preapproved research designs. All data recovery (Phase 3) research designs for federally reviewed projects need to be preapproved by sponsoring and reviewing agencies, as usually required in a memorandum of agreement.

Once the project begins, investigators are expected to address the stated objectives and follow the methods outlined in the research design. Deviations from the research design should be discussed with supervising agencies prior to implementation. Research designs should be flexible and anticipate changing field conditions and unexpected discoveries.

Archival Review

Archival review is also called literature search, background research, records check, historical research, existing information inventory, and file search, depending on the state or the agency. There is no official phase designation in most states for the basic prefield archival review, although in the BLM-derived Class I terminology, a Class I inventory project includes, but goes beyond, an in-depth archival review.

If done properly, an archival review can eliminate the need for any fieldwork. An archival review examines existing sources in order to summarize what has been written and what is known about a given area or topic without fieldwork. Most archival reviews are performed prior to undertaking fieldwork but may be expanded during or after fieldwork.

Archival review can be used to help assess the need for survey, to determine what survey methods should be employed, to develop site locational models, to determine areas of previous terrain disturbance or land use, to provide historic context to help evaluate site significance, to provide background information for developing data-recovery plans, and to provide sufficient information for National Register nominations or site interpretation. Archival review can, and in some cases should, involve oral interviews with appropriate individuals such as landowners, local artifact collectors, tribal elders, or topical experts (e.g., flour milling, mining).

While an archival review is required as part of all archaeological project phases, it can result in a stand-alone exercise that by itself may fulfill all heritage management needs for a particular undertaking. It could demonstrate that an area or site has already been sufficiently archaeologically documented by past work or that an area has little potential to contain significant archaeological resources based on a thorough land-use history. If such is the case, no field survey may be needed.

Most states and agencies do not set an absolute time limit as to how long an archival review is valid with respect to adequately assessing land use and the presence or eligibility of known sites within a project area. However, if a significant period has passed before fieldwork is undertaken or a project finally proceeds, within which time additional sites have been located in a project area, archaeological surveys have been done in the general project vicinity, or pertinent new methods have been developed, the archival review portion of an archaeological project might be deemed inadequate.

Before an archaeological project is initiated, it is essential that the files located in the Office of the State Archaeologist, SHPO, and/or land-management agency offices be examined. Some states have their inventories online, although a fee is usually charged, and they are password protected. These days, most review agencies will not perform extensive database searches requested by contractors or researchers for archaeological projects without charging a fee.

Following examination of the official site inventory, you should examine reports, pertinent paper site files, and maps. Paper site files usually contain information not present in databases or on site forms, such as correspondence or newspaper accounts. Phase 1 and 2 archaeological reports provide details with regard to previous surveys in a given area. Phase 3 archaeological reports provide bibliographies, possible research questions, examples of artifact analyses, and regional culture histories. Do not rely exclusively on boundary depictions of sites on site inventory forms or agency maps, but examine the original source of information if possible to assess boundary justifications based on field methods, extent of surveys, landownership, and field conditions. Examining regulatory agency files constitutes the minimum standard for archival review for most CRM archaeological projects.

Many state archaeological journals have been published for almost a century or more and are available at most major libraries or online. Information on the natural environment of most states is widely accessible, including increasingly detailed paleoenvironmental and soil studies. These studies are available in numerous books and in journals such as *Quaternary Research*. Important record repositories include state historical societies and university research centers, as well as local facilities such as municipal libraries, county courthouses, and county or city historical societies. These repositories have local histories, local government documents, manuscripts, research files, and maps.

Maps are especially useful sources for archival review. Two key historical map references in many states are General Land Office (GLO) survey notes/maps and historical county plat maps. US Geological Survey (USGS) topographic maps are another essential archival research tool, although many are decades out of date and thus are essentially historical maps of what an environment used to look like.

Aerial photographs are very useful for reconstructing land-use histories and even locating archaeological sites. Systematic aerial photographs were first taken of many states by the US Department of Agriculture (USDA) beginning in the mid-1930s. Many historic aerial photographs and recent aerial photos for all states are available online on a variety of websites, including Google Earth.

Archival review is more than examinations of the written, mapped, and imaged record. It should also include consulting knowledgeable groups and individuals, such as local collectors, landowners, and topical experts. This is especially important if Indian traditional cultural properties (TCPs) may be included within the APE. Any significant consultations should be noted in the contract completion report, although some of the information obtained may have to be kept confidential.

Basic Field Procedures

Because field conditions and historic contexts vary greatly nationwide, there are no national guidelines for field methods. Archaeological field schools (which are usually run by academic institutions) and archaeological field method books (which are usually written by academics) tend to focus on large-scale, site-specific excavations rather than CRM-related reconnaissance and evaluative surveys. They often reflect the preferred methods of a single individual or an institution. Neumann and Sanford (2010) is one of the few method books specifically aimed at doing CRM archaeology. Site types, geomorphology, and degree of soil exposure can also vary greatly by geographic area. Archaeological field methods used for CRM projects are often very different from state to state.

In the mid-1970s, many states and some federal agencies began to issue brief guidelines for CRM-focused field methods. By the 1990s, many detailed "survey manuals" had appeared, some issued by federal agencies and others by state archaeological groups or officials. For the most part, these manuals are indeed guidelines and not hard-and-fast rules that you must follow. The methods outlined in these manuals cannot anticipate every field situation, so some innovation is expected. Field methods will vary by project scope, survey phase, environmental conditions, research objectives, landownership, and management needs. In general, field methods must be appropriate to address management needs and to answer the questions posed in the research design by project phase.

Phase 1 Fieldwork

Phase 1 surveys attempt to reasonably determine the presence or absence of archaeological sites within a specific area and, if a site is found, to initially define the site's horizontal and vertical limits. A Phase 1 survey provides enough information to allow consideration of avoidance if a site may be impacted by an undertaking, while gathering enough information to allow for detailed recommendations for more intensive work, should it be necessary. Phase 1 surveys can also make preliminary assessments as to a site's archaeological nature (e.g., context, function, condition, significance). You can indeed recommend that a site is eligible or ineligible after only doing an identification-level survey if such a finding is obvious (e.g., "Eligible: a Paleoindian site with some integrity").

Phase 1 surveys can involve the use of a great variety of archaeological field techniques, including visual inspection, surface walkover (pedestrian survey), controlled surface collection, shovel testing, stratigraphy pits, augering, coring, and electronic remote sensing. Field methods must reasonably but efficiently maximize the vertical and horizontal sampling of the project area without significantly harming site integrity. There is a great deal of variety among states and agencies as to what site discovery methods are reasonable (i.e., sufficient, adequate, minimally harmful) and represent a good faith effort to find sites within an area of potential effects. Adequate field methods for discovering terrestrial archaeological sites will vary according to the extent of soil exposure, the time of year, the geomorphic setting, and topographic factors such as degree of slope, amount of bedrock exposure, and presence of surface water. Underwater surveys have their own sets of guidelines based on local conditions and agency requirements.

In some western states (e.g., Utah), much of the soil cover is exposed due to arid conditions, and drainage systems have had thousands of years to deeply expose sediments in numerous locations. Most areas of these states need only be subjected to surface inspection surveys. Transect spacing, surveyor examination speed, and artifact provenience control are specified by many states and agencies for surface inspections. Collect/no-collect strategies are also an issue, depending on the sponsoring agency and landownership.

In states with extensive vegetative cover, shovel testing will probably be required if weathered soil exposure is limited and the upper 1 meter of soil has the potential to contain archaeological remains. Shovel test shapes, sizes, spacing, and screen size vary by state and agency. In Minnesota, we require shovel tests for site discovery purposes to be circular in shape, between 30 and 40 centimeters (12 to 15 inches) in diameter, and spaced at 15-meter (50-foot) intervals, with the soil screened through quarter-inch mesh. I have found square as opposed to round shovel tests to be more time-consuming with little increased benefit for stratigraphic description or provenience control, but some states require square shovel test holes.

If shovel tests cannot go deep enough to sample the entire cultural-potential soil column, such as in areas where modern fill, alluviation, or colluviation has deeply buried soils, specialized deep testing may be necessary. Some states utilize coring or augering devices in lieu of shovel tests, even in shallow (< 1 meter) soils, although soil volumes are considerably less than in standard shovel tests and vertical control of artifacts recovered from augered units is less exact. Mechanical coring or backhoe excavation to penetrate overburden may be necessary if soils are very deeply buried. If machine stripping or trenching is used to remove overburden, care must be taken not to excessively harm near-surface or deep sites that may be significant. It may also be necessary to consult a geomorphologist to confirm that deeply buried soils may exist in a particular location and at what depths.

In northern states and high mountain areas, winter fieldwork is rare due to frozen soils and snow cover. Most states and agencies expect winter surveys to follow the same standards as warm-season work, although methods may vary. If low-relief archaeological features are expected to be present in the survey area, a light snowfall often makes them more visible. Heavy snowfall will obscure low features, however, so surface reconnaissance will have to wait until after the snow has melted.

The exclusive use of electronic remote-sensing devices to document the presence/absence of buried archaeological sites is generally not acceptable in lieu of soil removal with screening, except in soil conditions and site types where such techniques have proven reliable. For example, in sandy soils, ground-penetrating radar (GPR) has been demonstrated to find shallowly buried prehistoric features and artifacts as confirmed by subsequent excavation. Various types of remote sensing (e.g., GPR, magnetometer) have been used to confirm the presence and extent of buried architectural features in urban settings and individual burials within historic cemeteries. Metal detectors can be very helpful in locating features and artifacts on some contact and postcontact sites. Reconnaissance surveys relying on remote sensing need to physically document the presence and character of archaeological materials if such are suggested and if they have a bearing on management decisions.

Field documentation requirements for identification surveys also vary by state and agency but normally include daily log forms, photographic logs, and sketch maps of any located archaeological sites. Because an area of potential effects may not be contiguous with site boundaries, Phase 1 surveys often will not completely define the horizontal limits of archaeological sites that extend beyond the APE, due to project need, agency guidelines, or lack of landowner permission. In these cases, project archaeologists should be encouraged to provide a "best guess" estimate of complete site boundaries based on topography, although these limits can only be confirmed by field survey. Unconfirmed boundaries should be clearly labeled as such on site inventory forms and project maps in reports.

Phase 2 Fieldwork

Phase 2 surveys primarily attempt to gather enough information to evaluate the importance of sites to determine National Register eligibility. They can also refine site limits both vertically and horizontally, provide enough understanding for developing and implementing Phase 3 research designs, and gather sufficient information for an NRHP nomination or formal site interpretation. Thus Phase 2 surveys can be used for both evaluation and characterization.

Phase 2 field methods must provide critical details with regard to the site's depositional setting, cultural contexts, integrity, artifact and feature densities, and potential to answer important research questions, without significantly harming site integrity. Phase 2 survey usually requires intensive fieldwork that involves the excavation of formal units (e.g., 1 square meter or larger) with careful provenience control and a level of analysis beyond identification surveys.

Controlled surface collections of sites with sufficient soil exposure to discover horizontal patterning, remote-sensing survey to find features, and coring to better document deeply buried **horizons** are also standard field techniques on **intensive surveys**.

The use of tight-grid (≤ 5-meter interval) shovel testing should also be carefully considered and justified in a Phase 2 research design because it can inappropriately damage the integrity of a site. This is especially true if the purpose of the intensive survey is just to assess eligibility. Shovel testing generally does not allow for precise vertical control or determining the presence of or identifying particular types of features. For characterization purposes, however, tight-grid shovel testing may be needed to locate features or find artifact concentrations. It may be advisable to use square, fairly large (e.g., 30 square centimeter) shovel tests in this instance to maintain better vertical control or use small core or auger units to do less damage.

The number of test units will vary by the contextual association of the site, the size of the site, the site's condition, and the survey objective. A single 1-square-meter unit may be enough to determine a site eligible if that unit clearly demonstrates its research potential and the site appears to possess sufficient and uniform integrity. In general, however, most archaeological sites will need multiple formal test units distributed across the site to assess eligibility, especially for ineligible findings.

Additional excavation units may be necessary to characterize a site for the purposes of developing a data-recovery plan. Characterization surveys need to fully assess the kinds, quantity, and quality of archaeological materials a site is capable of yielding, as well as vertical and horizontal distributions of activity areas, possible feature locations, artifact concentrations, and areas of extensive disturbance.

Phase 3 Fieldwork

For the purposes of CRM, a large-scale site excavation is considered to be the same as a Phase 3 archaeological project. It is sometimes called a *treatment activity* or a *data-recovery project* if it is being used to mitigate the adverse effects of a development project on an eligible archaeological site. The need for mitigation excavations is usually specified in a Section 106 memorandum of agreement.

Phase 3 projects usually involve intensive excavation or other forms of intensive field examination following a carefully developed research design. Phase 3 research designs are often called *data-recovery plans* if they are related to adverse effect mitigation. Treatment options can also include nonfieldwork alternatives such as preservation easements and National Register nomination. Treatment involving only intensive fieldwork is generally done for sites eligible only under Criterion D, while sites that are also eligible under Criterion A may require additional forms of mitigation (e.g., site banking, educational materials).

Phase 3 projects generally gather enough data from sites or portions of sites to mitigate adverse effects from development activities or to fulfill research objectives of voluntary projects. The ultimate objective is not just to recover data or preserve artifacts but to use the recovered data and artifacts to answer important research questions. Field methods must carefully but efficiently locate, define, and recover multiple forms of data from cultural horizons, use-areas, artifact concentrations, and features. Provenience data must be recorded carefully and in detail.

Archaeological Phase 3 investigations most often involve excavating extensive formal units, employing some fine-scale recovery techniques, and subjecting recovered artifacts to detailed analysis. Phase 3 work can also include completing controlled surface collections when only horizontal integrity remains at an eligible site. Archaeological monitoring of construction activities (e.g., grading) at eligible sites can be part of a treatment activity if called for in a data-recovery plan.

Site Monitoring

Monitoring can be thought of as another type of archaeological project, but it is used to accomplish the objectives embedded in one or more of the three field phases discussed above. Monitoring can refer to archaeological observation of machine stripping of soil or of construction-phase activities to discover or explore sites (e.g., exploratory trenching within the APE). Construction monitoring should not be recommended unless well justified and consistent with management and regulatory needs. Only qualified archaeologists should do archaeological monitoring.

Monitoring is not an appropriate reconnaissance, evaluation, or burial authentication field procedure in most states, except in instances where it is impractical to perform preconstruction subsurface testing (e.g., beneath an existing building or parking lot) or if it is used to rapidly examine private land projects not subject to formal environmental review procedures or state licensing. Monitoring often does not allow for options such as project redesign or site preservation in place if an eligible site or a burial site is uncovered, options that are essential to most environmental review regulations and affiliated community preferences.

Monitoring can be appropriate as part of a treatment (Phase 3) activity (e.g., monitoring machine stripping of the plow zone to expose features) or as a final check to make sure nothing important was overlooked by Phase 1 or 2 surveys that used limited-area hand-testing methods.

Archaeological monitoring generally does not include what is called *tribal monitoring*. The purpose of tribal monitoring should be to evaluate construction impacts on nonarchaeological aspects of Indian-related cultural resources such as traditional cultural properties. Tribal monitoring is discussed in chapter 13.

Recording and Recovery Considerations

The principal investigator is ultimately responsible for obtaining landowner permission to enter land. It is against the law in most states to enter private property without landowner permission even for informal, no-collect surface surveys. The principal investigator is responsible for obtaining all required federal, state, and local permits and licenses to undertake archaeological work on public or private property. Principal investigators also need to contact utility companies if field activities may encounter buried power lines, pipelines, fiber-optic cables, or the like.

Carefully documenting fieldwork while it is in progress is critical for proper analysis and reporting. Documentation needs vary by the phase of the archaeological project, but daily logs describing archaeological work should be kept during all phases. Sketch maps should be prepared for all work carried out within archaeological sites; these maps should show known site boundaries, significant landforms/ cultural features, and locations of excavation units. Maps should be tied into the real world through project stationing, addresses/legal locations, or GPS coordinates. Photographs should be taken to document site conditions, field methods, and significant features. Photographic logs should record the subject, date, direction of view, and photographer.

Archaeologists need to establish collection, retention, and curation policies prior to the initiation of fieldwork. Artifacts from federal land are federal property. Artifacts from nonfederal public land in most states are the property of that state. Artifacts collected on private property belong to the landowner.

Until recently, all artifacts found by professional archaeologists doing fieldwork were collected and retained, except where overwhelming numbers of artifacts were present on the surface, such as at large stone tool workshops or historic dumps. In cases of large numbers of surface artifacts, representative samples or diagnostic artifacts could be retained. Due to sharply rising curation costs and limited curation space, some agencies and private consultants are now utilizing no-collect policies.

Another retention consideration applies to surveys on private land where the landowner has requested all or selected artifacts. Every effort should be made to encourage private landowners to donate artifacts from professional surveys to public repositories or at least permit their temporary removal for thorough analysis. If landowners immediately want all recovered artifacts, it may be advisable to field-document and leave in place all surface artifacts. Digital cameras and highly accurate GPS or Total Station units have made field documentation of surface artifacts efficient and affordable, with image quality instantly confirmable and individual locations electronically recorded. Be sure to include a uniform scale and a detailed photolog if artifacts are photo-documented in the field but not retained.

The downside of no-collect policies is that artifacts are often the only physical evidence that a site exists in a particular location. They may be needed to convince officials or private developers that additional work or site avoidance is indeed advisable. It is certainly a reasonable policy that all artifacts from surface surveys need not be collected and retained. However, this does not apply to most excavated artifacts, as once removed, they cannot be restored to their original soil context. Artifacts are the also the keys to understanding site function, historic context, and research potential. Field personnel are often inadequately trained to undertake complex artifact analyses, especially when artifacts have not been properly cleaned or when comparative collections or experts are not readily available for consultation. Advanced techniques like residue analysis or use-wear analysis cannot be completed in the field.

Basic Laboratory Analysis and Curation

The amount and type of artifact analysis will vary by the project phase. The methods selected should be consistent with the research questions identified in the project's research design. While a focused orientation should be addressed in the initial phases of the analysis, it should not preclude a flexible approach to data as the project proceeds. In selecting analytical methods, the analyst should consider continuity of research by reviewing data from previous work in the area. All phases of archaeological projects must classify and tabulate recovered artifacts. For example, basic prehistoric ceramic classification should include vessel portion (e.g., rim, body), temper, surface treatment, and historical index type if possible. A concise, tabular record of specimens and their provenience must be prepared during the analysis.

Artifact cleaning techniques should be used that are appropriate to the material and must conform to agency and curation facility guidelines. Care should be taken not to remove or destroy coatings or encrustations that may contain important information (e.g., pigment on ground stone tools, charred organic matter on sherds, blood residue on chipped stone tools). Preservation of unstable or fragile materials should begin in the field.

If treatment in the field is not realistic, preservation in the laboratory should be performed immediately upon conclusion of fieldwork. Care should be taken to avoid contaminating potential radiocarbon samples both in the field and in the lab. Short- and long-term curation of various types of materials should be planned for in the research design with the requirements of the final repository considered before materials are processed. At a minimum, all materials must be stored in a manner that preserves provenience, ensures preservation, and allows convenient access for researchers.

A complete inventory must be maintained during the cataloging process. A copy of all written records, including field notes, must be curated at the same institution as the archaeological materials. Any significant data recorded on an electronic medium should also be printed and included with the material. All photographic documentation must be catalogued in a manner appropriate for curation. Photos should be cross-referenced on both photo logs and site forms and on all pertinent field and laboratory records. Storage techniques for photographs must consider long-term curation. Laboratory records must also be maintained for materials requiring special or intensive analysis.

Before a project can start, the contractor must arrange for the curation of archaeological artifacts with an appropriate institution along with the associated inventory information (notes, photographs, maps, catalog sheets). Long-term curation responsibilities should be acknowledged and agreed upon in writing prior to the beginning of fieldwork. Federally approved curational institutions must meet the standards set forth in 36 CFR 79.

Some larger curational institutions require complicated curation training and charge fees for curating archaeological materials and the associated records; this limits artifact-retention options. Local museums with less complicated requirements may be able to curate materials at little or no cost. However, they still need to meet the sponsoring agency's curation requirements and should always ensure that materials are secure, well preserved, and available to all qualified researchers. Materials recovered from postcontact archaeological sites usually present the greatest challenges with regard to collecting and curation policies, because historical artifacts can be very numerous, very large, and very difficult to preserve (e.g., ferrous materials prone to rust). Prehistoric bone beds or high-density lithic sites also pose artifact retention and curation issues.

Completing Site Inventory Forms
Site inventory forms to record site locations and site characteristics are utilized by all states and federal land-management agencies. Each state and each agency form is unique, although most contain the same basic information. Some federal agencies agree to use state inventory forms and use state assigned numbers. Usually these numbers follow the Smithsonian trinomial system, where the first two numbers represent the state rank alphabetically prior to Alaska and Hawaii statehood; Minnesota is number 21. The second two letters are the county abbreviation. The last number is a one-up inventory number unique to the county. The first site recorded in Murray County, Minnesota, is 21MU1.

Inventory forms should be completed for each previously unrecorded site that is documented by a project and perhaps for all previously recorded sites where significant additional information is gathered (e.g., expanded site limits, additional context definition, new artifact collections). If federal agencies want official state site numbers for sites on their property, they often must complete a state site inventory form instead of just submitting federal inventory forms.

Every state has its own policy for what should be recorded on a site inventory form during a survey based on its definition of an archaeological site. When I was Minnesota state archaeologist, I defined an archaeological site as "any location containing evidence of past human activity that holds significance for most archaeologists." In Minnesota, a site can contain a single artifact or just a clearly cultural surface or soil feature with no obvious artifacts; there is no minimum site size requirement. In Pennsylvania, a prehistoric site must contain multiple artifacts within an area of at least 15 meters in diameter. In Utah, an archaeological site must contain at least 10 artifacts of the same type (e.g., sherds) or 15 artifacts of multiple types within at least a 10-meter-diameter area.

Some "artifacts" recovered in the field are not really artifacts. An artifact from a single flake site should be examined by a lithics expert, as some flakes, especially those in cultivated fields, can be of nonarchaeological origin (e.g., plow-struck). Nonarchitectural surface features, such as possible mining pits, should be functionally designated only if their dimensions and locations are consistent with confirmed features of this type; there are many reasons for digging holes, some recent and some ancient. In most states, ancient animal bone finds are not assigned official site numbers unless stone artifacts are found directly associated with them or the bone shows clear signs of human use or modification. Extinct animal remains lacking cultural association are paleontological sites.

Reporting Archaeological Projects
Adequate reporting is as important to an archaeological project as adequate fieldwork and analysis. Reports document that archaeological work has been done at a specific site or on a specific project and provide enough detail to assess if the work was adequate to fulfill legal and management needs. Reports are also the foundation of archaeological research. Although most CRM reports are not widely distributed, they are available to researchers at OSAs, SHPOs, or sponsoring agencies. Most states and agencies provide detailed guidelines as to how

reports are formatted and what they should contain. The SISG also provides basic reporting guidance. Some states exclusively rely on the SISG reporting requirements.

Project sponsors, regulating agencies, or principal investigators directly submit project completion reports to review agencies. In the case of federal and state laws, it is the regulating agency's responsibility to ensure that the report is adequately completed and that archaeological personnel meet appropriate standards, although any work on nonfederal public land or involving nonfederal historic burials is subject to OSA licensing requirements.

Reports submitted to review agencies by development agencies should have an accompanying letter that states the overall effect finding recommendation as well as eligibility/significance opinions regarding any involved sites. Cover letters should also include the project name, a basic description of the scope of the project, and the scope of the archaeological work.

If a report discusses a site that was unnumbered prior to a survey, an official site number should be obtained prior to submission of the final report. Site numbers are needed to link reports to sites in databases. Occasionally, a site number cannot be obtained in time to complete a Phase 1 report if there is some urgency to project development, but this should be explained in the report and every effort made to obtain a number as soon as possible.

Other Aspects of Heritage Management Archaeology

Archaeologists do more than find, evaluate, and mitigate effects to archaeological sites in the environmental review process. They are involved in both strategic and tactical preservation planning, helping to design and write comprehensive state plans, cultural resource management plans for specific areas of land, and disaster management plans. Archaeologists also write National Register nominations, although, as discussed in chapter 5, not many archaeologists have actually done this, and the value of doing it varies by state and situation.

Heritage management archaeologists also play a major role in what has become the "new" public archaeology. When Charles McGimsey wrote *Public Archaeology* in 1972, the term had much the same meaning that CRM archaeology did when it was introduced a few years later. It meant doing all aspects of archaeology in response to public agency reactions to legal requirements and doing it with public money. Now public archaeology is focused on outreach and education to promote broad archaeological goals and participation in community life. The focus of public archaeology today is not archaeology for research purposes or even for standard heritage management. The emphasis of public archaeology is on doing archaeology for more idealistic but often less tangible purposes. Public archaeology is now archaeology *with* the public more than *for* the public. Although the benefits of public collaboration are real and worthwhile, some modern public archaeology has less of an emphasis on rigorous archaeological research focused on better understanding the past.

Summary

Archaeology attempts to make the cultural past more understandable by carefully looking at the physical remains of the past. The human past goes back at least 14,000 years in North America. Sometimes the remains are very ephemeral, making our reconstructions highly speculative. Other remains are very substantial, such as structural features that have not changed much since they were abandoned, with obvious functions related to still familiar human activities.

American archaeology has only been a profession for a little over 100 years. Over that century, the goals and methods of archaeology have greatly changed. In the early twentieth century, the focus was on helping historians and architects accurately reconstruct important places from the Euro-American past, as well as providing a basic outline of the technology of the prehistoric past. The availability of radiocarbon dating in the mid-twentieth century allowed us to develop an absolute chronology of the distant past. This coincided with a deeper understanding of past environments to help reconstruct past ways of life during particular periods.

At the beginning of the last third of the twentieth century, a few influential archaeologists dominated American archaeology by suggesting what they considered to be a revolutionary perspective, focusing on an explicitly scientific approach attempting to discern past cultural processes. This "new archaeology" coincided with the appearance of cultural resource management brought about by a number of federal laws. By the time processual archaeology was falling out of favor in academic circles in the late twentieth century, the processualists were firmly embedded in the federal heritage preservation system, where they fit well with planning and interdisciplinary initiatives.

Today, CRM archaeology dominates American archaeology in terms of funding and numbers of employed archaeologists. While each state and agency has its own particular requirements, terminology, and methods to fulfill CRM obligations, overall the system is very familiar to all heritage management archaeologists. We have developed standard methods to find archaeological sites, to assess their significance, and to deal with mitigating adverse effects to sites caused by development.

What hasn't changed in the century of American professional archaeology is the need to carefully recover information, carefully record what we do, and widely share what we have found with our peers and the public. Without peer sharing, what we do is not science and it is not relevant no matter how carefully it is done. Without public sharing, we risk losing public support for the legal requirements that have preserved thousands of important sites and filled many museums with irreplaceable objects.

Review Questions

1. What are the roots of American archaeology?
2. How did the "new archaeology" affect CRM practice?
3. What are the objectives of a Phase 1 survey?
4. What are the objectives of Phase 2 fieldwork?
5. What are the objectives of a Phase 3 project?

Supplemental Reading

General histories of American archaeology can be found in various textbooks (e.g., D. Thomas 1998; Kelly and Thomas 2013; Pauketat and Loren 2005). Thomas King provides a number of short overviews of the history of CRM archaeology (King 2013:6–32; King 1987; King, Hickman, and Berg 1977, chapter 2). McManamon (2014) presents an overview of archaeology's transition from reactive to proactive public archaeology in the 1970s. A good example of a state history of CRM archaeology is Peebles (2013).

CRM archaeological contracting methodology has been explained in detail by Neumann and Sanford (2011). Most states and some agencies have archaeological survey manuals that can be found online. Many agencies, especially large federal land-management agencies, have considerable information on their archaeological findings and policies on their websites. The ACHP has specific Section 106 archaeology guidance on its website. See Little (2002) for discussions of the public benefits of archaeology.

SIDEBAR

Implementing Heritage Management: A Revolution in the Dirt

Sometimes a very simple idea has revolutionary implications. This was true for a new site-discovery method introduced in the mid-1970s. North American archaeologists find most sites by walking over areas with good soil exposure. If the bare soil is sufficiently weathered by rain or wind, artifacts can be very visible, scattered across the land surface. This "surface collection" technique works well in the western United States, where naturally exposed surface soils and deep erosional cuts are common. It is implemented selectively in the eastern half of the country, where agricultural practices have seasonally exposed soil, but a considerable amount of land is still heavily vegetated throughout the year in forests and grasslands.

As I set out to do my first highway reconnaissance surveys for the Minnesota Historical Society (MHS) in the fall of 1975, one of my new colleagues gave me a phosphate testing kit and an Oakfield 1-inch soil coring tool. He told me when I thought an area with poor soil exposure had some potential to contain a site, I was to take a soil sample and then test for the presence of high phosphate content at various levels in the removed soil core. Some cultural activities associated with habitation sites were known to increase soil phosphate. If a phosphate test appeared clearly positive, I was to then dig a formal 1-square-meter test unit, screening the dirt.

My 1975 site-discovery technique for areas of poor soil exposure was totally inadequate for the job I was supposed to do. I had to review 1,000 county and city road projects every year, varying from short-length bridge replacements to new road alignments 20 miles long. About 10% of the projects (about 100)

each year required field survey because they involved significant disturbance of new terrain in areas of high or medium site potential. Half of these surveys were typically in vegetated areas. Soil phosphate tests were relatively fast, but they were subjective and inexact. Soil phosphate concentrations can be due to many natural as well as cultural processes. Many cultural processes don't increase soil phosphate at all. Soil phosphate tests were efficient but unreliable. Relying on them did not constitute a "reasonable and good faith effort" at site discovery.

On the other hand, excavating formal test units and screening the soil is a very accurate way to find most types of sites, but it is very slow. In my fieldwork prime, I could dig one formal unit to a depth of about 1 meter by myself in a hard day's work, providing I didn't hit any features and encountered only a modest number of artifacts. With some of my road projects miles long, there was no way I could excavate formal test units at short intervals to adequately sample the entire proposed construction zone. This was a good faith approach but not reasonable.

In 1974, William Lovis, a US Forest Service archaeologist in Michigan, attempted to find a better way to discover sites in vegetated areas. Using 100-yard intervals, he shovel-cut 1-square-foot holes in the light sod of the forest floor. He lifted back the soil mat, examining it for artifacts. He occasionally removed a shallow soil plug and visually examined it for artifacts. Lovis gave a paper at a regional archaeology conference in 1974 describing his technique and later published his results (Lovis 1976). He called the technique "shovel testing." Some "post-holing" had already been done at known sites, but it was only for finding features and artifact concentrations to guide the placement of excavation units.

Doug Birk, an MHS archaeologist, attended the 1974 conference and heard the Lovis paper. He modified the Lovis method on a survey in northern Minnesota the following year. He excavated 30-centimeter square units about 20 centimeters in depth at 5-meter intervals over a relatively small area where a new MHS building was proposed. Unlike Lovis, Birk carefully troweled the soil back into the holes. He excavated 114 shovel tests and recovered 403 artifacts (Birk and George 1976). Birk's improvements were to always dig to a depth below the top soil, to trowel back the soil rather than just quickly visually examining it, and to use a very tight interval between shovel tests. But Birk was only examining a small area and no doubt missed recovering many small artifacts.

Les Peterson, a colleague of mine and Birk's at MHS, ran the Minnesota Trunk Highway Archaeological Reconnaissance Survey. He tried a variation of Birk's method on several highway survey projects in wooded environments in 1975. Peterson used 45-centimeter-diameter round shovel tests spaced at 15-meter (50-foot) intervals. Once again, the soil was not deeply excavated and was troweled back into the holes. When artifacts were found, at least one formal 1-square-meter unit was excavated adjacent to the positive shovel test, and the test unit soil was screened through quarter-inch mesh. The following year, Peterson employed the same technique on several projects but reduced the hole diameter to 30 centimeters.

A collective lightbulb went off in all MHS archaeologists' heads, including mine, during the winter of 1976–1977 as we discussed Birk's and Peterson's methods. What if we added screening to all shovel tests; wouldn't this greatly increase artifact recovery without greatly increasing time? So we all tried it the next field season. This proved so workable for large survey areas and so successful at finding sites in the 1977 survey field season that the Council for Minnesota Archaeology (CMA) adopted the shovel-testing technique as the standard method for site discovery in vegetated areas in the first Minnesota archaeological survey manual (CMA 1977). Shovel tests were to be used where soil exposure was poor; they were to be 30 centimeters in diameter, spaced at 15-meter (50-foot) intervals, extend into subsoil, and screened through quarter-inch mesh.

The shovel-testing revolution swept through most of the country in the late 1970s, with variations independently invented in other states (e.g., King 1978:23), although many western states still relied on surface inspection. The shovel-testing method seems so obvious today, but early CRM archaeologists had been university-trained to dig sites, not to find them. There have been some complaints about its reliability (e.g., Shott 1989; Kvamme 2003), but shovel testing is clearly a reasonable and good faith approach to implementing Section 106 archaeological identification.

CHAPTER 12

Among the Professionals
History and Architecture

American historians have long feared they lack influence in public life.

—Ian Tyrrell

Architecture is my delight, and putting up and pulling down, one of my favorite amusements.

—Thomas Jefferson

Archaeology, history, and architecture are the three interior pillars of the American cultural heritage management structure. Other heritage management professionals, such as curators and **archivists**, provide critical support for the main professions by maintaining and making accessible artifacts and manuscripts, while planners and ethnographers make specialized contributions concerning a few property types and activities. It is archaeologists, historians, and architects who do most of the day-to-day work of heritage management with regard to protecting the tangible heritage resources found outside museums and libraries. This chapter provides an overview of the practice of history and architecture as they apply to the preservation and management of our tangible cultural heritage.

In American heritage management, history overlaps with both archaeology and architecture, certainly more than the latter two fields overlap with each other. Historians and architects in heritage preservation focus almost exclusively on the tangible aspects of heritage. Much of this focus is on the built environment, whose major elements are buildings, structures, and altered landscapes. Because of the significant overlap in interests and tasks, historic preservation historians and architects are grouped together in state historic preservation office (SHPO) program areas and instructional manuals. They are often combined into a compound word: "history-architecture."

Between history and architecture there is a hybrid profession. Architectural historians are rooted part in general history, part in art history, and part in architectural design. With regard to the larger profession, most academic architectural historians are trained in classics departments or schools of architecture, where they focus on architectural aspects of the world's built environment. While basically historians, architectural historians are generally not caught up in historians' methodological disputes or interpretive distractions. Architectural historians who practice American historic preservation develop a specialty in identifying and interpreting aspects of the American built environment. Although today some schools of architecture and even a few departments of history have programs for educating architectural historians as American historic preservation professionals, in the formative late-twentieth-century days of the historic preservation movement, most were educated in history departments and later adopted their specialty and developed their skills.

Like archaeologists, historians and architects have benefited from significant technological advances over the last 40 years. The introduction of personal computers in the late 1970s soon promoted a flood of word processing, desktop publishing, and database software, greatly facilitating research, analysis, and reporting. Digital scanners and cameras provided quicker and more economical ways of recording and sharing data, as well as safer and more convenient access to rare documents. Computer aided design (CAD) took much of the tedium out of representing and presenting architectural ideas.

The introduction of the World Wide Web (WWW) in the early 1990s allowed for rapid text and graphic communication. Internet resources rapidly expanded, allowing for quick and comprehensive access not only to secondary information like journal articles but also to primary sources like historic maps, historic photographs, old manuscripts, and government documents.

While these technological advances made doing and sharing history and architecture easier, as with archaeology, in and of themselves they are not a substitute for well-planned research, thorough fieldwork, thoughtful analysis, and well-considered conclusions and designs. As Carol Pursell (1991:115) has observed, "Expanding technologies are answer oriented. . . . [H]istorians should be specialists in questions."

Standards and Guidelines

In 1976, the secretary of the interior, through the National Park Service (NPS), issued *Preservation Project Standards* and, in conjunction with the Department of Housing and Urban Development (HUD), issued *Guidelines for the Preservation of Old Buildings*. These publications were meant to assist federal agencies and SHPOs with managing NPS grants-in-aid projects, federal tax act building certifications, and Department of Housing and Urban Development (HUD) historic building rehabilitations. In 1979, the secretary, through the newly formed Heritage Conservation and Recreation Service (HCRS), updated and expanded the standards and added guidelines for their implementation. These early standards and guidelines emphasized the treatment of historic buildings. In 1981, HCRS was disbanded, and historic preservation duties returned to the NPS.

In 1983, the NPS provided some of the first comprehensive and detailed guidance on how to do all major aspects of the day-to-day work of historic preservation as required by the National Historic Preservation Act (NHPA), particularly with respect to agency responsibilities in Section 110 added in 1980. This was in the *Secretary of the Interior's Standards and Guidelines for Archaeology and Historic Preservation* (SISG). According to longtime Minnesota SHPO historian Susan Roth, the 1983 SISG publication was the first "go-to" document that SHPOs used to broadly implement their duties and provide direction for federal agencies and practitioners. An overview of the various standards and guidelines for historic preservation is presented here because many of them have come to more directly impact the work of historians and architects than that of archaeologists.

The 1983 standards and guidelines contained the following major sections:

- Standards for preservation planning
- Standards for identification
- Standards for evaluation
- Standards for registration

- Standards for historical documentation
- Standards for architectural and engineering documentation
- Standards for archaeological documentation
- Standards for historic preservation projects
- Professional qualification standards

Each section except the last presented guidelines on how to carry out the standards. The professional qualifications standards pertained to five professions: history, archaeology, architectural history, architecture, and historic architecture.

The words "standards" and "guidelines" are not defined in the 1983 SISG publication or the numerous similarly titled publications produced by the NPS for the secretary before and since. *Standards* are issued by an authority to define an expected level of quality that is used as a basis for comparing actions performed by multiple practitioners. *Guidelines* are official advice on how to carry out a standard that allows some flexibility in application.

For example, there are three standards for identification of historic properties:

1. Identification of historic properties is undertaken to the degree required to make decisions.
2. Results of identification activities are integrated into the preservation planning process.
3. Identification activities include explicit procedures for record keeping and information distribution.

There are then multiple detailed guidelines for implementing these standards:

1. The role of identification in the planning process
2. Performing identification
3. Integrating identification results
4. Reporting identification results

Performing identification is then divided into the following tasks:

- Research design
- Archival research
- Reconnaissance survey
- Intensive survey

The purpose of reconnaissance survey is "characterization of a region's historic properties." Techniques to accomplish this include "windshield" or "walkover" surveys, with "a limited use of sub-surface survey." Reconnaissance survey is used to define particular property types or to estimate the distribution of historic properties in a given area to assist development of a historic context or help with regional site locational modeling. The purpose of intensive survey is identification and description of "specific historic properties in an area." It defines "precisely" what historic properties are present in that area and gathers information on these properties "sufficient for later evaluation and treatment decisions."

The focus of the 1983 document was clearly on planning, National Register of Historic Places (NRHP) nomination, treatment of structural historic properties for the purposes of grant eligibility and tax benefits, and federal agencies' responsibilities on their own land. The justifications for the standards and guidelines are NHPA Section 101(f–h), as well as Section 110 of the NHPA. Section 106 of the NHPA is mentioned only once in the 1983 document under "Planning—Developing Historic Contexts," noting that reports produced because of Section 106 may be a source of information for developing historic contexts. Section 106 is not mentioned under "identification" or "evaluation," although the majority of identification and evaluation activities are done because of Section 106.

The 1983 SISG document has never been updated as a whole, although the standards for historic preservation projects have been given considerable attention in more recent official documents and publications, as described below. The 1992 amendments to the NHPA effectively forced the broadening of historic preservation into heritage preservation. In response to this broadening, the NPS in 1997 proposed revision and expansion of the professional qualification standards. These draft standards formally divided archaeology into prehistoric and historic. They also added the professions of conservation, cultural anthropology, curation, engineering, folklore, historic preservation planning, and historic preservation. (King [2013:361] thinks standards for cultural resource managers should have also been included.) The 1997 professional qualification standards have never been formally adopted, so the 1983 standards for the five original professions are still in effect, although they really only apply strictly to SHPO staff.

The 1983 standards and guidelines were meant for all the major historic preservation professions and all major activities, but other standards and guidelines issued by the secretary of the interior are more specialized. The 1976 preservation project standards for the grants-in-aid program were for seven types of treatments: acquisition, protection, stabilization, preservation, rehabilitation, restoration, and reconstruction. In 1977, the *Secretary of the Interior's Standards for Rehabilitation and Guidelines for Rehabilitating Historic Buildings* were issued for application just to rehabilitation of buildings for tax purposes. The standards for rehabilitation were updated several times in the 1980s and 1990s.

In 1979 the *Secretary of the Interior's Standards for Historic Preservation Projects with Guidelines for Applying the Standards* was a first attempt to offer guidelines to apply basic standards for all types of treatments to all types of historic properties with regard to grant eligibility, focused mainly on buildings and structures. These were updated in 1985, 1992, 1995, 2011, and 2017. The 1992 version eliminated acquisition as a treatment and consolidated protection and stabilization under preservation, leaving the four types of treatment that still exist today: preservation, rehabilitation, restoration, and reconstruction. The 1995 version embedded rehabilitation with the other three standards for tax purposes and was codified as 36 CFR 68. The 2011 version included sustainability guidelines. The 2017 version included more modern building materials and systems that had exceeded the 50-year threshold needed to be considered historic. In 1996, the secretary of the interior issued *Standards for the Treatment of Historic Properties with Guidelines for the Treatment of Cultural Landscapes*. Some of the standards and guidelines list authors, and some do not.

The 1980 amendments to the NHPA introduced Section 110, which outlined federal agencies' responsibility for identifying and preserving historic properties on lands they managed. These amendments (16 USC 470[a]) also required the secretary of the interior to promulgate regulations to implement Section 110. These regulations were published in 1988 (53 FR 4727). The 1992 amendments of the NHPA required revision of the regulations, which were published in 1998 (63 FR 20496) as the *Secretary of the Interior's Standards and Guidelines for Federal Agency Historic Preservation Programs Pursuant to the National Historic Preservation Act*.

Today only SHPOs still seem to know and broadly use the 1983 SISG. While archaeologists initially used some of the 1983 guidance on project levels and reporting, most archaeologists now use the 1983 general standards and guidelines mainly for the professional qualification standards, although the entire document is often cited in their reports. Federal agencies focus on the Section 110 standards and guidelines. Historians and architects are the primary users of the *Secretary of the Interior's Standards and Guidelines for the Treatment of Historic Properties* in its various forms and publications as described in this chapter.

Note that "treatment" has at least three meanings as applied to American heritage management. Although all three usages are very important, treatment in general is not explicitly defined anywhere in the various standards and guidelines issued by the secretary of the interior and is not explicitly defined in the NHPA Section 106 regulations (36 CFR 800).

- *Treatment meaning 1*: For the purposes of SISG, treatment is one of four types of actions (preservation, rehabilitation, restoration, and reconstruction) used to carry out a particular historic preservation goal consistent with maintaining the integrity of a historic property for National Register eligibility, emphasizing preservation in place and usually done in conjunction with affirming historic preservation fund grant eligibility or eligibility for tax benefits.
- *Treatment meaning 2*: For the broad purposes of Section 106, treatment is a method of streamlining the Section 106 process by applying an Advisory Council on Historic Preservation (ACHP)–approved standard treatment as a program alternative.
- *Treatment meaning 3*: For a focused Section 106 purpose, treatment is the act of mitigating adverse effects to an archaeological site, such as implementing a treatment plan through a data-recovery excavation.

In this chapter, especially with regard to the duties of preservation architects, the third meaning of treatment dominates usage.

Historians

While archaeological methods rely on material culture to interpret the past, historical methods rely on recorded accounts, especially primary sources. *Historiography* is the analysis of methods, sources, and interpretations that historians have employed to undertake their profession.

Archaeologists rarely have to deal with the authenticity of the artifacts they find in the ground, although those found by nonprofessionals usually lack acceptable provenience upon which to base major observations or conclusions. Artifacts can be placed in cultural-historic contexts by relative vertical position in the ground, typological classification, or absolute dating methods such as radiocarbon.

Primary written records have usually passed through many hands before they are discovered by a historian or placed in an archive accessible to historians. Oral accounts, be they first person or passed down, are subject to the inaccuracy of memory, which increases with time, or to distortion by an informant with motivations other than providing an accurate account. Source veracity evaluation is the first critical step in doing history.

Historians must consider the authenticity of their sources, be they written, based on original interviews they conduct, or based on information that has been passed down orally to an informant. With regard to written records, they must determine the age of the information, the geographic location of its origin and its travels, the probable author, whether it is a copy of an earlier document, and whether it is a forgery. With regard to oral information, they must assess the reliability of the informant by getting corroboration from other knowledgeable informants and by considering the societal role of the informant and possible motives or explanations for his or her providing alternative information. Once sources have been deemed authentic and accurate, the historian must synthesize and summarize the information gained from them. What historians extract from their sources depends on their area of interest.

Finally, the historian can offer conclusions or interpretations that provide insight into the past. This insight is also informed by other historical studies of the same topic, region, or period as well as analogies to similar situations. The "noble dream" of most historians is to be objective and tell "what really happened" in the past (Novick 1988).

The History of History in Historic Preservation

In terms of formal education and the presence of support organizations, history is the oldest of the American heritage preservation professions. Just as Thomas Jefferson contributed some of the first scientific archaeological work in this country, his 1785 *Notes on the State of Virginia* is one of the country's earliest historical studies. While focused on his native state, Jefferson's *Notes* provide details about daily life in other infant American states and observations about American history and culture immediately after the Revolution and prior to ratification of the Constitution.

The Massachusetts Historical Society was founded in 1791, followed by the American Antiquarian Society in 1812. These early organizations provided repositories for manuscripts and a community of like-minded individuals to support historical endeavors. They were not established by or for professional historians because there were no professional historians in America until the second half of the nineteenth century, but this still predated professional archaeology by a half century.

The study of history was a component of some of the first college curricula in this country beginning as early as the late seventeenth century. American university graduate programs did not appear until the middle of the nineteenth century. They were modeled on the German university approach with a seminar method of instruction and completion of a written thesis as the final proof of competency. By the late nineteenth century, a number of American universities in the Northeast (Harvard, Columbia, Johns Hopkins) and the Midwest (Wisconsin, Michigan) were producing PhD-level history graduates.

In 1884, the American Historical Association (AHA) was founded. It was soon intellectually dominated by professional historians with freshly minted PhDs who contributed articles to the AHA's journal, the *American Historical Review*, which started publication in 1895. Most of the first professional American historians considered themselves practitioners of "scientific history," reflecting the German origins of their educational system as well as an American love of science. Scientific history was based on objective facts, careful document analysis, a search for evolutionary laws, the writing of long research manuscripts, and submission of articles to scholarly journals (Terrell 2005:25).

The practice of American history rapidly became specialized. By the end of the nineteenth century, practitioners were doing colonial history, frontier history, and agricultural history, although there were still attempts at broad synthesis. An early call for historic preservation was made by prominent nineteenth-century historian Albert Bushnell Hart in 1898. Although Hart focused on erecting markers and establishing archives, he also called for the preservation of important historic sites: "In America some of the stateliest and most memorable buildings have been sacrificed" (Hart 1898:2). This preservation work was to be done by private and local organizations with no anticipated role for the federal government other than some archival work at the Library of Congress.

The scientific history school gave way to the progressive history school in the early twentieth century. The progressive historians incorporated the ideas of the awakening social sciences, like anthropology, abandoning political history for social history in an effort to help make the world a better place for all social groups. They also continued to specialize. This approach peaked in the 1930s with the onset of the Great Depression and the New Deal response. The progressive historians were no more interested in comprehensive historic preservation than their scientific predecessors, but the peak of progressive influence in American history coincided with the sudden availability, created by New Deal programs, of jobs for historians outside the university.

The progressives also introduced the first phase of "public history." It was very different from current public history with its roots in the New Left of the 1960s and 1970s and its trunk the postmodernism of the late twentieth century. To the early twentieth-century progressives, public history was the application of history to understanding public life and the production of popular history. Unlike the modern version, it was not a collaborative effort with the public. The public history of the progressives was also known as "applied history," a distinction to make it more palatable to academics.

Early public history was forced upon professional historians in the 1930s by widespread employment outside the ivory tower of historians whose principal subject matter concerned the products and production of local history. The New Deal was mostly about employment. Professional archaeologists and historians were hired not so much to employ them but so they could supervise a great many non-professionals doing archaeology and history projects.

Most of these professionals were under NPS management both for projects within NPS and at various New Deal agencies. In 1931, Vern Chatelain was hired as the first NPS historian and, as chief historian, had some responsibility for discovering and interpreting history at 80 NPS historical parks and monuments. At first he had only two historians under him, both at newly established Colonial National Park, but soon he hired more. Within a few years, Chatelain had 60 historians on his staff supervising thousands of workers.

Most historians focused on projects that were not so much historic preservation as we understand it today but historic interpretation in parks and the indexing of historic records. Some, however, were involved in restoration projects within the national parks, where they worked directly with archaeologists and architects. Many professional historians stayed with or returned to NPS after World War II and also went to the National Archives, forsaking jobs in the academy for jobs in government.

Other federal relief activities unrelated to park development greatly benefited the practice of history and heritage preservation. The Historical Records Survey of the Works Progress Administration was an outgrowth of the Federal Writers Project in late 1935, which, at its peak, employed 4,000 workers (Tyrrell 2005:176). Its purpose was to discover, preserve, and list basic historical research materials for the benefit of officials, historians, and the public. It initially focused on county public records but expanded to include church records, newspaper indexes, maritime records, and even the records of the National Archives and Records Administration (NARA), which had been established in 1934. The original intent had been to publish indexes of all the county records for the entire nation, but only about a third were published when World War II ended the survey.

The Historic Sites Act became law in August 1935, authorizing the creation of a survey of nationally significant historic sites. The Historic Sites Survey began in the summer of 1936 to find properties that could eventually come under NPS ownership. Four NPS regional historians directed the survey with oversight from Ronald Lee in Washington, DC. An advisory board developed historical themes within which properties could be targeted for survey and evaluated for relative importance. By the beginning of World War II, when the survey ended, only 560 properties had been surveyed, of which about 40% were considered nationally significant (Sprinkle 2014:15).

In 1940, the American Association for State and Local History (AASLH) and the American Society of Architectural Historians (ASAH) were established. The founders of these organizations had benefited from the great expansion in the employment of heritage preservation professionals due to the federal relief programs of the 1930s. Then World War II put things on hold for a decade.

In the 1950s, the progressive view was replaced with a more conservative one in the field of history. It agreed with the Dwight D. Eisenhower administration's philosophy of limiting government size and government spending, as well as addressing moral issues and stopping communism. It didn't fret about class distinctions even though such distinctions were necessary to democratic capitalism. The belief that personal property rights were at the core of the American way, limiting government in public life and promoting industrialization and reurbanization, did not bode well for advancing historic preservation. The 1950s and early 1960s witnessed such rampant destruction of historic properties that even political conservatives saw a need to support government-sponsored historic preservation.

By the early 1960s, historic preservation was being reborn, not as the myopic programs of the 1930s but as a comprehensive approach to preserving all kinds of resources. It was not archaeologists or historians who originally sounded the alarm but journalists, economists, scientists, politicians, and the public, who saw widespread threats to the total human environment. History-architecture books of note are Jane Jacobs's *The Death and Life of Great American Cities* (1961), Martin Anderson's *The Federal Bulldozer* (1964), and Peter Blake's *God's Own Junkyard* (1964). Also in 1965, Charles Hosmer published *Presence of the Past*, the first of his three-volume history of early historic preservation.

Historians and the practice of history also began to change in the 1960s, influenced by the socially focused political agendas of the John F. Kennedy and Lyndon B. Johnson administrations and the rise of the New Left. The New Left historians were not so much socialist in their thinking as they were focused on the experiences of the general public writ large. They were concerned with the flaws in American society such as racism, sexism, and war making and how those flaws came about. Subfields such as women's history, black history, and urban history soon flourished.

The "new social history" of the 1960s and 1970s began to lose control of American history after the Vietnam War ended and another conservative federal government took office in 1980. Today, American historiography is a blend of its many earlier iterations. No one movement completely dominates, although the left-leaning "new" public history is perhaps still the most academically popular. The journal *Public Historian* was first published in 1978, and two years later the National Council on Public History (NCPH) was founded.

Public history in the twenty-first century is very different from that of the early and mid-twentieth century. The first version of public history in the 1930s was simply history done for public purposes outside the ivory tower; the name did not reflect a philosophical change of heart. The public history of the 1960s and 1970s was a broadening of the 1930s perspective that included the formal practice of historic preservation by government agencies and private consultants, but its basic definition was still "history done outside of academia" (Kelley 1978:16).

The public history of the late twentieth and early twenty-first centuries is difficult to define even for its practitioners. The NCPH came up with a definition as stated in its newsletter in 2007 and repeated on its website into early 2012: "a movement, methodology, and approach that promotes the collaborative study and practice of history." This definition has since disappeared from the NCPH website, although the collaborative approach is still stressed.

A look at public history textbooks (e.g., Cauvin 2016; Howe and Kemp 1988) shows that public history today is not history done with public funding, because of public laws, or for public entities; it is history done to tell the stories of diverse communities in collaboration with those communities. Public history today has very little to do with mainstream historic preservation, although it is sometimes done in conjunction with historic preservation activities. Historic preservation is usually mentioned in public history book chapters discussing federal government history or private contract history, but it is not the focus of the discussion in those chapters.

Historians were the original leaders of historic preservation in the federal government, beginning with Ronald Lee (see chapter 9 sidebar). Other historians of note who played important roles in developing American historic preservation were Jerry Rodgers, who had various key roles with NPS from 1967 through 2001; Robert Garvey, head of the National Trust (1960–1967) and first executive director of the ACHP (1967–2001); and Robert Utley, chief NPS historian (1964–1966), director of the Office of Archaeology and Historic Preservation (1967–1972), and assistant executive director of the ACHP (1976–1980).

Historians, as one would expect, have played a key role in writing the history of historic preservation in America, at least with respect to its early days. Charles Hosmer was first, with his three-volume history taking the story up to the founding of the National Trust in 1949 (Hosmer 1965, 1981). The story was then picked up by James Glass (1990), trained as an architectural historian, who focused on the passage of NHPA in 1966 and the immediate aftermath. No one has written a comprehensive follow-up to Glass.

Becoming a Heritage Management Historian

Historians differ from architectural historians in two principal aspects. First, most historians are educated in history departments, while many architectural historians are educated in architecture departments. This gives them different perspectives on what is worthy of study and how to go about it. Second, most historians study the entire scope of the historical record, while most architectural historians just focus on aspects of the built environment. With regard to historic preservation projects, historians look broadly at all aspects of the built environment, including buildings, structures, and landscapes, while architectural historians tend to focus on projects related just to buildings (i.e., constructs that house human activities).

The *Secretary of the Interior's Professional Qualifications Standards* for historians are less restrictive with regard to education and experience than those for archaeologists:

History
The minimum professional qualifications in history are a graduate degree in history or closely related field; or a bachelor's degree in history or closely related field plus one of the following:
1. At least two years of full-time experience in research, writing, teaching, interpretation, or other demonstrable professional activity with an academic

institution, historic organization or agency, museum, or other professional institution; or

2. Substantial contribution through research and publication to the body of scholarly knowledge in the field of history.

Most first-generation historic preservation historians had a bachelor's degree in history, although, like archaeologists, they received limited specialized education in the day-to-day work of historic preservation. Today, while the federal qualifications for historians have not changed, many agencies and most private consultants require or prefer their historians to have advanced degrees in history or historic preservation.

Today, most historians in the practice of historic preservation consider themselves public historians, or at least their university programs consider them as such. As of the end of 2017, a search of university "public history" programs listed on the National Council on Public History website sorted only by "historic preservation" gets 81 hits. There is a great deal of variety in these programs with regard to how they define public history, both explicitly on their webpages and implicitly in the programs and classes they offer. Some provide focused classes in practical skills needed for doing historic preservation history and have instructors experienced in doing comprehensive historic preservation, two critical elements in practically preparing historic preservation historians for their careers. Some important classes include completing the many aspects of a Section 106 review, undertaking a historic records search, writing a National Register nomination, and preparing historic structures or **adaptive reuse** reports.

The availability of written practical guidance for historic preservation historians is less satisfying. I have not been able to find a single textbook that describes how to do the day-to-day work of most government and private consultant historians working in historic preservation. The NPS and various SHPOs do provide advice and guidelines for doing the historian's job in historic preservation as it applies to their specific needs.

Three basic levels of education and training prepare you for doing a historian's job in historic preservation. These levels essentially overlap with other professions. The first is intensive education in your particular profession that helps you to understand what you are doing, teaches you the methodology to employ in doing it, and gives you an ethical basis to guide the actual practice of your work. Most undergraduate and graduate courses are concerned with this level. While most of this education is done in the classroom, for a historian it should include some fieldwork component, such as doing an identification survey of a specific area and a field evaluation of the significance and integrity of at least one building or even a district.

The second level focuses on obtaining broad knowledge to put the work you do into a particular historic preservation context. This would include knowing applicable laws, the history of historic preservation, and the variations that apply for federal, state, local, and private applications. For a historian this should also include understanding the geographical context (e.g., midwestern) and topical history (e.g., agricultural, mining) of the location where you will practice. Field experience is also necessary, such as looking at properties associated with different historic contexts.

The third level consists of learning methods and skills necessary to actually complete a particular job. For a historian this would include knowledge of geographic information systems, map interpretation, database input and management, and the availability of critical written sources pertaining to your area. The ability to communicate effectively is critical for all fields of heritage management. Writing well is a skill many professionals assume they possess, but some actually don't. Oral communication is important to obtaining information, sharing information, and even getting a job that allows you to practice your profession. Digital communication through multiple venues is increasingly important, combining both written and oral skills with technical knowledge. Fieldwork at this level intensively examines all aspects of identification, evaluation, and nomination for buildings, structures, and landscapes.

Architectural Historians

There is no federal Office of Personnel Management (OPM) classification for architectural historian. Under the OPM Historian 0170 series, architectural history is not mentioned as a specialty. Under the OPM Architecture 0808 series, there is no mention of a historical architect. The General Services Administration (GSA), the manager of federal buildings, has a "preservation architect" employment category that includes the following specialists: preservation architect, architectural **conservator**, architectural historian, and **historic landscape architect**.

The *Secretary of the Interior's Professional Qualifications Standards* are specific for both architectural historians and historical architects. For architectural historians they state,

> *Architectural History*
> The minimum professional qualifications in architectural history are a graduate degree in architectural history, art history, historic preservation, or closely related field, with coursework in American architectural history, or a bachelor's degree in architectural history, art history, historic preservation, or closely related field plus one of the following:
> 1. At least two years of full-time experience in research, writing, or teaching in American architectural history or restoration architecture with an academic institution, historical organization or agency, museum, or other professional institution; or
> 2. Substantial contribution through research and publication to the body of scholarly knowledge in the field of American architectural history.

Today, most American architectural historians are trained in architecture departments or specialty university programs in historic preservation. As of December 2017, there were 49 graduate school programs in historic preservation listed at PreservationDirectory.com. Of these, 33 were in architecture departments, 6 were in historic preservation departments, 5 were in history departments, and 5 were in other departments, including planning, American studies, and urban affairs. At the undergraduate level, PreservationDirectory.com listed 47 programs, of which 23 were in architecture departments, 19 were in stand-alone historic preservation programs, 3 were in other departments, and only 2 were in history departments. Many of the stand-alone historic preservation programs are at the community college level.

Architectural historians involved in historic preservation trained in university architecture departments become well versed in building construction methods, architectural styles, and the nomenclature of building parts. Most practicing architectural historians who were trained in history departments probably had no intention of becoming what they are today. One influential instructor and maybe only one focused architectural history class probably shaped their interest and initial expertise in the history of buildings.

The professional requirements for being a historian or an architectural historian are almost identical. Just as in history, most university programs in architecture do not offer multiple classes in architectural history that would be of direct benefit to American historic preservation practice. Like historians, most architectural historians in historic preservation learn the majority of their skills after university and on the job.

Architectural history did not emerge as a distinct discipline in American historic preservation until the late 1960s. Just prior to the passage of the NHPA, James Marston Fitch and Charles Peterson started a historic preservation graduate program at Columbia University, the first in the nation. At the time, architectural history as an academic pursuit still focused on European expressions. Fitch and Peterson had to contend with not only making American architecture worthy of historical study but making historic preservation a worthy field for architects.

When the American Society of Architectural Historians (ASAH) was founded in 1940, preservation of buildings was formally recognized as important. The American Institute of Architects (AIA) established a Committee on the Preservation of Historic Buildings in 1951. But few architectural historians or architects actually got involved in American historic preservation until well after the NHPA was passed in 1966 (Bluestone 1999). Prior to 1966 the journal of the ASAH includes relatively few articles about American historic preservation other than the restoration of Williamsburg. A notable exception is Fiske Kimball's 1941 article "The Preservation Movement in America." The first extensive discussion of American historic preservation in the *Journal of the Society of Architectural Historians* didn't appear until 1999.

While the academic side of American architectural history continued to ignore historic preservation, architectural historians were making significant contributions to historic preservation in the late twentieth century. Multiple academic programs in historic preservation expanded at American universities. The major textbooks on historic preservation used in both architecture and history classes were almost all written or edited by architectural historians. These include James Fitch (1982, 1990), Norman Tyler (1994, 2000), Robert Stipe (2003), and William Murtagh (1988, 1997, 2006). Confirmation of architectural history's importance to historic preservation was validated by the inclusion of "architectural historian" in the 1983 *Secretary of the Interior's Professional Qualifications Standards for Archaeology and Historic Preservation.*

There is a great diversity of opinion as to what architectural history is and what architectural historians do. There is also a great difference between what architectural historians teach at universities and what architectural historians do in historic preservation practice. The academic practice of architectural history has its roots in art history. When I took classical art history as an undergraduate, we spent a lot of time talking about the construction details of Greek and Roman buildings. The history of American architecture as taught in architecture departments is basically about stylistic changes through time.

According to the ASAH, "Architectural historians engage in research into, and the dissemination of knowledge about, the evolution of the art and craft of architecture and its place in the history of civilization." Architectural history in American historic preservation practice is principally about researching buildings and structures constructed in North America over the last 500 years and providing public agencies and private entities with the information and analysis necessary for documenting the structural history and structural elements. This information and analysis are then used for completing inventories, assessing significance, implementing treatments, and registering significant examples.

With regard to historic preservation, the practice of architectural history differs from that of architecture principally with respect to at what stage they interact with the NHPA processes and tax act initiatives. NHPA involvement concerns four primary areas for architectural historians: Section 106 project review, National Register nominations, historic preservation planning, and community-related initiatives.

Doing History in Historic Preservation

Most aspects of what historians and architectural historians do in historic preservation could be incorporated into four basic types of work: planning, property identification, property evaluation, and property treatment. All formal historical projects for the purposes of historic preservation result in some tangible product such as a written plan, a written report, a database, a letter, or even a map. These activities are associated with historic preservation initiatives at the federal, state, and local levels and with environmental review as required by multiple federal laws and some state laws. Historians' and architects' roles in heritage management differ significantly from archaeologists' with regard to satisfying the needs of federal grant eligibility and tax act certification, specifically in the treatment of historic properties for these purposes.

Planning Studies

Historic property surveys, historic context studies, historic structures reports, and reuse studies are all elements of heritage management planning, but some projects are explicitly about planning. Planning is a consideration of options to implement actions. If planning is serious and formalized, like that on the part of governments, it results in a written plan that recommends or requires a particular course of action.

Although I am broadly discussing planning under the section on historians, all heritage management professionals are involved in planning both formally and informally. For archaeologists, a research design is basically a plan for efficiently and effectively achieving objectives at all levels of archaeological work. Archaeologists are also leaders in cultural resource management plans (CRMPs) that often focus on an area of land mainly containing or thought to contain archaeological resources. For architects, design guidelines are a plan for maintaining historical integrity in a historic district while allowing necessary intrusions and improvements. In my experience as a SHPO staff member, however, historians have taken the lead in many aspects of planning that more broadly address all types of historic properties, such as statewide preservation plans and community preservation plans.

Planning has been a big part of heritage management since the passage of the National Historic Preservation Act in 1966, when the NPS was given federal oversight responsibilities for much of American heritage preservation. Planning had been important in the NPS since the 1920s, as the agency struggled to find a balance between its dual responsibilities for public visitation and resource preservation. Visitation initially got the upper hand, promoting the development of roads and public facilities within the parks. In the early 1930s, park master plans were introduced, outlining development strategies for each national park. The NPS enactment of Mission 66 in 1956 continued to encourage development over preservation.

By the time of the fiftieth anniversary of NPS in 1966, the mission had changed. Parks were now classified as natural, historic, or recreational, with natural parks receiving preservation priority. The passage of the NHPA the same year also promoted a preservation ethic for historic parks. The passage of the National Environmental Policy Act (NEPA) in 1969 encouraged an interdisciplinary approach and an explicit assessment of development options. In the 1970s, park planning was completely revised and, for the first time, included formal public input. Plans were completed by professional planners assisted by multidisciplinary teams (deFranceaux 1987). The NPS developed plans to manage all types of resources, not just the natural and cultural resources found in parks. Management plans included internal resources, such as economic, personnel, and political resources, that maintained the organization's ability to fulfill its mission.

The familiarity of the 1960s "new" archaeologists with methodological aspects of planning, especially interdisciplinary approaches, made them a good fit with the NPS as the NHPA began to be implemented. This wasn't as true of historians. In the 1930s, Vern Chatelain, the chief historian for NPS, had noted that the academically trained historians were of little use in planning (Tyrrell 2005:173). While historians dominated the NPS cultural resource efforts beginning in 1930s, archaeologists were dominant by the end of the 1970s, in part because of their familiarity with planning. Today, archaeologists may dominate budgets and agency heritage management staff, but they no longer dominate planning.

Types of Plans

There are two basic types of plans, *strategic* and *tactical*. Strategic plans address broad goals not specific to one area, one type of property, or one action. Tactical plans do focus on specific areas, property types, or actions. Examples of strategic plans are statewide preservation plans and community preservation plans. Examples of tactical plans are cultural resource management plans for specific landholdings and design guidelines for historic districts.

Many types of heritage management plans result from planning at many different levels. Some tightly focused tactical plans are the realm of archaeologists (e.g., data-recovery plans), or of architects (e.g., design guidelines), or of curators (e.g., disaster management plans). All professionals can play important roles in tactical cultural resource management plans depending on the area of land being managed and its cultural resources. Historians play particularly important roles in state comprehensive plans and community preservation plans.

State Comprehensive Plans

The 1966 National Historic Preservation Act in Section 101 authorized the secretary of the interior to provide grants to states for preparing comprehensive statewide historic plans. In Section 102, it required that all grants to states be made in accordance with a comprehensive statewide historic preservation plan that had been approved by the secretary. Most states didn't initially comply with this requirement of the act because it took a while for the NPS and the states to come up to speed on the provisions of act. In addition, there were no clear guidelines as to what a state comprehensive plan should contain.

In the late 1970s, the Heritage Conservation and Recreation Service of the National Park Service began to push the Resource Protection Planning Process (RP3). This eventually became known as comprehensive historic preservation planning, and each state was required to produce a comprehensive plan that was statewide in scope as originally required by the NHPA. The RP3 process added the requirement of including historic contexts in state plans. Many states began their comprehensive planning process with developing their historic contexts but once again paid little attention to actually completing a comprehensive plan. While the *Secretary of the Interior's Standards and Guidelines for Archaeology and Historic Preservation* issued in 1983 included a section on planning, it focused almost totally on context development as an aid to evaluation and interpretation.

Although a few state comprehensive plans appeared by 1980, by 1990 only 36% of the states and territories had completed their plans, with another 43% having partially completed them and 21% having no plan. The failure by most states to complete the comprehensive plan was due mostly to inadequate funding but also to a lack of SHPO interest (Morrison 2014). An NPS review of comprehensive planning progress in 2014 indicated 65% of states and territories (35 of 54) had failed to complete or make timely updates to their plans. Apparently, the only penalty for not having an NPS-approved state comprehensive plan is the requirement to submit two additional documents with the annual SHPO Historic Preservation Fund (HPF) grant application, a program overview (1–2 pages) and an action plan narrative (10–15 pages).

The requirements of a state comprehensive plan are outlined in the NPS *HPF Grants Manual* in chapter 6, Section G (NPS 2007). The manual defines a state comprehensive plan as "a document that articulates a vision of the future for historic preservation across the State and identifies goals and strategies for achieving them in the future. The State Plan is a tool for the State Historic Preservation Office and others throughout the State for guiding effective decision-making on a general level, for coordinating Statewide preservation activities, and for communicating Statewide preservation policy, goals, and values to the preservation constituency, decision-makers, and interested and affected parties across the State." The plan must be "a single, concise, printed document," although there is no required length or format. Some plans are only 30 pages long (e.g., Wisconsin), while some have almost 150 pages (e.g., Kentucky). There is no fixed time period for plan validity or a fixed update schedule; a plan need only be updated "as necessary." Some states have 5-year plans (e.g., Minnesota, Washington), some 7-year plans (e.g., Indiana), and some 10-year plans (e.g., Texas, Iowa). Most state comprehensive plans are produced in-house by SHPO staff. Besides variability in length, format, and timing, there is a great deal of variety in plan content between states. Common problems for denial of NPS certification are failure to obtain adequate public consultation, lack of interpretation of data, too much focus on SHPO operations, and failure to correlate issues with goals and objectives.

Context Studies

Although the initial focus of planning in the 1983 SISG was on the development of historic contexts, a review of major SHPO publications in 2017 indicates that today contexts no longer dominate any aspect of heritage management. A review of SHPO history-architecture manuals demonstrates that few of these manuals discuss historic contexts in any detail. The same is true for state comprehensive preservation plans. But historic contexts are still vital to American heritage management.

Most properties are eligible for inclusion in the National Register due not to their uniqueness but to their representativeness. These properties cannot be evaluated for their significance without comparing them to other similar properties. Most buildings, structures, historic sites, and historic districts are eligible for inclusion in the National Register under Criterion A for their association with important events and patterns of events. *Historic contexts* organize key interpretive data into a unified perspective based on shared spaces, times, themes, and ultimately property types.

For example, say you were assessing the significance of a 1930s headquarters building in a state park. Your research indicates it was built by a Civilian Conservation Corps (CCC) crew, it is done in a rustic style, and it was designed by a locally prominent architect. There may be a statewide historic context associated with recreation. There may be statewide thematic contexts associated with federal relief construction, with rustic-style architecture, and with the architect. If there is nothing special about the design or many better examples by that architect are still extant, it may not be eligible under Criterion C for its association with rustic-style architecture or buildings designed by the architect. If there are many more prominent and better-preserved buildings in state parks associated with recreation, it may not be eligible under Criterion A for its association with the statewide recreation historic context. However, if it is a well-preserved, exemplary, and rare example of a CCC-built headquarters building in a state park, it may be eligible under Criterion A for its association with the federal relief thematic context. Without knowledge about similar buildings in similar settings with similar construction histories, the significance of the building in question can't be adequately evaluated.

States first developed their own historic contexts in the late 1970s following NPS guidelines. Some states put more effort into the process than others. If statewide historic contexts are truly comprehensive, every property present in a state should fit under one or more of its statewide contexts. Despite the historic context sermons still preached by the National Register, most states mainly pay lip service to them, as indicated by statewide preservation plans. Fewer than 10 states include a list of their current historic contexts in their statewide plans.

There is great variety in the types of historic contexts for the historic period used by states. Most rely on some form of thematic contexts that are statewide in scope. For instance, Alaska has the following thematic contexts: population movements, exploration, and settlement; survival and adaption; military and government; industrial, commercial, and economic development; transportation and communication; intellectual and social institutions; and natural history and disasters. Some states (e.g., Idaho, Illinois, West Virginia) use many of the themes found in the areas of significance for National Register nominations (e.g., agriculture, architecture, commerce). Some use regions for organizing their contexts, both natural and cultural (e.g., Colorado, Kentucky, Pennsylvania).

Minnesota has divided its historic contexts into three periods: Precontact, Contact, and Postcontact. Precontact- and Contact-period properties are primarily archaeological. Historians use Postcontact contexts for most properties they evaluate. In Minnesota, the Postcontact period lasts from 1837 up to 1945 or 50 years since from the most recent context document (1995). There are only eight Postcontact historic contexts. As originally defined in 1990, they are

- St. Croix Triangle lumbering (1830s–1900s)
- Early agriculture and river settlement (1840–1870)
- Northern Minnesota lumbering (1870–1930s)
- Indian communities and reservations (1837–1934)
- Railroads and agricultural development (1870–1940)
- Minnesota's iron ore industry (1880s–1945)
- Minnesota tourism and recreation in the Lake regions (1870–1945)
- Urban centers (1870–1940)

Only the last five contexts deal with properties created in the second half of the twentieth century. Properties belonging to these five contexts are still being created today, and some of them may be eligible 50 years after they were created. The Minnesota SHPO has made no attempt to revise or expand its statewide historic contexts since the early 1990s, although what are known as thematic contexts have continued to expand.

Thematic contexts are a second tier of contexts based on property types that share common origins, purposes, and form. Current Postcontact thematic contexts in Minnesota are state-owned buildings, bridges, military roads, Red River trails, hydroelectric power facilities, federal relief properties, geographic features of historic and cultural significance, Finnish log architecture, and grain elevators. Thematic contexts often come out of Multiple Property Documentation Forms (MPDFs). Most MPDFs are written by historians, although Minnesota has a number written by archaeologists (e.g., Native American earthworks, Native American rock art).

A third tier of contexts are *local contexts*. These are typically done by historians for large landowning federal agencies (e.g., a national forest) or for certified local governments (CLGs) that are in the early stages of their preservation planning. Local contexts help agencies and local governments decide what types of properties to include in their historic property surveys and which properties may be eligible for listing in historic registers.

The geographic area for most local contexts is easy to define because it is congruent with the jurisdictional boundary of the governmental entity. The theme of a local context and its age are based on important local events, industries, people, commercial developments, cultural activities, recreation, and institutions. Cities tend to focus on historical-period themes, rarely including archaeology. As the roster of CLGs expands within every state, so will the need for historians to complete local context studies.

Community Preservation Plans

Community preservation plans are not required if a community is to become a certified local government, but having one is a hallmark of a good CLG. Some states (e.g., Pennsylvania) include provisions for historic preservation planning in municipal planning statutes. A local historic preservation plan is often part of a larger community comprehensive plan that includes zoning requirements and capital investment considerations.

A joint National Trust for Historic Preservation (NTHP) and American Planning Association publication (White and Roddewig 1994) first outlined guidelines for local comprehensive plans in detail in 1994 and suggested the following basic elements of a good plan:

- Statement of goals
- Definition of historic character
- Summary of past preservation efforts
- Historic resources survey
- Explanation of the legal basis for historic preservation
- Coordination of preservation with zoning, land use, and growth management
- Definition of public-sector responsibilities
- Incentives for preservation
- Definition of the relationship between preservation and education
- Agenda for future action

Most communities hire a planner or a historic preservation firm to assist with developing a historic preservation plan, but a historian's input is the most important. Historic preservation plans are also most effective when coordinated with other planning initiatives, like smart growth, context-sensitive design, and going green.

Archival Research

The most common historic preservation task of a historian is to complete archival research in order to assess the potential of a given area to contain historic properties and the types of properties that may be found. Agency and SHPO staff are constantly doing basic archival research for each project they propose or review. The archival review is critical to making decisions as to whether a field survey is needed, as well as determining what to look for if a survey is done. If an undertaking is large or complex or has good potential to contain historic resources, a private contract historian may be hired to provide more detail prior to recommending or doing the field reconnaissance. Beyond identification, archival research is also done for evaluation, treatment, registration, and most other historic preservation activities. Each type of literature search has its own needs and standards.

Archival research has already been discussed with respect to archaeological projects. As with archaeological projects, archival research for history projects begins with an examination of existing inventories maintained by review agencies or various units of government. In most states, the SHPO is the starting point for archival research. SHPOs maintain not only the history-architecture database for a state but also the archaeological databases in some states, especially where the state archaeologist is part of the SHPO. SHPOs also have files concerning property types, National Register nominations, historic context studies, and reports of previous investigations. They also have key personnel who can provide advice and guidance. Some SHPOs include written guidelines for conducting archival research in their survey manual.

Moving on to more detailed archival research, local repositories are critical, including libraries, government offices, and historical societies. Libraries have historical newspapers, maps, city directories, photographs, county and city histories, professional journals, and topical files. Basic property information can be found at a county recorder's office, while many cities maintain records of building and demolition permits. Cities that are certified local governments have often done extensive literature searches, context studies, and planning. Copies of the results of these CLG initiatives can usually be found at the SHPO.

Maps are especially useful sources for archival research. Key maps for entire states include General Land Office (GLO) survey notes/maps and historical county plat maps. For cities, fire insurance maps (e.g., Sanborn, Rascher) and historical plats are essential. Older aerial photographs are very useful for reconstructing land-use histories and even locating some types of historical sites (e.g., farmsteads, mining camps). Archival research should also include consulting knowledgeable individuals such as local historians and landowners.

Online resources have dramatically simplified, improved, and expanded archival research. These resources include current and historical aerial photographs, historic maps, GLO records, US Geological Survey maps, context studies, professional journals, National Register nominations and Multiple Property Documentation Forms, historical photographs, and, of course, a Google search on any topic. Many SHPOs have their statewide inventories online, although there may be a fee for obtaining online access, and access to archaeological data may be restricted to archaeologists.

Historic Properties Reconnaissance Surveys

Field surveys are done for multiple historic preservation purposes. They were initially focused on planning and registration needs at the state and local levels. The 1980 amendments to the NHPA added Section 110, which broadened survey to incorporate the planning and registration needs of federal agencies. After the 1969 passage of the National Environmental Policy Act and 1971's Executive Order 11593 declaring National Register–eligible properties equal to listed properties for Section 106 purposes, historic property surveys were needed for environmental review purposes.

Today, environmental review needs are the major focus of historic preservation surveys, although individual property evaluation surveys are still necessary for tax act purposes, and new certified local governments are required to survey their communities for properties to register and protect. With regard to planning, most states do little to continue the work of their statewide identification surveys, prominent in the 1980s, due mainly to a lack of funding but also to an attitude that most important built environment properties have already been identified, except perhaps in isolated rural areas. Most of the large landowning federal agencies still continue identification surveys of their land for NHPA Section 110 purposes, but many focus on archaeological properties. Some communities also sponsor identification surveys to find local properties that will promote heritage tourism, heritage education, and a better understanding of their own history.

Two types of identification surveys, reconnaissance and intensive, are mentioned in the 1983 SISG, as discussed earlier. Based on the 1983 guidelines that are still in place, a *reconnaissance survey* only characterizes the types and number of historic resources present in a given area, while an *intensive survey* provides detailed descriptions of each resource in the area, including sufficient information for "later evaluation and treatment decisions." Historic resources include any potentially significant historical sites, structures, buildings, objects, or districts within the area.

The first necessity for a historic properties survey is a clear idea of what needs to be recorded. Historians doing surveys should also start with a research design, but this process is usually less formal than in archaeology and is often referred to as a survey plan or survey methodology. The 1983 SISG stresses the need for three aspects of a research design: objectives, methods, and expected results. Few SHPO history-architecture manuals require a formal research design prior to survey, especially with regard to the necessity of expected results. For history-architecture identification surveys, the expected results of both levels of survey are pretty obvious. A reconnaissance survey is expected to find some potentially eligible properties in the survey area or it would not have been recommended in the first place. The expected result of an intensive survey is to find some eligible properties.

Basic objectives and methods needed to satisfy a history-architecture survey are usually evident from a review of the required inventory form. Most agencies and states and some CLGs have their own inventory forms, although they must meet the requirements set in the NPS *HPF Grants Manual* (2007:9–2). If the area you are surveying is not for an entity that has or requires a standard inventory form, it is easy enough to develop one of your own by looking at the many examples available online. If you are developing your own, make sure you have included all necessary data to fulfill the objectives of the survey and that its meets your SHPO's standards so that it can easily be used to add necessary data to the statewide inventory. Be aware of mapping and photographic needs as well as filling out the basic descriptive items on the form.

Field surveys for historical and architecture properties are almost universally labeled by SHPOs as "reconnaissance" and "intensive" in conformance with the 1983 SISG. Unlike archaeological surveys, history-architecture survey levels are rarely given formal phase or class names. However, SHPO history-architecture survey manuals almost universally go beyond the requirements for reconnaissance and intensive as described in the 1983 SISG and are identical to archaeological survey purposes labeled as Phase 1 and Phase 2. The purpose of reconnaissance survey for history architecture is to identify all *potentially eligible* properties in an area, while an intensive survey identifies all of the *eligible* and *ineligible* properties among those identified by the reconnaissance survey. Thus, an intensive survey is best discussed under evaluation.

Reconnaissance surveys are often called "windshield" or "walkover" surveys because they are limited to driving slowly around in a vehicle or walking relatively quickly through a survey area. These surveys are easiest in cities where you can get visual access to almost every building and structure by just driving or walking the city streets. You can fill out your form, take a few pictures, and do a sketch map without ever going on someone's private property. You don't have to ask anyone's permission to do the survey. A windshield or quick walkover survey provides basic information as to an individual property's age, historic context, and condition, thus allowing a very preliminary assessment of its potential eligibility and need to be recorded, even by you. It provides a baseline inventory.

Windshield surveys don't work well in rural areas because many properties are not immediately adjacent to public roads and those that are may be hidden behind dense vegetation. In order to do a windshield survey in most rural areas, you have to drive down farm entrance roads, get out of your car, and knock on doors to get permission to enter people's land. While this is time-consuming, you can also ask for basic information, such as when the house or other structure was built or when an addition was put on. This type of survey gives you a better assessment as to a property's significance and integrity. It can be used to better determine which properties in the survey area will need a more detailed examination for impact assessment, mitigation, or registration.

When you are doing a reconnaissance survey for buildings or structures, it is important to be able to immediately assess the approximate age of the building because, in most cases, only buildings that are about 50 years old need to be recorded. Sometimes dating can be done just by looking at historic aerial photographs, noting when structures appeared on a particular parcel. In long-developed areas, however, buildings come, buildings go, and other buildings come. Which building is which is not always clear in aerial views.

To date a building in the field, architects and historians usually first look at the style. American architectural styles are the subject of numerous books and guides (e.g., Blumenson 1981; Baker 1994; Whiffen 1992; Poppeliers and Chambers 2003; McAlester and McAlester 2011). Some styles were preferred for houses, some for commercial buildings, and some for government buildings (Figure 12.1). The styles were originally regional, with a variety of colonial styles including Spanish, New England, southern, French, and Dutch. The Georgian style was popular throughout the eighteenth century, being replaced with federal and then Greek revival styles in the early nineteenth century. A few somewhat elaborate styles typified the mid-1800s, including gothic, Italianate, and Renaissance revival. Late-nineteenth-century houses featured a great variety of styles, including French Second Empire, stick, Eastlake, shingle, and Queen Anne. Popular early twentieth-century house styles were neoclassical, bungalow, and prairie. Commercial buildings in the later part of the mid-twentieth century included international, art deco, and art moderne styles. Some states (e.g., Washington, Utah), cities (e.g., New Orleans, Orlando), and private organizations (e.g., Boston Preservation Alliance) provide style guides to help date local buildings.

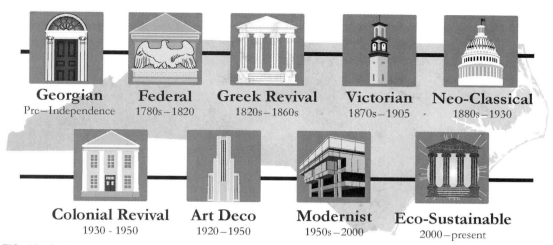

Georgian
Pre—Independence

Federal
1780s–1820

Greek Revival
1820s–1860s

Victorian
1870s–1905

Neo-Classical
1880s–1930

Colonial Revival
1930 - 1950

Art Deco
1920–1950

Modernist
1950s–2000

Eco-Sustainable
2000–present

FIG. 12.1 Major architectural styles of North Carolina courthouses (North Carolina Administrative Office of the Courts © Ava Barlow).

But styles come and go, and building styles are complicated and compromised by additions and renovations. Sometimes early styles are copied in later periods. As an archaeologist, I tend to date buildings by moving from the ground up. Foundation materials are clues to age, and foundations are less susceptible to replacement and stylistic copying than superstructure materials. Vermont even has a publication called *Stonewalls and Cellarholes: A Guide for Landowners on Historic Features and Landscapes in Vermont's Forests* (Sanford, Huffer, and Huffer 1995) to help identify remnants of architectural features.

In Minnesota, native stone foundations are the earliest, usually comprising tabular blocks of limestone, sandstone, or granite in urban areas and fieldstone in rural areas. The use of stone foundations had declined significantly by 1930. Cement blocks began to be used in the 1880s and are still popular, although block styles have changed through time. Brick foundations appeared about 1910 and stopped being used in the 1930s. Poured-concrete foundations first appeared in the 1930s using small-piece wooden forms, with large plywood forms and prefabricated forms appearing about 1960.

Window outer-frame (architrave trim) styles are a good indication of a building's age, even if the inner window frames have been replaced with aluminum or vinyl. Original exterior wall treatments, if visible, can also be roughly dated, with wood and stone cladding the earliest, followed by brick and stucco, and then a wide variety of asphalt, asbestos, aluminum, steel, vinyl, hardboard, and fiber cement siding. Roof shapes can also be used, although there are only a few basic shapes for most roofs, such as gabled, hipped, and flat. Mansard roofs are very distinctive, associated with the Second Empire style popular between 1860 and 1890. Flat roofs were not popular until the international style was introduced in the mid-twentieth century.

While residential, commercial, and governmental buildings can often be classified and dated by architectural style, other types of buildings and structures may be more difficult to date and classify. For example, farm-related buildings and structures require their own particular regional and topical expertise. They too have been the subject of multiple guides (e.g., Noble and Cleek 2009). Barns are the most studied farm buildings, with many regional styles and functions. There is a great variety of secondary farm buildings and structures, such as grain-storage facilities, small-animal shelters, and machine sheds. The Vermont SHPO has identified 48 different types of nonresidential farm buildings, including 10 types of barns (Jamele and Gilbertson 1991).

Remember not to get so focused on buildings that you forget about structures, objects, sites, and districts when you are doing a historic properties survey. The National Register defines *buildings* as constructions that house human activities. *Structures* are functional constructions for purposes other than human shelter. They include obvious items, like bridges, roads, and dams, but also vehicles, pieces of machinery, fences, and utility poles. *Objects* are relatively rare, especially in rural areas, and include outdoor sculpture, markers, and monuments. *Sites* are not exclusive to archaeology, being areas of land where the location itself possesses significance, such as where a significant event took place, a cemetery, or even natural features of cultural importance. *Districts* are related assemblages or concentrations of one or more of the four individual property categories, the most obvious being commercial and residential districts.

Landscapes are the most recent addition to history-architecture surveys and fit under the NRHP's "site" property category. Tischler (1979, 1980) discussed historic landscapes about a decade before they appeared on SHPO radars in the late 1980s, after the National Register issued Bulletin 18, *How to Evaluate and Nominate Designed Historic Landscapes* (Keller and Keller 1987). Within five years of Bulletin 18, the NRHP issued three other bulletins focused on historic landscapes: rural landscapes (Bulletin 30), battlefields (Bulletin 40), and cemeteries (Bulletin 41). Historic landscapes are also explicitly considered under bulletins that deal with mining properties (Bulletin 42) and traditional cultural properties (Bulletin 38).

All landscapes that are potentially eligible for inclusion in the National Register are now called *cultural landscapes* and consist of four types: historic sites, **designed landscapes**, **vernacular landscapes**, and ethnographic landscapes. The realm of historians includes the first three types, while the final type is a subject for anthropologists. A *designed landscape* is a landscape that was consciously designed or laid out by a landscape architect, master gardener, architect, or horticulturist according to design principles or by an amateur gardener working in a recognized style or tradition. A *vernacular landscape* is a landscape that evolved through use by the people whose activities or occupancy shaped that landscape. *Historic sites* as cultural landscapes have the same basic definition as "site" in terms of the National Register (areas of land significant for their association with a historic event, activity, or person), although the area of land often has multiple landscape elements both natural and cultural, such as a battlefield.

The secretary of the interior has issued *Standards for the Treatment of Historic Properties with Guidelines for the Treatment of Cultural Landscapes* (Birnbaum and Peters 1996). NPS Preservation Brief 36 deals with the protection of cultural landscapes (Birnbaum 1994). The Historic American Landscapes Survey (HALS) was established in 2000 by the NPS in association with the Library of Congress and the American Society of Landscape Architects (ASLA). Multiple books have been written on the subject of historic landscapes (e.g., Longstreth 2008; Alanen and Melnick 2000). Some landscape architects now specialize in historic landscapes. The NPS has an occupational category for **historical landscape architect**.

Intensive Surveys and Eligibility Evaluations

A big part of historians' heritage management duties is determining if properties are important enough to be documented, studied, registered, and preserved. National Register eligibility is the determinant of importance for most federal and state purposes. Local governments can set their own significance criteria for registration and preservation priorities.

The 1983 SISG emphasizes that an intensive survey is the second level of identification and is intended to provide enough information to eventually determine if a property is eligible. In the evaluation section of the SISG that follows the reconnaissance section, evaluation is inferred to be an office exercise, while in practice a formal evaluation of eligibility is usually the immediate outcome of an intensive survey. This is certainly the objective of an intensive survey as described in most SHPO history-architecture manuals.

Furthermore, the evaluation section in the 1983 SISG emphasizes only a property's significance with little mention of integrity, thus the extensive discussion of historic contexts within this section. Integrity is mentioned in relation to a property's appearance and condition. There is no discussion of the seven aspects of integrity required by the National Register, which seems to ignore integrity of setting and feeling dependent on a property's surroundings. Intensive surveys should include an explicit assessment of all seven aspects of integrity because a property lacking integrity is not eligible no matter how significant it once was.

The intensive survey requires a detailed examination of each potentially eligible property in the project area that will be impacted by a project or subject to registration for grant or tax benefit eligibility. While the integrity of a building's exterior is the critical factor in assessing eligibility, building interiors are increasingly of some importance. An intensive survey requires more detailed recording of features than the inventory form completed by initial reconnaissance surveys. While intensive surveys must provide substantial descriptive detail, the final report still relies on evaluating the significance within a historic context, within one or more of the significance criteria (A, B, C, D), and in terms of the integrity aspects appropriate for the selected significance criteria.

Property significance evaluations are critical not only for local governments and agencies to guide their surveys and preservation efforts but for environmental review, grant eligibility, and tax benefit certification. While landowning agencies and local governments can decide on their own what historic contexts to use for setting their own priorities, for the purposes of federal and state environmental review, National Register requirements have to be applied, and these generally rely on statewide historic contexts established by SHPOs. Chapter 5 discusses how the combination of significance and integrity is used for determining National Register eligibility.

The historian's role in determinations of eligibility (DOEs) for the Section 106 process is even more important than it is for nominations when it comes to applying National Register requirements to nonarchaeological properties. In addition, archaeological areas of potential effects (APEs) tend to be smaller than history-architecture APEs, so historians often have to deal with more properties, especially in urban areas. Over 90% of the properties subject to Section 106 consensus DOEs are never nominated to the National Register, although this is truer for archaeological sites, as sites don't receive much benefit from nomination. Buildings listed in the National Register can be eligible for federal and state tax credits or for grants that promote preservation.

Documentation

Although documentation can have a generic meaning, such as providing official information or evidence that serves as a record of a historic property (e.g., a National Register nomination), documentation in historic preservation practice is usually synonymous with a form of treatment used to mitigate adverse effects on a historic property due to development impacts. While the four standards treatments (preservation, rehabilitation, restoration, and reconstruction) noted in the various iterations of the SISG concern preservation in place, documentation as a treatment attempts to record as much as possible about a historic property before it is destroyed or significantly altered. Documentation may even need to be done prior to applying one of the four standard treatments.

There are separate standards and guidelines for historical documentation (four standards), architectural and engineering documentation (three standards), and archaeological documentation (four standards). The four standards for historical documentation are as follows:

- Standard I: Historical documentation follows a research design that responds to needs identified in the planning process.
- Standard II: Historical documentation employs an appropriate methodology to obtain the information required by the research design.
- Standard III: The results of historical documentation are assessed against the research design and integrated into the planning process.
- Standard IV: The results of historical documentation are reported and made available to the public.

According to the 1983 SISG for historical documentation, "Documentation is a detailed record, in the form of a report or other written document, of the historical context(s) and significance of a property. Historical research to create documentation uses archival materials, oral history techniques, ethnohistories, prior research contained in secondary sources and other sources to make a detailed record of previously identified values or to investigate particular questions about the established significance of a property or properties." Historical documentation is not merely recounting a property's construction and use but "generally results in both greater factual knowledge about the specific property and its values, and in better understanding of the property in its historical context. In addition to increasing factual knowledge about a property and its significance in one historical context, documentation may also serve to link the property to or define its importance in other known or yet-to-be defined historic contexts."

If the subject of the documentation is a building or structure, the historian may need to collaborate with a preservation architect or engineer to better understand its structural nature. If the subject is a historic landscape, the historian may need to collaborate with a landscape architect to better understand the various elements of the built environment. If the subject is a historical archaeological site, a historical archaeologist will play a critical or even dominant role in the documentation. Documentation is more than a written record; it must also include graphic recordation in the form of photographs, plans, and sketches.

National Register Nominations

Properties in any location can be nominated to the National Register of Historic Places. If they are listed in the National Register, they become registered historic properties. In some locations, properties can also be nominated to state or local historic registers.

Anyone can write a National Register nomination for a nonfederal property, but the nomination still has to go through SHPO review and be submitted to the Keeper of the National Register for review before it can be listed. If it is a privately owned property, the landowner can object and block the listing. Only federal agencies can nominate properties they control, and federal nominations go through a different vetting process than nonfederal nominations, but agencies usually hire an outside consultant to write the nomination. The elements of a National Register nomination and the nomination processes are described in chapter 5.

The 1983 SISG lists three standards for registration:

1. Standard I: Registration is conducted according to stated procedures.
2. Standard II: Registration information locates, describes and justifies the significance and physical integrity of a historic property.
3. Standard III: Registration information is accessible to the public.

The first standard states the obvious. The second standard contains the two basic requirements of any acceptable nomination and, unlike the evaluation discussion in the SISG, gives equal weight to integrity along with significance. The third standard is only recently being reasonably attained with internet access, although most nominations are not yet digitized and available online. Based on the planning and evaluation standards, there should have been a fourth standard under registration: "Registration is done within a historic context." Concern with historic contexts is embedded in two of the three planning standards and one of the four evaluation standards. It seems strange that a concern for historic contexts is not included in the registration standards.

Evaluation of a property's eligibility can be done somewhat informally as some properties are so obviously eligible that a prolonged discussion of historic context is unnecessary. For example, a state capitol building built a century ago is so important to the government of a state that its justification of significance and association with government is obvious just in the building's name. Within a nomination, however, that justification must be fully developed and the historic background described in detail. The building may also be eligible under more than one significance criterion, typically A and C, so the justification and description must focus on both. Justification within a historic context and description of structural elements and their integrity are the realms of a historian and an architectural historian.

Because National Register nominations should follow the guidelines outlined in NRHP bulletins, most require a certain amount of specialization in the area of significance and familiarity with National Register requirements for integrity as they apply to particular property types and applicable significance criteria. Considering the necessary specialized and technical knowledge needed to write a nomination and the fact that only 15% of the National Register listings are archaeological sites, professional historians and architectural historians are the most common authors of nominations. Because National Register requirements also commonly apply to state historic registers and some local historic registers, historians play a key role in these nominations too.

The Architectural Profession in Historic Preservation

Most schools of architecture offer two different specialties for historic preservation practice: architectural history and historic preservation architecture. For the first type of degree, you train as a historian and for the second as an architect. There is also landscape architecture, but at most universities there is currently no formal separation of historic preservation practice from just landscape architecture practice, although a landscape architect considering historic preservation practice can take specialty courses.

A History of Preservation Practice in Architecture

Thomas Jefferson not only made significant early contributions to American archaeology and American history but can also be thought of as the father of American architecture. Jefferson's most notable architectural design achievement was his own home, Monticello, into which he incorporated unique design elements with a basic European style (Figure 12.2). Jefferson also helped design the Virginia State Capitol and initial buildings at the University of Virginia, in addition to collaborating with Charles L'Enfant to design the landscape of Washington, DC. Monticello and the original University of Virginia campus were the first two American World Heritage sites.

While Jefferson may also be the father of American archaeology (he did the first scientific excavation) and the father of American history (he wrote the first history book), he is not the father of American architectural preservation. He once told an acquaintance, "Architecture is my favorite delight, and putting up and pulling down, one of my favorite amusements" (Rayner 1832:524). Jefferson was referring to his own work, not to historical structures, although in the late 1700s few Americans thought there was much historic value in American buildings. Jefferson was outraged by the intentional destruction of Roman ruins in France (Bowman 2013).

The first tangible successes in American historic preservation were carried out with the assistance of architects. In 1816, Independence Hall in Philadelphia had been saved from destruction and its steeple rebuilt in 1829 under the direction of architect William Strictland. Also in 1829, the Newport Synagogue was restored. Early intellectual guidance for historic preservation was also provided by architects, notably John Ruskin in his 1849 *The Seven Lamps of Architecture*, of which one lamp was the Lamp of Memory.

Architecture became a formal practice in America in the early nineteenth century, although designs for major American buildings were largely copied from British, Greek, and Italian forms. Most early federal buildings such as the White House (1801) and the Capitol Building (1831) were intentionally neoclassical to invoke the Greek and Roman roots of democracy. The School of Fine Arts (École des Beaux Arts) in Paris began training architects in the early nineteenth century and began accepting American students in the mid-nineteenth century. Early American students included Henry Richardson and Julia Morgan. Richardson's Marshall Field building (1887) in Chicago and Morgan's Hearst Castle (1919) in California were important in establishing American-based architecture.

The American Institute of Architects was founded in 1857, the same year Frederick Olmsted and Calvert Vaux submitted the winning design for Central Park in New York. In 1865, the Massachusetts Institute of Technology (MIT) began offering courses in architecture, followed by the University of Pennsylvania in

FIG. 12.2 Thomas Jefferson's Monticello, reflecting its owner-designer's interest in standard European and innovative American architecture (Library of Congress).

1869 and the University of Illinois in 1870. In 1881, the AIA acquired the 1799 Octagon House in New York for its headquarters, setting an early precedent for professional architects' support of historic preservation. The American Society of Landscape Architects was founded in 1899.

America developed its own distinctive architectural styles in the late nineteenth century, using steel and glass in high-rise buildings, assisted by the invention of the elevator by Elisha Otis. The Rand McNally Building, built in 1889 in Chicago, introduced the concept of the skyscraper. Chicagoan Louis Sullivan promoted the Chicago style in architecture, soon taken to its apex in the early twentieth century with the prairie style of Frank Lloyd Wright, a blend of the arts and crafts style with Japanese influences. French-influenced art deco styles were also popular until the stock market crash in 1929.

The Organic Act of 1916 established the National Park Service, charged with not only conserving natural objects and wildlife in national parks and monuments but preserving historic objects and scenery. This included archaeological sites, historic buildings, and cultural landscapes. The cultural landscapes aspect embedded in the "scenery" provision was not implemented by the NPS until the late 1970s. The early conception of cultural landscapes was largely limited to formal gardens, although the War Department had done an extensive survey of battlefields, a number of which became national parks.

In 1926, the restoration of Colonial Williamsburg began, creating considerable work for historical architects. Depression-era programs led to a great expansion of architects within the federal government. Landscape architect Charles Peterson was hired by NPS to oversee historic building reconstructions. Peterson started the Historic American Buildings Survey (HABS) in 1933 in cooperation with the AIA. With the passage of the Historic Sites Act in 1935, the National Survey of Historic Sites and Buildings was initiated. The American Society of Architectural Historians was founded in 1940, attesting to the great expansion of employment and interest in the topic.

World War II put a hold on most historic preservation activity, including HABS and the NPS Historic Sites Survey. After the war, the founding of the National Trust for Historic Preservation in 1949 was one of the first actions to revitalize architectural participation in American historic preservation. The year before, Hampton Mansion was designated a national historic site, the first historic property to be nationally recognized for its architectural design rather than its historic significance. The federal Housing Act of 1954 included a provision for historic preservation planning. HABS and the NPS Historic Sites Survey were reactivated in 1957, but at a much-reduced level of effort.

In the mid-twentieth century, German immigrants Walter Gropius and Mies van der Rohe moved American architecture to a modernist style, with an emphasis on glass, concrete, and steel and a lack of ornamentation. Modernism in America peaked with designs by Phillip Johnson and Louis Kahn. This coincided with major federal urban renewal efforts in the early 1960s, bringing the majority of "new construction" architects into direct opposition with "preservationist" architects. Some preservationist architects were leaders in the failed attempt to save New York's Penn Central Station in 1963.

The first Williamsburg Conference on historic preservation in 1963 brought focused professional attention to the crisis in historic preservation created by urban renewal and urban interstate highway construction. The principles that came out of the conference (Short 1966) formed the basis for the recommendations in *With Heritage So Rich* (Rains and Henderson 1966), which provided the foundation and justification for the National Historic Preservation Act in 1966. Another indication of the increase in historic preservation architectural interest in the mid-1960s was Columbia University's introduction of graduate work in historic preservation in 1964. The program was led by noted architectural historians James Fitch and Charles Peterson.

Besides the NHPA, a number of other federal laws promoted historic preservation of architecture: the Housing and Redevelopment Act of 1965, which created the Department of Housing and Urban Development; the Demonstration Cities and Metropolitan Development Act (DCMDA), which created the Model Cities Program; and the Architectural Barriers Act of 1968, which required handicapped accessibility for federal buildings.

Former NPS cultural resource personnel, who had been moved to the Interior Department's Heritage Conservation and Recreation Service (HCRS) in 1977, took their lead from the newly founded Alliance for Historic Landscape Preservation (AHLP) and began to officially acknowledge the need for historic landscape preservation. This was first couched as "rural preservation" (e.g., Stipe 1980; Melnick 1980; Tischler 1980). In 1981, after HCRS had been disbanded and the cultural resource unit moved back into NPS, the NPS officially recognized "cultural landscapes" in Director's Order 28.

In 1984, the NPS offered it first guidance on preserving rural landscapes (Melnick, Sponn, and Saxe 1984). In 1987, the National Register issued Bulletin 18 on designed historic landscapes (Keller and Keller 1987); two years later it issued Bulletin 30 on rural historic landscapes (McClelland et al. 1989). Historic landscapes had finally entered the mainstream of American historic preservation.

Building architects' relationship with historic preservation also changed in the 1970s. The *Secretary of the Interior's Standards for Rehabilitation and Guidelines for Rehabilitating Historic Buildings* were issued in 1977 in response to 1976 tax act changes. There were additional tax act changes in 1978, 1981, and 1986. The NTHP started its Main Street Program in 1980, encouraging the historic rehabilitation of central business districts in small towns. The Americans with Disabilities Act (ADA) of 1990 mandated handicapped access to all buildings open to the public, requiring innovative architectural solutions to maintain the integrity of historic buildings.

Architectural postmodernism in the late twentieth century brought back the use of more diverse materials and ornamentation to buildings. In the twenty-first century, no architectural style dominates. Architecture supports social movements like new urbanism, rightsizing, affordable housing, and sustainable (green) buildings. Much of this is implemented in the rehabilitation of older buildings.

Architects in Historic Preservation

"Historic architect" is basically synonymous with "preservation architect" and "conservation architect." (Note: these practitioners prefer "historic" to "historical"; I guess many of them are not only old but famous.) There has been a recent trend in architecture to move away from the use of "preservation architecture": it is confusing when applied to American heritage management as an architectural practice because preservation is a specific type of architectural treatment. The use of "conservation" in place of "preservation" as a description of the field of historic architecture has been promoted in some schools of architecture (Pybum 2005).

The *Secretary of the Interior's Professional Qualifications Standards* for historic architects are as follows:

Historic Architecture

The minimum professional qualifications in historic architecture are a professional degree in architecture or a State license to practice architecture, plus one of the following:

1. At least one year of graduate study in architectural preservation, American architectural history, preservation planning, or closely related field; or

2. At least one year of full-time professional experience on historic preservation projects. Such graduate study or experience shall include detailed investigations of historic structures, preparation of historic structures research reports, and preparation of plans and specifications for preservation projects.

A few university architecture programs specializing in historic preservation applications appeared in the mid-1960s, but their output and influence were limited. This coincided with the rapid destruction of the older built environment due to urban renewal and interstate highway construction. Most practicing architects were eager to participate in urban renewal as it gave them a chance to implement modernism on a large scale. It paid well too. A few architects were disturbed by the proposed demolition of landmark buildings such as Penn Station in New York and the Schiller Building in Chicago (Bluestone 1999:204).

A revolution in historic preservation architecture occurred when vernacular architecture suddenly became important in the late 1970s. This not only reduced the emphasis on style but socialized architecture by making it more concerned with political and cultural aspects. It also encouraged architects to become more interdisciplinary, a great asset in historic preservation. This occurred among practicing architects before academics, because there was work to be had in historic preservation but little fame or intellectual satisfaction. Historic preservation and vernacular architecture were simply ignored by most university architecture departments.

Financial incentives to rehabilitate older buildings became attractive with housing and tax acts in the 1960s and 1970s. In the mid-1970s, the NPS began to issue guidelines for historic building treatments in order to apply for NHPA grants-in-aid, HUD programs, and tax act eligibility. The first formal standards and guidelines issued by the secretary of the interior were for building rehabilitation in 1977. Standards and guidelines for other types of historic preservation projects soon followed. All of these standards and guidelines were consolidated into one document, the *Secretary of the Interior's Standards and Guidelines for Archaeology and Historic Preservation*, in 1983. Since 1983, the major clarification and expansion of the SISG has been with respect to building treatments, with a continuing focus on rehabilitation as it applies to tax credits.

In most architecture schools, historical architects continue to train first as architects, and then a few develop a specialty in historic preservation. Many of their preparatory classes are in design and drawing, especially computer-aided applications. With one or two classes in architectural history, most are ready to pursue a career in historic architecture. If they enter an agency at the state or federal level, they will have limited time and encouragement to pursue research and writing. If they become private contractors, their efforts will focus on specific projects, which may allow limited freedom to explore intellectual perspectives.

The Practice of Architecture in Historic Preservation

While ethnohistorians and archaeologists look broadly at a "cultural environment," architects focus on the "built environment." This is a human-made environment, ranging in scale from small structures to large cultural landscapes containing obvious human modifications and constructed features. In common historic preservation usage, the built environment does not include most prehistoric sites lacking major above-ground features or nonstructural alterations of a landscape such as the "voluntary" replacement of one native plant species with another.

Preservation architects are primarily concerned with treatments of historic buildings for the purposes of utilizing federal Historic Preservation Fund grants-in-aid, obtaining and implementing tax act certification, conducting Section 106 review of HUD urban development programs and projects, developing design guidelines for historic districts, and participating in historic structures reports.

Treatments of Historic Properties

As noted earlier, four distinct architectural treatments are applied to historic buildings as determined by the secretary of the interior: preservation, rehabilitation, restoration, and reconstruction. Federal definitions of these treatments first appeared in 1971 in conjunction with the availability of HPF grants. These grants could be used to fund state and local activities related to the "acquisition and development" of National Register–listed historic properties. A grants manual produced by NPS was issued in 1974 listing three types of development treatments: stabilization, restoration, and reconstruction. A 1976 revision of the grants manual defined seven eligible treatment activities: acquisition, protection, stabilization, preservation, restoration, rehabilitation, and reconstruction. The 1992 revision of the manual resulted in a reduction to four treatments that are still in place today: preservation, rehabilitation, restoration, and reconstruction.

The 1954 Housing Act had a provision for building rehabilitation, but it was seldom used to preserve historic properties and gave no specifics as to what rehabilitation entailed. The 1966 DCMDA authorized the newly created HUD to fund surveys to help identify historic properties that might be impacted by urban renewal programs, in addition to allowing for funding of acquisition and restoration of historic properties in blighted areas. However, both the 1954 and the 1966 housing acts did more to promote the destruction of historic properties than to preserve them. Passage of the Housing and Community Development Act in 1974 allowed HUD to provide block grants to cities and loans to individual property owners to rehabilitate buildings that were listed in or eligible for the National Register. As the grants were subject to Section 106 review, NPS and HUD issued *Guidelines for Rehabilitating Historic Buildings* in 1976 to guide compliance by HUD and HUD-designated local agencies for programs and projects.

The Tax Reform Act of 1976 created the Federal Historic Preservation Tax Incentive Program, which supported the rehabilitation of income-producing National Register–listed properties. The *Secretary of the Interior's Standards for Rehabilitation* were issued in March 1977 to provide guidance for the tax incentives program. They were revised in 1990, with additional NPS guidance provided in 2006 and 2011.

Grants-in-aid, HUD initiatives, and tax incentives were also subject to overview standards and guidelines for treatments issued by the secretary of the interior in 1977, 1983, 1985, 1992, and 2011. These standards and guidelines were consistent with the specific standards and guidelines issued separately that applied to grants-in-aid, HUD programs, and tax incentives. These treatment activities are largely the purview of historic architects.

"Treatment" is not defined by the secretary of the interior in the master document on treatments or in detailed documents on the four standard treatments, but the *Guidelines for the Treatment of Cultural Landscapes* define "treatment" as "work carried out to achieve a particular historic preservation goal." By inference with regard to the overall treatment guidelines, treatment means federally approved actions to promote the appropriate care of historic properties, resulting in their preservation, rehabilitation, restoration, or reconstruction. The appropriate treatment for a property is determined by level of significance, physical condition, proposed use, and the specific statutory application. Treatments can be applied to any property type but are mostly associated with buildings or structures. Archaeologists and historians can be major players in preservation as a treatment, but the other three treatments are almost exclusively the realms of architects.

Preservation

Preservation as a treatment allows for the least freedom of action because it literally means preserving as much of a property's historic fabric and historic look as possible. It includes all historic fabric, not just that associated with a particular period or style. As explained on the NPS Technical Preservation Services webpage, "Preservation is defined as the act or process of applying measures necessary to sustain the existing form, integrity, and materials of an historic property. Work, including preliminary measures to protect and stabilize the property, generally focuses upon the ongoing maintenance and repair of historic materials and features rather than extensive replacement and new construction. New exterior additions are not within the scope of this treatment; however, the limited and sensitive upgrading of mechanical, electrical, and plumbing systems and other code-required work to make properties functional is appropriate within a preservation project."

Preservation is a treatment most appropriate for buildings of national significance that are in good condition and whose intended use will closely approximate the original intended use or interpretation of that use. An example is a house museum associated with a president. A preservation requirement could be applied to HPF grants-in-aid action or NHPA Section 106 or 110 actions but would not be eligible for tax incentives or HUD grant programs. Because preservation involves minimal reconstruction, it is more the task of an architectural historian than a historic architect.

Rehabilitation

Rehabilitation recognizes the need to alter or add to the existing fabric and look of a historic property to meet new needs. As explained on the NPS Technical Preservation Services webpage, "Rehabilitation is defined as the act or process of making possible a compatible use for a property through repair, alterations, and additions while preserving those portions or features which convey its historical, cultural, or architectural values."

Rehabilitation is a treatment appropriate at any level of significance and applies to buildings that are in fair to poor condition whose intended use could be very different from the original intended use. An example is a factory being reused as housing. A rehabilitation requirement is most commonly associated with tax incentives and HUD grants but could also apply to HPF grants-in-aid, Section 106 reviews, or Section 110 actions. Rehabilitations are the most common historic preservation tasks of historic architects.

Of the 49 preservation briefs issued by the NPS, 45 concern historic building rehabilitation or restoration. The Association for Preservation Technology (APT) also provides extensive guidance on these treatment activities. The APT was founded in 1968 by American and Canadian preservationists. Its mission was "to advance the application of traditional and contemporary technology appropriate to conservation of the built environment and the cultural resources that contribute to its significance."

The application for a 20% tax credit for rehabilitation of a historic property entails a three-part process. For Part 1, an applicant must apply to the appropriate SHPO for certification that a building is indeed eligible for the National Register or is a contributing building within a listed historic district. If the building is not already listed, the SHPO evaluates the property and makes a written recommendation of eligibility that is sent to the NPS. If the NPS agrees a building is eligible, it directly notifies the building owner. The owner is then responsible for completion of an acceptable National Register nomination, and the SHPO will take it through the standard nomination process. A historian or architectural historian usually assists the building owner with the Part 1 requirements and National Register nomination.

For Part 2, the owner of the historic property must complete a description of rehabilitation. Here the owner will need the assistance of a historic architect to ensure that the project meets all 10 of the *Secretary of the Interior's Standards for Rehabilitation and Guidelines for Rehabilitating Historic Buildings*. The entire project as it affects the historic property must be described in detail. This includes interior and exterior details as well as effects to the setting. The property must be photographically documented prior to any construction activities actually applying the tax credits. A detailed description of alterations, accompanied by sketches and plans, must fully explain the proposed construction. The description of rehabilitation is submitted to the SHPO, and once the SHPO agrees it meets the standards, it is forwarded to the NPS. If the NPS agrees with the SHPO, a notice of certification is sent directly to the property owner. The property owner can start the construction prior to actual listing of the property in the National Register if Part 2 has been approved, although some owners are reluctant to start construction until they have a confirmation of listing. Construction should be carefully monitored by a historic architect to make sure the work is conforming to the standards.

Part 3 starts with a one-page form completed by the property owner that states all project work has been completed. Postconstruction photographs must accompany the form. The form is submitted to the SHPO. If the SHPO concurs that the work followed the Part 2 plan and meets the standards, it forwards the information to the NPS. If the NPS agrees, notification of certification is sent directly to the property owner. The owner then attaches a copy of the certification to a tax return to receive tax credits.

Restoration

Restoration results in the re-creation of the look and fabric an intact or partially intact historic property had during one particular period of its history. It requires the removal of elements and materials from other periods and often the significant addition of important lost elements. As explained on the NPS Technical Preservation Services webpage, "Restoration is defined as the act or process of accurately depicting the form, features, and character of a property as it appeared at a particular period of time by means of the removal of features from other periods in its history and reconstruction of missing features from the restoration period. The limited and sensitive upgrading of mechanical, electrical, and plumbing systems and other code-required work to make properties functional is appropriate within a restoration project."

Restoration is a treatment appropriate at any level of significance and applies to buildings that are in fair to poor condition whose intended use will be similar to the original intended use. An example is Colonial Williamsburg, although there was also considerable reconstruction involved with that project. A restoration requirement could be applicable to HPF grants-in-aid or to Section 106 or 110 actions. Restorations are usually directed by historic architects.

The first recognized participation for architects in historic preservation was the restoration of historic buildings. Building restoration itself had been the earliest historic preservation activity in America, dating back to two restorations in 1829: the steeple on Independence Hall in Philadelphia and the Touro Synagogue in Newport. Although Hosmer (1980) lists 29 early examples of historic building restorations, including such notable examples as Princeton's Nassau Hall in 1855, the Whipple House in 1898, and the Paul Revere House in 1905, architectural restoration didn't begin in earnest until the Williamsburg project started in 1926.

Almost all historic building restorations prior to the 1930s were done with private funds. NPS did its first restoration in 1931, of the Moore House at Yorktown, under the direction of Charles Peterson, but Depression-era historic preservation programs concentrated more on documentation than restoration. The opening of Colonial Williamsburg in 1934 was the major restoration event of the first half of the twentieth century, although of the 500 "period" buildings at Williamsburg, 88 have been restored and 412 reconstructed.

The basically conservative historic site approach the NPS developed in the 1930s carried over into its modern historic preservation policies. Conrad Wirth, the director of NPS, made a presentation at the first Williamsburg Conference in 1963, at which he discouraged building restoration unless four conditions were met:

1. There was very accurate knowledge of what the original looked like.
2. All continuity between the past and the present had been broken.
3. The restoration would play no important part in the surrounding landscape.
4. The restoration was critical to the well-being of the associated population (Wirth 1966).

The Williamsburg Conference adopted nine core principles for restoration that became the basis for the secretary of the interior's standards and guidelines a decade later.

Reconstruction

Reconstruction is the total or almost total re-creation of historic properties that were once present at a particular location but have been destroyed. The reconstruction must be based on sound archaeological and documentary evidence of what the property once looked like, using materials that would have been available in the designated time period. As explained on the NPS Technical Preservation Services webpage, "Reconstruction is defined as the act or process of depicting, by means of new construction, the form, features, and detailing of a non-surviving site, landscape, building, structure, or object for the purpose of replicating its appearance at a specific period of time and in its historic location."

Reconstruction is a relatively uncommon treatment, especially reconstruction supported by or conforming to federal tax benefits or grant eligibility requirements. It could be applied to the reconstruction of a building at a site of any level of significance. Historic property condition is not generally applicable, because the building is no longer present, although ruins and artifact distributions can help guide the reconstruction. The intended use of reconstruction is almost always interpretation. Example are the reconstruction of long-vanished forts or presidents' birthplaces. It could be an action associated with a grants-in-aid project.

Reconstruction is rarely a requirement of a federal action, although it could be used as a Section 106 mitigation. Reconstructions are usually planned by a historic architect with the assistance of archaeologists, historians, and architectural historians. If reconstructions are done appropriately at historic sites, they can be listed in the National Register under Criteria Consideration E. "Appropriate" means accurate in design and materials as well as setting.

Design Guidelines

Design guidelines are a method of clearly, reasonably, and consistently implementing a historic preservation ordinance within a historic district. The purpose of the guidelines is to restrict actions that would harm the appearance of individual historic properties within a historic district or harm the overall character of the district. Sometimes these may only involve keeping the historic facade of a building to maintain a streetscape (Figure 12.3). Design guidelines assist cities and property owners within historic districts in planning for acceptable improvements and obtaining long-term objectives, not just for historic preservation but for economic viability and neighborhood livability. They can also be used for educational purposes.

Design guidelines were initially developed as a reaction to the intrusion of modernist architecture into old neighborhoods. Following traditional NPS historic site practice and international standards like those in the Venice Charter of 1964, the *Secretary of the Interior's Rehabilitation Standards* issued in 1977 stressed the need to differentiate new construction from historic construction in historic districts. While modernist architecture was clearly distinct from earlier styles, it was too distinct to be compatible with most historic districts. The compromise was to limit the design of new construction within a historic district to either using distinct but familiar variations of older architectural styles or making some abstract reference to an earlier style within a new style (Semes 2007).

Design guidelines implement a historic preservation ordinance within a specific area (e.g., a residential neighborhood) or with regard to a specific type of construction (e.g., signage). The ordinance is the actual law, while the design guidelines help residents, property owners, developers, and city officials interpret and implement the law. Some cities just use the *Secretary of the Interior's Rehabilitation Standards* as their design guidance, while others have published individually tailored design guidelines.

There is limited federal advice for developing design guidelines for historic districts. The NPS webpages have a section titled "Creating and Using Design Guidelines," but it is restricted in scope and provides little detail on the process of completing the guidelines or the format of the final document. Many cities have completed design guidelines, however, so the first step in considering design guidelines should be for the members of a historic preservation commission (HPC) to consult multiple examples available online. Numerous private consulting firms specialize in or are experienced with doing design guidelines and have helpful information on their webpages. Some of the best advice can be found at Winter & Company (http://www.winterandcompany.net).

Nore Winter (2008) suggests design guidelines need to focus on identifying the key features of a historic district that have to be respected and retained, while allowing for some freedom of design within the district. Winter notes that the four standard features in the final document are a policy statement, a statement of design guidelines, supplementary information with additional suggestions, and illustrations

FIG. 12.3 Commercial building facade preservation in Memphis, Tennessee (author photo).

that clarify the guidelines, such as photographs and drawings of good and bad examples.

The process of establishing design review guidelines usually begins with discussions by the HPC and basic research such as looking at examples from other cities. A consulting team is then assembled made up of city officials from key departments (e.g., park board, engineering, code inspectors, city attorney), city residents, members of the HPC, and both agency-based (e.g., SHPO) and private preservation professionals. The team is often led by a planner or an architect as both have extensive design experience.

Initial design team meetings are usually described as "charrettes," which are intensive planning sessions intended to familiarize the team with the language of the ordinance, with the objectives of the design guidelines, and with the historical and current character of the district. The team identifies the most important features of the district that must be retained and elements that are open to change and innovation. The team then writes draft guidelines, preferably considering all four of the secretary of the interior's treatment standards. The draft is then widely circulated for public comment, before the team is reassembled to provide basic guidance to help write the final version. The final design guidelines are usually printed in book form and are made available online.

Every significant new development within the historic district is then considered under the guidelines. Project proposers appear before the HPC and make a presentation. Here, too, it would be helpful for the proposer to have obtained professional advice from architects or planners familiar with the guidelines. A written as well as an oral presentation should be completed. If the proposal meets the guidelines, a certificate of appropriateness can be issued by the city. If it does not meet the guidelines, the HPC can make suggestions for alterations that will bring it in line with the design guidelines. Local design guidelines do not necessarily meet the standards required for federal or state tax incentives for building rehabilitation.

On the cover of this book is a photograph of the St. Anthony Falls Historic District in Minneapolis. Note the ruins of the historic building on the right and the historic structures in the middle. A glass-walled building is built into the ruins, allowing an integration of the ruins into the view from every floor. Also note that on the left there is a building that is clearly outside the period of significance and has a very different architecture. This is the Guthrie Theater. It was designed by French architect Jean Nouvel and opened in June 2006. Nouvel's design was meant to invoke images of flour mills and grain elevators.

I was working for the Minnesota SHPO when the theater was first proposed to be located within the historic district. We had less of a problem with the new building in the historic district than we did with the demolition of the old (1963) building located well outside the district, but it had been designed by local architect Ralph Rapson. The new Guthrie clearly stands out and certainly doesn't imitate the architecture of the past, but it fits surprising well within its historic setting. This is a demonstration of how design guidelines for historic preservation purposes can allow a great deal of architectural freedom.

Historic Structures Reports

Slaton (2005:1) writes that a *historic structures report*

> provides documentary, graphic, and physical information about a property's history and existing condition. Broadly recognized as an effective part of preservation planning, a historic structure report also addresses management or owner goals for the use or reuse of the property. It provides a thoughtfully considered argument for selecting the most appropriate approach to treatment, prior to the commencement of work, and outlines a scope of recommended work. The report serves as an important guide for all changes made to a historic property during a project repair, rehabilitation, or restoration and can also provide information for maintenance procedures. Finally, it records the findings of research and investigation, as well as the processes of physical work, for future researchers.

The first formal historic structures report was completed by NPS architect Charles Peterson in 1935 for the Moore House at Yorktown. The Moore House was the first building restoration undertaken by NPS, and Peterson was the first NPS historical architect. He is best known for starting HABS in 1933.

NPS Preservation Brief 43 provides a good overview of the steps needed, the reporting format, and the value of a historic structures report. The brief states that such reports are valuable because they provide the following:

- A primary planning document for decision-making about preservation, rehabilitation, restoration, or reconstruction treatments
- Documentation to help establish significant dates or periods of construction
- A guide for budget and schedule planning for work on the historic structure
- A basis for design of recommended work
- A compilation of key information on the history, significance, and existing condition of the historic structure
- A summary of information known and conditions observed at the time of the survey
- A readily accessible reference document for owners, managers, staff, committees, and professionals working on or using the historic structure
- A tool for use in interpretation of the structure based on historical and physical evidence
- A bibliography of archival documentation relevant to the structure
- A resource for further research and investigation
- A record of completed work

The value of having a detailed understanding of a building's current structural condition, its history prior to restoration, and its function after restoration is now well established. Historic structures reports are used by many states, agencies, and even other countries. Each state and agency may have its own guidelines for completing a historic structures report. As Arbogast (2010) stresses, a historic structures report presents a workable plan to maintain as much of the historic fabric of a building as possible.

Minnesota has productively employed historic structures reports since the early days of the SHPO program. The Minnesota SHPO recently sponsored historic structures reports for buildings as complicated as the state capitol and a structure as simple as a lime kiln. They even assisted a CLG with a cultural landscapes report for an important vernacular landscape.

Reuse Studies

Most states, agencies, and historic preservation organizations promote the many advantages of reusing older buildings. Such rehabilitation is done not so much to win tax benefits or grant eligibility as to save a worthy historic property. Building reuse is green because it limits energy expenditures for making new materials and keeps old materials out of landfills. Building reuse is economically advantageous because rehabbing an old building is often cheaper than constructing a new building. Building reuse is good for historic preservation because it can save a significant building and help preserve the character of a neighborhood. The National Trust for Historic Preservation has even given building reuse in cities a new name: ReUrbanism.

In the early 1980s, the NTHP provided reuse assistance to states and cities in the form of a preservation advisory service team (PAST). A PAST would look in depth at a threatened historic property to see if a reasonable reuse could be found. In 1986, the Minnesota SHPO adapted the NTHP PAST model by developing historic property reuse teams that would attempt to find a reuse for imminently threatened properties listed in the National Register and recently abandoned. The report of the team was called a *reuse study*.

The NPS has a formal document called a historic structure reuse plan, which includes a structural evaluation, a cost analysis, and alternate strategies that can be reasonably and effectively employed. The scope of the study can be a single building or all buildings within a park unit. Because these NPS plans apply to NPS-owned structures, there is less threat of imminent demolition and more emphasis on preserving the structure, but the plan has to meet federal legal requirements. These plans are coordinated through the NPS Denver Service Center.

As with some complicated historic structures reports, a multidisciplinary team of professionals is assembled to undertake a reuse study. The team usually consists of architects, engineers, historians, real estate experts, and local preservationists. Other team members can be added based on the type of property (e.g., recreation specialists), legal complications that may arise (e.g., attorneys), and non-building-use needs (e.g., archaeologists, ethnographers). The team's objectives are to assess the preservation value of the property to the community, determine its market value in both its improved and unimproved states, develop practical alternatives for the property's future use, and rank the reuse options for viability. Immediate reuse may be the most preferred option, but mothballing might be the most viable current option.

Unlike a historic structures report, reuse studies require more than just professional assessment and advice. Reuse studies require input from nonprofessionals who have an interest in the property or its reuse. This should certainly include community members but may also include people who once had a special attachment to the property, such as a former owner, current neighbor, or former city official.

I served on the reuse team for an early Minnesota house built by a missionary to the Dakota Indians in the mid-nineteenth century. We invited Dakota elders to our consultation discussions. The first elder praised the missionary for helping his people through difficult times. We all felt great after his interview. The next day, another Dakota elder said the missionary was one of the worst enemies of the Dakota because he tried to destroy their religion, which was at the very heart of their culture. The team was quite dejected after hearing his testimony. In the end, the reuse of the property did not depend on the testimony of either Dakota elder, but the interviews certainly informed the city that it had to proceed carefully with publicity about the reuse and with any interpretation of the property's history.

The reuse study report can discuss these interpretation and publicity issues as well as standard economic issues, political issues, and design issues. Some confidentiality also needs to be maintained with regard to the results of the interview process. In the end, the reuse study may not save the building, but it provides a final chance to see if saving a property is viable and whether the community truly values a property. The process itself may create the political will to save the property or find a developer interested in completing the project.

Historic Landscape Architects

Historic landscape architects are among the most recent professionals to join the ranks of historic preservationists. With the exception of gardens, interest in preserving historic landscapes lagged behind the preservation of buildings and archaeological sites well into the 1970s. This was even true within the NPS, where the pre-NHPA Leopold Report (Leopold et al. 1963) had continued to emphasize the importance of restoring a "primitive" landscape in all national parks, even though the Organic Act creating the NPS in 1916 had included a provision to "conserve the scenery," not specifically the "natural" scenery. The preservation of Civil War battlefields in the late nineteenth century was done not overtly for landscape preservation but for historic site preservation on a landscape scale.

The first large-scale restoration of a historic landscape utilizing professionals took place in the late 1920s at Colonial Williamsburg, although it was mainly about formal gardens. The landscape architects were less concerned about the overall historical accuracy of the gardens than the restoration architects were with the buildings (see Figure 1.1). In the 1930s, HABS documentation included 40 historic landscapes in Massachusetts, but NPS didn't overly concern itself with landscapes in historical parks.

Landscape architect Frederick Olmsted Jr. had helped write the NPS Organic Act, no doubt inserting the phrase "conserve the scenery." In the late 1930s, Olmsted undertook a survey of Charleston, South Carolina, to assist the city with preserving its historical assets. Olmsted's 1940 report included landscape features: "the arrangements of buildings, wall, fences, gates, etc. and of trees, gardens, and other open spaces." But Olmsted's concern with historical landscapes would not reach the mainstream of historic preservation for more than 30 years.

In the early 1970s, NPS woke up with regard to cultural landscapes. In 1973, NPS defined a "historic scene" as "the overall appearance of all cultural resources and their surroundings as they were in the historic period." In 1975 NPS started using the word "cultural" instead of "historic" but still did not use "landscapes" as a type of cultural resource. In the late 1970s, a few members of the Association for Preservation Technology founded the Alliance for Historic Landscape Preservation (AHLP). The *APT Bulletin* also began to publish articles concerning the importance of historic landscapes (e.g., Tischler 1979).

In 1981, NPS first used the term "cultural landscape" in the second edition of NPS-28: Cultural Resource Management Guideline, noting four discrete types: historic sites, historic scenes, historic landscapes, and sociocultural landscapes. Three years later, NPS issued a publication on rural historic landscapes. In 1985, NPS-28 was revised to include three new types of landscape along with historic sites and historic scenes: **historic designed landscapes**, **historic vernacular landscapes**, and ethnographic landscapes. Historic scenes were finally eliminated in the late 1980s. By 1990, NPS was fully invested in cultural landscapes as demonstrated by two new National Register bulletins: *How to Evaluate and Nominate Designed Historic Landscapes* (1987) and *Guidelines for Evaluating and Documenting Rural Historic Landscapes* (1989).

In the early 1990s, NPS initiated a battlefield protection program and a cultural landscape inventory in its parks. In 1996, the secretary of the interior issued *Standards for the Treatment of Historic Properties with Guidelines for the Treatment of Cultural Landscapes*. The Historic American Landscapes Survey was established by NPS in 2000, joining HABS and the Historic American Engineering Record (HAER).

Private and international cultural landscape efforts also expanded in the 1990s. The Cultural Landscape Foundation was established by Charles Birnbaum in 1998. Birnbaum had written much of the early guidance on cultural landscapes for NPS. In 1992, the United Nations Educational, Scientific, and Cultural Organization (UNESCO) began to recognize cultural landscapes as World Heritage sites, defining cultural landscapes as "the combined works of nature and of man."

The Practice of Landscape Architecture in Historic Preservation

The 1983 SISG contains no professional qualification standards for historic landscape architects, probably because historic landscape architecture was still in its infancy when these standards were issued. They were included in the 1997 draft professional qualification standards but were never officially adopted. The federal Office of Personnel Management does have an occupation classification for landscape architecture (GS-0807) with duties that include "research[ing], conserv[ing], and recogniz[ing] visualizations of aesthetic, cultural, natural, and historical resources." OPM does not have a job classification for historic landscape architect.

The National Park Service has three occupational categories specifically for historical landscape architect: entry level, developmental level, and full performance level. The entry level requires a bachelor's degree in landscape architecture from an accredited program and an understanding of the NPS role in cultural landscape management; "basic knowledge of theories, principles, laws, practices and techniques of landscape architecture, particularly as they apply to the preservation of cultural landscapes"; and "basic knowledge of allied fields, such as planning, architecture, archeology, and the natural resource sciences, necessary to conduct project reviews, supervise contracts, and provide technical assistance and information." The developmental level requires the same education and knowledge as well as the demonstrated ability to apply the skills to NPS-specific programs. The full performance level requires a graduate degree in landscape architecture as well as expertise in cultural landscape management and the ability to resolve conflicts and solve complex problems.

Duties for historic landscape architects within NPS are listed under seven program areas:

1. Professional discipline: provides professional expertise in cultural landscape management
2. Preservation law, philosophy, and practice: provides professional direction on historic preservation law, philosophy, and practice as they apply to cultural landscape management
3. Research: conducts and coordinates complex cultural landscape research projects related to the identification, documentation, and analysis and evaluation of character-defining features
4. Treatment and preservation maintenance: serves as professional advisor regarding treatment and preservation maintenance of cultural landscapes; develops and implements treatment plans and preservation maintenance programs
5. Program and project management: serves as project manager for a wide variety of work including complex research, planning, design, and construction projects and assists in the ongoing development of a comprehensive cultural landscape program
6. Writing and communication: communicates, interprets, and presents cultural landscape preservation as an integral component of the National Park Service's mission
7. Training: delivers training regarding cultural landscape management

Privately employed historic landscape architects can do projects under contract with NPS assisting with all of the above-listed duties as well as HALS documentation. Historic landscape architects can play key roles in many of the historic preservation projects already discussed. This would include historic property surveys, community preservation plans, and design guidelines. Their expertise is particularly necessary for three types of projects: cultural landscape reports, cultural landscape management plans (CLMPs), and cultural landscape nominations to the National Register of Historic Places.

Cultural Landscape Reports

A cultural landscape report provides the essential historical background and descriptive information on a particular area. This report is the basis for making landscape treatment and management decisions for the area. As well as the narrative site history and a detailed description of current conditions, the report should contain an evaluation of National Register eligibility and recommendations for treatment, management, and use. Such an evaluation requires that the resources be understood within a historic context. Most reports follow the recommendations in *A Guide to Cultural Landscape Reports: Contents, Process, and Techniques* (Page, Gilbert, and Dolan 1998), with additional guidance from Birnbaum (1994), both produced by NPS.

Cultural Landscape Management Plans

Cultural landscape management plans describe basic strategies for maintaining and using cultural landscape resources within a particular area. The plan should include appropriate visitor use and recommended interpretation. The plan is dependent on a detailed understanding of cultural and natural resources in the area as they relate to the landscape. It must then consider the preservation and use of these resources as they apply to the mission of the managing entity and applicable statutes. The plan should be completed prior to any development activities. The CLMP provides the principal guidance for determining the treatment of all cultural landscape resources within the management unit. There is no detailed guidance on how to prepare a CLMP, although some basics are included in Birnbaum (1994) and other NPS publications.

Many examples of CLMPs at the national, state, local, and international levels are also available online. These provide helpful insight into common and unique management issues that need to be addressed in CLMPs. Because of the necessary inclusion of both cultural and natural resources within cultural landscapes, there is often a conflict between doing what is best for each type of resource and where to focus preservation efforts.

For instance, at Aztec Ruins National Monument, the general management plan (GMP) includes consideration of cultural landscapes. It defines three different cultural landscapes: the prehistoric designed landscape, the historic designed landscape, and the historic vernacular landscape. Because the primary purpose of Aztec Ruins is to protect and interpret the prehistoric past, the prehistoric designed landscape is given highest priority. The historic vernacular landscape is given the lowest priority, which means features like orchards and ornamental plantings are targeted for removal.

Like all good plans, CLMPs should be flexible. Global warming, changing mission, shifting understanding of resources, and newly discovered resources can all lead to changes in a CLMP. CLMPs also need to carefully consider who will implement them. Because basic maintenance is often at the core of a CLMP, maintenance staff's understanding of their responsibilities is critical to plan implementation and success. Reduced funding and staff cutbacks can severely hamper plan implementation and effectiveness.

Cultural Landscape National Register Evaluations and Nominations

The eligibility and listing of a cultural landscape can have a significant effect on its preservation and long-term viability. The National Register of Historic Places has

FIG. 12.4 The battlefield landscape at Yorktown containing elements of both the Revolutionary War and the Civil War (author photo).

provided two bulletins that address evaluation and registration of cultural landscapes: *How to Evaluate and Nominate Designed Historic Landscapes* (1987) and *Guidelines for Evaluating and Documenting Rural Historic Landscapes* (1989). *Designed historic landscapes* are one of the four basic types of cultural landscapes, while rural historic landscapes are generally classified as *historic vernacular landscapes*. Other NRHP bulletins that provide insights into designed and vernacular historic landscapes include those on historic residential suburbs and on cemeteries and burial places.

With regard to the other two types of cultural landscapes, the NPS Ethnography Program provides some guidance on ethnographic landscapes, as does National Register Bulletin 38 on traditional cultural properties (TCPs). The ACHP provides extensive guidance as to how consideration of cultural landscapes applies to the Section 106 process (http://www.achp.gov/na_culturallandscapes.html).

Much has been written by anthropologists and archaeologists about *ethnographic landscapes* (e.g., Basso 1996; Sundstrom 2003; Hardesty 2000). While these scholarly studies are not explicitly about determining the eligibility of ethnographic landscapes, they can be very helpful for gaining insight into the importance and discrete elements of this property type. Ethnographic landscapes are the one type of cultural landscape where an ethnographer rather than a historic landscape architect would take the lead in evaluation or nomination.

As for *historic sites* as cultural landscapes, battlefields are the most obvious example (Figure 12.4). The National Register bulletin titled *Guidelines for Identifying, Evaluating, and Registering Battlefields* provides basic instructions. Another example is homes of famous people such as presidents of the United States, although NRHP Bulletin 32 on this subject has no information pertaining to cultural landscapes. Visit Mount Vernon and you will spend much of your time walking the grounds.

Summary

Historians and architects both play key roles in American heritage management, but unlike archaeologists, heritage management professionals in history and architecture are less dominant in their respective fields as a whole. There are still probably as many academic historians as historic preservation historians, and new construction architects clearly outnumber preservation architects.

Compared with archaeologists and architects, historians in historic preservation tend to get the least specialized university education, with few history classes focusing on the methods of historic preservation and few universities offering a focused historic preservation specialty track within a department of history. Historic preservation often gets blended with public history within history departments, but most public history programs provide little comprehensive preparation for careers in historic preservation. Notable exceptions are Arizona State University, the University of Vermont, and the University of Maryland. Common duties for historians in historic preservation are historic context studies, literature searches, property identification surveys, property evaluation studies, HABS/HAER documentation, and treatment activities.

Historic architects almost always get specialized training in historic preservation within their departments of architecture. This includes overviews of key laws, common applications such as tax incentives and planning, specialized applications like reuse studies and historic structures reports, and the secretary of the interior's standards and guidelines for restoration. They are usually well grounded in the history of American architecture and changing architectural styles.

Landscape architecture specializations in historic preservation are the most recent. Recognition of cultural landscapes became explicit in the 1980s with several NPS publications. The Historic American Landscape Survey joined its HABS and HAER cousins in 2000. Historic landscape architects work on cultural landscape reports, management plans, and National Register evaluations and nominations.

Review Questions

1. What types of work do historians do in heritage management?
2. What types of work do architectural historians do in heritage management?
3. What types of work do historic architects do in heritage management?
4. What types of work do historic landscape architects do in heritage management?
5. What are the objectives of design guidelines?

Supplemental Reading

The development of history as an American profession is discussed by Novick (1988) and R. Townsend (2013). Historical overviews of historians' and architects' contributions to historic preservation can be found in Sprinkle (2014), Bluestone

(1999), Pyburn (2005), and chapter 5 of Allen (2007). Semes (2009) presents an architectural historian's perspective on historic preservation with the traditional emphasis on an international perspective.

With regard to doing the heritage management work of a historian and architectural historian, I have not found a good how-to book that comprehensively deals with major tasks such as completing thorough archival research and historic properties surveys. Some states provide guidance as to what resources should be examined in both the library and the field (e.g., Wisconsin, Florida). Obviously, familiarity with American architectural styles and features is required, and numerous books deal with these aspects, such as Whiffen (1992), Blumenson (1981), Baker (1994), and McAlester and McAlester (2011).

For building and landscape treatments, especially those with application to grant eligibility and tax benefits, the various secretary of the interior standards and guidelines are essential. They can be found on the NPS website under Technical Preservation Services.

For specialty projects done by historians and architects, guidance on completing a historic structures report can be found in Arbogast (2010) and Slaton (2005), as well as in various online examples. For reuse studies and planning studies, consult the NTHP and SHPO webpages. Architects involved with building rehabilitation and restoration must be very familiar with the secretary of the interior's guidelines for these activities. For design guidelines, see the NPS webpage and examples on city webpages, as well as Semes (2007) and Winter (2008). For activities associated with historic landscapes, see the NPS publications by Birnbaum (1994; Birnbaum and Peters 1996), as well as the website of Birnbaum's Cultural Landscape Foundation.

SIDEBAR

Implementing Heritage Management: The Road to Ruins

When I was a young survey archaeologist and totally focused on finding even ephemeral prehistoric sites, I would occasionally come upon a masonry ruin in the middle of nowhere. I would take a few pictures and make a quick sketch map. Even if the ruins weren't in my construction zone, I couldn't help but be curious about them. Ruins are where most archaeologists get their initial inspiration to become archaeologists. We are romantics for the Greek Acropolis, the Roman Forum, Norman castles in England, and our very own Mesa Verde.

We don't have many impressive ruins in Minnesota, and the ones we do have aren't really that old. Minnesota's prehistoric Indians didn't build with stone. French, British, and American traders used stone for their fur post fireplaces but not for their walls. The 1820 construction of Fort Snelling was the first significant masonry construction in Minnesota. When Euro-American settlers began arriving soon after Fort Snelling's completion, a few built with stone and with homemade bricks. Commercial brickmaking appeared in the 1850s. Fort Snelling was restored in the 1960s, so it is not a ruin. We have very few ruins dating prior to our 1858 statehood.

I didn't think much about the scarcity of ruins in Minnesota until I found the ruins of a large flour mill in a major city. It was scheduled to be demolished. I asked the city engineer why the city would get rid of such an impressive and picturesque remnant of its early history. He replied, "Because it's an attractive nuisance"—attractive not in a picturesque sense but to the wrong kinds of activity. Kids wanted to play on it and could get hurt. It was an insurance liability for the city. The lawyers and insurance underwriters wanted it down.

Soon after my city mill lesson, I started surveying a proposed parkway through the heart of old Minneapolis. Very few ruins were visible, but many were right beneath the surface. In an early meeting with the park board, I mentioned that my literature search suggested many important ruins were in the parkway's path, including ruins of the flour mills that had first brought Minneapolis fame and fortune—ruins of the beginnings of Pillsbury and General Mills. I expected the park board to be upset because I was making the parkway project more complicated and more expensive. But Bob Mattson, the lead planner, looked at me and said, "Do you think we could uncover them and have a Mill Ruins Park?" Bob nailed it. Modern ruins don't have to be attractive nuisances; they can simply be attractions. Today there is a Mill Ruins Park in the heart of Minneapolis.

Most historical or archaeological examinations of ruins concern themselves with ancient examples—ruins that epitomize the word "ruins." Ruins like we don't have in America, except in the desert Southwest. Most of studies of ruins as elements of the landscape (e.g., Ginsberg 2004; Yablon 2009) look at them from intellectual or philosophical perspectives, not as practical management issues or as properties that may be eligible for inclusion in the National Register.

What are ruins? There is no definition of "ruins" in National Register Bulletin 16A, although in the "Classification" section, under "Site," one of the examples is "ruins of historic buildings and structures" (p. 15), inferring that the property must be important (i.e., historic) not just old (i.e., historical). Bulletin 15, under "Categories of Historic Properties," states, "If a building has lost its basic structural elements, it is usually considered a ruin, and is categorized as a site" (p. 4).

Bulletin 36 (the archaeological bulletin) does define "ruins": "Ruins are defined by the National Register as buildings or structures that no longer possess original design or structural integrity. When there is considerable structural integrity still remaining, which is the case in many pueblos, the property should be classified as buildings rather than ruins" (p. 12). Page 3 of Bulletin 36 shows a picture of an excavated foundation of a Pueblo ruin that is described as a "feature." Thus a ruin can be a building, a structure, a site, or a feature within a site.

Modern ruins are even more problematic for both definition and classification. Are remains of wooden buildings ruins, or are ruins only made of more durable materials? What about foundations only: Are they ruins? Is a concrete foundation a ruin? Are bridge piers ruins? Are wooden dock pilings ruins? Is a collapsed metal framework of a structure a ruin? Masonry ruins of buildings seem to fit our image of ruins best, and in most cases they must be high- or low-wall ruins—that is, they must consist of more than just foundations.

Ruins have powerful interpretive potential, but they have many maintenance and safety issues, especially in temperate, urban areas. The freeze-thaw cycle quickly destabilizes masonry with cracks and gaps. Masonry walls need some sort of durable cap, as well as frequent tuck-pointing, which harms their integrity of materials and feeling. Large walls are tempting targets for graffiti, so constant monitoring, restricted access, and/or lighting is needed. High walls are attractive to climbers, leading to wall deterioration and safety issues. Litter can build up quickly in ruins. Ruins in urban areas can be convenient latrines.

Yet fencing off a ruin seriously harms its integrity of setting and prevents visitors from touching the walls or walking through the structural remnant, seriously reducing attractiveness. Some signage is needed to provide minimal interpretation, but too much signage harms integrity of setting and feeling. For industrial ruins, surrounding them with grass is aesthetically pleasing but historically inaccurate. How much stabilization, restoration, and reconstruction is allowable for a ruin to retain its National Register eligibility and aesthetic appeal?

America is a nation without castles and therefore without the ruins of castles. Yet some ruins from the recent past can serve as powerful and evocative reminders of that past. I have always been a proponent of signs that read "These are the ruins of . . . " rather than "This was the site of . . . " Ruins let you reach out and touch the past, not just imagine it.

CHAPTER 13

Tribal Matters
Tribes Matter

There is no such thing as "the Indians."

—Scott Anfinson

In many ways, this is the most difficult chapter for me to write and, for some of you, perhaps the most difficult to understand. Although I have a PhD in anthropology and have worked with Minnesota Indian reservations, communities, tribes, and individuals for over 40 years, I am still quite ignorant when it comes to tribal matters. Over these 40 years, I have changed greatly, tribes have changed greatly, the practice of archaeology has changed greatly, and the practice of heritage management has changed greatly. Most of these changes have been for the better.

Anytime you work with a culture other than your own, you must constantly be aware that you have an incomplete and possibly flawed understanding of that culture, sometimes woefully incomplete and fatally flawed. If you do not know the language and have not lived among a particular culture, you are at a huge disadvantage for understanding it. Even the very good American Indian ethnographers of the late nineteenth and early twentieth centuries, who did speak a language and did live among a people, were biased in their understandings and incomplete in their recordings.

More than the complications of understanding different cultures makes this chapter difficult to write. Applying standard cultural heritage management practices to tribes is very complicated. The application must be based on understanding something about tribal history, tribal lands, tribal law, tribal politics, and tribal traditional cultural properties (TCPs) before any attempt is made to do meaningful tribal consultation and accurate evaluation of tribal cultural properties.

Considering these inherent limitations, complexities, and my own possibly flawed perceptions, my objective in this chapter is not to provide comprehensive understanding of Indian tribal cultures or to be a standard reference for applying heritage management practices to tribes. I only hope to provide some practical advice for dealing with some tribal considerations that are now embedded in American cultural heritage management. Prior to the 1992 amendment of the National Historic Preservation Act (NHPA), we tiptoed around tribal issues, except for stumbling around the reburial controversy. Now we just as commonly consult with tribes and deal with tribal historic preservation offices (THPOs) as evaluate eligibility for the National Register of Historic Places (NRHP) or assess the effects of highway projects.

The 1992 amendments to the NHPA mainstreamed Indian tribes, Native Alaskans, and Native Hawaiians into the federal historic preservation process. As with all groups new to the process, there is a steep learning curve. Many indigenous groups are still figuring out the intricacies of heritage management processes and how they fit into them, just as agencies, state historic preservation offices (SHPOs), and consultants are trying to come up with best practices when dealing with tribes. While tribal groups are treated in a manner like no other consulting party due to their unique legal status (i.e., nation to nation), the same basic rules apply to tribes as to other groups. The evaluation of property importance is still a matter of applying National Register criteria, and Section 106 still means consider and consult, not necessarily preserve.

In this chapter, I will focus on Indian tribal matters in the lower 48 states. I know very little about Alaskan indigenous groups and almost nothing about indigenous Hawaiian culture. While the discussion in this chapter focuses on Indian tribes, many aspects of consultation, dealing with traditional cultural properties and sacred sites, and, to a limited degree, legal matters also apply to Native Hawaiians and Native Alaskans.

A note on terminology: Usually I refer to lower-48-state tribal groups collectively as Indians, not Native Americans. This is how the federal government and most state governments refer to them as a group, and in my Upper Midwest experience, most tribal individuals prefer to be called Indians rather than Native Americans, Indigenous Peoples, or First Nations. There are Indian treaties, not Native American treaties. The reservations are considered Indian Country, not First Nations Country. It is the Museum of the American Indian, not of Indigenous Americans. It is the Bureau of Indian Affairs. The term "Native American" has come to include American Indians, Native Alaskans, Native Hawaiians, and Native Pacific Islanders in the trust territories. In Canada, native residents are sometimes referred to as First Nations and sometimes as Aboriginal Peoples. I am not saying any term is the correct term, only explaining the term I will use here.

When my children were young and we were driving around Minnesota, they would point out the window and ask me, "What is the Indian name for that place?" I would reply, "What is the white name?" This would puzzle them until they were old enough to understand that there is no Indian name for anything. My children's European ancestors spoke many languages, as did the Indian inhabitants of Minnesota. There are many names for the same thing in many different Indian languages. Indian is not a language. Realistically, Indian is not even a culture.

In the early days of informal "Indian" consultation, before the 1992 amendments to NHPA, some archaeologists and agency officials thought that talking to any member of a tribal group constituted consulting with "the Indians." It was as if one individual represented and reflected the opinions of not only a whole community but a whole people. This was not only arrogant but also demonstrated a lack of common sense. They would have never thought the same way about representation of non-Indian groups. One resident of a town never represents the opinions of the whole town, not even the mayor.

Although I understand the term's usefulness to governments and others in talking about a group from a national perspective, for most heritage management purposes there is no such thing as "the Indians." The concept of pan-Indianism denotes a movement among peoples with some shared history, ancestry, and belief systems, who came together in the mid-twentieth century with a shared goal: bettering their living conditions and standing in American society. Indian peoples come from different tribes, different communities, different clans, and different families.

They have different languages. There are as many differences between tribal individuals as there are between individuals in other cultures and other groups. Agencies consult the tribes, not the Indians, and each tribal member is a unique individual.

Historical Background

To begin to understand tribal issues and tribal perspectives, you must first understand the history of indigenous peoples as a whole in this country and the history and ethnography of the particular tribes that live or once lived in your area. These are now passé topics for many university anthropology and history departments. They are not even covered broadly and in detail by most Indian studies departments. Today, my own University of Minnesota Anthropology Department has no courses in American Indian ethnography. Indian history courses in the History Department, if there are any, tend to be event oriented, focusing on treaties and wars. Indian culture courses in the Indian Studies Department tend to be politically or linguistically focused.

When I was an undergraduate at the University of Minnesota in the early 1970s, the Anthropology Department had multiple excellent professors in American Indian ethnography. They were the direct intellectual descendants of the brightest stars of American anthropology. E. Adamson Hoebel was an expert on Plains Indians, and Robert Spenser an expert on the Inuit. Hoebel was a student of Franz Boas at Columbia and Spenser of Alfred Kroeber and Robert Lowie at Berkeley. Even my archaeological advisor, Elden Johnson, had done his master's thesis on Yanktonai kinship and had worked for George Murdock on the Human Relations Area Files while at Yale as a doctoral candidate. As tribal consultation and traditional cultural properties hit my SHPO radar screen in the early 1990s, I felt very fortunate to have had an old-fashioned anthropological education with multiple ethnography classes.

In the Beginning

The age of the first human settlement in the Americas, what its cultural manifestation looked like, and the Old World origins of the population have become some of the most important questions in American archaeology. We now know with some certainty that people have been in North America for at least 14,000 years and that most, if not all, of these people originated in multiple areas of northeastern Asia. We strongly suspect that some people were here prior to the use of the diagnostic Clovis spear points, but we know little about their migration routes, material culture, and way of life.

Over the last 14,000 years or so, the people of the Americas multiplied, diversified, and occupied almost all habitable areas of North America, South America, and the Caribbean. They became the indigenes of the Americas. There were eventually at least 400 distinct languages spoken in North America alone, and these languages can be divided into at least 60 language families.

Precontact population sizes in North America are difficult to determine. You have to consider effects from the introduction of deadly European diseases, inter-tribal and European-tribal warfare, massive tribal migrations both in protohistoric and early historic times, and a paucity of reliable information about the continental interior. Estimates of the total North American population in 1491 run from less than 1 million (Kroeber 1934) to almost 20 million (Dobyns 1983). Ubelaker (2006) estimates a total North American population of 2.36 million at the time of Christopher Columbus's first visit to the Caribbean.

Although overall population estimates for pre-Columbian North America will probably always vary by millions of people, a regional or culture area approach is more insightful and more accurate for both estimating total population and examining population dynamics. It is clear that moving south from the Arctic, numbers and densities generally increased, except in some desert and mountain areas. Ubelaker (2006) states that the native populations in California and the Southeast had the highest density, and the populations in the Arctic, Subarctic, and Great Basin had the lowest based on climatic conditions and year-round subsistence resource availability.

The End of Prehistory

The European discovery of the Americas in 1492 began the rapid decline of most Indian cultures, languages, and numbers. Even if there is widespread disagreement as to total population decline, there is no argument as to the number of native languages that disappeared. Of the perhaps 400 different languages spoken in North America at the time of contact, only half that many survived by the end of the twentieth century. Today, only about one-quarter of the surviving languages have speakers in all age groups, making the other three-quarters vulnerable to extinction within a generation or so.

Most authors rely on estimated death rate percentages to estimate actual population numbers in the past. We know that epidemics of smallpox, measles, and influenza, beginning by at least 1600 and lasting into the late 1800s, led to dramatic native population declines in many areas of North America. There was perhaps a 95% reduction of the Indian population in California, a 90% reduction in the Southeast, and an 85% reduction on the Northwest Coast (Ubelaker 2006). Snow (1995) found no evidence of widespread and recurring epidemics in parts of the northeastern United States prior to the Revolutionary War, although major epidemics among tribes in the Chesapeake Bay area in the early 1600s may have reduced the local populations by as much as 80% (Tanner 1995).

Overall, Ubelaker (2006) estimates the North American Indian population had been reduced by 72% at its low point of 530,000 in 1900. It then began to slowly rebound. In the 2010 census, 5.2 million people in the United States identified themselves as American Indian or Native Alaskan. This population is much more heterogeneous than the 1900 population, however, as almost half the people in the 2010 census said they were also part of one or more other races. In Canada, 1,836,035 people identified themselves as Aboriginal in 2011. So if we add the United States and Canadian numbers together, there are now very likely more "Native Americans" than there were at the time of contact.

The Treaty Period: 1778–1871

More than just Indian peoples and Indian languages rapidly vanished after the coming of Europeans. The basic way of life for most tribes eventually disappeared, and entire tribes ceased to exist. The cultural change was not so much technological as it was socioeconomic and, to some degree, religious. Most of the socioeconomic change stemmed from the loss of land and traditional resources. Most tribes east of the Mississippi River were forcibly removed to locations west of the river in the nineteenth century. Most tribes west of the Mississippi signed treaties that gave them reservations, but these reservations, for the most part, were much smaller than their previous tribal territories and often included a land base poorer in the resources necessary for a thriving population.

The United States borrowed the idea of Indian treaties from the British. The first treaty between the United States and a tribal nation was signed with the Delaware in 1778. Indian treaties initially followed a basic European model: tribes were treated as sovereign nations, and the treaty was a process of negotiation to define territorial boundaries and prescribe behavior. Its objective was less to obtain land for white settlement than to maintain peace and order.

The George Washington, John Adams, and Thomas Jefferson administrations attempted to treat tribes in what they thought was a fair manner. Access to land for white settlement was to be obtained through purchase. The ultimate objective in federal government Indian policy after the Revolutionary War was to "civilize" the Indians—to have them adopt a Euro-American way of life dependent on an agricultural economy, trade, and a formal representative government.

Implementation of a uniform Indian policy was hindered by the differential governmental status of recently obtained British land between the Appalachians and the Mississippi. The land north of the Ohio River (the Northwest Territory) was seen as new federal land, while the land south of the Ohio was claimed by various adjacent southeastern states that also asserted their exclusive rights to Indian policy within this area. A uniform and fair Indian policy was also hindered by lingering animosity between many citizens of the United States and tribes, because most tribes had fought for the British in the Revolutionary War. This was reinforced when some of these tribes once again supported the British in the War of 1812.

After the War of 1812, the US government still relied on a policy that treated tribes as sovereign nations, but the ultimate objective was still to absorb the tribes into the American melting pot. To reinforce the elimination of British influence in the Northwest and to support white settlement in the new Louisiana Territory west of the Mississippi River, the federal government began to establish frontier forts. These forts housed not only military garrisons but Indian agents. Fort Snelling in Minnesota, where I was based for much of my career, was once one of these outposts.

With the coming of the Andrew Jackson administration, the government got more aggressive about tribal removal from the eastern United States. In 1830, the Indian Removal Act empowered the president to define areas for displaced eastern Indians to reside. In 1834, Congress formally defined this area, in what is now Kansas, Nebraska, and Oklahoma, as "Indian Territory." The first groups forced to occupy Indian Territory were from the Southeast. Known as the "Five Civilized Tribes," the Cherokee, Chickasaw, Choctaw, Creek (Muscogee), and Seminole were moved into what is now eastern Oklahoma. More northern tribes, including the Kickapoo, Miami, Delaware, and Shawnee, were moved into what is now eastern Kansas.

In the 1840s, the annexation of Texas, the opening of the Oregon Territory, and the California gold rush rapidly changed the idea that most of the area west of the Mississippi River could be reserved for exclusive Indian use. At first, only safe corridors were needed to allow overland routes from the Mississippi River to the West Coast. Most military forts were built along these routes. It wasn't long, however, before some white settlers began staying on the Great Plains.

As the frontier rapidly moved west, so did the need for more Indian treaties in order to "legally" obtain land and hopefully avoid armed conflict. Tribes were now treated as dependent domestic groups, and the treaties dealt mainly with the ceding of most of a tribe's land to the United States. Compensation was in the form of a reservation, a onetime cash payment to help establish schools and agricultural programs, and annual payments (annuities) to help support the tribe until it could become fully self-sufficient.

The Kansas-Nebraska Act of 1854 reduced Indian Territory to what is now just Oklahoma, excluding the panhandle. The onset of the Civil War temporarily delayed forcing tribes that had resettled in Kansas and Nebraska to move south into Oklahoma. The Five Civilized Tribes sided with the Confederacy during the war and had to cede the western half of their Oklahoma land as punishment. After the war ended, white settlement west of the Mississippi River greatly increased, and the reduction of reservations east of the Mississippi accelerated. The nomadic tribes of the Great Plains were resistant to giving up their way of life, and some refused to acknowledge reservations, but treaties were still implemented with annuity payments and forced land cessions.

By the end of the 1860s, tribal annuity payments were supporting over 100,000 tribal people, and there were over 1,000 federal employees in 77 Indian agencies. This was stressing the federal budget. Attempts to turn Indian reservations into self-supporting agrarian colonies had clearly failed. Tribes were resistant to becoming fully participating American citizens. A change in policy was needed.

Mainly for financial reasons, Congress in 1871 ended the use of formal Indian treaties, although congressional "agreements" with tribes were still implemented and informally referred to as treaties. Treaties as a legal instrument were now reserved for agreements with foreign nations. That year Congress also withdrew the tribal right to independent legal counsel. Other acts of Congress in the 1870s further reduced Indian rights. Many Indian children were forced to attend off-reservation boarding schools so they would "acculturate" more fully. Many of these schools were run by Christian religious organizations. The last major Indian wars on the Great Plains were fought in the late 1870s.

Allotment and Termination

In 1887, the Dawes Act attempted not only to resolve continuing federal financial burdens by forcing reservation residents to become self-sufficient but to reduce exclusive Indian access to valuable resources on many of the reservations. In Minnesota, the major incentive was to allow lumber companies access to white pine reserves on large northern Ojibwe reservations. The Dawes Act introduced allotment of reservation lands that had "agricultural potential." Each tribal member who was a head of household was given 160 acres, single adult individuals got 80 acres, and independent children got 40 acres.

The land allotted to tribal members could not be sold for 25 years, and for that period it was held in trust by the federal government. When an individual took possession of this fee title land, he became a full citizen of the United States. The reservation land not allotted to Indian individuals was considered "surplus" and put up for sale. Tribes in desert and mountainous areas of the West largely escaped allotment because of the limited agricultural potential of their lands. Reservations subjected to allotment soon were known as "checkerboards" due to the land division into many small parcels with diverse ownership.

By the turn of the twentieth century, the federal government was committed to the forced assimilation of tribes into American society. Allotments intensified in the first decade of the twentieth century as more reservations were made subject to the Dawes Act. Some allotted lands were even given to intermarried non-Indians or to nonreservation Indians. In 1906, Congress passed the Alaska Native Allotment Act, which gave each Native Alaskan 160 acres of land, although it was not taken from formal reservations.

The ultimate result of allotment was that two-thirds of all Indian reservation land had been transferred out of Indian ownership by 1934. The majority of land on many reservations was no longer tribally owned. Less than 5% of the Leech Lake Ojibwe Reservation in Minnesota was still owned by the tribe or tribal members after allotment ran its course.

In the 1920s, the attitude and policies of the federal government began to change from forced assimilation to acceptance of tribal identity. Boarding schools were gradually eliminated, and reservation children were encouraged to attend local public schools. Private organizations heavily criticized government mishandling of Indian education, Indian funds, and Indian lands. A report by the Brookings Institution (Meriam 1928) laid out many of the deficiencies of federal Indian policy. As the United States entered the Great Depression, the federal government under the Herbert Hoover administration began to comprehensively address Indian problems.

In 1934, the Indian Reorganization Act effectively rescinded the Dawes Act. Allotment ended with the restoration of unsold "surplus" land to the tribes. Tribes were allowed to form their own governments. Attempts to restore to the tribe as a whole all allotted land that was still owned by individual tribal members was taken out of the final bill, as was a provision for Congress to promote "the study of Indian civilization, including Indian arts, crafts, skills, and traditions."

Immediately after World War II, the Indian Claims Commission was established to investigate illegal takings of Indian land. This was soon followed by a reversion to the forced assimilation policies of the early twentieth century, including attempts to rescind the Indian Reorganization Act provisions for tribal self-government. Two acts of Congress in 1953 ended the prohibition on the sale of liquor on reservations and, in a number of states, placed tribal criminal and civil court jurisdiction for reservations under state courts. The federal government promoted the voluntary relocation of young tribal members from reservations to urban areas. The "termination" policy of the federal government in the 1950s attempted to end federal trusteeship for Indians.

The Rise of Modern Tribes and Modern Government Policy

The John F. Kennedy and Lyndon B. Johnson administrations in the 1960s reversed the federal Indian assimilation policy and greatly increased funding to tribes. The last quarter of the twentieth century witnessed the rise of pan-Indianism as individuals from diverse tribal groups formed organizations to promote policies for mutual benefit. The American Indian Movement (AIM) was founded in Minneapolis in 1968.

Congress too got into the act. The Alaska Native Claims Settlement Act (ANCSA) of 1971 repealed the Alaska Native Allotment Act of 1906 and transferred land to 12 regional corporations and over 200 village corporations. The Indian Self-Determination and Educational Assistance Act of 1975 allowed tribes to take over responsibilities previously reserved for the Bureau of Indian Affairs (BIA). The American Indian Religious Freedom Act (AIRFA) of 1978 protected Indian religious practices. Indian gaming was also allowed to be expanded according to each state's guidelines, allowing some reservations to finally reach the goal of economic self-sustainability. By the 1980s, the federal government had returned to the original "nation-to-nation" relationship with the surviving tribes.

During the settlement of North America by Euro-Americans and the assumption of sovereignty over tribes by the federal government, some tribal cultures were destroyed, most were greatly altered, and a few were amazingly resilient. Most tribal languages are still very vulnerable, but that is true of "minor" languages worldwide as electronic media, rapid transportation, and intertwined economic practices continue to make the world smaller and to favor limited forms of communication. In the end, it is amazing how many American Indian tribes have survived to once again become fully engaged in their own cultures, as well in American life as a whole, although many of these tribal cultures are still very vulnerable. Heritage preservation writ large is perhaps more critical to them than to any other group in America.

A Minnesota Tribal Story

Minnesota has seven Ojibwe reservations and four Dakota communities. Archaeologists can first archaeologically recognize the Dakota in east-central Minnesota about 1,000 years ago. They were woodland hunter-gatherers who made occasional forays onto the western Minnesota prairies to hunt bison. One of their staple foods was wild rice, a naturally occurring grain in the northern Midwest that could match the production capacity of cultivated maize and was much more nutritious. The first French encounters with the Dakota happened in the mid-1600s in west-central Wisconsin and east-central Minnesota. "Minnesota" is a Dakota word meaning sky-tinted waters.

In late prehistoric times, some Dakota followed their close relatives, the Lakota (Teton Sioux) and Nakota (Yankton and Yanktonai Sioux), and moved west onto the Great Plains, probably attracted by large bison herds. The Dakota of the woodlands continued to harvest wild rice, make birch-bark canoes, and follow a seasonal round that relied on movement in and out of the prairie-forest ecotone. Their art featured curvilinear floral designs. The Dakota of Minnesota's prairies gradually adopted a Plains way of life, with their access to northern forest resources gradually restricted by Ojibwe intrusion from the east. Dependence on corn horticulture increased. Their art soon reflected more typically Plains rectilinear patterns.

The Ojibwe began moving into northeastern Minnesota from the eastern and southern shores of Lake Superior by the mid-1700s. At first relations with the Dakota were peaceful, but as the Ojibwe pushed farther west and south into the heart of the old Dakota homeland, an intertribal war broke out that would last for a century. The remnant Dakota in the eastern and northern woodlands were soon forced south and west by the Ojibwe. The Ojibwe were also woodland hunter-gatherers, with fur trading now important to their economy. Their seasonal round featured spring maple sugaring, summer root, nut, and berry gathering, fall wild rice harvesting, and winter deer hunting. Stored foods like parched wild rice and maple sugar supplemented their diet. Fishing and hunting were important during all seasons. Trapping of beaver was an important activity mainly in the winter.

The first treaty with the Dakota was initiated by Zebulon Pike in 1805 as he ascended the Mississippi River to the junction of the Minnesota River. This was by then the new Dakota heartland, known as *mendota* (where the rivers meet). Soon ratified by Congress, the Pike Treaty gave the United States the right to occupy small areas on the Mississippi River near the Minnesota River junction. Fifteen years later, the army built Fort Snelling on the bluff overlooking the river junction. The Dakota signed two additional treaties in 1837 and 1851 that ceded the remainder of their Minnesota lands in exchange for a reservation on both sides of the upper Minnesota River and annuity payments. In 1858, the reservation was reduced by half to just lands on the south side of the Minnesota River.

In 1825 the Treaty of Prairie du Chien established a diagonal line through central Minnesota as the official boundary between Dakota and Ojibwe lands. Neither group paid much attention to this line, with raiding parties from both tribes frequently crossing it for another quarter century. The Prairie du Chien treaty also involved the Menominee, Ho-Chunk (Winnebago), Sac and Fox, Iowa, Potawatomi, and Ottawa groups, setting the boundaries of their lands. The treaty included a small slice of Ho-Chunk land in extreme southeastern Minnesota.

The Ojibwe signed their first treaty with the United States in 1837 and another in 1847, ceding the remnant of the old Dakota homeland in central Minnesota. Additional Ojibwe cessions occurred in 1854, 1855, 1863, 1864, 1866, 1867, 1889, and 1904. Some of the land now contained in the Red Lake Reservation was never formally ceded by the Ojibwe and was not subject to allotment. Originally, the government planned to move most Minnesota Ojibwe to a single reservation in northwestern Minnesota (White Earth), but many Ojibwe refused to leave their homes. They eventually retained seven reservations scattered across the northern half of the state, ranging in size from the 564,427-acre Red Lake Reservation to the 3,592-acre Mille Lacs Reservation.

Today the Dakota live in four small communities in the southern part of the state. They have communities rather than formal reservations because their treaties were abrogated after the US-Dakota War in 1862. The Dakota lost their reservations in Minnesota, and most Dakota were forcibly removed to reservations in Nebraska and South Dakota. A few Dakota remained in scattered Minnesota locations. Others gradually returned to the state in the late nineteenth century, living near their former villages on land purchased for them by private groups. Eventually, four Dakota communities were recognized as tribes by the federal government. They now have a small land base that is part owned by individual members, part owned by the community, and part held in trust by the federal government.

The Ojibwe occupy much of the old Dakota homeland, while the Dakota now occupy lands probably once controlled by the Iowa, the Oto, and the Omaha, groups that no longer live in Minnesota as tribal entities. The Dakota and Ojibwe have very different cultures with very different languages and very different histories in Minnesota. The Dakota have lived in some parts of the state for over 1,000 years, while the Ojibwe occupation is coeval with European intrusion. Until early historic times, the Dakota buried their dead in earthen mounds. The graves of their ancestors are scattered over much of the state. The Ojibwe did not build mounds in Minnesota, although they occasionally reused some Dakota ancestral mounds for burial purposes.

These late prehistoric and early historic tribal movements and behaviors have important implications for implementing modern heritage preservation laws. Under Section 106 of the NHPA, Dakota communities have to be consulted for most federal undertakings in Minnesota except in the far northeast. These areas are their ancestral lands, although they officially ceded only the southern part. If a burial mound is disturbed anywhere in the state, under the Native American Graves Protection and Repatriation Act (NAGPRA) on federal land and under state law (MS 307.08) on nonfederal land, the Dakota usually determine what should be done and how any removed remains are to be treated.

If an undertaking is in northern Minnesota, the Ojibwe also have to be consulted. If a disturbed mound in the northern half of the state is found to contain post-1800 artifacts, it may have been reused by the Ojibwe, so they too enter the decision-making process under NAGPRA or state law. Because the Red Lake Ojibwe refused to sign a treaty ceding their northwestern Minnesota lands, they have a slightly different relationship today with the federal government, with the state government, and even with the six other Minnesota Ojibwe reservations.

Many other groups that are still discrete tribal entities also once lived in Minnesota. Already mentioned are western Sioux tribes (Teton, Yankton, Yanktonai) and their linguistic relatives the Ioway, Oto, and Omaha. The Cheyenne probably lived in central Minnesota in prehistoric times, the Cree lived in northern Minnesota in early historic times, and in late historic times the Sauk and Ho-Chunk briefly occupied small government-assigned parcels in south-central and central Minnesota. All of these groups have the right to be consulted on federal undertakings on lands they once occupied but did not cede.

Every state was occupied by multiple tribes, and their homelands shifted even prior to European intrusion. The tribes of each state were treated somewhat differently by the federal and state governments depending on presidential and legislative attitudes and actions, as well as on how each tribe reacted to government actions. The only consistency from state to state today for heritage preservation is how the federal government deals with tribal matters concerning the NHPA and heritage preservation laws regarding federal lands.

Indian Lands

With the Gadsden Purchase in 1854 (southern Arizona and southwestern New Mexico), the federal government had acquired sovereignty over all the area that now makes up the southern 48 states. Alaska was acquired by purchase from Russia in 1867. Hawaii became a US territory in 1898. By 1900, the federal government, through treaties and agreements, had extinguished all primary tribal title to this land. Continental tribal lands still retain the status as having "original Indian title" for the purposes of land claims.

"Indian lands," as defined by Canby (2009:409), are "lands that are held by Indians or tribes under some restriction or with some attribute peculiar to the Indian status of its legal or beneficial owners." Indian land does not include land purchased by tribal individuals offered for public sale as fee title land. Canby (2009) also stresses that the concept of Indian lands is very different from that of reservations and "Indian Country." Indian lands are based on who holds title to the land, while reservations and Indian Country are based on government boundary definitions set through treaty, executive order, congressional agreement, or statute. As discussed under allotments above, much of the land now within some reservations is not Indian land.

The first basic legal category of Indian land is trust versus nontrust. *Trust land* is land held in trust for a particular tribe by the federal government. This applies to all unalloted reservation land or allotted land restored to tribes after 1934. Lands owned or purchased by a tribe or individual tribal members outside reservation boundaries can be put into trust with the consent of the owner and the secretary of the interior. Trust lands cannot be sold without the consent of the federal government and are not subject to state or local taxes or fees. This is called *restriction against alienation*. Because the federal government actually holds legal title to trust land, it is considered federal land for the purposes of heritage management laws and is not subject to most state laws. The BIA is the agency for trust land for purposes of federal heritage management.

Tribes have two types of nontrust land. *Restricted fee land* is tribally owned but has federal restrictions against alienation. *Unrestricted fee land* is land that has been purchased by a tribe and, if it is outside reservation boundaries, is not subject to federal restrictions. Within reservation boundaries, federal restrictions may be unclear, but the tribe itself may have restrictions on its status and disposition. Individual tribal members may also own both restricted and unrestricted fee land.

Indian land can also be subject to federal restrictions, even if it is not formally held in trust by the federal government, if a trust relationship exists between the tribe and the federal government. This is true with respect to New Mexico Pueblos due to their special status originating with previous Spanish authority. Alaska aboriginal lands also have a unique status due to a 1971 act of Congress that extinguished aboriginal title to all lands. The law provided for village or regional native corporations that could then select former aboriginal lands to which they would hold fee title. These lands are exempt from state and local taxes and were originally prohibited from sale for a set period, but the trust relationship with the federal government is now unclear.

Indian lands can be leased to non-Indians if the secretary of the interior approves the lease. This lease can be for mineral or oil extraction, farming, grazing, timber cutting, and many other activities. The lease period can vary but is typically for 25 or 99 years. The BIA supervises these leases, although they are often the subject of disputes about low fees, activities in violation of the lease agreement, or mismanagement.

Some tribes and the National Congress of American Indians (NCAI) have complained about the definition of "tribal lands" used by the Advisory Council on Historic Preservation (ACHP) in 36 CFR 800, which is how the definition appears in the NHPA:

(1) all land within the exterior boundaries of any Indian reservation; and
(2) all dependent Indian communities.

The NCAI and individual tribal complaints contend that tribal lands should include individual allotments now outside reservation boundaries and individual allotments for tribes that do not have reservations, even if these parcels of land are held in trust. Under the current NHPA definition, these individual allotments cannot be under the jurisdiction of a THPO because they are not within reservation boundaries. There are still over 10 million acres of individually owned lands that are held in trust for allotees and their heirs. Most of this land is within reservation boundaries and can be subject to THPOs.

Tribal Governments

As of January 2018, there were 567 federally recognized tribes in the United States, of which 229 are in Alaska. According to the BIA website, "A federally recognized tribe is an American Indian or Alaska Native tribal entity that is recognized as having a government-to-government relationship with the United States, with the responsibilities, powers, limitations, and obligations attached to that designation, and is eligible for funding and services from the Bureau of Indian Affairs. Federally recognized tribes are recognized as possessing certain inherent rights of self-government (i.e., tribal sovereignty) and are entitled to receive certain federal benefits, services, and protections because of their special relationship with the United States." Tribes have received official federal recognition through treaties, acts of Congress, presidential executive orders or other federal administrative actions, or federal court decisions. Treaties were eliminated in 1871 as a method for recognizing tribes. Some federally recognized tribes do not have a reservation.

Over 56 million acres of land are currently held in trust by the United States for Indian tribes and individuals (Figure 13.1). The great majority of this trust land is within about 325 areas variously described as reservations, pueblos, rancherias, missions, villages, associations, or communities. Included are 207 villages, corporations, and associations in Alaska, along with one Alaska reservation (Metlakatla). The largest Indian reservation is the 16-million-acre Navajo Reservation in Arizona, New Mexico, and Utah. Many of the smaller Indian land areas are less than 1,000 acres, with some only a few acres. Most reservations are remnants of a tribe's

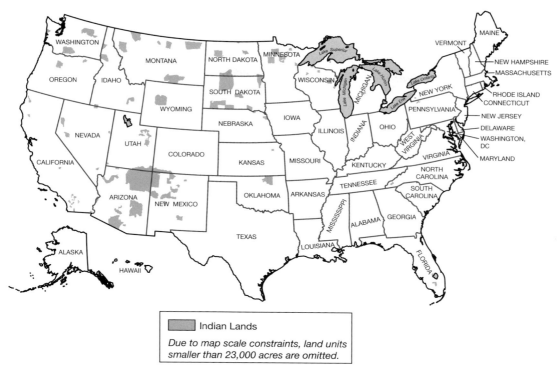

FIG. 13.1 Map of US Indian reservations (US Geological Survey–National Atlas).

original landholding that were retained as part of a treaty. Others (e.g., most Oklahoma reservations) were created for tribes relocated from their original homelands.

There are also state Indian reservations and state-recognized tribes. On some state-recognized reservations, lands can be held in trust by a state for a tribe. With state trust lands, title is held by the state on behalf of the tribe, and the lands are not subject to state property taxes, although they are subject to state laws. State trust lands originated from treaties or other agreements between a tribe and the state government or even a colonial government. States with formally recognized tribes include Alabama (9), Connecticut (3), Delaware (2), Georgia (3), Louisiana (10), Maryland (2), Massachusetts (1), New York (3), North Carolina (7), South Carolina (7), Vermont (4), and Virginia (11). Other states, like Kansas, Kentucky, Michigan, Missouri, and Oklahoma, recognize certain tribes less formally and do not have a state trust relationship with them.

The Indian Reorganization Act of 1934 not only ended allotment but allowed tribes to form their own governments by adopting a constitution and bylaws, as long as these measures were approved by the secretary of the interior. The model preferred by the federal government was the system outlined in the US Constitution, which features the three-part division of government. This did not mesh well with a traditional executive-only or small tribal council method of governance. Out of the 258 tribes that voted on the matter, 181 did form constitutionally based governments.

While fully democratic tribal governance was not universally adopted by the tribes and the constitutional model was ill-suited to most tribal ways of life, the 1934 act provided the legal basis for tribal governments, restored a significant amount of the tribal land base, and, most importantly, affirmed the right of tribes to exist as sovereign entities. This right to existence was challenged by House of

Representatives Resolution 108 in 1953, which attempted to terminate tribes as sovereign entities and end the special relationship with the federal government. Public Law 280 the same year gave five states (California, Nebraska, Minnesota, Oregon, Wisconsin) civil and criminal jurisdiction on reservations and gave other states the right to pass laws to assume that jurisdiction. The Civil Rights Act of 1968 reversed the state jurisdiction provision of Public Law 280.

Tribal governments have many of the powers reserved for states, except those reserved by the federal government (e.g., national defense) or those ceded in a treaty or agreement. These powers include the right to make and enforce laws (both civil and criminal), to tax, to establish and determine membership, and to license and regulate activities within their jurisdiction. They also have the right to bar nonmembers from entering tribal lands. The Indian Self-Determination and Education Act of 1975 allowed multiple federal agencies to directly contract with tribes for federal Indian programs without going through the BIA.

A tribal council with a chairperson form of government is still the most common on reservations. The council can also be called a reservation business committee. Most reservations still lack a large representative body. Tribal councils tend to be small. The 300,000-member Navajo Reservation has a 24-member council, while many small reservation councils have from 5 to 10 members. If tribal members disagree with council decisions, they have to wait for the next election of the tribal council to effectively express their dissatisfaction.

Maintaining law and order is one of the most important functions of a government. Most tribes have their own police forces, but only recently have many tribes developed their own court systems. Tribes also have their own departments of natural resources and business management departments. They may also have departments concerned with social services, education, health, and environmental protection.

The most divisive issue within tribes is who gets to be a member of the tribe. Most tribes use a "blood quantum" method, whereby an applicant has to prove a certain percentage of tribal ancestry. The blood quantum amount ranges from 1/2 to 1/64th. Some tribes also require that the applicant be born on the reservation. Being a tribal member is not just a matter of voting in tribal elections and being eligible for reservation services. Tribes that have successful businesses or gaming operations can directly share profits with members. These individual shares of gaming profits can represent hundreds of thousands of dollars for each member in smaller reservations with highly successful operations.

Indian-Specific Cultural Heritage Laws

Prior to 1990, there were no federal laws specifically protecting tribal historic properties, although trust lands received some protection under the 1906 Antiquities Act. Off Indian lands, Indian-related historic and archaeological sites were treated like any other historic or archaeological site. On nontrust Indian lands, you simply needed the permission of an individual or a tribe to enter the land. The American Indian Religious Freedom Act of 1978 gave some protection to traditional religious practices and provided access for practitioners to most religious sites on federal land but did not specifically protect the properties that the practices may have been associated with.

As discussed in chapter 4, in 1989 the Senate directed the National Park Service (NPS) to study the funding needs of historic preservation on Indian lands. NPS undertook consultation with tribes, federal agencies, and SHPOs to assess these needs. As a result, in 1990 NPS produced *Keepers of the Treasures: Protecting Historic Properties and Cultural Traditions on Indian Lands*. The report went far beyond just looking at funding, stressing that tribes viewed heritage preservation differently from most non-Indian historic preservationists and federal cultural resource managers. This is reflected in the title, which mentions *treasures* rather than *cultural resources*.

The most important heritage resources from tribal perspectives are not standing structures or ancient village sites but less tangible resources such as language, traditions, and practices. Preservation of these resources is critical to tribes' maintaining their identities, especially for tribal cultures that are in danger of disappearing. Dealing with intangible resources does not fit well into existing laws or agency and SHPO procedures and policies, which focus on tangible historic properties.

Keepers of the Treasures suggested altering federal cultural heritage management practices to comprehensively recognize tribal cultural resource needs and to use existing programs to deal with these needs. There were also specific legislative objectives, one of which directly led to the passage of the Native American Graves Protection and Repatriation Act in 1990. Another resulted in making tribal consultation a part of Section 106 review and the inclusion of THPOs as part of the 1992 amendment to NHPA.

Laws Concerning Indian Burials

The federal government normally defers to state governments for laws that protect human burials, although the federal government does have laws that protect federally owned cemeteries like veterans' cemeteries and graves on federal land. Until the late twentieth century, the federal government routinely gave archaeologists permission to excavate ancient Indian burial sites on federal property. The last burial mound excavation done for exclusively scientific purposes in Minnesota was in 1974 on a national wildlife refuge.

By the late 1970s, archaeologists were involved in a bitter internal debate as to whether it was ethical to excavate ancient Indian burials, especially without the permission of a local Indian tribe or Indian group with suspected affiliation. Minnesota passed its first law specifically protecting Indian burials on nonfederal public and private property in 1976. The federal government was slower to act, although the Antiquities Act and the Archaeological Resources Protection Act (ARPA) require federal permission to excavate any type of archaeological site, including ancient burials, on federal property.

Native American Graves Protection and Repatriation Act

The first congressional action in response to the *Keepers of the Treasures* report was the 1990 Native American Graves Protection and Repatriation Act. NAGPRA had three basic provisions:

- It required all federal agencies and nonfederal institutions that received federal funds after the passage of the act to compile a comprehensive inventory of human remains, grave goods, and significant tribal **cultural items** in their collections and then provide the list to all possibly interested tribes, so the remains and artifacts could be returned (repatriated) to tribes that requested them, if they could prove direct affiliation.
- It required consultation by federal agencies with appropriate tribes concerning potential and inadvertent impacts to burial sites on federal and tribal lands.

- It prohibited illegal trafficking of burial or sacred site artifacts, including materials that had been removed from federal or tribal lands or taken across state or international boundaries.

NAGPRA also provided for grants to assist institutions with compiling the inventories and tribes with repatriation. It required a committee within the Department of the Interior to review NAGPRA-related actions, develop regulations to implement NAGPRA, and complete an annual report to Congress. There were also penalties for violations of NAGPRA, including actions on tribal and federal lands and with regard to institutions that didn't comply with the inventory, consultation, and repatriation requirements.

The regulations for implementing NAGPRA (43 CFR 10) were first issued on July 24, 1994. Revisions to the regulations have been issued in 2003 (civil penalties), 2005 (technical amendment), 2010 (disposition of culturally unidentifiable human remains), 2013 (corrections and clarifications), and 2015 (disposition of unclaimed human remains, funerary objects, sacred objects, or objects of cultural patrimony). A civil penalties rule revision was issued on February 16, 2017, allowing for inflation adjustments. There is still one section (43 CFR 10.15[b]) of the NAGPRA regulations that remains to be finalized; it deals with the failure to claim objects or remains where no repatriation or disposition has occurred. There have been several attempts to revise NAGPRA, but none have been enacted.

Definitions are critical to the implementation of NAGPRA. Besides human remains (which were not defined but were considered cultural items), three other types of cultural items were to be included in the inventories: funerary objects (two kinds), sacred objects, and objects of cultural patrimony. The law defined these as

(A) "associated funerary objects" which shall mean objects that, as a part of the death rite or ceremony of a culture, are reasonably believed to have been placed with individual human remains either at the time of death or later, and both the human remains and associated funerary objects are presently in the possession or control of a Federal agency or museum, except that other items exclusively made for burial purposes or to contain human remains shall be considered as associated funerary objects.

(B) "unassociated funerary objects" which shall mean objects that, as a part of the death rite or ceremony of a culture, are reasonably believed to have been placed with individual human remains either at the time of death or later, where the remains are not in the possession or control of the Federal agency or museum and the objects can be identified by a preponderance of the evidence as related to specific individuals or families or to known human remains or, by a preponderance of the evidence, as having been removed from a specific burial site of an individual culturally affiliated with a particular Indian tribe.

(C) "sacred objects" which shall mean specific ceremonial objects which are needed by traditional Native American religious leaders for the practice of traditional Native American religions by their present day adherents.

(D) "cultural patrimony" which shall mean an object having ongoing historical, traditional, or cultural importance central to the Native American group or culture itself, rather than property owned by an individual Native American, and which, therefore, cannot be alienated, appropriated, or conveyed by any individual regardless of whether or not the individual is a member of the Indian tribe or Native Hawaiian organization and such object shall have been considered inalienable by such Native American group at the time the object was separated from such group.

Other critical definitions include the following:

(1) "burial site" means any natural or prepared physical location, whether originally below, on, or above the surface of the earth, into which as a part of the death rite or ceremony of a culture, individual human remains are deposited.
(2) "cultural affiliation" means that there is a relationship of shared group identity which can be reasonably traced historically or prehistorically between a present day Indian tribe or Native Hawaiian organization and an identifiable earlier group.
(15) "tribal land" means—
(A) all lands within the exterior boundaries of any Indian reservation;
(B) all dependent Indian communities;
(C) any lands administered for the benefit of Native Hawaiians pursuant to the Hawaiian Homes Commission Act, 1920, and section 4 of Public Law 86-3.

The definition of "tribal lands" is especially important, because it includes parcels not normally included under federal heritage management laws. Tribal lands under the NAGPRA definition encompass all types of land within the exterior boundaries of a reservation. Due to allotment, on many reservations this includes private lands owned by non-Indians as well as nonfederal public land under the control of state or local governments.

Additional definitions and some slightly revised definitions are provided in the NAGPRA regulations (43 CFR 10.2). The "Definitions" section in the regulations is divided into eight sections dealing with the following:

1. Who must comply with the regulations?
2. Who has standing to make a claim under the regulations?
3. Who is responsible for carrying out the regulations?
4. What objects are covered by the regulations?
5. What is cultural affiliation?
6. What types of lands do the excavation and discovery provisions of the regulations apply to?
7. What procedures are required by these regulations?
8. What are unclaimed items?

The NAGPRA regulations have an additional requirement for federal agencies. Agencies whose actions could result or have resulted in the discovery of human remains must develop a written plan of action (POA) produced as an outcome of tribal consultation. The POA must specify the kinds of objects considered, identification of tribal groups associated with the land in question, consultation procedures, an archaeological research design, and how any applicable cultural objects will be treated. The POA must be signed by the agency official and a copy given to the applicable tribes. As Tom King (2013:271) points out, the POA not only gives the agency an explicit methodology to follow but streamlines the process so there is no excessive delay in completing the undertaking due to NAGPRA issues.

The first NAGPRA task, the inventory, was to be completed within five years of the law's enactment, but this proved unrealistic. Many small institutions did not have the staff or expertise to do an adequate job. Many large institutions had huge collections that were not always well organized or well catalogued. The NPS did release a partial list of collections that had been submitted by 1995, but it was far from complete. According to the most recent NPS NAGPRA annual report, during fiscal year 2016 there were 100 new or amended NAGPRA inventories submitted. As of September 30, 2016, 1,341 lists from 1,111 institutions and federal agencies had been received by NPS since November 1990.

Real progress has been made over the first 27 years of the NAGPRA program. The NAGPRA database in late 2017 listed over 133,000 sets of human remains, as well as about 1.15 million associated funerary objects (many are individual beads), about 250,000 unassociated funerary items, 8,130 objects of cultural patrimony, and 1,162 sacred/cultural patrimony items. Over $45 million has been awarded in NAGPRA grants for assisting states, museums, and tribes.

The best way to understand NAGPRA is to apply a simplified version of how the "Definitions" section in the regulations is organized. Focus on where it applies, to what it applies, and to whom it applies, and then also consider when it does not apply to the where, what, and who.

For the where, NAGPRA applies to actions on federal or tribal lands and to federally supported (e.g., federal grants) repositories that are in possession and control of aboriginal cultural materials. NAGPRA does not apply to actions on lands that are off reservation and nonfederal. It does not apply to nonfederally supported curatorial institutions or institutions lacking applicable tribal or Native Hawaiian cultural materials. It does not apply to museums in other countries in possession of American aboriginal materials.

For the what, it applies to human remains, funerary objects, sacred objects, and objects of cultural patrimony. NAGPRA normally does not apply to everyday artifacts like arrowheads and potsherds that were not directly associated with a burial or obvious sacred practices. It does not apply to objects not originating in this country.

For the who, it applies to all federal agencies and all federally supported curation facilities (e.g., museums). NAGPRA does not apply to the Smithsonian Institution, institutions that have not received any federal funds or do not have any materials from federal or tribal lands, foreign institutions, and collections of private individuals if the materials were not obtained illegally or from federal or tribal lands.

It is also important to remember that NAGPRA, like ARPA, does not require the preservation of burial sites or forbid the excavation of burial sites on federal land. Agencies must consult with tribes about activities on federal lands that may disturb burial sites, but they do not have to concur with tribal recommendations. It would be rare these days, however, for a federal agency to ignore tribal preferences when it comes to burials that are likely affiliated with the tribe or even any burial of possible Indian affiliation. Also of note is that ARPA requires permanent federal curation of archaeological materials from federal lands, while agencies often cede these materials to tribes under NAGPRA.

One of the most difficult issues concerning NAGPRA is how to deal with unaffiliated remains. The 1990 law clearly distinguished between affiliated and unaffiliated remains and cultural objects. Within 10 years of passage, there was a major movement by tribes and many archaeologists to allow unaffiliated remains and associated grave goods to be returned to possible ancestors or to groups representing multiple tribes so that the remains and associated grave goods could be reburied. This caused considerable disagreement within the archaeological community, as discussed by David Hurst Thomas (2000).

The majority of remains in many collections could be classed as unaffiliated when NAGPRA first came out. Most institutions were very eager to rid their collections of human remains. A few institutions even gave them to any Indians who showed up at their door making a request in person, even if the requesting individuals had not proved direct lineal descent. Today, DNA testing can help determine affiliation, but it is expensive and only works some of the time. Because most states had the power to decide what to do about public collections from nonfederal lands, many have repatriated all human remains and associated grave goods from these collections. With the assistance of the state archaeologist (not me at the time), Minnesota repatriated all unaffiliated remains and associated grave goods in the possession of public institutions to the Minnesota Indian Affairs Council (MIAC) in 1999. Almost all of these remains have been reburied.

Some disagreements have ended up in court. The most famous NAGPRA case is that of Kennewick Man. In 1996, two private citizens found a human skull in the Columbia River near Kennewick, Washington. The county coroner thought the skull looked Caucasoid, but a bone fragment was submitted for radiocarbon dating. The skull was more than 9,000 years old. The Corps of Engineers (COE) then took possession of the skull as the river bottom was technically federal land. A number of anthropological/archaeological researchers sued the COE to prevent the skull from being repatriated under NAGPRA. A federal appeals court ruled in 2004 that the remains could not be firmly defined as "Native American" based on the skull's morphology and age and thus must be retained by the COE. DNA testing in 2015 determined that the skull was most closely related to North American Indians. An act of Congress in 2016 mandated the return of the Kennewick skull to a tribe, thus bypassing NAGPRA. The Kennewick skull was subsequently reburied.

The effects of NAGPRA were originally profound for archaeologists, physical anthropologists, and museum professionals, but the effects with regard to human remains are now basically confined to actions that have disturbed or may disturb burials on federal land. These are relatively rare. Objects of cultural patrimony and sacred objects are more problematic as they are not always obvious and museums are more likely to want to retain such objects as they are often considered objects of art or are of documented historic value. Furthermore, some tribes do not want some sacred objects repatriated to them because the objects are too "dangerous" for the tribes to handle as knowledge of their proper treatment has been lost.

In my 40 years as a practicing archaeologist, I never had to directly deal with NAGPRA. When I was a survey archaeologist (1975–1990), the law hadn't yet been passed. When I was a SHPO archaeologist (1990–2005), NAGPRA was not under my direct review authority, although I often reminded federal agencies of their responsibilities and helped tribes, agencies, and archaeologists decipher the law. As a state archaeologist (2006–2016), I spent almost half my time dealing with burial issues, but I had no authority on federal lands and maintained no collections of remains or objects from federal lands. Yet I have a thick folder of NAGPRA publications because there has been so much controversy and confusion about the law, and I need to explain it to students.

One of the great benefits of the NPS NAGPRA program is the online availability of a Native American Consultation Database (NACD). The database can be queried by tribe, state, county, contact name, reservation, or federal installation. Results show which tribes are interested in particular states or areas and provide up-to-date tribal contact information. This is helpful for the purposes of not only NAGPRA but other tribal consultation requirements, such as Section 106.

State Laws Protecting Indian Burials

State laws protecting burial sites have been discussed in chapter 10. Many states (e.g., Minnesota) have burial laws that offer stronger protection than NAGPRA or ARPA, as these state laws may actually forbid the disturbance of Indian burials without the consent of appropriate Indian groups or tribal authorities. State burial laws do not apply to federal land, however.

Federal Laws Concerning Sacred Sites

As noted earlier, in 1978 the American Indian Religious Freedom Act had several provisions meant to be consistent with the establishment clause (religious freedom) in the First Amendment to the Constitution. AIRFA was very brief in its language but broad in its scope. It provided access for practitioners to religious sites on federal property, provided for the use and possession of sacred items by Indian people, and affirmed the freedom to worship in traditional ways. But AIRFA was flawed. It had no implementing regulations, no definitions, and no enforcement provisions and only protected practices, not places. It was more a statement of support by Congress than a law to be implemented and enforced.

In 1988, AIRFA was challenged in *Lyng v. Northwest Indian Cemetery Protective Association* concerning a Forest Service road in northern California. The Supreme Court ruled against the tribes, finding that AIRFA lacked specificity to stop actions on federal lands that may harm sacred sites. A Supreme Court decision in an Oregon case two years later ruled against use of peyote in Indian religious ceremonies. Due to these decisions, AIRFA was amended in 1994 specifically to allow the use of peyote for religious purposes and to provide some definitions (e.g., "Indian," "Indian religion"), but "sacred site" remained undefined.

In 1996, President Bill Clinton issued Executive Order 13007. Unlike AIRFA, the emphasis of EO 13007 was on religious and sacred places, not practices. Once again, it only applied to federal land. It confirmed the reasonable right of access to sacred places, required agencies to avoid adverse impacts to those places, insured confidentiality of the locations, asked agencies to develop procedures (not regulations) concerning sacred sites on their lands, and required land-management agencies to report implementation results to the president within one year.

Unlike AIRFA, EO 13007 did include a definition of sacred site: "'Sacred site' means any specific, discrete, narrowly delineated location on Federal land that is identified by an Indian tribe, or Indian individual determined to be an appropriately authoritative representative of an Indian religion, as sacred by virtue of its established religious significance to, or ceremonial use by, an Indian religion; provided that the tribe or appropriately authoritative representative of an Indian religion has informed the agency of the existence of such a site." The definition reiterates the fact that the site must be on federal land and must be discrete and narrowly delineated. Thus large or inexactly delimited areas are excluded. It does, however, leave the decision of what is a sacred site solely up to tribes.

Most agencies apparently have not developed clear, stand-alone procedures for implementing EO 13007, although some, like the army, have embedded procedures in integrated cultural resource management plans (ICRMP) for specific areas or in larger documents implementing agency Indian policies. In 2012, the ACHP, Department of Defense, Department of the Interior, Department of Energy, and Department of Agriculture signed a memorandum of understanding (MOU) to promote tribal access to sacred sites and develop ways to better inform the public about the importance of preserving Indian sacred sites.

There have been a number of First Amendment conflicts with the applications of AIRFA and EO 13007. Some of these involve requiring federal agencies to provide exclusive Indian access to places that also have importance to the public. The most famous of these is Devils Tower National Monument in Wyoming, where the NPS can't exclude rock climbers when Indian religious practitioners want to hold ceremonies at the base of Devils Tower. NPS has asked climbers to refrain voluntarily from visiting on these ceremony days, and most climbers have complied.

Tribal Historic Preservation Officers

One recommendation in *Keepers of the Treasures* was to amend the National Historic Preservation Act "to establish a separate title authorizing programs, policies, and procedures for tribal heritage preservation and financial support." This was done in the 1992 amendment to NHPA, but full implementation with respect to Section 106 was delayed until 2004, when revised 36 CFR 800 regulations were finally adopted. The need for direct tribal participation in federal cultural resource management was one of the principal reasons for amending NHPA in 1992.

In the amended NHPA, tribes were given the right not only to be consulted on federal undertakings that might affect their historic properties (i.e., tangible cultural heritage) but to assume any or all of a SHPO's functions on tribal lands in individual states. In order to assume SHPO duties, they had to designate a tribal historic preservation officer, provide the NPS with an acceptable historic preservation plan, and have qualified staff or alternative procedures that allowed them to adequately carry out the assumed responsibilities.

Tribal historic preservation plans are somewhat different in content and organization from SHPO statewide plans. Tribes tend to emphasize the importance of traditional knowledge and living sources (i.e., elders) for this knowledge. Like state comprehensive plans, tribal plans do have to cover the basic duties that are being assumed by the THPO, including conducting a reservation-wide survey of historic properties. Tribal surveys tend to pay more attention to traditional cultural properties than SHPO statewide surveys.

THPO responsibilities as outlined in the NHPA are confined to the exterior boundaries of a specific reservation. Tribes, however, have a right to be consulted under Section 106 for undertakings inside and outside reservations. For most tribes that have THPOs, the THPO also handles off-reservation tribal consultation with regard to Section 106, NAGPRA, and other laws. Only federally recognized tribes have the right to have THPOs and to be consulted for the purposes of Section 106.

The first THPOs appeared in the mid-1990s. Two Minnesota Ojibwe tribes (Leech Lake and Mille Lacs) were among the first THPOs in the nation. As the Minnesota SHPO archaeologist at the time, I had to quickly get up to speed on the revised law, the proposed new 36 CFR 800 regulations, and Indian matters in general in order to help train the THPOs. By the end of 1999, there were only 17 THPOs in the nation, but 10 years later there were 100. As of the end of January 2017, 171 tribes in 30 states had appointed THPOs. This represents 30% of recognized tribes but half of the reservations. California has the most THPOs with 37, and Oklahoma is second with 19. Other states with double-digit numbers of THPOs include Minnesota (10), New Mexico (12), and Washington (15). The 20 states without THPOs are all east of the Mississippi River, with the exception of Missouri, Arkansas, Texas, and Hawaii.

Not all THPOs have assumed all of the SHPO duties within their reservations. Some prefer only to perform Section 106 reviews and educational functions. National Register nominations from tribes are infrequent. Tribes typically do not want to be responsible for certified local governments or tax act certifications. If a THPO only had the Section 106 responsibility, it could limit its professional staff to just an archaeologist and contract to perform less frequent duties associated with that function. THPOs have also taken responsibility for many other heritage preservation duties not directly related to duties outlined in NHPA, such as language preservation.

THPOs get a share of the Historic Preservation Fund (HPF) to assist them in carrying out their duties under the NHPA. As the number of THPOs has increased and the tribal allocation from the HPF has remained flat, the amount available for each THPO has fallen. In 2001, when there were only 27 THPOs, the average HPF grant to a THPO was about $155,000. In 2016, the 171 THPOs got an average grant of $60,000.

In 1998, the 15 existing THPOs formed the National Association of Tribal Historic Preservation Officers (NATHPO). NATHPO not only speaks for the THPOs as a whole but promotes "the preservation, maintenance and revitalization of the culture and traditions of Native peoples of the United States." The functions of the Tribal Historic Preservation Program at NPS include the regulation of THPO certification and the awarding of HPF grants to THPOs.

Like tribes in the lower 48 states, Native Alaskan groups can have THPOs, although only one of the 227 recognized "tribes" in Alaska does. For the purposes of the NHPA, Native Hawaiians are represented by the SHPO. There are currently no specific reserved native land areas under federal control in Hawaii. In 1921, the Hawaiian Homes Commission Act allowed Native Hawaiians to establish communities and farmsteads held under a trust relationship with the federal government, but this relationship was transferred to the state government when Hawaii became a state in 1959. The Department of Hawaiian Home Lands manages over 200,000 acres of state trust land. One further note: the government of Hawaii spells its name "Hawai'i," but the federal government still uses "Hawaii," so that is what I have used in this book.

Tribal Consultation

At least one book has been written on consultation for the purposes of American cultural heritage management (Nissley and King 2014). Almost all federal agencies now have guidelines for Indian consultation, although, as Claudia Nissley and Tom King point out, federal agency compliance often demonstrates the letter more than the spirit of the law.

The tribal aspect of consultation is what most practitioners immediately think of when they hear the word "consultation," but as discussed in chapter 5 specifically with regard to Section 106, consultation applies to anyone or any group with the right of input on an issue. Many of the same guidelines as to how to do consultation properly apply to both tribal and nontribal situations. If you work at an agency, it is important not to become so focused on your tribal consultation responsibilities that you forget about your broader consultation obligations with others.

Tribal consultation did not start with the 1992 NHPA amendments, but prior to this, federal consultation procedures and approaches were inconsistent and haphazard. Consultation with tribes is also required by the National Environmental Policy Act (NEPA), ARPA, AIRFA, and NAGPRA. It is also the foundation of Executive Orders 13007 and 13175. Nobody is a true national expert on tribal consultation because each of the 567 recognized tribes is different culturally, historically, and politically from the others. Cultural aspects are part ancient and part postcontact. Reservation politics are complex and can change rapidly. The unique history of each tribe determines its right to be proactively consulted for undertakings in specific areas.

If you want to make a detailed study of tribal consultation and its application with respect to particular laws, look at the numerous books and articles, as well as federal agency, NATHPO, and state agency guidance on the subject. Tom King in particular has lots of valuable insights and advice in various publications (e.g., 2003, 2007). Here I will emphasize some suggestions based on what I have learned over 40 years of mostly informal consultation with Dakota and Ojibwe tribes in Minnesota.

Before I make my suggestions for tribal consultation, some basic clarifications are in order. Consultation does not require collaboration. Collaboration is working together to achieve a common purpose. True collaboration is often difficult to obtain in implementing agency plans because collaboration is only possible when both parties want the same basic outcome. Most agencies have missions whose primary objectives do not include preserving tribal cultural heritage. The Federal Highway Administration (FHWA) helps build roads, the Department of Housing and Urban Development (HUD) assists community development, and the Department of Defense (DOD) defends the country from foreign aggression. Collaboration is good, but don't let it become an objective that gets in the way of effective consultation.

Consultation is not necessarily negotiation, a basic point made by Nissley (2011). Negotiation is between parties of almost equal standing. In the case of most federal cultural heritage laws, the federal agency makes unilateral decisions. As long as the agency follows the rules, it does not have to compromise, and it does not have to preserve important cultural sites. Nissley suggests that true negotiation is only feasible when nonagency project proposers and project opponents sit down without a federal oversight agency, even though the oversight agency is responsible for any formal consultation and makes all final decisions unilaterally.

Nissley (2011) also discusses impediments created for consultation due to issues of timing and ethics. Modern attempts at streamlining construction in order to save money and time may violate the requirement to make a good faith effort to consult by not allowing enough time for adequate discussion and consideration. She contends that those who are directly affiliated with a place or historic property have the right to decide if it is important to them. This does not mean, however, that the agency must agree or that the property is eligible. For historic properties, the National Register is the final arbiter of significance whether we like it or not.

In the end, reasonableness determines whether consultation was adequate and in good faith. Did you seek out everyone who should reasonably be consulted? Did you provide enough information for reasonable understanding of the scope of the project? Did you provide reasonable and convenient opportunities for meaningful interaction? Did you provide a reasonable amount of time for each step in the consultation process? Did you provide reasonable project alternatives at the beginning of consultation and reasonably consider other alternatives presented during the process? It is important to remember that consultation is a process not an event. It is an ethical as well as legal requirement.

As for my suggestions regarding tribal consultation, first and foremost, be respectful. Respect begins with acknowledging the nation-to-nation relationship of tribes and the federal government. Respect is also personal. No matter what your opinions as to tribal religious practices, the validity of oral history versus written history, or the perceived tribal motives for objections to an undertaking or action, you must respect those whom you consult and show respect for what they have to say.

An important element of respect is knowing what not to do based on a particular tribe's customs and social etiquette. Who in a tribe do you start consultation with? How do you address elders? Where should the meeting be held? How should you dress when attending meetings? What is your personal demeanor in a meeting? How should the room be arranged if it is at your office or in a neutral setting? Should you bring small gifts? Do you make direct eye contact when speaking, avoid turning your back on someone, and shake hands? These can all be elements of showing respect and vary by tribe. If you disagree, you must *respectfully* disagree. Know who makes the decisions for the tribe, but respect everyone who participates in consultation.

Second, I have learned, sometimes the hard way, that listening is more important than talking. Listening often takes a great deal of patience. In my meetings with Dakota people, sometimes the conversation started with a long story. Even if you don't understand the point of the story, don't fidget, don't look at your watch or cell phone, and don't interrupt. When you get to the nitty-gritty, avoid debating or arguing. Ask what parts of a conversation and what kinds of information should be kept confidential and from whom. When you do talk, always tell the truth. Sometime this means telling tribes what they don't want to hear but must in order to get an informed response. Don't make promises you can't keep.

Be well prepared for any meetings. Stay focused on the purpose of the meeting and avoid tangential issues if you can do so respectfully. Be ready for questions about the need for the project, the alternatives that will be considered, and what you already know about possible impacts to cultural properties that may be important to the tribe. Make your presentation short but comprehensive. Use plain language and avoid professional or governmental jargon. Do not claim to be an expert on anything tribal. Admit the limits of your knowledge. I avoid using greetings or other brief comments in a tribal language, as I may get the meaning wrong, mispronounce the words, or infer that I have the right to use them. However, if you are somewhat fluent in a tribal language, demonstrating it would be a great asset in demonstrating sincerity, understanding, and respect.

You must keep an open mind going into consultation, during consultation, and after formal consultation ends. You must demonstrate your sincerity in seriously considering tribal input by the language of your correspondence, your attitude during meetings, and the actions you take based on the consultation. Do not go into consultation with all decisions effectively already made and never suggest during consultation that major decisions have already been made.

Finally, I would stress that consultation is a two-way street. I find this suggestion lacking in most practitioner and agency guidance. Consultation should start with mutual respect. Tribes may be suspicious of your motives at the beginning of consultation, but they should still treat you as a guest if you are meeting with them at their reservation and treat you fairly if you are off the reservation. Tribal representatives should also have a somewhat open mind, which does not have to include compromising on what they truly think is worth preserving. They should be just as willing to see your point of view as you are to see theirs.

Beyond just doing consultation because you have to, consultation can help agencies avoid serious problems if they indeed make a "good faith" effort. It can help avoid litigation even if there isn't full agreement with consulting parties. Consultation can help avoid bad publicity and public demonstrations. It can help avoid significant project implementation delays. It can even help in court if an agency can demonstrate it undertook consultation in a comprehensive, timely, considerate, respectful, and fair manner. This is what a reasonable and good faith consultation is all about.

Recently, an increasing number of tribes have asked to be reimbursed by agencies or project developers for their travel expenses involved with consultation. Some tribes have even stated that they will charge a standard fee for every consultation, regardless of whether they travel or not. The ACHP released a director's memorandum in July 2001 titled "Fees in the Section 106 Review Process," which focused entirely on tribal applications. The ACHP director stressed that consulting parties are not required to provide input, and nothing in the 36 CFR 800 regulations requires agencies or applicants to reimburse tribes for consultation expenses. The ACHP has since recognized that in some instances reimbursement of consulting parties may be appropriate, but it had not released a revised director's memorandum addressing this as of the end of 2017. In its 2012 tribal consultation handbook, the ACHP stated that federal agencies can pay the expenses of tribes for expenses that "facilitate" all stages of Section 106 consultation, but they aren't required to. Most federal agencies (e.g., FHWA) have taken a similar position.

In my estimation, charging fees is not only counterproductive, because it creates bad feelings as to motive and responsibility, but goes against the spirit and purpose of the NHPA. The need to consult is based on the potential for an undertaking to harm heritage that someone holds dear. For those being consulted to ask for payment suggests they are putting monetary compensation ahead of protecting this heritage. Even if a tribe or other consulting party is short of funds, most consultation is just a matter of taking someone's time. If the consultation results in valuable heritage being protected, that time was well spent. With Facetime and Skype now available, not all consulting parties have to be in the same room with the agency. Distant travel is no longer required for effective consultation, although being in the same room can be helpful and promote better understanding.

Tribal Monitoring

In 1994, a major prehistoric site mitigation was done for a bridge replacement project in northern Minnesota. The Minnesota Department of Transportation (MnDOT) required the archaeological consultant to hire a respected Ojibwe elder from a nearby reservation to sit next to the active excavation unit every day and watch the archaeologists work in case any sacred items or burials were encountered (Figure 13.2). Although everyone on the archaeological crew enjoyed talking to the elder and he offered some helpful interpretation suggestions, the experienced crew was certainly competent to find any burials or unusual artifact concentrations and knew to stop excavating if such features were encountered. No sacred items or human remains were found. The Ojibwe as a tribe did not live in the area in prehistoric times, and there was no historic component at the site. So what was the real reason for this tribal monitoring?

As Minnesota SHPO archaeologist in the late 1990s, I reviewed a number of large northern Minnesota pipeline projects. These projects passed through several Ojibwe reservations. We requested that the Federal Energy Regulatory Commission (FERC) require comprehensive cultural resource surveys of the entire pipeline corridor. I remember asking that the surveys consider TCPs as well as archaeological sites and standing structures. FERC agreed, and the surveys were completed by private consulting firms led by archaeologists. Standing structures were

FIG. 13.2 Tribal monitoring at the McKinstry site (21KC2) in Minnesota in 1994 (author photo).

rarely impacted by pipeline projects, and most visual effects were temporary. For TCPs, the consultants just asked the tribes if there were any in the pipeline path.

Because TCPs were still relatively new to agencies, SHPOs, tribes, and consultants, the TCP identification process in the 1990s was not very thorough. Someone had come up with the idea of tribal monitoring to act as insurance in case something important had been missed by preconstruction review and to show the tribes that their cultural resource concerns were being carefully addressed. The concept was to have a knowledgeable tribal member present during the pipeline construction to see if any TCPs were encountered by the construction, although inadvertent discovery plans were already in place for archaeological and burial sites.

This seems a bit backward in retrospect, as this process did not encourage concerted attempts at finding and evaluating TCPs prior to construction so that they could be more easily avoided during construction. But as I said, TCPs and THPOs were both something new, and after the surveys were completed, we realized we had not thoroughly assessed TCP presence or absence during the project planning stages. The tribal monitoring idea seemed a reasonable way to cover a base we had not previously covered. The SHPO was happy with it, the tribes were happy with it, FERC was happy with it, the pipeline companies were happy with it, and the consultants were happy with it. It is rare that everyone is happy when it comes to Section 106 compliance, especially on a reservation.

Tribal monitoring was soon common in many states for many types of projects. As tribal monitoring became almost required for pipeline projects and recommended by various tribes for all large mitigation and construction projects, I started getting requests to help train tribal monitors to recognize archaeological materials. Many of these monitors were young tribal members who needed a summer job. I said I was not qualified to train a tribal monitor because the job of a tribal monitor is finding significant cultural properties that archaeologists had missed or did not recognize. If an archaeological survey had been adequately completed, a "reasonable and good faith effort" had already been made to identify archaeological sites. If a tribe suggested that not all archaeological sites in an area of potential effects (APE) had been found by an inadequate preconstruction survey, then a qualified archaeologist should be hired to do the monitoring.

Furthermore, I thought the job of a tribal monitor was to identify TCPs, and the great majority of these types of sites should have also been identified prior to project implementation. Finding a TCP other than a burial or special artifact concentration in an excavation trench is very rare. Archaeologists are trained to find burials and artifacts. Some other type of TCP may indeed take a tribal expert to identify, but it will generally not be found in an excavation trench and usually could only be recognized by a tribal member possessing significant elder knowledge.

As the job of tribal monitors became more widespread and lucrative, multiple tribes started demanding to have their own tribal monitors on projects, as many took place in areas with multitribe consultation. If the objective of a tribal monitor is to prevent the destruction of TCPs, this is a reasonable request because most TCPs are tribe specific. To find and recognize TCPs, elder knowledge is required, and this knowledge is becoming increasingly scarce. Suddenly, tribes were competing with other tribes for monitor positions, developers were being asked to pay for more than one monitor, and agencies, SHPOs, and consultants were increasingly conflicted as to what was required and appropriate. The period of universal tribal monitoring happiness ended.

Tribal monitoring is not a required activity under federal law or regulations. It is not explicitly discussed in 36 CFR 800, although in the 2012 ACHP tribal consultation handbook, fees for "services provided in the Section 106 process" are briefly discussed. These services are specifically linked to the identification and evaluation phase of Section 106. Agencies can pay for tribal surveys just as they pay for the services of other consultants, but they do not have to pay for the service if they did not request it. Monitoring is listed as an identification and evaluation activity (ACHP 2012:14).

Construction monitoring can be a requirement in programmatic agreements, but it is generally for archaeological materials or burials that may have been missed by or difficult to find during preconstruction surveys due to deep burial, limited access, or ephemeral presence. The implementation of tribal monitoring is typically an outcome of tribal consultation. A tribe will request it, and an agency will generally agree to it, if it doesn't affect project planning or scheduling and is not exceptionally expensive. Project proposers often accept it as a cost of doing business on or near reservations.

In order to justify tribal monitoring, a study should be done by some entity with broad authority and sufficient independence (e.g., ACHP) to see where and if tribal monitoring has resulted in significant findings. National or agency standards should be set for tribal monitors. Training courses should be developed to prepare tribal monitors to perform a unique duty that archaeologists can't or shouldn't do. Procedures should be developed to specify monitoring techniques and to evaluate who is qualified to monitor specific types of projects. Finally, tribal monitors or their supervisors should have to prepare reports like every other consultant so that performance and outcomes can be evaluated. California is the only state I know of that has professional standards for tribal monitors. The Standing Rock Sioux of South Dakota established a tribal monitoring training program in 2005.

There are benefits to tribal monitors besides just finding missed or hidden TCPs. Their use often improves relationships between agencies, archaeologists, developers, and tribes. They demonstrate agency and project proposer goodwill in the consultation process. They give tribes some assurance that they are being listened to. If done with an archaeological focus with qualified archaeologists mentoring tribal members, tribal monitoring can help establish trust between tribes and archaeologists and give tribal members insights into archaeological methods and objectives. Some tribes may even suggest tribal monitors primarily because of a lack of trust in archaeologists, developers, and agencies.

But tribal monitors should not be used as a substitute for thorough preconstruction surveys or as mitigation for harm to known TCPs. Tribes, agencies, and project sponsors should always ask whether tribal monitoring meets the "reasonable and good faith effort" standard for identification under Section 106. If cultural properties are found during monitoring, they should be evaluated for eligibility, although agencies can develop their own procedures to consider and preserve any kind of cultural property, eligible or not.

Traditional Cultural Properties

In 1990, the NRHP released Bulletin 38, *Guidelines for Evaluating and Recording Traditional Cultural Properties* (Parker and King 1990). While those of us with anthropology degrees previously knew such properties were out there and were very important to tribes, Bulletin 38 turned TCPs into a cultural heritage acronym and made them officially worthy of consideration, preservation, and registration.

Tom King has since written an entire book on TCPs (King 2003). For anyone dealing with TCPs in an official or educational capacity, King's book should be required reading. He provides the intellectual and bureaucratic background to the development of Bulletin 38. He offers a refined discussion of the intricacies of identifying, evaluating, treating, and consulting about TCPs. He uses numerous real-world examples to illustrate his points, not his usual tongue-in-cheek hypotheticals. He also talks about environmental review implications and management issues for this complicated property type.

The same year Bulletin 38 was released, I became the archaeologist for the Minnesota SHPO. Although National Register nominations were only one of my many duties (as I was the only archaeologist on staff), my actual title was National Register archaeologist. I remember receiving Bulletin 38 in the mail in the fall of 1990 and was excited to begin applying the anthropological part of my education. It had been of limited use so far in my career as a survey archaeologist. It didn't take long before I was also apprehensive about what TCPs would mean for Section 106 reviews. Agencies were apprehensive too.

When I started at the SHPO and instantly assumed major National Register responsibilities, at least I was one of few Minnesota archaeologists who had actually completed a National Register nomination. Writing a nomination had helped me sort out what was implied when you declared a site eligible for the National Register. I asked myself if I could have written nominations for all of the sites I had thought were eligible. Archaeologists think every site is important, but is every site significant in National Register terms? I also started thinking about boundaries, when Criterion A should be applied as well as just D, and the minimal number of aspects of integrity necessary. Furthermore, since I was mostly involved with surveys for Section 106 purposes, what were the implications for defining exact boundaries, choosing specific significance criteria, and determining individual aspects of integrity when the site was only going to be dealt with as a 106 issue and was not going to be nominated?

As TCP-related issues intensified, I began looking for a Minnesota TCP site that I could nominate, not only to get it listed as part of my SHPO responsibilities and offer some additional protection for the site under Minnesota law but so I could better understand the intricacies of finding, evaluating, and registering TCPs. I finally stumbled on a good candidate in the late 1990s: Maka Yusota (Boiling Springs). It had been threatened by a Department of Natural Resources (DNR) trail project I had reviewed. After initial consultation with several tribal officials of the nearby Shakopee Dakota community, I wrote the nomination in late 2002, and Maka Yusota was listed in the National Register in early 2003. I then got to assist with an additional TCP nomination, for Oheyawahi (Pilot Knob) in 2003, which didn't initially get listed due to landowner objection but was determined eligible by the Keeper. The nomination was resubmitted after a landowner change, and Oheyawahi was listed in the Register on March 14, 2017.

As I learned more about TCPs, I realized that 1990's Bulletin 38 was not the first federal acknowledgment of the importance of traditional cultural properties. As King stresses in numerous writings, cultural value has always been a reason for nomination, so many TCPs have always been eligible for inclusion in the National Register. King (2003:24) notes that he first officially encountered a TCP (Tahquitz Canyon in California) in 1971, and the location's traditional cultural value was critical in the ACHP's objection to a Corps of Engineers reservoir plan.

Many TCPs are listed in the National Register, although very few have been explicitly nominated and identified as TCPs. In Minnesota, Cannomoke, the Pipestone Quarry site (21PP2), was one of the first Register listings in the state (October 15, 1966). There is probably no more obvious TCP in Minnesota or even the nation. However, without its archaeological component and extensive mention in historical literature, it probably would not have been nominated at the time.

In the NPS journal *CRM Bulletin* in 1979, David Stuart discussed "non-artifactual cultural resources" and how they factored into NPS planning. The article was stimulated by the passage of AIRFA and the issuance of NPS's *Policy Guidelines for Native American Cultural Resources Management* in 1978. The NPS policy guidelines, as well as earlier NPS documents, stressed only the importance of archaeological, historical, and architectural resources, even though Interior Department guidance as early as 1973 had included properties important to indigenous cultures or communities "for traditional spiritual, religious, or magical reasons" (Stuart 1979:11).

In the opening paragraph of his 1979 article, Stuart states, "When the foci of Indian concerns coincide with recognized archaeological resources, few difficulties exist; the NPS policy of preservation (Management Policies 1878:V-2ff) is generally harmonious with preferences of the Indian community. Planning difficulties are more common when Native Americans identify locales of traditional importance that do not exhibit physical evidences of human behavior, i.e., there are no archaeological resources." Stuart went on to stress the implications for less tangible cultural resources under NEPA as well as the need to consider broad social impacts and to include Native American concerns in NPS planning. He even cited an early Tom King publication (King, Hickman, and Berg 1977).

In July 1985, the Minnesota SHPO received a copy from the ACHP of a document titled "Guidelines for Consideration of Traditional Cultural Values in Historic Preservation Review." Comments were to be sent to ACHP staff member Thomas F. King. Although King was not listed as an author, he discusses his authorship of the draft ACHP guidelines and the reasons for the document in his TCP book (King 2003:33). This 1985 ACHP document was the forerunner of Bulletin 38, although it uses the term "traditional cultural value" rather than "traditional cultural property." After the comment period ended in September 1985, the Interior Department required that the guidelines be incorporated into a National Register bulletin rather than as ACHP guidelines, because the document included evaluating historic property significance, a responsibility of the Register rather than the ACHP.

The application of Patricia Parker and Tom King's (1990) National Register bulletin on TCPs was and still is problematic for many agencies, tribes, and professional heritage management practitioners. There was great worry among the agencies that they would lose control of eligibility for TCPs if tribal opinions received the only consideration from the SHPOs and the Keeper. Tribes were concerned that knowledge of their most valuable places and most intimate stories would become public. Archaeologists were concerned that every prehistoric archaeological site would suddenly become a TCP and off-limits for excavation on public land without the permission of a tribe.

In 1992, the amendments to the NHPA mentioned in Section 101(c) properties that are considered to be inherently traditional cultural properties, although traditional cultural properties were not explicitly mentioned. The current language of the NHPA reads as follows:

302706. Eligibility for inclusion on National Register
(a) IN GENERAL.—Property of traditional religious and cultural importance to an Indian tribe or Native Hawaiian organization may be determined to be eligible for inclusion on the National Register.

Because the TCP bulletin was so innovative and TCPs are so subjective to find, evaluate, and register, every word was scrutinized, resulting in calls for revision from all directly involved parties and even largely uninvolved people and entities such as intellectually and socially interested academics. Minor revisions to Bulletin 38 were made in 1992 and 1998, but no changes were made in response to the 1992 NHPA amendments and the subsequent process of 36 CFR 800 regulation changes. The National Register dropped numbering the bulletins in 1997, so the 1998 revision of the TCP bulletin does not include the number "38," but most practitioners still refer to it this way, and I will continue to use "Bulletin 38" in this book as it is simpler than using the full bulletin title.

In April 2012, the NPS started soliciting comments to "update" Bulletin 38 with a comment end date of October 31, 2012. No mention was made as to who would be the author(s), although King (*CRM Plus* blog, September 22, 2013) reports that he was contacted by NPS to assist with reviewing comments and the ACHP was involved in initial conversations in order to produce a FAQ document regarding TCPs for Section 106 purposes.

Due to intense professional, agency, and tribal interest, the comment period was extended to April 2, 2013. The NPS presented multiple "webinars" and held several public meetings to discuss various TCP issues, including one on May 23, 2013, after the official comment period had ended. The ACHP subsequently dropped out of the process, apparently with no explanation, much to the consternation of King (*CRM Plus* blog, September 22, 2013).

The announcement of the Bulletin 38 update that appeared in the *Federal Register* on August 10, 2012, included the following list concerning what aspects of the bulletin commenters should focus on:

- What constitutes a "traditional" community
- "Continuity of use" by a traditional community
- Evolving uses of resources by a traditional community
- Multiple lines of documentary evidence
- Broad ethnographic landscapes
- Property boundaries
- Resource integrity

NPS was also seeking to identify and address any other "user-identified" TCP-related issues, as well as requesting comments and recommendations that specifically address the development of published guidance related to identifying, evaluating, and documenting National Register–eligible Native American landscapes.

The 28 comments received by NPS by the end of 2016 on the proposed Bulletin 38 revision illustrate the innovative, complex, and controversial nature of the original publication. Some comments entail only a single paragraph, while others involve many pages. The commenters have included three tribes, two Hawaiian organizations, two professional organizations, five federal agencies, two SHPOs, multiple contracting firms, several state agencies, a few academics, and a number of private individuals. Tom King commented three times (once for the Hopi), with his longest comment at 49 pages.

Most of the comments on Bulletin 38 deal with the seven issues presented in the 2012 *Federal Register* announcement. Almost a third, however, focus on the lack of specific environmental review guidance provided in the existing bulletin. This is ironic, considering that the original purpose of having Tom King work on the document in the mid-1980s was to provide the ACHP with guidance in implementing Section 106 and also that the ACHP dropped out of the revision discussions initiated in 2012.

At this writing in December 2017, a revised Bulletin 38 has not been produced, and the National Register webpage says if you still have any comments, "feel free" to submit them. I did not comment on the Bulletin 38 revision because I was no longer working at the Minnesota SHPO in 2012, and as state archaeologist my sole official concern was with historic properties of a strictly archaeological nature and those off federal land. Furthermore, Minnesota state law does not recognize TCPs or sacred sites as special properties in need of protection or acknowledgment, although anything listed in the National Register gets enhanced consideration in Minnesota's state environmental review process.

In actually applying Bulletin 38 to nominations, I noticed many tweaks that could be made. If I had commented on Bulletin 38 for the recent NPS review, I would have focused on only the following key points:

1. *Change the title.* I think that two important words are missing from Bulletin 38's title. Although "documenting" infers "identifying," it also encompasses what you record in the field, how you fill out an inventory form after you have identified a site, writing a report, how to go about mitigation, and how the information is stored in inventories. The word "documenting" should have been "identifying." The word "registering" is also missing from the title. After all, it is a National Register bulletin, regardless of the value of and problems with actually listing a TCP. In my view, the title should read, "Guidelines for Identifying, Evaluating, and Registering Traditional Cultural Properties."

2. *Avoid environmental review procedures.* I do not think the bulletin should get into Section 106, NEPA, or most management applications. These are responsibilities of the ACHP, federal agencies, and the NPS outside its National Register program. Let the National Register focus on identification, evaluation, and registration of TCPs as these topics are worry enough without getting into Section 106 or NEPA implications. Let the ACHP implement the original intent of Parker and King's initiative by issuing its own TCP guidance for Section 106 applications, but keep the guidelines focused on Section 106–related issues and outcomes, with perhaps some overlap on identification procedures as they specifically apply to 106 actions. The Council on Environmental Quality (CEQ) could offer NEPA guidelines. NPS, and other major federal landowners, should do TCP planning and management guidelines for their own properties. Other National Register bulletins don't focus on environmental review implications.

3. *Add some definitions.* Only one definition appears in Appendix I, and that is a brief discussion of the word "culture." The most critical missing definition in Bulletin 38 is "community." This definition is essential to the entire spectrum of TCP-related actions: identification, evaluation, registration, treatment, and management. Is there a community of motorcyclists that South Dakota should consult about the eligibility of Sturgis? I would say no, because I think community members need to reside together for more than just a week every year as required by Murdock's (1950:93) definition of "community."

   Another important definition that is needed is "traditional knowledge." Traditional knowledge in my view is "elder knowledge." It is critical cultural information passed from knowledgeable elders to appropriate members of a community's next generation. It is usually transmitted orally but can sometimes be found in ethnographies and other written texts. Identifying, evaluating, and treating TCPs all depend on traditional knowledge. Jan Vansina, a Belgian University of Wisconsin anthropologist, has some valuable insights into traditional knowledge in multiple publications (e.g., Vansina 1961, 1985). The people who have elder knowledge are not necessarily all older members of a group. Elders are respected members of a community who speak with deep knowledge and authority. There are elders, and there are "olders" in any community.

   Other definitions that could be included are "traditional," "traditional cultural property" (currently embedded in the Bulletin 38 text), "cultural practices," and "sacred site" (as a type and nontype of TCP). I have included suggestions for some of these definitions in Appendix D.

4. *Clarify professional qualifications.* The inclusion in Appendix II of Bulletin 38 of "Professional Qualifications: Ethnography" is clearly an afterthought or at least just a preliminary thought as to who is qualified to professionally undertake TCP identification and eligibility determination for the purposes of environmental review and registration. It does not require that the person be an ethnographer with an advanced degree in cultural anthropology. As currently listed in Bulletin 38, it simply requires a set of skills in linguistics, interviewing, and recording—basically standard academic ethnography skills. There is one glaring absence, however: experience in evaluating and registering. Because official blessing as to whether a TCP is eligible depends on application of National Register guidelines, this is an essential skill not possessed by most academic ethnographers or folklorists. In my experience, the lack of this skill has been a major flaw in many TCP evaluations for the purposes of Section 106. The other element often lacking in TCP identification and evaluation efforts is in-depth knowledge of a particular community's cultural practices, which involves much more than just familiarity with its language or having done a TCP evaluation for some other group.

What Are TCPs?

Bulletin 38 (Parker and King 1998:1) states, "A traditional cultural property . . . can be defined generally as one that is eligible for inclusion in the National Register because of its association with cultural practices or beliefs of a living community that (a) are rooted in that community's history, and (b) are important in maintaining the continuing cultural identity of the community." Like all National Register properties, TCPs can be buildings, structures, sites, objects, or districts. Although, since the first publication of Bulletin 38 in 1990, most attention has been focused on Indian TCPs, the bulletin stressed that TCPs can be associated with any community. Examples presented in the bulletin include an African American church and school in Kansas, the German Village Historic District in Ohio, sandbars in the Rio Grande near Sandia Pueblo in New Mexico, Chinatown in Honolulu, the Helkau Historic District in California's Six Rivers National Forest (a Tolowa-Yurok-Karuk-Hoopa Indian cultural landscape), a Shaker community in Massachusetts, and the shrine of Don Padrito Jaramillo in Texas.

First, note that a TCP must have both qualities listed under *a* and *b* above. The key questions are, Is there a living community directly associated with the property, and are the cultural practices that take place at the property or the historical associations with the property important to the community's cultural identity? Both of these qualifications are complex and dependent on definitions: What is a "living community"? What are "cultural practices"? What does "rooted in a community's history" mean? What does "important" mean? What is "maintenance"? What is "cultural identity"? Before you even start addressing most of the critical aspects involved with identification and evaluation noted in the 2012 NPS update request, you must first address these questions and answer them in an appropriate and convincing manner.

Second, it is important to distinguish sacred sites that may be eligible as TCPs from those that probably aren't. Broadly defined, sacred sites in general do not have to meet the rules of the National Register. Some are very personal and may have value only to one person. They do not have a minimum age requirement or need an explicit boundary. There are no restrictions on their being religious sites or cemeteries. Sacred sites simply have religious or spiritual significance to someone or some group. Sacred sites in and of themselves are treated as a special category of heritage resource on federal land under AIRFA and EO 13007. The whole world is sacred to some, but it is not eligible for the purposes of the National Register or Section 106.

Identifying and Recording TCPs

For identification of TCPs, Bulletin 38 first of all discusses *level of effort*. Section 106–related identification efforts connected with reviewing federal undertakings must be "reasonable and good faith efforts." This means you must first do a thorough literature search and make a concerted effort to locate consulting parties who may not only be interested in the project but have knowledge of potential TCPs in the project area. If identification is just for general planning or seeking properties to nominate, there is more time to find consulting parties, and their role is less formal than in a Section 106 action. Level of effort is also based on the nature of potential effects. Disturbing large, previously undisturbed areas requires a greater level of effort than a simple building rehabilitation. Bulletin 38 provides substantial consultation advice, including how to initiate contact with communities for TCP identification purposes.

Most TCPs will only be identified by asking appropriate members of associated communities. However, as with all cultural heritage investigations, finding TCPs begins with a literature search and preliminary analysis. This can help identify not only known examples or known types of TCPs in certain areas but also communities both in and out of the area that need to be consulted. When I was looking for a TCP to nominate in Minnesota, I started by compiling a list of important Dakota places in the Twin Cities area. This area was the core of the Dakota world at the time treaties were signed in the mid-nineteenth century. It has also been the area of most concentrated post-treaty land development in Minnesota and of the most concentrated threat to historic properties, including TCPs. I soon determined that many of the potential historic Dakota TCP locations had been totally destroyed, and others had been severely impacted by modern development.

The only way to determine if the impacted potential TCPs still had integrity was to begin consultation. When I worked for the SHPO in the 1990s, I went out to check a proposed addition to a 1950s building on a lake northwest of Minneapolis. As I walked through the adjacent woods, I came upon a small bronze plaque on the ground that read, "Red Rock Ancient Indian Shrine. Moved to this site in 1942 from 6 miles below St. Paul on the Mississippi River. Red Rock Camp Meeting." There was no rock or structure anywhere nearby.

I did some research and found that in 1805 Zebulon Pike had noted a large granitic boulder near the east bank of the Mississippi River that appeared to be important to the local Dakota Indians. The boulder was painted with red ochre, hence it became known to non-Dakota as the Red Rock, although a photograph from the early 1900s appears to show it painted with red and white stripes. To the Dakota it may have been known as *inyansa* (a literal translation of red rock) or more likely *inyan mani* (the rock that walks). Because it appeared to have religious importance to the Dakota, the first Protestant mission near St. Paul was located immediately adjacent to the Red Rock in 1837, no doubt to provide ready access to a group some Methodists thought were ripe for conversion to a new religion.

A small settler community grew up in the vicinity and took the name Red Rock. After the US-Dakota War in 1862, the Dakota were banished from Minnesota, so access to the Red Rock was essentially forbidden. In the late 1860s, a Methodist camp meeting assembly grounds was established at the site of the 1830s mission and the Red Rock. Over the next 70 years, the Red Rock was moved several times within Red Rock Camp in order to make it more accessible to campfire stories of Indian days and early mission history. It was not very accessible to the Dakota, although they had been gradually moving back into Minnesota.

In 1942, the Red Rock was moved to Medicine Lake northwest of Minneapolis when a new Methodist bible camp was established there. That was the reason for the plaque I found in the woods 50 years later. When the Methodists closed the camp in 1964 and built a new church on the bluff in Newport above the original Red Rock location, they moved the Red Rock to a spot in front of the church's front door (Figure 13.3). Some church members painted the rock again with red and white stripes similar to those shown in early photographs of the rock. That is where it was in 1995 when I first visited it. There was a large Minnesota Historical Society historical marker immediately adjacent to the rock. There is no view of the river from the rock, as the church is between the two. The original Red Rock location on the river is now covered with large oil tanks for a nearby refinery.

I asked a Dakota elder from the Shakopee community if he knew about the Red Rock. He got a sad look on his face and replied, "Ah, the Red Rock. When they moved it that is when things got really bad for us." I didn't ask him if it still was an important Dakota "sacred site." At the time, I was new to TCPs, and he would not have heard such sites referred to by that abbreviation. The Red Rock was clearly once very important to the Dakota, but the question remains, Does it have sufficient integrity to be eligible for inclusion in the National Register? Only the Dakota can answer that now. In 1995, I didn't know if any Dakota still visited it. In 2017, the Methodist church finally offered to give the Red Rock back to the Dakota.

Besides actually mentioning possible TCPs in historic and ethnographic literature, such sources also suggest places where certain landforms or certain resource areas have high TCP potential. For the Ojibwe, traditional wild ricing and maple sugaring locations are obvious, although not all groves of maple trees and current wild

FIG. 13.3 The Dakota Red Rock in front of the Newport, Minnesota, Methodist Church in 1995 (author photo).

rice beds are eligible. Many of these are what some would call traditional use-areas. For the Dakota, rock outcrops or large, lone boulders are good candidates.

Another clue is places that have recorded names in native languages and what the names mean. I did a study of Dakota place names in the Twin Cities area as part of a mitigation for the destruction of some small prehistoric sites for building construction (Anfinson 1995). *Inyan* is the Dakota word for rock, and I knew some of these places were very important to the Dakota, so I paid particular attention to the *inyan*-named places when looking for potential TCPs.

Doing fieldwork involves both looking at locations of known TCPs and attempting to find previously unrecorded ones. An initial walkover of an area can assess the extent of previous disturbance and locate obvious candidates, like certain types of buildings (e.g., churches), certain types of sites (e.g., burial grounds), and certain types of natural resources (e.g., maple trees, wild rice beds, rock outcrops). If you are on a reservation, be sure you have landowner permission for your survey and let reservation officials know what you are doing. For official tribal consultation for the purposes of a federal undertaking, the initial tribal contact has to be made nation to nation between agency officials and tribal officials of appropriate and approximately equal stature.

To record most potential TCPs located in the field, standard archaeological or building/structure inventory forms don't work well. There are too many unique categories of TCP information. You must also consider how and where the information will be stored. At the Minnesota SHPO, TCP information didn't fit well into either the archaeological or history-architecture inventories. Furthermore, some TCP information, especially that related to tribes, is even more sensitive than archaeological site locations and must be held in ultraconfidential locations with very limited access.

Bulletin 38 stresses that reconciliation may be needed regarding discrepancies between what a literature search suggests and what local informants know and say. An informant may even profess ignorance of a known TCP to guard sensitive information. One informant may say a place is important, while another may say it is not. An individual's access to traditional knowledge, motives, community standing, and personal values may all play into what he or she tells you.

Bulletin 38 skips around a bit when dealing with recording TCPs. It discusses fieldwork under the identification section (III) and has a separate section on documentation (V) that includes discussions of confidentiality, site characteristics, boundaries, setting, and registration. You can't do adequate fieldwork without documenting your findings, and prior to evaluation (III), you should have basic essential information already documented. There should be an entirely separate section in Bulletin 38 on registration, because some of the issues and needs are different from those for identification, recordation, and evaluation.

Evaluating TCPs

This step is more difficult and more controversial than the identification step. Because only eligible TCPs will be considered under Section 106 review and for National Register nomination, evaluation must be done carefully and thoroughly with regard to both significance and integrity.

With regard to significance, the necessary qualities are embedded in the definition of TCP on the first page of the bulletin: Is there a living community directly associated with the property, and does the property serve a function important to preserving the community's cultural identity?

Once the answer of general significance appears to be yes to the two-part definitional question, then standard National Register rules apply: Is the entity a property, meaning is it a site, building, structure, object, or district? Does it have definable or somewhat definable boundaries? The exact boundary question is more important for nomination than it is for initial environmental impact assessment. Construction or activity impacts to even a vaguely defined site can often be avoided through consultation with a community. If impacts are more difficult to assess, more exact boundaries may be necessary.

Once the entity is determined to be at least one of the National Register general property types and has a specific or general boundary defined, the next step is to determine which National Register significance criteria apply. Most tribal TCPs will be eligible under Criterion A, although some may also have Criteria B, C, and D qualities. I think Criterion B was pushed a bit too far in Bulletin 38, suggesting that association with an important deity was the same as association with an important person (think of all the Christian churches potentially eligible under B). The significance and integrity needs under Criterion A or B are about the same, meaning any adverse effect assessments are about the same, so I would not list B for association with a deity just to avoid First Amendment issues and other complications.

The seven National Register criteria considerations must also be applied to TCPs. Such considerations are often more complicated with TCPs than they are with other property types, especially with regard to religious properties (Consideration A), graves and cemeteries (Considerations C and D), and properties younger than 50 years (Consideration G). Bulletin 38 addresses all of these, so I won't go into them here, although be aware that they are controversial and received comments in response to the NPS 2012 request regarding updating Bulletin 38.

Once general significance, property assignment, boundary, and specific National Register significance criteria and criteria consideration applications have been determined, the next step is assessing a property's integrity. Bulletin 38 lumps the seven standard aspects of integrity into two aspects: *integrity of relationship* and *integrity of condition*. Relationship involves the standard aspects of association and feeling. Condition relates to setting, workmanship, materials, location, design, and to some degree, feeling. (See chapter 5 for a discussion of National Register integrity.)

Superficial integrity assessments that work well for archaeological sites and structures may not work well for tribal TCPs. Remember my Red Rock example. If the Red Rock had just been an artifact or a structure, moving it alone would have severely damaged its integrity of condition (i.e., location). The church ladies' painting it and its current location next to a Methodist church with no view of the river would have harmed qualities of condition (setting, feeling, workmanship, materials, and design). Integrity of relationship (i.e., association) for Red Rock is a matter for the Dakota to determine, although the justification for loss or retention must be explained in some detail.

To assist with both evaluating TCPs for eligibility and possibly registering eligible examples, when I was at the Minnesota SHPO I developed a worksheet (Appendix D) in 2010 to help me deal with the complicated questions and establish some consistency in my approach and conclusions. This is a very objective approach in dealing with very subjective information. I suppose this is typical for an American archaeologist educated in the 1960s and 1970s. I am well aware of the worksheet's possible failings but will nonetheless present it, as I think it brings some focus to answering the basic TCP questions and shows the state of the art in TCP evaluation 20 years after Bulletin 38 was first published.

Registering TCPs

Bulletin 38 has only a half page of instructions concerning registering TCPs—that is, how to nominate them for the National Register. This is very strange considering it is a National Register bulletin. Other property-type bulletins provide detailed instructions for completing each section of the nomination form. Bulletin 38 just provides a sentence or brief paragraph for each section. Mostly it just says follow the instructions in the bulletin *How to Complete the National Register Registration Form* (Bulletin 16A).

There should be an entirely separate section in Bulletin 38 just for dealing with registration. Issues of environmental review and registration with regard to TCPs should be kept separate due to separate needs for boundary definition, level of effort, intensity of consultation, and other aspects. Furthermore, as King often points out, the need for TCP registration is a very different question from the need for identification and evaluation of TCPs for environmental review purposes.

Final Thoughts about TCPs

Like Tom King, I could write an entire book on TCPs based on my own education, experiences, and thoughts about the subject over my almost 50 years of continuing anthropological education and heritage management practice. I don't have the energy for that, and King has already done it better than I could. Even while writing this heritage management book, I have constantly had to pull back and examine my perspective, for with expertise comes bias, with involvement comes position taking, and with authority comes responsibility. Constant self-examination is especially important when dealing with Indian issues and TCPs.

Because TCPs are so complicated and so dependent on external expertise that is difficult for agencies and professionals to access, it is easy to get lost. I think some TCP "experts" have certainly lost their objectivity as they have become involved in TCP controversies, representing or rendering opinions for one side or the other. Some proponents for the eligibility of certain properties seem to think that a tribal opinion is the only opinion that matters, even when their own knowledge of the property, the tribe, National Register evaluation, and the issues is superficial; some opponents give insufficient weight to the tribal position and oral histories, relying on familiar written methodologies and sources.

The most important thing to remember is that the abbreviation TCP and the environmental-review-policy term it stands for are a construct of the federal government for the purposes of National Register nomination and Section 106 consideration. As a general descriptive phrase, "traditional cultural property" can still be applied to ineligible properties as places that are important to communities as traditional use-areas. TCPs, as well as historic and archaeological sites, are not the exclusive purview of the federal government and environmental review. Their value to communities and their protection is not solely dependent on "expert" analysis and official blessing.

That said, potential for misuse or inappropriate use of TCPs with respect to attempting to stop development exceeds that of most other property types with the exception of suspected burials. Determining burial presence is ultimately a matter of archaeology. If decisions regarding TCP identification, boundary determination, and eligibility for the purposes of environmental review are solely left to communities, then federal agencies will be increasingly forced to disagree with communities, and future consultation will be impaired. There will also be no consistency in the review process from agency to agency, state to state, and community to community.

Communities must be carefully consulted with regard to TCPs, but in the end decisions about significance and treatment for the purposes of environmental review will always necessarily be bureaucratic. That is the way the current system works.

Summary

The 1992 amendments to the NHPA attempted to fully invest American Indian tribes, Native Alaskans, and Native Hawaiians in cultural resource management and historic preservation. These groups were given the ability to assume any or all of a SHPO's powers. There were also given access to the Historic Preservation Fund to help pay for running their preservation offices and in the form of grants to promote heritage preservation within their reservations and communities. As entities, even without formal preservation offices, these groups were also mainstreamed into the environmental review process by requirements in Section 106 that they be consulted by federal agencies for all undertakings that might impact properties in which they were interested.

Today, only about a third of recognized tribes have tribal historic preservation officers, but all tribes are consulted by all federal agencies that manage lands where· tribes once lived or that are involved in undertakings that may impact cultural heritage properties potentially valued by tribes. While tribes and federal agencies were slow to implement and understand the stipulations in the 1992 amendments to NHPA, both groups are now well aware of their obligations and opportunities, although there is still substantial disagreement about what represents "reasonable and good faith" identification and consultation.

Any heritage management professional who is preparing to participate in tribal heritage management must be aware not only of what the laws and regulations say but of tribal histories, federal and state legal intricacies involved with treaties and Indian landownership, and the current unique cultural manifestations of each tribe potentially dealt with. Consultation with tribes can be complicated and confusing. It may be required but can also be very rewarding when you are helping tribes to protect vital aspects of their tangible cultural heritage and gaining insight into intangible cultural heritage.

Understanding tribal histories and varying cultural perspectives is also critical to identifying and evaluating traditional cultural properties, but tribal knowledge and tribal perspectives must be applied to TCP analysis. Because TCP as an abbreviation and a property type are a federal construct for the purposes of federal actions, identification and evaluation must follow federal rules. TCPs must have some antiquity, they must have some kind of boundary that can be drawn on a map, and they must meet National Register requirements for significance and integrity, although these qualities are largely a matter for associated communities to define.

Review Questions

1. What characterizes the relationship of the federal government with tribes?
2. What is Indian land?
3. What does NAGPRA cover?
4. What do AIRFA and EO 13007 cover?
5. What are the keys to adequate tribal consultation?
6. What is tribal monitoring?
7. What are TCPs, and how do they differ from sacred sites?

Supplemental Reading

The best set of compiled references for understanding Indian history as a national story, as well as the histories and ethnographies of individual tribes, can be found in the *Handbook of North American Indians*, published in multiple volumes by the Smithsonian Institution. There are currently four general volumes: Volume 2: *Indians in Contemporary Society* (2008), Volume 3: *Environment, Origins, and Population* (2006), Volume 4: *History of Indian-White Relations* (1988), and Volume 17: *Languages* (1996). There are 12 regional volumes (5–15) summarizing the regional archaeology, history, and ethnography of various tribes and groups. Still to be completed are Volume 1: *Introduction*, Volumes 18–19: *Biographical Dictionary*, and Volume 20: *Index*.

Almost every agency now has guidance as to how to undertake consultation with tribes both for the purposes of Section 106 and for other reasons. The ACHP also has extensive guidance for tribal consultation on its website. Both HUD and NPS have consultation databases on their websites that help identify geographical areas tribes are interested in. For consultation in general with regard to cultural heritage resources, Nissley and King (2014) offer many suggestions and observations. Stapp and Burney (2002) offer perspectives on tribal cultural resource management.

Traditional cultural properties were introduced to American heritage management by National Register Bulletin 38 in 1990 (Parker and King 1990). It is still the essential guide to TCPs, although the need to update it is widely recognized, much anticipated, and unfortunately much delayed. See King (2003) for additional insight on TCPs.

◖ SIDEBAR ◗

Implementing Heritage Management: A Splash of Coldwater

During the 15 years I was SHPO archaeologist for Minnesota, I was involved with surprisingly few traditional cultural property issues with respect to both Section 106 project reviews and National Register nominations. The TCP National Register Bulletin 38 (Parker and King 1990) came out just as I started my SHPO job. After I read the bulletin, I thought, Uh, oh. This is going to be a big problem for a lot of federal agencies and SHPOs. It wasn't. Because TCPs were a relatively new property type and were very complicated to figure out, agencies weren't going to raise the TCP issue if SHPOs and tribes weren't.

I did have one major TCP Section 106 issue as a SHPO archaeologist. In 1998, the Minnesota Department of Transportation finally decided to rebuild a segment of Trunk Highway 55 (TH 55) near Fort Snelling. I say finally because MnDOT had initially proposed doing the work in the early 1960s. MnDOT had held public hearings on the project in 1965 prior to the passage of the National

Historic Preservation Act and the Department of Transportation Act (DOTA) in 1966. MnDOT did the first archaeological survey of the route in 1969 and a second one in 1971. Both were negative.

MnDOT then had to do an environmental impact statement (EIS) as required by the National Environmental Policy Act of 1969. The first EIS was rejected by the Federal Highway Administration in 1972, but federal funds were allocated for the TH 55 project in 1974. The main issue of concern was the effect on Minnehaha Park, one of the larger, earlier, and more famous Minneapolis parks. It was also listed in the National Register of Historic Places in 1969, the first district listed in Minnesota. This was not just a Section 106 and NEPA issue but a DOTA Section 4(f) issue, also in play by 1969. The southern end of the project also passed through the Fort Snelling Historic District, which had been listed as a National Historic Landmark (NHL) in 1960 and became a National Register district in 1971.

After negotiations with the Minneapolis Park Board and the Minnesota SHPO, a revised draft EIS was released in 1982. The SHPO asked for a third archaeological survey in 1983, but once again nothing was found. In December 1983, the SHPO issued an "adverse effect" finding due to impacts to Minnehaha Park. MnDOT concurred, so a memorandum of agreement (MOA) was enacted in 1984 that stipulated mitigative work in Minnehaha Park (a tunnel, additional archaeological survey) and archaeological monitoring of the construction in the Fort Snelling area. The final EIS for TH 55 was issued in February 1985. Some of the right-of-way was obtained by MnDOT, but no construction was initiated. This was all before my time at the SHPO.

In 1995, Congress voted to close the federal Bureau of Mines (BOM) and get rid of all BOM property. The BOM owned a major facility adjacent to the southern end of the TH 55 project. Because this was a Section 106 action, the SHPO (and I) got involved. We requested a historical and archeological survey, and the soon-to-be-defunct BOM complied. Most of the BOM buildings were found to be eligible for inclusion in the National Register for their role in developing the taconite iron ore process, which is very important to Minnesota. The archaeological survey determined most of the BOM property to be heavily disturbed except for a small area adjacent to the TH 55 right-of-way. It appeared to include remains of Camp Coldwater.

When Fort Snelling was first being constructed in the early 1820s, a temporary camp, known as Camp Coldwater due to the presence of a freshwater spring, was established near the proposed fort. The camp was soon abandoned by the military, but the buildings were reoccupied by early white settlers and a fur post. Most of the settlers abandoned Camp Coldwater as the military asserted control of its Fort Snelling reserve lands and better farmland was opened for settlement by treaties with the Dakota Indians in 1837 and 1851. In 1878, the army built a water reservoir at Camp Coldwater to supply an expansion of Fort Snelling. The army abandoned the Coldwater area in 1946 when Fort Snelling was closed. The Camp Coldwater land was given to the Veterans Administration (VA), which then gave most of it to the BOM. Both the VA and the BOM constructed large buildings on the site.

In 1998, MnDOT decided to finally build TH 55. Between 1985 and 1998, new residents had moved into the area. They opposed the road, but the EIS and Section 106 processes had already been completed. The residents asked a local Dakota group (not members of a recognized tribe) to assist them. The Mendota Dakota agreed, and soon we had a TCP complication. Based on the recent BOM survey findings, I didn't think the earlier archaeological surveys were adequate. MnDOT agreed, and a fourth survey was done. This survey too proved to be negative.

The Mendota Dakota claimed the spring was sacred and that four oak trees in the right-of-way were a burial site and also sacred. The actual pool/reservoir associated with the spring was outside the TH 55 project area. The state archaeologist (not me then) determined there were no burials under the oaks. I asked for a formal TCP analysis of the area, and MnDOT complied, conducting numerous interviews resulting in 200 pages of testimony. We could find no substantiation that the four oaks ever played an important role in Dakota culture. None of Minnesota's four recognized Dakota tribes objected. TH 55 was finally built in 2000.

But the BOM still had to determine if Coldwater Spring was a TCP. I had left the SHPO by then to become state archaeologist and had no jurisdiction on federal land. My brother John, who works for the National Park Service, inherited the problem. In the end, NPS did not find the spring to be eligible as a TCP but did concur that it could be a sacred site. Once again, the four recognized Dakota tribes in Minnesota did not object to this finding, but the Mendota Dakota and their supporters did. The spring is now protected and open to Dakota use for ceremonial purposes. NPS has torn down the BOM buildings and restored the early 1800s vegetation as part of a new NPS unit. Most parties are pleased with the outcome, TCP or not.

CHAPTER 14

Conclusions
Looking Back, Looking Forward

Make no mistake, my friends, these are dangerous times.
—Senator John McCain, February 2017

When I started writing this book in early 2016, my biggest concern was that I was not keeping up with current events in the wide world of heritage management. I had taken a leave of absence from teaching my heritage management class at the University of Minnesota for the first time in 15 years because I wanted to write this book and do a little traveling. I had just retired as Minnesota state archaeologist after 10 years of immersing myself in a state-centered perspective. I had already been slipping a bit with regard to federal heritage management, because I had been away from my state historic preservation office (SHPO) job for 10 years, but at least there had been no major changes in federal heritage management laws or procedures.

I coped with my peer-interchange and agency-contact isolation by frequently checking the Advisory Council on Historic Preservation (ACHP) and National Park Service (NPS) webpages and carefully scrutinizing emails I was still receiving from the National Association of State Archaeologists (NASA). I browsed professional journals for new articles and searched Amazon to see if there was some new book I should look at. I even regularly googled "historic preservation," "cultural resource management," and "heritage preservation" to see what popped up. I thought I was making a reasonable and good faith effort to keep current.

Just to keep me aware that major changes in practice could happen, the Minnesota legislature passed a law in early 2017 moving the SHPO from the Minnesota Historical Society (MHS) to the Minnesota Department of Administration. The SHPO had been at MHS for 50 years, since the very inception of the program. But this administrative relocation should not change the viability or the basic system of heritage management in Minnesota. The larger MHS organization was always more focused on expanding its membership, running its museum, and managing its visitor-oriented historic sites.

Then came the national election in November 2016. Suddenly keeping up with bureaucratic tweaks and practitioners' opinions seemed a relatively minor issue compared with the threat that everything I had learned over 40 years of heritage management practice might soon become totally irrelevant. The new wild-card administration and conservative Congress could rapidly and completely change the American heritage management structure as we have known it for the past half century. Hopefully, as you read this, my worst fears have not been realized. I hope the essential parts of the basic structure are still in place and this book is still relevant as a how-to book rather than a quaint historical perspective.

It would be somewhat ironic if the election of 2016 caused big changes in heritage protection. As I have previously mentioned, 2016 was a big anniversary year for heritage management. The NPS turned 100, and it had been 50 years since the passage of the National Historic Preservation Act (NHPA), the Department of Transportation Act (DOTA), and the Demonstration Cities and Metropolitan Development Act. How different American heritage management would be without the leadership and stewardship of NPS, the familiar preservation procedures of Section 106 and Section 4(f), and federal government support of urban historic preservation.

Examining the Structure of American Heritage Management

I have used two analogies in this book to help explain the structure of American heritage management. Like a cultural landscape, it is part organic and part constructed. The organic structure of American heritage management is a hybrid tree. The root system has some European heritage preservation practices based on the scientific method intertwined with some uniquely American practices based on democratic ideals. Onto these roots was grafted a trunk formed of the Constitution, explicitly promoting individual rights within a federalist structure. From the trunk grew five preservation limbs: the federal, state, local, tribal, and private. The private and local limbs were the first to emerge, but the federal limb is the central leader that gives the heritage preservation tree its shape and strength and determines how much fruit it will bear.

The constructed part of American heritage management is like a building. Its foundation, walls, and roof are built of laws passed by Congress, state legislatures, and city councils. Government regulations have added features and strength to the building's structural elements. Within the building are the offices of the agencies and professional entities that implement the laws and regulations. Some have bigger offices than others. Once again, federal offices are the largest and take up the ground floor, but the building's other occupants make the system work effectively, efficiently, and comprehensively.

Local and private heritage management efforts focus on cities and buildings. This started in eastern cities and with properties associated with the founders of our nation. Early heritage preservation was isolated and internalized. A museum was the place to learn about the past. With a few rare exceptions (e.g., Mount Vernon), preserving pieces of that past outdoors could only be done in communities with a will to save defining elements of their idealized past. These were usually limited to monumental public buildings and opulent private homes.

Heritage preservation at the state level was also initially internalized. Each state had a historical society with its small museum celebrating the conquest of nature and of Indians, who were then considered a force of nature, and the economic triumph of the new immigrants. State heritage management laws, just like federal law, had their beginnings in early twentieth-century antiquity acts focused on saving artifactual and structural remnants of a distant and puzzling prehistoric past. For much of the country just a century ago, the built environment was not that old, not much was worthy of preservation in the eyes of citizens, and the replacement of its existing fabric was slow and on the whole unthreatening to American heritage. The greatest danger to American heritage appeared to be to the pre-European aspects, which were vulnerable to pillaging by untrained or unscrupulous curiosity seekers.

It was not a military crisis that spurred federal leaders to broadly consider heritage preservation needs but an economic crisis: the Great Depression. The Historic Sites Act of 1935 authorized the creation of a survey of nationally significant historic sites, promoted cooperative agreements between the federal government and private entities for the maintenance of important historic sites, and empowered the secretary of the interior to accept new additions to the federally owned system of national historic sites. Within NPS, the Historic Sites Act promoted research, preservation, restoration, and interpretation, as well as the acquisition and management of culturally oriented park units. It also promoted the employment of heritage management professionals. The initiatives of this first broad federal historic preservation initiative were immediately coupled with archaeological, historical, and architectural employment initiatives of the new alphabet agencies, with NPS professionals coordinating most efforts.

The desperate struggle of World War II ended with a world that had become an American opportunity. It also changed heritage preservation in America into a desperate struggle against economic opportunism. Rampant freeway construction, broadly targeted urban renewal, and massive reservoir development became a "federal bulldozer" pushing away the past according to a shortsighted vision of the future. As the economy began to flourish, the environment began to fail. Rachel Carson's "silent spring" was becoming a reality. It would take a great societal effort to halt the destruction and restore as much as possible.

As the environmental movement gained momentum, so did the civil rights movement. Although the focus was on black lives, Indian peoples also came to the forefront. The American Indian Movement (AIM) was founded in 1968. AIM was concerned not only with the Indian present but the Indian past. One of the first major public actions by AIM was to disrupt an archaeological dig in Minnesota (see D. Thomas 2000:198–199). The 1990 NPS publication *Keepers of the Treasures* acknowledged the need to mainstream Indian participation in cultural heritage management, and the 1992 amendments to the NHPA took important steps to implement this. Today, tribes play a vital and increasing role in heritage preservation.

The American heritage management system has matured and to some degree stagnated. Many of the same preachers are talking to the same choirs, and both groups are aging. The tried-and-true aspects of environmental review (e.g., Section 106), government financial support (e.g., tax credits), and federal agencies' stewardship of their own properties (e.g., Section 110) remain the three essential elements of American heritage management. All have had considerable success in preserving important historic properties, but all three are threatened by senescence, a lack of funding, and the new owners of the political landscape.

Evaluating American Heritage Management

In 2016, the fiftieth anniversary of the National Historic Preservation Act logically resulted in some retrospectives on the act's effect on heritage management (e.g., Banks and Scott 2016). Most articles simply celebrate the NHPA, dwelling on successes or discussing "challenges and opportunities" in the future. A few give honest assessments of the major issues, such as problems with the 50-year rule and deficiencies in the training of the new generation of government heritage managers (e.g., Rood and Kintz 2016). After the election of 2016, as preservationists celebrated past successes, they were apprehensive about the future.

To evaluate the strengths and weaknesses of American heritage management, we can look at two major aspects of the system: who is responsible and how those responsible carry out their responsibilities. Performance can be judged according to two aspects: effectiveness and efficiency. Effectiveness examines how successful an entity is, and efficiency examines how well an entity uses the resources it is given. Both are closely tied to survivability in the post-2016 political world.

In this book, I have limited my criticisms of the American heritage management system in order to focus on how the system should be implemented as it currently exists. After doing heritage management for 40 years, however, I do have some observations for improving the system. Most of these suggestions could be implemented without significant additional funding or amendments to the laws. Many involve just changes to regulations and standard practice. Rather than critique the system top to bottom, I will focus on evaluating three key aspects: federal agencies, SHPOs, and the National Register of Historic Places (NHRP).

Federal Agencies

Federal agencies form the core of our heritage management structure. In order to evaluate agencies' effectiveness and efficiency, we need to understand their obligations and then apply some analysis to what they have done. Under environmental review laws, agencies must consider the effects of their actions on historic properties and consult with appropriate entities to fully understand what properties may be affected and how. Under Section 110 of the NHPA, agencies must constantly promote the preservation of historic properties under their control as land and building managers.

Comprehensive metrics evaluating agency compliance with laws are not easy to come by. SHPOs report some basic Section 106 review statistics to the NPS each year, and federal agencies also annually send their basic statistics on heritage management activities to NPS. NPS provides Congress with a summary of basic agency activity every four years, but this report does not summarize SHPO activity. Most SHPOs don't share their submitted NPS information with the public. A 2009 report by the National Academy of Public Administration noted that the ACHP has only limited information on day-to-day Section 106 reviews by federal agencies, SHPOs, and tribal historic preservation offices (THPOs). This report also noted the ACHP has no performance measures related to Section 106.

Even if we had all the statistics, they would only provide a superficial and incomplete measure of effectiveness. They might show the rate of agency compliance with the law but not the number of historic properties actually saved, because the "saving" takes place at so many different steps in the process. The majority of historic properties are saved by simple avoidance early in the process, so knowing the number of properties evaluated for National Register eligibility and the number of memoranda of agreements (MOAs) signed doesn't tell us how many unevaluated properties were avoided early in the process and thus saved.

I think the success of the environmental review process in protecting historic properties can be most effectively evaluated in a more subjective manner. When the system fails or even is controversial, we usually hear about it. Tom King in his many writings has told us about notable failures that led to or should have led to changes in law and practice. We are also now aware of complex property types like traditional cultural properties (TCPs) and cultural landscapes, as well as the need for input from all stakeholders in identification, evaluation, and treatment.

Despite what some may think, the highly publicized Dakota Access Pipeline and Cape Wind projects weren't failures of the current heritage management system.

The impacts of these developments were carefully considered by the review agencies. A reasonable and good faith effort was made to identify historic properties and consult with all stakeholders. The results certainly didn't please everyone, but the agencies involved followed the rules. The final judgement as to the effectiveness of our current heritage management system is that we don't hear about many failures regarding either the failure to save important historic properties from government actions or the failure of government agencies to fulfill their legal responsibilities.

As for evaluating efficiency, this too is dependent on both objective and subjective measures. The objective metrics are even more difficult to obtain. There is no central source to easily determine how much money each agency spends on heritage management. The amount is buried in each agency's budget, but even then it is difficult to determine the extent of funds actually spent on heritage management. How many employees are 100% dedicated to heritage management? What percentage of a line item in a budget is dedicated to heritage management? How much time and effort are spent on identification, evaluation, registration, and treatment? How much is spent on planning, curation, and education?

As for subjective measures, in my 40 years of practice I have personally seen both efficiency and waste by federal agencies with respect to heritage management. Sometimes both were due to an agency's culture, but most of the time it came down to personnel. Some people are good managers; some are not. Some people do their jobs because they believe in what they are doing; some just believe in having the job. Some people are just clueless when it comes to best practices; others provide the rest of us with valuable clues to improve our practices.

I also must note observations in Rood and Kintz (2016:203) that the ACHP and some agencies have been so concerned with demonstrating their commitment to diversity and inclusiveness that they are losing primary mission focus, favoring emotion and short-term feel-good outcomes over reasonable approaches and long-term preservation success. This can result in the impression that these agencies are inappropriately favoring the opinions of particular groups (e.g., tribes) to the detriment of professional analysis and a reasonable and balanced approach to heritage preservation.

The bottom line: federal agencies need to be more transparent. They need to do a better job of telling us how much money they are spending on heritage management, how many employees are fully dedicated to heritage management, and what kind of qualifications these employees have (e.g., put all staff resumes online). They need to produce succinct annual reports that summarize their heritage management activities, both successes and failures. They need to present a history of their heritage management programs on their webpages. This includes the agencies whose actions threaten historic properties and those charged with helping to avoid adverse impacts (e.g., ACHP). Federal preservation officers (FPOs) at many agencies need to become more involved in day-to-day heritage preservation. Most of all, agencies need to have qualified staff who not only understand the system but are willing to fairly apply it despite possible criticism from interest groups or politicians.

SHPOs

As with federal agencies, it is very difficult to evaluate SHPO performance with regard to both efficiency and effectiveness. There is certainly less potential to waste money at most SHPOs because most are underfunded and understaffed. SHPOs have had to go lean because the federal government has provided minimal financial assistance and most state legislatures don't make up the difference. These days, SHPOs have to dedicate most of their funding to the reactive rather than the proactive aspects of their responsibilities. Review and compliance staffs are usually the most robust in order to cope with the constant inflow of Section 106 projects and state environmental review responsibilities. National Register nominations are critical to tax credit and grant eligibility, so in most states commercial building nominations still dominate new listings. Certified local governments (CLGs) must receive 10% of Historic Preservation Fund (HPF) grants to a state, so SHPOs necessarily pay some attention to their activities and needs.

Proactive statewide resource surveys have fallen by the wayside in most states unless a state-supported funding mechanism is present. Minnesota has been very lucky over the last decade to receive substantial state funding due to a constitutional amendment that provides dedicated funding for the preservation of natural and cultural resources. We have restarted our statewide survey to examine poorly known areas and to do focused evaluation of certain property types (e.g., ruins, dams, Civilian Conservation Corps camps). States also have ignored updating and upgrading their historic context studies. If historic contexts are the key to protecting significant historic properties, why have most states basically ignored upgrading them for the last 20 years, and why do they pay so little attention to them in their current **state preservation plans**?

As for effectiveness, the biggest failure of SHPOs is their failure to evaluate their own performance when it comes to the review and compliance process. How many of the SHPO-recommended surveys are actually done by agencies? How many of these surveys find *significant* properties? How many evaluations result in determinations of eligibility? If eligible properties are adversely affected by undertakings, in all cases was eligibility confirmed by subsequent treatment activities? How effective are treatments in terms of accomplishing the stated objectives?

When I was SHPO archaeologist in Minnesota, I did some self-evaluation, and the results were both encouraging and discouraging. Almost every time I recommended an archaeological survey, the agency did it. When surveys were done, they were successful in finding sites over half the time, but in most cases the sites weren't eligible. My highest rate of negative results (i.e., surveys that did not find a site) was initially for cell tower surveys. In the 1990s, they were a new type of project, and there had been a few spectacular national failures (e.g., burial site impacts), so I was initially overly cautious. After careful analysis of my initial performance, I realized the great majority of cell tower locations were in very low-potential locations, and the great majority of surveys were indeed negative for significant sites. I subsequently dramatically cut the number of cell tower survey recommendations. I had no regrets about this major tactical change because strategically it was more efficient and economical, while still being sufficiently careful and effective.

I also examined my performance as a SHPO archaeologist with regard to archaeological excavations for mitigations of adverse effect. Like all archaeologists, I love research. If a site appeared to be eligible and we could get some major digging, analysis, and reporting done, I was all for it. After 10 years as a SHPO archaeologist, I reexamined all the major mitigations done with my concurrence on eligibility, my recommendation of adverse effect, and my advice on the final data-recovery plan. I looked at their cost, the competence of the archaeologists who did them, the quality of the analysis, the quality of the reporting, the availability of a public report, the effectiveness in answering the research questions from the data-recovery plan, whether they had really added important knowledge, and if the site was truly eligible based on reevaluation after the intensive examination. I scored each category from 0 to 3 (with 3 being the best) and added up the points. I then gave them a letter grade.

Out of 14 major mitigation excavations done in Minnesota in the 1990s, I counted one A, six Bs, five Cs, and two Ds. Most mitigations scored well on the quality of the work and competence of the staff. Most scored poorly on answering the research questions and cost-effectiveness. The worst scores were with regard to public reporting; I counted 1 two, 3 ones, and 10 zeros. Only 3 projects clearly confirmed a site's eligibility under Criterion D (potential to answer important questions), while 10 sites were probably eligible and 1 site probably was not eligible.

So what did I learn from this analysis? The first lesson was to do a better job with Phase 2/evaluation surveys, to not only firmly establish a site's eligibility but provide enough information to construct an appropriate data-recovery plan. The second lesson was to have a data-recovery plan focusing on only a few answerable and important questions, as well as staff competent to answer those questions. Finally, I came back to the Galileo conclusion: if data isn't made public, it is useless. While all the reports from the mitigation projects can be found at the SHPO, this is hardly the same as making them public. The reports will only be discovered if someone is doing a literature search for a future project in the same area and stumbles on them or they are cited in a research article by someone who was aware of the work. The need for some form of public reporting, or at least publicly available indexing, should be a part of every major treatment activity. This is certainly much easier and more possible with the internet.

The bottom line: most SHPOs do a good job of fulfilling their Section 106 agency responsibilities, but most do a poor job of analyzing their own performance. They keep recommending surveys regardless of past success, they keep saying the same kinds of sites are eligible regardless of their true significance and research potential, and they keep approving treatment activities regardless of their cost-effectiveness and value to heritage preservation. I think all SHPOs should have to do an annual report that is available on their websites. This report should not only include basic statistics but an honest analysis of the SHPO's performance in all program areas. SHPOs should also provide a history of their programs on their websites and in their state plans. This will not only help satisfy transparency requirements but allow SHPOs to better inform the public and improve their effectiveness and efficiency. This should also improve the public's support for what they do by giving SHPOs credit where credit is due for the predominantly hidden aspects of their successes.

National Register of Historic Places

I agree with Tom King about the limited value of archaeological nominations, but I have always been somewhat puzzled by his apparent antagonism toward the Register beginning in the early 1980s (e.g., King 1984). Most of King's complaints focus on its dual status as an honor roll and a planning tool. While I agree this does cause complications, I have never seen King provide a viable alternative. He thinks that the planning aspect of the National Register—determining the importance of historic properties and their treatment for the purposes of environmental review—should be handled at the community level, not by agencies, archaeologists, historians, or National Register staff (e.g., King 2011:544–547). He also thinks that consideration of cultural resources needs to include intangible aspects.

In my view, this would result in chaos and anarchy. There would be no universal standards from city to city and tribe to tribe, much less between states and agencies. Farmers would decide the eligibility of farm properties, tribes the eligibility of TCPs, and town hall meetings the eligibility of near and dear local buildings. A highway being built through multiple jurisdictions might encounter no review problems in one community and fierce opposition in another, resulting in properties eligible in one area and ineligible in the other, even if similar properties in both communities were essentially the same in significance and integrity. The highway would get built, but it would take more time, cost more money, and create bad feelings and mistrust. Local decision making for Register eligibility could be used to halt developments—a great tool for "not in my backyard" (NIMBY) activists.

The American Cultural Resources Association (ACRA) recently (September 28, 2016) stated on its webpage that consistent application of the Section 106 regulations is necessary to maintain the integrity of the process. A 2007 National Academy of Public Administration report called for "greater consistency by SHPOs and THPOs in conducting Section 106 reviews." The certified local government and historic preservation commission (HPC) structures already allow local governments a strong voice in the federal Section 106 review process, and local governments are already allowed to make local decisions as to the historical significance of their own properties with respect to the impacts of local developments.

The problem with the dual role of the National Register has only recently become a critical flaw in our heritage management system. For the first four decades of Section 106, the final arbiter of eligibility, the Keeper of the Register, was a professional historian. The Keeper had to make very few decisions because consensus was reached at the state level as to whether a property was eligible. I have no statistics, but I suspect that in more than 99% of instances in which a potentially eligible property might have been affected by a Section 106 undertaking, the Keeper was not consulted. If the Keeper was consulted, a decision could theoretically be made that was professional and consistent with the guidelines set forth in National Register bulletins.

Things began to change in the 1990s. First, new property types emerged that required new kinds of expertise. Cultural landscapes are very complex properties, often requiring input from architects, historians, ethnographers, and archaeologists. Traditional cultural properties need input from anthropologists and folklorists. While all the Register staff I have worked with over the years have been knowledgeable, thoughtful, and responsive, their expertise tends to be focused. Keepers and their small staff often don't have the breadth of knowledge and expertise to make appropriate analyses of all property types, especially newer varieties. For instance, almost all Register archaeologists have been historical archaeologists, most of them not trained to deal with the wide variety of prehistoric sites and with TCPs. There is not a single Register bulletin focused on prehistoric sites in general or on a specific prehistoric property type. The revision of the TCP bulletin was still not accomplished by the end of 2017, although it began in early 2012.

But the biggest problem with the Keeper being the final arbiter of eligibility became evident in 2005. The professional historian Keeper (Carol Shull) was replaced with a politically vulnerable deputy director of NPS (Janet Mathews). This was done for overtly political reasons. While Shull returned for a short time as acting Keeper following a presidential change, a deputy NPS director was soon made Keeper again. This politicizing of the heritage resources review process has happened at the state level too, with politically motivated SHPO appointments and SHPO removals (e.g., Ohio) by governors.

Having a politically responsive Keeper who is not a heritage management professional, assisted by a professional staff with limited expertise, is not an issue for almost all Register decisions for the honor roll function or even for the tax credit/grant eligibility function. But it could become an issue for the environmental review/planning aspect of the Register. If a project is controversial, then there will be political pressure from both sides. The side with political power will prevail, and properties will be saved or lost for political reasons, not due to their inherent significance and integrity.

The basic flaw is the lack of a fair and reasonable appeals process for National Register decisions involved with the environmental review process. A fair appeals process is a fundamental aspect of our system of government. Considering that eligibility decisions may become more politicized and more complicated for Register staff to deal with, I think the way to solve Tom King's issue is to take the Keeper out of making the final decision on eligibility for the purposes of environmental review. Considering how few Section 106 eligibility disagreements make it to the Keeper, an appeals board could be established at a national level or even at the level of each state or region. The board could be made up of agency officials, professional heritage management practitioners, tribal representatives, and experienced members of the public. They would meet only as necessary, and board makeup could change based on property type.

The bottom line: I think the National Register needs wider topical and regional expertise on its staff (e.g., cultural anthropologists, prehistoric archaeologists). The NRHP could even set up regional review boards to help with evaluating and registering difficult properties. The NRHP also needs to provide more guidance on key property types. How about a bulletin on lithic scatters or rock art? How about a bulletin that honestly assesses the archaeological research potential of post-1900 farmsteads? How about finishing the revision of the TCP bulletin emphasizing a reasonable and practical approach?

I also think we need to tighten eligibility requirements. I think it would be reasonable to restrict archaeological eligibility to 100 years, unless a careful analysis of properties younger than 100 years demonstrates a true potential to answer important research questions that can't be better or more completely answered using written or oral accounts. In all my years of doing and reviewing archaeological investigations of twentieth-century sites, I have seen very few that independently answered a question of importance. Perhaps the NRHP should add the qualifier "answerable" to its Criterion D requirement of "important" questions and better define what "important" means. Just as nonarchaeological properties listed or determined eligible under Criteria Consideration G can be less than 50 years old, exceptional archaeological properties could appeal a 100-year limit.

A Practical Approach

There are some aspects of a practical approach that are obvious and others that become apparent through practice, some as lightbulb moments when you realize there is an easier or better way of doing a common task. The obvious aspects of practicality are knowing what the key laws say, how these laws are applied, and the roles of the major players. These obvious aspects are all about the verbs found in the laws and in the procedures that implement them.

In the policy statement at the beginning of the NHPA (54 CFR 300101), the verbs are "foster," "provide," "administer," "contribute," "encourage," and "assist." Where are "identify," "preserve," "protect," and "save"? This is a classic federal government approach. The NHPA policy verbs are all about letting others do the actual work of preservation and giving them the freedom to decide what to do. *Foster* conditions that will promote preservation, *provide* leadership to help communities undertake preservation, *administer* federal funds and programs that assist preservation, *contribute* to efforts that make preservation happen, *encourage* public and private entities to use resources available to them, and *allow* federal agencies to assist others in making preservation happen.

The original verbs of implementation were "acquire," "preserve," and "protect." The post-1966 verbs of implementation are "plan," "identify," "record," "evaluate," "document," "register," "curate," "rehabilitate," "restore," "interpret," and "manage." To do any of this, you must *educate*—educate the public to support aggressive heritage management, educate legislators to pass laws that allow preservation to actually happen, and educate practitioners to implement the laws in an effective and efficient manner. The agencies that are given the responsibility under federal law to promote heritage preservation are led by two verbs: "consider" and "consult." They must consider how their actions impact significant historic properties (i.e., important tangible heritage resources) and consult with those who not only value those resources but know why they are important and what types of effects are truly adverse.

The not-so-obvious elements of a practical approach are knowing the purpose of heritage preservation, knowing the definitions of the key components, knowing the history of the practice, knowing the strengths and weaknesses of the current system, and knowing the tensions that exist within the system. Knowing the purpose allows evaluation of how well the system is working. Knowing the definitions of key terms allows focus on key elements and helps avoid distractions. Knowing how we got to where we are helps us understand what has and has not been accomplished and why. Knowing the roles and responsibilities of the key players enables focus to use those players to help accomplish what's possible. Knowing problems is the first step in providing strategies to address them.

Making a Reasonable and Good Faith Effort

When I worked as a survey archaeologist, within a few years I thought I knew the best ways to do a survey, but then agency needs, laws, funding, and technologies changed. When I was a SHPO archaeologist, I gradually figured out when to recommend a survey, when a site was eligible, and how to get a site listed in the National Register, but when I met my peers from other states I realized everyone did these basic cultural resource management (CRM) tasks somewhat differently. As a state archaeologist, I needed to develop standard procedures for the treatment of burial grounds, but I soon discovered that every burial case was unique. I also saw the need for each state to develop its own laws and procedures as a practical approach to its citizens' needs and wants, as well as its particular legal framework and history.

The biggest lesson I have learned in over 40 years of doing CRM archaeology is that there is no right way of doing things, but there are many wrong ways. That's why this book is more about helping you avoid wrong or inappropriate ways of doing things than telling you the right way. It offers advice on how to get your job done in a manner that is efficient, effective, and consistent with our American heritage management system and laws. Doing the job the right way is not necessarily doing it one particular way.

Overall, I think the American heritage management system does a pretty good job. The great majority of the time, important historic properties are protected from the adverse effects of development. The great majority of the time, there is widespread agreement on what is worth saving. Most agencies do make a reasonable and good faith effort to implement their responsibilities under multiple laws. Most federal agencies fulfill their Section 106 obligations, but some are delinquent in fulfilling those associated with Section 110.

Inadequate public funding continues to hamper effective heritage preservation. The Historic Preservation Fund has never been authorized at its targeted level. HPF support to states and tribes is nowhere near where it should be to accomplish the objectives Congress stated in the NHPA. Most states and cities do not make up the HPF shortfall in order to allow for comprehensive and proactive local heritage preservation. Private initiatives will always be dependent on economic variabilities and myopic visions.

The most difficult issue preventing better preservation is not the lack of funding or agency will. It is our uniquely American paranoia that private property is sacred in its own right. This leads to the assumption that private landowners know what's best for all of us and get to decide for all of us whether to preserve heritage resources on their property. Even if a nationally important historic property is privately owned, it will be difficult to save in the long run if the owner and the community where the property exists are not behind its preservation. While the "new" preservation that emerged in the late 1960s challenged some aspects of private owners' exclusive right to treat their historic properties as they saw fit, most private actions go unreviewed, so known and unknown historic properties are destroyed hourly in this country with no consideration and no consultation. This is especially true with regard to publicly invisible and officially unknown archaeological sites.

Heritage preservation is a constant battle. What is saved today because of Section 106 review can be destroyed tomorrow by an unreviewed action. Even very visible and prominent historic properties need maintenance and vigilance to keep them safe. Just like politics, all preservation is ultimately local. If a community does not want a property preserved, one or two very vocal supporters are not going to be able to preserve it by themselves, although their call to arms may lead the community to take them up.

In the end, practical means we can't save every important aspect of our cultural heritage, especially for the long term. It means that the majority of tangible heritage properties are not eligible for inclusion in the National Register and thus officially not worthy of preservation. It means we don't need to change the whole system because an agency occasionally misinterprets or fails to properly carry out its heritage management responsibilities. It means agencies, practitioners, and communities have to be reasonable in their approach, act in good faith in their relationships with each other, and be effective in fulfilling their obligations to protect important aspects of our heritage. If they do, heritage management will produce real results in the preservation of many important aspects of our cultural heritage. Eventually the public may realize that many aspects of our intangible heritage are worthy of preservation too, and we will develop practical ways to identify them, assess their relative importance, and protect them in meaningful and lasting ways.

SIDEBAR

Implementing Heritage Management: Being an Ethical Professional

Heritage management professionals have obligations that go beyond just fulfilling licensing requirements, agency expectations, and contract stipulations. They have ethical obligations. These obligations go beyond what their professional organizations require. Being a professional comes down to making a reasonable and good faith effort in every aspect of doing a project or a job. Being ethical means not only doing the job well but following basic professional standards in how you treat historic properties and basic moral standards in how you treat people.

The ethical standards of professional organizations tend to first focus on responsibilities that are at the core of a profession's mission. Archaeologists must preserve sites, artifacts, and information while considering the need to disturb original contexts. Historians must protect the integrity of the historical record and not be swayed by convenient politics in their interpretations. Architects must respect natural and cultural environments, yet try to make improvements. All professionals must be qualified to do a job they say they can do. All professionals must in some way serve the public and show respect for their peers and colleagues. They must publish significant findings and not plagiarize. Academic ethics include the fair treatment of all students.

Academic ethics in archaeology and history, as expressed by their major professional organizations, pay little attention to doing their professions outside the ivory tower, unless it is for the general public and basically of a community service nature. Most architects practice outside academic settings, so their ethical standards necessarily include aspects quite different from those of academic historians and archaeologists. All professionals' ethics rely on basic values of honesty, fairness, and respect, while considering obligations to clients and employers. These obligations include timeliness, confidentiality, and avoiding conflicts of interest. They also include maintaining objectivity. Your basic objective is to do what's best for historic properties, not necessarily what's best according to a client, an employer, a city, or a tribe.

Dealing with the dilemma of doing what's best for the profession as opposed to the company or the professional practitioner is a key standard missing from most professional ethical guidelines. This is true even of organizations whose membership is dominated by nonacademic practitioners, like the American Cultural Resources Association and the Register of Professional Archaeologists (RPA). The missing standard could simply read, "Professionals have an obligation to avoid charging for unnecessary work." This means that administrative pressures for obtaining contracts and increasing billable hours should only be followed if they are consistent with what is required to fulfill the contract objectives and the express instructions of the client.

This usually begins with offering an honest opinion on what work is really needed. When environmental review agencies (e.g., SHPOs) recommend surveys and project agencies agree, it does not mean that the entire project area must be field-surveyed or that any part of it really needs to be surveyed. It only means that some of the project area is thought to have some potential to contain historic properties based on known locations or the perceived nature of the environmental setting. This agency assessment is usually based on office-only review. Regardless of who recommends or requires a survey, professionals are obligated to make their own assessment of potential based on their archival research, a visual or virtual inspection of the area of potential effects (APE), the land-use history of the area, and their experience in similar settings. If you think an area has low potential to contain an eligible historic property, you should explain this to the sponsoring agency, the reviewing agency, and your client. If they still see a need for a survey, you are ethically good to go.

Identification work should only employ methods necessary to make a reasonable and good faith effort to find potentially eligible properties. Evaluation work should only employ the minimum effort needed to allow a reasonable assessment of a property's significance and integrity. Even if your research design calls for more work, once you have made a supportable decision as to an area's potential to contain historic properties or a known property's eligibility, you don't need to do additional fieldwork or research, unless the sponsoring agency or your client requires it after you have presented your preliminary conclusions. Archaeological site excavations for treatment purposes should recover sufficient data to accurately characterize and interpret a site according to important and answerable research questions posed in the data-recovery plan. When analyzing the materials obtained from fieldwork, archaeologists should only charge their sponsors for methods that directly address the pertinent research questions in a reasonable manner.

Official inventory forms should be filled out for all properties located during a survey even if a client is reluctant to share the information. Principal investigators are professionally obligated to complete written reports of their work even if a project is cancelled after a survey. Contract completion reports should cover all applicable federal and state reporting requirements but avoid including information that is not required or critical to the management objectives. As both a SHPO archaeologist and a state archaeologist, I have seen many reports that were clearly padded to increase billable hours, under the illusion that the longer a report was, the better it was. Publicly reporting significant findings is also a professional obligation.

I have always believed obligations are owed to your profession first and your employer second. The first is a matter of professional loyalty and ethics, the second of contractual loyalty and economics. I have rarely seen professionals putting profit ahead of site preservation or being intentionally dishonest about the presence or importance of a site. Most professionals err on the side of caution. This caution is more a matter of ignorance than deception. It is an ethical obligation to continue learning. Part of this learning process is realizing that every site may be important, but every site is not significant, just as many properties are historical but not historic.

APPENDIXES

A. Glossary: I do not attempt to define all the words I think are commonly used in heritage management; instead I define only those I think are especially important for students and professionals or require clarification for the purposes of my book. Tom King provides glossaries in many of his books, as do Hardesty and Little (2009), mainly for archaeologists. For "historian" and "architect," see glossaries in Murtagh (2006) and Tyler (1994).

B. List of Abbreviations: Heritage management exists in a world of abbreviations, acronyms, and initializations. You must know many of them to understand what agencies and professionals are talking about. You will use them yourself as shorthand to more efficiently do your job and communicate more efficiently with your peers. In my first class session each year, I provide my students with a list of acronyms and ask them to bring it to class every time. I tell them to keep track of the abbreviations and acronyms I use and how often I use particular ones. The top 10 might appear on an exam. If you note any missing abbreviations or acronyms that you think I should include, please let me know.

C. Chronology Chart: When summarizing or discussing something complex, I like to use an outline. For writing or discussing the histories of the various aspects of heritage management, I use chronology charts. I have compiled these for geographical areas (national, state of Minnesota, international), for important agencies (e.g., National Park Service, National Register of Historic Places), and for important heritage management subfields (e.g., archaeology, history-architecture). I hand a few of them out in class and have students highlight the items I discuss. These too can appear on my midterm exam. I have included my chart for American heritage management. If you see any critical dates I have missed or ones that are in error, please let me know. I am constantly tweaking these charts.

D. Traditional Cultural Property Evaluation Worksheet: I developed this worksheet in the late 1990s when I was Minnesota SHPO archaeologist to assist me with TCP identification and evaluation. This worksheet only provides guidance for making consistent determinations and should not be the only determinant for assessing a TCP's National Register eligibility. For any TCP, its importance to a community based on information obtained directly from that community is the key, although National Register requirements still need to be met. After all, the TCP as an official property type is a construct of the federal government for use with federal law. Also be aware that TCPs and sacred sites are not necessarily synonymous.

Glossary

Word meanings vary by usage and user. If a word may have multiple definitions for heritage management purposes, I have tried to include important variations. I use the following abbreviations to identify the sources of the definitions:

ARPA	Archaeological Resources Protections Act
CFR	Code of Federal Regulations
DOTA	Department of Transportation Act (1966)
ICOMOS	International Council on Monuments and Sites
NAGPRA	Native American Graves Protection and Repatriation Act
NEPA	National Environmental Policy Act (40 CFR 1500s)
NHPA	National Historic Preservation Act (1966)
NPS	National Park Service
NPS 28	National Park Service Cultural Resource Management Guideline
NRHP	National Register of Historic Places, given with the particular bulletin number (e.g., 16A)
SISG	*Secretary of the Interior's Standards and Guidelines for Archaeology and Historic Preservation*
UNESCO	United Nations Educational, Scientific, and Cultural Organization
US Legal Dictionary	An online law dictionary

A definition that includes the purpose comes from the law or regulation implementing that purpose. Definitions without attribution are by the author.

adaptive reuse   A use for a structure or landscape other than its historic use, normally entailing some modification of the structure or landscape.

affected environment   A description of the existing environment to be affected by [a] proposed action (NEPA).

agency   For Section 106 purposes, 5 U.S.C. 551 defines "agency" as each authority of the US government, whether or not it is within or subject to review by another agency; it does not include (1) the US Congress, (2) the US courts, (3) the governments of US territories or possessions, or (4) the government of the District of Columbia. For NAGPRA, "agency" does not include the Smithsonian Institution (43 CFR 10.2[a][1]).

alternative   A reasonable way to fix the identified problem or satisfy the stated need (NEPA), as in project alternatives.

archaeological resource   (1) Any material remains of past human life or activities which are of archaeological interest, as determined under uniform regulations promulgated pursuant to [the ARPA]. Such regulations containing such determination shall include, but not be limited to: pottery, basketry, bottles, weapons, weapon projectiles, tools, structures or portions of structures, pit houses, rock paintings, rock carvings, intaglios, graves, human skeletal materials, or any portion or piece of any of the foregoing items. Non-fossilized and fossilized paleontological specimens, or any portion or piece thereof, shall not be considered archaeological resources, under the regulations under this paragraph, unless found in an archaeological context. No item shall be treated as an archaeological resource under regulations under this paragraph unless such item is at least 100 years of age (ARPA). (2) Any material remains or physical evidence of past human life or activities which are of archeological interest, including the record of the effects of human activities on the environment (NPS 28).

archaeological site (1) The smallest unit of space dealt with by archaeologists (Willey and Phillips 1958). (2) A spatial clustering of artifacts, features, structures, or non-artifactual remains, such as animal and plant remains, that were manufactured, modified, or used by humans (Gibbon 1998). (3) A location of past human activity that can be studied by archaeologists (Tom King). (4) A discrete location containing evidence of past human activity that holds significance for archaeologists and is worthy of recording.

archaeologist (1) A federally qualified archaeologist has an advanced degree in archaeology or a closely related field, at least one year of supervisory experience, and at least four months of supervised experience doing North American archaeology (SISG). (2) A person educated in archaeological theory and methodology and trained to use physical methods to investigate archaeological sites and to scientifically interpret the materials present at or obtained from archaeological sites.

archaeology (1) The scientific study, interpretation, and reconstruction of past human cultures from an anthropological perspective based on the investigation of the surviving physical evidence of human activity and the reconstruction of related past environments (NPS 28). (2) The scientific study of important physical remnants of the cultural past.

architectural history The study of architecture through written records and the examination of structures in order to determine their relationship to preceding, contemporary, and subsequent architecture and events. An architectural historian is a historian with advanced training in this specialty (NPS 28).

architectural significance For National Register purposes, importance of a property based on physical aspects of its design, materials, form, style, or workmanship, and recognized by criterion C (NRHP 16A).

archival collection An accumulation of manuscripts, archival documents, or papers having a shared origin or provenance, or having been assembled around a common topic, format of record, or association (NPS 28).

archivist A professional responsible for managing and providing access to archival and manuscript collections (NPS 28).

area of potential effects (APE) For Section 106 purposes, the geographic area or areas within which an undertaking may directly or indirectly cause alterations in the character or use of historic properties, if any such properties exist. The area of potential effects is influenced by the scale and nature of an undertaking and may be different for different kinds of effects caused by the undertaking (36 CFR 800.16[d]).

artifact A natural or artificial article, object, tool, or other item manufactured, modified, or used by humans that is of archaeological interest (SA).

association   For National Register purposes, the link of a historic property with a historic event, activity, or person. Also, the quality of integrity through which a historic property is linked to a particular past time and place (NRHP 16A).

building   For National Register purposes, a resource created principally to shelter any form of human activity, such as house (NRHP 16A).

built environment   (1) All space purposefully shaped and manipulated by human activity; the result of conscious design decisions that can be both functional and aesthetic (Kuranda 2011:15; an architectural historian's definition). (2) The physical world that has been intentionally created through science and technology for the benefit of mankind (South African Built Environment Professions Bill; an engineer's definition). (3) An area where there are a lot of buildings (*Cambridge Dictionary*; an architect's definition) (4) An area where buildings or other structures, such as canals or dams, have been built (US Legal Dictionary; a lawyer's definition). (5) The human-made environment, ranging in scale from small structures (e.g., a fence, a shed) to large cultural landscapes (e.g., a farm) containing obvious modifications (e.g., cultivated fields) and constructed features; does not include most prehistoric sites lacking major above-ground features (e.g., a ruin) or nonstructural (i.e., built) alterations of a landscape, such as planting one type of tree to replace a type that naturally occurred at that location.

burial site   For NAGPRA purposes, any natural or prepared physical location, whether originally below, on, or above the surface of the earth, into which as a part of the death rite or ceremony of a culture, individual human remains are deposited (43 CFR 10.2[d][2]).

categorical exclusion (CATEX)   A category of actions that do not individually or cumulatively have a significant effect on the human environment and have been found to have no such effect in procedures adopted by a Federal agency pursuant to NEPA (40 CFR 1508.4).

certified local government (CLG)   A local government officially certified to carry out some of the purposes of the National Historic Preservation Act, as amended (NRHP 16A).

conservator   A person trained in the theoretical and practical aspects of preventive conservation and in performing treatments to prolong the lives of museum objects (NPS 28).

consideration   Under Section 106 of NHPA, an agency is required to act in a manner consistent with the procedures outlined in 36 CFR 800 to honestly and completely evaluate the effects of their undertakings on historic properties. Typical consideration failures include failure to adequately consult, to adequately identify and evaluate historic properties, and to adequately assess effects on historic properties.

consultation   The process of seeking, discussing, and considering the views of other participants, and, where feasible, seeking agreement with them regarding matters arising in the Section 106 process (36 CFR 800.16f).

contributing   For National Register purposes, this term applies to a building, site, structure, or object adding to the historic significance of a property (NRHP 16A).

Council on Environmental Quality (CEQ)   The Council on Environmental Quality oversees NEPA implementation, principally through issuing guidance and interpreting regulations that implement NEPA's procedural requirements. CEQ also reviews and approves Federal agency NEPA procedures, approves alternative arrangements for compliance with NEPA for emergencies, helps to resolve disputes between Federal agencies and with other governmental entities and members of the public, and oversees Federal agency implementation of the environmental impact assessment process and coordinates when agencies disagree over the adequacy of such assessments (https://www.whitehouse.gov/ceq).

criteria considerations For National Register purposes, additional standards applying to certain kinds of historic properties (NRHP 16A).

cultural affiliation (1) For National Register purposes, archeological or ethnographic culture to which a collection of sites, resources, or artifacts belong (NRHP 16A). (2) For NAGPRA purposes, a relationship of shared group identity which can be reasonably traced historically or prehistorically between a present day Indian tribe or Native Hawaiian organization and an identifiable earlier group (43 CFR 10.2[e]).

cultural heritage That which is valued due to its historical, archaeological, architectural, technological, aesthetic, scientific, spiritual, social, traditional, and other special cultural significance associated with human activity (New Zealand ICOMOS).

cultural items For NAGPRA purposes, these include human remains, funerary objects, and sacred objects (43 CFR 10 [d]).

cultural landscape A geographic area (including both cultural and natural resources and the wildlife or domestic animals therein) associated with a historic event, activity, or person or exhibiting other cultural or aesthetic values. There are four general types of cultural landscapes, not mutually exclusive: historic sites, historic designed landscapes, historic vernacular landscapes, and ethnographic landscapes (SISG).

cultural park A definable area that: a) is distinguished by historic property, prehistoric property, and land related to that property; and b) constitutes an interpretive, educational, and recreational resource for the public at large (NHPA).

cultural practice A pattern of behavior associated with a particular way of life.

Cultural practices are often associated with particular ecosystems, the use of natural resources, and the use or production of sites, structures, objects, and landscape features. Traditional forms of housebuilding, subsistence activities, religious, family, and community ceremonials, and expressive activities such as musical performance, craft production, and folklore are examples of cultural practices (NPS 28).

cultural resource (1) For National Register purposes, building, site, structure, object, or district evaluated as having significance in prehistory or history (NRHP 16A). (2) Those parts of the physical environment—natural and built—that have cultural value of some kind to some cultural group (King 1998:9). (3) Any resource that is of a cultural character generally tied up with a community's identity (King 2008:371). (4) Places, things, or practices that hold significant cultural value to communities.

cultural resource management (CRM) (1) The range of activities aimed at understanding, preserving, and providing for the enjoyment of cultural resources (NPS 28). (2) Practices concerned with the management of monuments and sites (ICOMOS). (3) The management both of cultural resources and of effects on them that may result from activities of the contemporary world (King 2009). (4) The identification, protection, and interpretation of archaeological sites, historic structures, and other elements of cultural heritage though survey, evaluation, and treatment strategies.

culture A system of behaviors, values, ideologies, and social arrangements. These features, in addition to tools and expressive elements such as graphic arts, help humans interpret their universe as well as deal with features of their environments, natural and social. Culture is learned, transmitted in a social context, and modifiable (NRHP 38).

cumulative effect (1) For NEPA, the incremental environmental impact or effect of [a] proposed action, together with impacts of past, present, and reasonably foreseeable future actions, regardless of what agency (Federal or non-Federal) or person undertakes such other actions. Cumulative effects can result from individually minor but collectively significant actions taking place over a period of time (40 CFR 1508.7). (2) Cumulative effects are mentioned in the Section 106 regulations (36 CFR 800.5) but are not defined.

curator A person professionally responsible for the management, preservation, and use of museum objects/specimens. Collection management responsibilities include acquisition and disposal, documentation and cataloging, preventive conservation, storage, access, interpretation and exhibition, and research and publication (NPS 28).

data recovery A recovery, through professional investigations and documentation, of significant cultural resource materials and data in lieu of in-place resource preservation (NPS 28). For archaeology, originally called "salvage"; also known as a "Phase 3 project."

de minimis impact (1) For historic sites, de minimis impact means that the Administration has determined, in accordance with 36 CFR part 800 that no historic property is affected by the project or that the project will have "no adverse effect" on the historic property in question. (2) For parks, recreation areas, and wildlife and waterfowl refuges, a de minimis impact is one that will not adversely affect the features, attributes, or activities qualifying the property for protection under Section 4(f) (DOTA).

design For National Register purposes, quality of integrity applying to the elements that create the physical form, plan, space, structure, and style of a property (NRHP 16A).

designed landscape A landscape that was consciously designed or laid out by a landscape architect, master gardener, architect, or horticulturist according to design principles, or an amateur gardener working in a recognized style or tradition (NPS Preservation Brief 36).

determination of eligibility An action through which the eligibility of a property for National Register listing is decided but the property is not actually listed; nominating authorities and federal agency officials commonly request determinations of eligibility for federal planning purposes and in cases where a majority of private owners has objected to National Register listing (NRHP 16A).

district For National Register and Section 106 purposes, a significant concentration, linkage, or continuity of sites, buildings, structures, or objects united historically or aesthetically by plan or physical development (NRHP 16A).

documentation Drawings, photographs, writings, and other media that depict cultural and natural resources (NPS 28).

effect For purposes of Section 106, alteration to the characteristics of a historic property qualifying it for inclusion in or eligibility for the National Register (36 CFR 800.16[i]).

eligibility (1) Ability of a property to meet the National Register criteria (NRHP 16A) or criteria established by state or local registers. (2) For Section 106 purposes, includes both properties formally determined as such in accordance with regulations of the Secretary of the Interior and all other properties that meet the National Register criteria (36 CFR 800.16).

environmental assessment (EA) A concise public document, prepared in compliance with NEPA, that briefly discusses the purpose and need for an action, alternatives to such action, and provides sufficient evidence and analysis of impacts to determine whether to prepare an environmental impact statement or finding of no significant impact (40 CFR 1508.9).

environmental consequences Environmental effects of project alternatives, including the proposed action, any adverse environmental effects which cannot be avoided, the relationship between short-term uses of the human environment, and any irreversible or irretrievable commitments of resources which would be involved if the proposal should be implemented (NEPA).

environmental impact statement (EIS) A detailed written statement required by Section 102(2)(C) of NEPA, analyzing the environmental impacts of a proposed action, adverse effects of the project that cannot be avoided, alternative courses of action, short-term uses of the environment versus the maintenance and enhancement of long-term productivity, and any irreversible and irretrievable commitment of resources (40 CFR 1508.11).

ethnographic landscape A landscape containing a variety of natural and cultural resources that associated people define as heritage resources. Examples are contemporary settlements, sacred religious sites, and massive geological structures. Small plant communities, animals, subsistence and ceremonial grounds are often components (NPS *Guidelines for the Treatment of Cultural Landscapes*).

ethnography Part of the discipline of cultural anthropology concerned with the systematic description and analysis of cultural systems or lifeways, such as hunting, agriculture, fishing, other food procurement strategies, family life festivals and other religious celebrations (NPS 28).

ethnohistory Systematic description (ethnography) and analysis (ethnology) of changes in cultural systems through time, using data from oral histories and documentary materials; anthropologists and historians conduct these studies (NPS 28).

ethnology Part of the discipline of anthropology concerned with the systematic and comparative analysis of cultures (NPS 28).

evaluation Process by which the significance and integrity of a historic property are judged and eligibility for National Register listing is determined (NRHP 16A).

feature (1) For archeology, a non-portable object, not recoverable from its matrix (usually in an archeological site) without destroying its integrity. Examples are rock paintings, hearths, post holes, floors, and walls (NPS 28). (2) For historic preservation, a prominent or distinctive aspect, quality, or characteristic of a historic property (NPS 28). (3) For landscape preservation, the smallest element(s) of a landscape that contributes to the significance and that can be the subject of a treatment intervention. Examples include a woodlot, hedge, lawn, specimen plant, allee, house, meadow or open field, fence, wall, earthwork, pond or pool, bollard, orchard, or agricultural terrace (SISG). (4) Nonartifactual evidence of human activity at an archaeological site usually expressed as noticeable soil disturbances such as pits and hearths. It can also refer to masonry walls and other structures at historical archaeological sites.

federal lands (1) For the purposes of NAGPRA, any land other than tribal lands which are controlled or owned by the United States, including lands selected by but not yet conveyed to Alaska Native Corporations and groups organized pursuant to the Alaska Native Claims Settlement Act of 1971 (43 CFR 10.2[f][1]). (2) For the purposes of ARPA, (A) lands which are owned and administered by the United States as part of (i) the national park system, (ii) the national wildlife refuge system, or (iii) the national forest system; and (B) all other lands the fee title to which is held by the United States, other than lands on the Outer Continental Shelf and lands which are under the jurisdiction of the Smithsonian Institution.

federal preservation officer (FPO) Official designated by the head of each Federal agency to be responsible for coordinating the agency's activities under the National Historic Preservation Act, as amended, including nominating properties to the National Register (NRHP 16A).

feeling For National Register purposes, the quality of integrity through which a historic property evokes the aesthetic or historic sense of past time and place (NRHP 16A).

finding of no significant impact (FONSI) A document prepared in compliance with NEPA, supported by an environmental assessment, that analyzes whether a federal action will have no significant effect on the human environment and for which an environmental impact statement, therefore, will not be prepared (40 CFR 1508.13).

foreclosure For the purposes of Section 106, an action taken by an agency official that effectively precludes the [Advisory] Council from providing comments which the agency official can meaningfully consider prior to the approval of the undertaking (36 CFR 800.16[j]).

guidelines Official advice on how to carry out a standard that allows some flexibility in application, such as advice issued by the secretary of the interior in various publications for heritage preservation purposes.

heritage (1) Everything that people want to save (Howard 2003:1); (2) Things we like (Mike Michlovic, personal communication 2016); (3) things passed down (common English usage); (4) for the purposes of the American heritage management system, tangible remnants of the past that are places deemed worthy of preservation because they are eligible for inclusion in the National Register of Historic Places or are cultural items required to be preserved or protected by law and standard professional practice.

heritage management Generally synonymous with cultural resource management (CRM) in its usage in the United States but infers a more anthropological perspective. In Europe, "heritage management" is more commonly used than historic preservation or CRM and can include both natural and cultural resources. For cultural resources, it includes both tangible and intangible aspects of heritage. As with CRM, heritage management involves the identification, protection, and interpretation of archaeological sites, historic structures, cultural landscapes, and other elements of cultural heritage such as traditional ways of life.

Heritage preservation commission See "historic preservation commission."

historian (1) A federally qualified historian has at least a bachelor's degree in history or a closely related field plus at least two years of full-time experience in research, writing, teaching, interpretation, or other demonstrable professional activity with an academic institution, historic organization or agency, museum, or other professional institution; or substantial contribution through research and publication to the body of scholarly knowledge in the field of history (SISG). (2) A specialist with advanced training in the research, interpretation, and writing of history (NPS 28). (3) A person educated in the theory and methodology of history and trained to use historic documents and other records to investigate and interpret the past.

historic (1) Famous or important in history, as in a historic occasion; thus a historic event is one that was very important (*Oxford English Dictionary*); (2) a period in which literate societies left primary texts that historians or historical archaeologists can study.

historic context (1) An organizing structure for interpreting history that groups information about historic properties which share a common theme, common geographical location, and common time period. The development of historic contexts is a foundation for decisions about the planning, identification, evaluation, registration, and treatment of historic properties, based upon comparative significance

(NRHP 16A). (2) A unit created for planning purposes that groups information about historic properties based on a shared theme, specific time period and geographical area (SISG).

historic designed landscape A landscape that was consciously designed or laid out by a landscape architect, master gardener, architect, engineer, or horticulturist according to design principles, or an amateur gardener working in a recognized style or tradition. The landscape may be associated with a significant person, trend, or event in landscape architecture; or illustrate an important development in the theory and practice of landscape architecture. Aesthetic values play a significant role in designed landscapes. Examples include parks, campuses, and estates (SISG).

historic district A geographically definable area, urban or rural, possessing a significant concentration, linkage, or continuity of sites, landscapes, structures, or objects, united by past events or aesthetically by plan or physical developments. A district may also be composed of individual elements separated geographically but linked by association or history (NRHP 15).

historic preservation (1) a) identification, evaluation, recordation, documentation, curation, acquisition, protection, management, rehabilitation, restoration, stabilization, maintenance, research, interpretation, and conservation; b) education and training regarding the foregoing activities; or c) any combination of the foregoing activities (NHPA). (2) Curatorial management of the built world (Fitch 2001). (3) The process of identifying resources of historic, cultural or architectural significance and then protecting, interpreting, maintaining, and/or rehabilitating such resources (Bronin and Rowberry 2014:2). (4) The practice of preserving man-made structures, sites, and objects because of their historical, aesthetic, or architectural importance (Glass 1990:ix). (5) A term used by

historians and architects to describe organized public and private efforts to protect, preserve, and rehabilitate historic properties.

Historic Preservation Fund (HPF) The Historic Preservation Fund established under section 303101 of Title 54 (NHPA).

historic preservation commission (HPC) (1) A board, council, commission, or other similar collegial body that is established by State or local legislation as provided in section 302503(a)(2) of Title 54. (2) All Commission members must have a demonstrated interest, competence, or knowledge in historic preservation. Unless State or local legislation provides for a different method of appointment, the chief elected local official must appoint all Commission members (36 CFR 61.6).

historic property (1) For National Register purposes, any prehistoric or historic district, site, building, structure, or object (NRHP 16A). (2) For Section 106 purposes, any prehistoric or historic district, site, building, structure, or object included in, or eligible for inclusion in, the National Register of Historic Places maintained by the Secretary of the Interior. This term includes artifacts, records, and remains that are related to and located within such properties. The term includes properties of traditional religious and cultural importance to an Indian tribe or Native Hawaiian organization and that meet the National Register criteria (36 CFR 800.16[l]).

historic site (1) The site of a significant event, prehistoric or historic occupation or activity, or structure or landscape whether extant or vanished, where the site itself possesses historical, cultural, or archeological value apart from the value of any existing structure or landscape (NPS 28). (2) A landscape significant for its association with a historic event, activity or person; examples include battlefields and presidential homes and properties (SISG).

historic vernacular landscape A landscape that evolved through use by the people whose activities or occupancy shaped it. Through social or cultural attitudes of an individual, a family, or a community, the landscape reflects the physical, biological, and cultural character of everyday lives. Function plays a significant role in vernacular landscapes. This can be a farm complex or a district of historic farmsteads along a river valley. Examples include rural historic districts and agricultural landscapes (SISG).

historical Concerning history or historical events, as in historical evidence; a historical event is something that happened in the past (*Oxford English Dictionary*).

historical archaeology A sub-discipline of archeology concerned with the remains left by literate societies (in contrast to prehistoric archeology, although the distinction is not always clear-cut). In the United States, historical archeology generally deals with the evidences of Euro-American societies and of aboriginal societies after major cultural disruption or material change from Euro-American contact (NPS 28).

historical architect Specialist in the science and art of architecture with specialized advanced training in the principles, theories, concepts, methods, and techniques of preserving prehistoric and historic structures (NPS 28).

Historic landscape architect Specialist in the science and art of landscape architecture with advanced training in the principles, theories, concepts, methods, and techniques of preserving cultural landscapes (NPS 28).

history The study of the past through written records, oral history, and material culture. Evidence from these is compared, judged for veracity, placed in chronological or topical sequence, and interpreted in light of preceding, contemporary, and subsequent events (NPS 28).

horizon (1) A technological or behavioral attribute with broad geographical distribution but not necessarily at the same time (e.g., fluted point horizon); (2) a particular layer within an archaeological site.

human environment The natural and physical environment and the relationship of people with the environment (NEPA).

identification (1) For National Register purposes, the process through which information is gathered about historic properties (NRHP 16A). (2) For Section 106 purposes, (a) the designation of the appropriate SHPO and/or THPO with whom to consult, and (b) the process of determining if potential historic properties are in an undertaking's area of potential effects.

impact (effect) A direct result of an action which occurs at the same time and place; or an indirect result of an action which occurs later in time or in a different place and is reasonably foreseeable; or the cumulative results from the incremental impact of the action when added to other past, present, and reasonably foreseeable future actions regardless of what agency or person undertakes such other actions (NEPA).

Indian lands Lands of Indian tribes, or Indian individuals, which are either held in trust by the United States or subject to a restriction against alienation imposed by the United States, except for any subsurface interests in lands not owned or controlled by an Indian tribe or an Indian individual (ARPA).

Indian tribe For purposes of Section 106, an Indian tribe, band, nation, or other organized group or community, including a native village, regional corporation or village corporation, as those terms are defined in section 3 of the Alaska Native Claims Settlement Act (43 U.S.C. 1602), which is recognized as eligible for the special programs and services provided by the United States to Indians because of their status as Indians (36 CFR 800.16[m]).

information potential For National Register purposes, the ability of a property to provide important information about history or prehistory through its composition and physical remains; importance recognized by criterion D (NRHP 16A). See also "tribal lands."

intangible cultural resources (1) The practices, representations, expressions, knowledge, skills—as well as the instruments, objects, artefacts and cultural spaces associated therewith—that communities, groups and, in some cases, individuals recognize as part of their cultural heritage (UNESCO). (2) Nonmaterial aspects of cultural behavior such as religious practices, subsistence-settlement preferences, social institutions, language, oral traditions, ceremonies, morals, values, and performing arts that can result in physical manifestations such as historic properties.

integrity For National Register purposes, authenticity of a property's historic identity, evidenced by the survival of physical characteristics that existed during the property's historic or prehistoric period (NRHP 16A).

intensive survey A systematic, detailed examination of an area designed to gather information about historic properties sufficient to evaluate them against predetermined criteria of significance within specific historic contexts (SISG).

inventory A list of cultural resources, usually of a given type and/or in a given area.

lead agency The agency or agencies responsible for preparing the environmental impact statement (NEPA).

level of significance For National Register purposes, the geographical level—local, State, or national— at which a historic property has been evaluated and found to be significant (NRHP 16A).

Light Detection and Ranging (LiDAR) A remote-sensing method that uses pulsed laser beams, usually sent from an airplane, to measure topographic elevation to a fine scale. It is highly valuable to archaeology for detecting earthworks such as ditches and mounds.

lithic Made of stone; lithic artifacts are generally manufactured either by chipping or flaking high-quality materials (e.g., chert, chalcedony) to produce tools such as knives, scrapers, and projectile points or by grinding or pecking granular rocks (e.g., sandstone, granite) to produce tools such as mauls, hammerstones, and axes.

lithic scatter A prehistoric site evidenced almost exclusively by the presence of stone tools and/or stone tool manufacturing debris and lacking ceramics and surface features.

local government For purposes of Section 106, a city, county, parish, township, municipality, borough, or other general purpose political subdivision of a State (36 CFR 800.16[n]).

local significance Importance of a property to the history of its community, such as a town or county (NRHP 16A).

location For National Register purposes, quality of integrity retained by a historic property existing in the same place as it did during the period of significance (NRHP 16A).

major federal action Actions with effects that may be major and which are potentially subject to Federal control and responsibility (NEPA).

management (1) The process of dealing with or controlling things or people (*Oxford English Dictionary*). (2) Good management is the effective and efficient utilization of an organization's resources to achieve its objectives.

materials For National Register purposes, quality of integrity applying to the physical elements that were combined or deposited in a particular pattern or configuration to form a historic property (NRHP 16A).

memorandum of agreement (MOA) The document that records the terms and conditions agreed upon to resolve the adverse effects of an undertaking upon historic properties (36 CFR 800.16[o]).

method (1) A subsystem of theory which is directed toward the solution of a particular class of problems (Dunnell 1971:199). (2) Methods are techniques of research (Lastrucci 1963:11). (3) A technique employed to help answer a research question.

methodology (1) How research questions are articulated with questions asked in the field (Clough and Nutbrown 2012:25). (2) The inquiry into the relationships between the theory of each of the sciences (Dunnell 1971:36). (3) The justification for a particular approach and the importance of the question.

mitigation (1) Planning actions taken to avoid an impact altogether, to minimize the degree or magnitude of the impact, reduce the impact over time, rectify the impact, or compensate for the impact (NEPA). (2) The full suite of activities to avoid, minimize, and compensate for adverse impacts to particular resources or values (NPS Energy and Climate Change Task Force 2014).

Multiple Property Documentation Form (MPDF) Official National Register form (NPS 10-900-b) used for documenting the contexts and property types for a multiple property listing (NRHP 16A).

multiple property listing A group of historic properties related by common theme, general geographical area, and period of time for the purpose of National Register documentation and listing (NRHP 16A).

National Historic Landmark (NHL) A historic property evaluated and found to have significance at the national level and designated as such by the Secretary of the Interior (NRHP 16A).

National Register of Historic Places Official federal list of districts, sites, buildings, structures, and objects significant in American history, architecture, archeology, engineering and culture (NRHP 16A).

national significance For National Register purposes, the importance of a property to the history of the United States as a nation (NRHP 16A).

Native Hawaiian For the purposes of Section 106, any individual who is a descendant of the aboriginal people who, prior to 1778, occupied and exercised sovereignty in the area that now constitutes the State of Hawaii (36 CFR 800.16[s]).

no action alternative The alternative where current conditions and trends are projected into the future without another proposed action (NEPA). Also known as a "no build alternative."

noncontributing Applies to a building, site, structure, or object that does not add to the historic significance of a property (NRHP 16A).

notice of intent (NOI) A notice that an environmental impact statement will be prepared and considered (NEPA).

object For National Register purposes, a construction primarily artistic in nature or relatively small in scale and simply constructed, such as a statue or milepost (NRHP 16A).

period of significance Span of time in which a property attained the significance for which it meets the National Register criteria (NRHP 16A).

Phase 1 survey Synonymous with a reconnaissance survey; a survey whose objective is to find archaeological sites, map the horizontal limits of the sites, and define the basic historic periods present. Also known as a Class 1 survey.

Phase 2 survey Synonymous with an evaluation survey; intensive fieldwork whose objective is to determine the significance of an archaeological site by assessing its research potential as demonstrated by the robustness of the identifiable historic contexts present and the integrity of artifacts and features associated with those contexts. Significance is generally equated with eligibility for inclusion in the National Register of Historic Places. Also known as a Class 2 or 3 survey.

Phase 3 project Synonymous with a treatment activity or site excavation; very intensive fieldwork generally done to mitigate the adverse effects of development upon a significant archaeological site through data recovery utilizing numerous formal excavation units or other intensive investigative methods. Also known as a Class 3 or 4 survey (SA).

planning (1) A basic management function involving formulation of one or more detailed plans to achieve optimum balance of needs or demands with the available resources (*Business Dictionary*). (2) The process of creating long-term visions for places and communities as small as an intersection and as large as a region (Boston Planning and Development Agency). (3) Planning is a consideration of options to implement an action often resulting in a written plan.

potential to yield important information For National Register purposes, likelihood of a property to provide information about an important aspect of history or prehistory through its physical composition and remains (NRHP 16A).

preservation (1) As a treatment of historic properties, the act or process of applying measures necessary to sustain the existing form, integrity, and materials of an historic property (SISG). (2) The act of saving something with an expectation of permanence.

programmatic agreement (PA) For the purposes of Section 106, a document that records the terms and conditions agreed upon to resolve the potential adverse effects of a Federal agency program, complex undertaking or other situations in accordance with 36 CFR 800.16[t]).

property For National Register purposes, area of land containing a single historic resource or a group of resources, and constituting a single entry in the National Register of Historic Places (NRHP 16A).

property type For National Register purposes, a grouping of properties defined by common physical and associative attributes (NRHP 16A).

protect (1) To prevent a person or thing from suffering harm or injury (*Oxford English Dictionary*). (2) To prevent harm to something with the intent that it should be kept safe.

reconnaissance survey An examination of all or part of an area accomplished in sufficient detail to make generalizations about the types and distributions of historic properties that may be present (SISG).

reconstruction As a treatment of historic properties, the act or process of depicting, by means of new construction, the form, features, and detailing of a non-surviving site, landscape, building, structure, or object for the purpose of replicating its appearance at a specific period of time and in its historic location (SISG).

record of decision (ROD) A concise public record of decision prepared by the Federal agency, pursuant to NEPA, that contains a statement of the decision, identification of all alternatives considered, identification of the environmentally preferable alternative, a statement as to whether all practical means to avoid or minimize environmental harm from the alternative selected have been adopted (and if not, why they were not), and a summary of monitoring and enforcement where applicable for any mitigation (40 CFR 1505.2).

registration Process described in 36 CFR Part 60 which results in historic or archeological properties being listed or determined eligible for listing in the National Register (NRHP 16A).

registration requirements Attributes of significance and integrity qualifying a property for listing in the National Register (NRHP 16A).

rehabilitation As a treatment of historic properties, the act or process of making possible a compatible use for a property through repair, alterations, and additions while preserving those portions or features which convey its historical, cultural, or architectural values (SISG).

research design A statement of proposed identification, documentation, evaluation, investigation, or other research that identifies the project's goals, methods and techniques, expected results, and the relationship of the expected results to other proposed activities or treatments (NPS 28).

resource For National Register purposes, any building, structure, site, or object that is part of or constitutes a historic property (NRHP 16A).

resource type The general category of property—building, structure, site, district, or object—that may be listed in the National Register (NRHP 16A).

restoration As a treatment of historic properties, the act or process of accurately depicting the form, features, and character of a property as it appeared at a particular period of time by means of the removal of features from other periods in its history and reconstruction of missing features from the restoration period. The limited and sensitive upgrading of mechanical, electrical, and plumbing systems and other code-required work to make properties functional is appropriate within a restoration project (SISG).

scope The range of actions, alternatives, and impacts to be considered in an environmental impact statement (NEPA).

scoping An early and open process for determining the extent and variety of issues to be addressed and for identifying the significant issues related to a proposed action (NEPA).

Section 4(f) property Publicly owned land of a public park, recreation area, or wildlife and waterfowl refuge of national, State, or local significance, or land of an historic site of national, State, or local significance (DOTA).

setting For National Register purposes, quality of integrity applying to the physical environment of a historic property (NRHP 16A).

significance Importance of a historic property as defined by the National Register criteria in one or more areas of significance (NRHP 16A).

significant (1) Use in NEPA requires consideration of both context and intensity (40 CFR 1508.27): Context—significance of an action must be analyzed in its current and proposed short- and long-term effects on the whole of a given resource (e.g. affected region). Intensity—Refers to the severity of the effect. (2) Use in Section 4(f) of DOTA denotes an adverse impact to, or occupancy of, a Section 4(f) property. There are three conditions under which use occurs: Permanent Incorporation, Temporary Occupancy, and Constructive Use (23 CFR 774.17).

significant date Date of an event or activity related to the importance for which a property meets the National Register criteria (NRHP 16A).

site For National Register purposes, the location of a significant event, a prehistoric or historic occupation or activity, or a building or structure, whether standing, ruined, or vanished, where the location itself possesses historic, cultural, or archeological value regardless of the value of any existing structure (NRHP 16A).

standards Principles issued by an authority to define an expected level of quality that are used as a basis for comparing actions performed by multiple practitioners, such as those issued in various publications of the secretary of the interior for heritage preservation purposes.

state historic preservation office (SHPO) Office in State or territorial government that administers the preservation programs under the National Historic Preservation Act (NRHP 16A).

state historic preservation officer (SHPO) The official designated by the Governor to administer the State's historic preservation program and the duties described in 36 CFR Part 61 including nominating properties to the National Register (NRHP 16A).

state preservation plan Document that sets forth the process by which a State develops goals, priorities, and strategies for preservation planning purposes (NRHP 16A).

state review board A board, council, commission or other collegial body appointed by the SHPO to review the eligibility of nominated properties and the adequacy of nomination documentation (NRHP 16A).

structure For National Register purposes, a functional construction made for purposes other than creating shelter, such as a bridge (NRHP 16A).

tangible cultural heritage (1) Physical artefacts of a group or society that are inherited from past generations, maintained in the present and bestowed for the benefit of future generations. Tangible heritage includes buildings and historic places, monuments, artifacts, etc., which are considered worthy of preservation for the future. These include objects significant to the archaeology, architecture, science or technology of a specific culture (UNESCO). (2) For the purposes of most American heritage laws, this includes remnants of the past that are either places deemed worthy of preservation because they are eligible for inclusion in the National Register of Historic Places or cultural items such as archaeological artifacts required to be preserved by law.

theme A trend or pattern in history or prehistory relating to a particular aspect of cultural development, such as dairy farming or silver mining (NRHP 16A).

traditional cultural property (TCP) A property that is eligible for inclusion in the National Register because of its association with cultural practices or beliefs of a living community that (a)

are rooted in that community's history, and (b) are important in maintaining the continuing cultural identity of the community (NRHP 38).

treatment (1) One of four types of action (preservation, rehabilitation, restoration, and reconstruction) to carry out a particular historic preservation goal consistent with maintaining the integrity of a historic property for National Register eligibility, emphasizing preservation in place and usually done in conjunction with affirming eligibility for Historic Preservation Fund grants or tax benefits. (2) A method of streamlining the Section 106 process by applying an ACHP-approved standard treatment as a program alternative. (3) The act of mitigating adverse effects to an archaeological site, such as implementing a treatment plan through a data-recovery excavation.

tribal historic preservation officer (THPO) The tribal official appointed by the tribe's chief governing authority or designated by a tribal ordinance or preservation program who has assumed the responsibilities of the SHPO for purposes of section 106 compliance on tribal lands in accordance with section 101(d)(2) of the National Historic Preservation Act (36 CFR 800.16[w]).

tribal lands (1) For the purposes of Section 106, all lands within the exterior boundaries of any Indian reservation and all dependent Indian communities (36 CFR 800.16[x]). (2) For the purposes of NAGPRA, (A) all lands within the exterior boundaries of any Indian reservation; (B) all dependent Indian communities; (C) any lands administered for the benefit of Native Hawaiians pursuant to the Hawaiian Homes Commission Act of 1920, and section 4 of Public Law 86-3 (43 CFR 10.2[f][2]).

undertaking For the purposes of Section 106, a project, activity, or program funded in whole or in part under the direct or indirect jurisdiction of a

Federal agency, including those carried out by or on behalf of a Federal agency; those carried out with Federal financial assistance; and those requiring a Federal permit, license or approval (36 CFR 800.16[y]).

vernacular landscape A cultural landscape that evolved through use by the people whose activities or occupancy shaped that landscape (Cultural Landscape Foundation).

workmanship For National Register purposes, the quality of integrity applying to the physical evidence of the crafts of a particular culture, people, or artisan (NRHP 16A).

APPENDIX B

Cultural Heritage Management Abbreviations

This list contains the following kinds of abbreviations:

- Federal agencies that play significant roles in heritage management (HM)
- State agencies that play significant roles in HM
- Federal laws and regulations
- International organizations that play significant roles in HM
- Private organizations that play significant roles in HM
- Standard HM or other terms familiar to multiple agencies

All agencies and programs have their own lists of acronyms and abbreviations. Many of these can be found on their websites or in their key heritage management documents.

106	Section 106 of the NHPA
110	Section 110 of the NHPA
4(f)	Section 4(f) of the Department of Transportation Act (1966)
AAM	Association of American Museums
AASHTO	American Association of State Highway and Transportation Officials
AASLH	American Association for State and Local History
ABPP	American Battlefield Protection Program
ACHP	Advisory Council on Historic Preservation
ACRA	American Cultural Resources Association
ADPA	Archaeological Data Preservation Act (1974) (aka AHPA or Moss-Bennett)
AFC	American Folklife Center
AFPA	American Folklife Preservation Act (1976)
AFPC	American Folklife Preservation Center (Library of Congress)
AHA	American Historical Association
AHLP	Alliance for Historic Landscape Preservation
AHPA	Archaeological and Historic Preservation Act (same as ADPA)
AIA	American Institute of Architects
AIM	American Indian Movement
AIRFA	American Indian Religious Freedom Act (1978)
AMS	accelerator mass spectrometry (radiocarbon dating)
ANCSA	Alaska Native Claims Settlement Act (1971)
APE	area of potential effects

APT	Association for Preservation Technology (international)
ARPA	Archaeological Resources Protection Act (1979)
ASA	Abandoned Shipwrecks Act (1987)
ASAH	American Society of Architectural Historians
BAE	Bureau of American Ethnology (SI)
BIA	Bureau of Indian Affairs
BLM	Bureau of Land Management
BOEM	Bureau of Ocean Energy Management
BOM	Bureau of Mines
BOR	Bureau of Reclamation (also BUREC)
BRAC	Base Realignment and Closure Commission (DOD)
BUREC	Bureau of Reclamation (also BOR)
CA	comprehensive agreement (NAGPRA)
CAD	computer aided design
CATEX	categorical exclusion (NEPA) (also CX)
CBD	central business district (also central business area, or CBA)
CCC	Civilian Conservation Corps (1933–1942)
CDBG	Community Development Block Grant (HUD)
CEF	considered eligible finding (National Register Section 106 consensus)
CEQ	Council on Environmental Quality (NEPA)
CERCLA	Comprehensive Environmental Response, Compensation, and Liability Act (1980)
CFR	Code of Federal Regulations
CLG	certified local government
CLI	cultural landscape inventory (NPS)
CLMP	cultural landscape management plan
CLR	cultural landscape report (NPS)
CNAE	conditional no effect determination (106)
COE	Corps of Engineers (also USACE)
CRAR	Committee for the Recovery of Archaeological Remains (1945–1972)
CRM	cultural resource management (also customer relations management)
CRMP	cultural resource management plan (see also HRMP)
CSD	context-sensitive design
CWA	Cape Wind Associates, LLC
CWA	Civil Works Administration (1933–1934)
CWA	Clean Water Act (1948, 1972)
DAPL	Dakota Access Pipeline
DCA	Department Consulting Archaeologist (NPS)
DCMDA	Demonstration Cities and Metropolitan Development Act
DEIS	draft environmental impact statement
DHS	Department of Homeland Security
DNR	Department of Natural Resources (state agency)
DOC	Department of Commerce
DOD	Department of Defense
DOE	Department of Energy
DOE	determination of eligibility (by the Keeper of the NRHP)
DOI	Department of the Interior (also USDI)
DOT	Department of Transportation (federal and state)
DOTA	Department of Transportation Act (1966)
EA	environmental assessment (NEPA)
ECS	ecological classification system
EDA	Economic Development Agency
EIS	environmental impact statement

EJ	environmental justice
EO	executive order (federal and state)
EPA	Environmental Protection Agency
ERA	Emergency Relief Agency
ERTA	Economic Recovery Tax Act
FAA	Federal Aviation Administration
FAST	Fixing America's Surface Transportation Act (2015)
FCC	Federal Communications Commission
FEMA	Federal Emergency Management Agency
FERA	Federal Emergency Relief Administration (1933–1935)
FERC	Federal Energy Regulatory Commission
FHA	Federal Housing Administration
FHWA	Federal Highway Administration
FLPMA	Federal Land Policy and Management Act (1976)
FONSI	finding of no significant impact (NEPA)
FPI	Federal Preservation Institute (NPS)
FPO	federal preservation officer
FR	*Federal Register*
FRA	Federal Records Act (1950)
FWS	Fish and Wildlife Service (US)
FY	fiscal year
GAO	General Accounting Office
GIS	geographic information system
GLO	General Land Office
GMP	general management plan (NPS)
GPR	ground-penetrating radar
GPRA	Government Performance Results Act (1993)
GPS	Geographic Positioning System
GSA	General Services Administration
HABS	Historic American Buildings Survey
HAER	Historic American Engineering Record
HALS	Historic American Landscapes Survey
HCRS	Heritage Conservation and Recreation Service (1978–1981)
HEW	Health, Education, and Welfare (now HHS)
HHS	Health and Human Services
HM	heritage management
HPC	heritage/historic preservation commission
HPF	Historic Preservation Fund
HPO	historic preservation officer
HRMP	historic resources management plan
HSA	Historic Sites Act (1935)
HSR	historic structures report
HUD	Housing and Urban Development
IASP	Interagency Archaeological Salvage Program
ICCROM	International Centre for the Study of the Preservation and Restoration of Cultural Property
ICOMOS	International Council on Monuments and Sites
ICRMP	integrated cultural resource management plan (DOD)
IRS	Internal Revenue Service
ISTEA	Intermodal Surface Transportation Efficiency Act (1991)
LEED	Leadership in Energy and Environmental Design (green buildings)
LiDAR	Light Detection and Ranging
LOA	letter of agreement

LOP	letter of permission (COE)
LOU	letter of understanding
MAP-21	Moving Ahead for Progress in the 21st Century Act (2012)
MFASAQHE	major federal action significantly affecting the quality of the human environment (NEPA, Tom King)
MFONSI	mitigated FONSI (NEPA)
MMS	Materials Management Service
MnDOT	Minnesota Department of Transportation
MOA	memorandum of agreement
MOU	memorandum of understanding
MPDF	multiple property documentation form (NRHP)
MRA	multiple resource area (NRHP)
MVHA	Mississippi Valley Historical Association
MVLA	Mount Vernon Ladies Association
MWAC	Midwest Archaeological Center (NPS)
NACD	Native American Consultation Database (NPS)
NADB	National Archaeological Database
NAGPRA	Native American Graves Protection and Repatriation Act (1990)
NAPC	National Alliance of Preservation Commissions
NARA	National Archives and Records Administration
NASA	National Association of State Archaeologists
NATHPO	National Association of Tribal Historic Preservation Officers
NCAI	National Congress of American Indians
NCHSB	National Council for Historic Sites and Buildings
NCPH	National Council on Public History
NCSHPO	National Conference of State Historic Preservation Officers (pronounced "nick-ship-o")
NEPA	National Environmental Policy Act (1969)
NHL	National Historic Landmark
NHLPA	National Historic Lighthouse Preservation Act (2000)
NHO	Native Hawaiian Organization
NHPA	National Historic Preservation Act (1966)
NHS	national highway system
NIMBY	not in my back yard
NOA	notice of availability
NOAA	National Oceanic and Atmospheric Administration
NOI	notice of intent
NPI	National Preservation Institute (private)
NRC	National Research Council
NRCS	Natural Resources Conservation Service (old SCS)
NRHP	National Register of Historic Places
NTHP	National Trust for Historic Preservation (private)
NWI	National Wetlands Inventory
NWR	National Wildlife Refuge
OAH	Organization of American Historians
OAHP	Office of Archaeology and Historic Preservation (1967–1978)
OFAP	Office of Federal Agency Programs (ACHP)
OMB	Office of Management and Budget
ONAA	Office of Native American Affairs (ACHP)
OPM	Office of Personnel Management (federal)
OSA	Office of the State Archaeologist
PA	programmatic agreement
PAST	Preservation Advisory Service Team (NPS)

PBS	Public Building Service (GSA)
PC	program comments (ACHP) (also politically correct)
PEIS	programmatic environmental impact statement
PI	principal investigator
PL	public law (federal)
POA	plan of action (NAGPRA)
R&C	review and compliance
R/W	right of way
RBS	River Basin Surveys (SI)
RFP	request for proposals
RFQ	request for qualifications
RFRA	Religious Freedom Restoration Act (1993)
RHPO	regional historic preservation officer (federal, GSA)
ROD	record of decision (NEPA)
RP3	Resource Protection Planning Process (HCRS)
RPA	Register of Professional Archaeologists
RSA	Reservoir Salvage Act (1960)
RTC	rehabilitation tax credit
RUS	Rural Utility Service
SAA	Society of American Archaeology (also Society of American Archivists)
SAFETEA	Safe, Accountable, Flexible, Efficient Transportation Equity Act (2005)
SCS	Soil Conservation Service (defunct; now in NRCS)
SDP	site development plan (NPS)
Section 10	Section 10 Rivers and Harbors Act of 1899 (COE permit for undertakings in navigable waters)
Section 404	Section 404 Clean Water Act (COE permit for wetland filling)
SEIS	supplemental environmental impact statement
SEPA	state environmental policy act (any state; also known as mini-NEPAs)
SHA	Society of Historical Archaeology
SHFG	Society for History in the Federal Government
SHPO	state historic preservation office; state historic preservation officer (pronounced "ship-o")
SI	Smithsonian Institution
SIA	social impact assessment (NEPA)
SISG	*Secretary of the Interior's Standards and Guidelines for Archaeology and Historic Preservation*
SLO	state liaison officer (now SHPO)
SLR	supplemental listing record (NRHP)
SMCA	Sunken Military Craft Act (2004)
SOW	scope of work
SRB	state review board
ST	shovel test
STB	Surface Transportation Board
TAC	technical advisory committee
TAP	Transportation Alternatives Program (FHWA)
TCP	traditional cultural property
tDAR	the Digital Archaeological Record
TE	transportation enhancement (FHWA)
TEA-21	Transportation Equity Act for the Twenty-First Century (1998)
THPO	Tribal Historic Preservation Office; tribal historic preservation officer (pronounced "tip-o")

TR	thematic resource (NRHP)
TU	test unit
TVA	Tennessee Valley Authority
UNESCO	United Nations Educational, Scientific, and Cultural Organization
USACE	United States Army Corps of Engineers (also COE)
USC	United States Code
USDA	United States Department of Agriculture
USDI	United States Department of the Interior
USFS	United States Forest Service
USGCB	US Green Building Council (LEED standards)
USGS	United States Geological Survey
USPS	United States Postal Service
VA	Veterans Administration
WAC	World Archaeological Congress
WASO	Washington Support Office (NPS)
WHL	World Heritage List (UNESCO)
WHS	World Heritage site (UNESCO)
WMA	Wildlife Management Area (federal)
WPA	Works Progress Administration (1935–1943; called Work Projects Administration from 1939)
WWW	World Wide Web

APPENDIX C

American Cultural Heritage Preservation Chronology

I have organized this list by periods related to major military conflicts in which the United States has been involved. Be aware that other major events and periods have had telling effects on heritage management, such as the Depression the Cold War, and the baby boom. Note also that the political leanings of Congress and the president have major effects on heritage management, although these can't simply be categorized as liberal or conservative, Democratic or Republican. Both political parties as well as the Left and the Right have had positive and negative effects on American heritage management. I include the election of Donald Trump because he is a wild card, not really affiliated with mainstream politics, and his election could have major implications for our present heritage management system.

Post–Revolutionary War

1781	Battle of Yorktown; Congress authorizes Yorktown Victory Monument (built 100 years later).
1784	Treaty of Paris officially ends Revolutionary War; Thomas Jefferson mound excavation takes place.
1785	Thomas Jefferson publishes *Notes on the State of Virginia*.
1788	Constitution ratified.
1789	Treasury Department founded, with responsibilities for federal buildings.
1790	Residence Act authorizes construction of the White House and Capitol; Hampton Mansion built.
1791	Massachusetts Historical Society founded; Bill of Rights ratified.
1793	President George Washington lays cornerstone for Capitol Building.
1800	Library of Congress established.
1809	Thomas Jefferson finishes Monticello construction.
1811	Construction starts on the National Road.
1812	American Antiquarian Society founded.
1814	British troops burn public buildings in Washington, DC, including the Library of Congress.
1815	Thomas Jefferson's personal library becomes the new Library of Congress.
1816	Local citizens in Philadelphia save Independence Hall.
1820	William Pell buys Fort Ticonderoga ruins.
1824	Bureau of Indian Affairs created in War Department.

1829   Independence Hall steeple rebuilt; Newport Synagogue restored; James Smithson bequeaths funds for founding of Smithsonian Institution; Capitol completed (wooden dome).

1830   Indian Removal Act passed.

1834   Indian Intercourse Act creates Indian Territory in the central and southern Plains.

1836   Construction begins on the US Treasury Building in Washington, DC.

1842   Bunker Hill Monument erected.

1843   Jens Worsaae publishes *Primeval Antiquities of Denmark*.

1846   Smithsonian Institution enabling legislation passed; Indian Affairs moves from War Department to Interior Department.

1848   Ephraim Squier and Edwin Davis publish *Ancient Monuments of the Mississippi Valley*.

1849   Department of the Interior established; John Ruskin publishes *The Seven Lamps of Architecture*.

1850   State of New York buys Hasbrouck House (George Washington's Revolutionary War headquarters).

1853   Mount Vernon Ladies' Association (MVLA) founded; federal Bureau of Construction established.

1855   Princeton's Nassau Hall restored; Smithsonian Institution opens.

1856   State of Tennessee buys Andrew Jackson's Hermitage.

1857   American Institute of Architects established; Frederick Olmsted and Calvert Vaux submit plan for Central Park.

1858   MVLA purchases Mount Vernon.

1861   Civil War begins.

1862   Department of Agriculture established.

1863   John Hancock's house in Boston demolished; Gettysburg National Cemetery established; cast-iron dome on US Capitol completed.

1864   US Army acquires Arlington House property (Custis-Lee Mansion) for use as a national cemetery; Gettysburg Battlefield Memorial Association founded; George Marsh publishes *Man and Nature*.

Post–Civil War

1865   Civil War ends; Massachusetts Institute of Technology architecture program founded.

1868   US Capitol extensions finished; Peabody Museum established.

1869   Transcontinental railroad completed; US Treasury Building completed; University of Pennsylvania architecture program founded.

1870   University of Illinois architecture program founded.

1872   Yellowstone becomes first national park.

1873   Financial panic erupts.

1876   Philadelphia Centennial Exposition held.

1879   Smithsonian's Bureau of Ethnology (later the Bureau of American Ethnology), the Anthropological Society of Washington, and the Archaeological Institute of America established.

1881   Arts and Industries Building erected in Washington, DC; Yorktown Victory Monument built.

1884   American Historical Association founded.

1886   Frederick Putnam publishes *On the Methods of Archaeological Research in America*.

1887   Illinois puts Abraham Lincoln's Springfield homestead in trust for pres-
         ervation; Dawes Act requires allotment of most Indian lands within
         reservations.
1888   American Folklore Society founded.
1889   Act protecting Casa Grande ruins (Arizona) from settlement or sale
         passed; W. H. Holmes hired by the Smithsonian (first federal archaeol-
         ogist); Association for the Preservation of Virginia Antiquities buys Wil-
         liamsburg building; Rand McNally Building built in Chicago.
1890   Chickamauga Battlefield becomes first national military park; Massa-
         chusetts Trustees of Reservations established.
1892   Executive order (EO) permanently protects Casa Grande.
1893   McLean House at Appomattox demolished; Chicago holds World's
         Columbian Exposition; Tarsney Act allows federal government to hire
         private architects.
1894   Harvard grants first American PhD in archaeology; Cyrus Thomas's
         Report on the Mound Explorations of the Bureau of Ethnology dispels
         Mound Builders myth.
1895   Trustees of Scenic and Historic Places and Objects of New York created;
         Gettysburg National Military Park established; *American Historical
         Review* starts publication.
1896   US Supreme Court says no to railroad through Gettysburg Battlefield.
1898   United States gives Spanish Governor's Palace (1611) to Territory of
         New Mexico; Whipple House restored; American Institute of Architects
         (AIA) moves into historic Octagon House in Washington, DC.
1899   Rivers and Harbors Act passed (COE Section 10 permits); American
         Society of Landscape Architects established; Washington, DC, post office
         built.
1901   New York group renames itself American Scenic and Historic Preserva-
         tion Society.
1902   McMillan Plan for Washington, DC, drafted; Reclamation Act passed.
1904   Louisiana Purchase Exposition held in St. Louis; Baltimore build-
         ing-height restriction law passed.
1905   Private group restores Paul Revere House in Boston; US Forest Service
         established.
1906   Antiquities Act passed; Mesa Verde becomes a national park; congressio-
         nal charter for Archaeological Institute of America issued; Alaska Native
         Allotment Act passed; El Morro becomes the first cultural national
         monument.
1907   Hartford, Connecticut, starts first city planning commission in the United
         States; Indian Territory abolished with Oklahoma statehood; Mississippi
         Valley Historical Association (MVHA) founded.
1908   Restoration of Fort Ticonderoga by private group begins; first Model T
         automobile produced.
1909   Daniel Burnham and Edward Bennett publish *Plan of Chicago*.
1910   Society for the Preservation of New England Antiquities established;
         New York's Penn Central Station opens.
1911   Frederick Taylor publishes *The Principles of Scientific Management*.
1912   Tarsney Act repealed; Nels Nelson perfects stratigraphic method for
         archaeological excavation.
1913   Public Buildings Act creates Public Buildings Commission.
1914   Ford starts mass-producing cars on assembly line; American Association
         of State Highway and Transportation Officials established.

1916   The Organic Act establishes the National Park Service (NPS).

1917   Alice Smith and D. E. Smith publish *The Dwelling Houses of Charleston, South Carolina*; United States enters World War I.

Post–World War I

1918   World War I ends.

1920   Army War College conducts historical survey of battlefields.

1921   First professional archaeologist hired at NPS (Mesa Verde).

1923   Thomas Jefferson Memorial Foundation acquires Monticello.

1924   Congress appropriates money for the restoration of Arlington House; Alfred Kidder publishes *An Introduction to the Study of Southwestern Archaeology.*

1925   Army War College study identifies over 3,400 battle sites in the United States; Metropolitan Museum of Art builds American wing; Vieux Carré Commission established in New Orleans (first historic preservation commission); Carl Sauer publishes *The Morphology of Landscape* (first mention of cultural landscapes).

1926   Colonial Williamsburg restoration begins, funded by John D. Rockefeller; Greenfield Village historic park in Dearborn, Michigan, started by Henry Ford; Study and Investigation of Battlefields Act passed; Public Buildings Act leads to construction of neoclassical Federal Triangle.

1927   Pan American Airways begins international flights; Pecos archaeological conference held.

1928   California historic sites survey begins; Archive of Folk Culture at Library of Congress established; Lewis Meriam issues report titled *The Problem of Indian Administration* critical of federal Indian policy.

1929   Horace Albright becomes director of NPS; War Department restores Arlington House; stock market crashes; Mount Vernon Memorial Highway (renamed the George Washington Memorial Parkway) construction begins; dendrochronology used to date Puebloan ruins in American Southwest.

1930   George Washington's Birthplace National Monument (Wakefield) established; Congress authorizes Colonial National Park (Yorktown, Jamestown); excavations at Wakefield find structural remains of Washington's birth cabin; Library of Congress Pictoral Division of Early American Architecture established; NPS hires landscape architect Charles Peterson; mid-continental drought begins; Rivers and Harbors Act authorizes Mississippi River locks and dams.

1931   Moore House restoration begins at Yorktown; first city historic district and historic preservation planning and zoning commission established (Charleston, South Carolina); NPS hires first historians (Elliot Cox and Vern Chatelain); California establishes State Register of Historic Landmarks; Yorktown celebrates its sesquicentennial; Athens Charter for the Restoration of Historic Monuments issued by First International Congress of Architects and Technicians of Historic Monuments.

1932   Archaeological work on William Penn's house promotes accurate reconstruction; Emergency Relief Agency (ERA) established; construction begins on Cass Gilbert–designed New York federal courthouse.

1933   Historic American Buildings Survey (HABS) conducted; ERA renamed Federal Emergency Relief Administration (FERA); first archaeology performed under FERA; EO 6166 transfers all federal historic sites to NPS; department consulting archaeologist position established at NPS (first filled by Jesse Nusbaum); NPS acquires Morristown as first national historic park; Greenfield Village opens; Civilian Conservation Corps (CCC) established; Tennessee Valley Authority established; EO 6166 changes NPS to Office of National Parks, Buildings, Reservations.

1934   NPS says uniqueness equals significance; AIA works with NPS on historic building documentation; Colonial Williamsburg opens to the public; NPS purchases Jamestown site; Society for American Archaeology (SAA) founded; Civil Works Administration (CWA) conducts widespread federal relief archaeology; National Archives and Records Administration established; National Housing Act creates Federal Housing Administration; Office of National Parks, Buildings, Reservations returns to NPS; Indian Reorganization Act passed.

1935   Historic Sites Act passed; Works Progress Administration (WPA) established; CCC performs excavations at Jamestown; Jefferson National Expansion Memorial established in St. Louis; *Philadelphia* shipwreck recovered from Lake Erie; Ronald Lee becomes chief NPS historian; Historical Records Survey initiated under WPA.

1936   National Survey of Historic Sites and Buildings begins (NPS); Louisiana passes constitutional amendment to help protect New Orleans French Quarter; first WPA archaeology conducted.

1937   California issues Historic Sites Policy; NPS issues guidelines for preservation of archaeological data; federal Housing Act passed.

1938   Natural Gas Act requires Federal Energy Regulatory Commission approval of interstate gas pipelines.

1939   Massive building demolition on St. Louis riverfront for Jefferson National Expansion Memorial; *Philadelphia* shipwreck moved to Smithsonian; National Research Council Committee on Basic Needs in Archaeology established; Public Works Branch transferred from Treasury to Federal Works Agency; American University (Washington, DC) starts program in archival administration.

1940   American Association for State and Local History and American Society of Architectural Historians established; Frederick Olmsted Jr. conducts architectural survey of Charleston, South Carolina.

1941   Pearl Harbor attacked; United States enters World War II; Frederick Douglas and René d'Harnoncourt publish *Indian Art of the United States*.

1942   *Collaborative Justification for Reconstruction of the McLean House at Appomattox* report issued demonstrating benefits of collaboration between architects, historians, and archaeologists; HABS and NPS Historic Sites Survey suspended due to war; NPS main office moves to Chicago; last WPA archaeology performed.

1943   Independence Hall designated a national historic site.

1944   Flood Control Act passed; National Congress of American Indians founded.

Post–World War II

1945   Committee for the Recovery of Archaeological Remains established; World War II ends.

1946   Interdisciplinary conference on archaeology held at Yorktown; River Basin Surveys begin; soil resistivity remote sensing first used at an archaeological site.

1947   First national historic preservation conference in Washington, DC, founds National Council for Historic Sites and Buildings; Pennsylvania historic sites survey includes archaeological sites; NPS moves back to Washington from Chicago; *American Heritage* magazine starts publication.

1948   War Department declares many military posts as surplus property; Hampton Plantation declared a national historic site and sold to a private trust; Walter Taylor publishes *A Study in Archaeology*; scuba equipment becomes commercially available.

1949   National Trust for Historic Preservation (NTHP) chartered by Congress (National Council for Historic Sites and Buildings); Federal Property and Administrative Services Act passed; Housing Act promotes urban renewal; Institute of Preservation and Interpretation of Historic Sites and Buildings established at Williamsburg; General Services Administration (GSA) founded; radiocarbon dating developed.

1950   Federal Records Act passed; Korean War begins.

1951   NTHP acquires Woodlawn Plantation.

1952   NTHP establishes *Historic Preservation* (now *Preservation*) magazine.

1953   Korean War ends; NTHP and NCHSB merge.

1954   Federal Housing Act includes historic preservation planning; Hague Convention for Protection of Cultural Property adopted; IBM 650 computer developed.

1955   Museum Properties Management Act and Presidential Libraries Act passed.

1956   Federal-Aid Highway Act passed; NPS Mission 66 begins; international symposium on "Man's Role in Changing the Face of the Earth" held; Philadelphia Historical Commission gets citywide authority.

1957   HABS and NPS Historic Sites Survey reactivated; Ivor Noel Hume becomes first Williamsburg professional archaeologist; NPS assumes full responsibility for River Basin Surveys; Jacob Morrison publishes *Historic Preservation Law.*

1958   Gordon Willey and Phillip Phillips publish *Method and Theory in American Archaeology*; first commercial photocopier released; metal detector used to investigate Little Bighorn Battlefield; first proton magnetometer surveys conducted; *Archaeometry* journal starts publication.

1959   UNESCO heritage training program called International Centre for the Study of the Preservation and Restoration of Cultural Property (ICCROM) starts in Rome; Public Buildings Act gives GSA responsibility for federal construction.

1960   Reservoir Salvage Act passed; National Historic Landmarks Program begins (NPS); first Conference on Historic Sites Archaeology held.

1961   Housing Act Urban Renewal Program founded; Jane Jacobs publishes *The Death and Life of Great American Cities.*

1962   Bureau of Outdoor Recreation created; Rachel Carson publishes *Silent Spring*; NPS adopts arrowhead symbol; Daniel Moynihan publishes *Guiding Principles for Federal Architecture*; Lewis Binford publishes "Archaeology as Anthropology"; Stuart Struever publishes article on the archaeological flotation method.

1963   Penn Central Station demolished in New York City; first Williamsburg Conference on "Principles and Guidelines for Historic Preservation in the United States" held; Stewart Udall publishes *The Quiet Crisis*; SAA holds session titled "The Meaning of Historical Sites Archaeology"; NPS issues Leopold Report.

1964   Columbia University starts graduate course in historic preservation architecture; International Monuments Year declared (UNESCO); Venice Charter founds the International Council on Monuments and Sites (ICOMOS) and sets basic standards for historic preservation; federal Land and Water Resources Conservation Fund Act (LAWCON) and Wilderness Act passed; Martin Anderson publishes *The Federal Bulldozer*; Peter Blake publishes *God's Own Junkyard*.

1965   First ICOMOS meeting held; US Conference of Mayors report issued; New York Landmarks Law passed; Special Committee on Historic Preservation created by Congress; Charles Hosmer publishes *Presence of the Past*; St. Louis Jefferson National Expansion Memorial Arch completed; Housing and Redevelopment Act forms Department of Housing and Urban Development (HUD); White House Conference on Natural Beauty held; George Marsh's 1864 *Man and Nature* reprinted by Harvard University Press; MVHA becomes the Organization of American Historians.

1966   NTHP begins publishing *Historic Preservation Today*; Rains Committee publishes *With Heritage So Rich*; National Historic Preservation Act (NHPA), Department of Transportation Act, and Demonstration Cities and Metropolitan Development Act (Model Cities Program) passed.

1967   First state liaison officers appointed; first meeting of the Advisory Council on Historic Preservation (ACHP) in July; William Murtagh becomes first Keeper of the National Register; Office of Archaeology and Historic Preservation (OAHP) at NPS includes National Register of Historic Places (NRHP) and Divisions of History, Archaeology, and Architecture; Society for Historical Archaeology founded; SYMAP GIS developed; second NTHP Williamsburg Conference looks at post-NHPA procedures; Klein side-scan sonar used in underwater archaeology.

1968   Association for Preservation Technology founded; first National Register list released; ACHP opposes power plant near Saratoga due to indirect effects; ACHP adopts first Section 106 guidelines; American Indian Movement founded; Sally Binford and Lewis Binford publish *New Perspectives in Archaeology*; Wild and Scenic Rivers Act and National Trails System Act passed; Architectural Barriers Act requires accessibility in federal buildings; Statistical Package for the Social Sciences software released.

1969   National Environmental Policy Act (NEPA) passed; Historic American Engineering Record established; first National Register of Historic Places listing published; first federal matching grants for local historic preservation projects; National Conference of State Historic Preservation Officers founded; New Mexico Cultural Properties Act passed.

1970   Postal Reorganization Act replaces Post Office Department with US Postal Service; first Corps of Engineers archaeologist hired; Robert Schuyler publishes "Historical and Historic Sites Archaeology as Anthropology."

1971   Nixon issues EO 11593; first Historic Preservation Fund (HPF) grants disbursed to states; NPS Denver Service Center established; Society for Industrial Archaeology founded; UNESCO Convention on Illicit Import/Export adopted; *Calvert Cliffs* decision handed down regarding NEPA; Total Station survey equipment developed; Alaska Native Claims Settlement Act passed; first NTHP National Conference on Preservation Law held; Norman Newton publishes *Design upon the Land: The Development of Landscape Architecture*; first HPF grants-in-aid issued for acquisition and development of NRHP-listed properties.

1972   World Heritage Convention held (UNESCO); Charles McGimsey publishes *Public Archaeology*; Hester Davis publishes "The Crisis in American Archaeology" in *Science*; Clean Water Act passed (COE Section 404 permits); ACHP issues revised guidelines for Section 106; Marine Protection, Research, and Sanctuaries Act passed (COE Section 103 permits; marine sanctuaries); federal Art in Architecture program founded; Landsat-1 satellite launched.

1973   First National Historic Preservation Week held; ACHP opposes highway in Hawaii's Mauna Loa Valley (traditional cultural property); *Old House Journal* begins publication; OAHP *11593* newsletter begins; NPS issues *HPF Grants-in-Aid Policies and Procedures* manual; Peter Drucker publishes *Management*; Texas Instruments releases SR-10 handheld calculator.

1974   Housing and Community Development Act and Archaeological and Historic Preservation Act passed; decision handed down in *U.S. v. Diaz* (Antiquities Act definitions vague); first Section 106 regulations issued by ACHP (nonbinding); Denver cultural resource management (CRM) conference and Arlie House archaeology conference held; Columbia University offers MA in historic preservation; state liaison officers become state historic preservation officers (SHPOs); Amtrak Improvement Act passed; shovel testing introduced; term "CRM" first used.

Post–Vietnam War

1975   Indian Self-Determination and Education Act passed; Vietnam War ends; term "public history" first used; ground-penetrating radar developed.

1976   NHPA amended, including NRHP "eligible" same as "listed" for purposes of Section 106, ACHP established as an independent agency, HPF; LAWCON amended to provide historic preservation funds; Tax Reform Act allows deductible easements to protect historically significant sites; first National Register regulations (36 CFR 60) and *Secretary of the Interior's Standards for Rehabilitation and Guidelines for Rehabilitating Historic Buildings* issued; Federal Land Policy Management Act, National Forest Management Act, American Folklife Preservation Act, Public Buildings Cooperative Use Act, and Mining in National Parks Act passed; public history program starts at University of California, Santa Barbara.

1977   First National Register bulletin issued; Japan conference on historic landscapes held; Apple II computer released; EO 11991 directs CEQ to develop regulations to implement NEPA; Lewis Binford publishes *For Theory Building in Archaeology*; Stanley South publishes *Method and Theory in Historical Archaeology*.

1978   American Indian Religious Freedom Act passed; Supreme Court hands down *Penn Central* decision; Bureau of Outdoor Recreation and NPS-OAHP joined to become Heritage Conservation and Recreation Service (HCRS); Federal Revenue Act passed; *Public Historian* journal begins publishing; *CRM* magazine starts (NPS); Carter Executive Memorandum gives ACHP rule-making authority; NTHP conference in Chicago looks at future directions; NEPA regulations (40 CFR 1500) issued by CEQ; EO 12072 requires federal agencies to give priority to central business district locations; Alliance for Historic Landscape Preservation founded.

1979   Archaeological Resources Protection Act passed; highest appropriated HPF funding reaches $60 million; ACHP issues its Section 106 procedures as legally binding regulations (36 CFR 800); third NTHP Williamsburg Conference focuses on private historic preservation; Christopher Alexander publishes *The Timeless Way of Building*; NPS acquires Hampton National Historic Site; Vernacular Architecture Forum held; WordStar word-processing software released.

1980   NHPA amended (Section 110, SHPO duties in 101; NPS four-year SHPO audits); NTHP starts Main Street Program; National Council for Preservation Education founded by National Trust; dBASE software program released; peak HPF funding reached; Archaeological Conservancy established; National Council on Public History founded.

1981   HCRS disbanded, with its historic preservation duties passed back to NPS; HPF cut in half (to $26 million); Economic Recovery Tax Act passed; Niquette archaeological contracting guidelines issued; IBM PC computer introduced; NPS codifies term "cultural landscape" in revised NPS 28: Cultural Resource Management Guideline (2nd); Epson HX-20 portable computer released.

1982   James Fitch publishes *Historic Preservation: Curatorial Management of the Built World*; Ian Hodder publishes *Symbolic and Structural Archaeology*; ARC/INFO GIS released; AutoCAD introduced; Roy Dickens publishes *The Archaeology of Urban America*; first widespread availability of Accelerator Mass Spectrometry for radiocarbon dating.

1983   *Secretary of the Interior's Standards and Guidelines for Historic Preservation* issued; Supreme Court's *People Against Nuclear Energy (PANE)* decision limits NEPA's social effects; first Archaeology Week held (Arizona); National Alliance of Preservation Commissions formed; Office of Personnel Management professional qualification standards issued for archaeologists, historians, and anthropologists; civilian GPS becomes available.

1984   First national heritage area established (I&M Canal); National Archaeological Database (NADB) created; Robert Stipe publishes *New Directions in Rural Preservation*; remote sensing joined with portable computers.

1985   Commission for the Preservation of American Heritage Abroad established; first commercial ground-penetrating radar available for archaeological use; NPS 28: Cultural Resource Management Guideline (3rd) issued.

1986   36 CFR 800 revised; Tax Reform Act passed; NPS database of large historic vessels created.

1987   ICOMOS meets for the first time in the United States; NRHP Bulletin 18 (designed historic landscapes) and Bulletin 20 (shipwrecks) issued; lowest HPF appropriated funding reached ($24 million); first World Archaeology Congress held; NPS archaeological management database and computerized curation catalog system established; desktop publishing programs released.

1988   Supreme Court hands down *Lyng* decision (free exercise of Indian religion); first NTHP Most Endangered list issued; NHPA Section 110 guidelines released; Abandoned Shipwrecks Act passed.

1989   NTHP publishes *Saving America's Countryside*; Congress directs NPS to study Indian historic preservation needs; NRHP Bulletin 30 (rural historic landscapes) issued; Apple Macintosh portable computer released.

1990   Native American Graves Protection and Repatriation Act (NAGPRA) passed; NPS publishes *Keepers of the Treasures*; 36 CFR 79 (curation standards) passed; NTHP issues Charleston Principles; Americans with Disabilities Act passed; Civil War Sites Advisory Commission authorized by Congress; Photoshop 1.0 released; Department of Defense Appropriations Act funds Legacy Resource Management Program.

1991   Intermodal Surface Transportation Efficiency Act (ISTEA) passed; World Wide Web first becomes available; NPS American Battlefield Protection Program (ABPP) created; Microsoft PowerPoint released.

1992   NHPA amended to include tribal consultation and tribal historic preservation officers (THPOs); NRHP Bulletin 38 (traditional cultural properties); NPS initiates Cultural Landscape Inventory; portable document file (pdf) format developed; Energy Policy Act requires enhanced efficiency standards for federal buildings; UNESCO recognizes and promotes the preservation of cultural landscapes.

1993   NRHP Bulletin 36 (historical archaeological sites) issued; US Green Building Council established; Congress for New Urbanism formed.

1994   National Maritime Heritage Act passed; Soil Conservation Service becomes Natural Resources Conservation Service; Disney historical park proposed in Virginia; NRHP Bulletin 30 (rural landscapes) published; NPS Preservation Brief 36 (cultural landscapes); NPS 28: Cultural Resource Management Guideline (4th) issued.

1995   American Cultural Resources Association established; NAGPRA regulations (43 CFR 10) passed; end of NPS four-year SHPO audits; NPS nationwide programmatic agreement reached with ACHP.

1996   EO 13007 (Indian sacred sites) and EO 13006 (use of federal urban historic buildings) issued; American Battlefield Protection Act passed; Kennewick Man skeleton found; Canon Powershot digital camera released; *Secretary of the Interior's Standards for the Treatment of Historic Properties with Guidelines for the Treatment of Cultural Landscapes* issued.

1997   Laser scanning introduced for historic buildings.

1998   Federal funding for NTHP ends; Save America's Treasures program begins; Institute for Environmental Conflict Resolution established; Transportation Equity Act for the Twenty-First Century passed; NHPA Section 110 guidelines revised; NPS 28: Cultural Resource Management Guideline (5th) issued; Cultural Landscape Foundation established.

1999   Revised 36 CFR 800 issued in response to 1992 NHPA amendment; LiDAR mapping of Red River Valley; GSA publishes *Held in Public Trust: PBS Strategy for Using Historic Buildings*.

2000   Federal Preservation Institute established (NPS); EO 13175 (nation-to-nation relationship with tribes for consultation) issued; National Historic Lighthouse Preservation Act passed; National Mining Association files lawsuit to halt implementation of new 36 CFR 800; Historic American Landscapes Survey conducted; first LEED standards (green buildings) issued; NPS reorganized (new associate director for cultural resource stewardship and partnerships); high-precision GPS available.

2001   UNESCO Convention on the Preservation of Underwater Cultural Heritage adopted; peak HPF funding reaches $94 million; 9/11 terrorist attacks; 3G cell phones released.

Post-9/11: The War on Terror

2002   NTHP publishes *Historic Preservation and Affordable Housing*; Smart Growth in the United States founded.

2003   EO 13278 authorizes "Preserve America" initiative.

2004   Revised 36 CFR 800 fully implemented after court decisions; National Museum of the American Indian established; Sunken Military Craft Act passed; federal appeals court hands down *Kennewick* decision; Federal Real Property Profile established (includes historic status).

2005   Keeper of National Register (Carol Shull) replaced by NPS associate director (Janet Mathews); ACHP reorganized; Denver ACHP office closed; Safe, Accountable, Flexible, Efficient Transportation Equity Act amends Department of Transportation Act (DOTA) Section 4(f) to include de minimis impacts; ACHP Department of Defense Base Realignment and Closure Commission (BRAC) task force established.

2006   "Preserve America" summit held in New Orleans; NHPA amended (minor).

2007   ACHP policy on human remains issued; CEQ issues *A Citizen's Guide to NEPA*.

2008   ACHP policy on archaeology and heritage tourism issued; NPS-ACHP programmatic agreement revised; Presidential Historical Records Preservation Act passed; the Digital Archaeological Record (tDAR) established; US Capitol Visitor's Center opens; commercial unmanned aerial vehicles/drones available.

2009   ACHP releases *Handbook on Indian Consultation*; ACHP expert panel issues recommendations; US ratifies 1954 Hague Convention for Protection of Cultural Property; LEED standards issued for building rehabilitation; American Recovery and Reinvestment Act passed.

2010   Consultation terminated on Cape Wind project; Apple releases first iPad.

2011   ACHP adopts Traditional Cultural Landscapes Plan; ACHP conducts Economic Impacts of Historic Preservation Study; ACHP reviews Section 106 regulations; NADB files transferred to tDAR.

2012   ACHP and four federal agencies sign memorandum of understanding on Indian sacred sites; HUD web-based tribal consultation tool developed; Department of Transportation publishes final rules for DOTA 4(f); NPS reorganized (new Cultural Resources, Partnerships and Science Directorate).

2013   Internal Revenue Service issues guidance on historic rehabilitation tax credit; ACHP and CEQ issue handbook on Section 106 and NEPA coordination.

2014   ACHP releases *Section 106 Applicant Toolkit*, *Guidance on Agreement Documents*, *Preservation and Rightsizing in America*, and policy on federal relationships with THPOs; NHPA amended (reorganized and renumbered sections in conformance with USC Title 54 for NPS-related laws); Unified Federal Review for Disasters issued by FEMA; NTHP issues *Preserving Native American Places*.

2015   ACHP unifies federal review process for infrastructure projects; Fixing America's Surface Transportation Act passed.

2016   Fiftieth anniversary of NHPA and DOTA; hundredth anniversary of NPS; Dakota Access Pipeline controversy erupts; NHPA amended (ACHP chair to be full-time, National Association of Tribal Historic Preservation Officers chair to be on ACHP, HPF reauthorized to 2023); Old Post Office in Washington converted to Trump Hotel; Kennewick Man reburied.

2017   Donald Trump becomes president.

Traditional Cultural Property Evaluation Worksheet

Name of Property

_____

Project or Current

Threats_____

Location

_____

Associated Community

_____

Type of Place

_____

Associated Practice/Belief

_____

Period of Significance

_____

Reviewer_____

Review Date_____

Answer the following questions yes, maybe, or no. Any no answer means the property is probably not eligible for the National Register, and multiple no answers may confirm this. A property determined to be ineligible may still be important to a community and may even be regarded as a sacred site, especially on federal land as defined by Executive Order 13007. This worksheet only provides guidance for making consistent determinations and should not be the only determinant for assessing eligibility.

_____ 1) Is the suspected TCP a *property*? (Is it a site, district, structure, building, or object as defined by the National Register with *definable boundaries*?)

_____ 2) Is a *living community* directly associated with the property?

_____ 3) Is there reasonable evidence that the property achieved its significance more than 50 years ago, or if it is younger than 50 years, is it of *exceptional* significance for its association with a critical *practice* or *belief*?

_____ 4) Does the property retain integrity of *condition* (location, design, setting, materials, workmanship, and feeling)?

_____ 5) Is the *cultural practice* or the *belief* attributed to the property based on oral accounts of knowledgeable members of the associated community or on reliable written documentation? In other words, does the property retain integrity of *relationship* (association)?

_____ 6) Is the property the only location or one of the few locations where a critical cultural *practice* can occur, or does the *belief* associated with the property have a unique and important association with that particular place?

_____ 7) Is the *cultural practice* that occurs at the property or the *belief* directly associated with the property critically important in maintaining the cultural identity of the community?

Comments:

Assessing the reliability of the evidence. (The *majority* of the answers should be yes.)

Oral Evidence

_____ Do multiple members of the associated community suggest the property is important?

_____ Are these community members widely respected in the community for their knowledge of the community's history and cultural beliefs?

_____ Is the oral evidence *traditional knowledge* as opposed to *experiential knowledge*?

_____ If the property was first identified by community members or others reacting to a proposed undertaking, is there evidence that its presence had been previously known to the community and was not openly discussed to protect its cultural or physical integrity?

_____ Prior to the proposal of the undertaking, is there evidence to suggest the property was of critical value to the community or that community members used/ attempted to use it for an important cultural practice?

_____ Does the place have a *traditional name* that is well known in the community or by respected members of the community?

Comments:

Written Evidence

_____ Is the written evidence over 50 years old?

_____ Is the written evidence based on accounts of knowledgeable observers?

_____ Is the written evidence specific enough to identify the location and the nature of the associated practice or event/function?

_____ Does the written evidence contain a name for the location that reflects its traditional use or importance? Is the written name similar to current names or names in oral accounts?

_____ Is there good reason to believe that the written evidence is relatively unbiased (e.g., the reason for the writing did not relate to a current political objective; the writer was relatively open-minded)?

Comments:

Suggested Boundary and Justification: (attach map)

TCP Evaluation Definitions

Boundary: The line delineating the geographical extent or area of a historic property (NRHP 16A). On the National Register nomination form, the boundary has to be both precisely described and explained. A TCP boundary need not be based on a tangible cultural manifestation (e.g., artifact distribution) and can be based on a general distribution of a resource (e.g., trees) or the approximate limits of a geographic feature (e.g., hill). Regardless of how the boundary is defined and justified, a line still has to be drawn on a map.

Cultural landscape: A geographic area (including both cultural and natural resources and the wildlife or domestic animals therein) associated with a historic event, activity, or person or exhibiting other cultural or aesthetic values. There are four general, not mutually exclusive types of cultural landscapes: historic sites, historic designed landscapes, historic vernacular landscapes, and ethnographic landscapes (NPS).

Culture: The traditions, beliefs, practices, lifeways, arts, crafts, and social institutions of a community (NRHP 38:1); includes language, oral traditions, written records, artifacts, and the built environment.

Ethnographic landscape: A landscape containing a variety of natural and cultural resources that associated people define as heritage resources. Examples are contemporary settlements, sacred religious sites, and massive geological structures. Small plant communities, animals, and subsistence and ceremonial grounds are often components (NPS). Most ethnographic landscapes are associated with indigenous peoples and are often less obvious as they contain fewer major human alterations, while cultural landscapes can be associated with any type of community or group, and most contain major elements of a built environment. An ethnographic landscape can be a TCP, and vice versa.

Experiential knowledge: Insight relating to recent experiences or opinions of living individuals: "I had a dream . . . ," "I have a feeling . . . ," "I know . . . , " "I saw . . . "

Fifty-year rule: In order to be eligible for inclusion in the National Register, properties generally must have achieved their initial significance over 50 years before; while a particular practice or belief may be older than 50 years, it must have been associated with a discrete location for at least 50 years for that location to be eligible. There are instances, however, when use of a place has been discontinued for a time due to inaccessibility, but there must be good evidence for the original use in the more distant past and good justification for the lack of recent access. A few properties may have achieved *exceptional* significance in less than 50 years, but such properties must be very well documented and well justified in order to be eligible as specified in NRHP Criteria Consideration G.

Living community: (1) "The maximal group of persons who normally reside together in face-to-face association" (Murdock 1950:93). (2) "The largest socio-cultural system manifest as a visible whole for the individual and that portion of his culture which most profoundly affects his identity; a discrete settlement that most often shares a common economic resource base and a system of economic production whose identity as a community may at times be corporately reaffirmed through public social and ritual activity" (Brown et al. 1982:18). (3) "A geographically localized population distinguished by extensive social interaction, relative self-sufficiency, and a common culture or identity" (Winthrop 1991). (4) A small social unit whose members share a common culture, live in or once lived in a discrete geographical area, and frequently gather to reinforce the bonds that historically and socially unite them, such as a tribe, reservation, town, religious group (e.g., Amish).

Period of significance: The span of time in which the property attained the significance for which it meets National Register criteria (NRHP 16A:42).

Sacred site: (1) "Any specific, discrete, narrowly delineated location on Federal land that is identified by an Indian tribe, or Indian individual determined to be an appropriately authoritative representative of an Indian religion, as *sacred* by virtue of its established religious significance to, or ceremonial use by, an Indian religion; provided that the tribe or authoritative representative of an Indian religion has informed the agency of the existence of such a site" (Executive Order 13007). (2) "Any geophysical or geographical area or feature which is sacred by virtue of its traditional cultural or religious significance or ceremonial use, or by virtue of a ceremonial or cultural requirement, including a religious requirement that a natural substance or product for use in Indian tribal or Native Hawaiian organization ceremonies be gathered from that particular location" (Sacred Lands Act, HR 2419 2003, not passed). (3) Any place having religious or spiritual importance to any group.

Traditional cultural property: "A property that is eligible for inclusion in the National Register because of its association with cultural practices or beliefs of a living community that are a) rooted in that community's history, and b) are important in maintaining the continuing cultural identity of the community" (NRHP 38:1).

Traditional knowledge: Cultural/historical information passed between generations primarily by word of mouth: "My grandfather told me . . . " or "There is a family story that says . . . "

Traditional use area: An area containing resources economically and culturally important to a group but not necessarily demonstrating long-term use. Some resources may be somewhat ephemeral in any given area (e.g., wild rice bed, maple trees, sweet grass clump, grove of birch trees).

Traditions: "Beliefs, customs, and practices of a living community of people that have been passed down through generations, usually orally or through practice" (NRHP 38:1).

References

Brown, Theodore, Kay Killen, Helen Simons, and Virginia Wulfkuhle
    1982 *Resource Protection Planning Process for Texas*. Texas Historical Commission, Austin.
Murdock, George
    1950 *Outline of Cultural Materials*. Human Relation Area Files. Yale University, New Haven, CT.
Winthrop, Robert
    1991 *Dictionary of Concepts in Cultural Anthropology*. Greenwood Press, New York.

NRHP 38 refers to the National Register of Historic Places bulletin *Guidelines for Evaluating and Documenting Traditional Cultural Properties* (originally numbered as Bulletin 38), first published in 1990 and revised in 1992 and 1998. The authors are Patricia Parker and Thomas King.

NRHP 16A refers to National Register of Historic Places Bulletin 16A, *How to Complete the National Register Nomination Form.*

NPS means the National Park Service, with the definition taken from the NPS website.

Definitions and comments without attribution are by the author, Scott Anfinson.

REFERENCES CITED

Advisory Council on Historic Preservation (ACHP)

1976 *The National Historic Preservation Program Today*. Report prepared for the Committee on Interior and Insular Affairs, United States Senate. US Government Printing Office, Washington, DC.

1980 *Treatment of Archaeological Properties: A Handbook*. ACHP Archaeology Task Force, Washington, DC.

2001 Summary Report: Caring for the Past, Managing for the Future: Federal Stewardship and America's Historic Legacy. ACHP. http://www.achp.gov/stewsum.html.

2012 *Consultation with Indian Tribes in the Section 106 Review Process: A Handbook*. ACHP Native American Program, Washington, DC.

2015 Section 106 Reviews for the United States Army Corps of Engineers Permits and Undertakings with Small Federal Handles, Office of Federal Agency Programs. ACHP. http://www.achp.gov/docs/fapc.pdf.

Alanen, Arnold, and Robert Melnick (editors)

2000 *Preserving Cultural Landscapes in America*. Johns Hopkins University Press, Baltimore.

Allen, David

2007 *The Olmsted National Historic Site and the Growth of Historic Landscape Preservation*. Northeastern University Press, Boston.

American Association of State Highway and Transportation Officials (AASHTO)

2016 *Consulting under Section 106 of the National Historic Preservation Act*. AASHTO's Practitioners Handbook 06. Center for Environmental Excellence.

Anderson, Martin

1964 *The Federal Bulldozer*. McGraw-Hill, New York.

Anderson, Richard

2004 *Guidelines for Recording Historic Ships* (3rd edition). National Park Service, Washington, DC.

Anfinson, Scott

1984 Cultural and Natural Aspects of Mound Distribution in Minnesota. *Minnesota Archaeologist* 43:9–30.

1989 Archaeology of the Central Minneapolis Riverfront (Part 1). *Minnesota Archaeologist* 48 (entire volume).

1990 Archaeology of the Central Minneapolis Riverfront (Part 2). *Minnesota Archaeologist* 49 (entire volume).

1994 Thematic Context: Lithic Scatters. Draft manuscript on file, Minnesota State Historic Preservation Office, St. Paul.

1995 *The Junction of Rivers: A Teacher's Guide to the American Indian Geography of the Twin Cities Area*. Minnesota Historical Society, St. Paul.

1996 The Wreck of the USS *Essex*. *Minnesota History* 55:94–103.

1997a *Southwestern Minnesota Archaeology: 12,000 Years in the Prairie Lake Region*. Minnesota Historical Society Press, St. Paul.

2001 *SHPO Manual for Archaeological Projects in Minnesota*. Minnesota State Historic Preservation Office, St. Paul.

2006 The Education of Government Archaeologists. *SAA Archaeological Record* 6(4):27–29.

2011 *State Archaeologist's Manual for Archaeological Projects in Minnesota*. Office of the State Archaeologist, St. Paul.

Anfinson, Scott (editor)
1979 *A Handbook of Minnesota Prehistoric Ceramics*. Minnesota Archaeological Society, St. Paul.

1993 *Archaeological and Historical Studies of Minnesota's Lake Superior Shipwrecks*. Minnesota State Historic Preservation Office, St. Paul.

1997b *History Underwater: Studies of Submerged Cultural Resources in Minnesota*. Minnesota State Historic Preservation Office, St. Paul.

Anfinson, Scott, Michael Michlovic, and Julie Stein
1978 *The Lake Bronson Site: A Multi-component Prehistoric Site on the Prairie-Woodland Border in Northwestern Minnesota*. Occasional Publications in Minnesota Anthropology No. 3. Minnesota Archaeological Society, St. Paul.

Anfinson, Scott, and Leslie Peterson
1979 Minnesota's Highway Archaeological Programs. *Minnesota Archaeologist* 38:86–104.

Arbogast, David
2010 *How to Write a Historic Structures Report*. W. W. Norton and Company, New York.

Austin, Robert
2002 Beyond Technology and Function: Evaluating the Research Significance of Lithic Scatters. In *Thinking about Significance*, edited by Robert Austin, Kathleen Hoffman, and George Ballo, pp. 153–185. Florida Archaeological Council, Riverview.

Austin, Robert, Kathleen Hoffman, and George Ballo
2002 *Thinking about Significance*. Florida Archaeological Council, Riverview.

Baker, John
1994 *American House Styles*. W. W. Norton, New York.

Baldwin, Pamela (editor)
2005 *Federal Land Management Agencies*. Novinka Books, New York.

Banks, Kimball, and Jon Czaplicki (editors)
2014 *Dam Projects and the Growth of American Archaeology*. Left Coast Press, Walnut Creek, CA.

Banks, Kimball, and Ann Scott (editors)
2016 *The National Historic Preservation Act: Past, Present, and Future*. Routledge, New York.

Banks, Larry
1976 Archaeology and the Corps of Engineers. *Great Plains Journal* 15:144–148.

Barlow, Ava
2013 *Architecture Styles in North Carolina Courthouses*. North Carolina Administrative Office of the Courts, Raleigh, NC.

Basso, Keith
1996 *Wisdom Sits in Places*. University of New Mexico Press, Albuquerque.

Beaumont, Constance
1991 Local Incentives for Historic Preservation. *CRM* 14(7).

Bell, Charlotte
1987 Historic Preservation: A New Section 106 Process. *Environmental Law Reporter*. (January News and Analysis).

Benjamin, Roger
1977 Strategy versus Methodology in Comparative Research. *Comparative Political Studies* 9(4):475–484.

Bettis, Arthur, and Dean Thompson
1981 Holocene Landscape Evolution in Western Iowa: Methods and Implications for Archaeology. In *Current Directions in Midwestern Archaeology: Selected Papers from the Mankato Conference*, edited by Scott Anfinson, pp. 1–14. Minnesota Archaeological Society, St. Paul.

Binford, Lewis
  1962 Archaeology as Anthropology. *American Antiquity* 28(2):217–225.

Birk, Douglas, and Douglas George
  1976 A Woodland Survey Strategy and Its Application in the Salvage of a Late Archaic Locus of the Smith Mounds Site (21KC3), Koochiching County, Minnesota. *Minnesota Archaeologist* 35(3):1–30.

Birnbaum, Charles
  1994 *Preservation Brief 36: Protecting Cultural Landscapes: Planning, Treatment and Management of Historic Landscapes*. National Park Service, Washington, DC.

Birnbaum, Charles, and Christine Peters
  1996 *Standards for the Treatment of Historic Properties with Guidelines for the Treatment of Cultural Landscapes*. National Park Service, Washington, DC.

Blake, Peter
  1964 *God's Own Junkyard*. Holt, Rinehart and Winston, New York.

Bluestone, Daniel
  1999 Academics in Tennis Shoes: Historic Preservation and the Academy. *Journal of the Society of Architectural Historians* 58(3):300–307.

Blumenson, John
  1981 *Identifying American Architecture: A Pictorial Guide to Styles and Terms, 1600–1945*. W. W. Norton and Company, New York.

Briuer, Frederick, and Clay Mathers
  1996 *Trends and Patterns in Cultural Resource Significance: An Historical Perspective and Annotated Bibliography*. US Army Corps of Engineers, Vicksburg, MS.

Bronin, Sara, and Ryan Rowberry
  2014 *Historic Preservation Law in a Nutshell*. West Academic Publishing, St. Paul.

Brown, Theodore, Kay Killen, Helen Simons, and Virginia Wulfkuhle
  1982 *Resource Protection Planning Process for Texas*. Texas Historical Commission, Austin.

Bureau of Land Management
  2004 *Manual 8100—The Foundations for Managing Cultural Resources*. Department of the Interior, Bureau of Land Management, Cultural Resource Management Program, Washington, DC.
  2014 *2014 Preserve America Progress Report*. Department of the Interior, Bureau of Land Management, Cultural Resource Management Program, Washington, DC.

Burke, Heather, Claire Smith, and Larry Zimmerman
  2009 *The Archaeologist's Field Handbook: North American Edition*. Alta Mira Press, Lanham, MD.

Canby, William
  2009 *American Indian Law in a Nutshell* (5th edition). West Publishing, St. Paul.

Carmichael, David, Robert Lafferty, and Brian Molyneaux
  2003 *Excavation*. Archaeologist's Toolkit 3. Alta Mira Press, Lanham, MD.

Carnett, Carol
  1991 Legal Background of Archaeological Resources Protection. Technical Brief Number 11. National Park Service.
  1995 *A Survey of State Statutes Protecting Archaeological Resources*. National Trust for Historic Preservation, Washington, DC.

Carson, Rachel
  1962 *Silent Spring*. Houghton Mifflin Company, New York.

Carter, Jimmy
  2013 *Public Papers of the Presidents of the United States: Jimmy Carter, 1980–1981*. National Archives of the United States, Washington, DC.

Cauvin, Thomas
  2016 *Public History: A Textbook of Practice*. Routledge, New York.

Clark, Ray, and Larry Canter (editors)
  1997 *Environmental Policy and NEPA: Past, Present, and Future*. St. Lucie Press, Boca Raton, FL.

Clough, Peter, and Cathy Nutbrown
2012 *A Student's Guide to Methodology* (3rd edition). Sage Publications, Thousand Oaks, CA.

Cofrise, Lina, and Rosetta Radtke
2003 Local Preservation Programs: Preservation Where It Counts. In *A Richer Heritage: Historic Preservation in the Twenty-First Century*, edited by Robert Stipe, pp. 117–156. University of North Carolina Press, Chapel Hill.

Collins, James, and Brian Molyneaux
2003 *Archaeological Survey*. Archaeologist's Toolkit 2. Alta Mira Press, Lanham, MD.

Council for Minnesota Archaeology
1977 *Archaeological Survey Standards for Minnesota*. Adopted May 10, 1977. Manuscript in possession of the author.

Council on Environmental Quality
2007 *A Citizen's Guide to the NEPA: Having Your Voice Heard*. NEPA. gov. https://www.energy.gov/nepa/downloads/citizens-guide-nepa-having-your-voice-heard-ceq-2007.

Cunningham, Robert
1974 Impact of Another New Archaeology. *Journal of Field Archaeology* 1:365–369.

deFranceaux, Cynthia
1987 National Park Service Planning. *Trends* 24(2):13–19.

Dickens, Roy
1982 *Archaeology of Urban America: The Search for Pattern and Process*. Academic Press, New York.

Dickens, Roy, and Carole Hill (editors)
1978 *Cultural Resources: Planning and Management*. Social Impact Assessment Series 2. Westview Press, Boulder, CO.

Dobyns, Henry
1983 *Their Number Becomes Thinned: Native American Population Dynamics in Eastern North America*. University of Tennessee Press, Knoxville.

Douglas, John
1999 Historic Preservation on the Public Domain: The Bureau of Land Management. *CRM* 4:24–28.

Drucker, Peter
1973 *Management*. Harper Collins, New York.

Dunnell, Robert
1971 *Systematics in Prehistory*. Free Press, New York.

Environmental Protection Agency (EPA)
2016 *Promising Practices for EJ Methodologies in NEPA Review*. Report of the Federal Interagency Working Group on Environmental Justice and NEPA Committee. EPA. https://www.epa.gov/sites/production/files/2016-08/documents/nepa_promising_practices_document_2016.pdf.

Fagette, Paul
1996 *Digging for Dollars: American Archaeology and the New Deal*. University of New Mexico Press, Albuquerque.

Federal Emergency Management Agency (FEMA)
2005 *Integrating Historic Property and Cultural Resource Considerations into Hazard Mitigation Planning*. State and Local Mitigation Planning How-To Guide, FEMA 389-6.

Federal Highway Administration
2012 *Section 4(f) Policy Paper*. Office of Planning, Environment and Realty Project Development and Environmental Review, Washington, DC.

Federal Preservation Institute
2007 Patterns in Determinations of National Register Eligibility, 1987–2006. National Park Service. https://www.nps.gov/fpi/Documents/Patterns%20in%20DOE.pdf.

Fitch, James
1990 *Historic Preservation: Curatorial Management of the Built World*. University of Virginia Press, Charlottesville (original 1982).

Flannery, Kent
1982 The Golden Marshalltown. *American Anthropologist* 84(2):265–278.

Fontana, Bernard
1965 On the Meaning of Historic Sites Archaeology. *American Antiquity* 31:61–65.

Foppes, Ellen, and Robert Utley
2002 Present at the Creation: Robert M. Utley Recalls the Beginnings of the National Historic Preservation Program. *Public Historian* 24(2):60–82.

Fowler, Don
1982 Cultural Resource Management. In *Advances in Archaeological Method and Theory*, Vol. 5: 1982, edited by Michael Schiffer, pp. 1–50. Academic Press, New York.
1986 Conserving America's Archaeological Resources. In *American Archaeology Past and Future*, edited by David Meltzer, Don Fowler, and Jeremy Sabloff, pp. 135–182. Smithsonian Institution Press, Washington, DC.

Friedman, J. L. (editor)
1985 A History of the Archaeological Resources Protection Act: Laws and Regulations. *American Archaeology* 5(2):82–119.

General Services Administration
1999 *Held in Public Trust: PBS Strategy for Using Historic Buildings.* US Government Printing Office, Washington, DC.
2004 *Extending the Legacy: GSA Historic Building Stewardship.* US Government Printing Office, Washington, DC.

Ginsberg, Robert
2004 *The Aesthetics of Ruins.* Rodopi, New York.

Glass, James
1987 *The National Historic Preservation Program, 1957–1966.* PhD dissertation, Cornell University, Ithaca, New York.
1990 *The Beginnings of a New National Historic Preservation Program, 1957 to 1969.* American Association for State and Local History, Nashville.

Gorte, Ross
2005 The National Forest System. In *Federal Land Management Agencies*, edited by Pamela Baldwin, pp. 25–35. Novinka Books, New York.

Gossett, Tanya
1998 The American Battlefield Protection Program: Forging Preservation Partnerships at Historic Battlefields. *George Wright Forum* 15(2):61–69.

Granger, Susan, and Scott Kelly
2005 *Historic Context Study for Minnesota Farms, 1820–1960* (3 vols.). Gemini Research. Contract report prepared for the Minnesota Department of Transportation, St. Paul.

Hardesty, Donald
2000 Ethnographic Landscapes: Transforming Nature into Culture. In *Preserving Cultural Landscapes in America*, edited by Arnold Allen and Robert Melnick, pp. 169–185. Johns Hopkins University Press, Baltimore.

Hardesty, Donald, and Barbara Little
2009 *Assessing Site Significance: A Guide for Archaeologists and Historians* (2nd edition). Alta Mira Press, Walnut Creek, CA.

Harmon, David, Francis McManamon, and Dwight Pitcaithley (editors)
2006 *The Antiquities Act: A Century of American Archaeology, Historic Preservation, and Nature Conservation.* University of Arizona Press, Tucson.

Hass, Daniel
1998 *Federal Archaeology Program: Secretary of the Interior's Report to Congress, 1994–1995.* Department of the Interior, National Park Service, Washington, DC.

Hart, Albert
1898 The Historical Opportunity in America. *American Historical Review* 4(1):2–20.

Heizer, Robert, and John Graham
1967 *A Guide to Field Methods in Archaeology.* National Press, Palo Alto, CA.

Hodsoll, Frank, William Leighty, and David Morgan
2007 *Back to the Future: A Review of the National Historic Preservation Program.* National Academy of Public Administration, Washington, DC.

Hoffman, Teresa, and Shireen Lerner
1988 Arizona Archaeology Week: Promoting the Past to the Public. Technical Brief 2. Archaeological Assistance Program, National Park Service, Washington, DC.

Hofsommer, Don
2009 Railroads and the Minneapolis Milling District. *Minnesota History* (summer):249–259.

Hole, Frank, and Robert Heizer
1965 *An Introduction to Prehistoric Archaeology.* Holt, Rinehart and Winston, New York.

Hosmer, Charles
1961 *Old Houses in America: The Preservation Movement to 1926.* PhD dissertation, Columbia University, New York.
1965 *Presence of the Past: The History of the Preservation Movement in the United States before Williamsburg.* Putnam and Sons, New York.
1981 *Preservation Comes of Age: From Williamsburg to the National Trust, 1926–1949* (2 vols.). University of Virginia Press, Charlottesville.

Howard, Peter
2003 *Heritage: Management, Interpretation, Identity.* Continuum, London.

Howe, Barbara, and Emory Kemp
1988 *Public History: An Introduction.* Robert Krieger, Malabar, FL.

Hufford, Mary
1991 *American Folklife: A Commonwealth of Cultures.* American Folklife Center, Library of Congress, Washington, DC.

Hutt, Sherry
1994 The Civil Prosecution Process of the Archaeological Resources Protection Act. Technical Brief Number 16. National Park Service, Washington, DC.

Hutt, Sherry, Elwood Jones, and Martin McAllister
1992 *Archaeological Resource Protection.* Preservation Press, Washington, DC.

Hutt, Sherry, Marion Forsyth, and David Tarler
2006 *Presenting Archaeology in Court.* Alta Mira Press, New York.

Interorganizational Committee on Principles and Guidelines for Social Impact Assessment
2003 Principles and Guidelines for Social Impact Assessment in the USA. *Impact Assessment and Project Appraisal* 21(3):231–250.

Jackson, R., M. Boynton, W. Olsen, and R. Weaver
1988 California Archaeological Resource Identification and Data Acquisition Program: Sparse Lithic Scatters. Office of Historic Preservation, Sacramento, CA.

Jacobs, Jane
1961 *The Death and Life of Great American Cities.* Random House, New York.

Jamele, Suzanne, and Elsa Gilbertson
1991 *Agricultural Resources of Vermont.* Multiple Property Documentation Form. Vermont State Historic Preservation Office, Montpelier.

Jarvis, T. Destry
2008 *The National Forest System: Cultural Resources at Risk—an Assessment and Needs Analysis.* National Trust for Historic Preservation, Washington, DC.

Jefferson, Thomas
1785 *Notes on the State of Virginia.* John Stockdale, London.

Jennings, Jesse
1985 River Basin Surveys: Origins, Operations, and Results, 1945–1969. *American Antiquity* 50(2):281–296.

Kanefield, Adina
1996 *Federal Historic Preservation Case Law, 1966–1996: Thirty Years of the National Historic Preservation Act.* Advisory Council on Historic Preservation, Washington, DC.

Keller, J. Timothy, and Genevieve Keller
1987 *How to Evaluate and Nominate Designed Historic Landscapes*. Bulletin 18. National Park Service, National Register of Historic Places, Washington, DC.

Kelley, Robert
1978 Public History: Its History, Nature, and Prospects. *Public Historian* 1(1):16–20.

Kelly, Robert, and David Thomas
2013 *Archaeology* (6th edition). Wadsworth, Belmont, CA.

Keune, Russell, National Trust for Historic Preservation (editor)
1984 *The Historic Preservation Yearbook*. Adler and Adler, Bethesda, MD.

Kidder, Alfred
1924 *An Introduction to the Study of Southwestern Archaeology*. Yale University Press, New Haven, CT.

Kiersz, Andy
2014 Here's How Much Land Military Bases Take Up in Each State. *Business Insider*, November 10.

Kimball, Fiske
1941 The Preservation Movement in America. *Journal of the Society of Architectural Historians* 1(3–4):16.

King, Thomas
1978 *The Archaeological Survey: Methods and Uses*. Heritage Conservation and Recreation Service, Department of the Interior, Washington, DC.
1984 Is There a Future for the National Register? In *The Historic Preservation Yearbook*, edited by Russell Keune, National Trust for Historic Preservation, pp. 74–77. Adler and Adler, Bethesda, MD.
1987 Prehistory and Beyond: The Place of Archaeology. In *The American Mosaic: Preserving a Nation's Heritage*, edited by R. E. Stipe and A. J. Lee, pp. 236–264. US/ICOMOS. Preservation Press, Washington, DC.
1998 *Cultural Resource Laws and Practice: An Introductory Guide*. Alta Mira Press, Walnut Creek, CA.
2000 *Federal Planning and Historic Places: The Section 106 Process*. Alta Mira Press, Walnut Creek, CA.
2002 *Thinking about Cultural Resource Management: Essays from the Edge*. Alta Mira Press, Walnut Creek, CA.
2003 *Places That Count: Traditional Cultural Properties in Cultural Resource Management*. Alta Mira Press, Walnut Creek, CA.
2004 *Cultural Resource Laws and Practice: An Introductory Guide* (2nd edition). Alta Mira Press, Walnut Creek, CA.
2005 *Doing Archaeology: A Cultural Resource Management Perspective*. Left Coast Press, Walnut Creek, CA.
2007 *Saving Places That Matter: A Citizen's Guide to the National Historic Preservation Act*. Left Coast Press, Walnut Creek, CA.
2008 *Cultural Resource Laws and Practice: An Introductory Guide* (3rd edition). Alta Mira Press, Walnut Creek, CA.
2009 *Our Unprotected Heritage: Whitewashing the Destruction of Our Cultural and Natural Environment*. Left Coast Press, Walnut Creek, CA.
2013 *Cultural Resource Laws and Practice: An Introductory Guide* (4th edition). Alta Mira Press, Walnut Creek, CA.

King, Thomas (editor)
2011 *A Companion to Cultural Resource Management*. Wiley-Blackwell, Chichester, UK.

King, Thomas, Patricia Parker Hickman, and Gary Berg
1977 *Anthropology in Historic Preservation: Caring for Culture's Clutter*. Academic Press, New York.

Knudson, Ruthann
1986 Contemporary Cultural Resource Management. In *American Archaeology Past and Future*, edited by David Meltzer, Don Fowler, and Jeremy Sabloff, pp. 395–413. Smithsonian Institution Press, Washington, DC.

Knudson, Ruthann, and Francis McManamon
1992 The Secretary of the Interior's Report to Congress on the Federal Archaeology Program. *Federal Archaeology Report* 5(2):4–10.

Kroeber, Alfred
1934 Native American Population. *Current Anthropology* 36(1):1–25.

Kuranda, Kathryn
2011 Studying and Evaluating the Built Environment. In *A Companion to Cultural Resource Management*, edited by Thomas King, pp. 13–28. Wiley-Blackwell, Chichester, UK.

Kvamme, Kenneth
2003 Geophysical Surveys as Landscape Archaeology. *American Antiquity* 68(3):435–457.

Lastrucci, Carlos
1963 *The Scientific Approach: Basic Principles of the Scientific Method.* Schenkman, Cambridge, MA.

Lee, Ronald
1970 Hampton and the Founding of the National Trust. National Park Service. https://www.nps.gov/parkhistory/online_books/hamp/notes/appe.htm.

Leopold, Aldo, Stanley Cain, Clarence Cottam, Ira Gabrielson, and Thomas Kimball
1963 *Wildlife Management in the National Parks: The Leopold Report.* Advisory Board on Wildlife Management. National Park Service, Washington, DC.

Lipe, William
1974 A Conservation Model for American Archaeology. *Kiva* 39(3/4):213–245.

Lipe, William, and Alexander Lindsay (editors)
1974 *Proceedings of the 1974 Cultural Resource Management Conference, Federal Center, Denver, Colorado.* Museum of Northern Arizona Technical Series Number 14. Flagstaff, AZ.

Little, Barbara
1997 Nominating Archaeological Sites to the National Register: What's the Point? *CRM* 7:3–4, 39.
1999 Nominating Archaeological Sites to the National Register: What's the Point? *SAA Bulletin* 17(4):19.

Little, Barbara (editor)
2002 *Public Benefits of Archaeology.* University Press of Florida, Gainesville.

Little, Barbara, Erika Seibert, Jan Townsend, John Sprinkle, and John Knoerl
2000 *Guidelines for Evaluating and Registering Archaeological Properties.* National Park Service, National Register of Historic Places, Washington, DC.

Longstreth, Richard (editor)
2008 *Cultural Landscapes.* University of Minnesota Press, Minneapolis.

Loomis, Ormond
1983 *Cultural Conservation: The Protection of Cultural Heritage in the United States.* American Folklife Center and National Park Service, Washington, DC.

Lovis, William
1976 Quarter Sections and Forests: An Example of Probability Sampling in the Northeastern Woodlands. *American Antiquity* 41(1):364–372.

Lowenthal, David
1998 *The Heritage Crusade and the Spoils of History.* Cambridge University Press, Cambridge, UK.
2004 The Heritage Crusade and Its Contradictions. In *Giving Preservation a History*, edited by Max Page and Randall Mason, pp. 19–43. Routledge, New York.
2015 *The Past Is a Foreign Country—Revisited.* Cambridge University Press, New York.

Lowenthal, David (editor)
2003 *George Perkins Marsh: Prophet of Conservation.* Weyerhaeuser Environmental Books, University of Washington Press, Seattle.

Lyon, Edwin
1996 *A New Deal for Southeastern Archaeology*. University of Alabama Press, Tuscaloosa.

Lyon, Elizabeth
1987 The States: Preservation in the Middle. In *The American Mosaic: Preserving a Nation's Heritage*, edited by Robert Stipe and Antoinette Lee, pp. 82–111. US/ICOMOS. Preservation Press, Washington, DC.

Lyon, Elizabeth, and David Brook
2003 The States: The Backbone of Preservation. In *A Richer Heritage: Historic Preservation in the Twenty-First Century*, edited Robert Stipe, pp. 81–116. University of North Carolina Press, Chapel Hill.

MacDonald, Douglas
2008 Interstate Variation in Cultural Resource Law and Application. *SAA Archaeological Record* 8(2):25–29.

Mackintosh, Barry
1985 *The Historic Sites Survey and National Historic Landmarks Program: A History*. National Park Service, Washington, DC.
1986 *The National Historic Preservation Act and the National Park Service: A History*. National Park Service, Washington, DC.

McAlester, Virginia, and Lee McAlester
2011 *The Field Guide to American Houses*. Alfred Knopf, New York.

McClelland, Linda, J. Timothy Keller, Genevieve P. Keller, and Robert Z. Melnick
1989 *Guidelines for Evaluating and Documenting Rural Historic Landscapes*. National Register of Historic Places, Washington, DC.

McDonald, Travis
1994 *Preservation Brief 35: Understanding Old Buildings: The Process of Architectural Investigation*. National Park Service, Washington, DC.

McGimsey, Charles
1972 *Public Archaeology*. Seminar Press, New York.

2004 *CRM on CRM*. Arkansas Archaeological Survey Research Series 61, Fayetteville.

McGimsey, Charles, and Hester Davis
1977 *The Management of Archaeological Resources: The Arlie House Report*. Special Publication of the Society for American Archaeology, Washington, DC.

McMahon, Edward, and Elizabeth Watson
1992 In Search of Collaboration: Historic Preservation and the Environmental Movement. National Trust for Historic Preservation (NTHP) Information Series No. 71. NTHP, Washington, DC.

McManamon, Francis
1991 The Federal Government's Recent Response to Archaeological Looting. In *Protecting the Past*, edited by George Smith and John Ehrenhard, pp. 261–269. CRC Press, Boca Raton, FL.
2000a Archaeological and Historic Preservation Act. In *Archaeological Method and Theory: An Encyclopedia*, edited by Linda Ellis, pp. 60–62. Garland Publishing, New York.
2000b The Archaeological Resources Protection Act of 1979. In *Archaeological Method and Theory: An Encyclopedia*. edited by Linda Ellis, pp. 62–64. Garland Publishing, New York.
2014 From RBS to CRM: Late Twentieth Century Developments in American Archaeology. In *The National Historic Preservation Act: Past, Present, and Future*, edited by Kimball Banks and Ann Scott, pp. 228–252. Routledge, New York.

Marling, Karal Ann
1988 *George Washington Slept Here: Colonial Revivals and American Culture, 1876–1986*. Harvard University Press, Cambridge, MA.

Marsh, George
1864 *Man and Nature*. Charles Scribner and Company, New York.

Melnick, Robert
1980 Protecting Rural Cultural Landscapes: Finding Value in the Countryside. *George Wright Forum* 3(1):15–30.

Melnick, Robert, Daniel Sponn, and Emma Saxe
1984 *Cultural Landscapes: Rural Historic Districts in the National Park System*. National Park Service, Washington, DC.

Meriam, Lewis
1928 *The Problem of Indian Administration*. Johns Hopkins Press, Baltimore.

Messenger, Phyllis, and George Smith (editors)
2010 *Cultural Heritage Management: A Global Perspective*. University Press of Florida, Gainesville.

Miller, Diane
1994 National Register Information Is a Hidden Treasure. *CRM Bulletin* 17(2):13.

Miller, Julia
2008 *A Layperson's Guide to Historic Preservation Law*. National Trust for Historic Preservation, Washington, DC.

Morrison, Lindsey
2014 SHPO Perspectives: Program Analysis of Statewide Historic Preservation Planning. National Park Service. https://www.nps.gov/preservation-planning/downloads/Morrisonreport2014.pdf.

Moynihan, Daniel
1962 *Guiding Principles for Federal Architecture*. US House Committee on Public Works, Report to the President by the Ad Hoc Committee on Public Office Space, 87th Congress, Second Session.

Murdock, George
1950 *Outline of Cultural Materials*. Human Relations Area Files. Yale University, New Haven, CT.

Murray, Alan
2010 *The Wall Street Journal Essential Guide to Management*. Harper, New York.

Murtagh, William
2005 *Keeping Time: The History and Theory of Preservation in America* (3rd edition). Main Street Press, Pittstown, NJ (previous editions 1988, 1997).

National Academy of Public Administration
2007 *Back to the Future: A Review of the National Historic Preservation Program*. Prepared for the National Park Service, Washington, DC.

2009 *Towards More Meaningful Performance Measures for Historic Preservation*. Prepared for the National Park Service, Washington, DC.

National Park Service
1990 *Keepers of the Treasures: Protecting Historic Properties and Cultural Traditions on Indian Lands*. Interagency Resources Division, Washington, DC.

2007 *HPF Grants Manual*. National Park Service. https://www.nps.gov/preservation-grants/hpf_manual.pdf.

2010 *The Goals and Accomplishments of the Federal Archeology Program*. Federal Archaeology Program: Secretary of the Interior's Report to Congress, 1994–1995. Department of the Interior, National Park Service, Washington, DC.

2012 *Historic Preservation Tax Incentives*. Technical Preservation Services, Washington, DC.

2016a *Federal Tax Incentives for Rehabilitating Historic Buildings*. Annual Report for Fiscal Year 2015, Washington, DC.

2016b Notes on Title 54 of the United States Code "National Park Service and Related Programs." National Park Service. https://www.nps.gov/subjects/historicpreservation/upload/title54notes.pdf.

National Oceanic and Atmospheric Administration
1994 *Guidelines and Principles for Social Impact Assessment*. Prepared by the Interorganizational Committee on Guidelines and Principles for Social Impact Assessment.

US Department of Commerce, Washington, DC.

2003 *Principles and Guidelines for Social Impact Assessment in the USA.* Prepared by the Interorganizational Committee on Guidelines and Principles for Social Impact Assessment. US Department of Commerce, Washington, DC.

National Register of Historic Places

1997a *How to Apply the National Register Criteria for Evaluation.* Bulletin 15. National Park Service, Washington, DC.

1997b *How to Complete the National Register Registration Form.* Bulletin 16A. National Register of Historic Places, Washington, DC.

1999 *How to Complete the National Register Multiple Property Documentation Form.* Bulletin 16B. National Register of Historic Places, Washington, DC.

Natural Resources Conservation Service

2003 *National Cultural Resources Procedures Handbook.* US Department of Agriculture, Washington, DC.

National Trust for Historic Preservation

1980 *Preservation: Toward an Ethic in the 1980s.* Preservation Press, Washington, DC.

Nelson, Lee

1988 *Preservation Brief 17: Architectural Character—Identifying Visual Aspects of Historic Buildings as an Aid to Preserving Their Character.* National Park Service, Washington, DC.

Neumann, Thomas, and Robert Sanford

2010 *Practicing Archaeology: A Training Manual for Cultural Resources Archaeology* (2nd edition). Alta Mira Press, Lanham, MD.

Neumann, Thomas, Robert Sanford, and Karen Harry

2010 *Cultural Resources Archaeology: An Introduction* (2nd edition). Alta Mira Press, Walnut Creek, CA.

Nissley, Claudia

2011 Consultation and Negotiation in Cultural Resource Management. In *Companion to Cultural Resource Management*, edited by Thomas King, pp. 439–453. Wiley-Blackwell, Oxford, UK.

Nissley, Claudia, and Thomas King

2014 *Consultation and Cultural Heritage: Let Us Reason Together.* Left Coast Press, Walnut Creek, CA.

Noble, Allen, and Richard Cleek

2009 *The Old Barn Book: A Field Guide to American Barns and Other Farm Structures.* Rutgers University Press, New Brunswick, NJ.

Novick, Peter

1988 *That Noble Dream: The Objectivity Question and the American Historical Profession.* Cambridge University Press, New York.

Olmsted, Frederick, Jr.

1940 Olmsted Report to Regional Planning and Advisory Committee. Manuscript in possession of the City of Charleston, SC.

Orser, Charles E., Jr.

2017 *Historical Archaeology* (3rd edition). Routledge, New York.

Page, Max, and Randall Mason (editors)

2004 *Giving Preservation a History: Histories of Historic Preservation in the United States.* Routledge, New York.

Parker, Patricia, and Thomas King

1990 *Guidelines for Evaluating and Recording Traditional Cultural Properties.* Bulletin 38. National Register of Historic Places, Washington, DC.

Pauketat, Timothy, and Diana DiPaolo Loren (editors)

2005 *North American Archaeology.* Blackwell Publishing, Malden, MA.

Peebles, Giovanna M.

2013 Looking Back at Archaeology and Cultural Resources Management in the United States and Vermont through a Forty-Year Mirror. *Journal of Vermont Archaeology* 13:19–62.

Poppeliers, John, and S. Allen Chambers
2003 *What Style Is It: A Guide to American Architecture*. John Wiley and Sons, New York.

Pursell, Carol
1991 Preservation Technologies: As Answers Get Easier, Questions Remain Hard. *Public Historian* 13(3):113–115.

Pyburn, Jack
2005 Historic Preservation in Architectural Education. *Future Anterior* 2(2):45–51.

Rains, Albert, and Lawrence Henderson (editors)
1966 *With Heritage So Rich*. Random House, New York (reprinted by the National Trust for Historic Preservation in 1983 and 1999).

Ramirez, Constance
1993 The Legacy Program: A Model for Federal Agencies: Enhancing the Management of Natural and Cultural Resources. *Forum Journal* 7(5) (September/October):62–71.
1997 A Summary History of the Army's Preservation Program. *CRM* 20(13):6–10.

Rayner, B. L.
1932 *Sketches of the Life, Writings, and Opinions of Thomas Jefferson*. Francis and Boardman, New York.

Rieth, Christina (editor)
2008 Small Lithic Sites in the Northeast. Bulletin Series 508. New York State Museum, Albany.

Richman, Jennifer, and Marion Forsyth
2004 *Legal Perspectives on Cultural Resources*. Alta Mira Press, New York.

Rodgers, Jerry
1987 The National Register of Historic Places: A Personal Perspective on the First Twenty Years. *Public Historian* 9(2):91–104.
2016 The National Historic Preservation Act: Fifty Years Young and Still Going Strong. In *The National Historic Preservation Act: Past, Present, and Future*, edited by Kimball Banks and Ann Scott, pp. 9–17. Routledge, New York.

Rood, Ronald, and Kimberley Kintz
2016 Perspectives from the Intermountain West and the Great Basin. In *The National Historic Preservation Act: Past, Present, and Future*, edited by Kimball Banks and Ann Scott, pp. 199–212. Routledge, New York.

Rosenberg, Ronald
1981 Archaeological Resource Preservation: The Role of State and Local Governments. *Utah Law Review* 4:755–802.

Ruskin, John
1849 *The Seven Lamps of Architecture*. Smith, Elder, and Company, London.
1876 *The Complete Works of John Ruskin*. George Allen, London.

Ryberg-Webster, Stephanie
2015 Urban Policy in Disguise: A History of the Federal Historic Rehabilitation Tax Credit. *Journal of Planning History* 14(3):204–223.

Sanford, Robert, Don Huffer, and Nina Huffer
1995 *Stonewalls and Cellarholes: A Guide for Landowners on Historic Features and Landscapes in Vermont's Forests*. Vermont Agency of Natural Resources, Waterford.

Santayana, George
1905 *The Reason of Common Sense*. Charles Scribner's Sons, New York.

Sebastian, Lynne, and William Lipe
2010 *Archaeology and Cultural Resource Management: Visions for the Future*. School for Advanced Research, Santa Fe.

Schiffer, Michael, and George Gumerman (editors)
1977 *Conservation Archaeology: A Guide for Cultural Resource Management Studies*. Academic Press, New York.

Schuyler, Robert
1970 Historical and Historic Sites Archaeology as Anthropology: Basic Definitions and Relationships. *Historical Archaeology* 8:83–89.

Semes, Steven
  2007 "Differentiated" and "Compatible": Four Strategies for Additions to Historic Settings. In *Sense of Place: Design Guidelines for New Construction in Historic Districts*, pp. 4–11. Preservation Alliance for Greater Philadelphia, Philadelphia.
  2009 *The Future of the Past*. W. W. Norton and Company, New York.
Short, James (editor)
  1966 *Historic Preservation Today: Essays Presented to the Seminar on Preservation and Restoration, Colonial Williamsburg*. National Trust for Historic Preservation and Colonial Williamsburg, University of Virginia Press, Charlottesville.
Shott, Michael
  1989 Shovel-Test Sampling in Archaeological Survey: Comments on Nance and Ball, and Lightfoot. *American Antiquity* 54:396–404.
Shrimpton, Jeffrey
  1998 State Historic Preservation Legislation Database. National Conference of State Historic Preservation Officers, Washington, DC.
Shull, Carol
  1987 The National Register after 20 Years. *CRM Bulletin* 10(3):4–6.
  2002 Irreplaceable Heritage: Archaeology and the National Register of Historic Places. In *Public Benefits of Archaeology*, edited by Barbara Little, pp. 195–201. University Press of Florida, Gainesville.
Slaton, Deborah
  2005 *Preservation Brief 43: The Preparation and Use of Historic Structure Reports*. National Park Service, Washington, DC.
Slaughter, Mark, Lee Fratt, Kirk Anderson, and Richard Ahlstrom
  1992 Making and Using Stone Artifacts: A Context for Evaluating Lithic Sites in Arizona. Report submitted to Arizona State Parks, State Historic Preservation Office. SWCA Inc., Tucson, AZ.

Smith, Alice, and D. E. Smith
  1917 *The Dwelling Houses of Charleston, South Carolina*. J. P. Lippincott, Philadelphia.
Snow, Dean
  1995 Migration in Prehistory: The Northern Iroquois Case. *American Antiquity* 60(1):59–79.
South, Stanley
  1977 *Method and Theory in Historical Archaeology*. Academic Press, New York.
  2005 *An Archaeological Evolution*. Springer, New York.
Sprinkle, John
  1994 Research, Stewardship, Visibility, and Planning: Four Reasons to Nominate Archaeological Sites to the National Register. *CRM Bulletin* 17(2):12.
  2011 "A Careful Inventory and Evaluation": The Origins of Executive Order 11593. *Journal of Heritage Stewardship* 8:80–102.
  2014 *Crafting Preservation Criteria: The National Register of Historic Places and American Historic Preservation*. Routledge, New York.
  2015 Section 110: An Introduction. *Preservation Leadership Forum Blog*. Preservation Leadership Forum, July 2.
Spude, Robert, and Jerry Rodgers
  2005 The Power of the Llano Estacado: Jerry Rodgers, Historian, Museum Director, and Federal CRM Leader. *Public Historian* 27(2):113–141.
Squier, Ephraim, and Edwin Davis
  1848 *Ancient Monuments of the Mississippi Valley*. Contributions to Knowledge 1. Smithsonian Institution, Washington, DC.
Stapp, Darby, and Michael Burney
  2002 *Tribal Cultural Resource Management: The Full Circle of Stewardship*. Alta Mira Press, Walnut Creek, CA.
Stipe, Robert
  1972 Why Preserve? *Preservation News* 12(7):5–8.

Stipe, Robert (editor)
1980 *New Directions in Rural Preservation.* Department of the Interior, Washington, DC.
2003 *A Richer Heritage: Historic Preservation in the Twenty-First Century.* University of North Carolina Press, Chapel Hill.

Stipe, Robert, and Antoinette Lee (editors)
1987 *The American Mosaic: Preserving a Nation's Heritage.* US/ICOMOS. Preservation Press, Washington, DC.

Struever, Stuart
1968 Flotation Techniques for the Recovery of Small-Scale Archaeological Remains. *American Antiquity* 33(3):353–362.

Stuart, David
1979 Non-artifactual Cultural Resources and NPS Planning. *CRM Bulletin* 2(2):11–12.

Sundstrom, Linea
2003 Sacred Islands: An Exploration of Religion and Landscape in the Northern Plains. In *Islands on the Plains: Ecological, Social, and Ritual Use of Landscape*, edited by Marcel Kornfeld and Alan Osborn, pp. 258–300. University of Utah Press, Salt Lake City.

Surovell, Todd, Jason Toohey, Adam Myers, and Jason LaBelle
2017 The End of Archaeological Discovery. *American Antiquity* 82(2):288–300.

Tanner, Helen (editor)
1995 *The Settling of North America. The Atlas of the Great Migrations into North America from the Ice Age to the Present.* John Wiley and Sons, New York.

Taylor, Frederick
1911 *The Principles of Scientific Management.* Harper and Brothers, New York.

Taylor, Walter
1948 *A Study of Archaeology.* Memoir 69. American Anthropological Association, Menasha, WI.

Terrell, Ian
2005 *Historians in Public.* University of Chicago Press, Chicago.

Terrell, Michelle
2005 *Historical Archaeology of Minnesota Farmsteads: Historic Context Study for Minnesota Farms, 1820–1960*, Vol. 4. Two Pines Resource Group. Contract report prepared for the Minnesota Department of Transportation, St. Paul.

Thiessen, Thomas
1999 Emergency Archaeology in the Missouri River Basin. Midwest Archaeological Center Special Report No. 2. National Park Service, Lincoln.

Thomas, Cyrus
1894 Mound Explorations of the Bureau of Ethnology. *Twelfth Annual Report of the Bureau of Ethnology.* Smithsonian Institution, Washington, DC.

Thomas, David
1998 *Archaeology* (3rd edition). Harcourt Brace, Fort Worth, TX.
2000 *Skull Wars.* Basic Books, New York.

Thompson, Raymond
1974 Institutional Responsibilities in Conservation Archaeology. In *Proceedings of the Cultural Resource Management Conference*, edited by William Lipe and Alexander Lindsey, pp. 13–24. Museum of Northern Arizona Technical Papers Number 14. Flagstaff, AZ.

Tischler, William
1979 The Landscape: An Emerging Historic Preservation Resource. *Bulletin of the Association for Preservation Technology* 11(4):9–25.
1980 The Role of Historic Preservation in Tomorrow's Rural Landscape. In *New Directions in Rural Preservation*, edited by Robert Stipe, pp. 25–31. Department of the Interior, Washington, DC.

Townsend, Jan
1994 Archaeology and the National Register. *CRM Bulletin* 17(2):10–12.

Townsend, Jan, John Sprinkle, and John Knoerl
1993 *Guidelines for Evaluating and Registering Historical Archaeological Sites and Districts*. National Register Bulletin 36. National Register of Historic Places, Washington, DC.

Townsend, Robert
2013 *History's Babel*. University of Chicago Press, Chicago.

Tyler, Norman
1994 *Historic Preservation: An Introduction to Its History, Principles, and Practice*. W. W. Norton and Company, New York (reprinted in 2000).

Tyler, Norman, Ted Ligibel, and Ilene Tyler
2009 *Historic Preservation: An Introduction to Its History, Principles, and Practice* (2nd edition). W. W. Norton and Company, New York.

Tyrrell, Ian
2005 *Historians in Public: The Practice of American History, 1890–1970*. University of Chicago Press, Chicago, IL.

Ubelaker, Douglas
2006 Population Size, Contact to Nadir. In *Handbook of North American Indians*. Vol. 3: *Environment, Origins, and Population*, edited by Douglas Ubelaker, pp 694–701. Smithsonian Institution, Washington, DC.

Udall, Stewart
1963 *The Quiet Crisis*. Holt, Rinehart, and Winston, New York.

US Department of Defense
1994 *The Benefits of Cultural Resource Conservation: Commander's Guide*. Legacy Resource Management Program, Washington, DC.
2014 *Department of Defense Response to Executive Order 13287, "Preserve America," Section 3: Reporting Progress on the Identification, Protection, and Use of Federal Historic Properties*. September 2014. Washington, DC.

US Department of the Interior
1983 *Secretary of the Interior's Standards and Guidelines for Archaeology and Historic Preservation*. Washington, DC.

US Government Printing Office
2017 *United States Government Manual*. Washington, DC.

Vansina, Jan
1961 *Oral Tradition: A Study in Historical Methodology*. Aldine Publishing Company, Chicago.
1985 *Oral Tradition as History*. University of Wisconsin Press, Madison.

Walka, Joseph
1979 Management Methods and Opportunities in Archaeology. *American Antiquity* 44(3):575–582.

Weeks, Kay, and Anne Grimmer
1995 *The Secretary of the Interior's Standards for the Treatment of Historic Properties with Guidelines for Preserving, Rehabilitating, Restoring, and Reconstructing Historic Buildings*. US Department of the Interior, National Park Service, Washington, DC.

Weiland, Paul
1997 Amending the National Environmental Policy Act: Protection in the Twenty-First Century. *Journal of Land Use and Environmental Law* 122:275–305.

Wendorf, Fred
1962 *A Guide for Salvage Archaeology*. Museum of New Mexico Press, Santa Fe.

Whiffen, Marcus
1992 *American Architecture since 1780* (revised edition). MIT Press, Boston.

White, Bradford, and Richard Roddewig
1994 *Preparing a Historic Preservation Plan*. American Planning Association, Washington, DC.

White, Gregory, and Thomas King
2007 *The Archaeological Survey Manual*. Taylor and Francis, New York.

Willey, Gordon, and Phillip Phillips
1958 *Method and Theory in American Archaeology*. University of Chicago Press. Chicago.

Williams, Gerald
2005 *The USDA Forest Service: The First Century*. US Forest Service, Office of Communication, Washington, DC.

Wilson, Paul, and James Winkler
1971 The Response of State Legislation to Historic Preservation. *Law and Contemporary Problems* 36(3):329–347.

Winter, Nore
2008 *The Benefits of Design Review*. Winter and Company, Boulder, CO.

Winthrop, Robert
1991 *Dictionary of Concepts in Cultural Anthropology*. Greenwood Press, New York.

Wirth, Conrad
1966 Comment. In *Historic Preservation Today: Essays Presented to the Seminar on Preservation and Restoration, Colonial Williamsburg*, pp. 185–198. National Trust for Historic Preservation and Colonial Williamsburg. University of Virginia Press, Charlottesville.

Wolfe, Mark
2014 Guidelines for Consulting with the Texas State Historic Preservation Officer to Meet Requirements of 24 CFR 58.5(a) and Section 106 of the National Historic Preservation Act. Memo dated June 2014. Texas Historical Commission, Austin.

Woodbury, Richard
1973 Getting Round Archaeologists Out of Square Holes. In *Research and Theory in Current Archaeology*, edited by Charles Redman, pp. 311–317. Wiley-Interscience, New York.

Worsaae, Jens
1843 *Primeval Antiquities of Denmark* (English translation 1849 by William Thoms). J. H. Parker, London.)

Yablon, Nick
2009 *Untimely Ruins. An Archaeology of American Urban Modernity, 1819–1919*. University of Chicago Press, Chicago.

Zenzen, Joan M.
1998 *Battling for Manassas: The Fifty-Year Preservation Struggle at Manassas National Battlefield Park*. Pennsylvania State University Press, University Park.

INDEX